Advances in Intelligent Systems and Computing

Volume 731

Series editor

Janusz Kacprzyk, Polish Academy of Sciences, Warsaw, Poland
e-mail: kacprzyk@ibspan.waw.pl

The series "Advances in Intelligent Systems and Computing" contains publications on theory, applications, and design methods of Intelligent Systems and Intelligent Computing. Virtually all disciplines such as engineering, natural sciences, computer and information science, ICT, economics, business, e-commerce, environment, healthcare, life science are covered. The list of topics spans all the areas of modern intelligent systems and computing such as: computational intelligence, soft computing including neural networks, fuzzy systems, evolutionary computing and the fusion of these paradigms, social intelligence, ambient intelligence, computational neuroscience, artificial life, virtual worlds and society, cognitive science and systems, Perception and Vision, DNA and immune based systems, self-organizing and adaptive systems, e-Learning and teaching, human-centered and human-centric computing, recommender systems, intelligent control, robotics and mechatronics including human-machine teaming, knowledge-based paradigms, learning paradigms, machine ethics, intelligent data analysis, knowledge management, intelligent agents, intelligent decision making and support, intelligent network security, trust management, interactive entertainment, Web intelligence and multimedia.

The publications within "Advances in Intelligent Systems and Computing" are primarily proceedings of important conferences, symposia and congresses. They cover significant recent developments in the field, both of a foundational and applicable character. An important characteristic feature of the series is the short publication time and world-wide distribution. This permits a rapid and broad dissemination of research results.

Advisory Board

Chairman

Nikhil R. Pal, Indian Statistical Institute, Kolkata, India
e-mail: nikhil@isical.ac.in

Members

Rafael Bello Perez, Universidad Central "Marta Abreu" de Las Villas, Santa Clara, Cuba
e-mail: rbellop@uclv.edu.cu

Emilio S. Corchado, University of Salamanca, Salamanca, Spain
e-mail: escorchado@usal.es

Hani Hagras, University of Essex, Colchester, UK
e-mail: hani@essex.ac.uk

László T. Kóczy, Széchenyi István University, Győr, Hungary
e-mail: koczy@sze.hu

Vladik Kreinovich, University of Texas at El Paso, El Paso, USA
e-mail: vladik@utep.edu

Chin-Teng Lin, National Chiao Tung University, Hsinchu, Taiwan
e-mail: ctlin@mail.nctu.edu.tw

Jie Lu, University of Technology, Sydney, Australia
e-mail: Jie.Lu@uts.edu.au

Patricia Melin, Tijuana Institute of Technology, Tijuana, Mexico
e-mail: epmelin@hafsamx.org

Nadia Nedjah, State University of Rio de Janeiro, Rio de Janeiro, Brazil
e-mail: nadia@eng.uerj.br

Ngoc Thanh Nguyen, Wroclaw University of Technology, Wroclaw, Poland
e-mail: Ngoc-Thanh.Nguyen@pwr.edu.pl

Jun Wang, The Chinese University of Hong Kong, Shatin, Hong Kong
e-mail: jwang@mae.cuhk.edu.hk

More information about this series at http://www.springer.com/series/11156

M. N. Hoda · Naresh Chauhan
S. M. K. Quadri · Praveen Ranjan Srivastava
Editors

Software Engineering

Proceedings of CSI 2015

 Springer

Editors
M. N. Hoda
Bharati Vidyapeeth's Institute of Computer
 Applications and Management
 (BVICAM)
New Delhi, Delhi
India

Naresh Chauhan
Department of Computer Engineering
YMCAUST
Faridabad, Haryana
India

S. M. K. Quadri
Department of Computer Science
University of Kashmir
Srinagar, Jammu and Kashmir
India

Praveen Ranjan Srivastava
Department of Information Technology
 and Systems
Indian Institute of Management Rohtak
Rohtak, Haryana
India

ISSN 2194-5357   ISSN 2194-5365 (electronic)
Advances in Intelligent Systems and Computing
ISBN 978-981-10-8847-6   ISBN 978-981-10-8848-3 (eBook)
https://doi.org/10.1007/978-981-10-8848-3

Library of Congress Control Number: 2018940631

This Springer imprint is published by the registered company Springer Nature Singapore Pte Ltd.
part of Springer Nature
The registered company address is: 152 Beach Road, #21-01/04 Gateway East, Singapore 189721,
Singapore

Preface

The last decade has witnessed remarkable changes in IT industry, virtually in all domains. The 50th Annual Convention, CSI-2015, on the theme "Digital Life" was organized as a part of CSI@50, by CSI at Delhi, the national capital of the country, during December 2–5, 2015. Its concept was formed with an objective to keep ICT community abreast of emerging paradigms in the areas of computing technologies and more importantly looking at its impact on the society.

Information and Communication Technology (ICT) comprises of three main components: infrastructure, services, and product. These components include the Internet, infrastructure-based/infrastructure-less wireless networks, mobile terminals, and other communication mediums. ICT is gaining popularity due to rapid growth in communication capabilities for real-time-based applications. New user requirements and services entail mechanisms for enabling systems to intelligently process speech- and language-based input from human users. CSI-2015 attracted over 1500 papers from researchers and practitioners from academia, industry, and government agencies, from all over the world, thereby making the job of the Programme Committee extremely difficult. After a series of tough review exercises by a team of over 700 experts, 565 papers were accepted for presentation in CSI-2015 during the 3 days of the convention under ten parallel tracks. The Programme Committee, in consultation with Springer, the world's largest publisher of scientific documents, decided to publish the proceedings of the presented papers, after the convention, in ten topical volumes, under ASIC series of the Springer, as detailed hereunder:

1. Volume # 1: ICT Based Innovations
2. Volume # 2: Next Generation Networks
3. Volume # 3: Nature Inspired Computing
4. Volume # 4: Speech and Language Processing for Human-Machine Communications
5. Volume # 5: Sensors and Image Processing
6. Volume # 6: Big Data Analytics

7. Volume # 7: Systems and Architecture
8. Volume # 8: Cyber Security
9. Volume # 9: Software Engineering
10. Volume # 10: Silicon Photonics & High Performance Computing

We are pleased to present before you the proceedings of Volume # 9 on "Software Engineering." The title on "Software Engineering" aims at informing the readers about state of the art of software engineering by publishing high-quality papers that represent results of consolidated research and innovations in software engineering and related areas. It helps the practitioners, researchers, and academicians understand the issues involved in designing, developing, evolving, and validating complex software systems. It provides excellent coverage for developing professional careers in software engineering.

The title "Software Engineering" also provides insights into various research issues such as software reliability, verification and validation, security, extensibility, model and component-based development, software process models and process-driven systems, and human–computer collaborative systems.

By taking above point of view, this volume is published, which would be beneficial for researchers of this domain.

The volume includes scientific, original, and high-quality papers presenting novel research, ideas, and explorations of new vistas in domains like component-based software engineering, knowledge-based software engineering, agile methodologies, CASE tools. The aim of this volume is to provide a stimulating forum for sharing knowledge and results in model, methodology, and implementations of speech and language processing tools. Its authors are researchers and experts of these domains. This volume is designed to bring together researchers and practitioners from academia and industry to focus on extending the understanding and establishing new collaborations in these areas. It is the outcome of the hard work of the editorial team, who have relentlessly worked with the authors and steered up the same to compile this volume. It will be useful source of reference for the future researchers in this domain. Under the CSI-2015 umbrella, we received over 300 papers for this volume, out of which 70 papers are being published, after a rigorous review processes, carried out in multiple cycles.

On behalf of organizing team, it is a matter of great pleasure that CSI-2015 has received an overwhelming response from various professionals from across the country. The organizers of CSI-2015 are thankful to the members of *Advisory Committee, Programme Committee, and Organizing Committee* for their all-round guidance, encouragement, and continuous support. We express our sincere gratitude to the learned *Keynote Speakers* for support and help extended to make this event a grand success. Our sincere thanks are also due to our *Review Committee Members* and the *Editorial Board* for their untiring efforts in reviewing the manuscripts, giving suggestions and valuable inputs for shaping this volume. We hope that all the participated delegates will be benefitted academically and wish them for their future endeavors.

We also take the opportunity to thank the entire team from Springer, who have worked tirelessly and made the publication of the volume a reality. Last but not least, we thank the team from Bharati Vidyapeeth's Institute of Computer Applications and Management (BVICAM), New Delhi, for their untiring support, without which the compilation of this huge volume would not have been possible.

New Delhi, India   M. N. Hoda
Faridabad, India   Naresh Chauhan
Srinagar, India   S. M. K. Quadri
Rohtak, India   Praveen Ranjan Srivastava
December 2017

The Organization of CSI-2015

Chief Patron

Padmashree Dr. R. Chidambaram, Principal Scientific Advisor, Government of India

Patrons

Prof. S. V. Raghavan, Department of Computer Science, IIT Madras, Chennai
Prof. Ashutosh Sharma, Secretary, Department of Science and Technology, Ministry of Science of Technology, Government of India

Chair, Programme Committee

Prof. K. K. Aggarwal, Founder Vice Chancellor, GGSIP University, New Delhi

Secretary, Programme Committee

Prof. M. N. Hoda, Director, Bharati Vidyapeeth's Institute of Computer Applications and Management (BVICAM), New Delhi

Advisory Committee

Padma Bhushan Dr. F. C. Kohli, Co-Founder, TCS
Mr. Ravindra Nath, CMD, National Small Industries Corporation, New Delhi
Dr. Omkar Rai, Director General, Software Technological Parks of India (STPI), New Delhi

Contents

About the Editors

Prof. M. N. Hoda is a Professor of Computer Science and Director of BVICAM, New Delhi. He has over 22 years of academic experience in different capacities. Prior to joining the academic world, he initially worked in the corporate sector as a Software Engineer. He is an expert member of several board-level committees of DST, CSIR and MHRD, and various universities. His current areas of research are Information System Audits, Software Engineering, Computer Networks, Artificial Intelligence, ICTs and Innovative Pedagogies for 21st Century Teaching Learning Systems. He is a Senior Member of IEEE, CSI, IE(I), ISTE, ISCA and ACM, and a fellow of IETE.

Prof. Naresh Chauhan is a Professor and Chairman in the Department of Computer Engineering at YMCA University of Science and Technology, Faridabad (India). He received his Ph.D. (Computer Engineering) from MD University, Rohtak; his M.Tech. (Information Technology) from GGSIP University, New Delhi; and his B.Tech. (Computer Engineering) from NIT, Kurukshetra. He has 23 years of experience in education and the industry. Previously, he served at Bharat Electronics Ltd and Motorola India Ltd. His research interests include Internet Technologies, Software Engineering, Software Testing, and Real-Time Systems. He has published two books on Software Testing and Operating Systems from Oxford University Press, India.

Prof. S. M. K. Quadri is a Professor and Head of the Department of Computer Science, University of Kashmir, Srinagar. He received his master's degree from Aligarh Muslim University (AMU) and his M.Tech. in Computer Applications from the Indian School of Mines (ISM), Dhanbad. He completed his doctorate in Computer Science at the University of Kashmir, Srinagar. He is a widely travelled researcher and a member of many prestigious national-level committees of India, e.g., NAAC, AICTE, and CSI. He has published many research papers in Elsevier and Emerald journals and for IEEE conferences. His main research interests are Software Testing and Reliability Engineering.

Dr. Praveen Ranjan Srivastava is an Assistant Professor and Head of the Department (Area Chair) in the Information Technology and Systems Group at the Indian Institute of Management (IIM), Rohtak, India. He is currently pursuing research in the area of Software Engineering and Management using novel nature-inspired techniques. His primary research areas are Software Testing, Data Analytics, Quality Management, Expert Systems, and Decision Science. He has published more than 120 research papers in various leading international journals.

A Multi-agent Framework for Context-Aware Dynamic User Profiling for Web Personalization

Aarti Singh and Anu Sharma

Abstract Growing volume of information on World Wide Web has made relevant information retrieval a difficult task. Customizing the information according to the user interest has become a need of the hour. Personalization aims to solve many associated problems in current Web. However, keeping an eye on user's behavior manually is a difficult task. Moreover, user interests change with the passage of time. So, it is necessary to create a user profile accurately and dynamically for better personalization solutions. Further, the automation of various tasks in user profiling is highly desirable considering large size and high intensity of users involved. This work presents an agent-based framework for dynamic user profiling for personalized Web experience. Our contribution in this work is the development of a novel agent-based technique for maintaining long-term and short-term user interests along with context identification. A novel agent-based approach for dynamic user profiling for Web personalization has also been proposed. The proposed work is expected to provide an automated solution for dynamic user profile creation.

Keywords Context aware · Dynamic · Multi-agents · User profiling
Web personalization

1 Introduction

Recent years have seen an exponential increase in size of World Wide Web and thereby led to many bottlenecks in accessing the required and relevant material from the pool of available information. Web personalization (WP) offers a solution to the information overload problem in current Web by providing the users with a personalized experience considering their interest, behavior, and context [1]. Thus, there is

A. Singh · A. Sharma (✉)
MMICT&BM, MMU, Ambala, India
e-mail: anu@iasri.res.in

A. Singh
e-mail: Singh2208@gmail.com

© Springer Nature Singapore Pte Ltd. 2019
M. N. Hoda et al. (eds.), *Software Engineering*, Advances in Intelligent Systems and Computing 731, https://doi.org/10.1007/978-981-10-8848-3_1

1

an increasing demand to devise adaptive techniques of Web personalization which may analyze user interests from his/her Web Surfing Behavior (WSB). However, considering the size of WWW and number of users accessing Internet, it is really hard to keep an eye on every user's behavior on Internet manually. Moreover, an individual's interests and requirements are major contributing factors toward his/her WSB and both these factors keep on changing with difference of time span.

An individual's interests may be classified as long-term interests (LTIs) and short-term interests (STIs). LTI reflects user's personality or may be a part of his/her professional profile and do not change rapidly, e.g., interest of a person in a particular sport, particular type of art, or research interest in a particular field. STIs are generated from dynamic requirements or may result from changing moods of a person such as watching movie, tour and travel plans, shopping for goods or accessory. Thus, any WP technique must focus on dynamic mechanism to capture user behavior so as to generate a digital user profile accurately. Some other important issues related to user profiling are accuracy, inference/reasoning of user interest, scalability, privacy, and user model interoperability [2].

User modeling (UM) is referred to as gathering and exploiting the information about the individual user. UM consists of various tasks described in detail in Sect. 2. Further, the automation of these tasks is highly desired considering large size and high intensity of users involved. Intelligent agents may be deployed for this purpose, since they may work autonomously, can monitor their environment continuously without being tired, and can learn user behavior. A multi-agent-based approach Web content mining based on semantic technology has been applied by Singh [3]. Further, a study to identify the scope of agents in Web usage mining has been undertaken by Singh and Mishra [4]. This provided us the motivation for the present work. This work presents an agent-based framework for dynamic user profiling for personalized Web experience. This paper is structured as follows: Sect. 2 elaborates user modeling techniques along with its inherent challenges. Section 3 presents the literature review with problem identification. Section 4 presents proposed framework, and Sect. 5 elaborates detailed working of framework along with detailed algorithmic procedure for each agent. Section 6 describes the flow diagram, and Sect. 7 concludes the work and presents future research directions.

2 User Modeling Techniques

UM is referred to as gathering and exploiting the information about the individual user. Information for creating user profile may be collected explicitly by asking the user to provide information or implicitly by observing the user behavior [5]. User profiles that may adapt themselves to change in user interests and preferences are called as dynamic user profile, whereas a static profile contains information that does not change with the time. There are three phases of user profile construction as given below.

2.1 Information Gathering

This phase consists of mainly gathering the information about the Web user. Two methods for collecting information about the user are explicit and implicit.

Explicit Information Collection

This deals with asking for user input and feedback for gathering knowledge about the user. This is an accurate method for identifying the user interest items. This method requires the explicit user intervention for specifying the complete interest and preferences. Another shortcoming of explicit user profile is that after some time the profile becomes outdated. Yahoo Personalized Portal explicitly asks the user for specifying his preferences and then customizes the home page layout as per interests of the user.

Implicit Information Collection

This deals with observing the user activities to identify the user information without explicitly asking for it. Thus, it removes the burden from user to enter the information. Various implicit information collection techniques are browsing cache, proxy server, browser agents, desktop agents, Web logs, and search logs. Most of these techniques are client-side based, except Web and search logs which are based on server side [6].

2.2 User Profile Representation

Some of the important techniques for representing user profiles are sets of weighted keywords, semantic networks, or weighted concepts, or association rules:

Keyword-Based Profile

User profiles are most commonly represented as sets of keywords. These can be automatically extracted from Web documents or directly provided by the user. Numeric weights are assigned to each keyword which shows the degree of user's interests in that topic [7, 8].

Semantic Network Profiles

Keyword-based profiles suffer from polysemy problem. This problem is solved by using weighted semantic network in which each node represents a concept [9].

Concept Profiles

Concept-based profiles are similar to semantic network-based profile. However, in concept-based profiles, the nodes represent abstract topics considered interesting to the user, rather than specific words or sets of related words. Concept profiles are also similar to keyword profiles in that often they are represented as vectors of weighted features, but the features represent concepts rather than words or sets of words. Mechanisms have been developed to express user's interest in each topic, e.g., assigning a numerical value, or weight, associated with each topic [10].

2.3   User Profile Construction

Various machine learning techniques are applied on collected information to build user profile [11]. Keyword-based profiles are constructed by extracting the keywords from the Web pages in search histories. Each extracted word is also assigned a weight which shows its relative importance with respect to interest. A vector of extracted keyword thus represents the user interest. Moukas [8] have extracted the top few keywords implicitly from WSB and used single keyword for each of user interest. But this approach could not represent the true user behavior as multiple user interests are represented as single vector. So, in another approach, a user profile is represented as multiple vectors with each vector corresponding to a separate user interest category. Number of user's interests to be included in the profile are either specified as fixed number or by using a similarity threshold. One keyword vector per interest instead of single keyword is represented by Chen and Sycara [7]. This is a more accurate method of user profile construction.

Semantic net user profiles are created by adding the keywords to a network of nodes. This profile is more accurate than keyword-based as it eliminates the ambiguity and synonymy in natural language. Concept-based profiles use available taxonomies to represent weighted concept hierarchies. These profiles are constructed by mapping the extracted keywords to the existing concepts in taxonomy. If the same concept is shown again, then its weight is increased by one.

3   Related Work

An extensive study for identifying scope, applicability, and state of the art in applying semantics to WP is undertaken by Singh and Anand [12]. Semantically enhanced and ontological profiles are found [13–15] more appropriate for representing the user profile. Ontological profile allows powerful representational medium along with associated inference mechanism for user profile creation. A brief review of work on semantically enhanced and ontological dynamic user profiles is given below.

A generic ontology-based user modeling architecture (OntobUM) for knowledge management had been proposed by Razmerita et al. [16]. Ontology-based user modeling architecture has three different ontologies namely user, domain, and log ontologies. User ontology structures the different characteristics of users and their relationships. Domain ontology defines the domain and application-specific concepts and their relationships. Log ontology defines the semantics of the user interaction with the system.

An ontology-based user profile creation by unobtrusively monitoring user behavior and relevance feedback has been proposed by Middleton et al. [14]. The cold start problem is addressed by using external ontology to bootstrap the recommendation system. This work considers only is-a type relationship in ontology and may be further extended to include other types of relationships in ontology. Further, there is scope for using external software agents and adding contextual information in task modeling. The techniques for the improvement of ontological user profile have been investigated by Trajkova and Gauch [17]. The authors investigated that ranking the concepts in the profiles by number of documents assigned to them rather than by accumulated weights provides better profile accuracy. The ordering of the concepts was also considered along with detecting non-relevant concepts and pruning them from the profile. But, this work does not include user's contextual and temporal information in user profile. In an approach, user context is modeled by using ontological profiles in Web search. The existing concepts in domain ontology are assigned implicitly derived interest scores [18]. A spreading activation algorithm has been used for maintaining and incrementally updating the weights based on the user's ongoing behavior. This approach may be further improved by observing the ontological profile over time for ensuring the true requirements of user as seen from interest scores. A dynamic model for user modeling by applying clustering techniques on Web usage data off-line has been proposed by Saeed et al. [19]. This model is adjusted periodically through new transaction and thus solves the problem of maintaining the accuracy of user model. But this does not use software agents and ontology.

A hybrid approach is adopted by Bhowmick et al. [13] by considering the features of static and dynamic user profiling techniques. Static user profile specifies the user's interest in a much focused manner, and dynamic user profiling adds the feature of adaptability into it. But this approach is limited to the school curriculum-related topics and also does not consider context and location while generating recommendations. Sosnovsky and Dicheva [15] had combined together research from two different fields—user modeling and Web ontology—to demon-strate how recent semantic trends in Web development can be combined with the modern technologies of user modeling. They have also highlighted the use of software agents and ontology. Users' behavior and characterization of users' needs for context-aware applications had been analyzed by Skillen et al. [20]. The cre-ation of a user profile ontology for context-aware application personalization within mobile environments was described. An approach for personalizing the Web using user profile ontology has been proposed by Vigneshwari and Aramudhan [21]. These ontologies are created dynamically using the server log file through classi-fication and clustering techniques. A global ontology is also created by identifying the word pairs that have occurred in most of the documents. An automatic mech-anism for ontology creation which is found useful in WP was proposed by Singh and Anand [12]. A multi-agent-based knowledge-oriented personalized search engine framework was suggested by Middleton [14].

Some other works on generating user profile dynamically are given by Hawalah and Fasli [18], Li et al. [22], Vigneshwari and Aramudhan [21]. A strategy for maintaining the LTI and STI of the user through user topic tree and Page-History Buffer (PHB) had been proposed by Li et al. [22]. Although the study considers the dynamic adaption of user profile, it does not use software agents to automate the tasks in user modeling. A multi-agent approach to solve this has been proposed by

Hawalah and Fasli [18] for building a dynamic user profile that is capable of learning and adapting to user behavior. But, it does not consider the contextual information in recommendations. An agent-based Web search personalization approach using dynamic user profile has been proposed by Li et al. [22]. The user query is optimized using user's profile preferences and the query-related synonyms from the WordNet ontology. The search results obtained from a set of syntactic search engines are combined to produce the final personalized results. However, this approach is limited to Web search personalization. In another work, Woerndl and Groh [23] has proposed a framework for multi-agent-based personalized context-aware information retrieval from distributed sources considering the privacy and access control. An agent-based interface is proposed which optimizes the user query using WordNet and user profile preferences and fetches the personalized search results from various search engines like Google, Yahoo. Although it includes the contextual information, it does not describe the detailed implementation of various agents and also does not include temporal aspects in context.

A critical analysis of the literature reveals that many research attempts have been made in using software agents and ontology for dynamic profile creation considering contextual information. Some of these studies are oriented toward search results personalization, while generic UM approaches do not consider contextual information. So, there is a need to consider some issues like adding the contextual information for creating dynamic user profile efficiently. This work aims to propose a framework for agent-oriented context-aware dynamic user profiling for personalized recommendations for the user. Our contribution in this work may be summarized as follows:

1. A novel agent-based technique has been developed for maintaining LTI and STI at client-side layer. User activities at his desktop are monitored by an agent and then incorporated in STI.
2. A novel agent-based approach has been developed for user context identification at client-side layer.
3. A novel agent-based approach has been developed for dynamic user profiling for WP.

The next section describes the proposed framework in detail.

4 Proposed Framework for Multi-agent-Based Dynamic User Profiling

The core idea for user profiling is based on the assumption that some characteristics of individual user affect the usefulness of recommendations. This framework considers three main dimensions of user modeling as given below:

- *Background*: This includes the basic information about the user.
- *Interest directed user information*: Information about multiple sites browsed and search queries by user helps in determining user's interest dynamically.
- *Context*: Spatial and temporal context plays an important role in generating useful recommendations to users. A user may choose different recommendations at different locations at different points of time in a day.

Various components of this approach are distributed and autonomous, which is the motivation behind using intelligent agents in it. These agents can communicate asynchronously and work simultaneously without interfering with other agents. This framework comprises of two layers namely client-side layer and server-side layer for collecting various types of data useful for profile creation. These layers work on client side and server side, respectively. These help in the automation of complex and tedious processes involved in user profiling and in efficient execution of the various tasks with reduced computation time. The high-level architecture of the proposed work is given in Fig. 1.

Three agents, at client side, gather the information about user namely user context identification agent (UCIA), user behavior tracking agent (UBTA), and user desktop agent (UDA). Detailed working of these agents is given in Sect. 5. These agents collect the data, and this information is sent to the agents working at server side.

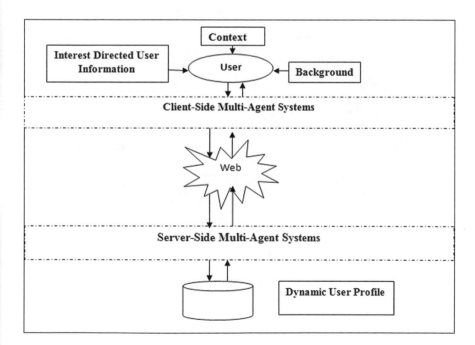

Fig. 1 High-level architecture of proposed framework

There are three agents working at server side namely user query analyzer agent (UQAA), profile manager agent (PMA), and cluster agent (CA). Detailed working and description of these agents are given in Sect. 5. These agents process the explicit and implicit information about the user and apply text processing and clustering techniques for generating and storing user profile. They also apply the semantic technologies for user profiling and generating better recommendations.

The next section explains in detail the flow of information, purpose of each agent, and their algorithms.

5 Detailed Description of Framework

The proposed multi-agent framework comprises of three agents at client side and three agents at server side as shown in Fig. 2

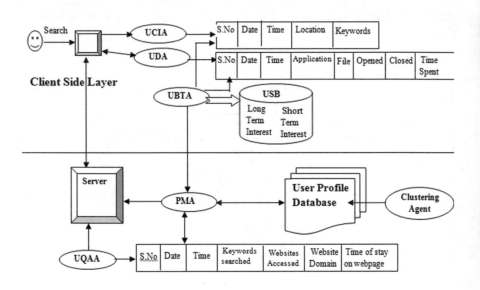

Server Side Layer

Fig. 2 Detailed view of architecture of proposed framework

5.1   Client-Side Agents

Various agents operating at client side are as follows:

- **UCIA**: Temporal information about the user is collected from system date and time settings. It receives the location data of the user from current Wi-fi/IP addresses utilizing the available location databases. Whenever the user enters a query in browser and selects the context, this agent copies this query for later analysis. It maintains a table containing keywords searched, context of search along with date and time of search.
- **UDA**: This agent is responsible for monitoring the user activities on desktop. It monitors the applications and files opened and used by user. It maintains a list of this usage along with time spent on them by the user, in a specified folder to maintain user privacy. This helps in observing the potential interest areas of the user.
- **UBTA**: This agent is responsible for summarizing user behavior and creating user profile based on short-term and long-term interests of the user. For this, it analyzes and processes tables maintained by UCIA and UDA. This agent also estimates the user's interest in Web pages by considering the five parameters namely text selection, text tracking, link clicking, link pointing, and scrolling. Detailed procedure can be seen from [24]. Filtered Web pages are then classified as STI and LTI based on their usage occasionally or daily. This agent is also responsible for communicating user's STI and LTI to server-side agent for their incorporation in user profile.

5.2   Server-Side Agents

- **PMA**: This agent is responsible for managing dynamic profile of the user by collaborating with UBTA of particular user. It receives LT and ST interests of a user from UBTA and maintains it in its database. Further, it also analyzes online WSB of the user, recorded on server side by UQAA, and keeps user profile updated.
- **UQAA**: This agent analyzes keywords of queries received from a particular user or IP address. It also saves the Web pages scrolled by the user using search engine or by requesting particular URL, along with time spent on each page. It also records hyperlinks accessed from one page to the other.
- **CA**: This agent is responsible for clustering the users based on similar interest areas so that similar recommendations may be provided to them. It works on the user profile database maintained by the PMA.

The algorithms for various agents involved in the framework are given in Figs. 3, 4, 5, 6, 7 and 8.

```
User_Context_Identification_Agent()
Input: User Client Machine
Output: Location, Temporal and search keywords database for user -
USER_CONTEXT
{
After time t elapsed
Activate ();
Scans the SYSTEM_TIME;
Temp= GET the Temporal Parameters;
Scan the IP Address/WiFi Network;
loc=GET the Location of the user;
keyword= Extract Keywords entered in search;
Insert into USER_CONTEXT values (Temp, loc, keyword)
Return USER_CONTEXT;
}
```

Fig. 3 User context identification agent

```
User_Desktop_Agent()
Input: Set D(F) = {F₁, F₂ ..Fₙ} Where n is the total number of files
in the folder
Output: A database of user activities at client-side - USER_INTEREST
{
After time t elapsed
Activate();
For each Fi in D(F)
  Fdate=SYSTEM_DATE;
  FTime=SYSTEM_TIME;
  FType=Find File Type;
  FName= Actual File Name;
  FOpen= Number of times the file is opened;
  FClose= Number of times the file is closed;
  FTimeSpent=Time Spent on File;
  Insert into USER_INTEREST values (Fdate, FTime, FType, FName,
FOpen, FClose, FTimeSpent);
End For
Return(USER_INTEREST);
}
```

Fig. 4 User desktop agent

```
User_Behaviour_Tracking_Agent()
Input: User Browser Cache
Output: Long term and short term interests based on user browsing ac-
tivities
{
    After time t elapsed
    Activate();
    Upload browser cache;
    Scan the browser cache;
    Until the end of Browser cache
    {
For each visited site
{
Find Date, Time, URL, Time_Open, Time_Close, Time Spent;
Insert into USER_INTEREST values (Date, Time, URL, Time_Open,
Time_Close, Time Spent);
}
    }
    Open Table  USER_INTEREST;
    For Each Record R in   Table  USER_INTEREST
    If (application="Web Page"
Bool  flag = Call IsInteresting(R);
          If flag = true then
Store R in Table TEMP_WEB; //This a temporary file having same struc-
ture as USER_INTEREST
 Else
Store R in Table TEMP_FILE; //This a temporary file having same struc-
ture as USER_INTEREST
End If
    End For
For Each Record R in   Table TEMP_WEB and TEMP_FILE;
   HitCounter =Find the number of times a web page is accessed in a
period;
          Fetch  MetaData associated with web page
        String S=MetaData and Title;
        Ts = Find words in S;
 If (HitCounter >10) then
     Insert into WSB(LongTermInterest) values Ts;
          Elseif (HitCounter<7 and HitCounter>4)
     Insert into WSB(ShortTermInterest) values Ts;
        else
     Delete Ts from WSB for given user;
          End If
 End For
 }
 Return(WSB);
}
```

Fig. 5 User behavior tracking agent

```
IsInteresting()
Input: Web Page
Output: Yes if interested and no otherwise
{
  Ws = 6.0;
  Find t;  // t is time spent in tracing;
  Wt = 1*t; Wc = 10; Wp = 6.9;
  Calculate the scrolling speed v;
  V1 = 2400; V2 =4800; V3 = 9600;  V4 = 14400;
  If ( v=0)
    Δ = 0;
  Elseif (v>V1 and v<V2) then
    Δ = 0.004 * v-9.2
  Elseif (v>V3 and v<V4)
    Δ = -0.001*v +14.8;
  Wf = Ws+Wt+Wc+Wp+Δ;
}
```

Fig. 6 Algorithm for checking user's degree of interest on Web page

```
User_Query_Analyzer_Agent()
Input: Web log of visited sites/pages
Output: Database of User Interested Web Site along with keywords
searched - USER_QUERY
{
After time t elapsed
Activate();
For each visited web page W in Web Server Logs
{
Find Date, Time, Keywords, URL, Domain,Time Spent;
Extract Meta Data and Title from Web page;
 Insert into USER_QUERY values (Date, Time, Keywords, URL, Domain,
Time Spent);
}
Return USER_QUERY;
}
```

Fig. 7 User query analyzer agent

```
Profile_Manager_Agent()
Input: Short Term and Long Term User Interest from client and server
side
Output:  User Profile Database Creation
{
  Receive LT and ST interest from WSB and USER_QUERY Database;
  Receives the USER_CONTEXT from UCIA;
  Create and update USER_PROFILE database;
  }
```

Fig. 8 Profile manager agent

Fig. 9 Flow diagram of the proposed framework

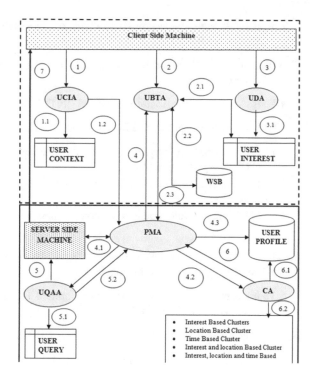

6 Flow Diagram of the Proposed Work

The flow diagram given in Fig. 9 illustrates the working of the proposed framework. UCIA, UDA, and UBTA work simultaneously on client side to gather the information about user's contexts and interests periodically.

1. UCIA accesses the client machine and is responsible for performing two tasks:

   1.1 It extracts the time, location, and searched keywords and stores them in table.
   1.2 It passes this information to PMA which stores the contextual information in user profile database.

2. UBTA accesses the client machine to collect the browsing history of user. It performs the following tasks:

   2.1 It extracts the various parameters from browser cache and stores them into USER_INTEREST table.
   2.2 It accesses the USER_INTEREST table and identifies the user degree of interest in Web page/file by using isInteresting() function. It also identifies the STI and LTI from USER_INTEREST table and prepares a database WSB for storing short-term and long-term interests.

2.3 It sends the database WSB to PMA after receiving a request from PMA to access WSB.

3. UDA accesses the files in a specified folder in client machine and extracts various parameters.

   3.1 It stores this information in USER_INTEREST table.

4. PMA sends a request to UBTA to access WSB.

   4.1 PMA sends a request to UQAA to access the information from USERY_QUERY table.
   4.2 PMA sends the USER_PROFILE database to CA after receiving a request from CA.
   4.3 PMA creates and updates a database named USER_PROFILE for storing user profile.

5. UQAA accesses server-side machine to access Web server logs. It parses the information contained in the log files.

   5.1 It stores this information in a table named USER_QUERY.
   5.2 It sends the USER_QUERY to PMA.

6. CA sends a request to PMA for accessing the USER_PROFILE database.

   6.1 After its request is authenticated, it is given access to USER_PROFILE database.
   6.2 Using USER_PROFILE database, CA creates the clusters of users on various parameters like time, location, and interests.

7. Recommendations are given from server side to client considering STI, LTI, and other contextual parameters.

7   Conclusion and Future Work

This study proposes a framework for multi-agent-based dynamic user profile generation considering contextual information. The proposed framework uses a number of autonomous software agents for automating the various tasks in profile generation. Detailed algorithms for working of each of the agents have been described along with flow of information between system components. Use of automated agents makes the proposed system more efficient than other available methods. The current work may be further extended by comparing and specifying various mechanisms for detailed representation of the user profile. Further, the actual implementation of the framework can be undertaken in future research.

References

1. Singh, A.: Wisdom web: the WWW generation next. Int J. Advancements Technol. **3**(3), 123–126 (2012)
2. Jammalamadaka, K., Srinivas, I.V.: A survey on ontology based web personalization. Int. J. Res. Eng. Technol. **2**(10), 163–167 (2013)
3. Singh, A.: Agent based framework for semantic web content mining. Int. J. Advancements Technol. **3**(2), 108–113 (2012)
4. Singh, A., Mishra, R.: Exploring web usage mining with scope of agent technology. Int. J. Eng. Sci. Technol. **4**(10), 4283–4289 (2012)
5. Carmagnola, F., Cena, F., Gena, C.: User model interoperability: a survey. User Model. User-Adap. Inter. **21**(3), 285–331 (2011)
6. Kelly, D., Teevan, J.: Implicit feedback for inferring user preference: a bibliography. ACM SIGIR Forum **37**(2), 18–28 (2003)
7. Chen, L., Sycara, K.: WebMate: a personal agent for browsing and searching. In: Proceedings of the 2nd International Conference on Autonomous Agents, Minneapolis/St. Paul, 9–13 May, pp. 132–139. ACM Press, New York (1998)
8. Moukas, A.: Amalthaea: information discovery and filtering using a multiagent evolving ecosystem. Appl. Artif. Intel. **11**(5), 437–457 (1997)
9. Minio, M., Tasso, C.: User modeling for information filtering on INTERNET services: exploiting an extended version of the UMT shell. In: UM96 Workshop on User Modeling for Information Filtering on the WWW; Kailua-Kona, Hawaii, 2–5 Jan 1996
10. Bloedorn, E., Mani, I., MacMillan, T.R.: Machine learning of user profiles: representational issues. In: Proceedings of AAAI 96 from Portland, 4–8 Aug, Oregon, vol. 1, pp. 433–438 (1996)
11. Gauch, S., Speretta, M., Chandramouli, A., Micarelli, A.: User profiles for personalized information access. In: Brusilovsky, P., Kobsa, A., Nejdl, W. (eds.) The Adaptive Web. LNCS 4321, pp. 54–89. Springer, Berlin, Heidelberg (2007)
12. Singh, A., Anand, P.: Automatic domain ontology construction mechanism. In: Proceedings of IEEE International Conference on Recent Advances in Intelligent Computing Systems (RAICS) from 19–21 Dec, pp. 304–309. IEEE Press, Trivandrum, Kerala, India (2013)
13. Bhowmick, P.K., Sarkar, S., Basu, A.: Ontology based user modeling for personalized information access. Int. J. Comput. Sci. Appl. **7**(1), 1–22 (2010)
14. Middleton, S.E., Shadbolt, N.R., Roure, D.C.D.: Ontological user profiling in recommender systems. ACM Trans. Inf. Syst. **22**(1), 54–88 (2004)
15. Sosnovsky, S., Dicheva, D.: Ontological technologies for user modelling. Int. J. Metadata Semant. Ontol. **5**(1), 32–71 (2010)
16. Razmerita, L., Angehrn, A., Maedche, A.: Ontology based user modeling for knowledge management systems. In: Brusilovsky, P., Corbett, A., Rosis, F.D. (eds.) User Modeling 2003. LNCS, vol. 2702, pp. 213–217. Springer, Berlin, Heidelberg (2003)
17. Trajkova, J., Gauch, S.: Improving ontology-based user profiles. In: Proceedings of RIAO 2004 on 26–28 Apr, pp. 380–389, France (2004)
18. Hawalah, A., Fasli, M.: A multi-agent system using ontological user profiles for dynamic user modelling, In: Proceedings of International Conferences on Web Intelligence and Intelligent Agent Technology, pp. 430–437, IEEE Press, Washington (2011)
19. Aghabozorgi, S.R., Wah, T.Y.: Dynamic modeling by usage data for personalization systems, In: Proceedings of 13th International Conference on Information Visualization, pp. 450–455. IEEE Press, Barcelona (2009)
20. Skillen, K.L., Chen, L., Nugent, C.D., Donnelly, M.P., Burns, W., Solheim, I.: Ontological user profile modeling for context-aware application personalization. In: Bravo, J., López-de-Ipiña, D., Moya, F. (eds.) Ubiquitous Computing and Ambient Intelligence. LNCS, vol. 7656, pp. 261–268. Springer, Berlin, Heidelberg (2012)

21. Vigneshwari, S., Aramudhan, M.: A novel approach for personalizing the web using user profiling ontologies. In: IEEE Fourth International Conference on Advanced Computing ICoAC, pp. 1–4. IEEE Press, Chennai (2012)
22. Li, L., Yang, Z., Wang, B., Kitsuregawa, M.: Dynamic adaptation strategies for long-term and short-term user profile to personalize search. In: Dong, G., Lin, X., Wang, W., Yang, Y., Yu, J.X. (eds.) Advances in Data and Web Management. LNCS, vol. 4505, pp. 228–240. Springer Berlin, Heidelberg (2007)
23. Woerndl, W., Groh, G.: A proposal for an agent-based architecture for context-aware personalization in the semantic web. In: Proceeding of IJCAI Workshop Multi-agent information retrieval and recommender systems, Edinburg, UK-IJCAI (2005)
24. Hijikata, Y.: Estimating a user's degree of interest in a page during web browsing. In: Proceedings of IEEE SMC '99 Conference, vol. 4, pp. 105–110. IEEE Press, Tokyo (1999)
25. Moawad, I.F., Talha, H., Hosny, E., Hashim, M.: Agent-based web search personalization approach using dynamic user profile. Egypt. Inf. J. 13, 191–198 (2012)
26. Sieg, A., Mobasher, B., Burke, R.: Learning ontology-based user profiles: a semantic approach to personalized web search. IEEE Intel. Inf. Bull. 8(1), 7–18 (2007)
27. Singh, A., Alhadidi, B.: Knowledge oriented personalized search engine: a step towards wisdom web. Int. J. Comput. Appl. 76(8), 1–9 (2013)
28. Singh, A., Sharma, A., Dey, N.: Semantics and agents oriented web personalization: state of the art. Int. J. Serv. Sci. Manag. Eng. Technol. 6(2), 35–49 (2015)
29. Yahoo Personalized Portal. http://my.yahoo.com/

Implementation of Equivalence of Deterministic Finite-State Automation and Non-deterministic Finite-State Automaton in Acceptance of Type 3 Languages Using Programming Code

Rinku, Chetan Sharma, Ajay Kumar Rangra, Manish Kumar and Aman Madaan

Abstract An automaton is used where information and materials are transformed, transmitted, and utilized for performing some processes without direct involvement of human. A finite automaton (both deterministic and non-deterministic) is used to recognize a formal regular language. In this paper, we will represent the acceptance of a formal regular language (Type 3 according to Noam Chomsky) by both deterministic and non-deterministic automaton. We are using a simple algorithm to implement finite-state automaton in a middle-level language and demonstrate that deterministic finite-state automation provides a best and unique solution in comparison to non-deterministic finite-state automaton. More important that if a problem solved by Non-deterministic finite state automation can be easily solved using equivalent deterministic finite state automaton.

Keywords Finite-state automaton · Formal regular language · Deterministic Non-deterministic · Equivalence

Rinku (✉) · C. Sharma · A. K. Rangra · M. Kumar · A. Madaan
Chitkara University, Kalujhinda, Himachal Pradesh, India
e-mail: rinku.cse@chitkarauniversity.edu.in

C. Sharma
e-mail: chetan.sharma@chitkarauniversity.edu.in

A. K. Rangra
e-mail: ajay.rangra@gmail.com

M. Kumar
e-mail: manish.kumar@chitkarauniversity.edu.in

A. Madaan
e-mail: amanmadaan90@gmail.com

© Springer Nature Singapore Pte Ltd. 2019
M. N. Hoda et al. (eds.), *Software Engineering*, Advances in Intelligent Systems and Computing 731, https://doi.org/10.1007/978-981-10-8848-3_2

1 Introduction

The word 'formal' means that all the rules for the language are explicitly stated in terms of what string of symbols can occur, and a formal language can be viewed as a set of all strings permitted by the rules of formation. Finite automatons are the simplest model of an automatic machine. If we see the history of designing of the automatic machines, the first calculating device was the abacus first time used in China. Abacus was used to perform some arithmetic operations like addition, multiplication on positive integers. This was the first initiation toward the designing of calculating devices. Further, we found several enhancements, and presently, we have numerous calculating devices. Today, all automatic machines are designed based on some kind of models. One great example of this machine is the computer system and finite automation are its abstract model.

Finite automaton is mainly used for modeling the reactive systems. System which changes its actions, outputs, and conditions/status in reply to reactions from within/outside it is known as reactive system. A reactive system is a situation-driven/control-driven system continuously having to react to external and/ or internal reaction. In general, finite automatons are useful models to explain dynamic behaviors of reactive systems.

Automaton (finite) consists of a finite memory called input tape, a read-only head, and a finite control. The input is written on tape, and head reads one symbol at a time on the tape and moves forward into next state and goes on until the last symbol of input string. The movement of head and transition into next state are decided by finite control. When input is read, the finite automaton decided the validity or acceptability of the input by acceptance or rejection. It does not write its output on the tape, which is a limitation of this model.

The input tape is divided into compartments, and each compartment contains 1 symbol from the input alphabets. The symbol '$' is used at the leftmost cell, and the symbol 'Ψ' is used at the rightmost cell to indicate the beginning and end of the input tape. It is similar to read-only file in a computer system, which has both beginning and end.

2 Finite Acceptors

Inputs are transformed into outputs with help of an information processing device. With a device, only two alphabets are associated: A is taken as input for communicating, and alphabet B is taken as output for receiving answers. Let us consider a device that accepts input as English sentence and outputs the corresponding sentence in French language. Once whole input is read out, then each input alphabet is processed step by step, and if after reading last alphabet of input string we reach to final state, then the output is yes and we can say A* is accepted else rejected. By the above procedure, A* is divided into two subparts: The 'true' subset is called as machine accepted language, and the 'no' subset is called as machine rejected language. The device that operates such thing is called as acceptor. The mathematical model is described below:

Finite automaton is of two types:

- *DFA*
- *NDFA.*

Deterministic finite acceptor A is explained with five tuples of information:

$A = (\Sigma, Q, S, \delta, F)$, Σ consists of a finite alphabet, a finite set Q of states, and a function: $Q \times \Sigma \rightarrow Q$, defined as the transition function and a set F of acceptance states. The set Q contains an element s and a subset F, and the set of acceptance states.

3   Algorithm to Implement DFA

DFA Algorithm:
```
     s <- s0 { start from the initial state }
     c <- next_char { get the next character from the input
string }
     while (c != eos) do { do until the end of the string }
     begin
     s <- move(s,c) { transition function }
     c <- next_char
     end
     if (s ∈ F) then { if s is an accepting state }
  return "y"      else      return "n"
```

NFA Algorithm:
```
     S <- e-closure({q0})
     c <- next_char
     while (c != eos) {
     begin
     s <- e-closure(move(S,c)) { set of all states can be ac-
cessible from a state in S by a transition on c }
     c <- next_char
     end
     if (S intersect F != 0) then { if S contains an accepting
state }   return "yes"      else      return "no"
```

4   Programming Code to Implement DFA and NFA

Programming Code for implementing DFA.

```
#include<stdio.h>
#include<conio.h>
int nlnp;
int checkfun(char,int );
int ddfa[22][22];
char p[12], dfaString1[12];
main()
{ int ndfastats, ndfafinals;
int fal[12];
int x,y,S=0,fdfa=0;
printf("NO. of states ");
scanf("%d",&Ndfastats);
printf("count of inp.");
scanf("%d",&nlnp);
printf("\n write inp.\t");
for(x=0; x<nlnp; x++)

{ printf(" %d symbols inp \t", x+1);
printf("%c",p[x]=getch()); } printf("\n\n
Enter No. of F.s of Dfa\t");
scanf("%d",&Ndfafinals);
for(x=0;x<Ndfafinals;x++){
printf("final ddfa is %d : q",x+1);
scanf("%d",&fal[x]);}
for(x=0; x<nlnp; x++)
  { for(y=0; y<Ndfastats; y++)
{printf("\n(q%d , %c ) = q",j,p[x]);
scanf("%d",&ddfa[x][y]);}}
 do{ x=0;
scanf("%s",dfaDfaString);
while(dfaDfaString[x]!='\0')
if((S=check(DfaString[x++],S))<0) break;
```

Programming Code for implementing NFA.

```
#include<stdio.h>
#include<conio.h>
IntFa[20][20][20],States1[12][12],Curr,Nf
aRow=0;
int Nfacolumn=0,Nfa_sir=0,Sc=0,ht=0,In;
char *Str;
int Nfa(char *string,int State)
 {int k3,k4;
for(k3=0;k3<=NfaRow;k3++)
{  if(*string){
Curr=Fa[State][*string-97][k3];
 if (Curr==-1)  break;
 if(Nfa(string+1,Curr))
  return 1;} else    {
  if(States1[1][k3]==-1)
  break;
if(State==States1[1][i])
return 1;}} return 0;}
main()
{ FILE *fp;
int k3,k4,k,Flag=0;
char C,hc;
fp=fopen("Nfa.txt","r");
for(k3=0;k3<2;k3++)   for(k4=0;k4<10;k4++)
States1[k3][k4]=-1; for(k3=0;k3<10;k3++)
for(k4=0;k4<10;k4++) for(k=0;k<10;k++)
Fa[k3][k4][k]=-1;
while(fscanf(fp,"%d",&In)!=EOF)
{ fscanf(fp,"%c",&C);
if(flag) { States1[Nfa_sir][Sc++]=In;
if(C=='\n') {
Nfa_sir++;   Sc=0; } }
```

```
for(x=0 ;x<Ndfafinals ;x++)

if(Fs[x] ==S)

Final7=1;

if(Final7==1)

printf("true");

else

printf("false");

getch();

printf("for another response?(U/T) ");}

while(getch()=='T');

getch();

}

  int checkfun(char Vlk,int ftr)

{   int k

; for(k=0; k<nlnp; k++)

if(Vlk==p[k])

return(ddfa[ftr][k]);

  return -1; }
```

```
else if(C=='#')

{ Flag=1;

Fa[NfaRow][Nfacolumn][ht]=In;

printf("\n
Fa[%d][%d][%d]=%d",NfaRow,Nfacolumn,ht,Fa
[NfaRow][Nfacolumn][ht]);

}else if(!Flag) {

Fa[NfaRow][Nfacolumn][ht]=In;

printf("\n
Fa[%d][%d][%d]=%d",NfaRow,Nfacolumn,ht,Fa
[NfaRow][Nfacolumn][ht]);

if(C==',') {ht++; }

else if(C=='\n')

{Nfacolumn=0; NfaRow++;  ht=0; }

else if(c!=',')

{ Nfacolumn++; ht=0; } } }

printf("\n\n enter  string : \n");

scanf("%s",Str);

if(Nfa(Str,States1[0][0]))

printf("\nString Is Accepted");

else

printf("\nString Not Accepted");

getch();

  return 0;}
```

5   Regular Languages or Type 3 Grammars

Type 3 languages are described by Type 3 grammars. The LHS of a Type 3 grammar is a single non-terminal. The RHS is empty or consists of a single terminal, or it can have a single terminal which is followed by a non-terminal. Type 3 grammars are represented by the productions A $\rightarrow$ aB or A $\rightarrow$ a. Type 3 languages are recognized using finite-state automata (FA). The following is an example of a regular grammar:

$$A \rightarrow aA \quad A \rightarrow e \quad A \rightarrow bB \quad B \rightarrow bB \quad B \rightarrow e \quad A \rightarrow c$$

6 Equivalence of NFA to DFA on Acceptance of Regular Language

```
#include <stdio.h>
#include <string.h>
#define STATES1363
#define REGSYMB120
int n_REGSYMB;
int NfA_States;
char *nFAtab1[STATES1][REGSYMB1];
int autostat;
int dFAtab[STATES1][REGSYMB1];
void put_Dfa_table(
   int tab1[][REGSYMB1],     int Nstates,
   int NREGSYMB)
   { int x, y;
for (x = 0; x < NREGSYMB; x++) printf("
%c  ", '0'+x);
printf("\n-----");
for (x = 0; x < NREGSYMB; x++) printf("---
");
for (x = 0; x < Nstates; x++) {
printf("  %c  | ", 'A'+x); /* state */
for (y = 0; y < NREGSYMB; y++)
printf("  %c  ", 'A'+tab1[x][y]);
} } /*
void init_nFA_table()
{
nFAtab1[0][0] = "12"; nFAtab1[0][1] =
"13";
nFAtab1[1][0] = "12"; nFAtab1[1][1] =
"13";
nFAtab1[2][0] = "4";   nFAtab1[2][1] = "";
nFAtab1[3][0] = "";    nFAtab1[3][1] = "4";
nFAtab1[4][0] = "4";   nFAtab1[4][1] =
"4";
nFA_states = 5;      autostat = 0;
n_REGSYMB = 2; }
void Combine_str12(char *l, char *m)
   int v = 1;
   char Stat_nxt[STATES1];
int j; strcpy(statename[0], "0");
for (x = 0; x < v; x++) {
for (y = 0; y < v_Sym; y++) { /
get_next_state(Stat_nxt, Statename[x],
nFa, n_nFa, y);
   Dfa[x][y] = ind_stat(Stat_nxt, Stat-
ename, &v);
      }   }   return v; }
```

```
{   char temporary_ddfa[STATES1],
*asdf=temporary_ddfa, *qwerty=l;
   while (*qwerty && *m) {
      if (*qwerty == *m) {
         *asdf++ = *qwerty++; m++;
      } else if (*qwerty < *m) {
         *asdf++ = *qwerty++;
      } else        *asdf++ = *m++;   }
   *asdf = '\0';
   if (*qwerty) strcat(r, qwerty);
   else if (*t) strcat(r, m);
   strcpy(l, temporary_ddfa);}
void get_next_state1(char *Stat_nxts, char
*Stat_current,*nFa[STATES1][REGSYMB1], int
n_nFa, int Symbol)
{ int x;
   char temporary_ddfa[STATES1];
   temporary_ddfa[0] = '\0';
   for (x= 0; x< strlen(Stat_current); x++)
string_merge(temporary_ddfa,
nFa[Stat_current[x]-'0'][Symbol]);
strcpy(Stat_nxts, temporary_ddfa);}
int ind_stat(char *State, char Stat-
ename[][STATES1], int *np)
{  int x;
if (!*state) return -1;
  for (x= 0; x< *np; x++)
if (!strcmp(state, statename[x]))
return x;
   strcpy(statename[x], state);
   return (*np)++; }
int ddfa_from_nonfa(char
*nFa[STATES1][REGSYMB1], int n_nFa,
   int n_Sym, int Dfa[][REGSYMB1])
{ char Statename[STATES1][STATES1];
   int x = 0;

main() {
init_nFA_table();
autostat = nfa_to_dfa(nFAtab, nFA_states,
n_REGSYMB, DFAtab);
put_Dfa_table(dFAtab, autostat,
n_REGSYMB);
}
```

The given above code shows the logical programming implementation of deterministic as well as non-deterministic automaton along with its equivalence.

Now there is some example executed based on the above-given algorithm and code with some test cases.

7 Example of NFA to DFA with Test Cases

Consider an NFA with few states along with some inputs shown in figure

Equivalent DFA for above NFA can be created easily as per the algorithm

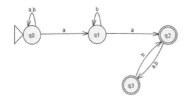

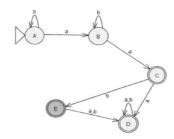

8 Algorithm for Conversion of NFA to DFA

Let Mn = (Q, Σ, δ, q$_0$, F) be NFA which identifies any language L then equivalent DFA Md = (Q, Σ, δ′, q′$_0$, F′) which satisfies the respective conditions recognizes L. Q = 2Q i.e. the set of all subsets of Q.

To obtain equivalent DFA, we follow the following procedure.

Step 1: Initially Q = Ø.

Step 2: {q$_0$} is the initial state of the DFA M and Put q$_0$ into Q.

Step 3: For each state q in Q following steps are needed: add this new state, add δ (q,a) = U p ϵ q δ(p, a) to δ, where δ on the right-hand side (R.H.S) is that of NFA M$_n$.

Step 4: Repeat step 3 till new state are there to add in Q; if there is new state found to add in Q, then process is terminated. All the states of Q which contain accepting state of M$_n$ are accepting state of M.

Important: Not reachable states are not included in Q (Not reachable means states which are not reached from initial state).

8.1   Test Case 1 for NFA and Its Equivalent DFA

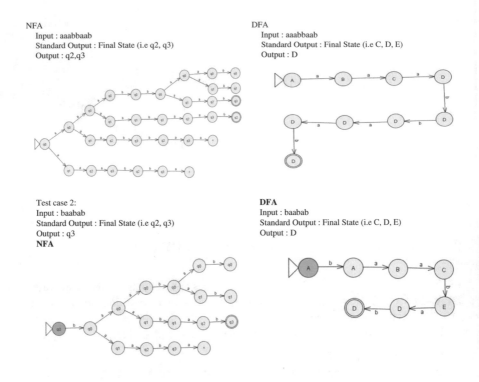

NFA
   Input : aaabbaab
   Standard Output : Final State (i.e q2, q3)
   Output : q2,q3

DFA
   Input : aaabbaab
   Standard Output : Final State (i.e C, D, E)
   Output : D

Test case 2:
Input : baabab
Standard Output : Final State (i.e q2, q3)
Output : q3
NFA

DFA
Input : baabab
Standard Output : Final State (i.e C, D, E)
Output : D

9   Result and Conclusion

In this paper, we have discussed distinction between deterministic and non-deterministic finite-state automaton. Using a simple algorithm, we can implement a deterministic as well as non-deterministic finite-state automaton in an executable format to find the solution of various problems. Here, we have also discussed the equivalence of deterministic and non-deterministic finite-state automaton with the use of various examples. This example shows the concern of non-deterministic finite-state automaton and gives equivalent deterministic finite-state automaton along with some suitable test cases to be measured. This concluded that non-deterministic finite-state automation may have different solution of given problems, but deterministic finite-state automaton provides the best unique solution to find the solution to a problem.

References

1. Goldsmith, J.A.: *Towards a new empiricism*, vol. 36. 2007
2. Bátfai, N.: Recombinations of busy beaver machines. http:arxiv.org/pdf/0908.4013 (2009)
3. Žilinskas, A., Žilinskas, J.: Interval arithmetic based optimization in nonlinear regression. Informatica (2010)
4. Sergeyev, Y.D.: Numerical point of view on Calculus for functions assuming finite, infinite, and infinitesimal values over finite, infinite, and infinitesimal domains. *Nonlinear Analysis Series A: Theory, Methods & Applications* (2009)
5. Sharma, C., Shakya, R.: Computational complexity in language string processing and theory of halting problem in deterministic turing machine accepting context sensitive language, context free language or regular language, 2015. In: 2nd International Conference on Computing for Sustainable Global Development (INDIACom), New Delhi, pp. 2091–2096 (2015).
6. Nagpal, C.K.: Formal Languages and Automata Theory. April 2011
7. Pandey, A.K.: An Introduction To Automata Theory & Formal Languages (2013)
8. Prof. Kamala Krithivasan, Theory of Computation, 2011

A Multi-factored Cost- and Code Coverage-Based Test Case Prioritization Technique for Object-Oriented Software

Vedpal and Naresh Chauhan

Abstract Test case prioritization is a process to order the test cases in such a way that maximum faults are detected as earlier as possible. It is very expensive to execute the unordered test cases. In the present work, a multi-factored cost- and code coverage-based test case prioritization technique is presented that prioritizes the test cases based on the percentage coverage of considered factors and code covered by the test cases. For validation and analysis, the proposed approach has been applied on three object-oriented programs and efficiency of the prioritized suite is analyzed by comparing the APFD of the prioritized and non-prioritized test cases.

Keywords Object-oriented testing · Test case prioritization · Cost- and code coverage-based testing · Multi-factors-based test case prioritization

1 Introduction

Testing is one of the important phases of the software development life cycle. The testing of the software consumes a lot of time and efforts. Presently, the cost of testing the software is increasing very rapidly. According to finding of the sixth quality report [1], the share of the testing budget is expected to reach 29% by 2017. Every software industry mainly concerns the reduction of the testing cost and detection of the bug by taking the minimum time. For delivering the quality software, it is necessary to detect all the possible errors and fix them. There are various factors that indicate the quality of the software. These factors are functionality, correctness, completeness, efficiency, portability, usability, reliability, integrity,

Vedpal (✉) · N. Chauhan
Department of Computer Engineering, YMCA University of Science and Technology, Faridabad, India
e-mail: ved_ymca@yahoo.co.in

N. Chauhan
e-mail: nareshchauhan19@gmail.com

© Springer Nature Singapore Pte Ltd. 2019
M. N. Hoda et al. (eds.), *Software Engineering*, Advances in Intelligent Systems and Computing 731, https://doi.org/10.1007/978-981-10-8848-3_3

maintainability, etc. Due to the advancement of technology and expectation of the customer, it is very challenging task to deliver the quality software within allocated budget.

The quality of the software also depends on the skills and experience of the developer. Nowadays, various languages are used by the developer. Every language has various features which provide the different functionalities. Many packages are also available in the markets which are directly imported in the software. If the different features of the language and packages are not used efficiently, then error-prone software may be produced. If the developers are not aware of the conditions of the software developed, then it will surely produce the bug. Sometimes, the implemented functionality is error-free, but it may consume more memory and execution time. High consumption of the memory and execution time affects the quality of the software. So there should be a technique to identify the factors which are most capable of introducing the error, increasing the execution time of software, and consuming more memory. The test case prioritization should be done in a way that the maximum errors can be detected as earlier as possible.

In this paper, a test case prioritization technique is presented. The proposed technique prioritizes the test cases on the basis of the cost and code covered by the test cases. To calculate the cost of the path, various factors are considered. For experimental validation and analysis, the proposed approach has been applied on the various examples that were implemented in the C++ language. The results show effectiveness of the proposed approach.

2   Related Work

The size of the test suits is increased as the software evolves. Test cases are used to test the existing program. If the software gets modified due to the addition of new functionality, new test cases may be added to the existing test cases. There are many constraints on the industry like resource, time, and cost. So, it is important to prioritize the test cases in a way that probability of error detection is higher and earlier. In this section, an overview of various researchers is discussed.

Shahid and Ibrahim [2] proposed a new code-based test case prioritization technique. The presented approach prioritizes the test cases on the basis of the code covered by the test case. The test cases that covered the maximum methods have the highest probability to detect the errors earlier. Abdullah et al. [3] presented the findings of the systemic review conducted to collect evidence testability estimation of object-oriented design. They concluded that testability is a factor that predicts that how much effort will be required for testing the software.

Huda et al. [4] proposed an effective quantification model of object-oriented design. The proposed model uses the technique of multiple linear regressions between the effective factors and metrics. Structural and functional information of object-oriented software has been used to validate the assessment of the effectiveness of the factors. The model has been proposed by establishing the correlation between effectiveness and object-oriented design constructs. The quantifying ability of model is empirically validated.

Chhikara and Chhillar [5] presented a set of metrics. The presented metrics are used to order the programs based on their complexity values. They concluded that there should be compromise among internal attributes of software to maintain the higher degree of reusability. Patwa et al. [6] presented the factors of coding phase that effect the testing of object-oriented software. These factors are programmer and tester skills, programmer and tester organization, development team size, program workload (stress), domain knowledge, and human nature (mistake or work omission). Analysis of factors and place of these factors according to their impact on the software are identified by using the relative weight method and ANOVA test.

Bruntink et al. [7] analyzed the relation between classes and their JUnit test cases. They demonstrated a significant correlation between the class-level metrics and test-level metrics. They also discussed how various metrics can contribute to testability. They conducted the experiments using the GQM and MEDEA framework. The results are evaluated using Spearman's rank-order correlation coefficient.

Malviya and Singh [8] presented some observation on maintainability estimation model for object-oriented software in requirement, design, coding and testing phases. The presented work is about increasing the maintainability factors of the MOOD metrics.

Hao et al. [9] presented a unified test case prioritization approach. The presented approach includes two models. They showed that there is a spectrum of test case prioritization techniques. The spectrum is generated by the model that resides between the techniques using purely total or purely additional strategies. They proposed extensions to enable the use of probabilities that test cases can detect errors for methods and use the dynamic coverage information in place of static coverage information.

3 Proposed Work

The presented approach prioritizes the test cases on the basis of the cost and the coverage of the code covered by the test case. For accurately finding out the cost of the test case, some factors are considered in Table 1. The proposed approach works at two levels. At the first level, all the considered factors existed in the source code are identified. After identification and counting the factors, all independent paths of the source code are resolute; then, the value of the cost of each path is determined on the basis of the coverage of the identified factors. Test cases are selected corresponding to independent paths. The cost of the test case can be calculated by using Formula 1. The code coverage of test case is determined by counting lines of code executed by the test case. At the second level, pairs of cost and code value of each test case are created. In this way by using the value of the cost and code coverage, the test cases are prioritized. The following scenario is used for the prioritization of the test cases:

Table 1 Proposed factors

S. No.	Proposed factor
1	Operators
2	Variables
3	External system call
4	Predicate statement
5	Assignment statement
6	Use of libraries/packages
7	Virtual function
8	Exception handling

(1) Highest code coverage and cost will have highest priority.
(2) Second priority should be given to test case that has highest cost value.
(3) Third priority should be given to test case that has highest code coverage.
(4) Test cases with the equal code coverage and cost should be ordered.

The overview of the proposed approach is shown in Fig. 1.

The cost covered by the test case can be calculated by applying the Formula 1 as given below:

$$\text{Cost}(T_i) = \text{SF}(T_i)/\text{TF} \tag{1}$$

where SF is the sum of the factors covered by the ith test case, and TF is the sum of the all existing factors in source code.

Fig. 1 Overview of the proposed approach

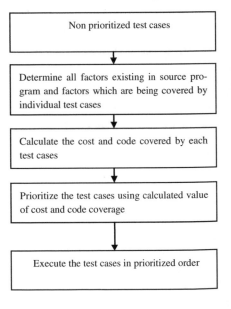

3.1 Considered Factors for Prioritized Test Cases

Table 1 shows the considered factors that are used to prioritize the test cases. The factors are considered by the structural analysis of the program. The considered factors may affect the testing process in terms of consumption of memory, execution time, and the possibility of introducing the error in program.

These are factors related to object-oriented program affecting the prioritization of test cases. There are a total of eight object-oriented software-related factors included in this work. The algorithm of the proposed approach is given in Fig. 2.

4 Result and Analysis

For the experimental validation and evaluation, the proposed approach has been applied on the three programs. The programs are implemented in the C++ language. For the experimental analysis, intentionally faults are introduced in the programs. The program one has 170 lines of code, program [10] two has 361 lines of code, and program three has 48 lines of code.

Table 2 shows the various factors covered by the test cases, Table 3 shows the line of code covered by the test cases, Table 4 shows the calculated cost of all test cases that are used to test the software, and Table 5 shows the various pairs of cost and code covered by the test cases.

The prioritizing order of test cases as determined by the proposed approach is TC6, TC2, TC1, TC4, TC8, TC5, TC3, TC7.

4.1 Faults Detected by Test Cases in Non-Prioritized Order

The faults are identified in the non-prioritized order as shown in Table 6.

Let T be is the list of non prioritized test cases and T' be the list of the prioritized test cases.
While (T not empty)
Begin
Step 1. Identify and Count all the considered factors that are used in the source code.
Step 2. Determine the factors and line of code being covered by the test cases.
Step 3. Calculate the cost by applying the formula on test cases.
        $Cost (T_i) = SF(T_i) / TF$
Where SF is the sum of factors covered by the test case and TF is the sum of the factors in the source code
End
Step 4. Determine the all possible pairs of the code coverage value and cost value of each test cases
            Pair = (Cost , Code Coverage)
Step 5. Prioritized the test cases in the following scenarios
(1) Highest the value of cost and code covered by the test case have highest priority
(2) Second priority should be given to test case that has highest cost value.
(2) Third priority should be given to test case that has highest code coverage.
(3) Test cases with the equal value of the code coverage and cost should be prioritized in the random order.
Create T' the list of prioritize test cases.

Fig. 2 Algorithm of the proposed approach

Table 2 Factors covered by test cases

Factors	TC1	TC2	TC3	TC4	TC5	TC6	TC7	TC8
Operators	4	4	0	0	1	7	0	0
Variable	3	3	1	4	2	3	1	4
Native method	0	0	0	0	0	0	0	00
Control statement	0	1	0	0	0	2	0	0
Assignment	3	2	0	0	1	2	0	0
SF	10	10	1	4	4	12	1	4

Table 3 Line of code covered by test cases

	TC1	TC2	TC3	TC4	TC5	TC6	TC7	TC8
Line of code	36	42	31	36	34	48	31	36

Table 4 Calculated cost of test cases

	TC1	TC2	TC3	TC4	TC5	TC6	TC7	TC8
Factor coverage (TFC)	10	10	1	4	4	12	1	4
Total factors (TF)	35	35	35	35	35	35	35	35
Cost	28.57	28.57	2.85	11.42	11.42	34.28	2.85	11.42

Table 5 Pairs of the cost and code coverage by test cases

S. No.	Test case	Pairs
1	TC1	(36, 28.57)
2	TC2	(42, 28.57)
3	TC3	(31, 2.85)
4	TC4	(36, 11.42)
5	TC5	(34, 11.42)
6	TC6	(48, 34.82)
7	TC7	(31, 2.85)
8	TC8	(36, 11.42)

Table 6 Faults detected by test cases in non-prioritized order

	TC1	TC2	TC3	TC4	TC5	TC6	TC7	TC8
F1	*	*	*	*	*	*	*	*
F2				*				*
F3								*
F4					*			
F5						*		
F6						*		
F7				*				
F8	*							
F9		*						
F10		*						

Table 7 Faults detected by test cases in prioritized order

	TC6	TC2	TC1	TC4	TC8	TC5	TC7	TC3
F1	*	*	*	*	*	*	*	*
F2				*	*			
F3					*			
F4						*		
F5	*							
F6	*							
F7				*				
F8			*					
F9		*						
F10		*						

4.2 Faults Detected by Test Cases in Prioritized Order

Table 7 shows the faults detected by the test cases when they executed in prioritized order.

For simplicity of the approach, the faults are detected for only one program.

4.3 Comparison of APFD Graphs Prioritized and Non-prioritized Order of Test Cases for Three Programs

Figure 3 shows the comparison of APFD graphs for program one, Fig. 4 shows the comparison of APFD graphs for program two, and Fig. 5 shows the comparison of APFD graphs for program three. The test cases are executed in prioritized order obtained after applying the proposed approach and non-prioritized approach [11, 12].

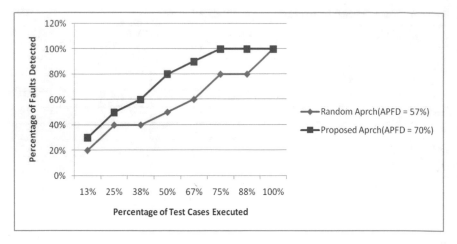

Fig. 3 Comparison of APFD detected by random and prioritized test cases for program one

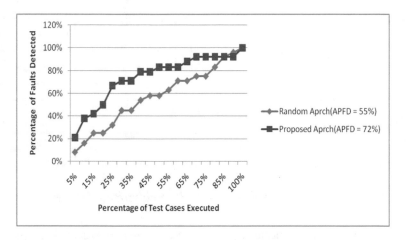

Fig. 4 Comparison of APFD detected by random and prioritized test cases for program two

4.4 Effectiveness of the Proposed Approach

Effectiveness of the proposed approach is measured through APFD metric, and its value is shown in Table 8 [13]. The APFD value of prioritized order of test cases obtained by applying the proposed approach is better than random ordering of test cases. Therefore, it can be observed from Table 8 prioritized test cases has higher fault exposing rate than the non-prioritized test cases.

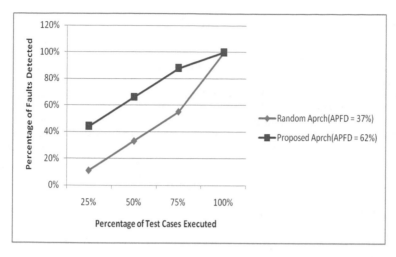

Fig. 5 Comparison of APFD detected by random and prioritized test cases for program three

Table 8 Compared result of test cases for prioritized and non-prioritized order

Case study	Non-prioritized test cases (APFD) (%)	Prioritized test cases (APFD) (%)
Program one	57	70
Program two	55	72
Program three	37	62

5 Conclusion

In the proposed approach, a test case prioritization technique for object-oriented software is presented. The approach prioritizes the test cases based on coverage of determined cost and lines of code. It works at two levels. At the first level, cost and code covered by the test cases are determined. Costs are calculated by using the proposed factors that are covered by the test case. At the second level, test cases are prioritized on the basis of determined cost and code covered by the test case. For experimental validation and evaluation, it has been applied on three object-oriented programs. The experimented results show that the proposed approach leads to improve the rate of fault detection early in comparison with non-prioritized order of test cases. The significant characteristic of the proposed approach is that it helps to reduce the testing cost by detecting the faults in short time.

References

1. Decouz Hester.: Capgemini world quality report. (2014) www.worldqualityreport.com
2. Shahid, M., Ibrahim, S.: A new code based test case prioritization technique. Int. J. Softw. Eng. Appl. **8**(6), 31–38 (2014)
3. Abdullah, D., Srivastava, R., Khan, M.H.: Testability estimation of object oriented design: a revisit. Int. J. Adv. Res. Comput. Commun. Eng. **2**(8) (2013)
4. Huda, M., Arya, Y.D.S., Khan, M.H.: Evaluating effectiveness factor of object oriented design: a testability perspective. Int. J. Softw. Eng. Appl. (IJSEA) **6**(1), 41 (2015)
5. Chhikara, A., Chhillar, R.S.: Analyzing complexity of java program using object oriented software metrics. IJCSI Int. J. Comput. Sci. **9**(1), 3 (2012). ISSN:1694-0814
6. Patwa, S., Malviya A.K.: Impact of coding phase on object oriented software testing. Covenanat J. Inf. Commun. Technol. (CJICT) **2**(1) (2014)
7. Bruntink, M., Van Deursen A.: Predicting class testability using object oriented metrics. In: 4th IEEE International Workshop on Source Code Analysis and Manipulation, pp. 136–145. Chicago, IL, US (2004)
8. Malviya, A.K., Singh V.: Some observation on maintainability estimation model for object oriented software in requirement, design, coding and testing phases. Int. J. Adv. Res. Comput. Sci. Softw. Eng. **5** (3) (2015). ISSN: 2277 128X
9. Hao, D., Zhang, L., Zhang, L., Rothermel, G., Mei, H.: A unified test case prioritization approach. In: ACM Trans. Softw. Eng. Methodol. **9**(4) (2010)
10. http://cppprojectcode.blogspot.in/2010/09/income-tax-calculation.html
11. Meyers S.: More effective C++. Addison-Wesley, Professional Computing Series
12. Jain R., Aggarwal N.: Additional fault detection test case prioritization. BIJIT-BVICAM's Int. J. Inf. Technol. **5**(2) (2013)
13. Chauhan, N.: Software testing principles and practices. Oxford University Press, Oxford (2010)

A Novel Page Ranking Mechanism Based on User Browsing Patterns

Shilpa Sethi and Ashutosh Dixit

Abstract Primary goal of every search engine is to provide the sorted information according to user's need. To achieve this goal, it employs ranking techniques to sort the Web pages based on their importance and relevance to user query. Most of the ranking techniques till now are either based upon Web content mining or link structure mining or both. However, they do not consider the user browsing patterns and interest while sorting the search results. As a result of which, ranked list fails to cater the user's information need efficiently. In this paper, a novel page ranking mechanism based on user browsing patterns and link visits is being proposed. The simulated results show that the proposed ranking mechanism performs better than the conventional PageRank mechanism in terms of providing satisfactory results to the user.

1 Introduction

The World Wide Web is an interlinked collection of trillions of Web documents accessed via Internet. To retrieve the desired information from such a huge collection, Web search engines can be used [1]. The basic components of every search engine are: crawler, indexer, user interface, and query processor. The Crawler browses the Web automatically at a specified interval, downloads the Web page from different Web servers, and provides the information to indexer. The indexer further indexes Web documents in search engine database. The query processor executes the user query on search engine database and finds the documents which matches with the user query and ranks them according to some relevance factors. Many ranking algorithms have been proposed in past. Among them, PageRank

S. Sethi (✉) · A. Dixit
Department of Computer Science, YMCA University of Science and Technology, Faridabad, India
e-mail: munjal.shilpa@gmail.com

A. Dixit
e-mail: dixit_ashutosh@rediffmail.com

© Springer Nature Singapore Pte Ltd. 2019
M. N. Hoda et al. (eds.), *Software Engineering*, Advances in Intelligent Systems and Computing 731, https://doi.org/10.1007/978-981-10-8848-3_4

Table 1 Overview of web mining techniques

Features	WCM	WSM	WUM
Mining focus	Within the document	Within as well as between the documents	User navigational patterns
Input data	Txt, HTML documents	Hyperlinks	Query logs, server log files
Representation of data	Bags of words for unstructured data HTML tags for semistructured data, ontology	Structured summary of web pages in the form of web graph	Relational tables
View of data	Semi- and unstructured	structured	Event triggers
Method	NLP and machine learning	Proprietary algorithms	Personalization algorithms, association rules, NLP

(PR) [2, 3], Weighted PageRank (WPR) [4], and Hypertext Induced Topic Search (HITS) [5], PageRank based on link visit (PRLV) [6] are some of the popular ranking algorithms. All these algorithms are based on Web mining concept.

Web mining is a branch of data mining techniques that discover the useful patterns from Web documents. Web content mining (WCM), Web structure mining (WSM), and Web usages mining (WUM) are three main categories of Web mining. [7, 8] PR, WPR, and HTTS are purely based on Web structure mining, whereas PRLV is based on Web structure as well as Web usages mining. Table 1 gives the overview of these Web mining techniques. The proposed mechanism captures the user interest in an efficient way by applying the concept of Web usages and Web structure mining.

The rest of the paper is organized as follows: In next section, Web structure mining and popular algorithms of this area have been discussed. Section 3 describes the proposed ranking mechanism in detail with example illustrations. Section 4 depicts the complete working of proposed system. Concluding remarks are given in Sect. 5.

2 Related Work

This section describes an overview of Web structure mining and some popular PageRank algorithms with examples illustration. Web structure mining means generating the link summary of Web pages and Web server in the form of Web graph by using the concept of hyperlink topology between different documents as well as within the same document [8]. A Web graph is directed labeled graph where nodes represent the Web pages and edges represents the hyperlinks between the pages. There are many algorithms based on Web structure mining. Some of them which form the basis of proposed work are discussed in following sections.

2.1 PageRank

The PageRank algorithm was developed by Google and named after Larry Page, [3]. The link structure of Web page is used to find out the importance of a Web page. The importance of a page P can be obtained by evaluating the importance of pages from which the page P can be accessed. Links from these pages are called as inbound links. According to this algorithm, if the inbound links of a page are important, then its outbound links also become important. The PageRank of a page P is equally divided among its outbound links which further propagated to pages corresponding to these outbound links. The PageRank of a page X can be calculated by Eq. (1) as follow

$$PR(X) = (1-d) + d\left(\frac{PR(P_1)}{O(P_1)} + \frac{PR(P_2)}{O(P_1)} \cdots \frac{PR(P_n)}{O(P_n)}\right) \qquad (1)$$

where:

- P_1, P_2, ... P_n represent the inbound links of page X
- $O(P_1)$, $O(P_2)$ ... $O(P_n)$ are no. of outbound links of page P_1, P_2 ... Pn, respectively
- d is the damping factor which is a measure of probability of user following direct link. Its value is usually set to 0.85.

To explain the working of PR method, Let us take a small Web structure as shown in Fig. 1a consisting of four pages, namely P_1, P_2, P_3, and P_4, where page P_1 is inbound link of page P_2 and P_4, page P_2 is inbound ink of page P_4 and P_3, P_3 is inbound link of P_1, P_2, and P_4, and P_4 is inbound link of P_1. According to Eq. (1), PageRank of page P_1, P_2, P_3, and P_4 can be computed as follows:

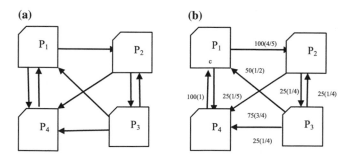

Fig. 1 a Sample web structure, **b** sample web structure with link visits and link weight

$$PR(P_i) = [(1d) + d(PR(P_3)/3 + PR(P_4)/1)] \tag{1a}$$

$$PR(P_2) = [(1 - d) + d(PR(P_1)/2 + PR(P_3)/3)] \tag{1b}$$

$$PR(P_3) = [(1 - d) + d(PR(P_2)/2)] \tag{1c}$$

$$PR(P_4) - [(1 - d) + d(PR(P_1)/2PR(P_2)/2 + PR(P_3)/3)] \tag{1d}$$

Initially considering the PageRank of each page equal to 1 and taking the value of $d = 0.85$, calculating PageRank of each page iteratively until their vales becomes stable as shown in Table 2.

From Table 2, it may be noted that $PR(P_1) > PR(P_4) > PR(P_2) > PR(P_3)$. These PR values are extracted by crawler while downloading a page from Web server, and these values will remain constant till the Web link structure will not change. In order to obtain the overall page score of a page, the query processor adds the precomputed PageRank (PR) value associated with the page with text matching score of page with the user query before presenting the results to the user.

2.2 Page Ranking Algorithm Based on Link Visits (PRLV)

Duhan et al. [6] proposed the extension of PageRank method in which the PageRank of a page is computed on the basis of no. of visits to Web page. They pointed out that traditional PR method evenly distributes the PageRank of page among its outgoing links, whereas it may not be always the case that all the outgoing links of a page hold equal importance. So, they proposed a method which assigns more rank to an outgoing link that is more visited by the user. For this purpose, a client side agent is used to send the page visit information to server side agent. A database of log files is maintained on the server side which store the URLs of the visited pages, its hyperlinks, and IP addresses of users visiting these hyperlinks. The visit weight of a hyperlink is calculated by counting the distinct IP addresses clicking the corresponding page. The PageRank of page 'X' based upon visit of link is computed by the Eq. (2)

Table 2 Calculation of PageRank by PR method

Steps	PR(P$_1$)	PR(P$_2$)	PR(P$_3$)	PR(P$_4$)
1	1.2805	2.1205	0.575	1.2805
2	1.4863	0.9422	1.052	1.8434
3	2.0147	1.0795	0.5504	1.4799
4	1.5639	1.1622	0.6088	1.6209
5	1.7000	0.9871	0.6439	1.4725

$$PR(X) = (1-d) + d \sum_{P_i \in I(X)} \frac{PR(P_i) * L(P_i, X)}{TL(P_i, O(Pi))} \qquad (2)$$

Where:

- PR(X) is PageRank of page X calculated by Eq. (1).
- I(X) is set of incoming links of page X.
- $L(P_i, X)$ is no. of link visits from P_i to X.
- $TL(P_i, O(P_i))$ is total no. of user visits on all the outgoing links of page P_i.

Let us consider the same hyperlinked structure as shown in Fig. 2 with no. of visits and visit weight (written in bracket) shown in Fig. 3. By taking the value of $d = 0.85$, the PageRank based on visit of link can be easily obtained by using Eq. (2) and iteration method as shown in Table 3.

By comparing the results of PR with PRLV, it is found that rank order of pages has been changed. By using PRVOL, $PRVOL(P_1) > PRVOL(P_2) > PRVOL(P_4) > PRVOL(P_3)$. A critical look at the available literature indicates that although dividing the PageRank of a page among its outgoing links based on link visit solved the problem of finding the importance of a page within the Web, it has been observed that the user who visits on a particular page may not necessarily find the page useful. Therefore, the time spent and action performed such as print, save may be considered as vital parameter while determining the relevance of a page with respect to the user. The proposed ranking mechanism discussed in the next section overcomes the above shortcomings by incorporating the user page access information to the link structure information of a Web page.

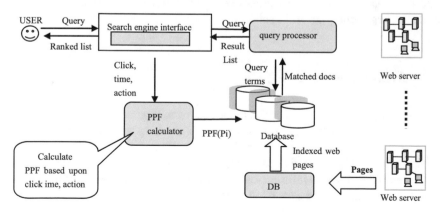

Fig. 2 Proposed system

Fig. 3 DB builder

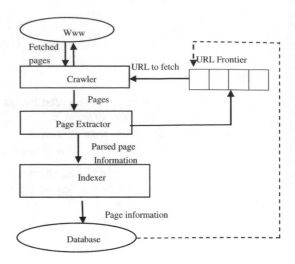

Table 3 Calculation of PageRank by PRLV method

Steps	PRVOL (P_1)	PRVOL (P_2)	PRVOL (P_3)	PRVOL (P_4)
1	1.141	0.560	0.256	0.569
2	0.669	0.944	0.209	0.622
3	0.708	0.392	0.250	0.822
4	0.884	0.408	0.191	0.352
5	0.476	0.464	0.193	0.333

3   Proposed Page Ranking Mechanism

An efficient search model based on user page access information is being proposed here as shown in Fig. 2. It consists of four main components: search engine interface, PPF calculator, query processor, and DB builder. The detailed description of each component is given in subsequent sections.

3.1   Search Engine Interface

The user enters the query at search engine interface. It passes these query words to query processing module and sends a signal 'something to record' to PPF calculator. At the end of search operation, it receives the sorted list of documents from query processor to present back to the user. When the user clicks a page in the result list, it sends the hit(click) information to its corresponding Web server which in turn stores this information in server log files.

3.2 PPF Calculator

After receiving the signal 'something to record' from search engine interfaces, it observes and records certain facts about the activity of user on a particular page. For this, it assigns the page probability factor (PPF) to each page clicked by the user. The page probability factor $PPF(P_i)$ can be computed as per the equation given in (3)

$$PPF(P_i) = CLICK_{wt}(P_i) + TIME_{wt}(P_i) + ACTION_{wt}(P_i) \qquad (3)$$

where:

- $CLICK_{wt}(P_i)$ denotes the importance of page P_i with respect to all the pages clicked by user u_i for query q_i in the current search session.
- $TIMESCORE(P_i)$ denotes the time spent by user 'u' on the page P_i
- $ACTION_{wt}(P_i)$ denotes the action performed on the page P_i

The computation of each of these factor used in Eq. (3) is given below.

Calculation of click weight on page P_i: When a user clicks a page, the click weight of page P increases as if the user votes for this page [9]. For any more clicking by the same user, the click weight of page will not be affected. To find the importance of page P with respect to query q, the click weight is defined by Eq. (4) given below.

$$CLICK_{wt}(P_i) = \frac{C}{|CLICK(q, *, u)|} \qquad (4)$$

where

- $click(q, *, u)$ denotes the total no. of clicks made by user u on all the pages for query q in current session.
- C is no. of vote for a page. It is set to 1 for clicked pages and 0 otherwise.

Let us consider a user clicked three pages $P_1, P_2 \ldots P_{10}$. Click weight of each clicked page can be computed by Eq. (4) as shown below. The $CLICK_{wt}$ of all other pages is set to zero as they did not get any click from user.

$$CLICK_{wt}(P_1) = \frac{1}{1+1+1} = 0.33 \qquad (4a)$$

$$CLICK_{wt}(P_2) = \frac{1}{1+1+1} = 0.33 \qquad (4b)$$

$$CLICK_{wt}(P_5) = \frac{1}{1+1+1} = 0.33 \qquad (4c)$$

Calculation of time weight on page P: Time is also an important factor as more time the user spent on something, more he is interested in it [10]. Time weight of document P_i is computed by analyzing its relevancy w.r.t document p whose view time is maximum. For query q in current session as given in Eq. (5). Let us consider the user spent 3 min, 2 min, and 9 min on page P_1, P_2, and P_5, respectively. The time weight of page P_1, P_2, P_5 can be computed by Eq. (5).

$$\text{TIME}_{wt}(P_i) = \frac{\text{Time spent}(P_i)}{\text{Highest Time Spent}(P)} \tag{5}$$

$$\text{TIME}_{wt}(P_1) = \frac{3}{9} = 0.33 \tag{5a}$$

$$\text{TIME}_{wt}(P_2) = \frac{2}{9} = 0.22 \tag{5b}$$

$$\text{TIME}_{wt}(P_5) = \frac{9}{9} = 1 \tag{5c}$$

Calculation of action weight on page P_i: Action that user may carry on any Web document is listed in Table 4 along with the weights. The weight is assigned according to the relevancy of the action where relevancy is determined based on user feedback in response of a survey. It is observed in the survey that if someone is printing the page means, it has higher utility at present, saving is less scored as the user will require it later on, bookmark come next, and sending comes at last in priority list as page is used by some other user. If a user performs more than one action, then only the higher weight value is considered. For example, if user perfume printing as well as saving, then only the printing weight is assigned to the page.

Let us consider the user takes no action on page P_1 and P_2 but performs the save action on page P_5. So, $\text{ACTION}_{wt}(P_5) = 0.3$, $\text{ACTION}_{wt}(P_1) = 0$, and $\text{ACTION}_{wt}(P_2) = 0$. This PPF information related to each clicked page is updated in search engine database. Initially, PPF of all pages is set to zero. It is computed and updated every time; a user selects the page in the result list.

Table 4 Action weight

Action	Weight
Print	0.4
Save	0.3
Bookmark	0.2
Send	0.1
No action	0

3.3 DB Builder

This component is responsible for extracting the pages from www and storing their information into search engine database. The main subcomponents are as follows: page extractor, crawler, and indexer as shown in Fig. 3. The working of each component is discussed in following subsections.

Crawler: It extracts the URL from the URL frontier and downloads the pages at specified interval [11] from the different Web server. URL frontier is a queue that contains URLs of the pages that need to be downloaded. The structure of URL frontier is shown in Fig. 6. The downloaded pages are passed to page extractor. Table 5 gives description of different fields of URL frontier.

Page extractor: It parses the fetched page and divides it into no. of terms. All the nonfunctional terms such as at, on, the are removed. It stores the term information related to parsed page in Term_info table. It also extracts the link information of page and stores it into Link_info. The structure of Term_info and Link_info is shown in Fig. 4. The different fields of Term_info and Link_info are described in Table 6.

Indexer: It first calculates the link weight of a page using Eq. (2) by taking the link information from Link_info then indexes every term of parsed page in search engine database. The structure of database is shown in Fig. 6. The page probability

Table 5 URL frontier description

Field	Description
URL	URL of the page yet to be downloaded by the crawler, e.g., http://www.snapdeal.com/ domain name system
Priority	The numeric value based on revisit interval of a page assigned by the crawler
Depth	The numeric value indicates how deep the crawler visits the hyperlinks of a page and downloads them
Server name	The web server name of the URL. For example, in the above-mentioned URL, the server name is snapdeal.com

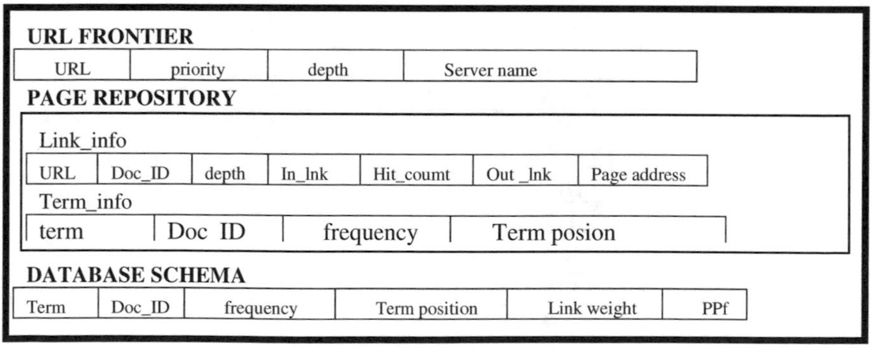

Fig. 4 Data structures for used by DB builder

Table 6 Description of page repository

Field	Description
Term	The word extracted from page
Doc_ID	A unique number or alphanumeric no. is assigned to each page such as D_1, D_2, D_3
Frequency	No. of occurrences of term in page
Position	It is a numeric value which tells the position of term in the page; e.g., graphics at 53rd position indicates that it is 53rd term of the parsed page D_i
URL	The URL of the page being parsed
Depth	The depth of URL
In_lnks	The URL of incoming link
Hit_count	The no. of link visit from incoming URL to parsed page URL
Out_lnks	URL of outgoing links
Page address	It specifies the memory location of page on the server site

Table 7 Organization of data in search engine database

Term	Doc ID	Frequency	Position	Link_weight	PPF
Prime	D_3	5	4, 12, 23, 56	7	4.5
Prime	D_8	3	7, 45, 89	9	7
–	–	–	–	–	–
Factors	D_3	6	5, 13, 24, 57, 79, 99	7	4.5
Minister	D_8	3	8, 46, 90	9	7

factor, PPF, of each new page is initially set to zero and updated by PPF calculator when ever the page is clicked by user in result list. Let us consider the sample data shown in Table 7 for understanding the organization of information in search engine database. The information is stored as vocabulary (terms list) and postings as shown in Fig. 5.

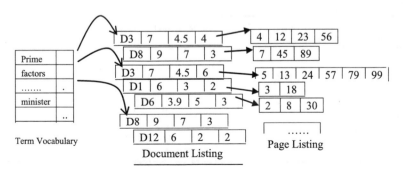

Fig. 5 Organization of information in search engine database

```
Algorithm: Query processor (  )
Input     : user query
Outpu     : Sorted list of pages
Variables: user query (Q),index repository(D),Array for storing func-
tional words (KW[n]),Two dimensional array to store URL name and total
rank of each URL(URL_Score[m])
Method: Begin
Read the user query Q ;
KW[n]←Stopword_removal(Q) ;              //Remove stop words and create stems
KW[n] ←Porter algorithm (Q);
For each term, ti belongs to D{if (ti  Є KW[n])
                            {Extract the PPF and LinkScore ofpage pi;
                            Total_Ran(Pi)←PPF(Pi)+Link_Score (Pi;}
                            URL Score[i] ←Total Rank(Pi) }
Sort the URL Score[i] and return the sorted list to search engine inter-
face to be presented to user;
End
```

Fig. 6 Algorithm for query processor

As shown in Table 7, the term 'Prime' occurs at four different places: 4, 12, 23, and 56 in document D_3 in row1. The link_weight of D_3 is 7, and PPF score is 4.5. Likewise, the information about the other terms is also stored.

3.4 Query Processor

It executes the user query on search engine database and fetches the pages whose text matches with the query terms. It calculates the overall_page_score of each selected page by adding the precomputed Link_weight to PPF and returns the sorted list of pages to search engine interface. The algorithm of query processor is shown in Fig. 6.

4 Example

Let us consider the scenario depicted in Fig. 7 to have a complete understanding of proposed page ranking mechanism.

5 Conclusion

In this paper, an efficient page ranking mechanism based on user browsing pattern has been presented. These patterns are used to deduce the importance of a page with respect to other candidate pages for a query. The technique is automatic in nature,

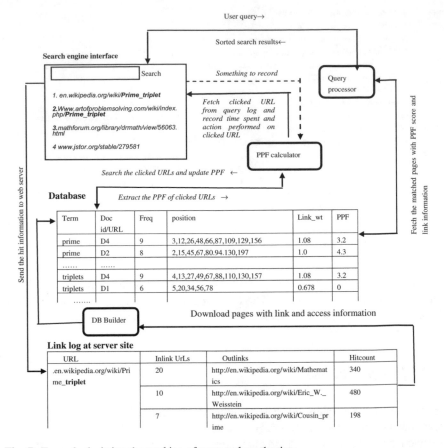

Fig. 7 Example depicting the working of proposed mechanism

and no overhead is involved at the part of user. The technique does not create each user profile; instead, collective interests are used to find the relevancy of a page. So, optimized approach is adopted. The technique proves to provide more relevant results as compared to regular search engine.

References

1. Sethi S., Dixit A.: Design of presonalised search system based on user interest and query structuring. In: Proceedings of the 9th INDIACom; INDIACom 2nd International Conference on Computing for Sustainable Global Development, 11–13 March 2015
2. Brin, S., Page, L.: The anatomy of a large scale hypertextual web search engine. Comput. Netw. ISDN Syst. **30**(1–7), 107–117 (1998)
3. Page, L., Brin, S., Motwani, R., Winograd, T.: The pagerank citation ranking: bringing order to the web. In: Technical report, Stanford Digital Libraries SIDL-WP-1999-0120 (1999)

4. Xing W., Ghorbani A.: Weighted pagerank algorithm. In: Proceedings of the Second Annual Conference on Communication Networks and Services Research (CNSR'04)0-7695-2096-0/ 04 $20.00 © 2004
5. Pal, S., Talwar, V., Mitra, P.: Web mining in soft computing framework: relevance, state of the art and future directions. IEEE Trans. Neural Netw. **13**(5), 1163–1177 (2002)
6. Gyanendra, K., Duahn, N., Sharma A.K.: Page ranking based on number of visits of web pages. In: International Conference on Computer and Communication Technology (ICCCT)-2011, 978-1-4577-1385-9
7. Markov, Z., Larose, D.T.: Mining the web: uncovering patterns in web content, structure, and usage data. Wiley, New York (2007)
8. Sethi, S., Dixit, A.: A comparative study of link based pge ranking algorithm. Int. J. Adv. Technol. Eng. Sci. (IJATES) **3**(01) (2015). ISSN: 2348-7550
9. Tyagi, N. et al. Weighted page rank algorithm based on number of visits of web page. Int. J. Soft Comput. Eng. (IJSCE) **2**(3) (2012). ISSN: 2231-2307
10. Mittal, A., Sethi, S.: A novel approach to page ranking mechanism based on user interest. Int. J. Adv. Technol. Eng. Sci. (IJATES) **3**(01) (2015). ISSN: 2348-7550
11. Dixit, A., Sharma, A.: A mathematical model for crawler revisit frequency. In: IEEE 2nd International Advanced Computing Conference (IACC), pp. 316–319 (2010)

Indexing of Semantic Web for Efficient Question Answering System

Rosy Madaan, A. K. Sharma, Ashutosh Dixit and Poonam Bhatia

Abstract Search engine is a program that performs a search in the documents for finding out the response to the user's query in form of keywords. It then provides a list of web pages comprising of those keywords. Search engines cannot differentiate between the variable documents and spams. Some search engine crawler retrieves only document title not the entire text in the document. The major objective of Question Answering system is to develop techniques that not only retrieve documents, but also provide exact answers to natural language questions. Many Question Answering systems developed are able to carry out the processing needed for attaining higher accuracy levels. However, there is no major progress on techniques for quickly finding exact answers. Existing Question Answering system is unable to handle variety of questions and reasoning-based question. In case of absence of data sources, QA system fails to answer the query. This paper investigates a novel technique for indexing the semantic Web for efficient Question Answering system. Proposed techniques include manual constructed question classifier based on <Subject, Predicate, Object>, retrieval of documents specifically for Question Answering, semantic type answer extraction, answer extraction via manually constructed index for every category of Question.

Keywords Information retrieval · Question Answering · Semantic web

R. Madaan (✉)
Department of Computer Science and Engineering, GD Goenka Univeristy, Sohna, Gurgaon, India
e-mail: madaan.rosy@gmail.com

A. K. Sharma
Department of Computer Science and Engineering, BSAITM, Alampur, Faridabad, India
e-mail: ashokkale2@rediffmail.com

A. Dixit · P. Bhatia
Department of Computer Engineering, YMCA University of Science and Technology, Faridabad, India
e-mail: dixit_ashutosh@rediffmail.com

P. Bhatia
e-mail: poonambhatia0401@gmail.com

© Springer Nature Singapore Pte Ltd. 2019
M. N. Hoda et al. (eds.), *Software Engineering*, Advances in Intelligent Systems and Computing 731, https://doi.org/10.1007/978-981-10-8848-3_5

1   Introduction

Question Answering (QA) is a technology that aims at retrieving the answer to a question written in natural language from the large collections of documents. Indexing is a technique of formation of indexes for the fast retrieval of the information needed by the Question Answering system to answer the query of the user. The user in the question categorization module selects the category of the Question which makes the system understand that it has to search in that particular category index; we have different index for different category of the Question.

2   Related Work

The evolution of the QA system was through closed domain because of their less complexity. Previously used QAs were BASEBALL and LUNAR. BASEBALL [1] QA gives information about the US baseball league for one year. LUNAR QA gives information about the geographical analysis of rocks given by the Apollo moon missions. Both QA systems were very powerful in their own domains. LUNAR was examined at a lunar science, and it was able to answer approximately 90% of the questions in its domain posed by people who are not trained on this system. The common feature of all these systems is that they had knowledge database or knowledge systems that were implemented by experts of the chosen domain.

SHRDLU [2] was a Question Answering system that has been developed by Terry Winograd. It was basically developed to offer for the user to ask the robot questions. Its implementation was done using the rules of the physics encoded in computer programming. The Question Answering systems developed to interface with these expert systems produced more repeatable and valid responses to questions within an area of knowledge. The system answered questions related to the Unix OS. It had a knowledge base of its domain, and its target is to phrase the answer to accommodate various types of users. LILOG [2] is a closed-domain Question Answering system and is basically a text understanding system. This system gives tourism information in a German city. Other system also helps the system in linguistic and computational processing.

QUALM (story understanding system) [3] works through asking questions about simple, paragraph length stories. QUALM [3] system includes a question analysis module that links each question with a question type. This question type guides all further processing and retrieval of information (see Table 1).

Kupiec (a simple WH question model) [3] Question Answering system performs similar function but it rather solves simpler who question models to build a QA system. This QA used the interrogative words for informing the kinds of information required by the system. Table 2 lists the Question categories and Answer type.

Table 1 QUALM question categories

Question type	Example question
Causal antecedent	How did the cloud formed?
Goal orientation	Rohan left for what reason?
Causal consequent	What happened after John left?
Disjunctive	Was Rohan or Mary here?
Verification	Did Rohan leave?

Table 2 Kupiec question categories

Question type	Answer type
Who/whose	Person
What/which	Thing, Person, location
Where	Location
When	Time
How many	Number

AnswerBus Question Answering system [4] is an open-domain Question Answering system based on sentence-level Web information retrieval. It accepts users' natural language questions in English, German, French, Spanish, Italian and Portuguese and provides answers in English. It can respond to users' questions within several seconds. Five search engines and directories (Google, Yahoo, WiseNut, AltaVista and Yahoo News) are used to retrieve web pages that contain answers. AnswerBus takes a user question in natural language, i.e. in English. A simple language recognition module will determine whether the question is in English, or any other five languages. If the question language is not in English, AnswerBus will send the original question and language information about the question to AltaVista's translation tool and obtain the question that has been translated into English and accordingly answer is provided to the user.

AskMSR Question Answering system [3] is to take the query as input and rewrite the query into the form the system can support. The rewrites generated by the system are simple string-based manipulations. AskMSR does not use a parser or part-of-speech tagger for query reformulation, but use a lexicon for a small percentage of rewrites, in order to determine the possible parts of speech of a word as well as its semantic variation. It created the rewrite rules and associated weights manually for the current system, and it may be possible to learn query to answer reformulations and their weight [4–6].

Query Reformulation in AskMSR is done as follows: Given a question, the system generates a number of weighted rewrite strings which are likely substrings of declarative answers to the question. For example, "When was C discovered?" is rewritten as "C was discovered". We search through the collection of documents in search of such patterns. Since many of these string rewrites will result in no matching documents, we also produce less decisive rewrites that have a much greater chance of finding matches. For each query, we generate a rewrite which is not having any stop word in the resultant query [7, 8].

3 Proposed Architecture

This Question Answering system is a system that is developed with an objective to answer question posed by a user in a natural language [9, 10]. The architecture of this system is shown in Fig. 1. The following are the functional modules of the proposed system:

- Query interface,
- Query processing,
- Document retrieval processing,
- Result processing.

The query interface is a dialogue to the Question Answering system that the user's natural language can be entered into and the output is given to the user. The knowledge base of this system consists of a stop words list, a synonym knowledge base, a Question Answer database (in the form of documents), a question term (index words), technology information knowledge database.

3.1 Query Interface Module

Query interface in Question Answering system is the module responsible for executing the query given by the user. It receives input queries in the form of plain text, parses and optimizes them and completes the execution of the query by performing different techniques on the query to retrieve the answer to the query posed by the user [11, 12]. So, the user query is the query posed by the user in plain text which is considered as a string of words.

3.2 Query Processing Module

Query processing is done in the manner as shown in Fig. 2.

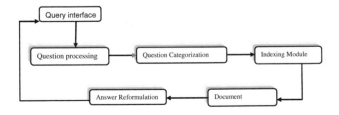

Fig. 1 Proposed architecture

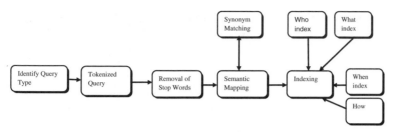

Fig. 2 Query processing framework

a. Identification of the query: This component is used to identify the type of the query entered by the user.
b. Tokenization of the query: In the first step, query is tokenized into bag of words or string of words.
c. Stop word Removal: Removing stop word is necessary to improve the efficiency of the query. Adjusting the stop word list to the given task can significantly improve results of the query.

3.3 Question Categorization Module

In this module, user has to select the category of the Question, i.e. who, what, when so that the system can identify the expected answer to the user query [13].

3.4 Question Analysis Module

Question analysis (see Fig. 3) is also referred to as "Question Focus". Classifying the question and knowing its type are not enough for finding answers to all questions. The "what" questions in particular can be quite ambiguous in terms of the information asked by the question. It reduces the ambiguity, analyses the Question and identifies its focus which is necessary [14, 15]. For example, if the user enters the query "Who is the Founder of C", focus must be on the "founder" and "C".

See Fig. 3 for Question analysis.

3.5 Question Categorization

Question categorization improves the performance of the retrieving the answer by the Question Answering system. If the category the user selected is "who", then the

Fig. 3 Question analysis

Question	Type	Subject	Predicate	object
Who discover C	Who	Person*,organization	Discover	C
Who is the founder of C	who	Person*,organization	Founder	C
Who found C	who	Person*,organization	found	C
Who develop C	who	Person*,organization	develop	C
Who invented C	who	Person*,organization	invent	C
What is the history of C	what	Paragraph(Content)	history	C
History of C	-	-	History	C
Brief history of C	-	-	History	C
C language history	-	C language	history	-
What is C Language	What	Paragraph(content)	-	C language
Intro to C	-	Intro	-	C

Table 3 Question categorization

Question	Type
Who discover C	who
Who is the founder of C	who
Who found C	who
Who develop C	who
Who invented C	who
What is the history of C	what
History of C	–

expected answer can be name of person or some organization. Table 3 lists the questions along with their type.

3.6 Semantic Mapping in Question Answering System

Dealing with difficult question involves the identification of semantic mapping of the query. Firstly, we need to recognize the answer type that is expected which is an affluent semantic structure. Secondly, we need to identify the Question class and patterns. Thirdly, we need to model the scenario that what sort of information is needed by the query.

Three concepts are needed to identify the answer type:

a. Question class.
b. Relationship between the subject and object, i.e. <Subject, Predicate, Object>.
c. Semantic mapping of the Question.

Let us take a question: What is the description of C? For this question, by knowing only the category of the question it is difficult to judge the answer to the query; we have to create a semantic relation between the query and the answer type. Query formulation is done on the basis of <Subject, Predicate, Object> "Subject" tell what contains the paragraph of the "object" C description judges the relationship between the subject and the object [16].

Table 4 General index

Term	Document ID
Founder	Doc1
C	Doc1, Doc2
Dennis Ritchie	Doc1
General purpose	Doc2

3.7 Indexing Module

Indexing is a technique of formation of indexes for the fast retrieval of the information needed by the Question Answering system to answer the query of the user [17]. The user in the question categorization module selects the category of the Question which makes the system understand that it has to search in that particular category index; we have different index for different category of the Question. The indexing module helps the QA system to locate the terms with the document id for fast processing. The indexing technique used in the QA system is manually locating the term with the document id. With the indexing module, the QA system identifies the matched document related to the query term for finding the candidate answers. After the identification of the matched documents, result processing module will process the result back to the user interface. Table 4 shows a general index.

3.8 Result Processing Module

After the documents are indexed, the documents having the matched query answers are processed to the query processor and finally the output of the query is given to the user. Figure 4 shows the process how result processing module works.

The proposed algorithm is shown in Fig. 5.

Algorithm for query processing is shown in Fig. 6.

Fig. 4 Result processing module

Fig. 5 Proposed algorithm of result processing module

Step 1: Take query as input as entered by the user
Step 2: Identify the category of the question.
Step 3: a) If category="Who" then check with who-index.
         b) If category="What" then check with what-index.
         c) If category="When" then check with when-index.
         d) If category="Why" then check with why-index.
         e) If category="how" then check with how-index.
         f) If category="Where" then check with where-index.
Step 4: If category="not found" then check with main-index.
Step 5: Return the candidate answer generated by matching the documents.

Step 1: Query=Input.
Step 2: Split query into Tokens.
Step 3: Check for Stop words
      a)   If found remove them.
Step 4: Set terms as tokens and return
Step 5: Identify the Subject, Predicate, Object for the query to find the relationship bet ween the subject and object.
Step 6: If term in the query does not match with the index term then find the synonym of the query term and replace the synon ym with the query term in the index.
Step 7: Identify the number of documents that match the query terms.
Step 8: Processing of result for the match documents is done.
Step 9: Processed Result is given to the query interface.

Fig. 6 Algorithm: query processing

4 Experimental Evaluation

The approaches taken have given satisfactory results up to a great extent. There are many types of question for which the answers are relevant and accurate. There is a scope of improvement in many areas but things have been achieved as per the proposed work. Whenever you want to know about a question "who is the founder of C?" you will be expecting the name of the person or an organization as the category of the Question is who. The answer will contain the name of the person and some description about the person. Snapshot of the proposed system is shown in Fig. 7.

This Question Answering system is able to answer a variety of questions accurately. As can be seen in the snapshots, the answers are formatted according to the Question requirements. This section calculates the relevancy of various answers.

It is worth noting that the answers follow a true positive result orientation, i.e. all the relevant results are coming. In some cases, other relevant information that might be useful is also coming in results. Performance is calculated on the basis of relevant result given by the system. Formula for calculating the performance is:

Fig. 7 Snapshot of the proposed system

Performance $\% = ($Answer processed by the system$)/($Expected relevant answer$)$
$$* 100$$

Let us take examples of some questions in Table 5:
Apart from this Question like:

a. Question: How to become self-educated?

Answers expected are:

1. Stepwise method to perform the task.

Accuracy from answers from this method entirely depends on the user experience. If those results meet the user expectation, then it is 100% else it cannot be computed.

b. Question: Convert metre to centimetre?

Answers expected are:

1. Conversion technique comes in the category of "how".

QA System Accuracy = $1/1*100 = 100\%$
This method relies on the current conversion data, so accuracy is 100%. See Fig. 8 for the plot of system accuracy.

Table 5 Example questions, expected answer type(s) and QA system accuracy

Question	Expected answer type(s)	QA system accuracy
Who is the founder of C?	1. Name of the person 2. Name of the organization	$2/2*100 = 100\%$
What is description of C?	1. Description about the topic	$1/1*100 = 100\%$
Where is Qutab Minar situated?	1. Location (i.e. city, state, country) 2. Location compared to other locations	$2/2*100 = 100\%$
When did India got independence?	1. Date and the place 2. Also some description about the past 3. Information about the condition when the event takes place	$2/3*100 = 66.6\%$
Which holiday fall on December 31?	1. All the holidays which fall on that date.	$1/1*100 = 100\%$
When was Mahatma Gandhi born?	1. Birth date	$1/1*100 = 100\%$
What event happened on 26 January?	1. All the event happened on that date	$1/1*100 = 100\%$

Fig. 8 Bar graph showing system accuracy of various QA systems

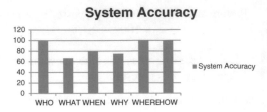

5 Conclusions and Future Scope

This Question Answering system is above its counterparts in giving relevant answers to many type of questions. By selecting the category of Question for the query, the indexing retrieval is done at a fast rate. As seen by the results and the views of the users, these facts have come out as its bright feature. Information about a person, word, location, birth date, death date, holidays, event, etc., available to the user is accurate and relevant to the need of the particular user, and according to the survey, many users are satisfied by it. The algorithm designed for the retrieval is fast in most of the cases. It is getting faster day by day. System's main aim was to have index retrieval fast so as to improve the complexity of the Question. QA system mapping of the query into <S,P,O> and creating the relationship between the subject and object improve the efficiency of the Question Answering system. By first selecting the category of the question QA system able to know what type of answer is expected from the user. These things conclude that the proposed Question Answering system is fast, efficient and relevant up to a great extent. Further work can be done to improve the quality of the results and on reasoning-type questions.

References

1. Question Answering System Wikipedia
2. Hirschman, L., Gaizauskas, R.: Natural Language Question Answering System (2001)
3. Allam, A.M.N., Haggag, M.H.: The question answering systems: a survey. Int. J. Res. Rev. Inf. Sci. (IJRRIS) (2012)
4. Zheng, Z.: AnswerBus question answering system. School of Information, University of Michigan (2001)
5. Greengrass, E.: Information Retrieval: A Survey, DOD Technical Report TR-R52-008-001 (2000)
6. Brin, S., Page, L.: Computer Networking and ISDN System, pp. 107–117 (1998)
7. John, B., Claire, C., Vinay, C., Robert, G., Sanda, H., David, I.: Issues, Tasks and Program Structuresto Roadmap Research in Question & Answering (Q&A) (2003)
8. Narayana, S., Harabagaiu, S.: Question Answering based on Semantic Structure (2005)
9. Andrenucci, A., Sneiders, E.: Automated Question Answering: Review of the Main Approaches (2005)
10. Soergel, D.: Indexing and retrieval performance. In: Srihari, R., Li, W. (eds.) A Question Answering System Supported by Information Extraction (1994)

11. Hammo, B., Abu-Salem, H., Lytinen, S.: QARAB: A Question Answering System to Support the Arabic Language (2002)
12. Mudgal, R., Madaan, R., Sharma, A.K., Dixit. A.: A Novel Architecture for Question Classification and Indexing Scheme for Efficient Question Answering (2013)
13. Moldovan, D., Paşca, M., Harabagiu, S., Surdeanu, M.: Performance Issues and Error Analysis in an Open-Domain Question Answering System (April 2003)
14. Lim, N.R., Saint-Dizier, P.: Some Challenges in the Design of Comparative and Evaluative Question Answering Systems (2010)
15. Suresh kumar, G., Zayaraz, G.: Concept Relation Extraction Using Naïve Bayes Classifier for Ontology-Based Question Answering Systems (13 Mar 2014)
16. Kapri, d., Madaan, R., Sharma, A.K., Dixit, A.: A Novel Architecture for Relevant Blog Page Identification (2013)
17. Balahur, A., Boldrini, E., Montoyo, A., Martínez-Barco, P.: A Comparative Study of Open Domain and Opinion Question Answering Systems for Factual and Opinionated Queries (2009)

A Sprint Point Based Tool for Agile Estimation

Rashmi Popli and Naresh Chauhan

Abstract In agile environment, the software is developed by self-organizing and cross-functional teams. Agile promotes ad hoc programming, iterative, and incremental development and a time-boxed delivery approach. Agile is always flexible to changes. Estimation approaches of agile are very different from traditional ones. However, research involving estimation in agile methodologies is considerably less advanced. This paper focuses on the estimation phase of agile software development which probably ranks as the crucial first step. Poor decisions related to estimation activity can cause software failures. In agile environment in order to support estimation, some delay-related factors are proposed that can delay the release date of the project and also a new Sprint-point based estimation tool (SPBE) is designed and developed in excel. The proposed tool is based on the Sprint-point based Estimation Framework and place major emphasis on accurate estimates of effort, cost, and release date by constructing detailed requirements as accurately as possible.

Keywords Agile software development · Agile alliance · Sprint-point
Planning poker · Agile estimation

1 Introduction

Agile software development (ASD) methodology is presently considered as the main methodology for software development in organizations [1]. The word "agile" means flexible and responsive. The ASD has the ability to survive in rapid changing

R. Popli (✉) · N. Chauhan
Department of Computer Engineering, YMCA University of Science and Technology, Faridabad, India
e-mail: rashmipopli@gmail.com; rashmimukhija@gmail.com

N. Chauhan
e-mail: nareshchauhan19@gmail.com

© Springer Nature Singapore Pte Ltd. 2019
M. N. Hoda et al. (eds.), *Software Engineering*, Advances in Intelligent Systems and Computing 731, https://doi.org/10.1007/978-981-10-8848-3_6

environment. ASD is a lightweight approach to most aspects of software development in contrast to traditional methods of producing applications.

1.1 Estimation

Estimation of size, effort, cost, and duration of an agile software project is a complicated task. Exact estimations of software are critical for software developers and management. Ignorance of estimation approaches causes dangerous effects like exceeding budget of project, not delivered on time, poor quality, and not right product [2, 3]. Popular agile methods are expert opinion, planning poker, analogy based, top-down approach, and bottom-up approach [1], etc. But these methods are not so efficient because in expert opinion the result is always based on the observation of expert and his/her experience. Similarly analogy-based method depends on the historical data or on previous projects. However in absence of historical data or in case it is a new project, it becomes difficult to estimate by existing agile estimation methods. Therefore, there is a need of some estimation tool that calculates estimates in agile environment effectively.

2 Sprint-point based Estimation Framework in SPBE Tool

2.1 Sprint Estimation

When planning about first sprint, at least 80% of the backlog items are estimated to build a reasonable project map. These backlog items consist of user stories grouped in sprints and user stories based on estimation is done using story points. When a software developer estimates that a given work can be done within 10 h, it never means that work will be completed in 10 h. Because no one can sit in one place for the whole day and there can be a number of factors that can affect story points and hence decrease the velocity. To estimate cost and time, it is a big challenge [4].

To resolve this problem, the concept of Sprint-point is proposed. A Sprint-point basically calculates the effective story points. Sprint point is an evaluation or estimation unit of the user story instead of story point. By using Sprint points, more accurate estimates can be achieved. Thus, the unit of effort is Sprint Point (SP) which is the amount of effort, completed in a unit time.

In the proposed Sprint-point based Estimation Framework, requirements are first gathered from client in the form of user stories. After requirement gathering, a user story-based prioritization algorithm is applied to prioritize the user stories. Consequently, story points in each user story are calculated and uncertainty in story points is removed with the help of three types of story points proposed. Then, these story points are converted to sprint-points based on the proposed agile estimation factors. Afterwards, sprint-point based estimation algorithm is applied to calculate cost, effort, and time in a software project.

If there is requirement of regression testing in agile, then defect data is gathered based upon the similar kinds of projects, which is used to calculate rework effort and rework cost of a project. Finally, the sprint-point based estimation algorithm using regression testing is applied to calculate the total cost, effort, and duration of the project.

This Sprint-point based Estimation Framework as shown in Fig. 1 performs estimation in scrum using below steps:

Step 1: User stories are prioritized by using User story-Based Prioritization Algorithm (will be discussed in Sect. 2.2).
Step 2: Uncertainty in story point is removed (will be discussed in Sect. 2.3).
Step 3: Story points are converted into sprint-points by considering agile delay factors. Delay factor is being proposed that affects the user stories and thus affects the cost, effort, and duration of a software project. Sprint-point based estimation is done by using the proposed Sprint-point based estimation using delay-related factors (will be discussed in Sect. 2.4).

2.2 *User Story-Based Prioritization Algorithm*

In agile software development method, the requirements from the customer are taken in the form of user stories. The proposed prioritization rule is "Prioritize the

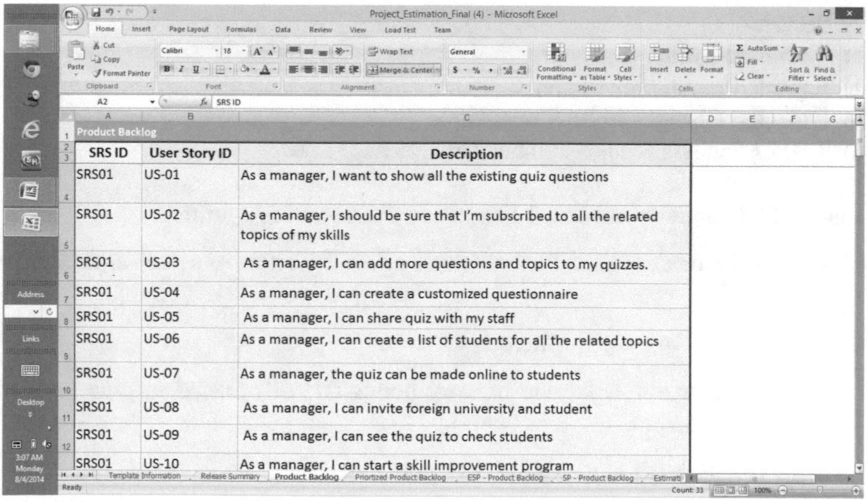

SRS ID	User Story ID	Description
SRS01	US-01	As a manager, I want to show all the existing quiz questions
SRS01	US-02	As a manager, I should be sure that I'm subscribed to all the related topics of my skills
SRS01	US-03	As a manager, I can add more questions and topics to my quizzes.
SRS01	US-04	As a manager, I can create a customized questionnaire
SRS01	US-05	As a manager, I can share quiz with my staff
SRS01	US-06	As a manager, I can create a list of students for all the related topics
SRS01	US-07	As a manager, the quiz can be made online to students
SRS01	US-08	As a manager, I can invite foreign university and student
SRS01	US-09	As a manager, I can see the quiz to check students
SRS01	US-10	As a manager, I can start a skill improvement program

Fig. 1 User stories

user stories such that the user stories with the highest ratio of importance to actual effort will be prioritized first and skipping user stories that are "too big" for current release" [5].

Consider the ratio of importance as desired by client to actual effort done by project team (I/E) as in Formula 1.

$$\text{Prioritization of user stories} = \frac{\text{Importance of user stories}}{\text{Effort per user stories}} \tag{1}$$

2.3 Managing Uncertainty in Estimating User Stories

The technique of managing uncertainty in estimation reduces uncertainty by following approach of reducing uncertainty in estimating user stories [6].

2.4 Sprint-Point Based Estimation Using Delay-Related Factors

Looking toward the various unaddressed problems of estimation, a new Sprint-point based Estimation Framework in agile has been proposed that helps to estimate the accurate cost, time, and effort [7, 8].

In this project, some delay-related factors have been proposed that can affect the estimation of cost and effort of the project. These factors are as below:

(1) Complexity
(2) Security
(3) Technical Ability
(4) Expected Ambiguity in Detail
(5) Expected Changes in Environment
(6) Team Members Responsibilities Outside the Project

Algorithm 1 Sprint-point based Estimation Framework Algorithm

- Identify the delay-related factors which effect the effort in scrum environment where

  $P = \{p_1, p_2, \ldots p_i, \ldots p_n\}$ where $1 < i <= n$

- Identify the unadjusted value of story points (UVSP) related to each level in scrum environment

  where UVSP $= \{p_1 + p_2 + p_3 + \cdots + p_n\}$
  where L_i ($1 <= i <= 3$)

- Compute the estimated story points (ESP) as

  $$ESP = BSP + 0.1(UVSP)$$
  where BSP is baseline story points

- Compute velocity from first iteration as

  Velocity = ESP/story point completed in one iteration

- Compute new velocity by considering delay-related factors

  $$V = \text{velocity} * d$$

- Estimated Development Time (EDT) = ESP/Velocity (in Days)
- Release Date = Start date + EDT

In the proposed algorithm, firstly the delay-related factors in agile scrum environment are calculated on the basis of which the UVSP is determined. With the help of UVSP, the story points are estimated. These estimated story points are then used in the calculation of the development time and the release date of the project.

2.5   Sprint-Point Based Estimation Tool

As agile projects are of small duration, so the team has not so much amount of time to apply the mathematical algorithms. To resolve this issue, a new sprint-point based estimation tool (SPBE) is designed and developed in Excel to automate the Sprint-point based Estimation Framework. The proposed SPBE tool for estimation place major emphasis on accurate estimates of effort, cost and release date by constructing detailed requirements as accurately as possible. This tool is used as a vehicle to validate the feasibility of the project. The proposed tool is a set of individual spreadsheets with data calculated for each team separately. The estimation tool is created to provide more accuracy in velocity calculations, as well as better visibility through burn down charts on all stages including planning, tracking, and forecasting. The proposed estimation tool first decides the priority sequence of user stories that dictates the implementation order. The priority of user story is decided based on the importance of user stories to the client and the effort of the scrum team. After prioritization product, backlog is prepared which is the most important artifact for gathering the data. After selecting a subset of the user stories, the sprint backlog is prepared and the period for the next iteration is decided.

Table 1 Contents of SPBE tool

S. No.	Spreadsheet name	Description
1.	Release summary	This spreadsheet contains the information about the overall planned and realized size of each release
2.	Product backlog	This spreadsheet lists all the user stories in prioritized order
3.	ESP-product backlog	This spreadsheet lists all the user stories and the story points in each user story
4.	TSP-product backlog	This spreadsheet lists all the user stories and the sprint-points in each user story
5.	Estimation summary	This spreadsheet calculates the total estimated effort, cost, and time for the release
6.	Sprint backlog	This spreadsheet is a list of tasks identified by the scrum team to be completed during the particular sprint
7.	Sprint summary	This spreadsheet contains information like start date, end date of sprint
8.	Defect	This spreadsheet describes the summary of defects, bug status, bug assignee, and bug reporter and also the date of bug creation
9.	Worklog	This spreadsheet involves the various resources involved in the project and also the type of work allocated to them
10.	Metric analysis	This spreadsheet shows the various metrics like rework effort, defect density ratio, effort variance

2.5.1 Contents of SPBE Tool

The SPBE tool contains the components. There is a separate spreadsheet for each component as in Table 1 like release summary, capacity management, product backlog, sprint backlog, sprint summary, defect, work log, and metric analysis. The backlog sheet contains all the user stories. The sprint summary sheet contains the information about the sprint like release date, start date.

2.6 Case Study

All the proposed approaches have been numerically analyzed on a case study named as enable quiz. The user stories of case study are in Table 2. As agile projects are of small duration so the team has not so much amount of time to apply the mathematical algorithms for estimation of cost, effort, and time. For resolving this problem, a new Sprint–point based estimation tool (SPBE) has been designed and developed to automate the Sprint-point based Estimation Framework. The

Table 2 User stories of case study

Story	Importance (I)	Effort (E)	I/E
1. As a manager, I want to browse my existing quizzes	10	7	10/7 = 1.42
2. As a manager, I can make sure that I am subscribed to all the necessary topics for my skills audit	4	3	4/3 = 1.33
3. As a manager, I can add additional technical topics to my quizzes	1	16	1/16 = 0.0625
4. As a manager, I want to create a custom quiz bank	8	8	8/8 = 1
5. As a manager, I want to create a quiz so I can use it with my staff	5	4	5/4 = 1.25
6. As a manager, I want to create a list of students from an Excel file so I can invite them to take the quiz	7	5	7/5 = 1.4
7. As a manager, I want to create a list of students online	6	8	6/8 = 0.75
8. As a manager, I want to invite a set of students	3	8	3/8 = 0.375
9. As a manager, I want to see which students have completed the quiz	9	6	9/6 = 1.5
10. As a manager, I want to see how the students scored on the test so I can put in place a skills improvement program	2	16	2/16 = 0.125

proposed SPBE tool for estimation places major emphasis on accurate estimates of effort, cost and release date by constructing detailed requirements as accurately as possible [9–11]. This tool may be used as a vehicle to validate the feasibility of the project.

2.7 Results

By using delay-related factors, decelerated velocity is calculated on the basis of which effort and cost is calculated. For simplicity, only 10 user stories are taken. The project start date is assumed as January 1, 2014, and initial velocity is 5 SP/day. The delay-related factors are taken at medium level. By using the Sprint-point based estimation tool the following results as shown in Table 3 are calculated.

The snapshots of the results in SPBE tool are as in Figs. 1, 2 and 3.

Table 3 Results

Unadjusted value (UV). All the six factors at medium level so UV = 6	UVSP = 6*6 = 36
Total user stories	10
BSP	300
Project start date	1st January, 2014
Estimated story points (ESP) = BSP + 0.1 (UVSP)	300 + 0.1 (36) = 303.6
Initial velocity	5 SP/Day
AvgVF = Average of VF of all the 6 factors	0.95667
Decelerated velocity (DV) = V * AvgVF	5 * 0.95667 = 4.78330 SP/Day
Estimated development time (EDT) = ESP/DV	303.6 * 8/ 4.78330 = 507.76 h
Project end date	14 Jan 2014

Capacity Planning for Release: Release-1						
Release Start Date	01-Jan-14			No. of User Stories		0
Release End Date	14-Jan-14			Baseline Story points		300
S. No	Resource Name	Allocation %	Factor	Competency	Start Date	Date→
						Day→
						Daily Max Hrs
			0.8			Capacity Hrs
1	Rajesh	100.00%	0.8	Developer	01-Jan-14	70.4
2	Akhil	100.00%	0.8	Developer	01-Jan-14	70.4
3	Tarun	100.00%	0.8	Developer	01-Jan-14	70.4
4	Amit	100.00%	0.8	Developer	01-Jan-14	70.4
5	Sachin	100.00%	0.8	Developer	01-Jan-14	70.4
6	Naresh	100.00%	0.8	Developer	01-Jan-14	70.4
7				Select		
8				Select		
9				Select		

Fig. 2 Capacity planning for release

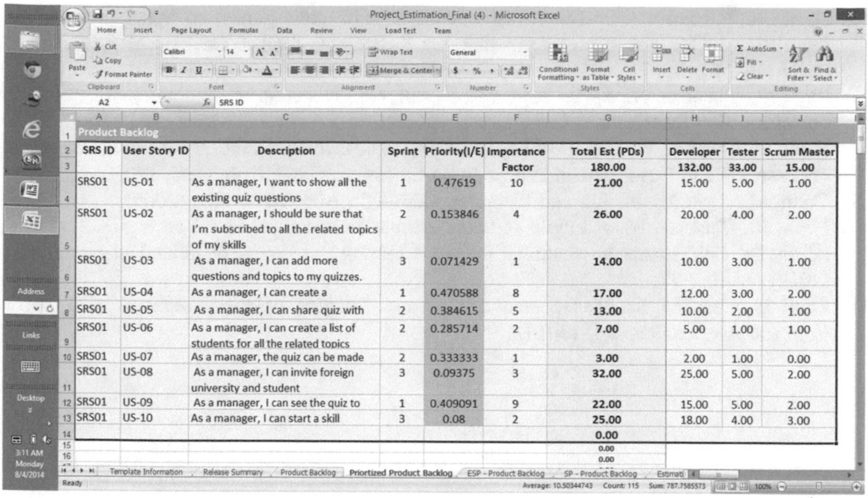

Product Backlog

SRS ID	User Story ID	Description	Sprint	Priority(I/E)	Importance Factor	Total Est (PDs)	Developer	Tester	Scrum Master
						180.00	132.00	33.00	15.00
SRS01	US-01	As a manager, I want to show all the existing quiz questions	1	0.47619	10	21.00	15.00	5.00	1.00
SRS01	US-02	As a manager, I should be sure that I'm subscribed to all the related topics of my skills	2	0.153846	4	26.00	20.00	4.00	2.00
SRS01	US-03	As a manager, I can add more questions and topics to my quizzes.	3	0.071429	1	14.00	10.00	3.00	1.00
SRS01	US-04	As a manager, I can create a	1	0.470588	8	17.00	12.00	3.00	2.00
SRS01	US-05	As a manager, I can share quiz with	2	0.384615	5	13.00	10.00	2.00	1.00
SRS01	US-06	As a manager, I can create a list of students for all the related topics	2	0.285714	2	7.00	5.00	1.00	1.00
SRS01	US-07	As a manager, the quiz can be made	2	0.333333	1	3.00	2.00	1.00	0.00
SRS01	US-08	As a manager, I can invite foreign university and student	3	0.09375	3	32.00	25.00	5.00	2.00
SRS01	US-09	As a manager, I can see the quiz to	1	0.409091	9	22.00	15.00	5.00	2.00
SRS01	US-10	As a manager, I can start a skill	3	0.08	2	25.00	18.00	4.00	3.00
						0.00			
						0.00			
						0.00			

Fig. 3 Priortized product backlog

3 Conclusion

The main focus of this paper is to propose a new sprint point based estimation tool which improve accuracy of release planning and monitoring. The estimation tool is created to provide more accuracy in velocity calculations, as well as better visibility through burn down charts on all stages including planning, tracking, and forecasting. This tool is used as a vehicle to validate the feasibility of the project. The approach developed is really simple and easy to understand and can be effectively used for release date calculation in agile environment. By this method, release date of small and medium size project can be calculated efficiently.

References

1. Cockburn, A.: Agile Software Development, Pearson Education. Asia Low Price Edition (2007)
2. Stober, T., Hansmann, U.: Agile Software Development Best Practices for Large Software Development Projects. Springer Publishing, NewYork (2009)
3. Awad, M.A.: A comparison between agile and traditional software development methodologies. Unpublished doctoral dissertation, The University of Western Australia, Australia (2005)
4. Maurer, F., Martel, S.: extreme programming. rapid development for web-based applications. IEEE Internet Comput. **6**(1), 86–91 (2002)
5. Popli, R., Chauhan, N.: Prioritizing user stories in agile environment. In: International Conference on Issues and Challenges in Intelligent Computing Techniques, Ghaziabad, India (2014)

6. Popli, R., Chauhan, N.: Managing uncertainity of story-points in agile software. In: International Conference on Computing for Sustainable Global Development, BVICAM, Delhi (2015)
7. Popli, R., Chauhan, N.: Sprint-point based estimation in scrum. In: International Conference on Information Systems and Computer Networks, GLA University Mathura (2013)
8. Popli, R., Chauhan, N.: Impact of key factors on agile estimation. In: International Conference on Research and Development Prospects on Engineering and Technology (2013)
9. Cohn, M.: Agile Estimating and Planning. Copyright Addison-Wesley (2005)
10. Popli, R., Chauhan, N.: An agile software estimation technique based on regression testing efforts. In: 13th Annual International Software Testing Conference in India, Bangalore, India (2013)
11. Popli, R., Chauhan, N.: Management of time uncertainty in agile environment. Int. J. Softw. Eng. and Applications **4**(4) (2014)

Improving Search Results Based on Users' Browsing Behavior Using Apriori Algorithm

Deepika, Shilpa Juneja and Ashutosh Dixit

Abstract World Wide Web (WWW) is decentralized, dynamic, and diverse. It is growing exponentially in size. To improve search results, various ranking methods are being used. Due to vast information on the Web, there is a need to build an intelligent technique that automatically evaluates Web pages that are of user interest. In this paper, interest of a user in a particular Web page can be estimated by his browsing behavior without incurring additional time and effort by the user. It can also adapt to changes in user's interests over time. A page ranking mechanism is being proposed which takes user's actions into account. For this, a Web browser has been developed to store user's behavior. Apriori algorithm is applied on the data collected by Web browser which results in most frequent actions out of all actions. A calculated confidence value has been used to calculate weight of the Web page. Higher the weight, higher the rank.

Keywords World wide web · Apriori algorithm · Browsing behavior
Actions · Web browser · PageRank

1 Introduction

With the advent increase in information over the Web, people are now more interested and inclined toward Internet to get their data. Each user has its own interest and accordingly his expectations from search engine vary. Search engines play an important role in getting relevant information. Search engines use various

Deepika (✉) · S. Juneja · A. Dixit
Department of Computer Engineering, YMCA University of Science and Technology,
Faridabad, India
e-mail: deepikapunj@gmail.com

S. Juneja
e-mail: shilpajuneja1189@gmail.com

A. Dixit
e-mail: dixit_ashutosh@rediffmail.com

© Springer Nature Singapore Pte Ltd. 2019   73
M. N. Hoda et al. (eds.), *Software Engineering*, Advances in Intelligent Systems
and Computing 731, https://doi.org/10.1007/978-981-10-8848-3_7

ranking methods like HITS, PageRank but these ranking methods do not consider user browsing behaviors on Web. In this paper, a PageRank mechanism is being devised which considers user's browsing behavior to provide relevant pages on the Web. Users perform various actions while browsing. These actions include clicking scrolling, opening a URL, searching text, refreshing, etc., which can be used to perform automatic evaluation of a Web page and hence to improve search results. The actions have been stored in a database; an algorithm named Apriori has been applied upon these actions stored in database to calculate weight of a particular Web page. Higher the weight higher will be the rank of that page.

1.1 Introduction to Apriori Algorithm

Apriori algorithm [1] is an algorithm used in mining frequent itemsets for learning association rules. This algorithm is designed to operate on large databases containing transactions, e.g., collection of items purchased by a customer. The whole point of an algorithm is to extract useful information from large amount of data. This can be achieved by finding rules which satisfy both a minimum support threshold and a minimum confidence threshold.

The support and confidence can be defined as below:

- Support count of an itemset is number of transactions that contain that itemset.
- Confidence value is the measure of certainty associated with discovered pattern.

Formally, the working of Apriori algorithm can be defined by following two steps:

i. Join Step

- Find the frequent itemsets, i.e., items whose occurrence in database are greater than or equal to the minimum support threshold;
- Iteratively find frequent itemsets from *1* to *k* for *k*-itemsets.

ii. Prune Step

- The results are pruned to find the frequent itemsets.
- Generate association rules from these frequent itemsets which satisfy minimum support and minimum confidence threshold.

2   Related Work

In order to get relevant results, a search engine has to modify their searching pattern. Crawlers are the module of search engine which are responsible for gathering Web pages from the WWW. There are many design issues related to designing of crawler [2]. Crawlers search on the basis of content or structure of a Web page [3]. But here, after getting Web pages from the crawler, now it is responsibility of search engine to show the users according to his interest. To show the results to the user, its interest should be taken into consideration. Users' browsing behavior actions should be involved for showing results. Much work has been done in this area. Some are discussed below:

Ying [4] classified the users' browsing behavior into three categories:

(a) Physical Behavior like eye rotation, heart rate changes.
(b) Significant behavior like save page, print page, open.
(c) Indirect behaviors like browsing time, mouse–keyboard operation.

According to this paper, indirect behaviors are most important in analyzing the user interest.

Morita and Shinoda [5], Konstan [6], and Claypool et al. [7] conclude that user spend much time on the page which is of his interest. The longer the user spends time on some page, the more interested he is in the page.

On contrary, Weinreich et al. [8] found that in nearly 50% cases user spend much time in deciding whether to move to the next page or not rather in reading the content. It showed that time spent alone cannot be the important action in considering users' interest.

Goecks and Shavlik [9] proposed an approach for an intelligent Web browser that is able to learn a user's interest without the need for explicitly rating pages. They measured mouse movement and scrolling activity in addition to user browsing activity (e.g., navigation history). It shows somewhat better result as compared to the previous work.

Xing et al. [10] suggested that some actions like scrolling, mouse clicking should be included in the total browsing time. They worked on user browsing history and analyze documents which user has visited. On analysis he concludes that browsing time and printing are important actions in showing users' interest.

Tan et al. [11] focused on user behavior to optimize the structure of network and Web site server configuration. By analyzing user browsing behavior, they found what type of information should broadcast instead of all. Thus, improving Internet usage and reducing Internet overhead. In this, users' browsing behavior was used for utilizing network resources in efficient manner.

Yang et al. [12] proposed personalized teaching software based on students interest. Students' interest was calculated by analyzing their browsing behavior. By knowing their interest, they developed the software and cater the need of students in efficient way.

From the above literature survey, it may conclude that existing system does not give relevant results in terms of users' interest. Many works has been done in this area. Many researchers worked on users' interest by analyzing their browsing behavior on Web pages [13, 14]. Some concluded browsing time has great impact in showing users' interest while some take such type of patterns that showed users' interest. But most of them do not consider enough behavior patterns.

3   Working Methodology

The main purpose of proposed approach is to find relevant pages by estimating user's interest implicitly. The proposed technique starts by developing a Web browser to record user's actions [2]. Actions include duration on Web page, number of mouse clicks, number of key ups and down, save, print, number of scrollbar clicks, reload, save, open URL, stop loading, add to favorites, back, forward, copy, search text, hyperlink, active time duration, etc. The proposed browser also pops up a window at the time of closing the Web page that asks the user to rate that Web page. Whenever user performs above-mentioned actions, their details will be stored in database. Apriori algorithm will then be applied on above-collected data. This algorithm will result in most frequent actions and confidence values of subsets of frequent actions. The values satisfying minimum confidence threshold will be used to calculate weight of the Web page. The flow of proposed work is shown in Fig. 1.

The detailed description of each step is discussed below:

Step 1: Developing User Interface: A Web browser was proposed in first step. Normally, a Web browser does not store actions performed by a user, whereas the proposed Web browser automatically stores various actions performed by different users. When a user opens this browser a unique id is provided to him and his actions get stored in accordance with his id.

Step 2: Storing Actions performed by user in database: All actions performed by user get stored in database. A user can view summary of all actions by clicking on "User Stats" on the interface. User stats show the frequency of every action that is performed by different users.

Fig. 1 Structure of proposed approach

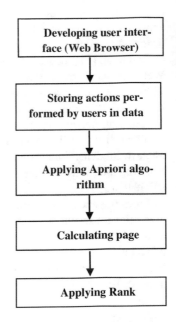

Step 3: Applying Apriori: Apriori is applied on stored actions to get most frequent actions. For each page, most frequent patterns are generated. These patterns are then used for calculating the page weight.

Step 4: Calculate Page Weight and PageRank: After applying Apriori on actions, frequent patterns are obtained. Confidence values of each pattern are taken to calculate page weight. Confidence value can be calculated as per Eq. (1):

$$\text{Confidence value} = \text{support\_count (most frequent action)}/\text{support\_count (sub set of most frequent action)} \tag{1}$$

where support count of an itemset is number of transactions that contain that itemset.

Based on the confidence value of each subset, the weight can be calculated by the following formula:

$$P_{wt} = C_1 + C_2 + C_3 + \ldots\ldots\ldots + C_i = \sum C_i \tag{2}$$

where C_1, C_2, C_3…. are the confidence values of subsets of frequent occurring actions which satisfy minimum confidence threshold.

Step 5: Apply Rank: Higher the page weight, higher its rank. It means the weight of the page which is calculated from above step is considered for PageRank. The page which has highest weight is assigned higher rank.

4 Example

In this section, an example is taken to show the working of proposed work. For this, actions performed by 40 users on two pages page $P1$, page $P2$ were stored in database. Database also stored number of times users visited those pages at different times. Users perform actions on those pages according to their needs. Their actions will be stored in a database. Apriori will be applied on those actions. For applying Apriori, minimum support of 20% and minimum confidence threshold of 60% were considered. Result of Apriori shows that most frequent actions on $P1$ were save as, add to favorites, number of scrollbar clicks, and most frequent actions on another page $P2$ were number of mouse clicks and print. With the help of this, the confidence values of pages were calculated.

Step 1: A Web browser is developed to store the user actions. The interface of proposed Web browser is shown in Fig. 2.

Step 2: All the actions performed by 40 users get stored in database and screenshot of which is shown in Fig. 3.

Deepika et al.

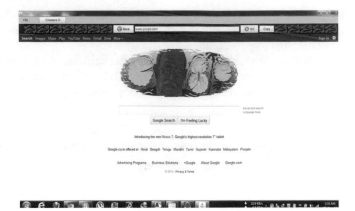

Fig. 2 Proposed bowser

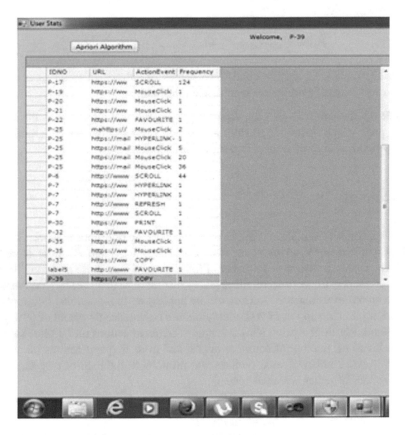

Fig. 3 Storing actions in database

Step 3: After applying Apriori on stored actions, frequency of actions can be calculated and then find out frequent patterns. The snapshot of this step is shown in Fig. 4.

Step 4: The confidence value of a page is calculated by putting the values in Eq. (1): First of all, we will calculate confidence values of most frequent actions of page $P1$.

$C1$ = sc {Save As, Add to Favorites, Number of Scrollbar Clicks}/sc {Save As} = 2/2 = **100%**

$C2$ = sc {Save As, Add to Favorites, Number of Scrollbar Clicks}/sc {Add to Favorites} = 2/6 = **33%**

$C3$ = sc {Save As, Add to Favorites, Number of Scrollbar Clicks}/sc {Number of Scrollbar Clicks} = 2/4 = **50%**

$C4$ = sc {Save As, Add to Favorites, Number of Scrollbar Clicks}/sc {Save As, Add to Favorites} = 2/3 = **67%**

$C5$ = sc {Save As, Add to Favorites, Number of Scrollbar Clicks}/sc {Save as, Number of Scrollbar Clicks} = 2/2 = **100%**

$C6$ = sc {Save As, Add to Favorites, Number of Scrollbar Clicks}/sc {Add to Favorites, Number of Scrollbar Clicks} = 2/3 = **67%**

Secondly, we will calculate confidence values of most frequent actions of page $P2$

$C1'$ = sc {Number of Mouseclicks, Print, Add to Favorites}/sc {Number of ouseclicks} = 2/3 = **67%**

$C2'$ = sc {Number of Mouseclicks, Print, Add to Favorites}/sc {Print} = 2/6 = **33%**

$C3'$ = sc {Number of Mouseclicks, Print, Add to Favorites}/sc {Add to Favorites} = 2/4 = **50%**

$C4'$ = sc {Number of Mouseclicks, Print, Add to Favorites}/sc {Number of Mouseclicks, Add to Favorites} = 2/2 = **100%**

Fig. 4 Frequency of actions performed by users

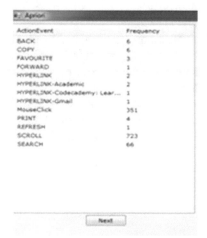

Table 1 Confidence values of subsets of most frequent actions

Confidence values	Selection
$C1 = 1$	✓
$C2 = 0.33$	✗
$C3 = 0.5$	✗
$C4 = 0.67$	✓
$C5 = 1$	✓
$C6 = 0.67$	✓
$C1' = 0.67$	✓
$C2' = 0.33$	✗
$C3' = 0.5$	✗
$C4' = 1$	✓
$C5' = 0.5$	✗
$C6' = 0.67$	✓

$C5'$ = sc {Number of Mouseclicks, Print, Add to Favorites}/sc {Number of Mouseclicks, Print} = 2/4 = **50%**

$C6'$ = sc {Number of Mouseclicks, Print, Add to Favorites}/sc {Print, Add to Favorites} = 2/3 = **67%** (Table 1)

Since minimum confidence threshold is 60%, confidence values $C2$, $C3$, $C2'$, $C3'$, $C5'$ will be rejected in page weight calculation.

Therefore, weight of page $P1$ is calculated as per Eq. (2):

P_{wt} = $C1$ + $C4$ + $C5$ + $C6$ = 1+0.67 + 1+0.67 = **3.34**

Weight of page $P2$ is:

P_{wt}' = $C1'$ + $C4'$ + $C6'$ = 0.67 + 1+0.67 = **2.34**

Step 5: Since page $P1$ has higher weight than page $P2$, rank of page $P1$ will be higher.

Page weight by Hit Count will be calculated by taking average of frequency of their visit on a particular page. Table 2 shows page weight of $P1$, $P2$ by Apriori, and Hit Count.

Star rating is calculated by user by explicitly asking while closing the Web page.

By the use of Table 2, we can give a graphical representation in Fig. 5 which shows the comparison between page weights calculated by both Apriori and Hit Count.

It is observed that Apriori is performing better than Hit Count as proposed work calculates higher relevance score. By explicitly asking users' interest also shows that proposed method predicts more accurate interest than Hit Count method.

Table 2 Comparison between page weight by Apriori, Hit Count, and star rating (by user)

Pages	Pwt (Apriori)	Pwt (Hit Count)	Star rating (by user)
Page P1	3.34	1.34	3
Page P2	2.6	2.2	2

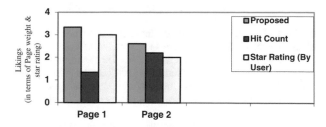

Fig. 5 Comparison between page weight by Apriori and by Hit Count

5 Conclusion

In this proposed approach, users' browsing behavior is used to find relevant pages. While past researches consider on user visit history and observing their time spent on a Web page, whereas above-mentioned mechanism shows that there are other user browsing behavior can also be consider to find the user's interest. The proposed mechanism identifies several implicit indicators that can be used to determine a user's interest in a Web page. In addition to previously studied implicit indicators, several new implicit indicators are also taken into consideration. The indicators examined are complete duration on a Web page, active time duration, search text, copy, print, save as, reload, number of key up and down, number of mouse clicks, number of scrollbar clicks, add to favorites, hyperlink, back, and forward. These implicit indicators prove to be more accurate than any indicator alone. To show that proposed results are more accurate, explicit indicator is also used to find more relevant pages. The explicit indicator used here is by asking from user to rate the page according to its interest, and then comparison is done with proposed work. The comparison shows that proposed is much closer to explicit indicators and is more accurate.

References

1. Agrawal, R., Ramakrishan, S.: Fast Algorithms for mining Association Rules. IBM Almaden Research Center (1994)
2. Deepika, Dixit, A.: Capturing User Browsing Behaviour Indicators. Electr. Comput. Eng. Int. J. (ECIJ) **4**(2), 23–30 (2015)

3. Deepika, Dixit, A.: Web crawler design issues: a review. Int. J. Multidiscip. res. Acad. (IJMRA) (2012)
4. Ying, X.: The research on user modeling for internet personalized Services. Nat. Univ. Def. Technol. (2003)
5. Morita, M., Shinoda Y.: Information filtering based on user behavior analysis and best match text retrieval. In: Proceedings of the 17th Annual International ACM SIGIR Conference on Research and Development in Information Retrieval (SIGIR), pp. 272–281 (1994)
6. Miller, B.N., Ried, J.T., Konstan, J.A.: GroupLens: applying collaborative filtering to usenet news. Commun. ACM, March (1997)
7. Claypool, M., Le, P., Waseda, M., Brown, D.: Implicit interest indicators. In: Proceedings 6th International Conference on Intelligent User Interfaces, ACM Press (2001)
8. Weinreich, H., Obendort, H., Herder, E., Mayer, M.: Off the beaten tracks: exploring three aspects of web navigation. In: WWW Conference 2006, ACM Press (2006)
9. Goecks, J. Shavlik, J.: Learning users' interests by unobtrusively observing their normal behavior. In Proceedings 5th International Conference on Intelligent User Interfaces, pp. 129–132 (2000)
10. Xing, K., Zhang, B., Zhou, B., Liu, Y.: Behavior based user extraction algorithm. In: IEEE International Conferences on Internet of Things, and Cyber, Physical and Social Computing (2011)
11. Tan, S.H., Chen, M., Yang, G.H.: User Behavior Mining on Large Scale Web Log Data. In: Apperceiving Computing and Intelligence Analysis (ICACIA) International Conference (2010)
12. Yang, Q., Hao, H., Neng, X: The research on user interest model based on quantization browsing behavior. In: The 7th International Conference on Computer Science and Education (ICCSE) Melbourne, Australia (2012)
13. Agrawal, R., Faloutsos, C., Swami, A.: Efficient similarity search in sequence databases. In: Proceedings of the Fourth International Conference on Foundations of Data Organization and Algorithms, Chicago, October (1993)
14. Kim, H., Chan, K.: Implicit indicators for interesting web pages. In: Web Information System and Technologies WEBIST 2005 (2005)

Performance Efficiency Assessment for Software Systems

Amandeep Kaur, P. S. Grover and Ashutosh Dixit

Abstract Software quality is a complex term. Various researchers have various different views for defining it. One common point in all is that quality is required and is indispensable. It should not only be able to meet the customer requirements but should exceed it. Customers not only mean the external customers but the internal ones too. Performance efficiency characteristic is one of the vital software quality characteristics. If we improve the performance efficiency, then it will definitely have a positive effect on the software quality. In this paper, we have identified various sub-characteristics that can affect the performance efficiency of the software and proposed a performance efficiency model. We assessed the performance efficiency of the software systems by using one of the multi-criteria decision making (MCDM) methods, namely analytical hierarchy process (AHP). Results suggest that the proposed model is consistent and may be used for comparing the software system.

Keywords Software quality · Software quality models · Performance efficiency
Optimized code · Analytical hierarchy process

A. Kaur (✉)
GTBIT, New Delhi, India
e-mail: amandeep.gtbit@gmail.com

P. S. Grover
KIIT Group of Colleges, Gurgaon, India
e-mail: drpsgrover@gmail.com

A. Dixit
YMCA University of Science and Technology, Faridabad, India
e-mail: dixit_ashutosh@rediffmail.com

© Springer Nature Singapore Pte Ltd. 2019
M. N. Hoda et al. (eds.), *Software Engineering*, Advances in Intelligent Systems and Computing 731, https://doi.org/10.1007/978-981-10-8848-3_8

1   Introduction

As per IEEE Std 610.12-1990, IEEE Standard Glossary of Software Engineering Terminology, "Software Quality" is defined as the degree to which a system, component, or process meets specified requirements and customer needs [1]. This definition was modified in IEEE Std 1633-2008, IEEE Recommended Practice on Software Reliability. It defines "Software Quality" as

1. The totality of features and characteristics of a software product that bears on its ability to satisfy given needs, such as conforming to specifications.
2. The degree to which software possesses a desired combination of attributes.
3. The degree to which a customer or user perceives that software meets his or her composite expectations.
4. The composite characteristics of software that determine the degree to which the software in use will meet the expectations of the customer.

This definition of software quality not only covers the objective but also the subjective part of quality. But one thought-provoking question that arises is that "Who is the Customer?". First thing that comes to the mind is the external customers. That is, those people who are external to the organization and who receive our product (software) and services. Another category of customers who are often forgotten or taken for granted are the internal customers. These are the people in the next phase of the software development life cycle and who are the internal customers of our work done.

Quality cannot be added later into the system as an afterthought. Rather, it needs to be built into the system from the very beginning. For building the software quality, we need to build an efficient system in terms of not only time and resources but efficiency of the code should also be a parameter. That is, we need to consider the expectations of not only external customers but also our internal customers.

2   Related Work

Inadequate quality of the software systems may lead to many problems like difficult maintenance, low performance efficiency, low reusability or frequent program change. From time to time, several researchers have proposed various software quality models in order to measure the quality of the software products. Latest software quality standard is ISO/IEC 25010 which was prepared by ISO/IEC JTCI after technically revising the earlier software quality model ISO/IEC 9126-1:2001. Various amendments were made in order to address the weaknesses of ISO/IEC 9126 in the newly revised quality model division ISO/IEC 2501n [2].

As per this latest International Standard ISO 25010, software product quality model enumerates eight characteristics. These characteristics are further subdivided into sub-characteristics which can be measured internally or externally [3]. Briefly, these quality characteristics are as follows:

1. Functional suitability: "the degree to which the software product provides functions that meet stated and implied needs when the software is used under specified conditions." It consists of functional completeness, functional correctness, and functional appropriateness as its sub-characteristics.

2. Reliability: "the degree to which software product performs specified functions under specified conditions for a specified period of time." It consists of maturity, fault-tolerance, recoverability, and availability as its sub-characteristics.

3. Usability: "the degree to which software product can be used by specified users to achieve specified goals with effectiveness, efficiency, and satisfaction in a specified context of use." It consists of appropriateness, recognizability, learnability, operability, user error protection, user interface aesthetics, and accessibility as its sub-characteristics.

4. Security: "degree to which a software product protects information and data so that persons or other products or systems have the degree of data access appropriate to their types and levels of authorization." It consists of confidentiality, integrity, non-repudiation, accountability, and authenticity as its sub-characteristics.

5. Performance Efficiency: "the capability of the software product to provide appropriate performance, relative to the amount of resources used, under stated conditions." It consists of time behavior, resource utilization, and capacity as its sub-characteristics.

6. Maintainability: "the degree of effectiveness and efficiency with which a software product can be modified by the intended modifiers." It consists of modularity, reusability, analyzability, modifiability, and testability as its sub-characteristics.

7. Portability: "the degree of effectiveness and efficiency with which a software product can be transferred from one environment to another." It consists of adaptability, installability, and replaceability as its sub-characteristics.

8. Compatibility: "the degree to which the software product can exchange information with other software products and/or perform its required functions, while sharing the same hardware or software environment." It consists of co-existence and interoperability as its sub-characteristics [2].

One major amendment done by ISO 25010 software quality model is in relation to efficiency characteristic of the software quality.

Earlier in ISO 9126 model, efficiency characteristic was one of the six software quality characteristics and was defined as "the capability of the software product to provide appropriate performance, relative to the amount of resources used, under stated conditions." It consists of time behavior, resource utilization, and efficiency compliance as its sub-characteristics.

Later in ISO 25010 model, efficiency was renamed to performance efficiency and capacity sub-characteristic was added to it along with time behavior and

resource utilization. Capacity as per ISO 25010 is the degree to which the maxi
mum limits of a product or system parameter meets requirements.

3 Proposed Performance Efficiency Model

Performance is an indication of the responsiveness of a system to execute specified
actions in given time interval. Performance efficiency can be defined as the performance relative to the amount of resources used under the stated conditions.

David Parnas quoted "For much of my life, I have been a software voyeur,
peeking furtively at other people's dirty code. Occasionally, I find a real jewel, a
well- structured program written in a consistent style, free of kludges, developed so
that each component is simple and organized, and designed so that the product is
easy to change."

Writing an optimized code has a positive effect on performance in terms of less
response time, increased throughput, reduced memory consumption, and reduced
network bandwidth consumptions.

According to Pressman "More books have been written about programming
(coding) and the principle and concepts that guide it than about any other topic in
the software process."

Sommerville also identified efficiency as one of the four generalized attributes
which is not concerned with what a program does, but how well the program does it
[4].

3.1 Performance Efficiency in Quality Models

Various software quality models have been reviewed in order to understand the
perspective for taking the performance efficiency as a characteristic for defining the
quality.

In 1977, Jim McCall identified three main perspectives (product revision, product transition, and product operations) for characterizing the quality attributes of a
software product and considered efficiency as one of the quality factors under
product operations. It defined one or more quality criteria for each quality factor, in
order to assess the overall quality of software product. According to McCall's
quality model, the quality criteria for efficiency are execution efficiency and storage
efficiency [5].

In 1978, Barry Boehm proposed a software quality model with seven quality
attributes according to the three fundamental uses (As-is utility, maintainability, and
portability) of the software which may affect the quality of the software product. It
identified efficiency as a quality attribute under As-is utility. According to Boehm's
quality model, the factors that affect efficiency are accountability, device efficiency,
and accessibility [3].

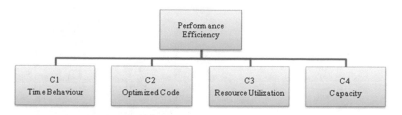

Fig. 1 Proposed performance efficiency model

In 1993, ISO 9126 software quality model was proposed and composed of six quality characteristics in relation to the internal and external quality. It identified efficiency as one of the quality characteristics and specifies three quality attributes that affect the efficiency of software are time behavior, resource behavior, and efficiency compliance [6].

In 2009, Kumar extended the ISO/IEC 9126 quality model and proposed aspect-oriented programming-based software quality model, viz aspect-oriented software quality (AOSQUAMO) model. It added code reducibility as a sub-characteristic under efficiency quality characteristic. Hence, the quality attributes that affect the efficiency according to AOSQUAMO model are time behavior, resource behavior, and code reducibility [7].

In 2011, although in ISO/IEC 25010 the problems related to efficiency were addressed, but still one area is untouched [2].

Use of solid coding techniques and good programming practices while developing high-quality optimized code plays an important role in software quality and performance. Code written while consistently applying well coding standard and proper coding techniques is not only an optimized code in terms of time, effort, cost (resources) but also is easier to comprehend and maintain. Hence, it will serve the expectation of our internal customers. The missing point in ISO 25010 model is that while estimating efficiency of software, no weightage is given to how efficiently code is written and how much optimized it is.

In this section, we propose a performance efficiency model as performance efficiency is a vital part for improving the software quality (Fig. 1).

4 Assessment of the Proposed Performance Efficiency Model

Analytic hierarchy process (AHP) method is one of the multi-criteria decision making (MCDM) methods that was developed by Dr. Thomas L. Saaty so as to make decisions in an organized and structured manner. Hence, AHP method works as a decision support tool that is used to solve various complex decision problems [8, 9].

Fig. 2 Problem
decomposition

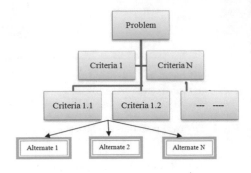

Table 1 Comparison matrix

	C_1	C_2	***	***	***	C_n
C_1	w_1/w_1	w_1/w_2	...	...	...	w_1/w_n
C_2	w_2/w_1	w_2/w_2	...	...	...	w_2/w_n
***	...	...	...	...	...	...
***	...	...	...	...	...	...
***	...	...	...	...	...	...
C_n	w_n/w_1	w_n/w_1				w_n/w_n

where C_1, C_2 ... C_n denote the criteria and w_1, w_2 ... w_n their
calculated weights

AHP is a four-step process:

Step 1: Define the problem and state the goal or objective.
Step 2: Define the criteria/factors that affect the goal or objective, and structure
them into levels and sub-levels (Fig. 2).
Step 3: Use paired comparisons of each criterion with respect to each other, and
find the matrix with calculated weights, eigenvectors, and consistency measures
(Table 1).

Saaty advised consistency index (CI) and consistency ratio (CR) as two measures for verifying the consistency of the comparison matrix [10].

$$\text{CI (Consistency Index)} = \frac{(\lambda \max - n)}{n - 1} \quad \text{and} \quad \text{CR(Consistency Ratio)} = \frac{\text{CI}}{\text{RI}}$$

As per Saaty, for $n \geq 5$, i.e., for 3×3 matrix if Consistency Ratio is greater
than 0.05: for 4×4 matrix if Consistency Ratio is greater than 0.08 and for all
larger matrixes If Consistency Ratio is greater than 0.1 than our set of judgment is
inconsistent.

Step 4: Synthesize the rank of alternatives until final choice is made.

5 Case Study

Step 1: Structuring the hierarchy for performance efficiency (Fig. 3).
Step 2: Calculating weights for each criterion.

Next step after decomposing the performing efficiency characteristics into a hierarchy of sub-characteristics, namely time behavior, optimized code, resource utilization, and capacity is to calculate the weights corresponding to these sub-characteristics. For this, a survey was conducted in which ten participants from software industry background participated [11, 12]. A survey form composed of six comparisons was provided to each participant. It constituted of pairwise comparison of the sub-characteristics. The participants were asked to assign a relative value in the range of 1–9 for every pairwise comparison. After collecting the same input from the participants, the mean value is calculated and shown in Fig. 4.

Step 3: Eigenvector and eigenvalue calculation.

Eigenvector is calculated by squaring the comparison matrix and then calculating the row sum which is then normalized.

I Iteration

The iteration is repeated till the time difference between the current eigenvector and previous eigenvector becomes negligible (Figs. 5 and 6).

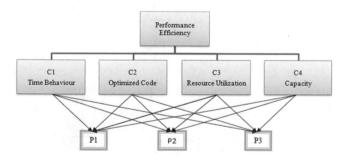

Fig. 3 Hierarchy for performance efficiency

		C1	C2	C3	C4
	C1	1.0000	1.5950	2.1400	1.8858
A=[a$_{ij}$]=	C2	0.6270	1.0000	3.0867	2.6243
	C3	0.4673	0.3240	1.0000	2.3575
	C4	0.5303	0.3811	0.4242	1.0000

Fig. 4 Comparison matrix with calculated weights

		C1	C2	C3	C4
	C1	4.0000	4.6019	10.0031	13.0024
$A^2=$	C2	4.0879	4.0000	8.6282	13.7077
	C3	2.3878	2.2916	4.0000	6.4464
	C4	1.4977	1.7453	3.1593	4.0000

Fig. 5 Squaring the A matrix

Fig. 6 Row sum matrix and eigenvector

Row Sum		Eigenvector
31.6074		0.3610
30.4238		0.3475
15.1259		0.1727
10.4024		0.1188
Row Total= 87.5594	Total=	1.0000

II Iteration

See Figs. 7 and 8.

III Iteration

After the third iteration, the difference between the current and the previous eigenvector is approaching to zero. Hence, these values can be accepted as our final values (Figs. 9 and 10).

		C1	C2	C3	C4
	C1	78.1713	82.4320	160.8103	231.5851
$A^4=$	C2	73.8355	78.5090	153.2247	218.4349
	C3	38.1252	40.5726	80.0248	114.0316
	C4	26.6601	28.0948	55.3153	79.7643

Fig. 7 Squaring the A^2 matrix

Row Sum		Eigenvector		Difference
552.9987		0.3592		0.0018
524.0041		0.3404		0.0071
272.7541		0.1772		-0.0044
189.8346		0.1233		-0.0045
Row Total= 1539.5915	Total=	1.0000		

Fig. 8 Row sum matrix, eigenvector, and difference

		C1	C2	C3	C4
	C1	24502.1669	25946.3020	50880.3759	72919.0117
$A^8=$	C2	23233.7919	24603.6880	48247.6013	69144.0854
	C3	12067.0475	12778.5585	25059.3028	35912.6987
	C4	8393.8838	8888.5931	17430.8257	24981.0151

Fig. 9 Squaring the A^4 matrix

Fig. 10 Row sum matrix,
eigenvector, and difference

Row Sum		Eigenvector		Difference
174247.8565		0.3593		-0.0001
165229.1666		0.3407		-0.0003
85817.6075		0.1769		0.0002
59694.3177		0.1231		0.0002
Row Total= 484988.9482	Total=	1.0000		

Fig. 11 Eigenvalues, λ, and
λ_{max}

Eigenvalues	λ
1.5135	4.2124
1.4351	4.2125
0.7454	4.2124
0.5185	4.2124

λ max	4.2125

Step 4: Consistency measures calculation

According to Saaty, matrix A is consistent matrix if $\lambda_{max} \geq n$ and consistency ratio (CR), the ratio of consistency index to random matrix, is significantly small, i.e., less than 10%. If not, then there is still scope of improvement in consistency. As for our case study, an equal to four hence to be consistent λ_{max} should be greater than or equal to four (Fig. 11).

$$\text{Consistency index (CI)} = \frac{(\lambda\max n)}{n-1} = \frac{(4.2125 - 4)}{4 - 1} = 0.0708$$

And

$$\text{Consistency Ratio (CR)} = \frac{\text{CI}}{\text{RI}} = \frac{0.070833}{0.9} = 0.0787$$

Now as λ_{max} is 4.2125 which is greater than 4 and consistency ratio is 0.0787 which is less than 0.1, hence matrix A is consistent.

6 Conclusion and Future Scope

In this paper, we assess the performance efficiency characteristic of the software systems. Firstly, we identified the criterion/factors that could affect the performance efficiency and structured them into levels and proposed the performance efficiency model. After this, in order to assess the proposed model, we conducted the survey. Ten participants from software industry background participated in the survey. We applied AHP method for insuring the consistency of the proposed performance efficiency model. Result showed that the chosen quality sub-characteristics are consistent and the relative ranking of the quality attributes for performance efficacy is in the order of time behavior, optimized code, resource utilization, and then capacity. In future, this model may be used for comparing the performance efficiency of different software systems.

References

1. Pressman, R.S.: Software Engineering: A Practitioner's Approach, 5th edn. Mc Graw Hill, New York (2005)
2. ISO/IEC 2010; ISO/IEC 25010: Systems & software engineering—system and software quality requirements and evaluation (SQuaRE)—system and software quality models (2010)
3. Boehm, B., et al.: Quantitative evaluation of software quality. In: IEEE International Conference on Software Engineering, pp. 592–605 (1976)
4. Sommerville, Ian (2004). Software Engineering (Seventh ed.). Pearson. pp. 12–13. ISBN 0-321-21026-3
5. McCall, J.A., Richards, P.K., Walters, G.F.: Factors in Software Quality, vols. I, II, and III. US Rome Air Development Center Reports. US Department of Commerce; USA (1977)
6. ISO 2001; ISO/IEC 9126-1: Software Engineering—Product Quality—Part 1: Quality Model. International Organisation for Standardisation, Geneva Switzerland (2001)
7. Kumar, A.: Analysis & design of matrices for aspect oriented systems. Ph.D. Thesis, Thapar University (2010)
8. Saaty, T.L.: Analytic Hierarchy Process. Mc Graw Hill (1980)
9. Kaur, A., Grover, P.S., Dixit, A.: Quantitative evaluation of proposed maintainability model using AHP method. In: 2nd International Conference on computing for sustainable global development, pp. 8.159–8.163 (2015)
10. Kaur, A., Grover, P.S., Dixit, A.: An improved model to estimate quality of the software product. YMCAUST Int. J. Res. 1(2), 01–06 (2013)
11. Kaur, A., Grover, P.S., Dixit, A.: Analysis of quality attribute and metrics of various software development methodologies. In: International Conference on Advancements in Computer Applications and Software Engineering, pp. 05–10 (2012)
12. Grady, R., et al.: Software Metrics: Establishing a Company-Wide Program, p. 159. Prentice Hall (1987)

Impact of Programming Languages on Energy Consumption for Sorting Algorithms

Tej Bahadur Chandra, Pushpak Verma and Anuj Kumar Dwivedi

Abstract In today's scenario, this world is moving rapidly toward the global warming. Various experiments are performed, to concentrate more on the energy efficiency. One way to achieve this is by implementing the sorting algorithms in such a programming language which consumes least amount of energy which is our current area of research in this paper. In this study, our main goal is to find such a programming language which consumes least amount of energy and contributes to green computing. In our experiment, we implemented different sorting algorithms in different programming languages in order to find the most power-efficient language.

Keywords Programming language · Sorting algorithms · Power consumption Joulemeter

1 Introduction

Energy efficiency is a critical aspect in battery-operated devices like sensor nodes, Internet of things (IoT) devices, and many other devices engaged in space research operations. As data size grows in battery-operated devices, so does the power consumption, and it ultimately reduces the device's uptime. Not only is the hardware blamed for energy consumption, however, the software is equally responsible for same. We, on this paper, focus on the energy consumption of three standard programming languages, Visual Basic 6.0, Java, and C#.Net by implementing four

T. B. Chandra (✉) · P. Verma
School of Information Technology, MATS University, Raipur, Chhattisgarh, India
e-mail: tejbahadur1990@gmail.com

P. Verma
e-mail: verma.pushpak@gmail.com

A. K. Dwivedi
Govt. Vijay Bhushan Singh Deo Girls Degree College, Jashpur 496331, Chhattisgarh, India
e-mail: Anuj.ku.dwivedi@gmail.com

© Springer Nature Singapore Pte Ltd. 2019   93
M. N. Hoda et al. (eds.), *Software Engineering*, Advances in Intelligent Systems and Computing 731, https://doi.org/10.1007/978-981-10-8848-3_9

sorting algorithms, bubble sort, insertion sort, selection sort, and Quick sort. We simulate the energy consumption of sorting algorithms when implemented in different programming languages in order to come up with energy-efficient programming.

Our interest area in this paper is to promote green computing by coming up with such programming languages and sorting algorithms into limelight which require least energy.

2 Related Works

The IT industries have been focusing on energy efficiency of hardware and evolved their devices for better efficiency [1]. Green computing is the environmental-friendly use of available computing resources without sacrificing performance [2]. A very few researches have been performed in this field due to constrained hardware resources and extensive cost. Researchers had concluded that the most time and energy-efficient sorting algorithm is Quick sort [3]. It is also found that the energy consumption greatly depends on time and space complexity of the algorithms [4]. A programmer can develop application-level energy-efficient solutions if he uses energy-efficient language [5]. Algorithms also have great impact on the energy consumption and ultimately on green computing [6]. Several researches have already been performed on hardware and concluded that home server hardware together with well-tuned, parallelized sorting algorithms can sort bulk amounts of data and is noticeably more energy-efficient than older systems [7]. Bunse, C. concluded that, different software has the different energy payload; also, his studies show that different algorithms have different energy requirements [8].

3 Role of Programming Language in Energy Efficiency

A lot of researches had already been performed to gain the energy efficiency which mostly focuses on algorithm designs, hardware architectures (VLSI designs), operating systems, and compilers, etc., but investigations show that the programming language design and good programming practice may be one perspective to reduce power consumption [9]. Distinct programming languages handle the same situation differently and require discrete number of operations to accomplish the same task. In general, compiled language is typical to code but runs faster; on the other hand, interpreted languages are easier to program but take longer to run. There is some difference in the energy consumption between different loops (such as *For Loop* and *While Loop*) when the number of operations needed in increasing the loop counter variables and checking termination conditions are significant between the two alternatives. Energy consumption by an application can be further cut down by using *'vector operations'* in a vector register where possible. Code execution time can also be reduced by taking advantage of multiple threads and cores, resulting in increased idle time that in turn leads to power conservation. The inefficient codes force the CPU to draw more from the processor and consume more electricity [10]. Performance-to-power relationship can be improved by loop unrolling. Use of idle-power-friendly programming language implementations and libraries may improve the power saving [11]. Based on several researches, researchers estimated that between 30 and 50% energy savings can be achieved by selecting energy-aware software solutions and even more could be achieved by proper combination of both software and hardware [12].

4 Sorting Algorithms

It is a very efficient way which helps in performing important task of putting the element list in order. For example, sorting will arrange the elements in ascending or descending [13]. When it comes to battery-operated devices, use of energy-efficient sorting is a prime requirement. The text follows contains the sorting algorithms that were used in our research. Table 1 shows the complexities of various sorting algorithms.

4.1 *Bubble Sort*

It is a simple algorithm, which begins at the start of the data, bubbles the largest element to the end of the data set on each pass, and in next cycle it repeats the same with one reduced cycle [14].

Table 1 Sorting algorithm complexity

Sorting name	Average case	Worst case	Best case	Stability
Bubble	O(n^2)	O(n^2)	O(n)	Yes
Insertion	O(n^2)	O(n^2)	O(n)	Yes
Quick sort	O(nlog n)	O(n^2)	O(n log(n))	No
Selection	O(n^2)	O(n^2)	O(n^2)	No

4.2   Selection Sort

It is also referred as comparison sort, is best known for its simplicity, and has pretty good performance over complicated algorithms. It is not as good as insertion sort which works in a similar way as the selection sort [15].

4.3   Insertion Sort

Insertion sort separates the data list into two parts: one part which is in sorted section and the other which is in the unsorted section. When a new element is inserted, all the existing elements are required to be shifted to right [16].

4.4   Quick Sort

The Quick sort is an advanced form of Quick sort. Some modifications are made in the internal loops of Quick sort to make it very well optimized and short. It is also abbreviated as Median Hybrid Quick sort.

5   Programming Language

It is a specially designed instruction set that is used to represent algorithms in machines' understandable format and control its behavior. There exist many different programming languages that suit to different environments. Being a programmer, it is very essential to focus on the latest programming trends that contribute to power conservation. Following are some computer languages that are used in our study [17].

5.1   Java [18]

Java is a platform-independent, open-source programming language mainly designed to operate on the distributed environment of the Internet. It uses all the best parts of C and C++ by introducing many new things in it. Microsoft version of Java is known as visual J++.

5.2   Visual Basic 6.0

It provides a complete GUI-based high-level integrated programming environment for developing Windows application. It is based on event-driven programming and is derived from language called BASIC. Visual Basic provides easy application development by using structured programming approach and can be easily debugged and modified [19].

5.3   C#.Net

C# is a modern language which is type-safe and completely object-oriented programming language from Microsoft. C# embodies both the power of C++ and comfort of Visual Basic. C# uses C++ as base while incorporating features that make it familiar to Java programmers. C# is designed to work on Microsoft platform [20].

6   Experimental Setup

Here in this study, we used a simulator tool named "Joulemeter" [21] from Microsoft Corporation to simulate power consumption of various sorting algorithms implemented in three languages: Java, C#.NET, and Visual Basic 6.0.

We used Intel Core i5 and 4th generation CPU with Windows 8.1 (Version 6.3.9600) operating system to perform our experiment. Figure 1 shows the model for experimental setup.

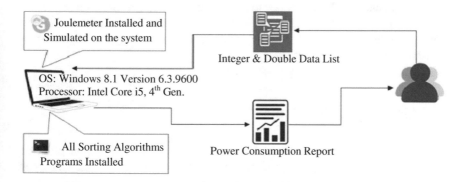

Fig. 1 Experimental setup for calculation of power consumption

– **Joulemeter**

It is a software tool which was introduced by Microsoft. It is used to view the overall power consumption by the whole system and also the key components which are to be monitored. The user has to calibrate the Joulemeter in order to estimate the power consumption of an idle system. After the calibration, the total power consumption can be monitored and obtained by adding up values (in watt) for duration of interest. It can also be converted to other units like kW h/W h by using the following conversion:

$$
\begin{aligned}
1\,\text{kW h} \quad &= 1000\,\text{W} \times 1\,\text{h} \\
&= 1000\,\text{W} * 3600\,\text{s} \\
&= 3,600,000\,\text{J}.
\end{aligned}
$$

$$
\begin{aligned}
\text{i.e.} \quad \text{Watt} \quad &= \text{J/s}. \\
\text{Thus,} \quad 1\,\text{Joule} \quad &= 1/3,600,000\,\text{kW h.} \ [3]
\end{aligned}
$$

– **Sorting Algorithm Programs**

In our study, we implemented four sorting algorithms in three different languages: Visual Basic 6.0, C#.Net, and Java. All these sorting programs provide sorting on both integer and double data sets with sixty thousand elements.

7 Experimental Run

In our experiment, we have compared the four sorting algorithms implemented in three different languages on the basis of their power consumption over sixty thousand integer as well as double data elements. We performed four test runs on same data set and took their average to find average power consumption per second on each programming language for all sorting algorithms discussed here. To verify which programming language requires lesser amount of energy for which sorting algorithm, we plotted a bar graph.

8 Experimental Result and Analysis

After comparing the above sorting algorithms implemented in different programming languages over sixty thousand data for both integer and double data types. The values are calculated on the basis of power consumption represented in Watt per second.

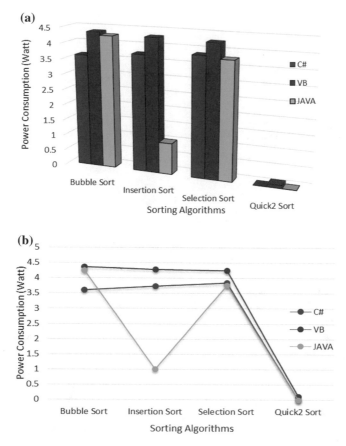

Fig. 2 **a** Average power consumed for integer data set (in W/s). **b** Average power consumed for integer data set (in W/s)

In Fig. 2a, b, we noted that different programming languages consume different amount of power for each sorting algorithm and also the power consumption depends on selection of sorting algorithms.

In Fig. 3a, b, we observed that in case of sorting the elements of double data type also, Java is most power efficient and Visual Basic consumes more power.

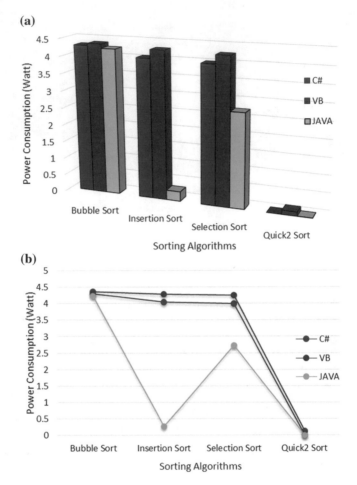

Fig. 3 **a** Average power consumed for double data set (in W/s). **b** Average power consumed for double data set (in W/s)

9 Conclusion

Our research enlightens on such measurements and calculations, which results in selection of such programming language which consumes least power and leads to increased uptime of battery-operated devices and ultimately results in green computing. In this paper, we mainly focus on the power efficiency of programming languages used to implement sorting algorithms. Based on our experiment, we found that Java is most power-efficient programming language while Visual Basic 6.0 consumes more power than the other two languages which are used in our study. Also, sorting the data elements of type double consumes more power than that of data set of integer type.

References

1. Raza, K., Patle, V.K., Arya, S.: A review on green computing for eco-friendly and sustainable IT. J. Comput. Intell. Electron. Syst. **1**(1), 3–16 (2012)
2. Saha, B: Green computing. Int. J. Comput. Trends Technol. **14**(2) (2014)
3. Chandra, T.B., Patle, V.K., Kumar, S.: New horizon of energy efficiency in sorting algorithms: green computing. In: Proceedings of National Conference on Recent Trends in Green Computing. School of Studies in Computer in Computer Science & IT, Pt. Ravishankar Shukla University, Raipur, India, 24–26 Oct 2013
4. Bunse, C., Höpfner, H., Roychoudhury, S., Mansour, E.: Choosing the "best" sorting algorithm for optimal energy consumption. In: ICSOFT (2), pp. 199–206 (2009)
5. Liu, Y. D.: Energy-aware programming in pervasive computing. In: NSF Workshop on Pervasive Computing at Scale (PeCS) (2011)
6. Narain, B., Kumar, S.: Impact of algorithms on green computing. Int. J. Comput. Appl. (2013). ISSN No. 0975-8887
7. Beckmann, A., Meyer, U., Sanders, P., Singler, J.: Energy-efficient sorting using solid state disks. In: Proceedings of IEEE Green Computing Conference (2010)
8. Bunse, C., Hopfner, H., Mansour, E., Roychoudhury, S.: Exploring the energy consumption of data sorting algorithms in embedded and mobile environments. In: Tenth International Conference on Mobile Data Management: Systems, Services and Middleware, 2009. MDM'09, pp. 600–607. IEEE (2009)
9. Liu, Y.D.: Energy-aware programming in pervasive computing. In: NSF Workshop on Pervasive Computing at Scale (PeCS) (2011)
10. Francis, K., Richardson, P.: Green maturity model for virtualization. Archit. J. **18**(1), 9–15 (2009)
11. Energy-Efficient Software Guidelines. https://software.intel.com/en-us/articles/partner-energy-efficient-software-guidelines
12. Code green: Energy-efficient programming to curb computers power use, http://www.washington.edu/news/2011/05/31/code-green-energy-efficient-programming-to-curb-computers-power-use/
13. Sareen, P.: Comparison of sorting algorithms (on the basis of average case). Int. J. Adv. Res. Comput. Sci. Softw. Eng. **3**(3), 522–532 (2013)
14. Research Paper on Sorting Algorithms. http://www.digifii.com/name-jariya-phongsai-class-mac-286-data-structure_22946/. Accessed on 26 Oct 2009
15. Nagpal, H.: Hit sort: a new generic sorting algorithm
16. Khairullah, M.: Enhancing worst sorting algorithms. Int. J. Adv. Sci. Technol. **56** (2013)
17. Singh, T.: New software development methodology for student of Java programming language. Int. J. Comput. Commun. Eng. **2**(2), 194–196 (2013)
18. Gosling, J.: The Java language specification. Addison-Wesley Professional (2000)
19. Hassan, A.B., Abolarin, M.S., Jimoh, O.H.: The application of Visual Basic computer programming language to simulate numerical iterations. Leonardo J. Sci. **5**(9), 125–136 (2006)
20. Benton, N., Cardelli, L., Fournet, C.: Modern concurrency abstractions for C#. ACM Trans. Program. Lang. Syst. (TOPLAS) **26**(5), 769–804 (2004)
21. Joulemeter. http://research.microsoft.com/en-us/downloads/fe9e10c5-5c5b-450c-a674-daf55565f794

Crawling Social Web with Cluster Coverage Sampling

Atul Srivastava, Anuradha and Dimple Juneja Gupta

Abstract Social network can be viewed as a huge container of nodes and relationship edges between the nodes. Covering every node of social network in the analysis process faces practical inabilities due to gigantic size of social network. Solution to this is to take a sample by collecting few nodes and relationship status of huge network. This sample can be considered as a representative of complete network, and analysis is carried out on this sample. Resemblance of results derived by analysis with reality majorly depends on the extent up to which a sample resembles with its actual network. Sampling, hence, appears to be one of the major challenges for social network analysis. Most of the social networks are scale-free networks and can be seen having overlapping clusters. This paper develops a robust social Web crawler that uses a sampling algorithm which considers clustered view of social graph. Sample will be a good representative of the network if it has similar clustered view as actual graph.

Keywords Social graph · Sampling · Social web crawler · OSNs

1 Introduction

Social networks provide an open platform to analyse and understand the behaviour of users, their interaction patterns and propagation of information. An explosive growth of Online Social Networks (OSNs) has assured possibility of prominent

A. Srivastava (✉) · Anuradha
Department of Computer Engineering, Y.M.C.A. University of Science and Technology,
Faridabad, India
e-mail: atul.nd2@gmail.com

Anuradha
e-mail: anuangra@yahoo.com

D. J. Gupta
Department of Computer Science and Engineering, D. I. M. T, Ambala, India
e-mail: dimplejunejagupta@gmail.com

© Springer Nature Singapore Pte Ltd. 2019
M. N. Hoda et al. (eds.), *Software Engineering*, Advances in Intelligent Systems
and Computing 731, https://doi.org/10.1007/978-981-10-8848-3_10

outcomes of social network analysis. Facebook, a social networking site, crossed 1.3 billion monthly active users and Twitter, also called SMS of Internet, 284 million monthly active users putting 500 million tweets per day [1, 2].

Although OSNs provide easily available data for analysis, the size of OSNs is gigantic that hinders researchers to understand the structure of graphs. Huge size of OSNs brings two major challenges: first, it is difficult to collect complete graph. Reasons being, the administrator of the network is not willing to give data or the users on the site have different restrictions on visibility of their data. Time required to acquire complete graph makes it impossible. Secondly, if somehow the data of complete graph is gathered at one place, it requires expensive and well-equipped computers and large overhead in terms of time, storage and computation [3]. Alternatively, sampling of graph suggests a prominent and inexpensive solution. A subset of graph is considered representative of the original graph. A good sampling cuts short the scale of the original graph, yet maintains its characteristics.

While sampling can, in principle, draw accurate results in comparatively very small observations, the accuracy majorly depends on the representativeness of the sample. Recent work in the area of sampling focuses on resemblance of statistical properties a sample holds. Sampling algorithms are based on the facts that nodes are connected to one another via some relationship in social graph. Hence, a sample of social graph can be collected easily by crawling. Earlier efforts in sampling were made with the techniques like BFS/Snowball-type approaches [4]. These algorithms are fed with seed node (starting point), and then connected nodes are explored recursively. But these techniques came up with a well-known anomaly called biasing. Sample collected through these techniques may be biased towards high-degree nodes due to which the sample exhibits poor statistical properties [5]. Recent work focuses on unbiased sampling techniques mostly based on random walks [6–11] in the social network.

2 Related Work

Several sampling algorithms have been proposed for social graph sampling. These algorithms can be put into two categories: first, which focuses on nodes and second, which focuses on edges. In algorithms in former category, the sampling decision-making process is executed on nodes, e.g., BFS [4, 12], MHRW [4, 9, 10] and UGDSG [13]. The latter class of algorithms acquires edges in sample and nodes as the end points of the edges are selected, e.g., FS [13].

BFS has been used widely to study user behaviour of OSNs [4] and analysing topological characteristics of social graphs [14]. But BFS suffers from biasing [4, 14]. It visits nodes with higher degree more frequently. Due to which BFS obtains higher local clustering coefficient than the original ones [paper].

MHRW is based on Markov Chain Monte Carlo (MCMC) model that selects random nodes' samples according to degree probability distribution of the nodes [9, 10]. MHRW designs a proposal function based on probability distribution which is randomly accepted or rejected. Probabilities are modified during transition by which sample achieves convergence at probability distribution. Selection of next node from the current node is made on the basis of another independent event, i.e., random number generation, p, from uniform distribution $U(0, 1)$. If p < probability ratio of current node and proposed node, then proposed node is selected as next node. So if degree of the proposed node is small (small chance to be selected), there will be a high probability that the proposal will be accepted. MHRW was originally designed for undirected graphs. Another method USDSG [ ] is developed that is based on MHRW and works with directed graphs. USDSG considers all the uni-directional edges as bidirectional edges. To apply UGDSG, a directed graph is changed to symmetric graph. This methodology is also used in Frontier Sampling (FS) [1]. FS is an edge sampling algorithm based on Random Walk. FS selects one node v as seed node from set of seed nodes S, with the probability defined as:

$$P(v) = \frac{k_v}{\sum_{u \in S} k_v}$$

An edge (v, w) is selected uniformly from node v's outgoing edges, and v will be replaced with w in the set of seed nodes. Edge (v, w) is added to the sample. FS does not perform well if clustering coefficient is small [13].

Corlette et al. [15] proposed event-driven sampling that focuses active part of the network. Event-driven sampling is similar to the process used by various search engines to refresh their repository by including new Web pages and eliminating expired ones. However, multigraph sampling [16] considers social network dis-tributed in clusters. The sampling is carried out on multiple relations among users in social network.

3   Problem Description

Generally, social Web crawling has distinct steps; crawler starts with seed node, explores and collects its directly connected nodes, selects few of explored nodes as sample for further exploration, and this process is repeated. After fetching any information of one node completely, crawler needs next node to crawl and that is selected by sampling algorithm.

Almost every social network is scale-free and can be seen as unevenly formed; i.e., the network is denser at some places and sparse at others. These denser portions can be considered as clusters or people/actors in these denser portions exhibit some kind of similar characteristics, e.g., same workplace, same hometown, same study place or same country or same continent. Hence, social network is not uniform but it is collection of overlapping clusters (few clusters can be stand-alone also).

We consider a social graph $G = (V, E)$, where V is collection of nodes and E is collection of edges representing associations among nodes. Due to scale-free per-sona of social graphs, we can consider the graph has several overlapping clusters

$CL_1, CL_2, CL_3 \ldots CL_k$ such that $G = \bigcup_{1 \le i \le k} CL_i$. There is a possibility that few of these clusters may not be overlapping of completely disjoints. Here, clusters can be said former form of communities or less-restricted communities. There is a greater possibility that each community that is excavated from sample of the graph definitely has a parent cluster. Let graph $G_s = (V_s, E_s)$ be the sample of graph G. $Co_1, Co_2, Co_3 \ldots Co_m$ be the communities detected in G_s, such that $G_s = \bigcup_{1 \le j \le m} Co_j$. Then, following predicate is always true

$$\forall_j [Co_j \rightarrow \exists_i [CL_i \text{ is parent of } Co_j], \text{ where}, 1 \le j \le m \text{ and } 1 \le i \le k$$

Here, we propose an algorithm that focuses on the above-stated fact with assumption that there is no disjoint cluster in the social graph. The sample reflects almost exact overlapping clustered view of original network only if the above predicate holds.

4 Cluster Coverage Sampling (CCS) Methodology

A crawling framework proposed in this paper uses adaptive sampling which aims at potential limitations or challenges evident in several existing sampling algorithms which will be discussed along with the explanation of proposed framework. The crawling framework is briefly shown in Fig. 1. The framework assumes that the social graph is undirected, crawler is interested in only publically available information, and graph is well connected (graph can be disconnected if it has stand-alone clusters which will be ignored by the crawler). Social Web is apparently huge and is in the form of overlapping clusters which is demonstrated by intersecting bubbles in the social Web cloud.

Social Web is clustered which overlaps by having common actors. The crawler while digging into the network and collecting sample must ensure that it touches every cluster. Crawler starts with a seed node and proceeds further by hoping to its friends (directly connected nodes). In Fig. 1, social Web is shown having clusters which overlap. Crawler can start at any cluster to which seed node belongs.

Crawling proceeds further with following algorithms:

Algorithm 1
Crawler (S_n)
        Input: Seed_Node S_n.
    Start
        Perform login with credentials of S_n;
        Initialize Sample_Date_Set and Sparse_Data_Set;
           $C_n[] \leftarrow S_n$;
           Crawling $(C_n[])$;
    End

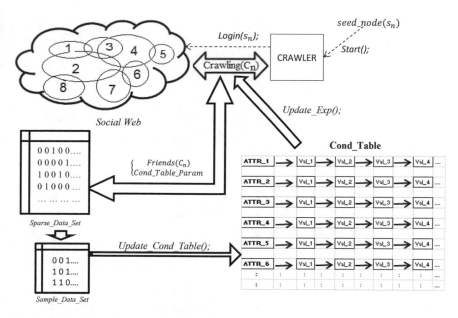

Fig. 1 Crawler framework based on CCS

As shown in Algorithm 1, crawler enters in the network via seed node S_n. Most of the OSNs require username and password, provided to the crawler to login. Two data sets are maintained by the framework. First, Sparse_Data_Set that contains every node explored by the crawler and identified links between them. Out of many explored nodes, few are selected for further exploration. Connectivity among nodes is known for only those nodes which are visited by the crawler. Thus, Sparse_Data_Set contains many nodes among which the relationship status is not known and hence considered unrelated nodes (there may exist connectivity in real network). Therefore, another data set, Sample_Data_Set is also maintained that contains only those nodes among which the relationship is known. $C_n[]$ is the list of nodes, which will be crawled by the crawler next.

Algorithm 2
Crawling $(C_n[])$
   Input: Nodes_To_Crawl_List $C_n[]$.
Start
      Update (Sample_Date_Set, $C_n[]$, Sparse_Data_Set);

```
      While (Cₙ[]!empty)
      {
              Pₙ ← Select_&_Remove (Cₙ[]);    //Pₙ is current node being
processed.
              E_Nodes ← Find_Friends (Pₙ);
              Competing_Nodes ← Find_Redundancy(E_Nodes, id_Table);
              Update (Sparse_Data_Set, Competing_Nodes); //nodes explored
and their connections are saved.
              Cond_Table ← Fetch_Attr_Values (Pₙ);
      }
      EXP ← Expression_Generator(Cond_Table);
      Cₙ[] ← Sample_Nodes (Competing_Nodes, EXP);
      Crawling (Cₙ[]); //Recursive call.
  End
```

Algorithm 2 exploits actual crawling process. List of sampled nodes $C_n[]$ is fed to crawling process. Nodes contained in $C_n[]$ are visited by the crawler one by one so these nodes are stored in Sample_Data_Set. E_Nodes contains direct friends of the node currently being visited by the crawler. E_Nodes may contain redundancy if sampled nodes have common friends or sampled nodes have friends which have already been sampled. id_Table contains every node sampled by the crawler so far. Such redundancies are eliminated in Competing_Nodes. Sparse_Data_Set is updated with every new node their connections explored through current node being processed, P_n.

Cond_Table contains attributes of user (node) and their possible values which are refined along with the crawling. For instance, suppose Facebook is being crawled. Any user in the network has attributes like 'Lives in', 'Work', 'Study Places'. Possible values of such attributes have huge range as it depends on cluster of the gigantic social graph which the crawler is in. As the crawling process proceeds and crawler visits nodes, attributes (if found any new) and their possible values (if found any new) are updated. Selection expression EXP is generated on attributes and their values in Cond_Table. Nodes which satisfy EXP are sampled next.

EXP is a Boolean expression. It contains several attributes with their one possible value ANDed or ORed, thereby forming a nested Boolean expression. One combination of attribute and its value is considered as an 'Atom' ($Atom_k$ can be defined as $(ATTR_k == Value_j(ATTR_k)), 1 \leq j \leq$ total num of possible values of $ATTR_k$). AND and OR (Between_Atom_Op_List) are binary operators, used between atoms, and NOT (On_Atom_Op_List) is unary operator used on any Atom optionally. Values of attributes Between_Atom_Operator and On_Atom_Operator are selected randomly. Algorithm 3 is used to generate (first time) and update EXP.

```
Algorithm 3
  Expression_Generator(Cond_Table)
  Start
    k = 0;
    while(k < Num_Of_Attributes(Cond_Table))
    {
        Atom_k ← Select_Value(ATTR_k);
        On_Atom_Op_k ← Select_Op(On_Atom_Op_List);
        Between_Atom_Op_k ← Select_Op(Between_Atom_Op_List);
        Update(EXP, On_Atom_Op_k, Atom_k, Between_Atom_Op_k);
    }
    Return EXP;
  End
```

Algorithm 4 represents how next nodes are selected from Competing_Nodes. Number of nodes to be sampled is limited by a threshold value which is decided by the size of Competing_Nodes. Nodes are selected randomly from Competing_Nodes but only those nodes which satisfy EXP are sampled. If the algorithm fails to find desired number of nodes which satisfy EXP, it completes requirement by randomly selecting remaining number of nodes from Competing_Nodes.

```
Algorithm 4
  Sample_Nodes (Competing_Nodes, EXP)
  Start-
    s_count = 0; r_count = 0; //To count number of sampled nodes and
    randomly selected nodes
    while(s_count < Threshold(Competing_Nodes)  &  r_count < SizeOf
    (Competing_Nodes))
    {
        r_count ++;
        P_n ← RandomSelect_&_Remove (Competing_Nodes); //P_n is
    current node being processed
        If(P_n holds EXP)
        {
            s_count ++;
            add(Node_List, P_n);
```

```
       }
    }
    while(s_count < Threshold(Competing_Nodes))
    {
       Add(Node_List, RandomSelect_&_Remove(Competing_Nodes));
       s_count ++;
    }
    Append(id_Table, Node_List);
    Return Node_List;
 End
```

Let us assume that the crawler has sampled nodes of cluster 2 of social graph shown in Fig. 1. Nodes lying in the area of cluster 2 that is not overlapped by any other cluster have similar characteristics and probably can satisfy the current EXP. If EXP is altered at few Atoms, there might be a possibility that nodes lying in the area of cluster 2 overlapped by any other cluster (1, 3, 4, 7 or 8). By sampling nodes lying in overlapping area of clusters, crawler migrates from one cluster to other cluster. Hence, the sample will have nodes covering almost every cluster of the social network rather than having nodes of just few adjacent clusters.

5 Experiments and Result Analysis

The proposed model in this paper has been tested on a synthetic social network created on local server. The synthetic network has identical characteristics as any other social network in terms of power law of degree distribution, clustering coefficient, etc. The synthetic social network is created using logs of e-mail conversations of students and faculty members in YMCA UST, Faridabad, India. The nodes in synthetic social network exhibit some inherent attributes such as place of birth, place of work, education, political orientation, birthday. These attributes of each user and their values are used for creating Boolean expression EXP. The description of the data set is shown in Table 1.

The attributes of each node in the network are created anonymously. The algorithm is executed on the network in two phases. In first phase, the algorithm is executed for some time and paused. First sample is gathered that is called sample 1. Then algorithm is resumed again and another sample is gathered as sample 2. Table 2 shows statistics of sample 1 and sample 2.

Table 1 Data set statistics

Data set statistics	
Nodes	1539
Edges	20,234

Table 2 Samples statistics

Sample	Nodes	Edges
Sample 1	257	1332
Sample 2	513	4442

The collected samples are analysed against degree distribution and compared with the original network to ensure if the samples collected represent the original network. Degrees of nodes in the networks are normalized by the median of the degrees; therefore, complete degree distribution falls in range of 0–2.

$$\text{Normalized\_Degree}_j = \frac{\text{Degree}_j}{M}$$

where M is median of degrees in the network and $1 \leq j \leq$ total number of nodes.

Degree distribution is shown in Fig. 2. X-axis denotes degree distribution and y-axis denotes fraction of nodes. The graph clearly represents that the original network as well as the two samples follows power law of degree distribution that is first evidence of correctness of the algorithm.

Figure 3 shows original network. Figures 4 and 5 represent sample 1 and sample 2, respectively. It is clearly evident the original network is clustered which overlaps. Similar overlapping clustered view can be seen in sample 1 and sample 2.

In Fig. 6, the Normalized Mean Square Error (NMSE) for a node degree has been taken as a metric to demonstrate the behaviour of the sampling algorithms on a bar graph. For the estimation of node degree distribution, we need to first calculate the NMSE of node degree k, using the below-given formula [13]

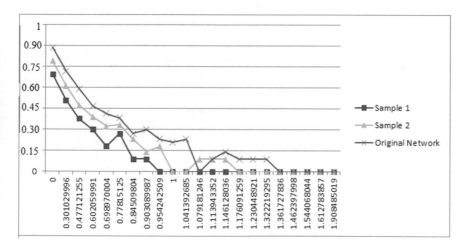

Fig. 2 Degree distribution of samples and original network

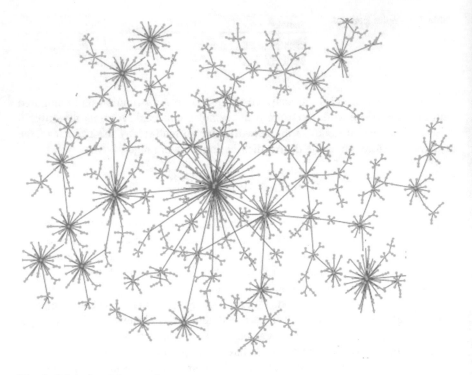

Fig. 3 Original social network

Fig. 4 Sample 1

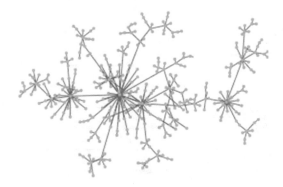

$$\text{NMSE}(k) = \frac{\sqrt{E\left[\left(\hat{\theta}_k - \theta_k\right)^2\right]}}{\theta_k}$$

where $\hat{\theta}_k$ is the estimation of θ_k based on the sampled graph. NMSE(k) metric is defined in order to show the difference between the degree distribution of the

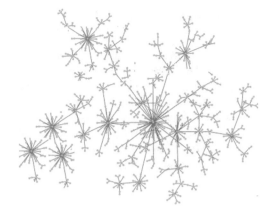

Fig. 5 Sample 2

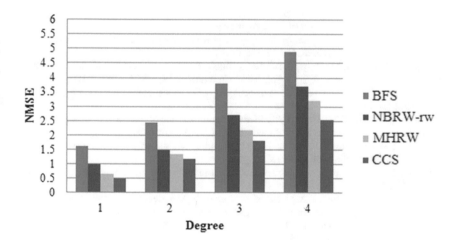

Fig. 6 NMSE comparison graph

sampled graphs and the original one. The lower the NMSE value of an algorithm, the better is the performance of the sampling algorithm in the social network graph.

Above analysis clearly shows that algorithm proposed in this paper tends to migrate from one cluster to another. Therefore, we had taken two clusters at different intervals to make sure if the algorithm is leaving one cluster and getting into other. It also implies that the representation extent of cluster is directly proportional to the time for which the algorithm is run if the size of the graph is finite. But evidently, we have gigantic online social network whose size is near to infinite. In that case, we can set a threshold on the number of nodes crawled. When sufficient number of nodes and their relationship edges has been gathered, the algorithm can be stopped. The collected sample will have clustered view similar to the original network, thereby giving maximum possible representation of the network.

6 Conclusion and Future Scope

This paper presents a crawler that works on cluster coverage sampling algorithm for selection of next node. The algorithm benefits clustered structure of most of the social networks. The algorithm is tested on a synthetic network that has clustered structure like many social networks and scale-free distribution of nodes. The results are promising. As future prospect, the algorithm is to be tested on some online social network like Facebook. Social graph dynamism is also a burning area in the field of social network analysis. Cluster coverage sampling algorithm also shows promising possibilities of its application in tackling social graph dynamism.

References

1. http://www.socialbakers.com/statistics/facebook/
2. http://www.socialbakers.com/statistics/twitter/
3. Srivastava, A., Anuradha, Gupta, D.J.: Social network analysis: hardly easy. IEEE Int. Conf. Reliab. Optim. Inf. Technol. **6**, 128–135 (2014)
4. Gjoka, M., Kurant, M., Butts, C.T., Markopoulou, A.: Practical recommendations on crawling online social networks. IEEE J. Sel. Areas Commun. **29**(9), 1872–1892 (2011)
5. Lee, S.H., Kim, P.-J., Jeong, H.: Statistical properties of sampled networks. Phy. Rev. E **73**, 016102 (2006)
6. Gjoka, M., Kurant, M., Butts, C.T., Markopoulou, A.: Walking in facebook: a case study of unbiased sampling of OSNs. In: Proceedings of IEEE INFOCOM (2010)
7. Ribeiro, B., Towsley, D.: Estimating and sampling graphs with multidimensional random walks. In: Proceedings of ACM IMC (2010)
8. Cho, M., Lee, J., Lee, K.M.: Reweighted random walks for graph matching. ECCV 2010, Part V, LNCS 6315, pp. 492–505 (2010)
9. Lee, C.H., Xu, X., Eun, D.Y.: Beyond random walk and metropolis-hastings samplers: why you should not backtrack for unbiased graph sampling. ACM (2013)
10. Li, R.H., Yu, J.X., Qin, L., Mao, R., Jin, T.: On random walk based graph sampling. IEEE ICDE Conference (2015)
11. Ribeiro, B., Wang, P., Murai, F., Towsley, D.: Sampling directed graphs with random walks. In: Ribeiro, B., Wang, P., Murai, F., Towsley, D. (eds.) UMass CMPSCI Technical Report UMCS (2011)
12. Wilson, C., Boe, B., Sala, A., Puttaswamy, K.P.N., Zhao, B.Y.: User interactions in social networks and their implications. In: Proceedings of ACM EuroSys (2009)
13. Wang, T., Chen, Y., Zhang, Z., Xu, T., Jin, L., Hui, P., Deng, B., Li, X.: Understanding graph sampling algorithms for social network analysis. In: 2011 31st International Conference on Distributed Computing Systems Workshops (ICDCSW), pp. 123, 128, 20–24 June 2011
14. Ahn, Y., Han, S., Kwak, H., Moon, S., Jeong, H.: Analysis of topological characteristics of huge online social networking services. In: Proceedings of WWW (2007)
15. Corlette, D., Shipman, F.: Capturing on-line social network link dynamics using event-driven sampling. In: IEEE International Conference on Computational Science and Engineering (2009)
16. Gjoka, M., Butts, C.T., Kurant, M., Markopoulou, A.: Multigraph sampling of online social networks. IEEE J. Sel. Areas Commun. **29**(9), 1893–1905 (2011)

Efficient Management of Web Data by Applying Web Mining Pre-processing Methodologies

Jaswinder Kaur and Kanwal Garg

Abstract Web usage mining is defined as the application of data mining techniques to extract interesting usage patterns from Web data. Web data provides the information about Web user's behavior. Pre-processing of Web data is an essential process in Web usage mining. This is used to convert the raw data into processed data which is necessary for Web mining task. In this research paper, author proposed the effective Pre-processing methodology which involves field extraction, significant attributes selection, data selection, and data cleaning. The efficient proposed methodology improves the quality of Web data by managing missing values, noise, inconsistency, and incompleteness which is usually found attached with data. Moreover, obtained results of pre-processing will be further used in frequent pattern discovery.

Keywords Web log file · Web server · Web usage mining · Pre-processing Data cleaning

1 Introduction

Data mining is a process of discovering interesting and useful pattern from raw data, also known as knowledge discovery in databases. This technology analyzes the data and helps to extract useful information. It is used in various areas such as retail industry, intrusion detection, and financial data analysis. Generally, Web mining is used in World Wide Web that continues to grow both in the huge volume of traffic and the size and complexity of Web sites, where it is difficult to identify the relevant information present in the Web [1]. In the proposed model, researcher

J. Kaur (✉) · K. Garg
Department of Computer Science & Applications, Kurukshetra University,
Kurukshetra, Haryana, India
e-mail: kaurjazz84@gmail.com

K. Garg
e-mail: gargkanwal@yahoo.com

© Springer Nature Singapore Pte Ltd. 2019
M. N. Hoda et al. (eds.), *Software Engineering*, Advances in Intelligent Systems and Computing 731, https://doi.org/10.1007/978-981-10-8848-3_11

used Microsoft Excel and SQL Developer software to perform the pre-processing process. Through this process, raw Web log data is transformed to processed data. The main objective of this model is to remove irrelevant data and improve data quality.

Author has organized this paper in following sections: In Sect. 2, researcher reviewed the pre-processing related work. Section 3 gives a description of the proposed model of pre-processing technique. Section 4 shows experimental results of the effective proposed system. Section 5 concludes the discussion.

2 Literature Review

Web usage mining provides useful information in abundance which makes this area interesting for research organizations and researchers in academics. Rathod [2] focuses on the pre-processing tasks that are data extraction and data filtering which were performed on combined log file; in this, one of the popular platform ASP.NET 2010 is used to implement the above tasks. Priyanka and Ujwala [3] proposed two algorithms for field extraction and data cleansing; latter is used in removing the errors and inconsistencies and improves the quality of data. Ramya et al. [4] explored the concept of merging of log files from different servers and is used in data pre-processing process, after which, data cleaning removes request concerning non-analyzed resources. Prince Mary et al. [5] clarified that people are more interested in analyzing log files which can offer more useful insight into Web site usage, thus data cleaning process is used in data analysis and mining. Data cleaning involved the following steps such as robot cleaning, elimination of failed status code, elimination of graphics records, videos. Chintan and Kirit [6] proposed novel technique that was more effective as compared to existing techniques, data extraction, data storage, and data cleaning technique included in data pre-processing to convert the Web log file in database. During data cleaning, only noise is removed from log file. Ramesh et al. [7] stated that data pre-processing is a significant process of Terror Tracking using Web Usage Mining (TTUM), which was effectively done by field extraction, data cleaning, and data storage tasks. Pooja et al. [8] explored the records which are not suitable for identifying the user's navigational behavior, such as access from the Web robot, e.g., Googlebot, access for images and access for audio files. These records are removed during data cleaning module.

3 Data Pre-processing on Web Log File

Web usage mining is a significant part of Web mining. It is used to extract user's access patterns from Web data over WWW in order to understand the user's browsing behavior, and it helps in building of Web-based applications. Web usage mining depends on different source of data such as Web Server Side, Proxy Side, and Client Side. Generally, raw Web log contains irrelevant, noisy, incomplete, duplicate, and missing data. Data pre-processing is the most important phase of Web usage mining in order to clean Web log data for discovering patterns.

The log files are stored in the Web server and may suffer from various data anomalies such data may be irrelevant, inconsistent, and noisy in nature. In the present research work, the researcher removes the said anomalies by following data pre-processing steps as shown in Fig. 1.

3.1 Field Extraction

The server's log entry contains different fields like IP address, date and time, request and user agent that should be separated out before applying data cleaning process. Field extraction is the process to separate the fields from single entry of the log file.

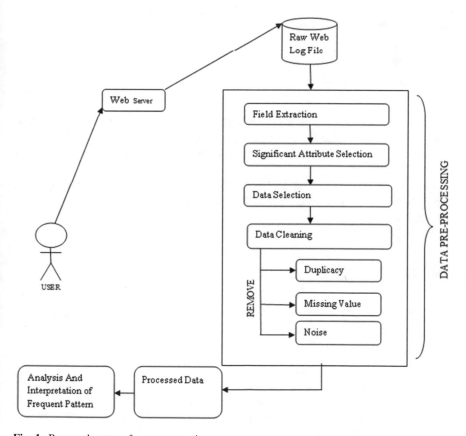

Fig. 1 Proposed system for pre-processing

Researcher performed field extraction process on log file using Microsoft Excel which is explained as follows.

Open Microsoft Excel, using open option select the log file, use characters such as space or comma as delimiter to separate each field. These separated attributes are stored in different heading according to the input Web log file such as IP address, username, date, request, status code, referrer. Now, this file can be saved with .xls extension, this concludes the field extraction process.

3.2 Significant Attributes Selection

Researcher had analyzed the Apache Web server log file and obtained the important attributes of Web log files which were IP address, date, time, request line, or URI stem, status code, referrer, and user agent [9]. These attributes provide valuable information about visitor's behavior, traffic pattern, navigation paths, Web browser, errors, etc.

Using the above analysis, only significant attributes which were identified are selected for further processing.

3.3 Data Selection

When a Web server receives a HTTP Request, it returns back a HTTP Response code to the client. These HTTP status codes are three-digit numbers such as 1xx, 2xx, 3xx. All these records with the status code below 200 and above 299 are not used for analysis.

Filtering of records is done in Microsoft Excel sheet which was obtained after significant attributes, by keeping records with status code >=200 and status code <=299.

3.4 Data Cleaning

Data cleaning is the fourth step of pre-processing to remove irrelevant records. Following three kinds of records are required to be removed.

a. Records having duplication.
b. Records with missing value.
c. Access for images, audio files, video files, and css files; they are identified by checking extensions in request field such as .gif, .mp3, .avi. In addition to this, the records with irrelevant information created by spiders, crawlers, Web robots like Googlebot, can be found in request or user agent field.

3.4.1   Remove Duplicacy

In Microsoft Excel file, select range of the cell then select Data tab and perform 'Remove Duplicates' in Data Tools Group to remove the duplicate records.

3.4.2   Missing Value

Find out the blank cell with the help of Find and Replace dialog box. Remove these tuples.

3.4.3   Noise

After removing missing value, obtained Microsoft Excel file is imported in Oracle SQL Developer remove noise from log file.

Proposed procedure:

Step 1: Create new database connection in Oracle SQL Developer.
Step 2: Under this new database connection, using SQL command create a database table.
Step 3: Import obtained Microsoft Excel file after removing missing value into this newly created database table.
Step 4: Using SQL command, remove noise present in the request field and user agent field such as images, audio files, video files, page style files, and robots. Completion of this will create a database table having processed data.
Step 5: Save and close the SQL Developer.

After performing all the above steps, processed data will be used for further analysis and interpretation of frequent pattern.

4   Results and Interpretation

In this section, effectiveness and efficiency of the proposed model mentioned above are proved, and researcher has applied several experiments with the Web log file. Apache Web log file is used and is from April 08, 2012, to July 08, 2012, with a file size of 958 kB at the beginning.

Researcher performed experiments on a 2.40 GHz Intel Core processor, 4.00 GB RAM, 64-bit Windows 2007 Home Premium Operating System, SQL Developer 4.1.0, and Java SE Development Kit JDK 8. Oracle SQL Developer 4.1.0 is a free Oracle database integrated development environment (IDE). SQL Developer provides GUI to help the DBA and database; user saves time while performing the database task. Oracle database 10g, 11g, 12c is supported by SQL Developer and requires Java-supported platforms (OS) for operation.

Figure 2 shows Web log file imported in Microsoft Excel. Each field is separated by using space character as delimiter. As explained different attributes are stored in separate headings. Initial Web log file entries were 6000.

According to the analysis, only six attributes are significant out of nine attributes those are IP address, date and time, request, status code, referrer, and user agent attributes. These six attributes help in identifying the user navigational behavior and are of at most importance for Web usage mining. Outcomes from Web usage mining are implemented to enhance the characteristics of Web-based applications. After performing the data selection step, only 3674 rows were left.

First step in data cleaning removes duplicate records from log file. Thus, 11 duplicates values were identified and 3663 unique values remain. During second step, the fields with missing values were deleted as this does not provide any useful information for Web mining. Total 23 cells containing missing value in this log file were deleted. 3640 tuples are left on completion of this step.

In addition to above, researcher found noise in log file such as .gif, robot, and Web spider, example of which is 'GET/icons/compressed.gif.'

In Fig. 3, Microsoft Excel file is imported in SQL Developer to perform further action; SQL Query is executed to remove noise from Web log file such as .gif, .rm, . mp4, robot, and spider. Result obtained contains only 2458 rows.

Finally, pre-processed Web log file is obtained. Furthermore, this processed file will be used in analysis and interpretation of frequent pattern of log file.

According to Table 1, this clearly indicates that the application of pre-processing on the Web log file helps in removing irrelevant data and improves the quality of data.

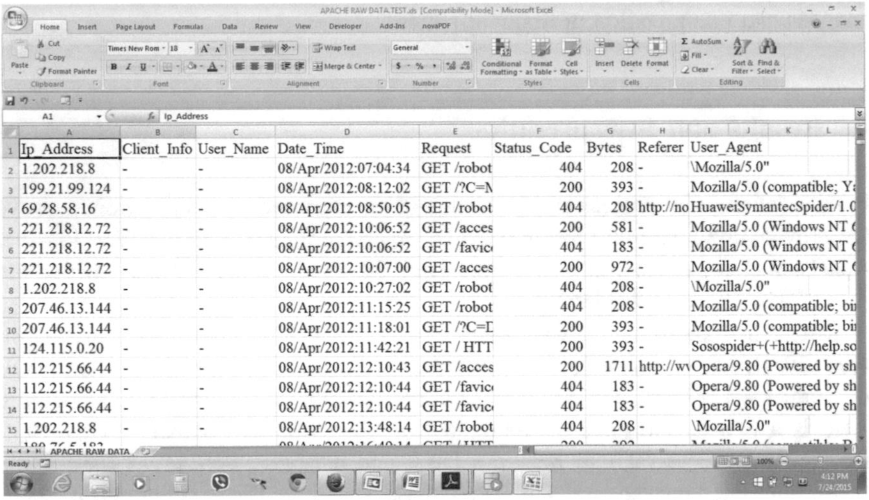

Ip_Address	Client_Info	User_Name	Date_Time	Request	Status_Code	Bytes	Referer	User_Agent
1.202.218.8	-	-	08/Apr/2012:07:04:34	GET /robot	404	208	-	\Mozilla/5.0"
199.21.99.124	-	-	08/Apr/2012:08:12:02	GET /?C=N	200	393	-	Mozilla/5.0 (compatible; Y
69.28.58.16	-	-	08/Apr/2012:08:50:05	GET /robot	404	208	http://no	HuaweiSymantecSpider/1.0
221.218.12.72	-	-	08/Apr/2012:10:06:52	GET /acces	200	581	-	Mozilla/5.0 (Windows NT
221.218.12.72	-	-	08/Apr/2012:10:06:52	GET /favic	404	183	-	Mozilla/5.0 (Windows NT
221.218.12.72	-	-	08/Apr/2012:10:07:00	GET /acces	200	972	-	Mozilla/5.0 (Windows NT
1.202.218.8	-	-	08/Apr/2012:10:27:02	GET /robot	404	208	-	\Mozilla/5.0"
207.46.13.144	-	-	08/Apr/2012:11:15:25	GET /robot	404	208	-	Mozilla/5.0 (compatible; bi
207.46.13.144	-	-	08/Apr/2012:11:18:01	GET /?C=D	200	393	-	Mozilla/5.0 (compatible; bi
124.115.0.20	-	-	08/Apr/2012:11:42:21	GET / HTT	200	393	-	Sosospider+(+http://help.so
112.215.66.44	-	-	08/Apr/2012:12:10:43	GET /acces	200	1711	http://w	Opera/9.80 (Powered by sh
112.215.66.44	-	-	08/Apr/2012:12:10:44	GET /favic	404	183	-	Opera/9.80 (Powered by sh
112.215.66.44	-	-	08/Apr/2012:12:10:44	GET /favic	404	183	-	Opera/9.80 (Powered by sh
1.202.218.8	-	-	08/Apr/2012:13:48:14	GET /robot	404	208	-	\Mozilla/5.0"

Fig. 2 Imported Web log file in Microsoft Excel

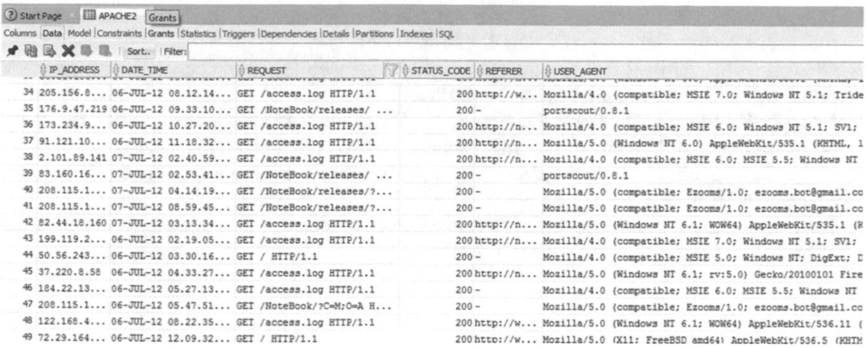

	IP_ADDRESS	DATE_TIME	REQUEST	STATUS_CODE	REFERER	USER_AGENT
34	205.156.8...	06-JUL-12 08.12.14...	GET /access.log HTTP/1.1	200	http://w...	Mozilla/4.0 (compatible; MSIE 7.0; Windows NT 5.1; Tride
35	176.9.47.219	06-JUL-12 09.33.10...	GET /NoteBook/releases/ ...	200	-	portscout/0.8.1
36	173.234.9...	06-JUL-12 10.27.20...	GET /access.log HTTP/1.1	200	http://n...	Mozilla/4.0 (compatible; MSIE 6.0; Windows NT 5.1; SV1;
37	91.121.10...	06-JUL-12 11.18.32...	GET /access.log HTTP/1.1	200	http://n...	Mozilla/5.0 (Windows NT 6.0) AppleWebKit/535.1 (KHTML, 1
38	2.101.89.141	07-JUL-12 02.40.59...	GET /access.log HTTP/1.1	200	http://n...	Mozilla/4.0 (compatible; MSIE 6.0; MSIE 5.5; Windows NT
39	83.160.16...	07-JUL-12 02.53.41...	GET /NoteBook/releases/ ...	200	-	portscout/0.8.1
40	208.115.1...	07-JUL-12 04.14.19...	GET /NoteBook/releases/?...	200	-	Mozilla/5.0 (compatible; Ezooms/1.0; ezooms.bot@gmail.co
41	208.115.1...	07-JUL-12 08.59.45...	GET /NoteBook/releases/?...	200	-	Mozilla/5.0 (compatible; Ezooms/1.0; ezooms.bot@gmail.co
42	82.44.18.160	07-JUL-12 03.13.34...	GET /access.log HTTP/1.1	200	http://n...	Mozilla/5.0 (Windows NT 6.1; WOW64) AppleWebKit/535.1 (K
43	199.119.2...	06-JUL-12 02.19.05...	GET /access.log HTTP/1.1	200	http://n...	Mozilla/4.0 (compatible; MSIE 7.0; Windows NT 5.1; SV1;
44	50.56.243...	06-JUL-12 03.30.16...	GET / HTTP/1.1	200	-	Mozilla/4.0 (compatible; MSIE 5.0; Windows NT; DigExt; D
45	37.220.8.58	06-JUL-12 04.33.27...	GET /access.log HTTP/1.1	200	http://n...	Mozilla/5.0 (Windows NT 6.1; rv:5.0) Gecko/20100101 Fire
46	184.22.13...	06-JUL-12 05.27.13...	GET /access.log HTTP/1.1	200	-	Mozilla/4.0 (compatible; MSIE 6.0; MSIE 5.5; Windows NT
47	208.115.1...	06-JUL-12 05.47.51...	GET /NoteBook/?C=M;O=A H...	200	-	Mozilla/5.0 (compatible; Ezooms/1.0; ezooms.bot@gmail.co
48	122.168.4...	06-JUL-12 08.22.35...	GET /access.log HTTP/1.1	200	http://w...	Mozilla/5.0 (Windows NT 6.1; WOW64) AppleWebKit/536.11 (
49	72.29.164...	06-JUL-12 12.09.32...	GET / HTTP/1.1	200	http://w...	Mozilla/5.0 (X11; FreeBSD amd64) AppleWebKit/536.5 (KHTM

Fig. 3 Processed database table after pre-processing

Table 1 Resultant data set size after data pre-processing

	Raw Web log file	Significant attribute selection	Data selection	Data cleaning	Result
No. of tuples	6000	NA	3674	2458	2458
No. of attributes	09	06	NA	NA	06

5 Conclusion

In the present research work, the researcher has taken raw Web log file for its empirical analysis and concludes that data pre-processing is an essential step to remove anomalies; lies in data for the purpose. The researcher has proposed data pre-processing methodology which improved the quality of data. After applying the said methodology, the procedure proves that only six attributes are significant out of nine available attributes and similarly out of 6000 original instances only 2458 are meaningful. The resultant itemset surely will be useful for the discovery of frequent pattern.

References

1. Jayalatchumy, D., Thambidurai, P.: Web mining research issue and future directions—a survey. IOSR J. Comput. Eng. (IOSR-JCE) **14**, 20–27 (2013)
2. Rathod, D.B.: Customizable web log mining from web server log. Int. J. Eng. Dev. Res. (IJEDR), 96–100 (2011)
3. Priyanka, P., Ujwala, P.: Preprocessing of web server log file for web mining. World J. Sci. Technol. **2**, 14–18 (2012)
4. Ramya, C., Shreedhara, K.S., Kavitha, G.: Preprocessing: a prerequisite for discovering patterns in web usage mining process. Int. J. Inf. Electron. Eng. **3**, 196–199 (2013)

5. Prince Mary, S., Baburaj, E.: An efficient approach to perform pre-processing. Indian J. Comput. Sci. Eng. (IJCSE) **4**, 404–410 (2013)
6. Chintan, H.M., Kirit, R.R.: An efficient technique for web log preprocessing using microsoft excel. Int. J. Comput. Appl. **90**, 25–28 (2014)
7. Ramesh, Y., Mayuri, D., Tejali, N., Trupti, K.: Unauthorized terror attack tracking using web usage mining. Int. J. Comput. Sci. Inf. Technol. (IJCSIT) **5**, 1210–1212 (2014)
8. Pooja, K., Jyotsna, N.: Data preprocessing: a milestone of web usage mining. Int. J. Eng. Sci. Innovative Technol. (IJESIT) **4** (2015)
9. Kaur, J., Garg, K.: Analyzing the different attributes of web log files to have an effective web mining. Int. J. Adv. Sci. Tech. Res. **3**, 127–134 (2015)

A Soft Computing Approach to Identify Multiple Paths in a Network

Shalini Aggarwal, Pardeep Kumar and Shuchita Upadhyaya

Abstract This paper presents a modified technique to generate the probability table (routing table) for the selection of path for an ant in AntNet algorithm. This paper also uses the concept of probe ant along with clone ant. The probe ant identifies the multiple paths which can be stored at destination. Overall purpose of this paper is to get an insight into the ant-based algorithms and identifying multiple optimal paths.

Keywords AntNet · ACO · ABC · Probe ant · Clone ant · Link goodness

1 Introduction

Routing is an important aspect in computer networks as it controls the traffic between one node to another depending on various parameters. Routing is the basic process for determining the performance of a network in terms of quality and quantity. For performing routing, routers are required. The basic purpose of routers is to update the routing table via an algorithm. Most of the traditional routing algorithms transmit the data by minimizing the cost function which may be distance, delay, jitter, etc. They find the shortest path which may become congested over time and/or may become expensive later on. Sometimes, a path which is better on the basis of more than one metric such as distance, delay, bandwidth, jitter is required. Then sometimes, there is a trade-off between those metrics. Therefore, it is necessary to get an optimal solution based on more than one metric.

S. Aggarwal (✉) · P. Kumar · S. Upadhyaya
Department of Computer Science and Applications, Kurukshetra University,
Kurukshetra, India
e-mail: shaliniagg07@gmail.com

P. Kumar
e-mail: mittalkuk@gmail.com

S. Upadhyaya
e-mail: shuchita_bhasin@yahoo.com

© Springer Nature Singapore Pte Ltd. 2019
M. N. Hoda et al. (eds.), *Software Engineering*, Advances in Intelligent Systems
and Computing 731, https://doi.org/10.1007/978-981-10-8848-3_12

For getting such optimal solution, nowadays a number of studies are going on to identify routing alternatives using heuristic techniques. One of such techniques is Ant Colony Optimization (ACO). In ant-based routing, the artificial ants, while moving from source to destination, deposit some artificial pheromone in terms of numeric value and store some information in the form of routing table at the intermediate nodes. This information is used by newly generated ants for accepting or rejecting a path. Another important aspect of routing is increasing need of multi-path routing. The main reason for the need of multi-path routing is the data transmission in Internet. When a video or audio streaming is required, very high bandwidth is required. With single path routing, it might not be possible, hence arise the need of multi-path routing. When multi-path routing is combined with multi-metric routing, it becomes a perfect candidate for use of heuristic techniques. Therefore, ACO can prove to be a very effective technique for this type of routing.

2 Related Work

According to [1], an ant not only finds the shortest path for searching its food source but also conveys this shortest path to other ants. In the ACO, this intelligence of ants is intermixed with various optimization techniques to identify optimum routes in a computer network. In this paper, various mechanisms to solve the problem to identify optimum path using ACO were explained and compared with different traditional algorithms of routing.

This paper throws light on a critical review in four different groups for applying ACO in routing, which are (i) Ant-Based Control (ABC) Systems, (ii) AntNet System, (iii) Ant System with other variations, and (iv) Multiple Ant Colony Systems.

Schoonderwoerd et al. [2, 3] applied ACO to routing in telecommunication networks based on circuit-switching. The algorithm was termed as Ant-Based Control (ABC). In the ABC algorithm, all the nodes in a network follow various features [2] such as capacity, probability of being a destination, pheromone table, and routing table, on the basis of which criteria for choosing next node is decided. But the main problem of Schoonderwoerd et al. approach is that it can only be applied when the network is symmetric in nature.

For packet-switched networks routing, Caro and Dorigo's [4–6] designed AntNet Routing. Although it is inspired by ACO meta-heuristic, yet have additional changes as desired for a network.

In [7], a new version of AntNet was generated and was named as AntNet-FA or AntNet-CO. In this version, backward ants performed a number of tasks such as, (a) estimating the trip time using various metrics, (b) updating local traffic statistics, and (c) determining and depositing the pheromone for estimating the probability of reinforcement. As backward ants are using real-time statistics for determining the amount of reinforcement, the information for routing was found to be more correct and up-to-date. The results of this version are found to be better than AntNet algorithm which are proved by experiment performed in this paper.

Oida and Sekido [8] proposed Agent-based Routing system (ARS) in which they suggested for supporting various types of bandwidth requirement, the forward ants move in a network, which is based on bandwidth constrained. The probability of selection of outgoing link depends on routing table as well as bandwidth constraints.

Although adaption has been proved to be one of the better techniques for identifying the optimum paths, but one of the major problems that can be attached with AntNet is stagnation [9]. Due to this problem, local optimum solution might be obtained and diversity of the population might also be lost. In this paper, the concept of multiple ant colonies was applied to the packet-switched networks. Upon comparison with AntNet algorithm with evaporation, it was found that by using multiple ant colonies throughput can be increased. No improvement was found in delay. But the basic problem was the need of large resources for multiple ant colonies.

3 AntNet Routing Algorithm

In an AntNet algorithm [1], an ant explores the path and updates the routing and probability tables, so that other ants can use the tables to know which path is better than others. Some statistical traffic model is also used to help the ants to identify the better path.

A routing table is maintained which is a local database. The routing table contains information about all possible destinations along with probabilities to reach these destinations via each of the neighbours of the node.

Another data structure that each node carries is termed as local traffic statistics. This structure follows the traffic fluctuations as viewed by the local node.

The AntNet algorithm as proposed by Di Caro and Dorigo is dependent on two types of ants named as forward ant and backward ant. The forward ant collects the information regarding the network, while the backward ant uses this information to update the routing tables on their path.

Working of the algorithm is given as follows:

(i)   Initially to generate a routing table, a forward ant is initiated from every node towards the destination node after a fixed time interval to find low-cost path to that node and load status of the network is also explored, and accordingly, priorities of the paths are set. These priorities are used by the forward ants to transmit the data.

(ii) The forward ants store the information about their paths in a stack.

(iii) At each node, decision is made to select a node for reaching towards destination with the help of probabilities using pheromone values. The nodes which are unvisited are only considered for selection or from all the neighbours in case all of them have found to be previously visited.

(iv)   When the forward ant moves towards destination, if at any time any cycle is detected, all the nodes in that cycle's path are popped. Also all of the information about them is also deleted.

(v)   When the forward ant reaches its destination, then it generates another ant named as backward ant. It transfers all of its memory to it and dies.

(vi)   The backward ant as its name indicates will travel to the opposite direction that of forward ant. The backward ant uses stack formed by forward ant and pops the element in the stack to reach the source node. The backward ant use high-priority queues to reach source so that information can be quickly transmitted to the source node. The information collected by forward ant is stored in the routing table by the backward ants.

(vii) The backward ant basically updates the two data structure, i.e. routing table and the local traffic model for all the node in its path for all entries starting from the destination node.

Limitations of AntNet Routing

AntNet has performed very well as compared to the traditional routing algorithms as visible from various experiments performed by different researchers. But still there are problems associated with the algorithm. This algorithm takes into account the probabilities to identify the path for destination. As more and more pheromone will be deposited on that path, most or all of the traffic will travel through the same path, and hence making that path congested. Also as probability of that path is very high, other path may never be explored, and hence, the diversity of solution may be lost. This basically is the problem of stagnation [1]. Although some work has been done on stagnation, but still a lot of effort is required to make this algorithm better.

4   Proposed AntNet Modifications

In this work, a new type of forward ant named as probe ant [10] along with its clone is proposed. The probe ants are generated to replace the forward ants from source node to explore the path. The probe and clone probe ants are generated depending on the paths selected at a particular node. Only a little additional overhead is required for generating clone ants. The multiple paths are selected according to the probabilities in the pheromone table and a threshold value of bandwidth. These probe and clone ants [11] will reach to the destination according to proposed strategy. The advantage will be that instead of one optimal path more than one optimal path are identified. The paths will be identified only with the help of a single ant, other ants being the clone ant. The major advantage of this technique is saving of the overhead taken by number of forward ants in AntNet algorithm.

The proposed modifications are briefly explained below:
The structure of probe ant is defined as follows:

S	D	I	Aid	PT	MB	TD	HC

Structure of Probe Ant

Here,

S   Source node,
D   Destination node,
I   Intermediate node from which ant has arrived recently,
Aid   Ant Identification Number
PT   Path Traversed so far
MB   Minimum Bandwidth of the path traversed
TD   Total Delay of the path
HC   Hop Count

In this work, a threshold bandwidth is considered. Any link having bandwidth less than that threshold value is discarded. The remaining links are considered for the purpose of identifying the multiple paths. The process works in a similar manner to AntNet algorithm, except that queue length is taken into account for selecting a path in case of AntNet algorithm, while in the proposed work, two metrics, i.e. delay and bandwidth, are considered for selecting a path. Another important difference in this case is that instead of selecting a single path, multiple (quite similar) paths are being selected for data transmission. Various paths are identified at the destination and stored in an array and from these paths some optimal paths are chosen using some intelligent approach. For selecting the paths based on two metrics, a new metric named as link goodness is proposed and is denoted by G_L. The value of G_L can be calculated with the help of following formula:

$$G_L = \frac{\alpha}{D_L + 1} + (1 - \alpha) * B_L$$

where

D_L Delay of a Link,
B_L Bandwidth of a Link

α is a constant having value between 0 and 1, i.e. $0 < \alpha < 1$.

At each node, two tables named as pheromone table and routing table will be maintained. The pheromone table will be initialized with equal pheromone value distributed to each link from a node except the discarded link. The second table is the routing table consisting of probabilities for selecting the next node in the path. The structure of both the tables is as shown below:

Destination nodes				
Neighbouring nodes	τ_{11}	τ_{12}	...	τ_{1n}
	τ_{21}	τ_{22}	...	τ_{2n}
	.	.	.	.
	.	.	.	.
	.	.	.	.
	τ_{11}	τ_{12}	...	τ_{1n}

Pheromone table

In the above table, τ_{nd} is the pheromone value of link from node n when destination node is d. The τ_{nd} value lies in the interval [0, 1] and sums up to 1 (as the probabilities can not exceed 1) along each destination column:

$$\sum_{n\in Nk} \tau_{nd} = 1, d \in [1, N], N_k = \{\text{neighbours}(k)\}$$

The routing table can be represented as follows:

Destination node					
Neighbour nodes		1	2	...	n
	1	p_{11}		...	p_{1n}
	2	p_{21}	p_{22}	...	
	.	.	.	.	.
	.	.	.	.	.
	.	.	.	.	.
	1	p_{11}		...	p_{1n}

Routing table

In the above table, blank cells indicate that particular neighbour node is discarded for a particular destination.

P_{sd} = probability of creating a probe ant at node s with node d as destination.

At each node i, a probe ant computes probability P_{ijd} of selecting neighbour node j for moving towards its destination d by adding $\tau_{ijd} * G_{ij}$ to the pheromone value τ_{ijd} and then subtracting this value dividing equally from each of the remaining valid neighbours. This process must be followed for each of the neighbours in parallel.

Using these probabilities, multiple paths from source to destination can be identified, and the information about paths will be stored in probe ants. At destination, paths can be stored in an array of paths. From this array, some of the better paths on the basis of various metrics can be found using some intelligent approach.

5 Conclusion

In this paper, a modified approach for generating the probabilities for routing table has been proposed. In this approach, the probabilities have been calculated of the basis on two metrics instead of a single metric. Another important feature that has been used in this paper is the use of a threshold value of bandwidth. Only one ant will be generated at the source, while other ants will be the clone ants with a little additional overhead. With the help of this technique, multiple paths can be generated which can be stored at destination via probe ants. These paths can be further refined using some intelligent approach, and multiple paths for a better transmission of data packets can be identified.

References

1. Sim, K.M., Sun, W.H.: Ant colony optimization for routing and load-balancing: survey and new directions. IEEE Trans. Syst. Man Cybern. Part A Syst. Hum. **33**(5) (2003)
2. Schoonderwoerd, R., Holland, O., Bruten, J., Rothkrantz, L.: Ants for Load Balancing in Telecommunication Networks. Hewlett Packard Lab., Bristol, U.K., Tech., pp. 96–35 (1996)
3. Schoonderwoerd, R., Holland, O., Bruten, J., Rothkrantz, L.: Ant-based load balancing in telecommunications networks. Adapt. Behav. **5**(2) (1996)
4. Caro, G.D., Dorigo, M.: AntNet: distributed stigmergetic control for communications networks. J. Artif. Intell. Res. **9**, 317–365 (1998)
5. Caro, G.D., Dorigo, M.: Ant colonies for adaptive routing in packet-switched communications networks. In: Proceedings of 5th International Conference on Parallel Problem Solving from Nature, Amsterdam, The Netherlands, 27–30 Sept 1998
6. Caro, G.D., Dorigo, M.: An adaptive multi-agent routing algorithm inspired by ants behavior. In: Proceedings of 5th Annual Australasian Conference on Parallel Real-Time Systems, pp. 261–272 (1998)
7. Caro, G.D., Dorigo, M.: Two ant colony algorithms for best-effort routing in datagram networks. In: Proceedings of 10th IASTED International Conference on Parallel Distributed Computing Systems, pp. 541–546 (1998)
8. Oida, K., Sekido, M.: An agent-based routing system for QoS guarantees. In: IEEE International Conference on Systems, Man, and Cybernetics, pp. 833–838 (1999)
9. Tekiner, F., Ghassemlooy, Z., Al-khayatt, S.: Investigation of Antnet Routing Algorithm by Employing Multiple Ant Colonies for Packet Switched Networks to Overcome the Stagnation Problem
10. Devi, G., Upadhyaya S.: Path identification in multipath routing. JGRCS J. Glob. Res. Comput. Sci. **2**(9) (2011)
11. Richa, S., Upadhyaya, S.: Identifying multiple optimal paths in Antnet routing algorithm with negligible overhead. Int. J. Comput. Sci. Netw. Secur. **9**(2), 314–320 (2009)

An Efficient Focused Web Crawling Approach

Kompal Aggarwal

Abstract The amount of data and its dynamicity makes it very difficult to crawl the World Wide Web (WWW) completely. It is a challenge in front of researchers to crawl only the relevant pages from this huge Web. Thus, a focused crawler resolves this issue of relevancy to a certain level, by focusing on Web pages for some given topic or a set of topics. This paper deals with survey of various focused crawling techniques which are based on different parameters to find the advantages and drawbacks for relevance prediction of URLs. This paper formulates the problem after analysing the existing work on focused crawlers and proposes a solution to improve the existing focused crawler.

Keywords Focused crawler · Page relevance · Web crawler

1 Introduction

World Wide Web (WWW) contains a large amount of information, and every second, new information is added such that the Web size is of order tens of billions of pages. Web crawler is the most important component of search engine. It continuously downloads pages, and these pages are indexed and stored in database. So, it becomes very difficult for a crawler to crawl entire Web and keep its index fresh. Because of limitation of various computing resources and time constraints, focused crawlers are developed. A focused crawler is web crawler that downloads only those Web pages which are considered to be relevant for specific topic or set of topics.

A focused crawler can be implemented in various ways [1]. Some of the approaches are shown below.

K. Aggarwal (✉)
Department of Computer Science, Government College, Chhachhrauli, India
e-mail: kompalagg@gmail.com

© Springer Nature Singapore Pte Ltd. 2019
M. N. Hoda et al. (eds.), *Software Engineering*, Advances in Intelligent Systems
and Computing 731, https://doi.org/10.1007/978-981-10-8848-3_13

Priority-Based Focused Crawler In a priority-based focused crawler, the priority queue is used for storing retrieved pages instead of a normal queue. The priority is assigned to each page based on a function which uses various factors to score a page. Thus, in every iteration, a more relevant page is returned.

Structure-Based Focused Crawler In structure-based focused crawlers, to evaluate the page relevance, we have to take into account the Web page structure. The strategy used is predefined formula for computation of page relevance score. After that, link relevance score can be predicted, and then from the queue of URLs to be crawled, the authority score is determined. The priority is determined from relevance score and authority sore.

Context-Based Focused Crawler To avoid filtering out unwanted data, context-based focused crawler tries to understand the context of the user's needs by interacting with user and comprehending the user profile. The crawler then gets adapted to such contexts and uses them for future search requests.

Learning-Based Focused Crawler Learning-based focused crawler is a new approach based on learning. It is used for improving relevance prediction in focused Web crawler. First of all, a training set is built. The purpose of training set is to train the system, and it contains four relevance attribute values: URL, parent page, anchor text, and surrounding text relevancy. Secondly, classifier (NB) is trained by using training set. The trained classifier is used for predicting the relevancy of URL which is still unvisited [2, 3].

The architecture of focused Web crawler is shown in Fig. 1. URL queue is initialized with a list which is not visited and maintained by a crawler and starts off with seed URLs. The module Web page downloader extracts URLs from the queue which is used for storing URLs and retrieves the pages as specified by retrieved

Fig. 1 Architecture of focussed web crawler

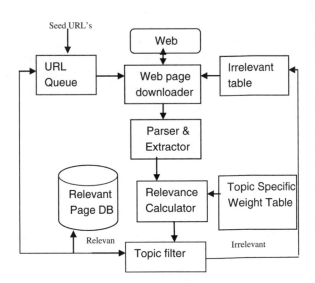

URL from the Internet [4]. The parser module retrieves various information such as the text, terms, and the out links URLs from the page which is being downloaded. The relevance calculator module calculates relevance of the parsed page with respect to topic, and relevance score is assigned to URLs. Topic filter module determines whether the page content which is being parsed is related to topic specified or not. If the parsed page is found to be relevant, the URLs retrieved from it will then be updated in the queue which is used for storing URLs; otherwise, page will be discarded and added to the irrelevant matrix.

2 Related Work

De Bra et al. [5] proposed "fish search" for predicting page relevance in which the system takes as input a set consisting of seed pages and search query, and it considers only those Web pages whose content matches a given search query and their neighbourhoods (pages pointed to by these matched pages). Fish-search algorithm treats Web as a directed graph where Web page is considered as node, and hyperlink can be taken as edge, so the way of searching is similar to the search operation in directed graph. For each node, we have to judge whether the node is relative or irrelative (1 represents relevant, and 0 represents irrelevant). In the fish-search algorithm, for storing URL of page to be searched, a list is maintained. If the fish finds a relevant page based on query, it continues to look for more links from the same page. If the page is not found to be relevant, then his child receives a low score. The various URLs have different priority; the higher priority URL will be stored at the front of the list and will be searched earlier in comparison with others. It associates a relevance score in a discrete manner (1 stands for relevant; 0 or 0.5 stands for irrelevant). The drawback of the fish-search algorithm is that the differentiation among priority that exists among the pages in the list is very low.

Michael et al. [6] proposed shark search which is the modification made to fish search. In this algorithm, a child derives a discounted score from its parent. The inherited discounted score is combined with a value which is based on anchor text that exists around the link in the Web page. One improvement is that it replaces binary with fuzzy score. Binary value of document relevance can be relevant or irrelevant. "Fuzzy" score is a score lying between 0 (no similarity) and 1 (perfect "conceptual" match). It uses a vector space model [7] for calculating the relevance score in which the similarity between a search string and a document is a function of the distance existing among the vectors. The cosine similarity measure is commonly used measure for this purpose. But this algorithm neglects information of link structure.

Batra [1] proposes a method based on link scoring in which the crawler also checks and crawls the unvisited links up to a certain threshold that is included in irrelevant pages. The various approaches have been suggested by many researchers which are based on link analysis; for example, one of effective focused crawling which is based on both content and link structures has been proposed. This crawling method is based on URL score, links, and anchor scores. The link scores can be calculated by the crawler using the following equation and a decision is made regarding fetching of pages as specified by links or not. The link score can be calculated as [1, 8]:

$$\text{LinkScore}(i) = \text{URLScore } (i) + \text{Anchorscore}(i) + LinksFromRelevantPageDB(i)$$
$$+ [\text{Relevance}(p_1) + \text{Relevance}(p_2) + \cdots + \text{Relevance}(p_n)].$$

LinkScore (i) represents score of link i, *URLScore*(i) is the relevance that exists between the HREF information of i and the topic keywords, and *AnchorScore*(i) is the relevance that exists between the anchor text of i and the topic keywords.

LinksFromRelevantPageDB(i) is the number of links from relevant crawled pages to i; P_n is the ith parent page of URL n. Parent page is a page from which a link was extracted. Thus crawler spends some time on crawling relevant pages and also crawl relevant pages, those are children of an irrelevant page.

In a crawling process, the effectiveness of the focused crawler [8] can be determined from the speed of the crawling process and not only from the maximum amount of fetched relevant pages. The speed of a crawler is determined from the number of inserted URLs which are considered to be relevant.

Therefore, URL optimization mechanism is used by the crawler to select relevant links which helps for the removal of certain links whose link scores lie below a predefined threshold. For URL optimization, two methods used for evaluating relevant pages link score are used.

- Same as above equation which is used for irrelevant pages.
- Naive Bayes (NB) classifier which is used to compute link scores [2, 8].

Diligenti et al. [9] proposes a method based on link analysis of forward links and backward links of the page. In this method, priority value is assigned to Web page based on Pvalue which is the difference between FwdLnk and BkLnk. The priority is directly proportional to the page having the highest Pvalue.

$$\text{Pvalue} = \text{FwdLnk} - \text{BkLnk}$$

The URLs had been classified in the above categories by using the parameters backward link count (BkLnk) and the forward link count (FwdLnk). The values of forward link count (FwdLnk) can be calculated by the server after returning the number of links in the page after parsing it and without downloading it. The values of BkLnk can be calculated by the server after calculation of how many pages are referring to this page by using the existing database which is built by various crawler machines. After that, the crawler will sort the list of URLs according to descending order of Pvalue of URLs received from the repository. This sorted list of URLs will be sent to maintain quality of crawling. This method gives weightage to current database and helps in building a database of higher-quality indexed Web pages even when the focus is on crawling the entire Web. This method would also be used for broken links, growing and matured stage of databases. A URL having zero value for FwdLnk and nonzero value of BKLnk is assigned low priority as Pvalue will always be negative [9].

Kaur and Gupta [10] proposed weighted page rank method, in which weight of Web page is calculated on the basis of the number of incoming and outgoing links, and the importance of page is dependent on the weight. The relevancy comes out by using this technique is less as page rank is calculated on the basis of weight of the Web page calculated at the time of indexing [2].

This algorithm is an updated version of page rank as important pages have been assigned more value instead of dividing the page rank value commonly among all outgoing links of that page [11].

The weighted page rank is thus given by:

$$PR(u) = 1 - d)/|D| + d(PR(V_1)W_{in}(V_1, u)W_{out}(V_1, u) + \cdots + PR(V_n)W_{in}(V_n, u) W_{out}(V_n, u))$$

where $W_{in}(v, u)$ = weight of link(v, u) can be calculated on the basis of number of inlinks of page u and the number of inlinks of all reference pages of page v $W_{out}(v, u)$ = weight of link(v, u) can be calculated on the basis of number of outlinks of page u and the number of outlinks of all reference pages of page v $PR(u)$ = page rank of page u.

Pal et al. [4] proposed a method for construction of topic-specific weight table. The topic name had been given to Google Web search engine, and based on the topic, first few results are retrieved. Each word had been assigned weight by $w_i = tf * df$, where tf is term frequency and df is document frequency After assigning weights to each word, their weights had been normalized by using the following equation

$$W_{i+1} = W_i / W_{max}$$

where W_{max} stands for the maximum weight that can be assigned to any keyword and W_{i+1} stands for the new weight assigned to every keyword. The page relevancy is calculated with the help of topic specific weight table and by using cosine similarity measure.

Kleinberg [12] proposes a method called Hyperlink-Induced Topic Search (HITS). It calculates the hubs as well as authority values of the relevant pages. The result given is the relevant as well as important page.

HIT is a link analysis algorithm for rating Web pages. The page which is pointed to many other pages is represented as good hub, and the page that was linked by many different hubs represented a good authority.

Selecting seed URL set is based on authority of Web pages. The rank is calculated by computing hub and authorities score. Authority score determines the value of the page content. Hub score determines the value of page links to other pages.

When comparing two pages having approximately the same number of citations, if one of these has received more citations from P_1 and P_2, which are counted as important or prestigious pages, then that page relevance becomes higher. In other words, having citations from an important page is better than from an unimportant one [13, 14].

Fujimura et al. [15] proposes Eigen Rumor Algorithm to solve the problem of increasing number of blogs on the Web. It is a challenge to the service providers to display quality blogs to users [13].

- The page rank algorithm decides very low page rank scores for blog entries so rank score cannot be assigned to blog entries according to their importance.
- The rank score can be provided to every blog by weighting the hub scores, and authority of the bloggers is dependent on the calculation of eigenvector.
- It is mostly used for blog ranking not for ranking the web pages.

3 Proposed Method

The proposed focused crawler starts with a seed URL. It does not download the page, instead it parses the page to extract the URLs and words of interest into that page [16].

To determine the importance of the page being parsed, the weight of keywords/ search string in whole Web page is calculated corresponding to the every keyword in the topics specific weight table. As occurrence of same words at various locations of a page has different importance and representing different information [17]. So, relevance of the page being parsed can be decided by considering its each component. For example, the title text is more informative for expressing the topic covered in a page as compared to the common text.

Here, we are computing the weight of oulinks/hyperlinks by the same procedure, i.e. to crawl an relevant page which is children of an irrelevant page [18, 19]. If the level of relevance crosses predefined threshold, only then the page will be downloaded and will be extracted and repository is updated with the page. The page will be discarded otherwise.

In this way, we save the bandwidth after discarding an irrelevant page and network load is reduced.

To obtain the overall weight (wkp) of keyword k in page p, the weights of keyword in different locations of page p can be added as shown below:

wkp = wkurl + wkt + wkb

wkp = l weight of keyword k in page p
wkurl = weight assigned to keyword k based on page URL
wkt = weight assigned to keyword k based on page title

wkb = weight assigned to keyword k based on page body
wko = weight assigned to keyword k based on page outlinks

furl = frequency of search string in url
fb = frequency of search string in body
ft = frequency of search string in title

Wurl = predefined weight of URL
Wb = predefined weight of body text
Wt = predefined weight of title text

Proposed Algorithm

1. Start
2. Add Seed URL to Queue
3. Pick URL from queue
4. Fetch the page
5. Parse the page
6. while (queue is not empty)
{
If (search string or keyword present in URL)
wkurl = furl*wurl
else
Return 0
If (search string or keyword present in title)
wkt = ft*wt
Else
Return 0
If (search string or keyword present in the body)
wkb = fb* wb
Else
Return 0
wkp = wkurl + wkt + wkb
If (wkp > threshold_value)
{
Add to output.
}
Insert all outlinks into the queue
}
7. Stop

4 Conclusion

Hence, by using the concept of page weight, we completely scan Web pages and compute the page weight. In this way, we can improve the efficiency of Web crawler, as URL list produced as output by this method is of great importance than traditional Web crawling method.

References

1. Batra, M.R.: A review of focused crawler approaches. Int. J. **4**(7), (2014)
2. Pant, G., Srinivasan, P.: Link contexts in classifier-guided topical crawlers. IEEE Trans. Knowl. Data Eng. **18**(1), 107–122 (2006)
3. www.wikipedia.org/web_crawler. Accessed 12 May 2010
4. Pal, A., Tomar, D.S., Shrivastava, S.C.: Effective focused crawling based on content and link structure analysis. **2**(1), (2009)
5. De Bra, P., Houben, G.-J., Kornatzky, Y., Post, R.: Information retrieval in distributed hypertexts. In: Proceedings of RIAO-94, Intelligent Multimedia, Information Retrieval Systems and Management, pp. 481–492 (1994)
6. Michael, H., Michal, J., Yoelle, M., Dan, P., Menachem, S., Sigalit, U.: The Shark-search algorithm—an application: tailored web site mapping. Comput. Netw. ISDN Syst. **30**(1–7), 317–326 (1998)
7. Hao, H.W., Mu, C.X., Yin, X.C., Lim, S., Wang, Z.B.: An improved topic relevance algorithm for focused crawling. In: IEEE (2011)
8. Mali, S., Meshram, B.B.: Focused web crawler with page change detection policy. In: 2nd International Conference and workshop on Emerging Trends in Technology (ICWET) Proceedings, International Journal of Computer Applications® (IJCA) 2011
9. Diligenti, M., Coetzee, F., Lawrence, S., Giles, C., Gori, M.: Focused crawling using context graphs. In: Proceedings of 26th International Conference on Very Large Databases (2000)
10. Kaur, S., Gupta, A.: A survey on web focused Information extraction Algorithms. Int. J. Res. Comput. Appl. Robot. **3**(4), 19–23 (2015)
11. Xing, W., Ghorbani, A.: Weighted pagerank algorithm, In: Proceeding of the Second Annual Conference on Communication Networks and Services Research (CSNR' 04), IEEE (2004)
12. Kleinberg, J.M.: Authoritative sources in a hyperlinked environment. J. ACM-SIAM Symp. Discrete Algorithm **46**(5), 604–632 (1999)
13. Sharma, D.K., Sharma, A.K.: A comparative analysis of web page ranking algorithms. Int. J. Comput. Sci. Eng. **02**(08), 2670–2676 (2010)
14. http://en.wikipedia.org/wiki/HITS_algorithm
15. Fujimura, K., Inoue, T., Sugisaki, M.: The EigenRumor algorithm for ranking blogs. In: WWW 2005 2nd Annual Workshop on the Web logging Ecosystem (2005)
16. Chain, X., Zhang, X.: HAWK: a focused crawler with content and link analysis. In: IEEE International Conference on e-Business Engineering (2008)
17. Avraam, I., Anagnostopoulos, I.: A comparison over focused web crawling strategies. In: 2011 IEEE Conference on Panhellenic Conference on Informatics, IEEE (2011)
18. Porter, M. F.: An algorithm for suffix stripping. Readings in information retrieval, pp. 313–316. Morgan Kaufmann Publishers Inc, San Francisco (1997)
19. Avraam, I., Anagnostopoulos, I.: A comparison over focused web crawling strategies. In: IEEE 15th Panhellenic Conferewnce Informatics, pp. 245–249 (2011)

A New Log Kernel-Based Possibilistic Clustering

Meena Tushir and Jyotsna Nigam

Abstract An unsupervised possibilistic (UPC) algorithm with the use of validity indexes has already been proposed. Although UPC works well, it does not show a good accuracy for non-convex cluster structure. To overcome this limitation, we have proposed a kernel version of UPC with a conditionally positive-definite kernel function. It has the ability to detect clusters with different shapes and convex structures because it transforms data into high-dimensional space. Our proposed algorithm, the kernelized UPC-Log(UKPC-L), is an extension of UPC, by introducing log kernel function, which is only conditionally positive-definite function. This makes the performance of our proposed algorithm better than UPC in case of non-convex cluster structures. This has been demonstrated by the results obtained on several real and synthetic datasets. We have compared the performance of UPC and our proposed algorithm using the concept of misclassification, accuracy and error rate to show its efficiency and accuracy.

Keywords Fuzzy c-means · Kernel functions · Possibilistic c-means
Conditionally positive-definite function

1 Introduction

Clustering [1, 2] is commonly used as one of the analytical techniques in the fields of pattern recognition, modelling of system, image segmentation and analysis, communication, data mining and so on. It sorts out the group of N observations or

M. Tushir (✉)
Department of Electrical and Electronics Engineering, Maharaja Surajmal
Institute of Technology, C-4, Janakpuri, New Delhi, India
e-mail: meenatushir@yahoo.com

J. Nigam
Department of Information Technology, Maharaja Surajmal Institute
of Technology, C-4, Janakpuri, New Delhi, India
e-mail: jyotsnaroy81@gmail.com

© Springer Nature Singapore Pte Ltd. 2019   139
M. N. Hoda et al. (eds.), *Software Engineering*, Advances in Intelligent Systems
and Computing 731, https://doi.org/10.1007/978-981-10-8848-3_14

data points into C groups or data clusters (number of clusters), and the objects in each group are more identical to one another than those in other groups. Data clusters on which clustering is to be performed can be well separated, continuous or overlapping. On the basis of cluster type, there are predominantly two types of clustering: hard and fuzzy. Traditional (hard) clustering has a constraint to it that each point of the dataset is restricted to only one cluster. The conception of fuzzy clusters was proposed by Zadeh [3]. It included the notion of partial membership where a data point in a dataset can simultaneously belong to more than one cluster. It gave rise to the thought of probabilistic theory in clustering. Clusters, which are well separated or continuous, give suitable results when processed with hard clustering techniques but sometimes objects in a cluster overlap each other and belong simultaneously to several clusters. Compared with hard clustering, fuzzy clustering has a superior clustering performances and capabilities. The membership degree of a vector x_k to the ith cluster (u_{ik}) is a value in the interval [0, 1] in fuzzy clustering. This idea was first introduced by Ruspini [4] and used by Dunn [5] to construct a fuzzy clustering method based on the criterion function minimization. This approach was generalized by Bezdek to fuzzy c-means algorithm by using a weighted exponent on the fuzzy memberships. Although FCM is a very competent clustering method, its membership does not always correspond well to the degrees of belonging of the data, and it carries certain constraints. The results of FCM may tend to be inaccurate in a noisy environment. Many spurious minima are generated due to the presence of noise in the datasets, which further aggravate the situation. FCM does not provide any method to handle this complication. To reduce this weakness to some extent, Krishnapuram and Keller [6] proposed possibilistic c-means algorithm. PCM uses a possibilistic approach, which uses a possibilistic membership function to describe the degree of belonging. It determines a possibilistic partition matrix, in which a possibilistic membership function measures their absolute degree of typicality of a point in a cluster. In contrast to FCM, possibilistic approach appeared to be more resilient to noise and outliers. PCM has a necessity to predefine the number of clusters and is sensitive to initializations, which sometimes generates coincident clusters. The condition to define the optimal c is termed as cluster validity. To overcome the limitations imposed by FCM and PCM, many new algorithms have been proposed which comprise of the ability to generate both membership and typicality for unlabelled data [7, 8]. However, it is inferred from the observations that these algorithms tend to give not so good results for unequal-sized clusters. In 2006, a novel fuzzy clustering algorithm called unsupervised possibilistic clustering algorithm (UPC) was put forward by Yang and Wu [9]. Unsupervised clustering can determine the number of clusters with the help of their proposed validity indexes. The objective function of UPC integrates the FCM objective function with two cluster validity indexes. The parameters used in UPC are easy to manoeuvre. UPC has many credits, like most enhanced visions, it only works for the convex cluster structure of the dataset. UPC fails to give desirable results when processed on non-convex structures of datasets. The kernel-based unsupervised algorithm proposed in this paper is an extension to the UPC. The data points in the proposed method (UKPC-L) are mapped to a higher dimensional space by kernel function, and the culminating clustering partition is obtained by optimizing the objective function of UKPC-L. The experimental results exhibit better results when compiled with the proposed kernel-based unsupervised algorithm.

The remainder of this paper is organized as follows. Section 2 provides background information on the fuzzy c-means, possibilistic c-means and unsupervised possibilistic clustering. In Sect. 3, the kernel-based approach and kernel trick are highlighted. In Sect. 4, the proposed kernelized version of UPC clustering model is formulated. Section 5 highlights the potential of the proposed approach through various synthetic and real datasets. Concluding remarks are presented in Sect. 6.

2 Literature Work

2.1 Fuzzy C-Means Clustering (FCM)

Most methodical clustering algorithms for clustering analysis are based on the optimization of basic c-means function. In datasets clustering the similarity norm used to group the object, which are identical in nature, is defined by the distance norm. A large family of clustering algorithms and techniques complies with the fuzzy c-means functional formulation by Bezdek and Dunn:

$$J(U; V) = \sum_{i=1}^{c} \sum_{k=1}^{n} u_{ik}^{m} \|x_k - v_i\|^2 \tag{1}$$

It is applicable to wide variety of data analysis problems and works well with them. FCM algorithm assigns membership values to the data points, and it is inversely related to the relative distance of a point to the cluster centres in the FCM model. Each data point in FCM is represented by x_k and v_i represents the centre of the cluster. Closeness of each data point to the centre of the cluster is defined as membership value u_{ik}. m is the weighting exponent who determines the fuzziness of the resulting clusters and it ranges from $[1, \infty]$.

The cluster centres and membership values are computed as

$$v_i = \frac{\sum_{k=1}^{n} u_{ik}^{m} x_k}{\sum_{k=1}^{n} u_{ik}^{m}} \tag{2}$$

$$u_{ik} = \frac{1}{\sum_{j=1}^{c} \left(\frac{x_k - v_i}{x_k - v_j}\right)^{\frac{2}{m-1}}} \tag{3}$$

For a given dataset $X = \{x, \ldots, x_n\}$, the fuzzy c-means algorithm partitions X into C fuzzy subsets by minimizing the objective function given above. It satisfies the condition:

$$\sum_{i=1}^{c} u_{ik} = 1$$

There are some limitations to the fuzzy c-means clustering method. Firstly, since it is based on fixed distance norm, it has a limitation that this norm forces the objective function to prefer clusters of certain shape even if they are not present in the data. Secondly, it is sensitive to noise and there is a requirement to predefine the number of clusters.

2.2   Possibilistic C-Means Clustering (PCM)

PCM works with the viewpoint of possibility theory. According to possibility theory, the membership values can be interpreted as the degree of compatibility or possibility of the points belonging to the classes. In variance to PCM, fuzzy possibilistic c-means clustering simultaneously produces both typicality and membership values. Due to low typicality, outliers are eliminated from the algorithm.

The objective function of PCM is [9]

$$P_m(T, V; X, \gamma) = \sum_{i=1}^{n} \sum_{k=1}^{c} t_{ik}^m d_{ik}^2 + \sum_{i=1}^{c} \gamma_i \sum_{k=1}^{n} (1 - t_{ki})^m \tag{4}$$

where t_{ik} is the typicality value for data point x_k whose cluster centre is v_i, d_{ki} is the distance measured between x_k and c_i, and γ denotes a user-defined constant. γ is greater than zero with the value of i lying in the range of 1 to c. PCM uses approximate optimization for additional conditions. The typicality of data point x_k and the centre of cluster v_i can be obtained by the following equations

$$t_{ki} = \frac{1}{\left(1 + \frac{d_{ki}}{\gamma_i}\right)^{\frac{1}{m-1}}}, \quad \forall i \tag{5}$$

$$v_i = \frac{\sum_{k=1}^{n} t_{ik}^m x_k}{\sum_{k=1}^{n} u_{ik}^m} \tag{6}$$

PCM does not hold the probabilistic constraint that the membership values of the data point across classes sum to one. It overcomes sensitivity to noise and overcomes the need to specify number of clusters. However, there are still some disadvantages in the PCM, i.e. it depends highly on a good initialization and it tends to produce coincidental clusters which are undesirable. The KPCM uses the KFCM to initialize the membership and avoids the above-mentioned weakness of the PCM.

2.3 Unsupervised Possibilistic C-Means Clustering (UPC)

In 2006, Yang and Wu proposed a new possibilistic clustering algorithm called unsupervised possibilistic clustering (UPC) [9]. The objective function of UPC is an extension to FCM objective function with partition coefficient (PC) and partition entropy (PE) validity indexes to make it robust to noise and outliers.

The objective function of UPC is

$$J_{\text{upc}}(U, V) = \sum_{i=1}^{c} \sum_{j=1}^{n} u_{ij}^m d_{ij}^2 + \frac{\beta}{m^2 \sqrt{c}} \sum_{i=1}^{c} \sum_{j=1}^{n} \left(u_{ij}^m \log u_{ij}^m - u_{ij}^m \right) \qquad (7)$$

where m is the fuzzy factor and c is the cluster numbers. The first term is identical to FCM objective function. The second term is constructed by analogue of PE and PC validity indexes.

Parameter β is the sample covariance defined as:

$$\beta = \frac{\sum_{j=1}^{n} \left\| x_j - \bar{x} \right\|}{n} \quad \text{where} \quad \bar{x} = \sum_{j=1}^{n} \frac{x_j}{n} \qquad (8)$$

Minimizing the objective function with respect to u_{ij} and setting it to zero, we get equation for membership value, i.e.

$$u_{ij} = \exp\left(-\frac{m\sqrt{c}\|x_j - v_i\|^2}{\beta} \right), \quad i = 1, \ldots, c, j = 1, \ldots, n \qquad (9)$$

Minimizing the objective function with respect to v_i, we get equation for membership value cluster centres, i.e.

$$v_i = \frac{\sum_{j=1}^{n} \mu_{ij}^m x_j}{\sum_{j=1}^{n} \mu_{ij}^m} \qquad (10)$$

3 Kernel-Based Algorithm

3.1 Kernel-Based Approach

A kernel function is generalization of the distance matrix that measures the distance between two data points as the data points are mapped into high-dimensional space in which they are more clearly separable [10, 11]. We can increase the accuracy of algorithm by exploiting a kernel function in calculating the distance of data points from the prototypes.

Kernel trick:

The kernel trick is a very interesting and powerful tool. It provides a bridge from linearity to nonlinearity to any algorithm that can express solely on terms of dot products between two vectors.

Kernel trick is interesting because that mapping does not need to be ever computed. The "trick" is wherever a dot product is used, it is replaced with a kernel function. The kernel function denotes an inner product in feature space and is usually denoted as:

$$K(x, y) = \langle \Phi(x), \Phi(y) \rangle$$

Given an unlabelled dataset $X = \{x_1, \ldots, x_n\}$ in p-dimensional space R^p, let Φ be nonlinear mapping function from this input space to high-dimensional feature space H:

$$\Phi : R^p \rightarrow H, x \rightarrow \Phi(x)$$

The dot product in high-dimensional feature space can be calculated through kernel function $K(x_i, x_j)$, in the input space R^p

$$K(x_i, x_j) = \Phi(x_i)\Phi(x_j) \tag{11}$$

Some examples of kernel function are as follows:

Example 1 (Linear kernel): $k(x, y) = x^T y + c$

Example 2 (Polynomial kernel): $K(x_i, x_j) = (x_i.x_j + c)^d$ where $c \geq 0, d \in N$

Example 3 (Gaussian basis kernel):

$$K(x_i, x_j) : \exp\left(-\frac{\|x_i - x_j\|^2}{2\sigma^2}\right) \quad \text{where } \sigma > 0$$

Example 4 (Hyperbolic tangent (sigmoid) kernel):

$$K(x, y) = \tanh\left(ax^T + c\right).$$

4 Proposed kernelized UPC-Log Algorithm

To further improve UPC, we have used a log kernel function. Log kernel function is conditionally positive-definite function, i.e. it is positive for all values of greater than 0. We named our proposed algorithm as UKPC-L.

Conditionally positive definite function:
Let X be a non-empty set. A kernel K is called conditionally positive definite if and only if it is symmetric and

$$\sum_{j,k=1}^{n} c_j c_k K\left(x_j, x_k\right) \geq 0 \tag{12}$$

For $n \geq 1, c_1,\ldots, c_n \in R$ with $\sum_{j=1}^{n} c_j = 0$ and

$$x_1, \ldots, x_n \in X$$

The log kernel function that we have proposed for our algorithm is:

$$K(x, y) = \log\left(1 + \left\|\alpha x_j - v_i\right\|^2\right) \tag{13}$$

Using our log kernel function, the objective function and the distance for UKPC-L clustering is as follows:

$$J_{\text{UKPC-L}} = \sum_{i=1}^{c}\sum_{j=1}^{n} u_{ij}^m D_{ij}^2 + \frac{\beta}{m^2\sqrt{c}} \sum_{i=1}^{c}\sum_{j=1}^{n}\left(u_{ij}^m \log u_{ij}^m - u_{ij}^m\right) \tag{14}$$

where

$$D_{ij}^2 = \left\|\Phi(x_i) - \Phi(v_i)\right\|^2 = -2\log\left(1 + \alpha\left\|x_j - v_i\right\|^2\right) \tag{15}$$

$$\beta = \frac{-2\sum_{j=1}^{n}\log(1 + \alpha\left\|x_j - v_i\right\|^2)}{n} \tag{16}$$

Minimizing the objective function with respect to v_i, we get equation for cluster centres

$$v_i = \frac{\sum_{j=1}^{n} u_{ij}^m x_j \left(\frac{1}{1 + \left(\alpha\left\|x_j - v_i\right\|^2\right)}\right)}{\sum_{j=1}^{n} \frac{u_{ij}^m}{1 + \left(\alpha\left\|x_j - v_i\right\|^2\right)}} \tag{17}$$

Minimizing the objective function with respect to u_{ij} and setting it to zero, we get equation for membership value

$$u_{ij} = \exp\left(\frac{2m\sqrt{c}}{\beta}\log\left(1 + \alpha\left\|x_j - v_i\right\|^2\right)\right) \tag{18}$$

The general form of our proposed algorithm is as follows:

*Fix the number of clusters C; fix(m) > 1; set the learning rate α;
*Execute a FCM clustering algorithm to find initial U and V;
*Set iteration count $k = 1$;
Repeat
Calculate objective function $J(u, v)$ using (14).
Compute β using (16).
Update v_i using (17).
Update u_{ik} using (18).
Until a given stopping criterion, i.e. convergence precision ε is satisfied.

5 Experimental Results

To demonstrate the efficiency and performance of our proposed algorithm, we applied the kernelized UPC-L and UPC to a number of widely used datasets. We used datasets with varying shapes, orientation and number of data points. The real-life datasets used in the experiments are Iris dataset and Seed dataset. For our experiments, we have chosen: $m = 2$, $\alpha = 2$, $\varepsilon = 0.00001$ and max_iter = 100.

5.1 Synthetic Datasets

1. *Gaussian Random Data with Noise*: The dataset generated is spherical with unequal radii. There are four clusters and, the data points in each cluster are normally distributed over two-dimensional space. Analysing the Fig. 1 closely, our proposed algorithm gives desired results with cluster centres located at their prototypical locations, while in the cases of UPC the cluster centres are slightly shifted from the ideal locations.

The respective covariance matrices are:

$$\begin{bmatrix} 0.40 \\ 00.8 \end{bmatrix}, \begin{bmatrix} 0.40 \\ 00.8 \end{bmatrix}, \begin{bmatrix} 0.40 \\ 00.8 \end{bmatrix} \text{ and } \begin{bmatrix} 10 \\ 01 \end{bmatrix}$$

The respective means for each cluster using the UPC clustering technique and our proposed algorithm are given as:

Fig. 1 Clustering by **a** UPC.
b UKPC-L

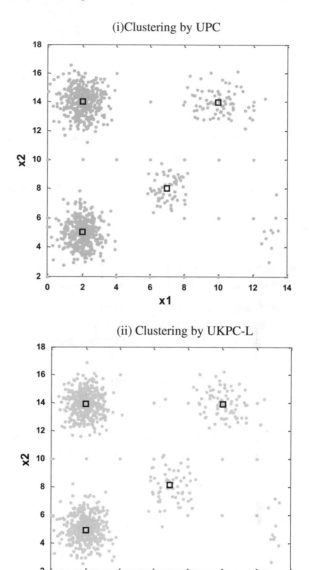

$$V_{\text{IDEAL}} = \begin{bmatrix} 2 & 5 \\ 2 & 14 \\ 7 & 8 \\ 10 & 14 \end{bmatrix}$$

$$V_{\text{UPC}} = \begin{bmatrix} 1.9947 & 5.0186 \\ 2.0138 & 13.9765 \\ 6.7874 & 8.1653 \\ 9.9408 & 13.8123 \end{bmatrix} \quad V_{\text{UKPC-L}} = \begin{bmatrix} 2.0146 & 4.9913 \\ 2.0007 & 13.9779 \\ 6.9814 & 8.0660 \\ 9.9735 & 14.0319 \end{bmatrix}$$

To show the effectiveness of our proposed algorithm, we also compute the error using:

$$E_* = ||V_{\text{ideal}} - V_*||^2$$

where $*$ is UPC/UKPC-L. $E_{\text{UPC}} = 0.00126$ and $E_{\text{UKPC-L}} = 0.00029$. Clearly we can see from error results that our proposed algorithm is better than UPC.

2. *R15 spherical dataset*: The next dataset consists of identical-sized spherical dataset with 15 clusters. UPC has misplaced all the inner cluster prototypes. Our proposed algorithm clusters the data points in the best way with all cluster centres at the required positions.

   The shift in the centres is clearly visible in Fig. 2.

3. *Random Gaussian dataset without noise*: The next dataset is a typical convex cluster dataset. In this dataset, the UPC algorithm detects only four clusters taking all as convex shapes, whereas our proposed algorithm detects five clusters and hence proves to work well all shapes as well (Fig. 3).

5.2   *High-Dimensional Real Datasets*

We now study the performance quality and efficiency of our proposed clustering algorithm on a few real datasets, namely Iris dataset and Seed dataset. The clustering results were concluded using Huang's accuracy measure [12] with the following formula:

$$r = \frac{\sum_{i=1}^{k} n_i}{n} \tag{19}$$

Fig. 2 Clustering by **a** UPC.
b UKPC-L using R15 dataset

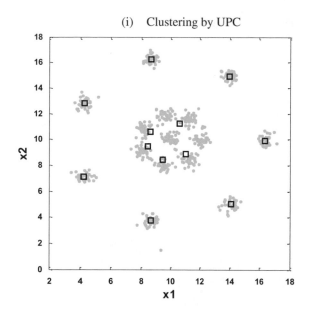

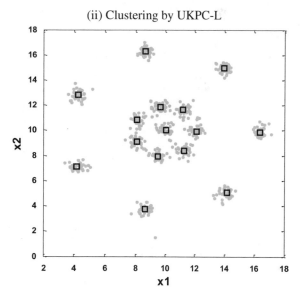

where n_i is the number of data occurring in both the ith cluster and its corresponding true cluster, and n is the number of data points in the dataset. According to
this measure, a higher value of r indicates a better clustering result with perfect
clustering yielding a value $r = 1$. Error has been calculated by using the measure:
$E = 1 - r$

Fig. 3 Clustering by **a** UPC.
b UKPC-L

(i) Clustering by UPC

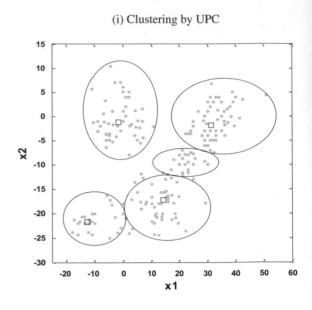

(ii) Clustering by UKPC-L

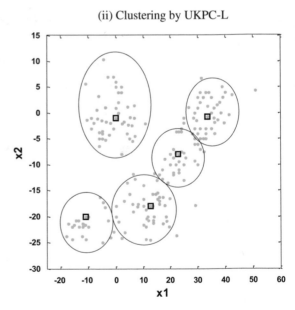

Table 1 Number of misclassified data, elapsed time, accuracy and error using UPC and UKPC-L

Clustering algorithm	Misclassifications	Elapsed time	Accuracy (%)	Error (%)
UPC	12	1.50	92.0	8.0
UKPC-L	10	0.71	93.3	6.6

Table 2 Number of misclassified data, elapsed time, accuracy and error using UPC and UKPC-L

Clustering algorithm	Misclassifications	Elapsed time	Accuracy (%)	Error (%)
UPC	25	0.28	88.57	11.42
UKPC-L	23	0.29	89.04	10.95

1. *Iris dataset*: This is a four-dimensional dataset containing 50 samples each of three types of Iris flowers. One of the three clusters (class 1) is well separated from the other two, while classes 2 and 3 have some overlap. We made several runs of UPC and our proposed method when these algorithms are initialized with FCM terminal prototypes. Table 1 compares the algorithms based on the optimization efficiency as judged by the above equation.

As can be seen in the Table 1, UPC has the higher error value with 12 samples assigned to incorrect labels. Comparing it with our proposed method, our algorithm shows better accuracy of 93.33% making only ten errors.

2. *Seed dataset*: This is a multivariate dataset with 7 attributes (dimensions) and 210 instances. The examined dataset comprised kernels belonging to three different varieties of wheat with 70 elements each.

As seen clearly from the Table 2, our proposed algorithm misclassifies only 23 elements into incorrect classes with 89.04% accuracy, which is slightly more efficient compared to UPC which misclassifies 25 elements.

6   Conclusions

In this paper, we have proposed a conditionally positive-definite log kernel-based possibilistic clustering. It performs well for different-shaped datasets, thereby overcoming the limitation of previously proposed unsupervised algorithm in terms of efficiency. Compared to UPC, our proposed method selects more desirable cluster centroids, thereby increasing the clustering accuracy. To check the accuracy of our algorithm, we have applied it on various real and synthetic datasets, and our proposed algorithm gives better performance results on various performance criteria like misclassification, accuracy and error rate.

References

1. Anderberg, M.R.: Cluster Analysis for Application. Academic Press, New York (1973)
2. Backer, E., Jain, A.K.: A clustering performance measure based on fuzzy set decomposition. IEEE Trans. Pattern Anal. Mach. Intell. **3**(1), 66–74 (1981)
3. Zadeh, L.A.: Fuzzy sets. Inf. Control **8**, 338–353 (1965)
4. Ruspini, E.H.: A new approach to clustering. Inform. Control **15**(1), 22–32 (1969)
5. Dunn, J.C.: A fuzzy relative of the ISODATA process and its use in detecting compact well-separated cluster. J. Cybern. **3**(3), 32–57 (1973)
6. Krishnapuram, R., Keller, J.M.: A possibilistic approach to clustering. IEEE Trans. Fuzzy Syst. **1**, 98–110 (1993)
7. Dave, R.: Characterization and detection of noise in clustering. Pattern Rec. Lett. **12**(11), 657–664 (1991)
8. Pal, N.R., Pal, K., Bezdek, J.C.: A mixed c-means clustering model. In: Proceedings of the IEEE International Conference on Fuzzy Systems, Spain, pp. 11–21 (1997)
9. Yang, M.S., Wu, K.L.: Unsupervised possibilistic clustering. Pattern Recogn. **39**(1), 5–21 (2006)
10. Christianini, N., Taylor, J.S.: An Introduction to SVMs and Other Kernel-Based Learning Methods. Cambridge University Press, Cambridge (2000)
11. Girolami, M.: Mercer kernel-based clustering in feature space. IEEE Trans. Neural Netw. **13** (3), 780–784 (2002)
12. Huang, Z., Ng, M.K.: A fuzzy k-modes algorithm for clustering categorical data. IEEE Trans. Fuzzy Syst. **7**(4), 446–452 (1999)

Fuzzy c-Means Clustering Strategies: A Review of Distance Measures

Jyoti Arora, Kiran Khatter and Meena Tushir

Abstract In the process of clustering, our attention is to find out basic procedures that measures the degree of association between the variables. Many clustering methods use distance measures to find similarity or dissimilarity between any pair of objects. The fuzzy c-means clustering algorithm is one of the most widely used clustering techniques which uses Euclidean distance metrics as a similarity measurement. The choice of distance metrics should differ with the data and how the measure of their comparison is done. The main objective of this paper is to present mathematical description of different distance metrics which can be acquired with different clustering algorithm and comparing their performance using the number of iterations used in computing the objective function, the misclassification of the datum in the cluster, and error between ideal cluster center location and observed center location.

Keywords FCM clustering · Euclidean distance · Standard euclidean distance Mahalanobis distance · Minkowski distance · Chebyshev distance

J. Arora (✉)
Department of Information Technology, Maharaja Surajmal Institute of Technology,
C-4, Janakpuri, New Delhi, India
e-mail: joy.arora@gmail.com

K. Khatter
Department of Computer Science, Ansal University, Gurgaon, India
e-mail: kirankhatter@ansaluniversity.edu.in

M. Tushir
Department of Electrical & Electronics Engineering, Maharaja Surajmal Institute
of Technology, C-4, Janakpuri, New Delhi, India
e-mail: meenatushir@yahoo.com

© Springer Nature Singapore Pte Ltd. 2019
M. N. Hoda et al. (eds.), *Software Engineering*, Advances in Intelligent Systems
and Computing 731, https://doi.org/10.1007/978-981-10-8848-3_15

153

1 Introduction

Clustering is a technique of finding similar characteristic data among the given set of data through association rules and classification rules resulting into separation of classes and frequent pattern recognition. Clustering is basically knowledge discovery process whose result can be used for future use, in various applications. A good cluster definition involves low interclass similarity and high intra-class similarity. In order to categorize the data, we have to apply different similarity measure techniques to establish a relation between the patterns which will group the data into different clusters with a degree of membership. In clustering, we have to evaluate a good distance metrics, in order to have high intra-class similarity. Several clustering algorithms with the different distance metrics have been developed in the past, some of them are used in detecting different shapes of clusters such as spherical [1], elliptical [2], some of them are used to detect the straight lines [3, 4], algorithms focusing on the compactness of the clusters [2, 5]. Clustering is a challenging field of research as it can be used as a separate tool to gain insight into the allocation of data, to observe the characteristic feature of each cluster, and to spotlight on a particular set of clusters for more analysis. Focusing on the proximity measures, we can find some work that compares a set of distance metrics; therefore, these could be used as guidelines. However, most of the work includes basic distance metrics as Grabusts [6] compared Euclidean distance, Manhattan distance, and Correlation distance with k-means on Iris dataset, similarly Hathaway [7] compared distance with different values of p, Liu et al. [8] proposed a new algorithm while changing the Euclidean distance with Standard Mahalanobis distance.

In this paper, we are presenting the survey of different distance metrics in order to acquire proximity measure to be followed by the clustering criterion that results in the definition of a good clustering scheme for dataset. We have included Euclidean distance, Standard Euclidean distance, Mahalanobis distance, Standard Mahalanobis distance, Minkowski distance, and Chebyshev distance and compared on the criteria of accuracy and misclassification, location of center which to our knowledge have not been discussed in such detail in any of the surveys till now.

The remainder of this paper is sectioned as follows. Section 2 provides related work which includes detail of fuzzy c-means algorithm and overview of different distance metrics, and Sect. 3 includes experimental results on different data types including synthetic and real datasets. Section 4 concludes the review.

2 Related Work

2.1 Fuzzy c-Means Algorithm

The notion of fuzzy sets was developed by Zadeh [9] is an attempt to modify exclusive clustering on the basis of their probability of any parameter on which clusters have been developed, which was further extended by Bezdek et al. [3] as fuzzy c-means algorithm (FCM) is the most widely used algorithm. This approach partitions a set of data $\{x_1, \ldots, x_n\} \subset R^s$ into c-clusters based on a similarity computed by the least square function of Euclidean distance metrics. The objective function of FCM is

$$J_{\text{FCM}}(X : U, V) = \sum_{j=1}^{c} \sum_{i=1}^{N} (u_{ij})^m \|x_i - v_j\|^2, 1 < m < \infty \tag{1}$$

where $m > 1$ is a fuzzification parameter, $v_j \in R^S$ is a cluster center, $u_{ij} \in [0, 1]$ is a degree to which data x belongs to cluster, defines partition matrix. $\|x_i - v_j\|^2$ is a Euclidean distance metrics. The partition matrix u_{ij} is a convenient tool for representing cluster structure in the data, where the fuzzy partition has constraint $\sum_{i=1}^{c} u_{ij} = 1$. The most effective method of optimization of Eq. (1) is by alternative optimization method used in conventional FCM. The equation of v_j and u_{ij} can be referred from [3].

2.2 Distance Measures

Important component of clustering algorithm is similarity measurement between the data points. There are different measures which have been used with different clustering algorithms in order to have clusters with desired properties. Some distance measures we will discuss are

2.2.1 Euclidean Distance

The Euclidean distance is the most intense similarity measure which is used widely in FCM. This formula includes two objects and compares each attribute of individual item with other to determine strength of relativity with each other. The smaller the distance is greater the similarity. The equation for Euclidean distance is

$$d_{x,v} = \sqrt{(x_1 - v_i)^2 + (x_2 - v_i)^2 \ldots (x_n - v_i)^2} \tag{2}$$

Euclidean distance as a measure of similarity, hyperspherical-shaped clusters of equal size are usually detected [10]. However, Euclidean distance degrades the performance in the presence of noise in the dataset. This is because the object to center dissimilarity term in (1) can place considerable membership to the outlying data and due to membership constraint.

2.2.2 Standard Euclidean Distance

The Standard Euclidean distance can be squared in order to place progressively greater weight on objects that are farther apart. In this case, the equation becomes

$$d_{x,v}^2 = (x_1 - v_i)^2 + (x_2 - v_i)^2 \ldots (x_n - v_i)^2 \tag{3}$$

This distance metrics is frequently used in optimization problems in which distances only have to be compared. Clustering with the Euclidean Squared distance is faster than clustering with the regular Euclidean distance.

2.2.3 Mahalanobis Distance

Mahalanobis distance is a measure of the distance between a given point and a distribution. It is a multi-dimensional generalization of the act of determining the number of standard deviations that a point x is away from the mean of the distribution. The equation of the Mahalanobis distance is given by

$$d_{x,v} = \overline{)(x_k - v_i)A^{-1}(x_k - v_i)} \tag{4}$$

In (4), A is a covariance matrix of data. The Mahalanobis distance is better adopted where the cluster required are nonspherical in shape. In [2], Cai has discussed in clustering algorithm, a modified Mahalanobis distance with preserved volume was used. It is more particularly useful when multinormal distributions are involved.

2.2.4 Standard Mahalanobis Distance

In Standard Mahalanobis distance, covariance matrix is replaced by correlation matrix. The equation of the Standard Mahalanobis distance is represented by

$$d_{x,v} = \overline{)(x_k - v_i)R^{-1}(x_k - v_i)} \tag{5}$$

In (5) R is a correlation matrix. In [8], Liu et al. has proposed new algorithm giving FCM-SM, normalizing each feature in the objective function, and all covariance matrix becomes corresponding correlation matrix.

2.2.5 Minkowski Distance

Minkowski distance termed as L_p is a generalized metric that includes special cases of p and introduced three distance metrics with $p = 1$(Manhattan distance), $p = 2$

(Euclidean distance), and $p = \infty$ (Chebyshev distance). The Minkowski distance of order p between data points and center points is represented by

$$d_{x,v} = \left(\sum_{i=1}^{n} \|x_i - v_i\|^p \right)^{1/p} \tag{6}$$

In [1, 2], different function of Minkowski distance with different value of p has been implemented with FCM showing results on relational and object data types.

2.2.6 Chebyshev Distance

Chebyshev distance (L_∞) is a distance metric specified on a vector space where the given two vectors are separated by a distance which is the largest of their differences measured along any coordinate dimension. Essentially, it is the maximum distance between two points in any single dimension. The Chebyshev distance between ant two points is given by (7)

$$d_{x,v} = \max |x_i - v_i| \tag{7}$$

3 Experiments' Results

The purpose of the experimental part was to test the operation of the FCM algorithm by applying different distance metrics on synthetic and real dataset. We used datasets with wide variety in the shape of clusters, numbers of clusters, and count of features in different data point. FCM is an unsupervised clustering so the number of clusters to group the data was given by us. We choose $m = 2$ which is a good choice for fuzzy clustering. For all parameters, we use $\varepsilon = 0.001$, max_iter = 200.

3.1 Synthetic Datasets

3.1.1 X_{12} Dataset

The first example involves X_{12} dataset as given in Fig. 1 contains two identical clusters with one outlier which is equidistant from both the clusters. We know FCM is very sensitive to noise, so we do not get the desired results. To show the effectiveness of different distance metrics, we have calculated the error E_*, by sum of the square of the difference between calculated center and the ideal center with every distance metrics as given in Eq. (8).

Fig. 1 Representation of X_{12} dataset

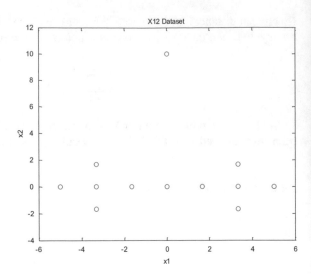

Different Volume Rectangle Dataset

By changing the volume of clusters in a pattern, we observe the effectiveness of different distance metrics. Figure 2 shows the representation of dataset with two identical clusters of different volume, ideal cluster center are defined by V_{RD}.

Table 1 shows that for X_{12} dataset, best results are shown with Euclidean distance, Minkowski distance, and Chebyshev distance but number of iterations used by Minkowski distance are more. The Standard Mahalanobis distance and

Fig. 2 Representation of rectangle dataset

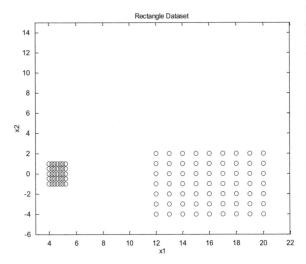

Table 1 Centers produced by FCM with different distance metrics, effectiveness and number of iteration for the X_{12} dataset and different volume rectangle dataset

Distance	Euclidean		Std. Euclidean		Mahalanobis		Std. mahalanobis		Minkowski		Chebyshev	
Center (V_{12})	2.98	0.54	2.67	2.15	2.97	0.55	−2.98	0.54	−2.98	0.54	−2.98	0.54
	−2.98	0.54	−1.51	0.08	−2.97	0.55	2.98	0.54	2.98	0.54	2.98	0.54
E_*	0.412		4.213		0.438		0.412		0.412		0.412	
No. of Iter.	10		10		10		9		17		10	
Center (V_{RD})	4.22	−0.02	7.42	0.30	5.90	−0.10	4.86	0.54	4.92	−0.01	4.76	−0.02
	16.30	−1.01	16.26	−2.02	16.42	−1.06	16.33	−0.94	16.33	−0.94	16.26	−1.00
E_*	0.349		3.53		0.5		0.211		0.059		0.062	
No. of Iter.	10		23		27		10		14		13	

Mahalanobis distance also show optimal results but Standard Euclidean distance shows poor results. Similarly in Different Volume Rectangle dataset, Minkowski distance and Chebyshev distance perform best as compared to other distance metrics. The highest number of iterations is used by Mahalanobis distance. The Standard Euclidean distance shows worst result with this dataset also. Both the above data comprises of clusters forming compact clouds that are well separated from one another, thus sum of squared error distance outperforms as compare to other distance and Standard Euclidean distance shows poor results. Mahalanobis distance due to calculation of covariance matrix for the data does not show accurate result.

$$E_* = \|V_{12}(\text{ideal}) - V_{12}(\text{dist})\|^2 \tag{8}$$

$$V_{12}(\text{ideal}) = \begin{bmatrix} -3.3400 & 0 \\ 3.3400 & 0 \end{bmatrix} \quad V_{RD}(\text{ideal}) = \begin{bmatrix} 5 & 0 \\ 16 & -1 \end{bmatrix}$$

3.2 High-Dimensional DataSets

We now examine the defined evaluation criteria with some well-known real datasets, namely Iris dataset, Wine dataset and Wisconsin dataset. We are going to analyze the clustering results using Huang' s accuracy measure (r) [11].

$$r = \frac{\sum_{i=1}^{k} n_i}{n} \tag{9}$$

where n_i is the number of data occurring in both the ith cluster and its corresponding true cluster, and n is the number of data points in the dataset. According to this measure, a higher value of r indicates a better clustering result with perfect clustering yielding a value of $r = 1$.

We made several runs of FCM with different distance metrics and calculated the misclassification, accuracy, number of iterations on all the three high-dimensional datasets. Here in Table 2, we find that how the algorithm shows different values of misclassification over the three datasets with the change of distance metrics. In this, we can see Chebyshev distance is giving good result with Iris and Breast Cancer dataset with an accuracy of 90 and 96% respectively, Standard Euclidean distance is giving best result with Wine dataset with an accuracy of 91%, however number of iterations used is very high.

Table 2 FCM with different distance metrics showing misclassification, accuracy and number of iteration with Iris, Wine, Breast Cancer (BC) dataset

Dataset	Distance					
	Euclidean	Std. Euclidean	Mahalanobis	Mahalanobis	Minkowski	Chebyshev
Misclassification$_{IRIS}$	17	27	43	27	17	15
Accuracy$_{IRIS}$	0.88	0.82	0.71	0.82	0.88	0.9
No. of Iter.$_{IRIS}$	18	41	67	22	25	20
Misclassification$_{WINE}$	56	16	79	55	55	56
Accuracy$_{WINE}$	0.68	0.91	0.55	0.69	0.69	0.68
No. of Iter.$_{WINE}$	47	113	9	46	86	61
Misclassification$_{BC}$	30	31	22	53	38	22
Accuracy$_{BC}$	0.95	0.95	0.96	0.92	0.94	0.96
No. of Iter.$_{BC}$	14	22	100	25	21	18

4   Conclusions

We described various distance metrics for FCM and examined the behavior of the algorithm with different approaches. It has been concluded from results on various synthetic and real datasets that Euclidean distance works well for most of the datasets. Chebyshev and Minkowski distances are equally suitable for clustering. Further exhaustive exploration on distance metrics needs to be done on various datasets.

References

1. Patrick, J.F., Groenen, U., Kaymak, J.V., Rosmalen: Fuzzy clustering with Minkowski distance functions. Econometric Institute Report, EI(24), (2006)
2. Cai, J.Y., Xie, F.D., Zhang, Y.: Fuzzy c-means algorithm based on adaptive Mahalanobis distance. Comput. Eng. Appl. 174–176(2010)
3. Bezdek, J.C., Coray, C., Gunderson, R, Watson, J.: Detection and characterization of cluster substructure. SIAM J. Appl. Math. 339–372 (1981)
4. Dave, R.N.: Use of the adaptive fuzzy clustering algorithm to detect lines in digital images. Intell Robots Comput. Vision VIII 1192, pp. 600–661 (1982)
5. Dunn, J.C.: A fuzzy relative of the ISODATA process and its use in detecting compact well separated clusters. J Cybern, 32–57(1973)
6. Grabusts, P.: The choice of metrics for clustering algorithms. In: International Scientific and Practical Conference Vol 2(8), pp. 70–76 (2011)
7. Hathaway, R.J., Bezdek, J.C., Hu, Y.: Generalised fuzzy c-means clustering strategies using L_P norm distance. IEEE Trans. Fuzzy Syst. 8(5), (2000)
8. Liu, H.C., Jeng, B.C., Yih, J.M., Yu, Y.K.: Fuzzy c-means clustering algorithm based on standard mahalanobis distance. In: International Symposium on Information Processing, pp. 422–427 (2009)
9. Zadeh, L.A.: Fuzzy sets. Inf. Control 8, 338–353 (1965)
10. Su, M.C., Chou, C.H.: A Modified means of K-Means algorithm with a distance based on cluster symmetry. IEEE Trans. Pattern Anal. Mach. Intell. 23, 674–680 (2001)
11. Tushir, M., Srivastava, S.: A new kernelized hybrid c-mean clustering with optimized parameters. Appl. Soft Comp. 10, 381–389 (2010)

Noise Reduction from ECG Signal Using Error Normalized Step Size Least Mean Square Algorithm (ENSS) with Wavelet Transform

Rachana Nagal, Pradeep Kumar and Poonam Bansal

Abstract This paper presents the reduction of baseline wander noise found in ECG signals. The reduction has been done using wavelet transform inspired error normalized step size least mean square (ENSS-LMS) algorithm. We are presenting a wavelet decomposition-based filtering technique to minimize the computational complexity along with the good quality of output signal. The MATLAB simulation results validate the good noise rejection in output signal by analyzing parameters, excess mean square error (EMSE) and misadjustment.

Keywords ECG signal · ENSS algorithm · LMS algorithm · Wavelet transform
EMSE · Misadjustment

1 Introduction

Electrocardiographic (ECG) signals are very low amplitude signals around 1 mV. ECG signal can be corrupted with either noises named as baseline wander (BW) or power line interface (PLI) noises. These two noises badly degrade the ECG signal quality and generate a resembling PQRST waveform and remove some tiny features which are important for diagnosis. ECG is commonly more affected by Baseline Wander (BW), which is the reason behind varying electrode skin impudence, patient's breath, and movement. This noise is a kind of sinusoid signal with random frequency and phase. Baseline wander reduction is very important step to process

R. Nagal (✉) · P. Kumar
Department of ECE, ASET, Amity University, Noida, Uttar Pradesh, India
e-mail: rnagal@amity.edu

P. Kumar
e-mail: pkumar4@amity.edu

P. Bansal
Department of CSE, MSIT, IP University, New Delhi, India
e-mail: pbansal89@yahoo.co.in

© Springer Nature Singapore Pte Ltd. 2019
M. N. Hoda et al. (eds.), *Software Engineering*, Advances in Intelligent Systems and Computing 731, https://doi.org/10.1007/978-981-10-8848-3_16

ECG signal. Finally, the work presents here with aim to find the clean signal from the undesired noisy signals so that the out coming signal can be used for easy diagnosis.

There are so many techniques used to enhance the quality of the signal in the research papers [1–9], those were used both adaptive and non-adaptive models. There were so many adaptive filters proposed for canceling noise from ECG signal. These adaptive filters minimize the error between the noisy ECG signal (considered as the primary input) and a reference signal which is somehow correlated with the noise present in primary ECG signal. To track the dynamic variations of the ECG signals, Thakor et al. [1] give the concept of an adaptive recurrent filter structure which acquired the impulse response of normal QRS. To track the QRS complexes in ECG signals with few parameters, an adaptive system has been proposed which is based on the Hermite functions [2]. To update the coefficient of the filter, there is always a need to have an adaptive algorithm. The task of this adaptive algorithm is to minimize the error obtained after subtracting the output of the filter and the addition of main signal and noise. The researcher also analyzed the error convergence when the reference input is deterministic signal. One of that kind works has been published by Olmos et al. [3], where they had derived the expression for steady-state misadjustment taking ECG as input signal. Costa et al. [4] proposed noise resilient variable step size LMS algorithm which is specially designed for biomedical signals. A software approach has also been developed by Brouse et al. [5] for detecting noises from ECG signal using wavelet decomposition of signals. But hardware implementation of this approach becomes costly for biomedical applications. So there are several adaptive algorithms, and there modification has been published [10–13].

This paper contributes by implementing error normalized step size least mean square (ENSS-LMS) algorithm with the help of wavelet transforms. In this paper, the adaptive structure of ENSS is presented to eliminate the baseline wander noise from ECG signals. MIT-BIH database is used to implement and analyze the performance of weight updating algorithm (ENSS) to eliminate the baseline wander noise from ECG signals. MATLAB simulations have been done to indicate substantial improvements of the quality if ECG signals by obtaining the good value of EMSE and misadjustment.

This paper is organized as follows: Sect. 2 gives the proposed Implementation of ENSS algorithm along with wavelet transform. Section 3 shows the simulation results. Section 4 concludes the work.

2 Proposed Implementation

2.1 ENSS Algorithm-Based ANC System

Adaptive noise cancellation is a technique used to remove the noise from the input signal. Figure 1 shows the primary input signal $x(n)$ which is basically the addition of original signal with some noise. If an original signal is say $s(n)$ and noise signal

Fig. 1 Block diagram of
proposed ENSS-based ANC
system

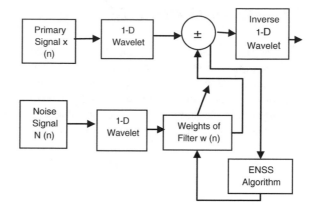

say $N1(n)$, then primary input $x(n)$ becomes $x(n) = s(n) + N1(n)$. There is also a reference signal taken which is related to the noise added with the original signal. The reference noise signal $N(n)$ will pass through a filter whose coefficient will be updated through ENSS-LMS algorithm.

2.2　1-D Wavelet Transform (Haar Wavelet Transform)

It has been seen that a signal is decomposed in terms of its sinusoids for spectral analysis, but it has also found that decomposing the signal in terms of its components for different frequency band spectrum is very good to reduce the complexity of transform like wavelet transform [14]. So we use discrete wavelet transform for spectral analysis of signal using a set of basic function defined in both frequency and time domain. Here we are using 'Haar' wavelet [15]. Haar wavelet is basically a sequence of rescaled square-shaped integral function on the unit interval represented in terms of an orthonormal function. It is generally used for the analysis of signals which suddenly changes [16]. The mother wavelet function for Haar wavelet is defined as:

$$\begin{bmatrix} X_\Psi(0,0) \\ X_\phi(0,0) \end{bmatrix} = \begin{bmatrix} \frac{1}{\sqrt{2}} & \frac{1}{\sqrt{2}} \\ \frac{1}{\sqrt{2}} & \frac{1}{\sqrt{2}} \end{bmatrix} \begin{bmatrix} x(0) \\ x(1) \end{bmatrix} \quad \text{or} \quad X = H_{n,0}x \qquad (1)$$

Its inverse function is defined as

$$x = H^T X \qquad (2)$$

2.3   ENSS-LMS Algorithm

Error normalized step size least mean square (ENSS) is an algorithm where instead of filter input the step size parameters vary. The step size parameters vary as a nonlinear function of the error vector. In error normalized step size algorithm, the variable step size is inversely proportional to the squared of the error vector. Also in this algorithm, the number of iteration and the length of the error vector are equal. The equation for updating the weights of ENSS is:

$$W(n+1) = W(n) + \frac{\mu}{1 + \mu \|e_n\|^2} e(n)x(n) \tag{3}$$

where

$$\|e_n\|^2 = \sum_{i=0}^{n-1} e^2(n-i) \tag{4}$$

is the squared of the error $e(n)$, which is used for the estimation of it for its entire updating. The step size equation is now defined as:

$$W(n+1) = W(n) + \frac{1}{\frac{1}{\mu} + \|e_n\|^2} e(n)x(n) \tag{5}$$

As the length of error vector $e(n)$ is equal to the number of iterations say n, the proposed variable step size $\mu(n)$ becomes nonlinear decreasing function of n. So, $\|e_n\|^2$ will be increasing function of n. Also, $\mu(n)$ is an increasing function of the parameter μ [17].

2.4   Implementation Steps

1. Import the ECG signal in the program to workspace which is $x(n)$; we consider this ECG signal with noise.
2. Following that baseline wander noise file is also imported from workspace, we call it as reference noise signal and denoted by $N(n)$.
3. A correlated noise is generated by passing the noise signals through a parameterized filter of some order.
4. Wavelet Transform of principle signal and baseline wander noise both will be taken. So the output of 1-D wavelet box shown in Fig. 1 is $x(n)\Psi(t)$ for primary signal and $N1(n)\Psi(t)$ for reference signal.
5. Weights, error, and other variables are initialized.

6. Now the wavelet coefficient obtained from signals will be processed through the FIR Wiener filter.
7. The step size is determined using its limit equation (3), where the error will be calculated by Eq. (5).
8. Output of the filter is calculated by multiplying the baseline noise signal with the computed tap weight. So Eq. (3) becomes

$$W(n+1) = W(n) + \left(\frac{\mu}{1 + \mu \|e_n\|^2} e(n)N1n)\Psi(n) \right). \tag{6}$$

9. The output of filter acts as a complementary to the noise present in the signal which when added to the corrupted signal cancels a part of the noise. This negative addition gives desired response from the ANC system.
10. The desired signal is a cleaned signal. This cleaned signal which when subtracted from the principal signal gives us an error signal.
11. The error signal is fed back into tap weight computing equation via ENSS-LMS algorithm using Eq. (3).
12. Finally, the inverse 1-D wavelet transform has been taken to get the final signal using Eq. (2).

The resulted signal is the clean ECG signal.

3 Simulation Results

The work presented here used database of 3600 samples of the ECG signal. This has been collected from the benchmark MIT-BIH arrhythmia database [18] (recording nos 101, 102, 103). The non-stationary real baseline wander noise is obtained from MIT-BIH Normal Sinus Rhythm Database (NSTDB). The arrhythmia database consists of ECG recordings obtained from 47 subjects (men and women of different age-groups). The recording has 11-bit resolution over a 10 mV range with 360 samples per second per channel. The performance of algorithm is evaluated in terms of EMSE and misadjustment as shown in Table 2.

After getting the database, the ECG recording (records 101, 102, 103), add baseline wander noise to generate primary signals. As shown in Fig. 1, wavelet transform of primary signal (addition of normal ECG and baseline wander) has been taken. Figure 2 shows the wavelet transform of primary signal using 'Haar' wavelet with level 1 decomposition. After this export the coefficient of wavelet to MATLAB workspace.

Now as per Fig. 1, the wavelet transform of reference noise needs to be taken using 'Haar' wavelet with level 1 decomposition. Figure 3 shows the wavelet decomposition of reference noise signal using wavelet 1-D transform. The coefficient of wavelet transform can be now export to MATLAB workspace for further processing.

Fig. 2 Wavelet
decomposition of primary
signal (ECG+ baseline
wander noise)

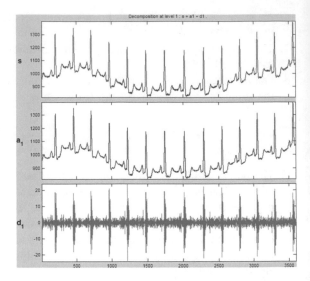

Fig. 3 Wavelet
decomposition of reference
noise signal (baseline wander
noise)

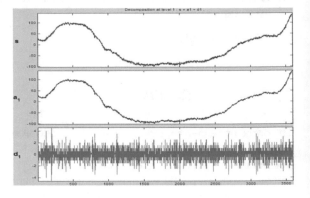

The wavelet decomposition allows the temporal addition of the ECG signal and
left the ECG signal with only one-fourth of the input signal size. Now the reference
signal will be passed through a FIR filter designed. The output of the filter will be
subtracted from the primary signal $x(n)$ [after wavelet decomposition it becomes sig
(n)], and an error signal has been generated, which will again fed back to the filter
via ENSS-LMS algorithm [using Eq. (1)] to update the weights of filter. Finally,
inverse wavelet transform is taken to get the cleaned signal shown in Fig. 4.

To validate the clean ECG signal shown in Fig. 4, the parameters EMSE and
misadjustment have been analyzed (refer Table 1). It is clear from Table 2 that
when recording 101 has been taken as input signal with noise, the EMSE reduced to
−30.665 dB which is great reduction as compared to LMS algorithm with value

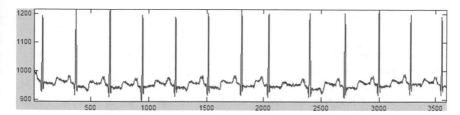

Fig. 4 Final ECG signal output after taking inverse wavelet transform

−7.788 dB for same recording for step size parameter $\mu = 0.025$. Now increasing the step size parameter with value $\mu = 0.05$, the value of EMSE reduced to −34.257 dB and to −18.752 dB for LMS algorithm so as misadjustment too. For step size parameter $\mu = 0.1$, EMSE has value −39.710 (ENSS) against −30.407 in case of LMS algorithm. To validate the model, the experiment was repeated for other ECG database recording too named as 101, 102, and many more. But because of space constraint, only the results of three recordings have been shown in Tables 1 and 2.

Table 1 EMSE and misadjustment values for different recorded ECG signals for ENSS-LMS algorithm

ENSS	Record 101		Record 102		Record 103		Average	
	EMSE (dB)	M	EMSE (dB)	M	EMSE (dB)	M	EMSE (dB)	M
$\mu = 0.025$	−30.665	0.5142	−31.543	0.5150	−31.658	0.6265	−30.666	0.5519
$\mu = 0.05$	−34.257	0.9337	−35.252	0.9299	−34.743	0.9501	−34.746	0.9379
$\mu = 0.1$	−39.710	0.7555	−41.324	0.8258	−42.101	0.7563	−41.045	0.7792

Table 2 EMSE and misadjustment values for different recorded ECG signals for LMS algorithm

LMS	Record 101		Record 102		Record 103		Average	
	EMSE (dB)	M	EMSE (dB)	M	EMSE (dB)	M	EMSE (dB)	M
$\mu = 0.025$	−7.788	0.908	−6.952	0.992	−7.129	0.912	−7.289	0.937
$\mu = 0.05$	−18.752	0.846	−17.842	0.878	−18.521	0.855	−18.371	0.859
$\mu = 0.1$	−30.407	−8.919	−29.107	−8.990	−30.203	−8.23	−29.905	−8.890

4 Conclusion

Wavelet decomposition-based method for improving the quality of ECG signal by removing baseline wander noise has been proposed in this paper. The simulation results show the effectiveness of this technique by decreasing the EMSE and misadjustment. Analyzing the result shown in Tables 1 and 2, we can say that stablishing the wavelet-based adaptive noise cancellation system with ENSS algorithm, taking ECG signal as input gives better results than LMS stablished ANC system. The average value of EMSE from recordings 101, 102, 103 gives -30.66 dB than -7.289 dB (LMS) for $\mu = 0.025$. Similar for misadjustment, the average value is 0.5519 (ENSS) than 0.937 (LMS) value for $\mu = 0.025$. Overall even for other values for $\mu = 0.025$, the proposed method behaves better and can be used as a performance optimization tool in biomedical signal processing.

References

1. Thakor, N.V., Zhu, Y.S.: Applications of adaptive filtering to ECG analysis: noise cancellation and arrhythmia detection. IEEE Trans. Biomed. Eng. **38**(8), 785–794 (1991)
2. Lagnna, P., Jan, R., Olmos, S., Thakor, N.V., Rix, H., Caminal, P.: Adaptive estimation of QRS complex by the Hermite model for classification and ectopic beat detection. Med. Biol. Eng. Comput. **34**(1), 58–68 (1996)
3. Olmos, S., Laguna, P.: Steady-state MSE convergence analysis in LMS adaptive filters with deterministic reference inputs for biomedical signals. IEEE Trans. Signal Process. **48**, 2229–2241 (2000)
4. Costa, M.H., Bermudez, C.M.: A noise resilient variable step-size LMS algorithm. Sig. Process. **88**, 733–748 (2008)
5. Brouse, C., Bumont, G.A., Herrmann, F.J., Ansermino, J.M.: A wavelet approach to detecting electrocautery noise in the ECG. IEEE Eng. Med. Biol. Mag. **25**(4), 76–82 (2006)
6. Leski, J.M., Henzel, N.: ECG baseline wander and power line interference reduction using nonlinear filter bank. Sig. Process. **85**, 781–793 (2005)
7. Meyer, C., Gavela, J.F., Harris, M.: Combining algorithms in automatic detection of QRS complexes in ECG signals. IEEE Trans. Inf. Technol Biomed. **10**(3), 468–475 (2006)
8. Kotas, M.: Application of projection pursuit based robust principal component analysis to ECG enhancement. Biomed. Signal Process. Control **1**, 289–298 (2007)
9. Mihov, G., Dotsinsky, I.: Power-line interference elimination from ECG in case of non-multiplicity between the sampling rate and the powerline frequency. Biomed. Signal Process. Control **3**, 334–340 (2008)
10. Floris, E., Schlaefer, A., Dieterich, S., Schweikard, A.: A fast lane approach to LMS prediction of respiratory motion signals. Biomed. Signal Process. Control **3**, 291–299 (2008)
11. Li, N., Zhang, Y., Yanling, H., Chambers, J.A.: A new variable step size NLMS algorithm designed for applications with exponential decay impulse responses. Sig. Process. **88**, 2346–2349 (2008)
12. Xiao, Y.: A new efficient narrowband active noise control system and its performance analysis. IEEE Trans. Audio Speech Lang. Process. **19**(7) (2011)
13. Leigh, G.M.: Fast FIR algorithms for the continuous wavelet transform from constrained least squares. IEEE Trans. Signal Process. **61**(1) (2013)

14. Kozacky, W.J., Ogunfunmi, T.: Convergence analysis of an adaptive algorithm with output power constraints. IEEE Trans. Circ. Syst. II Express Briefs **61**(5) (2014)
15. Das, R.L., Chakraborty, M.: On convergence of proportionate-type normalized least mean square algorithms. IEEE Trans. Circ. Syst. II **62**(5) (2015)
16. Sheetal, Mittal, M.: A Haar wavelet based approach for state analysis of disk drive read system. Appl. Mech. Mater. **592–594**, 2267–2271 (2014)
17. Narula, V. et al.: Assessment of variants of LMS algorithms for noise cancellation in low and medium frequency signals. In: IEEE Conference on Recent Advancements in Electrical, Electronics and Control Engineering, pp. 432–437 (2011)
18. http://www.physionet.org/cgibin/atm/ATM?database=mitdb&tool=plot_waveforms(MIT-BIHdatabase)

A Novel Approach for Extracting Pertinent Keywords for Web Image Annotation Using Semantic Distance and Euclidean Distance

Payal Gulati and Manisha Yadav

Abstract The World Wide Web today comprises of billions of Web documents with information on varied topics presented by different types of media such as text, images, audio, and video. Therefore along with textual information, the number of images over WWW is exponentially growing. As compared to text, the annotation of images by its semantics is more complicated as there is a lack of correlation between user's semantics and computer system's low-level features. Moreover, the Web pages are generally composed of contents containing multiple topics and the context relevant to the image on the Web page makes only a small portion of the full text, leading to the challenge for image search engines to annotate and index Web images. Existing image annotation systems use contextual information from page title, image src tag, alt tag, meta tag, image surrounding text for annotating Web image. Nowadays, some intelligent approaches perform a page segmentation as a preprocessing step. This paper proposes a novel approach for annotating Web images. In this work, Web pages are divided into Web content blocks based on the visual structure of page and thereafter the textual data of Web content blocks which are semantically closer to the blocks containing Web images are extracted. The relevant keywords from textual information along with contextual information of images are used for annotation.

Keywords Image search engine · Annotation · Semantic correlation
Semantic distance measure

P. Gulati
YMCA UST, Faridabad, Haryana, India
e-mail: gulatipayal@yahoo.co.in

M. Yadav (✉)
RPSGOI, Mahendergarh, Haryana, India
e-mail: manishayadav17@gmail.com

© Springer Nature Singapore Pte Ltd. 2019
M. N. Hoda et al. (eds.), *Software Engineering*, Advances in Intelligent Systems and Computing 731, https://doi.org/10.1007/978-981-10-8848-3_17

1   Introduction

WWW is the largest repository of digital images in the world. The number of images available over the Web is exponentially growing and will continue to increase in future. However, as compared to text, the annotation of images by means of the semantics they depict is much more complicated. Humans can recognize objects depicted in images, but in computer vision, the automatic understanding the semantics of the images is still the perplexing task. Image annotation can be done either through content-based or text-based approaches. In **text-based** approach, different parts of a Web page are considered as possible sources for contextual information of images, namely image file names (ImgSrc), page title, anchor texts, alternative text (ALT attribute), image surrounding text. In the **content-based** approach, image processing techniques such as texture, shape, and color are considered to describe the content of a Web image.

Most of the image search engines index images using text information associated with images, i.e., on the basis of alt tags, image caption. Alternative tags or alt tag provides a textual alternative to non-textual content in Web pages such as image, video, media. It basically provides a semantic meaning and description to the embedded images. However, the Web is still replete with images that have missing, incorrect, or poor text. In fact in many cases, images are given only empty or null alt attribute (alt = " ") thereby such images remain inaccessible. Image search engines that annotate Web images based on content-based annotation have problem of scalability.

In this work, a novel approach for extracting pertinent keywords for Web image annotation using semantic distance and Euclidean distance is proposed. Further, this work proposes an algorithm that automatically crawls the Web pages and extracts the contextual information from the pages containing valid images. The Web pages are segmented into Web content blocks and thereafter semantic correlation is calculated between Web image and Web content block using semantic distance measure. The pertinent keywords from contextual information along with semantic similar content are then used for annotating Web images. Thereafter, the images are indexed with the associated text it refers to.

This paper is organized as follows: Sect. 2 discusses the related work done in this domain. Section 3 presents the architecture of the proposed system. Section 4 describes the algorithm for this approach. Finally, Sect. 5 comprises of the conclusion.

2   Related Work

A number of text-based approaches for Web image annotation have been proposed in recent years [1]. There are numerous systems [2–6] that use contextual information for annotating Web images. Methods for exacting contextual information are (i) window-based extraction [7, 8], (ii) structure-based wrappers [9, 10], (iii) Web page segmentation [11–13].

Window-based extraction is a heuristic approach which extracts image surrounding text; it yields poor results as at times irrelevant data is extracted and relevant data is discarded. **Structure-based wrappers** use the structural information of Web page to decide the borders of the image context but these are not adaptive as they are designed for specific design patterns of Web page. **Web page segmentation** method is adaptable to different Web page styles and divides the Web page into segments of common topics, and then each image is associated with the textual contents of the segment which it belongs to. Moreover, it is difficult to determine the semantics of text with the image.

In this work, Web page is segmented into Web content blocks using vision-based page segmentation algorithm [12]. Thereafter, semantic similarity is calculated between Web image and Web content block using semantic distance measure. *Semantic distance* is the inverse of *semantic similarity* [14] that is the less distance of the two concepts, the more they are similar. So, *semantic similarity* and *semantic distance* are used interchangeably in this work.

Semantic distance between Web content blocks is calculated by determining a common representation among them. Generally, text is used for common representation. As per the literature review, there are various similarity metrics for texts [13, 15, 16]. Some simple metrics are based on lexical matching. Prevailing approaches are successful to some extent, as they do not identify the semantic similarity of texts. For instance, terms Plant and Tree have a high semantic correlation which remains unnoticed without background knowledge. To overcome this, WordNet taxonomy as background knowledge is discussed [17, 18].

In this work, the word-to-word similarity metric [19] is used to calculate the similarity between words and text-to-text similarity is calculated using the metric introduced by Corley [20].

3 Proposed Architecture

The architecture of proposed system is given in Fig. 1. Components of proposed system are discussed in following subsequent subsections.

3.1 Crawl Manager

Crawl manager is a computer program that takes the seed URL from the URL queue and fetches the Web page from WWW.

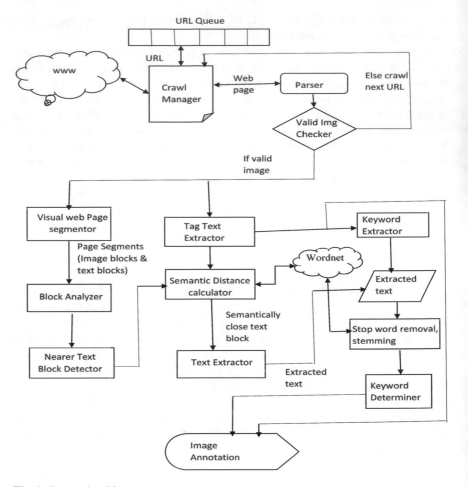

Fig. 1 Proposed architecture

3.2 URL Queue

URL queue is a type of repository which stores the list of URLs that are discovered and extracted by crawler.

3.3 Parser

Parser is used to extract information present on Web pages. Parser downloads the Web page and extracts the XML file of the same. Thereafter, it convert XML file into DOM object models. It then checks whether valid images are present on the

Web page or not. If valid image is present on the Web page, then the page is segmented using visual Web page segmenter; otherwise, next URL is crawled. The DOM object models which contain page title of Web page, image source, and alternative text of valid images present on the Web page are extracted from the set of object models of the Web page.

3.4 Visual Web Page Segmenter

Visual Web page segmenter is used for the segmentation of Web pages into Web content blocks. By the term segmentation of Web pages means dividing the page by certain rules or procedures to obtain multiple semantically different Web content blocks whose content can be investigated further.

In the proposed approach, VIPS algorithm [12] is used for the segmentation of Web page into Web content blocks. It extracts the semantic structure of a Web page based on its visual representation. The segmentation process has basically three steps: *block extraction, separator detection, and content structure construction.* Blocks are extracted from DOM tree structure of the Web page by using the page layout structure, and then separators are located among these blocks. The vision-based content structure of a page is obtained by combining the DOM structure and the visual cues. Therefore, a Web page is a collection of Web content blocks that have similar DOC. With the permitted DOC (pDOC) set to its maximum value, a set of Web content blocks that consist of visually indivisible contents is obtained. This algorithm also provides the two-dimensional Cartesian coordinates of each visual block present on the Web page based on their locations on the Web page.

3.5 Block Analyzer

Block analyzer analyses the Web content blocks obtained from segmentation. Further, it divides the Web content blocks into two categories: *image* blocks and *text* blocks. Web blocks which contain images are considered as *image* blocks and rest are considered as *text* blocks.

3.6 Nearest Text Block Detector

Nearest text block detector detects the nearest text blocks to an image block. For checking closeness, Euclidean distance between closest edges of two blocks is calculated. Distance between two line segments is obtained by using Eq. (1):

$$\text{Euclidean Distance} = \sqrt{(x_2 - x_1)^2 + (y_2 - y_1)^2} \qquad (1)$$

After the distance is calculated between each image block pair and text block pair, the text blocks whose distance from image block is below the threshold are assigned to that image block. In this way, each image block is assigned with a group of text blocks which are closer in distance with that image block.

3.7 Tag Text Extractor

In the proposed approach, tag text extractor is used for extracting text from the HTML tags. Parser provides the DOM object models by parsing a Web page. If the image present on this Web page is valid, i.e., it is not a button or an icon, which is checked by valid image checker, are extracted from metadata of image like image source (Imgsrc), alternative text (Alt). Page title of the Web page which contains this image is also extracted.

3.8 Keyword Extractor

In this work, keyword extractor is used to extract keywords from the metadata of images and page title. Keywords are stored into a text file which is further used for obtaining semantically close text blocks by calculating semantic distance.

3.9 Semantic Distance Calculator

Semantic distance calculator is used to determine the semantic correlation among the Web content blocks. As lexical matching between words does not provide better results, here the words are matched with concepts in a knowledge base and concept to concept matching is computed using WordNet.

Before computing text similarity between image metadata and text blocks, preprocessing of the text blocks is done. After preprocessing process, sentence detection is done. Then tokenization is done, and finally, a part of speech tagging is done for all the words using NLP. At last, stemming of the terms is done and thereafter, terms are mapped to WordNet concepts.

The similarity of text is calculated using Corley's approach. In this method, for every noun (verb) that belongs to image metadata, the noun (verb) in the text of text blocks with maximum semantic similarity is identified according to Eq. 2.

$$\text{sim}_{\text{Lin}} = \frac{2.\text{IC}(\text{LCS})}{\text{IC}(\text{Concept}_1) + \text{IC}(\text{Concept}_2)} \quad (2)$$

Here LCS is the least common subsumer of the two concepts in the WordNet taxonomy, and IC is the information content that measures the specificity for a concept as follows:

$$\text{IC}(\text{concept}) = -\log P(\text{concept}) \quad (3)$$

In Eq. 3, P(concept) is the probability of occurrence of an instance of concept in a large corpus. For the classes other than noun (verb), a lexical matching is performed. The similarity between two texts $T1$ (text of image metadata), $T2$ (text of text blocks) is calculated as:

$$\text{sim}(T_1, T_2)_{T_1} = \frac{\sum_{w_i \in T_1} \text{maxSim}(w_i, T_2).idf(w_i)}{\sum_{w_i \in T_1} idf(w_i)} \quad (4)$$

where $idf(w_i)$ is the **inverse document frequency** [19] of the word w_i in a large corpus. A directional similarity score is further calculated with respect to $T1$. The score from both directions is combined into a bidirectional similarity as given in Eq. 5:

$$\text{sim}(T_1, T_2) = \text{sim}(T_1, T_2)_{T_1}.\text{sim}(T_1, T_2)_{T_2} \quad (5)$$

This similarity score has a value between 0 and 1. From this similarity score, semantic distance is calculated as follows:

$$\text{dist}_{\text{sem}}(T_1, T_2) = 1 - \text{sim}(T_1, T_2) \quad (6)$$

In this way, semantic distance is calculated among image block and its nearest text blocks. The text block whose semantic distance is less is the semantically correlated text block to that image block.

3.10 Text Extractor

Text extractor is used to extract text from text blocks present on the Web page. Text of semantically close text block obtained in the previous step is extracted and buffered. This text along with the text extracted from image metadata and page title of Web page is used to extract frequent keywords.

3.11 Keyword Determiner

In this work, keyword determiner is used to extract keywords from the text stored in a buffer. Frequent keywords are determined by applying a threshold on the frequency count of keywords. Keywords whose frequency is above the threshold are extracted and used for annotating images.

3.12 Image Annotation

Page title of Web page, image source of image, alternative text of image, and frequent keywords extracted in the previous step—all of these describe the image best.

4 Algorithm

The algorithm for proposed system is automatic image annotation. This algorithm takes the URL of Webpage as input and provides the description of the Web page as output.

This algorithm is used here for annotating images present on the Web page. Firstly, parsing is done to extract page title, Img_Src, Alt Text of image. Secondly, Web page segmentation is performed using VIPS algorithm. Then validity of image is checked and for valid images find nearest text blocks using the algorithm given below. For closer text block list, semantic distance is calculated using bidirectional similarity between blocks. Then keywords are extracted from the semantically close text block. These keywords are used for image annotation process.

```
Automatic_Image_Annotation (Description of image)
     Begin
   Parse the Web page (URL)
   If contain valid image
        Text₁ = Extract Page_Title, Img_Src(valid image),
        alt( valid image)
      Web_Page_Segmentation (URL)
      For each valid image_block
           Text_block_list = Find_Nearest_text_block
           (ImageBlock Cartesian Coordinates, Text Blocks
           Cartesian Coordinates)
   least_distance = some_big_number;
   For each text block in Text_block_list
   Distance = Find_semantic_distance (Text Block, Text₁ )
```

```
If (least_distance > distance)
{
                Least_distance = Distance
    Return id_{text} ;
      }
      Extract keywords from text block ( id_{text} )
      End
End
```

Algorithm for obtaining nearest text blocks is find nearest text blocks. It takes image blocks and text blocks as input and provides a list of nearest blocks as output. This algorithm collects the nearest text blocks to an image block present on the Web page using closest edge Euclidean distance between Web content blocks. It uses the Cartesian coordinates of Web content blocks to calculate Euclidean distance.

```
Find_Nearest_Text_Block (List of Nearest Text Blocks)
    Begin
    For each Text Block
        {
                Distance = calculate Euclidean distance
                between image block and text block
      If (distance < threshold)
                {
                        Put the id of text block in a list
                }
        }
    End
```

5   Conclusion

This paper presents algorithm for the novel approach for extracting pertinent keywords for Web image annotation using semantics. In this work, Web images are automatically annotated by determining pertinent keywords from contextual information from Web page and semantic similar content from Web content blocks. This approach provides better results than method of image indexing using Web page segmentation and clustering [21], as in existing method context of image, it is not coordinated with the context of surrounding text. This approach will provide good results as closeness between image and Web content blocks is computed using both Euclidean distance and semantic distance.

References

1. Sumathi, T., Devasena, C.L., Hemalatha, M.: An overview of automated image annotation approaches. Int. J. Res. Rev. Inf. Sci. **1**(1) (2011) (Copyright © Science Academy Publisher, United Kingdom)
2. Swain, M., Frankel, C., Athitsos, V.: Webseer: an image search engine for the World Wide Web. In: CVPR (1997)
3. Smith, J., Chang, S.: An image and video search engine for the world-wide web. Storage. Retr. Im. Vid. Datab. 8495 (1997)
4. Ortega-Binderberger, M., Mehrotra, V., Chakrabarti, K., Porkaew, K.: Webmars: a multimedia search engine. In: SPIE An. Symposium on Electronic Imaging, San Jose, California. Academy Publisher, United Kingdom (2000)
5. Alexandre, L., Pereira, M., Madeira, S., Cordeiro, J., Dias, G.: Web image indexing: combining image analysis with text processing. In: Proceedings of the 5th International Workshop on Image Analysis for Multimedia Interactive Services (WIAMIS04). Publisher, United Kingdom (2004)
6. Yadav, M., Gulati, P.: A novel approach for extracting relevant keywords for web image annotation using semantics. In: 9th International Conference on ASEICT (2015)
7. Coelho, T.A.S., Calado, P.P., Souza, L.V., Ribeiro-Neto, B., Muntz, R.: Image retrieval using multiple evidence ranking. IEEE Trans. Knowl. Data Eng. **16**(4), 408–417 (2004)
8. Pan, L.: Image 8: an image search engine for the internet. Honours Year Project Report, School of Computing, National University of Singapore, April, 2003
9. Liu, B.: Web data mining: exploring hyperlinks, contents, and usage data. Data-Centric Syst. Appl. Springer 2007 **16**(4), 408–417 (2004)
10. Fauzi, F., Hong, J., Belkhatir, M.: Webpage segmentation for extracting images and their surrounding contextual information. In: ACM Multimedia, pp. 649–652 (2009)
11. Chakrabarti, D., Kumar, R., Punera, K.: A graphtheoretic approach to webpage segmentation. In: Proceeding of the 17th International Conference on World Wide Web, WWW'08, pp. 377–386, New York, USA (2008)
12. Cai, D., Yu, S., Wen, J.R., Ma, W.Y.: VIPS: a vision based page segmentation algorithm. Technical Report, Microsoft Research (MSR-TR-2003-79) (2003)
13. Hattori, G., Hoashi, K., Matsumoto, K., Sugaya, F.: Robust web page segmentation for mobile terminal using content distances and page layout information. In: Proceedings of the 16th International Conference on World Wide Web, WWW'07, pp. 361–370, New York, NY, USA. ACM (2007)
14. Nguyen, H.A., Eng, B.: New semantic similarity techniques of concepts applied in the Biomedical domain and wordnet. Master thesis, The University of Houston-Clear Lake (2006)
15. Voorhees, E.: Using WordNet to disambiguate word senses for text retrieval. In: Proceedings of the 16th Annual International ACM SIGIR Conference (1993)
16. Landauer, T.K., Foltz, P., Laham, D.: Introduction to latent semantic analysis. Discourse Processes **25** (1998)
17. Miller, G.A., Beckwith, R., Fellbaum, C., Gross, D., Miller, K.: WordNet: An on-line lexical database. Int. J. Lexicogr. **3**, 235–244 (1990)
18. Patwardhan, S., Banerjee, S., Pedersen, T.: Using measures of semantic relatedness for word sense disambiguation. In: Proceedings of the 4th International Conference on Computational Linguistics and Intelligent Text Processing, CICLing'03, pp. 241–257. Springer, Berlin, Heidelberg (2003)
19. Lin, D.: Automatic retrieval and clustering of similar words. In: Proceedings of the 36th Annual Meeting of the Association for Computational Linguistics and 17th International Conference on Computational Linguistics, vol. 2, ACL-36, pp. 768–774, Morristown, NJ, USA. Association for Computational Linguistics (1998); Sparck Jones, K.: A Statistical

Interpretation of Term Specificity and Its Application in Retrieval, pp. 132–142. Taylor Graham Publishing, London, UK (1988)

20. Corley, C., Mihalcea, R.: Measuring the semantic similarity of texts. In: Proceedings of the ACL Workshop on Empirical Modeling of Semantic Equivalence and Entailment, EMSEE'05, pp. 13–18, Morristown, NJ, USA, 2005. Association for Computational Linguistics (1998)

21. Tryfou, G., Tsapatsoulis, N.: Image Indexing Based on Web Page Segmentation and Clustering (2014)

Classification of Breast Tissue Density Patterns Using SVM-Based Hierarchical Classifier

Jitendra Virmani, Kriti and Shruti Thakur

Abstract In the present work, three-class breast tissue density classification has been carried out using SVM-based hierarchical classifier. The performance of Laws' texture descriptors of various resolutions have been investigated for differentiating between fatty and dense tissues as well as for differentiation between fatty-glandular and dense-glandular tissues. The overall classification accuracy of 88.2% has been achieved using the proposed SVM-based hierarchical classifier.

Keywords Breast tissue density classification · Texture feature extraction
Hierarchical classifier

1 Introduction

The most commonly diagnosed disease among women nowadays is breast cancer [1]. It has been shown that high breast tissue density is associated with high risk of developing breast cancer [2–10]. Mortality rate for breast cancer can be increased if detection is made at an early stage. Breast tissue is broadly classified into fatty, fatty-glandular, or dense-glandular based on its density.

Various computer-aided diagnostic (CAD) systems have been developed by researchers in the past to discriminate between different density patterns, thus providing the radiologists with a system that can act as a second opinion tool to

J. Virmani (✉)
Thapar University, Patiala, Punjab, India
e-mail: jitendra.virmani@gmail.com

Kriti
Jaypee University of Information Technology, Waknaghat, Solan, India
e-mail: kriti.23gm@gmail.com

S. Thakur
Department of Radiology, IGMC, Shimla, Himachal Pradesh, India
e-mail: tshruti878@yahoo.in

© Springer Nature Singapore Pte Ltd. 2019
M. N. Hoda et al. (eds.), *Software Engineering*, Advances in Intelligent Systems
and Computing 731, https://doi.org/10.1007/978-981-10-8848-3_18

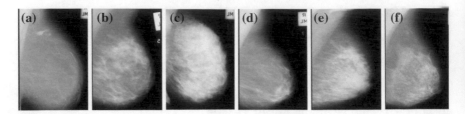

Fig. 1 Sample of mammographic images from MIAS database, **a** typical fatty tissue 'mdb132,' **b** typical fatty-glandular tissue 'mdb016,' **c** typical dense-glandular tissue 'mdb216,' **d** atypical fatty tissue 'mdb096,' **e** atypical fatty-glandular tissue 'mdb090,' **f** atypical dense-glandular tissue 'mdb100'

validate their diagnosis. Few studies have been carried out on Mammographic Image Analysis Society (MIAS) dataset for classification of breast tissue density patterns into fatty, fatty-glandular, and dense-glandular tissue types [3–10]. Among these, mostly the studies have been carried on the segmented breast tissue (SBT) and rarely on fixed-size ROIs [3–10]. Out of these studies, Subashini et al. [6] report a maximum accuracy of 95.4% using the SBT approach, and Mustra et al. [9] report a maximum accuracy of 82.0% using the ROI extraction approach.

The experienced participating radiologist (one of the authors of this paper) graded the fatty, fatty-glandular, and dense-glandular images as belonging to typical or atypical categories. The sample images of typical and atypical cases depicting different density patterns are shown in Fig. 1.

In the present work, a hierarchical classifier with two stages for binary classification has been proposed. This classifier is designed using support vector machine (SVM) classifier in each stage to differentiate between fatty and dense breast tissues and then between fatty-glandular and dense-glandular breast tissues using Laws' texture features.

2 Methodology

2.1 Description of Dataset

The MIAS database consists of total 322 mammographic images out of which 106 are fatty, 104 are fatty-glandular, and 112 are dense-glandular [11]. From each image, a fixed-size ROI has been extracted for further processing.

2.2 Selecting Regions of Interest

After conducting repeated experiments, it has been asserted that for classification of breast density, the center area of the tissue is the optimal choice [12]. Accordingly,

Fig. 2 ROI extraction protocol for mammographic image 'mdb216' with ROI marked

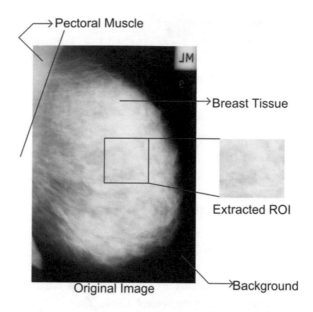

Pectoral Muscle

JM

→Breast Tissue

Extracted ROI

Original Image

→Background

fixed-size ROIs of size 200 × 200 pixels have been extracted from each mammogram as depicted in Fig. 2.

2.3 Proposed Method

Computer-aided diagnostic systems involve analysis of mammograms through computers which can be used by the radiologists as a second opinion tool for validating their diagnosis as these systems tend to improve the diagnostic accuracy by detecting any lesions that might be missed during subjective analysis [1, 3–10, 13, 14]. The block diagram is shown in Fig. 3.

Feature Extraction Module The texture descriptor vectors (TDVs) derived from Laws' texture analysis using Laws' masks of resolutions 3, 5, 7, and 9 have been used in the present work for design of SVM-based hierarchical classifier.

Feature Classification Module Support vector machine classifier has been extensively used for classification of texture patterns in medical images [1, 14–19]. In the present work, two binary SVM classifiers arranged in a hierarchical framework have been used for three-class breast tissue density classification. The SVM classifier is implemented using LibSVM library [20].

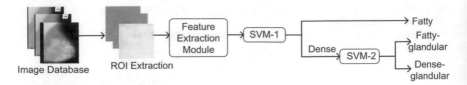

Fig. 3 Proposed classification system

3 Results

Various experiments were conducted to obtain the classification performance of Laws' texture features using hierarchical classifier built using two stages of binary SVM classifiers.

3.1 Classification Performance of Laws' Texture Features Using Hierarchical Classifier

In this work, the performance of TDVs derived using Laws' masks of length 3, 5, 7, and 9 is evaluated using SVM-based hierarchical classifier. The results obtained are shown in Table 1.

From Table 1, it can be observed that OCA of 91.3, 93.2, 91.9, and 92.5% is achieved for TDV1, TDV2, TDV3, and TDV4, respectively, using SVM-1 sub-classifier, and OCA of 92.5, 84.2, 87.0, and 90.7% is obtained for TDV1, TDV2, TDV3, and TDV4, respectively, using SVM-2 sub-classifier.

The results from Table 1 show that for differentiating between the fatty and dense breast tissues, SVM-1 sub-classifier gives best performance for features extracted using Laws' mask of length 5 (TDV2), and for further classification of dense tissues into fatty-glandular and dense-glandular classes, SVM-2 sub-classifier gives best performance using features derived from Laws' mask of length 3 (TDV1). This analysis of the hierarchical classifier is shown in Table 2. The OCA for hierarchical classifier is calculated by adding the misclassified cases at each classification stage.

Table 1 Performance of TDFVs derived from laws' texture features using hierarchical classifier

TDV (l)	Classifier	CM			OCA (%)
			F	D	
TDV1 (30)	SVM-1	F	43	10	91.3
		D	4	104	
	SVM-2		FG	DG	92.5
		FG	48	4	
		DG	4	52	
TDV2 (75)	SVM-1		F	D	93.2
		F	43	10	
		D	1	107	
	SVM-2		FG	DG	84.2
		FG	39	13	
		DG	4	52	
TDV3 (30)	SVM-1		F	D	91.9
		F	43	10	
		D	3	105	
	SVM-2		FG	DG	87.0
		FG	41	11	
		DG	3	53	
TDV4 (75)	SVM-1		F	D	92.5
		F	44	9	
		D	3	105	
	SVM-2		FG	DG	90.7
		FG	46	6	
		DG	4	52	

Note TDV: texture descriptor vector, l: length of TDV, CM: confusion matrix, F: fatty class, D: dense class, FG: fatty-glandular class, DG: dense-glandular class, OCA: overall classification accuracy

Table 2 Performance analysis of hierarchical classifier

Classifier	TDV (l)	CM			CA (%)	Misclassified cases	OCA (%)
			F	D			
SVM-1	TDV2 (75)	F	43	10	93.2 (11/161)	19/161	88.2
		D	1	107			
SVM-2	TDV1 (30)		FG	DG	92.5 (8/108)		
		FG	48	4			
		DG	4	52			

Note TDV: texture descriptor vector, l: length of TDV, CM: confusion matrix, F: fatty class, D: dense class, FG: fatty-glandular class, DG: dense-glandular class, CA: classification accuracy, OCA: overall classification accuracy

4 Conclusion

From the exhaustive experiments carried out in the present work, it can be concluded that Laws' masks of length 5 yield the maximum classification accuracy of 93.2% for differential diagnosis between fatty and dense classes and Laws' masks of length 3 yield the maximum classification accuracy 92.5% for differential diagnosis between fatty-glandular and dense-glandular classes. Further, for the three-class problem, a single multi-class SVM classifier would construct three different binary SVM sub-classifiers where each binary sub-classifier is trained to separate a pair of classes and decision is made by using majority voting technique. In case of hierarchical framework, the classification can be done using only two binary SVM sub-classifiers.

References

1. Kriti, Virmani, J., Dey, N., Kumar, V.: PCA-PNN and PCA-SVM based CAD systems for breast density classification. In: Hassanien, A.E., et al. (eds.) Applications of Intelligent Optimization in Biology and Medicine, vol. 96, pp. 159–180. Springer (2015)
2. Wolfe, J.N.: Breast patterns as an index of risk for developing breast cancer. Am. J. Roentgenol. 126(6), 1130–1137 (1976)
3. Blot, L., Zwiggelaar, R.: Background texture extraction for the classification of mammographic parenchymal patterns. In: Proceedings of Conference on Medical Image Understanding and Analysis, pp. 145–148 (2001)
4. Bosch, A., Munoz, X., Oliver, A., Marti, J.: Modeling and classifying breast tissue density in mammograms. In: Computer Vision and Pattern Recognition, IEEE Computer Society Conference, 2, pp. 1552–1558. IEEE Press, New York (2006)
5. Muhimmah, I., Zwiggelaar, R.: Mammographic density classification using multiresolution histogram information. In: Proceedings of 5th International IEEE Special Topic Conference on Information Technology in Biomedicine (ITAB), pp. 1–6. IEEE Press, New York (2006)
6. Subashini, T.S., Ramalingam, V., Palanivel, S.: Automated assessment of breast tissue density in digital mammograms. Comput. Vis. Image Underst. 114(1), 33–43 (2010)
7. Tzikopoulos, S.D., Mavroforakis, M.E., Georgiou, H.V., Dimitropoulos, N., Theodoridis, S.: A fully automated scheme for mammographic segmentation and classification based on breast density and asymmetry. Comput. Methods Programs Biomed. 102(1), 47–63 (2011)
8. Li, J.B.: Mammographic image based breast tissue classification with kernel self-optimized fisher discriminant for breast cancer diagnosis. J. Med. Syst. 36(4), 2235–2244 (2012)
9. Mustra, M., Grgic, M., Delac, K.: Breast density classification using multiple feature selection. Auotomatika 53(4), 362–372 (2012)
10. Silva, W.R., Menotti, D.: Classification of mammograms by the breast composition. In: Proceedings of the 2012 International Conference on Image Processing, Computer Vision, and Pattern Recognition, pp. 1–6 (2012)
11. Suckling, J., Parker, J., Dance, D.R., Astley, S., Hutt, I., Boggis, C.R.M., Ricketts, I., Stamatakis, E., Cerneaz, N., Kok, S.L., Taylor, P., Betal, D., Savage, J.: The mammographic image analysis society digital mammogram database. In: Gale, A.G., et al. (eds.) Digital Mammography. LNCS, vol. 1069, pp. 375–378. Springer, Heidelberg (1994)
12. Li, H., Giger, M.L., Huo, Z., Olopade, O.I., Lan, L., Weber, B.L., Bonta, I.: Computerized analysis of mammographic parenchymal patterns for assessing breast cancer risk: effect of ROI size and location. Med. Phys. 31(3), 549–555 (2004)

13. Kumar, I., Virmani, J., Bhadauria, H.S.: A review of breast density classification methods. In: Proceedings of 2nd IEEE International Conference on Computing for Sustainable Global Development (IndiaCom-2015), pp. 1960–1967. IEEE Press, New York (2015)
14. Virmani, J., Kriti.: Breast tissue density classification using wavelet-based texture descriptors. In: Proceedings of the Second International Conference on Computer and Communication Technologies (IC3T-2015), vol. 3, pp. 539–546 (2015)
15. Virmani, J., Kumar, V., Kalra, N., Khandelwal, N.: A comparative study of computer-aided classification systems for focal hepatic lesions from B-mode ultrasound. J. Med. Eng. Technol. 37(44), 292–306 (2013)
16. Virmani, J., Kumar, V., Kalra, N., Khandelwal, N.: SVM-based characterization of liver ultrasound images using wavelet packet texture descriptors. J. Digit. Imaging 26(3), 530–543 (2013)
17. Virmani, J., Kumar, V., Kalra, N., Khandelwal, N.: Characterization of primary and secondary malignant liver lesions from B-mode ultrasound. J. Digit. Imaging 26(6), 1058–1070 (2013)
18. Virmani, J., Kumar, V., Kalra, N., Khandelwal, N.: SVM-based characterization of liver cirrhosis by singular value decomposition of GLCM matrix. Int. J. Artif. Intel. Soft Comput. 3 (3), 276–296 (2013)
19. Virmani, J., Kumar, V., Kalra, N., Khandelwal, N.: PCA-SVM based CAD system for focal liver lesions from B-Mode ultrasound. Defence Sci. J. 63(5), 478–486 (2013)
20. Chang, C.C., Lin, C.J.: LIBSVM, a library of support vector machines. ACM Trans. Intell. Syst. Technol. 2(3), 27–65 (2011)

Advances in EDM: A State of the Art

Manu Anand

Abstract Potentials of data mining in academics have been discussed in this paper. To enhance the Educational Institutional services along with the improvement in student's performance by increasing their grades, retention rate, maintain their attendance, giving prior information about their eligibility whether they can give examination or not based on attendance, evaluating the result using the marks, predicting how many students have enrolled in which course and all other aspects like this can be analyzed using various fields of Data Mining. This paper discusses one of this aspect in which the distinction has been predicted based on the marks scored by the MCA students of Bharati Vidyapeeth Institute of Computer Applications and Management, affiliated to GGSIPU using various machine learning algorithms, and it has been observed that "Boost Algorithm" outperforms other machine learning models in the prediction of distinction.

Keywords Distinction prediction · Machine learning · Boost algorithm

1 Introduction

Every sector, every organization maintains large amount of data in their databases and powerful tools are designed to perform data analysis, as a result mining of data will result in golden chunks of "Knowledge." There are many misnomers of data mining like knowledge mining, knowledge discovery from databases, knowledge extraction, and pattern analysis that can be achieved using various data mining algorithms like classification, association, clustering, prediction. Data mining approach plays a pivot role in decision support system (DSS).

Educational data mining [1] is promising as a research area with a collection of computational and psychological methods to understand how students learn. EDM

M. Anand (✉)
Bharati Vidyapeeth Institute of Computers Application and Management (BVICAM),
New Delhi, India
e-mail: manu9910.anand@gmail.com

© Springer Nature Singapore Pte Ltd. 2019
M. N. Hoda et al. (eds.), *Software Engineering*, Advances in Intelligent Systems
and Computing 731, https://doi.org/10.1007/978-981-10-8848-3_19

develops methods and applies techniques from statistics, machine learning, and data mining to analyze data collected during teaching and learning [2–4]. In this paper, machine learning classification models have been used to predict distinction of students using marks of nine subjects that a student of MCA third semester scored in their End term exams of GGSIPU. Various subjects whose marks are considered in student dataset used for predicting distinction are theory of computation, computer graphics, Java programming, data communication and networking, C# programming, computer graphics laboratory, Java programming laboratory, C# programming laboratory, general proficiency. There are totally 112 records with 15 input variables. Some of the considered features like marks of all subjects, percentage, and distinction have higher importance than others like name, roll no. in predicting distinction. The student dataset is used by various machine learning models namely decision tree model, AdaBoost model, SVM model, linear model, neural network model [5].

2   Materials and Methods

2.1   Dataset and Its Features

In total, 112 student records having 15 input variables have been considered for data analysis. These student records are the original results of MCA students of the third semester in 2014, at Bharati Vidyapeeth Institute of Computer Applications and Management from GGSIPU. Table 1 describes the subjects associated with each code in the student dataset. In Table 2, student dataset sample is shown. Table 3 shows the correlation between each feature. In this, total marks scored by every student are calculated and then the percentage has been evaluated. Depending upon the percentage, the distinction has been set to 0 or 1.

Table 1 Features description

Feature	Subject title
201	Theory of computation
203	Computer graphics
205	Java programming
207	Data communication and networking
209	C# programming
251	Computer graphics laboratory
253	Java programming laboratory
255	C# programming laboratory
261	General proficiency

Table 2 Sample dataset

Roll_No.	Name	201	203	205	207	209	251	253	255	261
311604413	SANGEETA SINHA	55	60	67	53	66	78	84	80	81
411604413	PAWAN	50	66	62	73	60	80	83	80	78
511604413	GIRISH SHANKAR	33	63	62	72	52	78	86	82	78
611604413	TANU	55	76	75	82	73	78	89	84	70

Table 3 Correlation between each feature

Roll_No.	Total	Percentage	Distinction
311604413	624	69.33333	0
411604413	632	70.22222	0
511604413	606	67.33333	0
611604413	682	75.77778	1

2.2 Feature Measurement

In this analysis of distinction prediction, some of the basic calculations have been performed in the student dataset using simple method. First total marks have been evaluated by the summation of every mark scored by each and every student, followed by the calculation of percentage for each and every record. Then, the distinction has been marked as 0 or 1 based on the percentage a student has scored. If the percentage is greater than or equal to 75%, then the distinction is marked as 1 else it is marked as 0.

3 Methodology

The methodology is described in Fig. 1. In the first step, the result of MCA students of the third semester has been taken as the primary data for the prediction of distinction. After this, various features like their total of marks, percentage, and distinction have been evaluated by considering distinction as target value. The removal of extra fields was carried out which were not required in distinction prediction, while different algorithms were applied on the student dataset. There were totally 15 input variables, out of which 9 variables have been passed as an input to dataset for evaluation. Then, different algorithms have been applied on student dataset. In the fifth step, different models were trained and tested on the dataset with their default parameters. Finally, the evolution of the model is done on accuracy and sensitivity.

Fig. 1 Methodology used

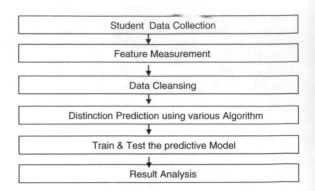

3.1 AdaBoost Algorithm

Adaptive boosting is a machine learning algorithm used in combination with other learning algorithms to improve their performance that represents final output of the boosted classifier which is represented by the output of the other learning algorithms ("weak learners") which is combined into a weighted sum.

Algorithm: Adaptive Boost pseudocode

Set uniform example weights.
   for Each base learner **do**
   Train base learner with weighted sample.
   Test base learner on all data.
   Set learner weight with weighted error.
   Set example weights based on ensemble predictions.
   end for

3.2 Feature Importance Using AdaBoost Algorithm

The AdaBoost is used to find the importance of each feature. To train a boosted classifier, AdaBoost algorithm is used. The basic representation of Boost classifier is as follows:

$$F_T(x) = \sum_{t=1}^{T} f_t(x)$$

where each f_t is a weak learner that takes an object x as input and returns a real-valued result indicating the class of the object. Predicted object class is identified with the sign of the output obtained with the weak learner.

For each sample in the training set, an output or hypothesis is produced by weak learner. While executing this algorithm, the main focus should be on the minimization of the resulting t-stage Boost classifier which is achieved with the selection of weak learner and by assigning a coefficient α_t.

$$E_t = \sum_i E[F_{t-1}(x_i) + \alpha_t h(x_i)]$$

Here, $F_{t-1}(x)$ is the boosted classifier that has been built up to the previous stage of training, $E(F)$ is some error function, and $f_t(x) = \alpha_t h(x)$ is the weak learner that is being considered for the addition to the final classifier.

3.3 Machine Learning Methods

Four machine learning models [5, 6] for distinction prediction have been used. Rattle has been used where all these models are available. The idea about this model is discussed below:

(a) Decision tree: It uses a recursive partitioning approach [7].
(b) Support vector machine: SVM searches for so-called support vectors which are data points that are found to lie at the edge of an area in space which is a boundary from one class of points to another.
(c) Linear model: Covariance analysis, single stratum analysis of variance, and regression are evaluated using this model.
(d) Neural net: It is based on the idea of multiple layers of neurons connected to each other, feeding the numeric data through the network, combining the numbers, to produce a final answer (Table 4).

Table 4 Parameters used for different algorithms

Model	Parameter setting
Decision tree	Min split = 30, max depth = 40, min bucket = 7
SVM	Kernel radial basis
LM	Multinomial
Neural net	Hidden layer nodes
Boost	Max depth = 30, min split = 20, no. of trees = 50

4   Model Evaluation

Classifier's performance has been measured using various parameters like accuracy, sensitivity, ROC. Sensitivity S_i for the class i can be defined as the number of patterns correctly predicted to be in class i with respect to the total number of patterns in class i. Consider p number of classes, and the value C_{ij} of size $p * p$ represents the number of patterns of class i predicted in class j, then accuracy and sensitivity can be calculated as follows:

$$\text{Accuracy} = \frac{\sum_{i=1,p} C_{ii}}{\sum_{i=1,p} \sum_{j=1,p} C_{ij}}$$

$$\text{Sensitivity} = \frac{C_{ii}}{\sum_{j=1,p} C_{ij}}$$

5   Experimental Result

This section deals with the analysis on prediction result of all the four machine learning classification models on the testing dataset. In Figs. 2 and 4, Precision parameter has been plotted for ada, SVM and verified for all other models. In

Fig. 2 Precision versus recall using ada algorithm

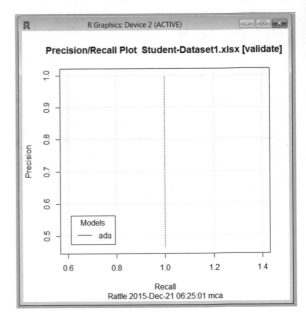

Fig. 3 Sensitivity versus
specificity using ada
algorithm

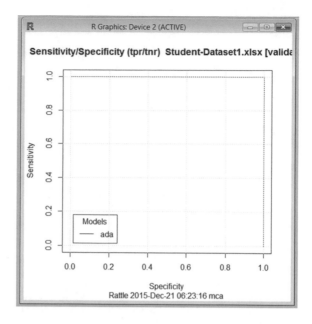

Figs. 3 and 5, sensitivity has been observed. Another parameter predicted vs observed also been plotted (Fig. 6).

Fig. 4 Precision versus recall
using svm algorithm

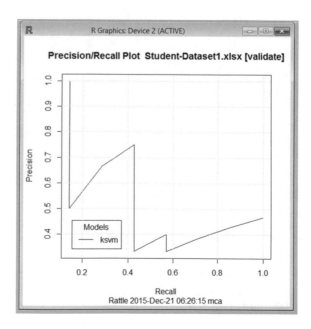

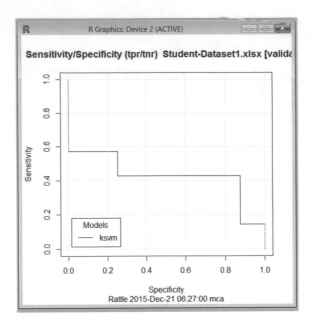

Fig. 5 Sensitivity versus specificity using svm algorithm

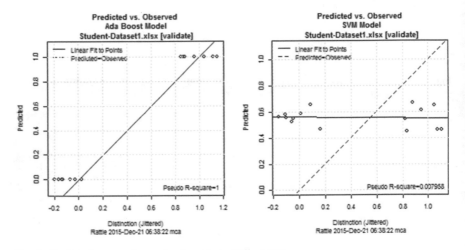

Fig. 6 Predicted versus observed using ada as well as svm

6 Conclusion and Future Scope

In this work, various machine learning classification models are explored with input variables to predict the distinction of students. The result indicates that Boost Algorithm outperforms the other classification models.

This work can be extended by inclusion of more parameters such as combining the distinction and attendance record of student to predict that "if a student attendance record is good, does it actually enhance the academic performance or not" and then different categories of student based on these parameters can be made that can be further used with some classification models. In this paper, individual models are applied on the dataset to predict the distinction, and we can also use ensemble approach.

References

1. Ayesha, S., Mustafa, T., Sattar, A., Khan, I.: Data mining model for higher education system. Eur. J. Sci. Res. **43**(1), 24–29 (2010)
2. Shovon, Md.H.I.: Prediction of student academic performance by an application of K-means clustering algorithm. Int. J. Adv. Res. Comput. Sci. Softw. Eng. **2**(7) (2012)
3. Sharma, T.C.: WEKA approach for comparative study of classification algorithm (IJARCCE). Int. J. Adv. Res. Comput. Commun. Eng. **2**(4) (2013)
4. Kumar, V., Chadha, A.: An empirical study of the applications of data mining techniques in higher education. Int. J. Adv. Comput. Sci. Appl. **2**(3), 80–84 (2011)
5. Quinlan, J.R.: Induction of decision trees. Mach. Learn. **1**(1), 81–106 (1986)
6. Keerthi, S.S., Gilbert, E.G.: Convergence of a generalized SMO algorithm for SVM classifier design. Mach. Learn. **46**(1), 351–360 (2002)
7. Fernandez Caballero, J.C., Martinez, F.J., Hervas, C., Gutierrez, P.A.: Sensitivity versus accuracy in multiclass problem using Memetic Pareto evolutionary neural networks. IEEE Trans. Neural Netw. **21**, 750–770 (2010)

Proposing Pattern Growth Methods for Frequent Pattern Mining on Account of Its Comparison Made with the Candidate Generation and Test Approach for a Given Data Set

Vaibhav Kant Singh

Abstract Frequent pattern mining is a very important field for mining of association rule. Association rule mining is an important technique of data mining that is meant to extract meaningful information from large data sets accumulated as a result of various data processing activities. There are several algorithms proposed for having solution to the problem of frequent pattern mining. In this paper, we have mathematically compared two most widely used approaches, such as candidate generation and test and pattern growth approaches to search for the better approach for a given data set. In this paper, we came to conclusion that the pattern growth methods are more efficient in maximum cases for the purpose of frequent pattern mining on account of their cache conscious behavior. In this paper, we have taken a data set and have implemented both the algorithms on that data set; the experimental result of the working of both the algorithms for the given data set shows that the pattern growth approach is more efficient than the candidate generation and test approach.

Keywords Association rule mining · Candidate generation and test
Data mining · Frequent pattern mining · Pattern growth methods

---

The research work is small part of supplementary work done by the author beside his base work on RSTDB an AI supported Candidate generation and test algorithm.

V. K. Singh (✉)
Department of Computer Science and Engineering, Institute of Technology,
Guru Ghasidas Vishwavidyalaya, Bilaspur, Chhattisgarh, India
e-mail: vibhu200427@gmail.com

© Springer Nature Singapore Pte Ltd. 2019
M. N. Hoda et al. (eds.), *Software Engineering*, Advances in Intelligent Systems
and Computing 731, https://doi.org/10.1007/978-981-10-8848-3_20

1 Introduction

With the increase in the use of computer, there is a situation where we are accumulating huge amount of data every day as a result of various data processing activities. The data that we are gaining can be used for having competitive advantage in the current scenario where the time to take important decisions has gone down. Today the need for systems that can help the decision makers to make valuable decision on the basis of some patterns extracted from historical data in form of some reports, graphs, etc., has increased. The branch of computer science that is in concern with the subject is data mining. Data mining is branch of computer science that is developed to combine the human's power of detecting patterns along with the computers computation power to generate patterns. The branch is having its utility in designing of decision support systems that are efficient enough to help the decision makers to make valuable decisions on time.

Data mining is used for a wide range of applications such as finance, database marketing, health insurance, medical purpose, bioinformatics, text mining, biodefense. There are several data mining tools that help the designer of the system to simulate such systems such as Intelligent miner, PRW, Enterprise miner, Darwin, and Clementine. Some of the basic techniques used for the purpose of data mining are association rule mining, clustering, classification, frequent episode, deviation detection, neural network, genetic algorithm, rough sets techniques, support vector machine, etc. For each of the above-mentioned techniques for data mining, there are algorithms associated which are used for implementation of each paradigm. In this paper, we are concerned with the association rule mining.

1.1 Association Rule Mining

An association rule is an expression of the form $X \rightarrow Y$, where X and Y are the sets of items. The intuitive meaning of such a rule is that the transaction of the database which contains X tends to contain Y. Association depends basically on two things:

- Confidence.
- Support.

Some of the algorithms used for finding of association rules from large data set include Apriori algorithm, partition algorithm, Pincer-Search algorithm, dynamic item set counting algorithm, FP-tree growth algorithm. In this paper, we have taken into account two types of approaches for mining of association rules. First is candidate generation and test algorithm and second approach is pattern growth approach. The two approaches are concerned with extraction of frequent patterns from large data sets. Frequent patterns are patterns that occur frequently in transactions from a given data set. Frequent pattern mining is an important field of association rule mining.

2 Literature Survey

In [1], Han et al. proposed the FP-tree as a pattern growth approach. In [2], Agarwal et al. showed the power of using transaction projection in conjunction with lexicographic tree structure in order to generate frequent item sets required for association rules. In [3], Zaki et al. proposed algorithm that utilizes the structural properties of frequent item sets to facilitate fast discovery is shown. In [4], Agarwal and Srikant proposed two algorithms for the purpose of frequent pattern mining which are fundamentally different. Empirical formula used in the paper showed that the proposed algorithm proved to be handy as compared to the previously proposed approaches. In [5], Tiovonen proposed a new algorithm that reduces the database activity in mining. The proposed algorithm is efficient enough to find association rules in single database. In [6], Savasere et al. proposed algorithm which showed improvement in the input–output overhead associated with previous algorithms. The feature proved to be handy for many real-life database mining scenarios. In [7], Burdick et al. proposed algorithm showed that the breakdown of the algorithmic components showed parent equivalence pruning and dynamic reordering were quite beneficial in reducing the search space while relative compression of vertical bitmaps increases vertical scalability of the proposed algorithm whereas reduces cost of counting of supports. In [8], Zaki and Gonda proposed a novel vertical representation Diffset. The proposed approach drastically reduces the amount of space required to store intermediate results. In [9, 10], the author proposed a new algorithm RSTDB which also works on the candidate generation and test mechanism. The algorithm is having a new module that makes it more efficient than the previous approach. In [11], a study of some of the pattern growth methods along with description of the new algorithm RSTDB for frequent pattern mining is shown. In [12], the algorithm RSTDB is compared from FP-tree growth algorithm. In [13], a cache conscious approach for frequent pattern mining is given. In [14, 15], candidate generation and test approach for frequent pattern mining is given. In [16], RSTDB is proposed as an application.

3 Experiment

In this paper for comparing the two approaches, we have taken two algorithms Apriori as a representative of candidate generation and test mechanism and FP-tree as representatives of pattern growth approach, since these two algorithms are the base algorithm that explains to the two approaches in best. In this section, we took Table 1 to explain the difference of the two algorithms. Table 1 is having 15 records and 9 distinct records having lexicographic property.

Table 1 Transaction
database consisting of 15
records and 9 distinct items

Transaction ID	Item set
T100	BDFG
T101	E
T102	EFG
T103	CEG
T104	BDH
T105	BC
T106	H
T107	DEG
T108	ACEG
T109	CEG
T110	BCI
T111	AEFH
T112	BCD
T113	EFH
T114	BFGI

In this section, we will consider one transaction database of Table 1 capable of holding 15 records and 9 distinct items A, B, C, D, E, F, G, H, I. We will see the working of both algorithms for the purpose of evaluation of FP-tree from the side of pattern growth methods as a more cache conscious effort. The minimum support for the transaction database is fixed at 20%, i.e., minimum of threshold value of 3 is required to be frequent. Here, now in Fig. 1, we have shown the working of the two approaches for the given data set according to Han and Kamber [17].

4   Result and Discussion

The total number of counters required for the finding of frequent item set in Apriori algorithm which is candidate generation and test approach is more.

If the number of counters is more, this implies that the total amount of space required will be more in the case of Apriori approach. Also for generation of candidate set at each step of the Apriori algorithm, the whole transaction database is to be scanned. Whereas in the case of FP-tree, once f-list is generated only once each record is to be scanned. Beside the above advantages, FP-tree structure could be accommodated in the memory and fast referencing is possible. The comparison we are making is for a small data set which shows difference in efficiency. Think in real-time scenario where the size is very large. The efficiency of the FP-tree would be far better than Apriori.

Apriori Algorithm a Candidate Generation and Test algorithm

FP-Tree Algorithm a Pattern Growth approach

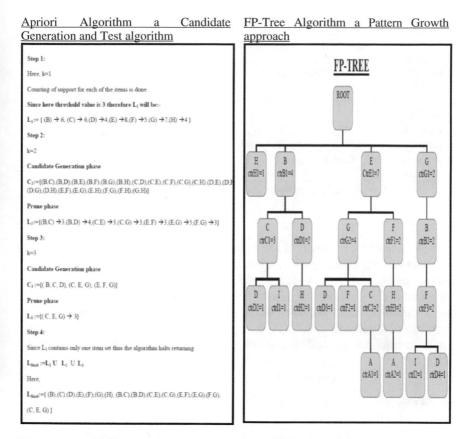

Fig. 1 Comparison of the working of the two algorithms in terms of space consumed for evaluation of frequent patterns

5 Conclusion

Considering to the fact that today's data mining algorithms are keener on having the data set required for computation in the main memory to have better performance outcome. From Table 2, it is clear that the amount of space required by the Apriori algorithm violates to need of the current scenario where time takes the peak position. From the above example of working of Apriori and FP-tree, it is clear that execution of Apriori will require considerable large amount of space compared to FP-tree. Thus, FP-tree employing tree structure easily fitting to the cache can be a better option despite of the complexity present. Thus, we propose that FP-tree which is a cache conscious effort as the size of the tree is good enough to reside in the memory for complete computation. As already discussed that we have taken FP-tree as a representative of the pattern growth algorithm and Apriori as a representative of the candidate generation and test algorithm, the result obtained is

Table 2 Comparison of apriori and FP-tree

Differentiating property	Apriori	FP-tree
Space required for processing	More space required for processing	Less space required for processing
Time required for operation	More time required for processing	Less time required for processing
TDB scanning required	More scanning of TDB required for generating final result	Less scanning of TDB required for generating final result
Complexity of programming	Less complex	More complex
Understandability	Simple to understand	Compared to Apriori difficult to understand

meant to give a general idea of the two approaches and also the result guides us that we should go for pattern growth approach when selecting algorithm for frequent pattern mining, which is also clear from its working that it is more cache conscious compared to the other one. Beside the above facts derived from the working of the two approaches, some positives which are drawn of Apriori algorithm are the simplicity of implementation which is very important and the approaches which are similar to candidate generation and test are easily understandable.

References

1. Han, J., Pei, J., Yin, Y.: Mining frequent patterns without candidate generation. In: Proceeding of the 2000 ACM SIGMOID International Conference on Management of Data, pp. 1–12. ACM Press (2000)
2. Agarwal, R.C., Aggarwal, C.C., Prasad, V.V.V.: A tree projection algorithm for generation of frequent item sets. J. Parallel Distrib. Comput. **61**(3), 350–371 (2001)
3. Zaki, M.J., Parthasarathy, S., Ogihara, M., Li, W.: New algorithms for fast discovery of association rules. In: Proceeding of the 3rd International Conference on Knowledge Discovery and Data Mining, pp. 283–296. AAAI Press (1997)
4. Agarwal, R., Srikant, R.: Fast algorithms for mining association rules. In: The International Conference on Very Large Databases, pp. 207–216 (1993)
5. Toivonen, H.: Sampling large databases for association rules. In: Proceeding of 22nd Very Large Database Conference (1996)
6. Savasere, A., Omiecinski, E., Navathe, S.: An efficient algorithm for mining association rules in large databases. In: Proceeding of the 21st Very Large Database Conference (1995)
7. Burdick, D., Calimlim, M., Gehrke, J.: MAFIA: a maximal frequent itemset algorithm for transaction databases. In: Proceeding of ICDE'01, pp. 443–452 (2001)
8. Zaki, M., Gouda, K.: Fast vertical mining using diffsets. In: Journal of ACM SIGKDD'03, Washington, D.C. (2003)
9. Singh, V.K., Singh, V.K.: Minimizing space time complexity by RSTDB a new method for frequent pattern mining. In: Proceeding of the First International Conference on Human Computer Interaction IHCI'09, Indian Institute of Information Technology, Allahabad, pp. 361–371. Springer, India (2009). ISBN 978-81-8489-404-2

10. Singh, V.K., Shah, V., Jain, Y.K., Shukla, A., Thoke, A.S., Singh, V.K., Dule, C., Parganiha, V.: Proposing an efficient method for frequent pattern mining. In: Proceeding of International Conference on Computational and Statistical Sciences, Bangkok, WASET, vol. 36, pp. 1184–1189 (2009). ISSN 2070-3740
11. Singh, V.K., Shah, V.: Minimizing space time complexity in frequent pattern mining by reducing database scanning and using pattern growth methods. Chhattisgarh J. Sci. Technol. ISSN 0973-7219
12. Singh, V.K.: Comparing proposed test algorithm RSTDB with FP-tree growth method for frequent pattern mining. Aryabhatt J. Math. Inf. 5(1), 137–140 (2013). ISSN 0975-7139
13. Singh, V.K.: RSTDB and cache conscious techniques for frequent pattern mining. In: CERA-09, Proceeding of Fourth International Conference on Computer applications in Electrical Engineering, Indian Institute of Technology, Roorkee, India, pp. 433–436, 19–21 Feb 2010
14. Singh, V.K., Singh, V.K.: RSTDB a new candidate generation and test algorithm for frequent pattern mining. In: CNC-2010, ACEEE and IEEE, IEEE Communication Society, Washington, D.C., Proceeding of International Conference on Advances in Communication Network and Computing, Published by ACM DL, Calicut, Kerala, India, pp. 416–418, 4–5 Oct 2010
15. Singh, V.K., Singh, V.K.: RSTDB a candidate generation and test approach. Int. J. Res. Digest, India 5(4), 41–44 (2010)
16. Singh, V.K.: Solving management problems using RSTDB a frequent pattern mining technique. In: Int. J. Adv. Res. Comput. Commun. Eng., India 4(8), 285–288 (2015)
17. Han, J., Kamber, M.: Data Mining: Concepts and Techniques. Morgan Kaufmann Publisher, San Francisco, CA (2001)

A Study on Initial Centroids Selection for Partitional Clustering Algorithms

Mahesh Motwani, Neeti Arora and Amit Gupta

Abstract Data mining tools and techniques allow an organization to make creative decisions and subsequently do proper planning. Clustering is used to determine the objects that are similar in characteristics and group them together. K-means clustering method chooses random cluster centres (initial centroid), one for each centroid, and this is the major weakness of K-means. The performance and quality of K-means strongly depends on the initial guess of centres (centroid). By augmenting K-means with a technique of selecting centroids, several modifications have been suggested in research on clustering. The first two main authors of this paper have also developed three algorithms that unlike K-means do not perform random generation of the initial centres and actually produce same set of initial centroids for the same input data. These developed algorithms are sum of distance clustering (SODC), distance-based clustering algorithm (DBCA) and farthest distributed centroid clustering (FDCC). We present a brief survey of the algorithms available in the research on modification of initial centroids for K-means clustering algorithm and further describe the developed algorithm farthest distributed centroid clustering in this paper. The experimental results carried out show that farthest distributed centroid clustering algorithm produces better quality clusters than the partitional clustering algorithm, agglomerative hierarchical clustering algorithm and the hierarchical partitioning clustering algorithm.

Keywords Partitional clustering · Initial centroids · Recall · Precision

M. Motwani (✉)
Department of Computer Science and Engineering, RGPV, Bhopal, India
e-mail: mahesh.bpl.7@gmail.com

N. Arora · A. Gupta
RGPV, Bhopal, India

© Springer Nature Singapore Pte Ltd. 2019
M. N. Hoda et al. (eds.), *Software Engineering*, Advances in Intelligent Systems and Computing 731, https://doi.org/10.1007/978-981-10-8848-3_21

1 Introduction

K-means [1–4] is a famous partition algorithm which clusters the n data points into k groups. It defines k centroids, one for each cluster. For this k, data points are selected at random from D as initial centroids.

The K-means algorithm has a drawback that it produces different clusters for every different set of initial centroids. Thus, the quality of clusters formed depends on the randomly chosen set of initial k centroids [5]. This drawback of K-means is removed by augmenting K-means with some technique of selecting initial centroids. We discuss in Sect. 2, the different such modifications published in the literature on modified K-means algorithm. These proposed algorithms do not perform random generation of the initial centres and do not produce different results for the same input data. In Sect. 3, we discuss the farthest distributed centroid clustering algorithm followed by its experimental results in Sect. 4. Section 5 contains conclusion, and finally, Sect. 6 has bibliography.

2 Study on Initial Centroid Selection for Clustering Algorithms

An algorithm proposed in [6] partitions the given set of points to be clustered in a cell. This cell is divided into two cells with the help of cutting plane. The cells are divided one at a time till they are equal to the number of clusters to be formed. The k initial centroids for the K-means algorithm are the centres of these k cells. The method proposed in [7] analyses the distribution and probability of data density to find the initial centroids. The given input dataset is divided into smaller parts in order to minimize the memory requirement needed for storing the given dataset. This results in superior clustering results from the refined initial centroids in comparison to randomly chosen initial centroids in K-means algorithm.

A global K-means clustering algorithm in [8] adds the cluster centre incrementally. It also performs several executions of the K-means algorithm which are equal to the size of the data set. An improved version of K-means proposed in [9] evaluates the distance between every pair of data points in order to determine the similar data points. Based on this determination of data points, initial centroids are finally chosen. This method creates better clusters in comparison to K-means algorithm.

The method in [10] distributes the initial centroids in order to widen the distances among them. An efficiently enhanced K-means method proposed in [11] uses a heuristic function. This function is chosen in a manner to perform less number of distance calculations. This helps in improving the execution time of the K-means algorithm. In this method, the determination of initial centroids is similar to that of the K-means algorithm. Thus, after every execution of the algorithm, it produces different clusters just like in the K-means algorithm. A smaller time complexity results in this method in comparison to K-means algorithm. By embedding hierarchical clustering into K-means clustering, a new algorithm [12] is proposed for finding the initial cluster centres.

The algorithm proposed in [13] selects the position of initial centroids calculated from the farthest accumulated distance metric between each data point and all previous centroids. A data point which has the maximum distance is thus selected as initial centroid. In the paper [14], the method of selection of the first initial centroid is from the given set of points which are going to be clustered. The remaining initial centroids are selected from rest of the points. The probability of selecting each of this point is proportional to square of the distance between this point and its nearest initial centroid.

The initialization method proposed in [15] depends on reverse nearest neighbour (RNN) search and coupling degree. RNN takes a query point p and fetches all points in a given dataset whose nearest neighbour is p. The coupling degree between neighbourhoods of nodes is defined as the amount of similarity between the objects. This method deals with three main sets: candidate set (CS), representative set (RS) and centroids set. The centroid initialization method proposed in [16] is based on the graph theory of Kruskal algorithm [17]. This algorithm uses the Kruskal algorithm to generate the minimum spanning tree of the all clustering objects at first and then deletes $(k - 1)$ edges according to the order of their weights. The K-mean values of objects in each connected sub-graph that is obtained are then taken as the initial clustering centres. Simulation experiment shows that this method gives better accuracy and clustering quality in comparison with K-means algorithm.

The method in [18] partitions the dataset into blocks so as to compress the dataset. The K-means is applied on this compressed dataset, to get the k points that are used as the initial centroids for the K-means on the full dataset. The method in [19] constructs a Voronoi diagram from the given data points. For a set of n points in a m-dimensional space, the Voronoi diagram [20] of these set of points is the division of the space into n cells in such a way that each point belongs to only one cell. The initial centroids are chosen from the points which lie on the Voronoi circles.

Teaching learning-based Optimization algorithm proposed in [21] has two steps. The first step explores the search space and finds the near-optimal cluster centres which are then evaluated by a function. The cluster centres with the minimum function values are taken in the second step as initial centroids for the K-means algorithm. The algorithm proposed in [22] defines two measures for refining initial clustering centres, to measure a point's local density. The clustering centre with local maximal density for each cluster is produced with the help of these measurements. After refinement, the K-means clustering algorithm converges to a better local minimum. Experiments demonstrate the efficiency of the proposed algorithm. The method in [23] takes the data and finds the high-density neighbourhoods from it. The central points of the neighbourhoods are now chosen as initial centroids for clustering. The high-density neighbourhoods are found by neighbourhood-based clustering [24]. A filtering method is used to avoid too many clusters from being formed.

A heuristic method is used in [25] to find a good set of initial centroids. The method uses a weighted average score of dataset. The rank score is found by averaging the attribute of each data point. This generates initial centroids that follow the data distribution of the given set. A sorting algorithm is applied to the score of each data point and divided into k subsets. The nearest value of mean from each subset is taken as initial centroid. This algorithm produces the clusters in less time as compared to K-means. A genetic algorithm for the K-means initialization (GAKMI) is used in [26] for the selection of initial centroids. The set of initial centroids is represented by a binary string of length n. Here n is the number of feature vectors. The GAKMI algorithm uses binary encoding, in which bits set to one select elements of the learning set as initial centroids. A chromosome repair algorithm is used before fitness evaluation to convert infeasible chromosomes into feasible chromosomes. The GAKMI algorithm results in better clusters as compared to the standard K-means algorithm.

Sum of distance clustering (SODC) [27] algorithm for clustering selects initial centroids using criteria of finding sum of distances of data objects to all other data objects. The algorithm uses the concept that good clusters are formed when the choice of initial k centroids is such that they are as far as possible from each other. The proposed algorithm results in better clustering on synthetic as well as real datasets when compared to the K-means technique. Distance-based clustering algorithm (DBCA) [28] is based on computing the total distance of a node from all other nodes. The clustering algorithm uses the concept that good clusters are formed when the choice of initial k centroids is such that they are as far as possible from each other. Once some point d is selected as initial centroid, the proposed algorithm computes average of data points to avoid the points near to d from being selected as next initial centroids.

The farthest distributed centroid clustering (FDCC) algorithm [29] uses the concept that good clusters are formed when the choice of initial k centroids is such that they are as far as possible from each other. FDCC algorithm proposed here uses criteria of sum of distances of data objects to all other data objects. Unlike K-means, FDCC algorithm does not perform random generation of the initial centres and produces same results for the same input data. DBCA and FDCC clustering algorithms produce better quality clusters than the partitional clustering algorithm, agglomerative hierarchical clustering algorithm and the hierarchical partitioning clustering algorithm.

3 Developed Farthest Distributed Centroid Clustering Algorithm

3.1 Basic Concept

The algorithm selects a good set of initial centroids such that the selected initial centroids are spread out within the data space as far as possible from each other. Figure 1 illustrates the selection of four initial centroids C1, C2, C3 and C4. As is evident, there are four clusters in the data space. The proposed technique selects a point d as the first initial centroid using a distance criteria explained in Sect. 3.2. Once this point d is selected as initial centroid, the proposed technique avoids the points near to d from being selected as next initial centroids. This is how C1, C2, C3 and C4 are distributed as far as possible from each other.

3.2 Farthest Distributed Centroid Clustering Algorithm

Let the clustering of n data points in the given dataset D is to be done into k clusters. In farthest distributed centroids clustering (FDCC) algorithm, the distance of each data point $di = 1$ to n in the given dataset D is calculated from all other data points and these distances are stored in a distance matrix DM. Total distance of each data point $di = 1$ to n with all other data points is calculated. The total distance for a point di is sum of all elements in the row of the DM corresponding to di. These sums are stored in a sum of distances vector SD. The vector SD is sorted in decreasing order of total distance values. Let P-SD is the vector of data points corresponding to the sorted vector SD; i.e., P-SD [1] will be the data point whose sum of distances (available in SD [1]) from all other data points is maximum, and

Fig. 1 Illustration of selecting a good set of initial centroids

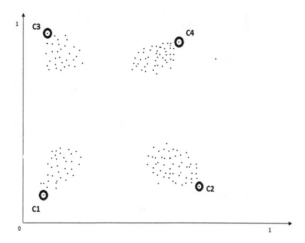

P-SD [2] will be the data point whose sum of distances (available in SD [2]) from all other data points is second highest. In general, P-SD [i] will be the data point whose sum of distances from all other data points is in SD [i].

The first point d of the vector P-SD is the first initial centroid. Put this initial centroid point in the set S of initial centroids. To avoid the points near to d from being selected as next initial centroids, variable x is defined as follows:

$$x = \text{floor}\ (n/k) \tag{1}$$

Here, the floor (n/k) function maps the real number (n/k) to the largest previous integer; i.e., it returns the largest integer not greater than (n/k).

Now discard the next x number of points of the vector P-SD and define the next point left after discarding these x numbers of points from this vector P-SD, as the second initial centroid. Now discard the next x number of points from this vector P-SD and define the next point left after discarding these x numbers of points from this vector P-SD, as the third initial centroid. This process is repeated till k numbers of initial centroids are defined. These k initial centroids are now used in the K-means process as substitute for the k random initial centroids. K-means is now invoked for clustering the dataset D into k number of clusters using the initial centroids available in set S.

4 Experimental Study

The experiments are performed on core i5 processor with a speed of 2.5 GHz and 4 GB RAM using MATLAB. The comparison of the quality of the clustering achieved with FDCC algorithm [29] is made with the quality of the clustering achieved with

1. Partitional clustering technique. The K-means is the partitional technique available as a built-in function in MATLAB [30].
2. Hierarchical clustering technique. The ClusterData is agglomerative hierarchical clustering technique available as a built-in function in MATLAB [30]. The single linkage is the default option used in ClusterData to create hierarchical cluster tree.
3. Hierarchical partitioning technique. CLUTO [31] is a software package for clustering datasets. CLUTO contains both partitional and hierarchical clustering algorithms. The repeated bisections method available in CLUTO is a hierarchical partitioning algorithm that initiates a series of k − 1 repeated bisections to produce the required k clusters. This effectively is the bisect K-means divisive clustering algorithm and is the default option in CLUTO named as Cluto-rb.

Recall and precision [32] are used to evaluate the quality of clustering achieved. Recall is the percentage of data points that have been correctly put into a cluster among all the relevant points that should have been in that cluster. Precision is the

Table 1 Average recall and average precision for real datasets

Algorithm	Corel5K		Corel (Wang)		Wine	
	Recall (%)	Precision (%)	Recall (%)	Precision (%)	Recall (%)	Precision (%)
FDCC	30.02	38.2	100	100	41.67	72
K-means	20.02	33.3	60.7	86.71	33.67	61
ClusterData	10.08	41	100	100	25.37	47
Cluto-rb	23.02	30.32	33.29	27.91	39.67	69

Fig. 2 Average recall for real datasets

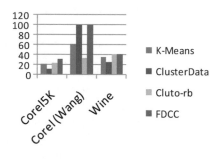

Fig. 3 Average precision for real datasets

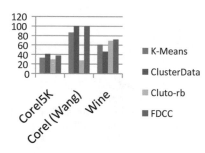

percentage of data points that have been correctly put into a cluster among all the points put into that cluster.

Three real datasets, namely Corel5K, Corel (Wang) and Wine, are used in the experiments [33]. Corel5K is a collection of 5000 images downloaded from Website [34]. We have formed ten clusters of these images using K-means, ClusterData, Cluto-rb and FDCC algorithm. Corel (Wang) database consists of 700 images of the Corel stock photo and is downloaded from Website [35] and contains 1025 features per image. We have formed ten clusters of these images using K-means, ClusterData, Cluto-rb and FDCC algorithm. The wine recognition dataset [36] consists of quantities of 13 constituents found in three types of classes of wines of Italy. The dataset consists of 178 instances. The number of instances in class 1, class 2 and class 3 are 59, 71 and 48, respectively. We have formed three clusters of these images using K-means, ClusterData, Cluto-rb and FDCC algorithm.

The average recall and precision using these algorithms is shown in Table 1. The graphs plotted for average recall and average precision in percentage using these techniques is shown in Figs. 2 and 3, respectively. The results show that the recall and precision of FDCC are better than that of K-means, ClusterData and Cluto-rb. Hence, the FDCC algorithm produces better quality clusters.

5 Conclusion

The initialization of k data points determines quality of clustering of K-means. The random selection of k initial centroids is the weakness of K-means. Several algorithms are developed to overcome this weakness of K-means algorithm. These algorithms select a good set of initial centroids to be used by K-means. We have discussed several such algorithms available in the literature. We have also discussed farthest distributed centroid clustering algorithm developed by the first two authors of this paper. The experimental results show that farthest distributed centroid clustering algorithm produces better quality clusters than the partitional clustering algorithm, agglomerative hierarchical clustering algorithm and the hierarchical partitioning clustering algorithm.

References

1. Han, J., Kamber, H.: Data Mining Concepts and Techniques. Morgan Kaufmann Publishers, Burlington (2002)
2. MacQueen, J.B.: Some methods for classification and analysis of multivariate observations. In: Proceedings of 5th Berkeley Symposium on Mathematical Statistics and Probability, Berkeley, University of California Press, pp. 281–297 (1967)
3. Dunham, M.: Data Mining: Introductory and Advanced Concepts. Pearson Education, London (2006)
4. Llyod, S.: Least Squares quantization in PCM. IEEE Trans. Inf. Theory **28**(2), 129–137 (1982)
5. Khan, S.S., Ahmed, A.: Cluster center initialization algorithm for k-means algorithm. Pattern Recogn. Lett. **25**(11), 1293–1302 (2004)
6. Deelers, S., Auwatanamongkol, S.: Engineering k-means algorithm with initial cluster centers derived from data partitioning along the data axis with the highest variance. In: Proceedings of World Academy of Science, Engineering and Technology, vol. 26, pp. 323–328 (2007)
7. Bradley, P.S., Fayyad, U.M.: Refining initial points for K-Means clustering. In: Proceedings of the 15th International Conference on Machine Learning, Morgan Kaufmann, San Francisco, CA, pp. 91–99 (1998)
8. Likas, A., Vlassis, N., Verbeek, J.J.: The global k-means clustering algorithm. Pattern Recogn. **36**, 451–461 (2003)
9. Yuan, F., Meng, Z.H., Zhang, H.X., Dong, C.R.: A new algorithm to get the initial centroids. In: Proceedings of the 3rd International Conference on Machine Learning and Cybernetics, Shanghai, pp. 26–29 (2004)

10. Barakbah, A.R., Helen, A.: Optimized K-means: an algorithm of initial centroids optimization for K-means. In: Proceedings of Soft Computing, Intelligent Systems and Information Technology (SIIT), pp. 63–66 (2005)
11. Fahim, A.M., Salem, A.M., Torkey, F.A., Ramadan, M.A.: An efficient enhanced k-means clustering algorithm. J. Zhejiang Univ. Sci. 7(10), 1626–1633 (2006)
12. Barakbah, A.R., Arai, K.: Hierarchical K-means: an algorithm for centroids initialization for K-means. Rep. Fac. Sci. Eng. 36(1) (2007) (Saga University, Japan)
13. Barakbah, A.R, Kiyoki, Y.: A pillar algorithm for K-means optimization by distance maximization for initial centroid designation. In: IEEE Symposium on Computational Intelligence and Data Mining (IDM), Nashville-Tennessee, pp. 61–68 (2009)
14. Arthur, D., Vassilvitskii, S.: K-means++: the advantages of careful seeding. In: Proceedings of the 18th Annual ACM-SIAM Symposium on Discrete Algorithms, Philadelphia, PA, USA, Society for Industrial and Applied Mathematics, pp. 1027–1035 (2007)
15. Ahmed, A.H., Ashour, W.: An initialization method for the K-means algorithm using RNN and coupling degree. Int. J. Comput. Appl. (0975–8887) 25(1) (2011)
16. Huang, L., Du, S., Zhang, Y., Ju, Y., Li, Z.: K-means initial clustering center optimal algorithm based on Kruskal. J. Inf. Comput. Sci. 9(9), 2387–2392 (2012)
17. Kruskal, J.: On the shortest spanning subtree and the travelling salesman problem. Proc. Am. Math. Soc, 48–50 (1956)
18. Fahim, A.M., Salem, A.M., Torkey, F.A., Ramadan, M.A, Saake, G.: An efficient K-means with good initial starting points. Georgian Electron. Sci. J. Comput. Sci. Telecommun. 19(2) (2009)
19. Reddy, D., Jana, P.K.: Initialization for K-mean clustering Voronoi diagram. In: International Conference on C3IT-2012, Hooghly, Procedia Technology (Elsevier) vol. 4, pp. 395–400, Feb 2012
20. Preparata, F.P., Shamos, M.I.: Computational Geometry—An Introduction. Springer, Berlin, Heidelberg, Tokyo (1985)
21. Naik, A., Satapathy, S.C., Parvathi, K.: Improvement of initial cluster center of c-means using teaching learning based optimization. Procedia Technol. 6, 428–435 (2012)
22. Yang, S.Z., Luo, S.W.: A novel algorithm for initializing clustering centers. In: Proceedings of International Conference on IEEE Machine Learning and Cybernetics, China, vol. 9, pp. 5579–5583 (2005)
23. Ye, Y., Huang, J., Chen, X., Zhou, S., Williams, G., Xu, X.: Neighborhood density method for selecting initial cluster centers in K-means clustering. In: Advances in Knowledge Discovery and Data Mining. Lecture Notes in Computer Science, vol. 3918, pp. 189–198 (2006)
24. Zhou, S., Zhao, J.: A neighborhood-based clustering algorithm. In: PAKD 2005. LNAI 3518, pp. 361–371 (1982)
25. Mahmud, M.S., Rahman, M., Akhtar, N.: Improvement of K-means clustering algorithm with better initial centroids based on weighted average. In: 7th International Conference on Electrical and Computer Engineering, Dhaka, Bangladesh, Dec 2012
26. Kwedlo, W., Iwanowicz, P.: Using genetic algorithm for selection of initial cluster centers for the K-means method. In: International Conference on Artificial Intelligence and Soft Computing. Springer Notes on Artificial Intelligence, pp. 165–172 (2010)
27. Arora, N., Motwani, M.: Sum of distance based algorithm for clustering web data. Int. J. Comput. Appl. 87(7), 26–30 (2014)
28. Arora, N., Motwani, M.: A distance based clustering algorithm. Int. J. Comput. Eng. Technol. 5(5), 109–119 (2014)
29. Arora, N., Motwani, M.: Optimizing K-Means by fixing initial cluster centers. Int. J. Curr. Eng. Technol. 4(3), 2101–2107 (2014)
30. MathWorks MatLab: The Language of Technical Computing (2009)
31. Karypis, G.: CLUTO: A Clustering Toolkit. Release 2.1.1, Tech. Rep. No. 02-017. University of Minnesota, Department of Computer Science, Minneapolis, MN 55455 (2003)
32. Kowalski, G.: Information Retrieval Systems—Theory and Implementation. Kluwer Academic Publishers (1997)

33. Veenman, C.J., Reinders, M.J.T., Backer, E.: A maximum variance cluster algorithm. IEEE Trans. Pattern Anal. Mach. Intell. **24**(9), 1273–1280 (2002)
34. Duygulu, P., et al.: Object recognition as machine translation: learning a lexicon for a fixed image vocabulary. In: Proceedings of the 7th European Conference on Computer Vision, pp. 97–112 (2002)
35. Wang, J.Z., Li, J., Wiederhold, G.: SIMPLIcity: semantics-sensitive integrated matching for picture libraries. IEEE Trans. Pattern Anal. Mach. Intell. **23**(9), 947–963 (2001)
36. Forina, M., Aeberhard, S.: UCI Machine Learning Repository (1991)

A Novel Rare Itemset Mining Algorithm Based on Recursive Elimination

Mohak Kataria, C. Oswald and B. Sivaselvan

Abstract Pattern mining in large databases is the fundamental and a non-trivial task in data mining. Most of the current research focuses on frequently occurring patterns, even though less frequently/rarely occurring patterns benefit us with useful information in many real-time applications (e.g., in medical diagnosis, genetics). In this paper, we propose a novel algorithm for mining rare itemsets using recursive elimination (RELIM)-based method. Simulation results indicate that our approach performs efficiently than existing solution in time taken to mine the rare itemsets.

Keywords Apriori · Frequent pattern mining · Rare itemset mining
RELIM · Maximum support

1 Introduction

With huge influx of data in every real-world application, data analysis becomes important and data mining helps in effective, efficient, and scalable analysis by uncovering many hidden associations among data which otherwise cannot be interpreted and is useful at the same time. Data mining is the non-trivial process of extraction of hidden, previously unknown and potentially useful information from large databases [1, 2]. It differs from retrieval tasks in the fact that knowledge (patterns) can be discovered through data mining. Pattern mining being a basic data mining task enables to extract hidden patterns from set of data records called

M. Kataria (✉)
Department of Computer Science and Engineering, Thapar University, Patiala, Punjab, India
e-mail: mohakkataria@outlook.com

C. Oswald · B. Sivaselvan
Department of Computer Engineering, Design and Manufacturing Kancheepuram,
Indian Institute of Information Technology, Chennai, India
e-mail: coe13d003@iiitdm.ac.in

B. Sivaselvan
e-mail: sivaselvanb@iiitdm.ac.in

© Springer Nature Singapore Pte Ltd. 2019
M. N. Hoda et al. (eds.), *Software Engineering*, Advances in Intelligent Systems and Computing 731, https://doi.org/10.1007/978-981-10-8848-3_22

transactions. The various data mining techniques involve association rule mining (ARM), classification, clustering, and outlier analysis. ARM is the process of finding frequent itemsets/patterns, associations, correlations among sets of items or objects in transactional databases, relational databases, and other information repositories [1].

The motivation for ARM emerged from market basket analysis, which is a collection of items purchased by a customer in an individual customer transaction [2], for example a customer's visit to a grocery store or an online purchase from Amazon.com. Huge collections of transactions are received from them. An analysis of the transaction database is done to find frequently occurring sets of items, or itemsets, that appear together. Frequent pattern (itemset) mining (FPM) is an important and non-trivial phase in ARM followed by rule generation [1]. Let $I = \{i_1, i_2, i_3, \ldots, i_m\}$ be a set of items, and a transaction database $TD = \langle T_1, T_2, T_3, \ldots, T_n \rangle$, where $T_i (i \in [1 \ldots n])$ is a transaction containing a set of items in I. The support of a pattern X, where X is a set of items, is the number of transactions containing X in TD. A pattern (itemset) X is frequent if its support is not less than a user-defined minimum support($min\ supp = \alpha$). FPM algorithms concentrate on mining all possible frequent patterns in the transactional database.

The second phase is relatively straightforward compared to the first phase. Algorithms for ARM have primarily focused on the first phase as a result of the potential number of frequent itemsets being exponential in the number of different items, although the actual number of frequent itemsets can be much smaller. Thus, there is a need for algorithms that are scalable. Many efficient algorithms have been designed to address these criteria first of which was Apriori [2]. It uses prior knowledge which is "*all non-empty subsets of a frequent itemset must also be frequent.*" A rule is defined as an implication of the form $X \Rightarrow Y$ where $X, Y \subseteq I$ and $X \cap Y = \emptyset$. The sets of items (for short itemsets) X and Y are called antecedent and consequent transactions containing only X of the rule, respectively. A rule which satisfies a minimum confidence threshold is said be an interesting rule. The rule $X \Rightarrow Y$ satisfy confidence c, where

$$c = \frac{\text{Number of transactions containing both } X \text{ and } Y}{\text{Transactions containing only } X}.$$

The paper is organized as follows. Related studies are presented in Sect. 2. Section 3 presents the proposed algorithm. Section 4 explains the proof of correctness of our algorithm. Details of the datasets, results, and performance discussion are given in Sect. 5. Section 6 concludes with further research directions.

1.1 Rare Itemset Mining

The current literature on mining is focused primarily on frequent itemsets only. But rare itemsets too find their place of high interest sometimes, especially in cases of biomedical databases. The above description applies to a vast range of mining situations where biomedical data are involved [3]. For instance, in pharmacovigilance, one is interested in associating the drugs taken by patients to the adverse effects the latter may present as a result (*safety signals or drug interactions in the technical language of the field*). A nice motivation given by Szathmary et al. is given below [4]. Given a database of drug effects on patients, rare itemset mining helps us in decoding the adverse effects of drugs on patients which may be rare but drastic. Mining on such data for frequent itemsets provides us with associations such as "{drug} ∪ {A}," where {A} is an itemset describing a kind of desirable effect. These frequent associations mean that a drug is working in the expected right way, whereas in case if it is a rare association, it represents an effect of drug which is abnormal, possibly undesirable. Discovering rare itemsets and rare association rules deriving from rare itemsets is particularly useful in the field of biology and medicine. Rare events deserve special attention because they have their own importance in a database full of hidden knowledge. In these examples, there lies the motivation of extracting the hidden rare itemsets within a database.

An itemset $X \subseteq \{x_1, \ldots, x_n\}$ is a rare itemset (RI) if $0 < \text{support}(X) \leq$ maximum support(*max supp*). An itemset X is non-present itemset (NPIs) if support $(X) = 0$. Moreover, all rare itemsets are infrequent but not all infrequent itemsets (IFI) are rare, i.e., $RI \subseteq IFI$. *min supp* differentiates between frequent itemsets (FIs) and infrequent itemsets(IFIs). So, *max supp* used for finding RIs will be less than *min supp* used for finding FIs, in fact $0 < max supp < max supp$. If *max supp* = 0, set of RIs will be $\emptyset$ and if *max supp* = *min supp* − 1, then RI = IFI. If we take a relatively higher value for *max supp*, then the cardinality of RIs will be more compared to smaller value of *max supp*. Mining all possible rare itemsets is termed as rare itemset mining.

If X is a RI, then $X' \supseteq X \in \{RI, NPI\}$ and the subsets of X may or may not be RI. For example, if $X = \{a, b, c\}$ is an RI with a support of 1 and $\{a, b, c, d\}$ is present in the database, then $\{a, b, c, e\}$ is not present in the database. So it is evident that $\{a, b, c, d\} \supset X$ and is a RI and its support will also be 1, and $\{a, b, c, e\} \supset X$ is not present in database, so its support will be 0. $\{a, b\}$ is a subset of X, but it may or may not be a RI, i.e., support($\{a, b\}$) ≥ support(X). The proposed work employs efficient strategies to mine rare itemsets in a time-efficient manner using RELIM algorithm, designed for FIM by Borgelt et al. [5]. The paper focuses on exhaustive listing of all the RIs present in the database subject to a value of *max supp*.

2 Related Work

The scarce literature on the subject of rare itemset mining exclusively adapts the general levelwise framework of pattern mining around the seminal Apriori algorithm to various forms of the frequent pattern algorithms like FP-growth, ECLAT, H-mine, Counting Inference, RELIM [2, 5–8]. A detailed survey of seminal

FP-based algorithms can be seen in [9]. These methods provide with a large itemset search space and associations, which are not frequent. But these associations will be incomplete either due to restrictive definitions or high computational cost. Hence, as argued by [10], these methods will not be able to collect a huge number of potentially interesting rare patterns. As a remedy, we put forward a novel and simple approach toward efficient and complete extraction of RIs. Mining for RIs has received enhanced focus of researchers, and in the recent past, few algorithms have been proposed.

Apriori-inverse algorithm by Y. S. Koh et al. uses the basic Apriori approach for mining sporadic rules (rules having itemsets with low support value and high confidence) [11]. This algorithm was the seminal work for RI mining. Laszlo Szathmary et al. proposed two algorithms, namely MRG-Exp, which finds minimal rare itemsets (mRIs) with a naive Apriori approach and a rare itemset miner algorithm (ARIMA) which retrieves all RIs from mRIs [3]. Rarity algorithm by Luigi Troiano et al. implements a variant Apriori strategy [12]. It first identifies the longest rare itemsets on the top of the power set lattice and moves downward the lattice pruning frequent itemsets and tracks only those that are confirmed to be rare. Laszlo Szathmary et al. have proposed Walky-G algorithm which finds mRIs using a vertical mining approach [3]. The major limitation of the existing algorithms is that they work with the assumption that all itemsets having support <*min supp* form the set of RIs. This notion states that all IFIs are RIs, while this is not the case. All IFIs may or may not be RIs, but all RIs are IFIs. RIs are those IFIs which are relatively rare.

The other limitation with the present algorithms is that they propose to find mRIs only; none of the algorithms except ARIMA and take into consideration the exhaustive generation of set of RIs. As these algorithms use Apriori levelwise approach, so generating the exhaustive set of RIs would be a very space and time expensive approach as is evident from the paper by Luigi Troiano et al., in which the authors took subsets of the benchmark datasets to analyze results of ARIMA and rarity algorithms [12]. Since the number of RIs produced is very large, the memory usage and execution time are high for such exhaustive RI generation. The proposed algorithm overcomes the repeated scan limitation of Apriori-based approaches based on the recursive elimination (RELIM) algorithm.

3 Proposed Rare Itemset Mining Algorithm

We introduce the RELIM algorithm for exhaustive generation of rare itemsets from given database. Like RELIM for frequent itemsets, this algorithm follows the same representation for transactions. In the first scan of the database, the frequencies of each unique item present in each transaction of database are calculated. The items are sorted in ascending order according to their frequencies. Items having same frequencies can be in any order. The relim prefix list for each item is initialized with their support value taken to be 0 and suffix-set list to $\emptyset$. The next step is to reorder the items in each transaction according to the ascending order got in the previous step. This step takes one more pass over the database. After sorting the transaction, $P = \text{prefix}[T']$; i.e., first item of the transaction is taken as the prefix for the sorted transaction T and the remaining items are taken as suffix-set for the transaction. Then the, suffix-set to suffix-set list of prefix P is inserted in relim prefix list for each transaction.

After populating the relim prefix list with all of the sorted transactions, iteration through the relim prefix list in the order of ascending order of frequencies of each unique item found in step 1 is done. For each prefix P in relim prefix list, and for each suffix-set $S(i)$ in the suffix-set list S of P, generate all of the possible subsets except empty set and store the subsets prefixed with P in a hashmap along with its support value. If a generated subset already exists in hashmap, its associated value is incremented. Now let $P' = \text{suffix-set}(S(i))$ is the prefix item of the suffix-set $S(i)$. The suffix-set from the suffix-set list of prefix P is removed. Let $S(i) = \text{suffix-set}(S(i))$. $S(i)$ to prefix P is added in the relim prefix list, and its corresponding support is incremented by 1. Once iteration through the suffix-set list of prefix P is over, all the candidate rare itemsets in a hashmap are obtained and on pruning the hashmap, and the rare itemsets prefixed with P are generated. Subset generation is done based on an iterative approach, and a hashmap data structure is used in the process of pruning itemsets to optimize on implementation.

3.1 Illustration

After scanning database and counting frequencies of unique items, seven unique items in sorted order remain, as shown in Fig. 1. Then, a prefix list of seven items is generated with initial support of 0. Now in next pass, the transactions in the order of frequencies of prefixes are sorted, and for each sorted transaction T and its prefix, suffix-set[T] is inserted into the suffix-set list of prefix[T] in the relim prefix list. In this case, the first transaction $\{a, d, f\}$ is converted to $\{f, a, d\}$ and $\{a, d\}$ being the suffix-set of the transaction is stored in suffix-set list of prefix f. The relim prefix list is populated with all the transactions and the recursive.

Algorithm 1 RELIM-based RI *Efficient Pruning-based RELIM based-Mining of Rare Patterns.*

Input: *D, max supp*
Output: RI's with support $\leq$ *max supp*.
Method:
Scan *D* once and retrieve all frequent 1-length itemsets in *Fi* .
Sort *Fi* in ascending order to get *F'* .

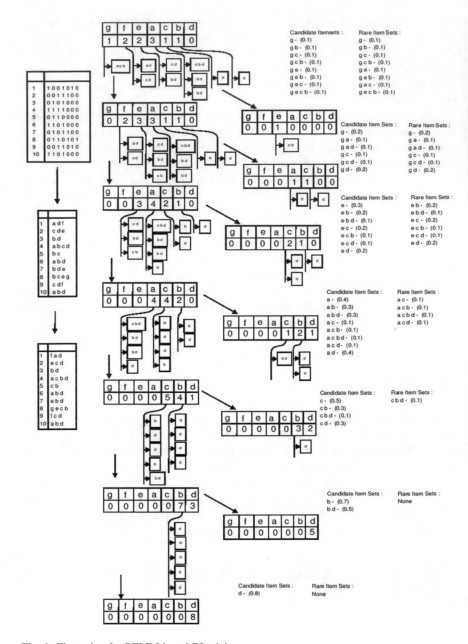

Fig. 1 Illustration for RELIM-based RI mining

```
for f ∈ F' do
    P ← prefix(f); P.support ← 0
    P.suffixsetlist
```

```
end for
call sort transaction and addto prefixlist();
for each prefix P ∈ P REFI X LI ST do
  candidate [P ] ← P .support
   for each suffixset.SS ∈ P .suffixsetlist do
    call calc support candidate subsets(SS, P);
    P' ← prefix(SS)
    P .suffixsetlist ← P .suffixsetlist – SS
    P .support–; SS' ← suffix(SS)
    if SS' = ∅ then
       P' .suffixsetlist ← P .suffixsetlist ∪ SS'
       P'.support ++;
    end if
  end for
end for
Rp ← prune candidatelist() //Set of RI's with prefix P
end for
```

Procedure *sort transaction and add to prefixlist(): Find the sorted transaction and add it to the prefix list*

```
Method:
for each transaction T ∈ D do
   T' ← ∅
   for each item I ∈ F' do
     if (I ∈ T) then
        T' ← ∪I
     end if
   end for
   P' ← prefix (T'); SS' ← suffix(T')
   P .suffixlist ← P .suffixsetlist ∪ SS'
   P .support ++;
end for
```

Elimination of each prefix is carried out. The first prefix is g with support (number of suffix-sets in the suffix-set list) of 1 and the only suffix-set being $\{e, c, b\}$. Now all possible subsets of this suffix-set are generated except empty set which are $\{b\}$, $\{c\}$, $\{e\}$, $\{e, b\}$, $\{e, c\}$, $\{b, c\}$, $\{e, c, b\}$, and their supports are calculated and are inserted in the candidate list. Candidate list is pruned, and RIs are retained. In this case, all the subsets generated of prefix g are rare.

After generating RIs, an extension for prefix g is created and all the suffix-sets of g as transactions are listed, and the same is inserted into extended relim prefix list for prefix g. The only suffix-set of g is $\{e, c, b\}$.

Procedure *calc support candidate subsets(SS, P)*: Find the support of candidate subsets

```
Method:
sub ← ∅
sub ← generate subsets(SS); //
Generate subsets of all items in suffixset and add it to a set of subsets
                              sub.
for each set S ∈ sub do
  Candidate[P ∪ S] ++;
end for
```

Procedure *prune candlist( )*: *prune the candidate list of rare itemsets*

```
Method:
R ← ∅
m ← count of RI's
for i ← 0 to candidate.end do
  if value [candidate.at(i)] ≤ max supp * # transactions then
      m + + ; R ← R ∪ candidate.at(i)
  end if
end for
Return R
```

So prefix[$\{e, c, b\}$] = e, and suffix-set[$\{e, c, b\}$] is $\{c, b\}$. Hence, suffix-set $\{c, b\}$ is added to prefix e suffix-set list, and support for e is incremented to 1 in the extended relim prefix list for prefix g. After populating this extended relim prefix list, the suffix-sets in the extended prefix list are added to the corresponding relim prefix list and the support values are added from the extended prefix list to the relim prefix list. So $\{c, b\}$ is added to the suffix-set list of e, and support for e is incremented. This process happens for every prefix in the main relim prefix list.

4 Proof of Correctness

Lemma 1 *The ascending order sorting of transactions leads to the generation of RIs with prefix tp collectively.*

Proof After sorting transactions in an ascending order of frequencies of unique itemsets, we ensure in relim data structure that all transactions with prefix P are in the suffix-set list of P. So generating all subsets of each suffix-set of P will generate candidate itemsets with prefix P only and the sorting ensure that P will not be a part of any suffix-sets of subsequent prefixes.

Lemma 2 *Let $X \subseteq \{x_1, \ldots, x_n\}$ is a rare itemset, then $X' \supseteq X$ is also a rare itemset or a non-present, where $X' \subseteq \{x_1, \ldots, x_n\}$.*

Proof If support $(X) = s$ and Y superset of X, then support $(y) \leq s$. The range for support (y) is $0 \leq$ support$(y) \leq s$. So either superset of RI is rare or its support is 0 and is non-present. This is the monotonicity property of Apriori lattice.

5 Simulation Results and Discussion

Simulation experiments are performed on an Intel Core i5-3230 M CPU 2.26 GHz with 4 GB main memory and 500 GB hard disk on Ubuntu 13.04 OS Platform and are implemented using C++ 11 standard. The standard frequent itemset mining (FIMI) dataset is taken for simulation [13]. Results presented in this section are over Mushroom dataset which contains 8124 transactions with varying number of items per transaction (maximum 119). The detailed results are tabulated in Table 1. In the simulation for this algorithm, various combinations of number of items per transactions and number of transactions of mushroom data set were used and the portion of data used from mushroom dataset was truncated using the first item and first transaction as pivot. There is a general trend, which we see that as we increase the dimension of the portion we use for getting RIs out of the mushroom dataset, the time taken to mine the RI increases.

Figure 2 highlights the comparison of natural logarithm of time taken to mine RIs with varying number of items per transaction by keeping number of transactions constant with RareRELIM and rarity algorithm approach. It can be clearly seen that time taken to mine RIs increases when we increase items per transaction keeping number of transactions constant. This is because of the fact that a larger data set leads to more candidate item sets and hence more time taken to prune RI's from candidate sets. For example, for 60 items per transaction, log(time taken) increases from 39.64 to 227.81 as we increase number of transaction from 1000 to 8124 for our approach.

Figure 3 showcases the comparison of natural logarithm of time taken to mine RIs with varying number of items per transaction by keeping number of transactions constant with RareRELIM and rarity algorithm approach. It can be clearly

Table 1 Detailed results for mushroom dataset for various *max supp*

max_supp (%)	Time taken_RELIM-based RI (s)	Time taken_Rarity (s)	# Candidate RI	# RI
#Items per transaction: 40 and no. of transactions: 5000				
20	7.02	9.5472	23,549	23,286
10	6.957	9.46152	23,549	22,578
5	6.91	9.3976	23,549	20,382
2.5	6.864	9.33504	23,549	17,128
1	6.848	9.31328	23,549	14,162
#Items per transaction: 40 and no. of transactions: 8124				
20	27.699	38.22462	785,887	785,847
10	27.409	37.82442	785,887	785,847
5	27.393	37.80234	785,887	785,575
2.5	30.701	42.36738	785,887	785,073
1	31.87	43.9806	785,887	781,829
#Items per transaction: 50 and no. of transactions: 5000				
20	17.004	23.46552	101,283	101,016
10	17.05	23.529	101,283	100,176
5	17.035	23.5083	101,283	97,258
2.5	19.422	26.80236	101,283	90,828
1	16.77	23.1426	101,283	78,158
#Items per transaction: 50 and no. of transactions: 8124				
20	28.938	40.80258	138,079	137,875
10	27.627	38.95407	138,079	137,109
5	28.065	39.57165	138,079	134,891
2.5	29.031	40.93371	138,079	128,895
1	28.314	39.92274	138,079	113,663
#Items per transaction: 60 and no. of transactions: 5000				
20	150.4	212.064	851,839	850,662
10	147.108	207.42228	851,839	845,550
5	147.862	208.48542	851,839	826,958
2.5	147.489	207.95949	851,839	782,490
1	145.018	204.47538	851,839	692,178
#Items per transaction: 60 and no. of transactions: 8124				
20	228.072	328.423.68	1,203,575	1,202,659
10	227.807	328.04208	1,203,575	1,198,659
5	232.191	334.35504	1,203,575	1,185,813
2.5	230.1	331.344	1,203,575	1,148,930
1	227.854	328.10976	1,203,575	1,050,463

seen that in this case also, time taken to mine RIs increases when we increase number of transactions keeping items per transaction constant because of the same reason that as data set increases, more candidates are generated and hence more

Fig. 2 Number of items per transaction versus log time taken for mushroom

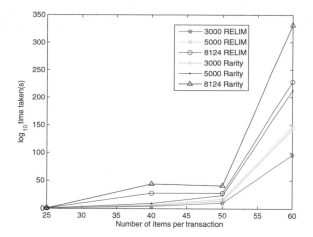

Fig. 3 Number of transactions versus log time taken for mushroom

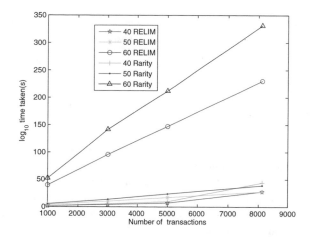

time is taken to prune RIs. For example, for 8124 transactions, log(time taken) increases from 0.7 to 230.1 as we increase number of items per transaction from 25 to 60 for our approach. But in general, RareRELIM algorithm takes less time than rarity algorithm because rarity approach takes into consideration candidate set and veto list, and it generates both of them and uses both of them to classify an itemset as rare or not. It takes more time to generate both candidate itemsets and veto lists.

Figure 4 highlights the comparison of number of RIs with varying support for a fixed portion of mushroom data set, i.e., 60/8124 (items per transaction/number of transactions). We see a general rise in trend of the graph because of the reason that, as we keep on increasing the maximum support value used to filter out the RIs from the database, the rarity of an itemset tends to increase and itemsets tend to be less frequent. As can be seen from the graph, as we increase *max supp* value from 1 to

Fig. 4 Maximum support versus number of rare itemsets for mushroom dataset

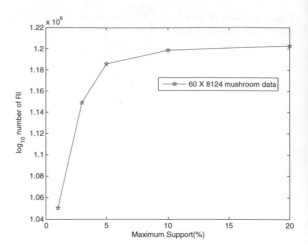

20%, the value of $\log_{10}$ #RIs increases from 1,050,463 to 1,202,659, an increase of 14%, leading to the conclusion that we got more number of RIs at higher *max supp* value.

6 Conclusion

The paper has presented a novel approach to mine rare itemsets, employing RELIM strategy. Efficient pruning strategies along with a simple data structure have been employed, and results indicate the significant decline in time taken to mine the rare itemsets. Future work shall focus on reducing the storage space taken for generating the RIs. Moreover, efforts shall be put in using the mined rare itemsets in other data mining strategies.

References

1. Han, J., Kamber, M.: Data Mining: Concepts and Techniques. Morgan Kaufmann, Los Altos (2000)
2. Agarwal, R., Srikant, R.: Fast algorithms for mining association rules in large databases. In: Bocca, J.B., Jarke, M., Zaniolo, C. (eds.) VLDB'94, Proceedings of 20th International Conference on Very Large Data Bases, pp. 487–499. 12–15 September 1994, Morgan Kaufmann, Santiago de Chile, Chile (1994)
3. Szathmary, L., Valtchev, P., Napoli, A., Godin, R.: Efficient vertical mining of minimal rare itemsets. In: CLA, pp. 269–280. Citeseer (2012)
4. Szathmary, L., Napoli, A., Valtchev, P.: Towards rare itemset mining. In: 19th IEEE International Conference on Tools with Artificial Intelligence, 2007, ICTAI 2007, vol. 1, pp. 305–312. IEEE (2007)

5. Borgelt, C.: Keeping things simple: finding frequent item sets by recursive elimination. In: Proceedings of the 1st International Workshop on Open Source Data Mining: Frequent Pattern Mining Implementations, pp. 66–70. ACM (2005)
6. Han, J., Pei, J., Yin, Y., Mao, R.: Mining frequent patterns without candidate generation: a frequent-pattern tree approach. Data Min. Knowl. Discov. **8**(1), 53–87 (2004)
7. Goethals, B.: Survey on frequent pattern mining (2003)
8. Bastide, Y., Taouil, R., Pasquier, N., Stumme, G., Lakhal, L.: Mining frequent patterns with counting inference. ACM SIGKDD Explor. Newsl **2**(2), 66–75 (2000)
9. Han, J., Cheng, H., Xin, D., Yan, X.: Frequent pattern mining: current status and future directions. Data Min. Knowl. Disc. **15**(1), 55–86 (2007)
10. Weiss, G.M.: Mining with rarity: a unifying framework. ACM SIGKDD Explor. Newsl **6**(1), 7–19 (2004)
11. Koh, Y.S., Rountree, N.: Finding sporadic rules using apriori-inverse. In: Advances in Knowledge Discovery and Data Mining, pp. 97–106. Springer (2005)
12. Troiano, L., Scibelli, G., Birtolo, C.: A fast algorithm for mining rare itemsets. In: 2009 Ninth International Conference on Intelligent Systems Design and Applications, pp. 1149–1155. IEEE (2009)
13. Dataset, F.: Frequent itemset mining implementation (fimi) dataset

Computation of Various Entropy Measures for Anticipating Bugs in Open-Source Software

H. D. Arora and Talat Parveen

Abstract Bugs could be introduced at any phase of software development process. Bugs are recorded in repositories, which occur due to frequent changes in source code of software to meet the requirements of organizations or users. Open-source software is frequently updated and source codes are changed continuously due to which source code becomes complicated and hence bugs appear frequently. Bug repair process includes addition of new feature, enhancement of existing feature, some faults or other maintenance task. Entropy measures the uncertainty, thus helpful in studying code change process. In this paper, bugs reported in various subcomponents of Bugzilla open-source software are considered; changes are quantified in terms of entropies using Renyi, Havrda–Charvat, and Arimoto entropy measures of each component for all changes in components. A linear regression model using SPSS is applied to detect the expected bugs in the Bugzilla subcomponents. Performance has been measured using goodness-of-fit curve and other R-square residuals.

Keywords Entropy measure · Bug detection · Bugzilla · Open-source software

1 Introduction

Software goes under regular maintenance and updation with introduction of new features, enhancement of existing features, and bug repair. Software use and dependency has increased over a time it required almost everywhere in current time. Ever-increasing user demand leads to tremendous changes in software, making it complex over time. The process of maintenance is crucial phase in software

H. D. Arora (✉) · T. Parveen
Department of Applied Mathematics, Amity Institute of Applied Sciences,
Amity University, Sector-125, Noida, Uttar Pradesh, India
e-mail: hdarora@amity.edu

T. Parveen
e-mail: talat.tyagi@gmail.com

© Springer Nature Singapore Pte Ltd. 2019   235
M. N. Hoda et al. (eds.), *Software Engineering*, Advances in Intelligent Systems
and Computing 731, https://doi.org/10.1007/978-981-10-8848-3_23

development cycle. When software undergoes maintenance, main changes occurred in source code are due to the introduction of new features, bug repair, and feature enhancement. It is necessary to record to all the changes in source code in a repository to access it in future for further study and understanding of code change process. Frequent source code change makes it complex and thus faulty and sometimes causes a failure. Software reliability and quality are affected by bugs lying dormant or introduced at any phase in the software development cycle. Bugs are introduced in the system by increased complexity of source code, advanced release pressure, no communication, or miscommunication among active developers and bugs introduced during software development process. Bugzilla [1] is most widely used bug-tracking system. It is the most commonly used bug reporting system which assists in bug-fix process. It was released by 'Netscape Communications' in 1998. Entropy is an important concept of information theory which is defined as the measure of randomness/uncertainty/complexity of code change. It tells us how much information is present in an event.

In this paper, we have developed an approach for predicting bugs in an open-source software system using entropy measures. We have applied the simple linear regression for predicting future bugs using entropy changes calculated using bug-tracking data from Bugzilla [1]. We have predicted the bugs using three different generalizations of Shannon's entropy [2], namely Renyi [3], Havrda–Charvat [4], and Arimoto [5]. Further, we analysed our results with the R-square measure calculated for each entropy measure. To do this work, we have taken our data from the Bugzilla bug-tracking system and we considered the bug report in the Bugzilla subsystem, arranged the data on yearly basis, and then applied simple linear regression using SPSS. This paper is organized as follows:

2 Literature Review

Hassan [6] applied information theoretic approach of measuring the amount of entropy as a measure of complexity of code change in a system, and he proposed to quantify the code change process in terms of entropy. Six open-source software systems FreeBSD, NetBSD, OpenBSD, KDE, KOffice, and PostgreSQL were considered for evaluating entropy-based metrics. Entropy-based measures proved to be better in prediction than the methods using number of changes and previous bugs. Singh et al. [7] used Hassan's [6] approach and applied entropy-based metrics to predict the bugs using simple linear regression (SLR) and support vector regression (SVR). Nagappan et al. [8] studied the effect of number of modified lines on the defect density in windows vista. It is concluded that code churn is better predictor than absolute churn. Ihara et al. [9] proposed bug prediction model which studies base and state metrics using the eclipse project gives improved performance than standard model. Maszczyk et al. [10], Shannon entropy in standard top-down decision trees, and Tsallis and Renyi entropies for modified C4.5 decision trees are compared for several data sets. They presented that this approach may be used in any decision tree and information selection algorithm. Menzies et al. [11] used NASA Metrics Data Program (MDP) for his study and concluded that learning algorithm used is more relevant than static source code metric. The effect of using metrics such as McCabe, LOC, and Halstead is compared with algorithms such as J48, OneR, and Naïve Bayes. Chaturvedi et al. [12] proposed a method of predicting the potential complexity of code changes in subcomponents of Bugzilla project using bass model. This approach helps in predicting the source code changes yet to be diffused in a system. D'Ambros et al. [13] have done extensive bug prediction along with releasing data set on their website consisting of many software systems. They have set a benchmark by comparing the approach developed by them with the performance of several existing bug prediction approaches. Giger et al. [14] introduced in a bug prediction a metric with number of modified lines using fine-grained source code changes (SCCs). Shihab et al. [15] proposed a statistical regression model to study the eclipse open-source software. This approach can predict post-release defects using the number of defects in previous version, and the proposed model is better over existing PCA-based models.

3 Information Theoretic Approach

Information theory has become a keyword in current era which is characterized by a quantitative approach to the notion of information. It is collection of statistics- and probability-based mathematical theories. Information theory is a probabilistic approach dealing with assessing and defining the amount of information contained in a message. The concept of entropy in information theory was developed by Shannon [16]. A measure of entropy known as Shannon's entropy was defined in Shannon [16]; in his research paper entitled 'A mathematical theory of communication', Shannon [16] proposed and investigated a mathematical model for communication system. He suggested a quantitative measure of average amount of information supplied by a probabilistic experiment. A systematic attempt to develop a generalization of Shannon [2] entropy was carried out by Renyi [2] who characterized a nonnegative and additive entropy of order α defined as follows:

$$H_\alpha(P) = \frac{1}{1-\alpha} \log \left(\sum_{i=1}^{n} p_i^\alpha \right) \tag{1}$$

where $\alpha \neq 1, \alpha > 0, P_i \geq 0, \sum_{i=1}^{n} P_i = 1$, α is a real parameter, n is the number of files, and value of n varies from 1 to n. P_i is the probability of change in a file, and the entropy is maximum when all files have same probability change, i.e. when $p_i = \frac{1}{n}, \forall i \in 1, 2, \ldots n$. The entropy would be minimum when element k has probability say, $P_i = 1$ and $\forall i \neq k, P_i = 0$. Havrda and Charvat [4] gave the first non-additive measure of entropy called structural β-entropy. This quantity permits simpler axiomatic characterizations too. It reduced to Shannon [16] when $\beta \to 1$. It lacks the additive property but satisfies the sum property and generalized recursive property.

$$H_\beta(P) = \left(2^{1-\beta} - 1\right)^{-1} \left[\sum_{k=1}^{n} p_k^\beta - 1\right] \tag{2}$$

where $\beta \neq 1, \beta > 0$—β is a real parameter.

Arimoto [5] defined generalized parametric entropy referred as γ-entropy. It is neither additive, nor satisfies recursive or sum property.

$$H_\gamma(P) = \left(2^{\gamma-1} - 1\right)^{-1} \left[\left(\sum_{k=1}^{n} p_k^{\frac{1}{\gamma}}\right)^\gamma - 1\right] \tag{3}$$

where $\gamma \neq 1, \gamma > 0$—$\gamma$ is a real parameter. Many generalizations of Shannon's entropy [2] had been developed so far by researchers such as Renyi [3], Aczel and Daroczy [17], Havrada and Charvat [4], Kapur [18], Arimoto [5], Sharma and Taneja [19], and Tsallis [2]. We have limited ourselves to three generalization of Shannon's entropy measure for our study which are Renyi [3], Havrda and Charvat [4], and Arimoto [5] entropy measure.

4 Basic Model for Entropy Measurement

In open-source software, source code changes frequently with the increasing demand of new feature addition and bug repair process. Changes are recorded in a repository, and complexity of source code increases with code change process. Shannon's entropy is used for studying code change process. Probability changes for a specific file are calculated, and thus, entropy is calculated. Time period could be considered in terms of year, half year, month, or a week [6].

For example, in a system let 14 changes be occurred in three different files over a different time period. If File1 has two changes, File2 and File3 have one change in time t_1. Table 1 represents the total changes in each file for respective time period t_1, t_2, and t_3. For time period t_1, total files in $t_1 = 4$. Thus, probability of File1 for

Table 1 Changes in File1, File2, and File3 with respect to time period t_1, t_2, and t_3

File1	✿	✿		✿	✿		✿
File2		✿			✿		✿
File3		✿		✿	✿	✿	✿	✿
		t_1			t_2		t_3

$t_1 = 2/5 = 0.4$, probability of File2 for $t_1 = 1/5 = 0.2$, and probability of File3 for $t_1 = 1/5 = 0.2$. Similarly, probabilities for time periods t_2 and t_3 could be calculated. Using the probabilities found by above-mentioned method, entropies for all time periods could be calculated. In this study, Renyi [3], Havrda–Charvat [4], and Arimoto [5] entropies are calculated using Eqs. (1)–(3). When there would be changes in all files, then the entropy would be maximum, while it would be minimum for most changes occurring in a single file.

5 Data Collection and Preprocessing

Bugzilla renders bug-tracking service to large number of organizations and projects. It is open-source software. Apache Project, Code Magus, Eclipse, GCC, KDE, NetBeans, Red Hat, W3C, and many other organization use public Bugzilla installation. In this paper, components from the Mozilla subsystem are selected. Bugzilla [1] is a bug-tracking system, and bug reports of few subcomponents are considered for the study. Bugs are extracted from the CVS repository: http://bugzilla.mozilla.org. We have considered subcomponents of Bugzilla project for our study. Data extracted is arranged considering changes in files of subsystem on yearly basis. In this paper, a fixed period as one year is taken from 2007 to July 2015. The number of files in each of these subsystems varied in the range of 21–157 files. Following subcomponents are selected, and a number of files in each component [1] are mentioned along with them (Table 2):

The data is available in the repository, and the data is collected from the repository and processed using following steps:

Step1   Select the project
Step2   Select the subsystem
Step3   Browse Bugzilla repository for tracking the bug reports
Step4   Collect the reported bug data from the repository for selected subcomponents
Step5   Arrange the data year-wise and calculate entropy using Eqs. (1)–(3)
Step6   Apply simple linear regression model with bugs $m(t)$ observed as dependent and entropy $H(t)$ calculated as independent variables.
Step7   Predict the future bugs using regression coefficients
Step8   Performance of the model is assessed through R^2 and other statistical performance measure

All changes in the subcomponents have been extracted by browsing the concurrent version repository of Bugzilla. Simple linear regression model is fitted for predicting the future bugs using the entropy measure of the historical changes.

Table 2 Bugzilla components and changes in files

XSLT	Reporter	XForms	General	Telemetry Dashboard	Verbatim	Geolocation	MFBT	MathML	X-Remote	Widget Android	XBL
131	27	87	19	31	57	66	126	91	21	58	157

6 Calculation of Arimoto, Havrda–Charvat, and Renyi Entropy

In this paper, subcomponents of Bugzilla software are considered and entropy variation in the system over a period of time ranging from 2007 to 2015 based on number of bugs calculated is studied Renyi [3]. Havrda–Charvat [4], and Arimoto [5] entropies are calculated based on data extracted for different subcomponents for α, β, γ ranging from 0.1 to 0.9, respectively. After collecting data for time period varying from 2007 to 2015 for different files as discussed above, Renyi, Havrda–Charvat, and Arimoto entropies are calculated using the calculated probabilities as depicted in Eqs. (1)–(3), respectively, following the method as described in Sect. 4. For Renyi, Havrda–Charvat, and Arimoto α, β, and γ are ranging from 0.1 to 0.9, respectively, as by the definition of these entropy measures the value parameter in Eq. (1)–(3) must be greater than 0 and not equal to 1.

Figures 1, 2 and 3 depict the entropy change in various subsystems over the time period ranging from 2007 to 2015 calculated using Renyi, Havrda–Charvat, and Arimoto entropy measures, respectively. Renyi, Havrda–Charvat, and Arimoto entropy decrease as we increase the value of α, β, γ from 0.1 to 0.9.

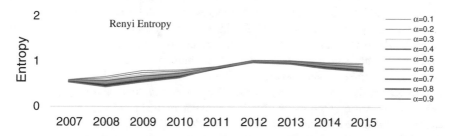

Fig. 1 Renyi entropy for α ranging from 0.1 to 0.9

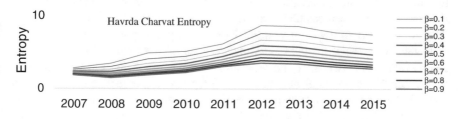

Fig. 2 Havrda–Charvat entropy for β ranging from 0.1 to 0.9

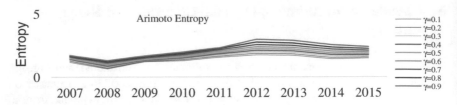

Fig. 3 Arimoto entropy for γ ranging from 0.1 to 0.9

7 Analysis and Bug Prediction Approach

The simple linear regression [19] is a statistical approach which enables predicting the dependent variable on the basis of independent variable which has been used to fit the entropy measure as independent variable $H(t)$ and bugs observed as dependent variable $m(t)$ using Eq. (4)

$$m(t) = \sigma_0 + \sigma_1 * H(t) \tag{4}$$

where σ_0 and σ_1 are regression coefficients. Once getting the regression coefficients σ_0 and σ_1 value, we predict the future bugs by putting the value of regression coefficients in Eq. (4). The simple linear regression model is used to study the code change process [20]. SLR is fitted for independent variable $H(t)$ and dependent variable $m(t)$ using Eq. (4). Here, $m(t)$ represents the number of bugs recorded for specified in the Bugzilla [1] subcomponent, namely XSLT, Reporter, XForms, General, Telemetry Dashboard, Verbatim, Geolocation, MFBT, MathML, X-Remote, Widget Android, and XBL. The regression coefficients σ_0 and σ_1 are calculated by varying the value of α, β, γ parameters in Eqs. (1)–(3) taking entropy as independent variable and number of recorded bugs as dependent variable. We varied the value of α, β, γ from 0.1 to 0.9, respectively, for each entropy measure and studied the effect of different entropy measure on bug prediction technique [21]. The values of R, R^2, adjusted R^2 standard error of estimate, and regression coefficients for the entropy measures, namely Renyi [3], Havrda–Charvat [4], and Arimoto [5] have been calculated by varying the parameter value in each entropy measure from 0.1 to 0.9 from year 2007 to 2015 and illustrated in Table 3.

R value determines the correlation between set of observed and predicted data, and its value lies between -1 and 1. R^2 also known as coefficients of determination determines the closeness of data to the fitted regression line, and it lies between 0 and 1. R-square estimates the percentage of total variation about mean, and its value close to 1 explains that data fits the model appropriately. Adjusted R^2 represents the percentage of variation based only on the independent variables which are affecting the dependent variable. The results of the simple linear regression are represented in Table 3, the table represents the value of R, R^2, adjusted R^2, standard error of estimate, and regression coefficients. The value of parameter α in Renyi's entropy [11] measure in Eq. (1) is varied from 0.1 to 0.9, and entropy is calculated for the

Table 3 Statistics and regression coefficients

Model	Parameter	R	R^2	Adjusted R^2	Std. error of the estimate	Regression coefficients	
						σ_0	σ_1
Equation 1 (α)	0.1	0.996	0.993	0.992	26.50367	−65.497	114.985
	0.2	0.996	0.992	0.991	26.91679	−62.751	117.442
	0.3	0.996	0.992	0.991	27.49703	−59.943	119.870
	0.4	0.996	0.992	0.991	28.21549	−57.126	122.240
	0.5	0.996	0.991	0.99	29.03881	−54.346	124.528
	0.6	0.995	0.991	0.989	29.93830	−51.639	126.705
	0.7	0.995	0.99	0.989	30.90207	−49.015	128.734
	0.8	0.995	0.989	0.988	31.96744	−46.437	130.525
	0.9	0.994	0.988	0.987	33.43824	−43.611	131.648
Equation 2 (β)	0.1	0.995	0.991	0.989	30.09957	−8.091	15.512
	0.2	0.995	0.99	0.988	31.54890	−10.639	17.875
	0.3	0.994	0.989	0.987	32.63041	−13.668	20.392
	0.4	0.994	0.988	0.987	33.38173	−17.109	23.041
	0.5	0.994	0.988	0.986	33.85169	−20.884	25.800
	0.6	0.994	0.988	0.986	34.09773	−24.905	28.642
	0.7	0.994	0.988	0.986	34.18984	−29.076	31.535
	0.8	0.994	0.988	0.986	34.23875	−33.263	34.429
	0.9	0.994	0.988	0.986	34.61405	−37.092	37.174
Equation 3 (γ)	0.1	0.994	0.989	0.987	32.80168	−58.873	72.152
	0.2	0.994	0.989	0.987	33.00622	−59.372	67.935
	0.3	0.994	0.989	0.987	32.90916	−59.629	64.082
	0.4	0.994	0.989	0.987	32.66821	−59.262	60.425
	0.5	0.995	0.989	0.987	32.42818	−58.201	56.908
	0.6	0.995	0.989	0.988	32.24788	−56.447	53.514
	0.7	0.995	0.989	0.988	32.12785	−54.053	50.238
	0.8	0.995	0.989	0.988	32.01330	−51.131	47.099
	0.9	0.995	0.99	0.988	31.61755	−48.045	44.227

time period varying from year 2007 to 2015. The entropy calculated is used to predict the bugs using simple linear regression model in SPSS. The regression coefficients and hence the predicted value for the future bugs are evaluated. It is observed that as the value of α progresses from 0.1 to 0.9, a decline in the value of R^2 is observed, which reduces from 0.993 for $\alpha = 0.1$ to 0.998 for $\alpha = 0.9$. The value of parameter β in Havrda–Charvat [4]'s entropy measure in Eq. (2) is varied from 0.1 to 0.9 and entropy for the period varying from year 2007 to 2008 is calculated. Then, the regression coefficients evaluated through SLR are used to predict the bugs to be appeared in system. A decline in the value of R^2 is observed as the β progresses from 0.1 to 0.9. It is seen that for $\beta = 0.1$ the value of R^2 is 0.991, while following continuous degradation as β value increases at $\beta = 0.9$, the

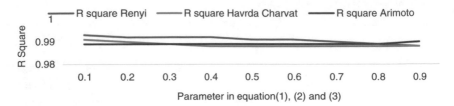

Fig. 4 Performance of simple linear regression model in bug prediction

R-square value is found to be 0.988. Similarly, for Arimoto [5] entropy in Eq. (3) similar to SLR approach is applied as is mentioned above, and hence, the regression coefficients are calculated. The predicted value is calculated, and hence, R^2 value is analysed. It is found that unlikely of Renyi [11] and Havrda–Charvat [4] entropy measure analysis with SLR in Arimoto [5] as we increased the value of γ from 0.1 to 0.9, the value of R^2 improved at $\gamma = 0.9$. The value of R^2 was similar for $\gamma = 0.1$ to 0.8, and it increased significantly at $\gamma = 0.9$.

A graph of R-square against the parameter value ranging from 0.1 to 0.9 in Eqs. (1)–(3) is plotted, and it is observed that the R-square value for the where R-square value for bugs predicted by Renyi [3] entropy measure is close to 1. It is observed that the simple linear regression approach predicts the future bugs with precision. The value of R-square indicates that the Renyi [3] entropy measure diffused in simple linear regression approach as independent variable provides the best predicted value of future bugs. While best R-square values for bugs predicted by Havrda–Charvat [4] and Arimoto [5] entropy are 99 and 99.1%, respectively. (Figure 4)

8 Result and Discussion

Goodness-of-fit curve has been plotted between observed and predicted values. Goodness of fit for simple linear regression depicts the fitting of the observed bug value with the predicted bug's value. Simple linear regression method significantly anticipates the future bugs using the number of bugs recorded from the subsystem of open-source software and entropy measure in Eqs. (1)–(3) by determining the regression coefficients. Figures 5, 6, and 7 represent this goodness-of-fit curve for each entropy measure considered for our study, i.e. Renyi [3], Havrda–Charvat [4],

Fig. 5 Goodness-of-fit curve for Renyi entropy

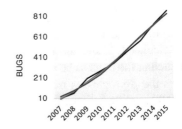

Fig. 6 Goodness-of-fit curve
for Havrda–Charvat entropy

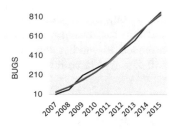

Fig. 7 Goodness-of-fit curve
for Arimoto entropy

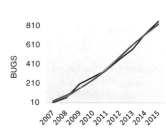

and Arimoto [5]. The predicted value is calculated, and hence, R-square value is analysed. It is found that in Renyi [3] and Havrda–Charvat [4] entropy measure analysis, the value of R-square degraded from 99.3 to 98.9 and 99.1 to 98.8% with the increase in value of parameter α and β from 0.1 to 0.9, respectively.

While in case of Arimoto [5] as we increased the value of γ from 0.1 to 0.9, the value of R-square improved at $\gamma = 0.9$ from 98.7 to 98.8%. The value of R-square was similar for $\gamma = 0.1$ to 0.8, i.e. shows 98.7% variability, and it increased significantly at $\gamma = 0.9$ to 98.8% variability.

9 Conclusion

Software is affected by code change process which leads to increased code complexity. Based on the data set statistics, Renyi [3], Havrda–Charvat [4], and Arimoto [5] entropies are calculated for different values of parameter α, β, and γ, respectively, ranging from 0.1 to 0.9 in Eq. (1)–(3) for 12 subcomponents of Mozilla open-source software (OSS). It is observed that Renyi [3], Havrda–Charvat [4], and Arimoto [5] entropies lie between 0.4 and 1, 1.8 and 9, 0.7 and 3, respectively. It could be analysed through Figs. 1, 2 and 3 that all entropy values decrease as we increase the value of α from 0.1 to 0.9. We have considered a bug prediction approach to predict the appearance of bugs in the OSS subsystem in coming years; hence, through comparative analysis of the R^2 value for each entropy measure, it is observed that Renyi [3] entropy measure provides the best R^2 value 99.3% for $\alpha = 0.1$. Goodness-of-fit curve has been plotted and represented in Figs. 1, 2, and 3. This study based on entropy measures is useful in learning the code change process in a system. In the future, entropy measures could be used to predict bug occurrence in the software and thus complexity of code changes that software has during a long maintenance period. In the future, our study could be extended to predict the potential complexity/entropy of code changes that the software will have during a long maintenance period.

References

1. The Bugzilla. http://bugzilla.mozilla.org
2. Tsallis, C.: Possible generalization of Bolzmann-Gibbs statistics. J. Stat. Phys. **52**, 479–487 (1988)
3. Renyi A.: On Measures of entropy and information. In: Proceedings of the Fourth Berkeley Symposium on Mathematical Statistics and Probability, pp. 547–561. University of California Press, Berkeley-Los Angeles (1961)
4. Havrada, J.H., Charvat, F.: Quantification method of classification process: concept of structural α -entropy. Kybernetika **3**, 30–35 (1967)
5. Arimoto, S.: Information-theoretical considerations on estimaton problems. Inf. Control **19**, 181–194 (1971)
6. Hassan A.E.: Predicting faults based on complexity of code change. In: The proceedings of 31st International Conference on Software Engineering, pp 78–88 (2009)
7. Singh, V.B., Chaturvedi, K.K.: Improving the quality of software by quantifying the code change metric and predicting the bugs. In: Murgante, B., et al. (eds.) ICCSA 2013, Part II, LNCS 7972, pp. 408–426. Springer, Berlin (2013)
8. Nagappan, N., Ball T.: Using software dependencies and churn metrics to predict field failures: an empirical case study. In: ESEM '07: Proceedings of the First International Symposium on Empirical Software Engineering and Measurement, pp. 364–373. Washington, DC, USA. IEEE Computer Society (2007)
9. Ihara, A., Kamei, Y., Monden, A., Ohira, M., Keung, J.W., Ubayashi, N., Matsumoto, K.: An investigation on software bug-fix prediction for open source software projects—a case study on the eclipse project. In: Software Engineering Conference (APSEC), 2012 19th Asia-Pacific, pp. 112–119. vol. 2 (2012)
10. Maszczk and Duch: Comparison of Shannon, Renyi and Tsallis entropy used in decision trees. Lect. Notes Comput. Sci. **5097**, 643–651 (2008)
11. Menzies, Tim, Greenwald, Jeremy, Frank, Art: Data mining static code attributes to learn defect predictors. IEEE Trans. Softw. Eng. **33**(1), 2–13 (2007)
12. Chaturvedi, K.K., Kapur, P.K., Anand, S.: Singh VB (2014) Predicting the complexity of code changes using entropy based measures. Int. J. Syst. Assur. Eng. Manag. **5**(2), 155–164 (2014)
13. D'Ambros M., Robbes R.: An extensive comparison of bug prediction approaches. In: MSR'10: Proceedings of the 7th International Working Conference on Mining Software Repositories, pp. 31–41 (2010)
14. Giger, E., Pinzger, M., Gall H.C.: Comparing fine-grained source code changes and code churn for bug prediction. In: Proceedings of the 8th Working Conference on Mining Software Repositories, pp. 83–92. MSR '11, New York, NY, USA. ACM (2011)
15. Shihab, E., Jiang, Z.M., Ibrahim, W.M., Adams, B., Hassan A.E.: Understanding the impact of code and process metrics on post-release defects: a case study on the eclipse project. In: ESEM '10: Proceedings of the 2010 ACM-IEEE International Symposium on Empirical Software Engineering and Measurement, pp. 1–10. New York, NY, USA. ACM (2010)
16. Shannon, C.E.: A mathematical theory of communication. Bell's Syst. Tech. J. **27**, 379–423 (1948)

17. Aczel, J., Daroczy, Z.: Charakterisierung Der Entrpien Positiver Ordung under Shannibscen Entropie; Acta Math. Acad. Sci. Hunger. **14**, 95–121 (1963)
18. Kapur, J.N.: Generalization entropy of order α and type β. Math. Semin. **4**, 78–84 (1967)
19. Weisberg, S.: Applied linear regression. Wiley, New York (1980)
20. Sharma, B.D., Taneja, I.J.: Three generalized additive measures of entropy. ETK **13**, 419–433 (1977)
21. IBM SPSS statistics for windows, Version 20.0. Armonk, NY: IBM Corp

Design of Cyber Warfare Testbed

Yogesh Chandra and Pallaw Kumar Mishra

Abstract Innovations doing fine in a predictable, controlled environment may be much less effective, dependable or manageable in a production environment, more so in cyber systems, where every day there is new technology in malware detection, zero-day vulnerabilities are coming up. Considering NCSP-2013, authors propose a realistic cyber warfare testbed using XenServer hypervisor, commodity servers and open-source tools. Testbed supports cyber-attack and defence scenarios, malware containment, exercise logs and analysis to develop tactics and strategies. Further, authors provide ways and means to train cyber warriors, honing their skills as well as maturing attack and defence technologies on this testbed.

Keywords Virtualization · Hypervisor · Metasploit · Malware
Container

1 Introduction

National Cyber Security Policy (NCSP) was announced in July 2013 with a mission to protect information and IT infrastructure in cyberspace, build capabilities to prevent and respond to cyber threats, reduce vulnerabilities and hence damage from cyber incidents through an arrangement of institutional structures, people, processes, technology and their collaboration. One of the objectives is to generate workforce of five lakhs cyber security professionals in coming five years through capacity building, skill development, training and use of open standards for cyber security [1]. National Institute of Standards and Technology (NIST) developed the framework for improving critical IT infrastructure cyber security in Feb 2014.

Y. Chandra (✉) · P. K. Mishra
Institute for Systems Studies and Analyses, Defence Research and Development
Organisation, Metcalfe House, Civil Lines, New Delhi, Delhi 110054, India
e-mail: yogeshchandra.drdo@gmail.com

P. K. Mishra
e-mail: pallaw.mishra@gmail.com

© Springer Nature Singapore Pte Ltd. 2019
M. N. Hoda et al. (eds.), *Software Engineering*, Advances in Intelligent Systems
and Computing 731, https://doi.org/10.1007/978-981-10-8848-3_24

While NCSP addresses the high-level perspective, the NIST framework helps organizations addressing actual cyber security risks.

The gap between threat and defence continues to expand as opponents use increasingly sophisticated attack technologies. Cyber Defense Technology Experimental Research (DETER) is an attempt to fill that gap by hosting an advanced testbed facility where top researchers and academicians conduct critical cyber security experiments and educational exercises. It emulates real-world complexity and scale essential to evolve advance solutions to help protect against sophisticated cyber-attacks and network design vulnerabilities [2] using Emulab software [3].

Cyber Exercise and Research Platform (KYPO) project aims to create an environment for R&D of new methods to protect critical IT infrastructure against cyber-attacks. A virtualized environment is used for emulation of complex cyber-attacks and analyse their behaviour and impact on the IT infrastructure [4]. Malware is a powerful, free and independent malware analysis service to the security community [5]. DARPA is setting up a virtual testbed named National Cyber Range to carry out virtual cyber warfare games for testing different scenarios and technologies in response to cyber-attacks.

2 Testbed Requirements

Cyber security experiments involve two or more contestants, due to the adversarial nature of the problem. Safe and isolated virtual network environment is needed to be attacked and penetrated as a means of learning and improving penetration testing skills. In conventional environment, investigator constructing the experiment is fully aware of both sides of the scenario and all components of the experiment are equally visible. This affects scenario realism and may foster experimental bias and may not be able to handle present-day attacks.

Testbed should support on-demand creation of experimental scenarios and advanced attack emulation. Scenarios generated are to be based on real-world exploitations. The requirements are network-related, hosts-related, monitoring, testbed control and deployment. The host monitoring set-up needs to get information about the node performance. It is to monitor processor and memory utilization, open connections, interface statistics and other characteristics of hosts.

3 Testbed Design

The testbed consists of four major systems, i.e. cluster of nodes and networks, attack system, defence system and data logger and report generation.

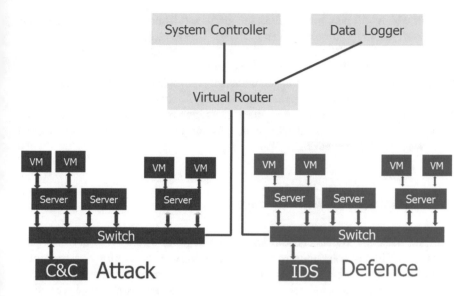

Fig. 1 Cyber warfare testbed

3.1 Design of Cluster

Testbed cluster comprises of many nodes in a laboratory connected using a programmable switch to construct any arbitrary topology. Some nodes may be used to emulate required link characteristics using network emulator (Netem).

Citrix XenServer serves the objective regarding setting up of underlying infrastructure for cyber warfare. Though the console is provided by XenCenter, but it is limited in use and functionality. More sophistication and high fidelity in creation of nodes and controlling them can be achieved through commercially available tools such as Cloudstack. Using these tools, a number of virtual nodes are created for both attack and defence system and testing them in requisite environment [6] (Fig. 1).

3.2 Composing Attack System

Based on the attacker objective, a number of sequences of attack in the form of attack graphs may be generated. Each attack graph will be evaluated based on the extent of objective achieved, time and resources used, the deception achieved and ease of launch. Though open-source software OpenVAS can be explored, authors have used Nessus framework for this and have found quite useful aid in generation of attack graph. The best attack sequence may be executed by the specifically built actuator which will pick next node in the graph and launch particular attack on the node. Individual attack tools such as LOIC for DDOS or hping for scanning can be utilized by starters. For the attack system, Metasploit Community Edition [7] in conjugation with Nmap and Wireshark may be used. Kali Linux (formerly Backtrack) by Offensive Security contains several tools aimed at numerous information security tasks, such as penetration testing, forensics and reverse engineering [8]. Using these tools, a number of attack techniques may be tried and matured on the cyber warfare testbed. Malware and malware generation tools can be sourced from Websites like vxheaven.org [9].

3.3 Composing Defence System

Intrusion detection systems (IDSs) and system logs may be used to detect several types of malicious behaviours that can compromise the security and trust of a computer system. This includes network attacks against vulnerable services, data-driven attacks on applications, host-based attacks such as privilege escalation, unauthorized logins and access to sensitive files, and malware (viruses, Trojan horses and worms). Provisions are given in IDS to configure rules according to the experiment. Authors used Snort for network-based intrusion detection and OSSEC for host-based intrusion detection. These will report various security-related system activities and logs to central console, e.g. insertion/removal of external media, changes in specified software. These alerts then can be correlated to have better awareness of cyber situation.

Formulation of proper response in case of such attack based on situation response technologies includes response recommenders that evaluate alternatives and recommend responses in light of the mission and response managers and actuators that implement the responses [10].

3.4 Data Logger and Report Generation

The data logger collects data in passive mode. There are no external linkages from the data logger during a live experiment. Interactive access is allowed to this only from report generation and post analyses modules. Depending on the experiment's risk rating, data collected by this module may have to be cleaned for malware before it can to be used by others.

Data logger retrieves information about the performance. Several tools are available under the various nomenclature, most popular being security information and event management (SIEM). Authors have used system information gatherer and reporter (SIGAR) for data logging and reporting. SIGAR API provides a portable code for collecting system information such as processor and memory utilization, open connections, interface statistics and other characteristics of hosts.

4 Operational Configuration

4.1 Scenarios

The testbed will facilitate a scenario-driven exercise designed to emulate expected player actions required to meet certain objectives. The exercise scenario may be built using adversaries with credible capabilities. The scenario will be built around a series of cyber-attack vectors that fall within the technical capabilities of the adversary (Fig. 2).

4.2 Attack Emulation

Bandwidth amplification attack, phishing, malware propagation and infection scenarios may be enacted to understand emerging mobile worms, viruses and other malware. Application layer DoS attacks such as Slowloris and Slow HTTP POST rely on the fact that the HTTP protocol requires requests to be completely received by the server before processing them. If an HTTP request is not complete, or if there is a very low transfer rate, the server keeps its resources busy waiting for the rest of the data. If the server keeps too many resources busy, this leads to denial of service. These attacks can easily be emulated in the proposed testbed using SlowHTTPTest tool. Malware containment may be achieved through virtualization, encryption and zone-based security segmentations (VLANs). Initially, malware analysis could be done in sandbox environment, before deploying it to the testbed.

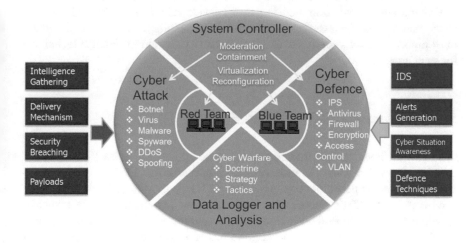

Fig. 2 Operational diagram

5   Analysis

A large number of exercises need to be conducted for various scenarios and their objectives to generate volume of data. This data are then analysed for specific objectives afterwards.

5.1   Identification of Measures of Effectiveness (MOEs)

Firstly, MOEs are identified, and the MOEs determine the attack strength, particular to a specific node on specific network configuration. MOEs for attack may be number of computers affected, data losses in terms of time and volume, target identification, number of targets engaged, number of attempts/mechanisms used to breach, targets missed, DOS induced in terms of time frame, number of routers attacked/compromised, number of antivirus/antimalware defeated, number of OS breached, number of Websites attacked, number of applications breached. Similarly, MOEs for defence may be time delay in detection of attack, value of asset before and after attack, data losses in terms of time and volume.

5.2   Vulnerability Analysis

Vulnerability analysis may be carried out using Common Vulnerability Scoring Scheme (CVSS). CVSS provides open framework for communicating the characteristics and severity of software vulnerabilities [11]. Authors have used this model to define slightly modified base, temporal and environmental metric groups.

Cyber security prediction models may be developed using history and nature of attack and models for assessment of system vulnerability, most probable attack, most probable target system, attack strength and evaluation of defence techniques for such attack [10].

5.3   Development of Strategy and Tactics

Statistical methods or data mining tools may be applied on data collected during exercises to evolve better defence techniques and attack-resilient network topologies. Added to it is behaviour analysis, which will help prevention against advanced persistent threat (APT), polymorphic malware, zero-day attacks, which otherwise are almost impossible to detect. It includes behaviour of both, malware as well as attacker. A good analysis of polymorphic malware from behavioural perspective has been carried out by Vinod et al. [12]. These analyses will help produce tactical rule book for senior IT managers and chief information security officers (CISOs).

6 Conclusion

The main tools of cyber defence are not the switches, routers or operating systems, but rather the cyber defenders themselves. The key benefits derived from the testbed would be enhancement of skills on cyber warfare, formulation of cyber warfare strategies and tactics, a training platform for the cyber warfare and analysis of vulnerability of the existing network system.

Innovations doing fine in a predictable and controlled environment may be less effective, dependable or manageable in a production environment. Without realistic, large-scale resources and research environments, results are unpredictable. The testbed as a mini-Internet emulates real-world complexity and scale.

The testbed can also host capture the flag (CTF) and attack–defence competitions, where every team has own network with vulnerable services. Every team has time for patching services and developing exploits. Each team protects own services for scoring defence points and hack opponents for scoring attack points. Exercise can take place on WAN and can be extended to multiple team configuration.

7 Future Scope

US military has indicated that it considers cyber-attack as an "Act of War" and will include cyber warfare for future conflicts engaging its Cyber Command. In future, a move from device-based to cloud-based botnets, hijacking distributed processing power may be witnessed. Highly distributed denial-of-service attacks using cloud processing may be launched. To counter such massive attacks, the testbed needs to be realized at much larger scale. Hence, the testbed also needs to be migrated to cloud platform [13]. Hybrid cloud solutions, e.g. OpenStack may be used as infrastructure-as-a-service (IaaS). Further efficiency may be achieved by harnessing operating system container technology. OS designed to run containers, such as Red Hat Atomic Host, Ubuntu Snappy, CoreOS and Windows Nano, can complement hypervisors, where containers (VMs without hypervisor) are lightweight virtual machines which are realized by OS kernel.

There is scope for simulating human behaviour related to cyber security using agent-based simulation toolkit. It will support for agent modelling of human security behaviour to capture perceived differences from standard decision making.

References

1. National Cyber Security Policy (NCSP-2013). http://deity.gov.in/content/national-cyber-security-policy-2013-1
2. The DETER Project. http://deter-project.org/
3. Emulab Software. https://www.emulab.net/
4. KYPO Project. http://www.muni.cz/ics/research/projects/23884/web/
5. Malware Analysis Service. https://malwr.com/
6. Citrix   Xenserver.   http://xenserver.org/overview-xenserver-open-source-virtualization/download.html
7. Metasploit Community Edition. http://www.metasploit.com/
8. Kali Linux. https://www.kali.org/downloads/
9. Source of Malware and Malware Generation Tools. http://vxheaven.org/
10. Mishra, P.K.: Cyber defence: an approach to defend cyber assets. In: Proceedings of 1st National Conference on Cyber Security 2012, DIAT Pune (2012)
11. Common Vulnerabilities Scoring Scheme. https://www.first.org/cvss
12. Vinod P., Laxmi, V., Gaur, M.S., Chauhan, G.: Malware analysis using non-signature based method. In: Proceedings of IEEE International Conference on Network Communication and Computer, ICNCC (2011)
13. Kouril, D., et al.: Cloud-based testbed for simulation of cyber attacks. In: Proceedings of the 2014 IEEE Network Operations and Management Symposium (2014)

Performance Evaluation of Features Extracted from DWT Domain

Manisha Saini and Rita Chhikara

Abstract The key task of Steganalyzer is to identify if a carrier is carrying hidden information or not. Blind Steganalysis can be tackled as two-class pattern recognition problem. In this paper, we have extracted two sets of feature vectors from discrete wavelet transformation domain of images to improve performance of a Steganalyzer. The features extracted are histogram features with three bins 5, 10, and 15 and Markov features with five threshold values 2, 3, 4, 5, 6, respectively. The performance of two feature sets is compared among themselves and with existing Farid discrete wavelet transformation features based on parameter classification accuracy using neural network back-propagation classifier. In this paper, we are using three Steganography algorithms outguess, nsF5 and PQ with various embedding capacities.

Keywords Discrete wavelet transformation · Neural network · Steganography Steganalysis · Histogram · Markov

1 Introduction

Steganography is a technique of information hiding in digital medium in such a way that it is imperceptible to human eyes. According to the survey [1], it is found that terrorists have been using Steganography techniques to pass information over Web sites and auction sites over a period of time. Most widely used digital medium over the Internet is image file in comparison with other digital objects. Steganography hides information in spatial domain and transform domain. Main difference among spatial and transform domain is that in spatial domain data embedding in pixels is

M. Saini (✉)
G D Goenka University, Gurgaon, India
e-mail: manisha.saini@gdgoenka.ac.in

R. Chhikara
The NorthCap University, Gurgaon, India
e-mail: ritachhikara@ncuindia.edu

© Springer Nature Singapore Pte Ltd. 2019 257
M. N. Hoda et al. (eds.), *Software Engineering*, Advances in Intelligent Systems and Computing 731, https://doi.org/10.1007/978-981-10-8848-3_25

done directly, whereas in transform domain images are first transformed [2, 3] to discrete cosine transform (DCT) or discrete wavelet transform (DWT) domain and then the message is embedded inside the image. So advantage of transform method over spatial method is that it is more protected against statistical attacks.

The misuse of Steganography has led to development of countermeasures known as Steganalysis [4]. The aim of forensic Steganalysis is to recognize the existence of embedded message and to finally retrieve the secret message. Based on the way methods are detected from a carrier, Steganalysis is classified into two categories: target and blind Steganalysis. (i) Target/specific Steganalysis where particular kind of Steganography algorithm which is used to hide the message is known and (ii) blind/universal Steganalysis where the particular kind of Steganography tool used to hide the message is not known.

In this paper, two sets of feature vectors are extracted from discrete wavelet domain of images to enhance performance of a steganalyzer. The features extracted are histogram features with three bins 5, 10, and 15 and Markov features with five different threshold values 2, 3, 4, 5, 6, respectively. The performance of two feature sets is compared with existing DWT features given by Farid [5] and with different parameters among themselves.

The rest of the paper is divided in the following sections. Section 2 discusses three Steganography algorithms outguess, nsF5, and PQ used in the experiment. In Sect. 3, proposed DWT feature extraction method is explained. Section 4 discusses neural network classifier used for classification. In Sects. 5 and 6, experimental results and analysis is described in detail. Finally, the paper is concluded in Sect. 7.

2 Steganography Algorithms

Our experiment employs three steganography algorithms: Outguess, nsF5, and PQ. Outguess [6] is an enhanced variant of Jsteg. It uses pseudorandom number generator (PRNG)-based scattering to obscure Steganalysis. Seed is required as additional parameter to initialize the pseudorandom number generator. nsF5 (no shrinkage F5 [7]) is enhanced version of F5, proposed in 2007. This algorithm was developed to improve the problem of shrinkage which exists in F5 algorithm by combining F5 algorithm with wet paper codes (WPCs). In perturbed quantization (PQ) algorithm [8], quantization is perturbed according to a random key for data embedding. In this procedure, prior to embedding the data, on the cover–medium, an information-reducing process is applied that includes quantization such as lossy compression, resizing, or A/D conversion. PQ does not leave any traces in the form that the existing Steganalysis method can grab.

3 Proposed DWT Feature Extraction

On applying discrete wavelet transformation (DWT) [9] on each image from image dataset, we obtain four different subbands at each level (up to level 3 decomposition is done), and we have obtained 12 sub-bands (cA1, cH1, cV1, cD1 at Level 1; cA2, cH2, cV2, cD2 at Level 2, and cA3, cH3, cV3, cD3 at Level 3, respectively) where CA is approximation coefficients and rest three subbands (cH, cV, cD) are detailed coefficients. Histogram and Markov features are extracted from the complete image, and 12 subbands are obtained after applying DWT.

3.1 Histogram

Histogram [10] is an approach of summarizing data that are calculated on an interval scale (either discrete or continuous). It partitions the range of feasible values in a dataset into groups. Features of histogram are extracted by binning the elements of all subbands into evenly spaced containers [11] and returning the number of elements in each container. The values are thereafter normalized by dividing each element by sum of all the elements.

$$H\_O = H\_O/\mathrm{sum}(H\_O) \tag{1}$$

We have extracted features calculated from original image +12 subbands (13 subbands) by using three different bins 5, 10, and 15.

3.2 Markov

Markov features show the difference between absolute values of neighboring coefficients. These features have been extracted in DCT domain by Pevný [12], but we have extracted Markov features in DWT domain [11]. We have calculated four difference arrays along horizontal, vertical, minor diagonal, and major diagonal direction using formula:

$$N_h(u, v) = N(u, v) - N(u+1, v) \tag{2}$$

$$N_v(u, v) = N(u, v) - N(u, v+1) \tag{3}$$

$$N_d(u, v) = N(u, v) - N(u+1, v+1) \tag{4}$$

$$N_m(u, v) = N(u+1, v) - N(u, v+1) \tag{5}$$

From difference array, we have calculated four transition probability matrices (TPMs) in horizontal, vertical, diagonal direction. We have extracted features from HL and LH subbands and averaged the four transition probability matrices (TPMs) to obtain features. We have applied different threshold values 2, 3, 4, 5, and 6, respectively.

3.3 Existing DWT Farid Features

Farid proposed 72 feature set [5]; four features that are extracted from subbands are mean, variance, skewness, and kurtosis formula which are shown below.

$$E(x) = \frac{1}{n} \sum_{k=1}^{n} x_k \tag{6}$$

$$\text{Var}(x) = \frac{1}{n-1} \sum_{i=1}^{n} (x_i - E(x))^2 \tag{7}$$

$$S(x) = E\left[\left(\frac{x - E(x)}{\sqrt{\text{Var}(x)}} \right)^3 \right] \tag{8}$$

$$K(x) = E\left[\left(\frac{x - E(x)}{\sqrt{\text{var}(x)}} \right)^4 \right] \tag{9}$$

The image decomposition used in Farid paper is based on separable quadrature mirror filters (QMFs) which contain vertical, horizontal, and diagonal subbands. A total of 72 features are extracted from level 3 decomposition.

4 Neural Network Classifier

We have used neural network back-propagation classifier to classify images into stego images and cover images [13]. Features extracted are given as input to input layer, and then, input propagates through network to output layer. Output is calculated and compared with target output. If actual output does not match with the target output, then error is generated and propagated back. Weights are adjusted till neural network classifier correctly classifies images.

Table 1 Embedding capacities

Images	Outguess	nsF5 (%)	PQ (%)
1–500	16 × 16	10	10
501–1000	32 × 32	25	25
1001–2000	48 × 48	50	50

Table 2 Proposed histogram features and Markov features

Histogram		Markov	
Bins [B]	Features	Threshold [T]	Features
5	65	$T = 2$	25
10	130	$T = 3$	49
15	195	$T = 4$	81
–	–	$T = 5$	121
–	–	$T = 6$	169

5 Experimental Results

We have created dataset of images consisting of 2,000 cover and 2,000 stego images of various sizes which are resized into 640 × 480. Stego images are obtained by applying three Steganography tools, Outguess, nsF5, and PQ. These 4000 images have been divided into training (2,800 samples), validation (600 samples), and testing (600 samples) sets. Features are extracted from image using DWT transform domain. Then, features are fed to neural network back-propagation classifier for detecting whether image is stego or clean image. The performance of classifier is compared on the basis of parameter classification accuracy. Various embedding capacities have been used to generate the dataset as shown in Table 1.

Accuracy of classifier is the fraction of test samples that are correctly classified. Firstly, we have compared the performance of proposed features extracted from wavelet domain among themselves and with existing DWT features. Next, experiment evaluates histogram features with different bins and finally Markov features with different threshold values.

Histogram features are extracted by binning the elements of all subbands into 5, 10, and 15 evenly spaced containers. Markov features are calculated after applying different threshold values 2, 3, 4, 5, and 6, respectively, as shown in Table 2.

6 Analysis

Comparison between various histogram features on the basis of parameter classification accuracy with 20 hidden neurons in Outguess, nsF5, and PQ Steganography algorithm is listed in Table 3. We can observe the following from Table 3. (i) In Outguess Steganography algorithm, accuracy obtained with 5 bins

Table 3 Comparison of accuracy in % of histogram features with 20 hidden neurons

	Outguess			nsF5			PQ		
	5 bin	10 bin	15 bin	5 bin	10 bin	15 bin	5 bin	10 bin	15 bin
Training	99.78	98.89	98.28	51.32	52.5	51.17	87.53	91.03	90.8
Validation	99.66	98.66	97.16	48.33	52	52.33	89	90	89.6
Testing	99.3	97.8	97.83	50.33	49.6	49.33	89.66	89.16	89.5

Table 4 Comparison of accuracy in % of various threshold values with 20 hidden neurons

	$T = 2$	$T = 3$	$T = 4$	$T = 5$	$T = 6$
Outguess					
Training	61.142	64.214	72.107	71.75	71.35
Validation	63	62	66.667	70.166	71.66
Testing	59.166	60.666	69.334	70.667	70
nsF5					
Training	87.5	92.142	93.214	95.785	96.714
Validation	87.166	90.166	92	92.833	93.667
Testing	87.166	89.166	90.667	93	94.667
PQ					
Training	86.892	92.464	95.5	99	98.5
Validation	86.166	91.667	95	98	98.166
Testing	88.833	91.334	94.666	97	97.5

(65 features) is much higher than obtained with 10 bins (130 features) and 15 bins (195 features). (ii) In nsF5 and PQ Steganography algorithm, we obtain equivalent results with 5 bin, 10 bin, and 15 bin, respectively.

From the experimental results of Table 4, we found that accuracy obtained after applying threshold value 5 is best in comparison with other threshold values in case of Outguess, but in nsF5 and PQ Steganography algorithm threshold value 6 gives more accuracy in comparison with others. Next, we evaluate the performance of the proposed features with existing DWT features based on parameter classification accuracy.

As shown in Fig. 1, we conclude that proposed histogram 65 features in DWT domain give best accuracy in comparison with Markov 121 features and existing Farid 72 DWT features for Outguess. This proves that this algorithm is more sensitive to histogram features and with reduced number of features we are able to obtain better accuracy.

We conclude from Figs. 2 and 3, that Markov 121 features are able to detect nsF5 and PQ Steganography algorithm more efficiently. However, the limitation is that histogram features (65) do not improve the accuracy much for these two algorithms.

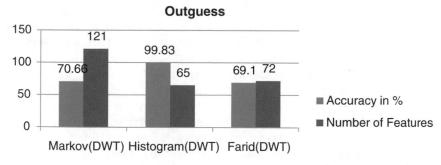

Fig. 1 Comparison of accuracy in % of proposed features with existing features for Outguess

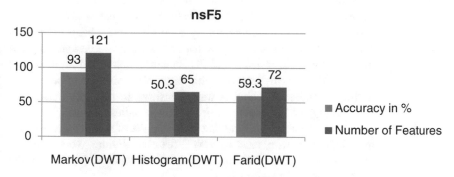

Fig. 2 Comparison of accuracy in % of proposed features with existing features for nsF5

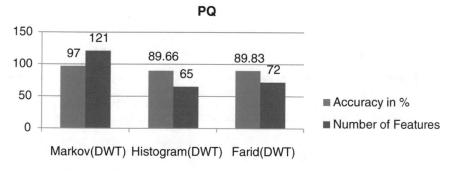

Fig. 3 Comparison of accuracy in % of proposed features with existing features for PQ

7 Conclusion

We have created image dataset consisting of 2000 cover images downloaded from various Web sites and digital photographs. Three Steganography algorithms (1) Outguess (2) nsF5 (3) PQ have been applied to obtain three sets of 2,000 stego images. Various embedding capacities have been used to generate the datasets. Three kinds of images with sizes of 16×16, 32×32, and 48×48 were embedded in image using Outguess Steganography algorithm. Different embedding ratio taken in nsF5 and PQ methods are 10, 25, and 50%. The reason for embedding diverse % of information is to test the performance with different percentage of information embedded. So total 4,000 images (cover plus stego) have been generated in each case. These 4000 images have been divided into training (2,800 samples), validation (600 samples), and testing (600 samples) by neural network classifier. After dividing the dataset into training, validation, and testing, the proposed DWT features (i) histogram, (ii) Markov are compared with existing Farid DWT features. We have compared the histogram features with different bins 5, 10, and 15, respectively, and Markov features with different threshold values 2, 3, 4, and 5, respectively. All the experiments are performed with neural network classifier. The results show 5 bins histogram features give best performance for Outguess, and in nsF5 and PQ Steganography algorithm, we obtain equivalent results with 5 bin, 10 bin, and 15 bin. Markov features with threshold value 5 gives best performance for Outguess; in nsF5 and PQ Steganography algorithm, we get better performance with Markov features with threshold value 6. Experimental results indicate that outguess algorithm is more sensitive to histogram statistical features and nsF5 and PQ can be detected with Markov statistical features. From the experimental result, we can also conclude that proposed set of features gives better performance in comparison with existing DWT features. Future work involves (a) applying proposed features on different embedding algorithms. (b) Finding the size of information hidden in a stego image.

References

1. Choudhary, K.: Image steganography and global terrorism. Glob. Secur. Stud. 3(4), 115–135 (2012)
2. Cheddad, A., Condell, J., Curran, K., Mc Kevitt, P.: Digital image steganography: survey and analysis of current methods. Signal Processing 90, pp. 727–752 (2010)
3. Johnson, N.F., Jajodia, S.: Steganalysis the investigation of hidden information. In: Proceedings of the IEEE Information Technology Conference, Syracuse, NY, pp. 113–116 (1998)
4. Nissar, A., Mir, A.H.: Classification of steganalysis techniques: a study. In: Digital Signal Processing, vol. 20, pp. 1758–1770 (2010)
5. Farid, H.: Detecting hidden messages using higher-order statistical models. In: Proceedings of the IEEE International Conference on Image Processing (ICIP), vol. 2, pp. 905–908 (2002)
6. Niels Provos. www.outguess.org
7. Fridrich, J., Pevný, T., Kodovský, J.: Statistically undetectable JPEG steganography: dead ends, challenges, and opportunities. In: Proceedings of the ACM Workshop on Multimedia & Security, pp. 3–14 (2007)
8. Fridrich, J., Gojan, M., Soukal, D.: Perturbed quantization steganography. J. Multimedia Syst. 11, 98–107 (2005)

9. Ali, S.K., Beijie, Z.: Analysis and classification of remote sensing by using wavelet transform and neural network. In: IEEE 2008 International Conference on Computer Science and Software Engineering, pp. 963–966 (2008)
10. Shimazaki, H., Shinomoto, S.: A method for selecting the bin size of a time histogram. Neural Comput. **19**(6), 1503–1527 (2007)
11. Saini, M., Chhikara, R.: DWT feature based blind image steganalysis using neural network classifier. Int. J. Eng. Res. Technol. **4**(04), 776–782 (2015)
12. Pevný, T., Fridrich, J.: Merging Markov and DCT features for multi-class JPEG steganalysis. In: Proceedings of the SPIE, pp. 03–04 (2007)
13. Bakhshandeh, S., Bakhshande, F., Aliyar, M.: Steganalysis algorithm based on cellular automata transform and neural network. In: Proceedings of the IEEE International Conference on Information Security and Cryptology (ISCISC), pp. 1–5 (2013)

Control Flow Graph Matching
for Detecting Obfuscated Programs

Chandan Kumar Behera, Genius Sanjog and D. Lalitha Bhaskari

Abstract Malicious programs like the viruses, worms, Trojan horses, and back-doors infect host computers by taking advantage of flaws of the software and thereby introducing some kind of secret functionalities. The authors of these malicious programs attempt to find new methods to get avoided from detection engines. They use different obfuscation techniques such as dead code insertion, instruction substitution to make the malicious programs more complex. Initially, obfuscation techniques those are used by software developers to protect their software from piracy are now misused by these malware authors. This paper intends to detect such obfuscated programs or malware using control flow graph (CFG) matching technique, using VF2 algorithm. If the original CFG of the executable is found to be isomorphic to subgraph of obfuscated CFG (under examination), then it can be classified as an obfuscated one.

Keywords Obfuscation · Decompilation · Optimization · Graph isomorphism
Control flow graph

1 Introduction

The obfuscation is a technique to convert a program to a new different version, while making their functionalities equal to each other [1]. Using this technique, the malware writers make their code harder to understand. A lot of malware is being designed every day and no full proof technique exists that can combat all of them.

C. K. Behera (✉) · G. Sanjog · D. Lalitha Bhaskari
Department of Computer Science & Systems Engineering, Andhra University,
Visakhapatnam, India
e-mail: ckb.iitkgp@gmail.com

G. Sanjog
e-mail: genius.sanjog@gmail.com

D. Lalitha Bhaskari
e-mail: lalithabhaskari@yahoo.co.in

© Springer Nature Singapore Pte Ltd. 2019
M. N. Hoda et al. (eds.), *Software Engineering*, Advances in Intelligent Systems
and Computing 731, https://doi.org/10.1007/978-981-10-8848-3_26

These malware authors try to find innovative techniques all the way for prevention of their codes from malware detection engines or delaying the analysis process of the malware, etc., by transforming their malicious programs into another format, which will be much for reverse engineer [2], i.e., by changing the syntax and making it more complex by using different obfuscation techniques.

Earlier, malware detectors were designed by using simple pattern-matching techniques. Some malware was then easily detected and removed through these antivirus software. These antivirus software maintain a repository of virus signatures, i.e., binary pattern characteristics of the malicious codes, and is used to scan the program for the presence of these fixed patterns. If the matches were found by the detectors, they used to alert them as malwares. But, eventually the malware writers learnt the weakness of these detectors, which is the presence of a particular pattern (the virus signature) and then the writers started changing the syntax or semantics of these malwares in such a way that, it would not get detected easily, but the basic behavior and functionality of such malwares remained the same [3, 4].

Section 2 discusses disassembling. In Sect. 3, some obfuscation techniques are listed out. Section 4 explains about control flow graphs. Finally, Sect. 5 proposes a framework, followed by the explanation with an example, which includes disassembly of suspected malware, its CFG generation, and matching. The last section is about the conclusion of the paper with future targets.

2 Disassembly of Executables

The disassembling process aims at achieving a program as identical as to the original program [5, 6]. Compilation process consists of translation process which converts any high-level language (HLL) code to machine code [7]. Then, with the help of linkers and loaders, executable code will be created. As we have the executable of any malware, the next process will be disassembling the executable. During this process, all the details regarding registers, individual instructions will be trimmed away. Finally, the intermediate representation will be prepared by replacing the jump instructions with loops and conditional statements, if available [8, 9]. The automatically generated assembly code from the executable will be lacking from significant comments, variable names, and function names used by the code writer. Because, after a series of transformations, the machine-specific metadata attached with the program semantics will be removed.

3 Obfuscation Techniques

Obfuscation was originally aimed at protecting programs against reverse engineering, illegal modifications, and protecting software from illegal usage at the stage of distribution (with the help of watermarks), but it has been broadly used by malware authors to defeat detection [2]. Some of the simple techniques are mentioned below, which can be used for obfuscating the code generally.

(a) *Replacement of instructions with equivalent instructions*: A technique in which instructions in the original code are replaced by some other equivalent instructions.
(b) *By introducing dead code instructions*: A technique in which a dead code is inserted into the original code.
(c) *Insert semantically NOP code*: By this technique, a NO operation code will be inserted in the original code to make the code lengthier as well as complex.
(d) *Insert unreachable code*: Some code will be inserted in the program, which is never going to be executed. In some cases, jumping is introduced to bypass it directly.
(e) *Reorder the instructions*: Technique which uses reordering of mutually exclusive statements such that the syntax changes from the original code but the output remains same.
(f) *Reorder the loops*: This technique reorders mutually exclusive loop statements in the program.
(g) *Loop unrolling*: This technique uses by moving the loop, and the statements written inside the loop body are rewritten as many number of times as the counter value.
(h) *Cloning methods*: This technique uses in different parts of the program in different ways, but for the same task.
(i) *Inline methods*: In this technique, the body of the method is placed into the body of its callers and the method will be removed.

4 Control Flow Graph

The control flow is driven by the execution of instructions with having various sequential instructions, conditional/unconditional jumps, function calls, returning statements, etc., of the program. The control flow graph (CFG) corresponds to all the possible paths, which must be covered during its execution of the program [10, 11].

4.1 Control Flow Graph Reduction

If the program is an obfuscated one, then various optimization techniques will be used on the CFG to reduce the number of basic blocks (if possible) [11]. The reduction of CFG can be done by concatenating consecutive instruction nodes, by removing the loops and jumps to handle possible permutation of the code or by merging consecutive conditional jumps.

4.2   Control Flow Graph Matching

The aim is to develop a detection strategy based on control flow graphs. In this paper, VF2 algorithm is used to find the subgraphs isomorphism [12]. For two graphs G and G', the algorithm goes down as a traversal of a tree data structure, and at each step, we try to match the next node of G with one of the nodes of G' and stop after traversal of all the nodes of G' (i.e., after finding a leaf). The matching is done for all the possible combinations, and if it does not end completely, then the graphs taken would not be isomorphic [13, 14].

5   Proposed Framework

To prove this framework, we perform the following steps:

Step 1. Get code of a simple program in high-level language, (in our case C language). Obfuscate it several times in that particular high-level language only, using one or more obfuscating transformations.

Step 2. Generate executables for both of these programs using C language compiler.

Step 3. Decompile both of these executables to produce assembly language programs using any decompiler.

Step 4. Make basic block of codes from both of the assembly language programs.

Step 5. Construct control flow graph from the basic blocks for both of these programs.

Step 6. Compare both of the CFGs for subgraph isomorphism using VF2 algorithm.

Since the obfuscated program is also derived from the original program, so both the CFGs of the original and obfuscated programs should match. For justifying correctness of the proposed framework, a simple C program has been taken for experiment, which finds the factorial of a number.

5.1   Explanation

A simple factorial calculation program in C language as shown in Fig. 1 is taken into consideration.

Thereafter, the above-mentioned program will be obfuscated, using various obfuscation techniques, and after that the original code can be transformed as Fig. 2.

Fig. 1 Snapshot of the original HLL program

```
 fact.c ×
#include <stdio.h>

int main()
{
    int c, n, fact = 1;

    printf("Enter a number to calculate it's factorial\n");
    scanf("%d", &n);

    for (c = 1; c <= n; c++)
        fact = fact * c;

    printf("Factorial of %d = %d\n", n, fact);

    return 0;
}
```

As, we can have the executable file of the malicious program, the executable code of both the programs is taken for this testing. Next, with the help of disassemblers, the assembly codes will be generated, from the machine codes of both the original and obfuscated programs (Fig. 3).

Then, the codes will be optimized by using by simply eliminating dead codes, removal of global common sub-expression, removal of loop invariant codes, eliminating induction variables, etc. Then, the control flow graph will be generated from the assembly codes. The structure of the CFGs is shown below, to understand the difference between both the CFGs, pictorially (Fig. 4).

By looking to all basic blocks and the jump, conditions, loops, and return statements, the graphs are prepared from both CFGs (Fig. 5).

Both of these CFGs are matched for subgraph isomorphism using the VF2 algorithm. As a result, the following steps are performed while comparing both of the graphs (Fig. 6).

```
#include <stdio.h>

int main()
{
    int c, n, obs_var1,obs_var2, fact = 1;        //obfuscation variables are added
    obs_var1 = 20 ;          //dead code insertion
    obs_var2 = 10 ;
    printf("Enter a.number to calculate it's factorial\n");
    scanf("%d", &n);

    for (c = 1; c <= n; c++)
    {
        obs_var1 = c;
        fact = fact * obs_var1;        //replacing original statement with similar meaning statement
        obs_var2 = obs_var2 ^ 0 ;      //NOP instruction
    }

    for(c=0;c<10;c++)        //this useless loop was added to obfuscate program several times
    {
        if(3<4)        //Always true statement added
            obs_var2 = obs_var2 * c;        //junk code inserted
    }

    printf("Factorial of %d = %d\n", n, fact);

    return 0;
}
```

Fig. 2 Snapshot of obfuscated HLL program

```
.file       "fact.c"                                        movl        $1,-16(%rbp)
            .section    .rodata                             jmp         .L2
            .align 8                             .L3:        movl        -12(%rbp), %eax
.LC0:       .string     "Enter a number to calculate it's factorial"    imull    -16(%rbp), %eax
.LC1:       .string     "%d"                                movl        %eax,-12(%rbp)
.LC2:       .string     "Factorial of %d = %d\n"            addl        $1,-16(%rbp)
            .text                               .L2:        movl        -20(%rbp), %eax
            .globl      main                                cmpl        %eax,-16(%rbp)
            .type       main, @function                     jle         .L3
main:                                                       movl        -20(%rbp), %eax
.LFB0:      .cfi_startproc                                  movl        -12(%rbp), %edx
            pushq       %rbp                                movl        %eax, %esi
            .cfi_def_cfa_offset 16                          movl        $.LC2, %edi
            .cfi_offset 6, -16                              movl        $0, %eax
            movq        %rsp, %rbp                          call        printf
            .cfi_def_cfa_register 6                         movl        $0, %eax
            subq        $32, %rsp                           movq        -8(%rbp), %rcx
            movq        %fs:40, %rax                        xorq        %fs:40, %rcx
            movq        %rax, -8(%rbp)                      je          .L5
            xorl        %eax, %eax                          call        __stack_chk_fail
            movl        $1, -12(%rbp)           .L5:
            movl        $.LC0, %edi                         leave
            call        puts                                .cfi_def_cfa 7, 8
            leaq        -20(%rbp), %rax                     ret
            movq        %rax, %rsi                          .cfi_endproc
            movl        $.LC1, %edi            .LFE0:        .size       main, .-main
            movl        $0, %eax                            .ident      "GCC: (Ubuntu 4.9.2-10ubuntu13) 4.9.2"
            call        __isoc99_scanf          .section    .note.GNU-stack,"",@progbits
```

Fig. 3 Assembly code after disassembling the executable of 'fact.c' program

```
.file       "obs_fact.c"                                    imull       -12(%rbp), %eax
            .section    .rodata                             movl        %eax, -16(%rbp)
            .align 8                                         addl        $1,-24(%rbp)
.LC0:       .string     "Enter a number to calculate  it's factorial"   .L2:  movl   -28(%rbp), %eax
.LC1:       .string     "%d"                                cmpl        %eax, -24(%rbp)
.LC2:       .string     "Factorial of %d = %d\n"            jle         .L3
            .text                                            movl        $0, -24(%rbp)
            .globl      main                                jmp         .L4
            .type       main, @function        .L5:        movl        -20(%rbp), %eax
main:                                                       imull       -24(%rbp), %eax
.LFB0:      .cfi_startproc                                  movl        %eax, -20(%rbp)
            pushq       %rbp                                addl        $1,-24(%rbp)
            .cfi_def_cfa_offset 16             .L4:        cmpl        $9,-24(%rbp)
            .cfi_offset 6, -16                              jle         .L5
            movq        %rsp, %rbp                          movl        -28(%rbp), %eax
            .cfi_def_cfa_register 6                         movl        -16(%rbp), %edx
            subq        $32, %rsp                           movl        %eax, %esi
            movq        %fs:40, %rax                        movl        $.LC2, %edi
            movq        %rax, -8(%rbp)                      movl        $0, %eax
            xorl        %eax, %eax                          call        printf
            movl        $1, -16(%rbp)                       movl        $0, %eax
            movl        $20, -12(%rbp)                      movq        -8(%rbp), %rcx
            movl        $10, -20(%rbp)                      xorq        %fs:40, %rcx
            movl        $.LC0, %edi                         je          .L7
            call        puts                                call        __stack_chk_fail
            leaq        -28(%rbp), %rax        .L7:
            movq        %rax, %rsi                          leave
            movl        $.LC1, %edi                         .cfi_def_cfa 7, 8
            movl        $0, %eax                            ret
            call        __isoc99_scanf                      .cfi_endproc
            movl        $1, -24(%rbp)          .LFE0:
            jmp         .L2                                 .size       main, .-main
.L3:        movl        -24(%rbp), %eax                     .ident      "GCC: (Ubuntu 4.9.2-10ubuntu13) 4.9.2"
            movl        %eax, -12(%rbp)                     .section    .note.GNU-stack,"",@progbits
            movl        -16(%rbp), %eax
```

Fig. 4 Assembly code after disassembling the executable of 'obfuscated fact.c' program

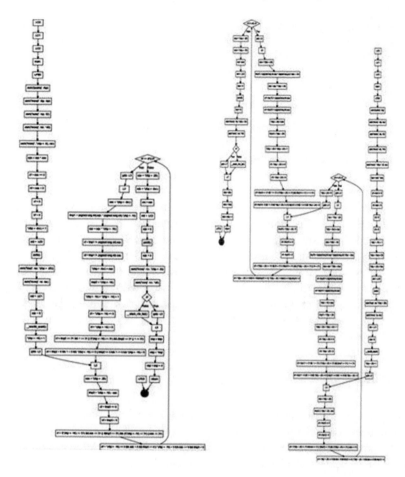

Fig. 5 Snapshots of the structures of the CFGs of the original and obfuscated program

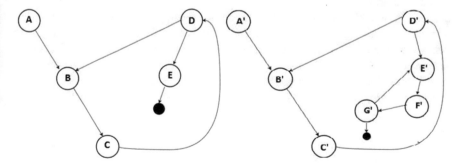

Fig. 6 Optimized CFGs G and G′ of the original and the obfuscated program

(a) Both of the empty graphs G and G' match
(b) Node A of G matches with A' of G'
(c) Node B of G matches with B' of G'
(d) Node C of G matches with C' of G'
(e) Node D of G matches with D' of G'
(f) Node E of G matches with E' of G'

After reaching the leaf node of graph G, no more nodes are left in it and so it can be declared that the graph G is isomorphic to a subgraph of graph G'. Thus, according to the observation, the CFG of the original program comes out to be isomorphic with a subgraph of the CFG of the obfuscated program. The result is as per our expectations.

The above exercise establishes the fact that our proposed framework works well as per its design and proved as it can be used for detection of advanced malware or any other software, over which obfuscation techniques have been performed. On the contrary, in existing systems only a comparison of the binary signature of both the programs will be done. Due to application of several obfuscation techniques on the original program, the binary pattern of the obfuscated program will vary hugely with that of original program. So the obfuscated program will not be alerted as a malware by existing antivirus engines.

6 Conclusion

In this paper, a framework has been proposed to detect the obfuscated programs or malware using control flow graph matching technique. This framework is verified, and its functionality has been proved through an example. After generating executables from both original and obfuscated programs, disassembling has been done on both the executables (as it is known that only malware executables were available, not their source code). Next, both the assembly codes and constructed CFGs of both executables have been optimized. Then, matching has been done between these CFGs for subgraph isomorphism using VF2 algorithm and found to be matched. This means, after obfuscating also, the proposed framework is able to detect the program. The future expectations are to maintain a database of CFGs of known malware and study matching issues (such as matching CFG of any new suspected program with a huge database of CFGs). For this, better graph storage and graph comparison techniques are to be implemented as continuation of this paper.

References

1. You, I., Yim, K.: Malware obfuscation techniques: a brief survey. In: International Conference on Broadband, Wireless Computing, Communication and Applications, IEEE Computer Society, pp. 297–300 (2010)
2. Sharif, M., et al.: Impeding malware analysis using conditional code obfuscation. In: Network and Distributed System Security Symposium (2008)
3. Walenstein, A., Lakhotia, A.: A transformation-based model of malware derivation. In: 7th IEEE International Conference on Malicious and Unwanted Software, pp. 17–25 (2012)
4. Durfina, L., Kroustek, J., Zemek, P.: Psyb0t malware: a step-by-step decompilation—case study. In: Working Conference on Reverse Engineering (WCRE), pp. 449–456. IEEE Computer Society (2013)
5. Ernst, M., et al.: Quickly detecting relevant program invariants. In: 22nd International Conference on Software Engineering, pp. 449–458 (2000)
6. Cordella, L.P., Foggia, P., Sansone, C., Vento, M.: Evaluating performance of the VF graph matching algorithm. In: Proceedings of the 10th International Conference on Image Analysis and Processing, pp. 1172–1177. IEEE Computer Society Press (1999)
7. Cordella, L.P., Foggia, P., Sansone, C., Vento, M.: An improved algorithm for matching large graphs. In: 3rd International Workshop on Graph-based Representations, Italy (2001)
8. McKay, B.D.: Practical graph isomorphism. Congressus Numerantium **30**, 45–87 (1981)
9. Messmer, B.T., Bunke, H.: A decision tree approach to graph and subgraph isomorphism detection. J. Pattern Recog. **32**, 1979–1998 (1999)
10. Gold, R.: Reductions of control flow graphs. Int. J. Comput., Electr. Autom. Control Inf. Eng. **8**(3), (2014)
11. Sadiq, W., Orlowska, M.E.: Analyzing process models using graph reduction techniques. Inf. Syst. **25**(2), 117–134 (2000)
12. Bondy, J.A., Murty. U.S.R.: Graph Theory. Springer, Berlin (2008)
13. Abadi, M., Budiu, M., Erlingsson, U'., Ligatti, J.: Control flow integrity principles, implementations, and applications. ACM Trans. Inf. Syst. Secur. **13**(1), 4:1–4:40 (2009)
14. Brunel, J., Doligez, D., Hansen, R.R., Lawall, J.L., Muller, G.: A foundation for flow-based program matching, using temporal logic and model checking POPL. ACM (2009)

A Novel Framework for Predicting Performance of Keyword Queries Over Database

Mujaffar Husain and Udai Shanker

Abstract In fast-growing information era, business or commercial RDBMS provides huge data access in the form of distributed database, and this data can be accessed by keyword queries very easily, because no need to know structured query languages which is problem for almost end user, and they do not know SQL but needs efficient result; with the help of keyword query interface (KQI), it is possible but often has problem like low ranking quality, i.e., low precision values or recall values, as shown in recent benchmarks. Because of ambiguity in keyword-based search, query result needs improvement. Effectiveness of keyword query should be decided based on query result. It attracts more improvement because huge data creates more complication, and for efficient results, query should be appropriate. Commercial database must support efficient approach to deal with such issues like low precision value of result; by existing methods, precision value is low because of ambiguous interpretation of queries, so in this paper, we try to rank the result according to similarity score based on mathematical model to find proper ranking of result to give efficient result of keyword-based queries.

Keywords Keyword query interface · Query effectiveness · Keyword query
Similarity score · Precision

1 Introduction

Keyword-based search was popularly useful for unstructured data but now going popular day by day for RDBNS because of end user requirement, so this field has attracted much efficient way to tackle problem related to keyword-based search. So many researchers have suggested different approaches for such papers [1–5]

M. Husain (✉) · U. Shanker
Department of Computer Science, MMMUT, Gorakhpur, India
e-mail: Mujaffarhn786@gmail.com

U. Shanker
e-mail: udaigkp@gmail.com

© Springer Nature Singapore Pte Ltd. 2019
M. N. Hoda et al. (eds.), *Software Engineering*, Advances in Intelligent Systems and Computing 731, https://doi.org/10.1007/978-981-10-8848-3_27

have different methods to deal with Keyword based search. Keyword query interface tries to find most appropriate and efficient result for each query. Each Keyword query may have different result because of which exact prediction is not possible in this scenario. We know day to day more users want to access data in all the forms available on the network, so they need their desired result by just typing simple keyword-based search because almost user does not aware about database languages. Different papers suggested different approach to deal with it like in papers [6–9] suggested how to get efficient result by using keyword queries like selecting top k result, semsearch- and index search-based results which is efficient to filter the efficient result for given query. Some related introductory information given for the different terminologies used in this paper is:

Structured Data: When data is stored in form of relational database and can easily retrieve by structured query language (SQL), it is called structured data. Unstructured data is some sort of data which is stored without any preimplementation logic in form of file, Web, etc., and cannot be retrieved easily [10]. Data mining is organized for application in the business community because it is supported by three technologies that are now sufficiently nature.

- Huge data collection added millions pages everyday;
- Powerful supercomputers with great computation power;
- Efficient data mining algorithms for efficient computation.

Business databases are developing at huge rate. According to Google, daily, millions of pages are added. Huge data creates complexity problems, so it needs more efficient strategies to manage and access. Today, a great many pages included in one day. In as indicated by a study, Internet every day included data of amount as about from today 2000 years before information is accessible throughout the day. The extra requirement for enhanced computational systems can now be met in a savvy way with parallel multiprocessor PC innovation. Information mining calculations embody systems that have existed for at smallest 10 years, however have 1 min prior have been actualized as settled, trustworthy, intelligible apparatus that always surpass more established factual techniques.

How much query is effective? "For any query, we can calculate how much query is efficient and we can suggest other query instead of hard query if precision value is low."

2 Related Work

Today, many application works on both structured data and unstructured data means where lots of users try to find answer to their queries with keyword search only. Commercial relational database management systems (RDBMSs) are nowadays providing way for keyword queries execution, so for this type of query it is not as simple as in SQL execution to get appropriate answer to the query, and so different approach like [1–9, 11, 12] is suggested by different researchers to get appropriate answer by just executing keyword queries in structured database. As we know, with the keyword queries, it is not possible to get exact answer, so ambiguity creates more answer for same queries, and so researchers suggested the different approach to rank the result according to relevance of result and also rank the performance of the queries performing on particular databases.

2.1 Post-retrieval Methods

These are the methods that work after each executed keyword query and help to get the efficient result.

2.2 Clarity Score Based

The strategies in view of the idea of clarity score accept that clients are occupied with a not very many points, so they figure a question simple in the event that its aftermath fit in with not very many topic(s) and along these lines, adequately recognize capable from different archives in the combination [7].

2.3 Popularity Based

The basic idea of popularity raking is to find the pages that are popular and rank them higher than other pages that contain specified keywords. This is mostly working in unstructured like Web-based keyword search. Example for this implementation is that most search engine uses this strategy like Google, Bing, etc.

2.4 Challenges in Information Retrieve in Structured Database with Keyword Query

Information retrieval is as much important as information because if we cannot get required information from database, there is no need of storing data. We have surveyed and have found the following big challenges:

- Proper interpretation of what a particular keyword query is hard.
- Ambiguity due to a Keyword Query, which type of information we want to search it's difficult to exactly find this.
- Information needed behind each keyword query may be different, but query may be same.

3 Proposed System

3.1 Objective

We study many methods used to get efficient result with the help of keyword query, but each method has some certain problem in our work we try to improve the performance of Keyword Query.

- Improve the performance of the keyword query on the basis of information needed behind keyword query.
- We try to find the similarity score between document and keyword query and rank the query as according to its performance which we calculate by precision value and recall value.
- We can suggest a user if he wants some certain information, then which keyword query will be useful.

In our proposed method, we create vector to map effectiveness of the query on database or structured data. This based on terms in particular document.

Vector space model is very useful in calculating distance between query and data. This model is used to deal with first unstructured data to get the appropriate result by executing keyword queries. This model provides just talk with the document set with the help of term present in the queries (Table 1).

With the help of this model, it is easy and effective to get ranking of the result as relevance of the result for particular query. So this model provides some mathematical calculation to get the efficient result in case of ambiguity in the interpretation of the query.

By and by, it is less demanding to ascertain the cosine of the point between the vectors, rather than the edge itself (Fig. 1):

$$\cos \theta = \frac{\mathbf{d_2} \cdot \mathbf{q}}{\|\mathbf{d_2}\| \|\mathbf{q}\|} \tag{1}$$

Table 1 Hierarchy of different model

Fig. 1 Vector representation
of query and documents

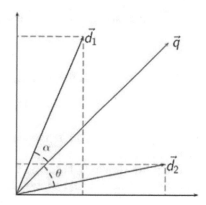

In above equation, $(d_2 \cdot q)$ is calculated as documents, $\|\mathbf{d_2}\|$ is the norm of vector d_2, and $\|\mathbf{q}\|$ is the norm of vector q. The norm of a vector is calculated as such:

$$\|\mathbf{q}\| = \sqrt{\sum_{i=1}^{n} q_i^2} \tag{2}$$

In this model, documents and queries are represented as vectors.

$$d_j = (w_{1,j}, w_{2,j}, \ldots, w_{t,j})$$

$$q = (w_{1,q}, w_{2,q}, \ldots, w_{n,q}) \tag{3}$$

In the given mathematical model, we try to calculate the weight of each matching text or word, and each document is represented in the form of algebraic terms, and query is also represented in same manner. The model is known as term recurrence backward record recurrence model. The weight vector for this particular example is calculated as in this report d is

$$\mathbf{v}_d = \left[w_{1,d}, w_{2,d}, \ldots, w_{N,d} \right]^{\mathrm{T}}$$

$$w_{t,d} = tf_{t,d} \cdot \log \frac{|D|}{|\{d' \in D | t \in d'\}|}$$

where $w_{t,d} = tf_{t,d} \cdot \log \frac{|D|}{|\{d' \in D | t \in d'\}|}$.

And $tf_{t,d}$ is frequency of term t in document d

$$\log \frac{|D|}{|\{d' \in D | t \in d'\}|}$$

The above ratio gives inverse document frequency

$$|D|$$

The term represents the total number of documents in document set;

$$|\{d' \in D | t \in d'\}|$$

The above parameter represents the total number documents in which term t present.

Using the similarity based on cosine model for calculation of similarity score between document d_j and query q can be calculated as:

$$\text{sim}(d_j, q) = \frac{\mathbf{d_j} \cdot \mathbf{q}}{\|\mathbf{d_j}\| \|\mathbf{q}\|} = \frac{\sum_{i=1}^{N} w_{i,j} w_{i,q}}{\sqrt{\sum_{i=1}^{N} w_{i,j}^2} \sqrt{\sum_{i=1}^{N} w_{i,q}^2}} \tag{4}$$

This is the method which is used to implement the keyword query ranking for database. When we see this method compared to other method which is already implemented, this method is performing very well and precision value is good.

This method is based on similarity-based score to get the efficient result (Fig. 2).

Step to get ranking module:

Example for method implementation by algebraic calculation:

Here is an improved case of the vector space recovery model. Consider a little accumulation C that comprises in the accompanying three records:

d_1: "tom cruise MIB"
d_2: "tom hunk future"
d_3: "cameroon diaz MIB"

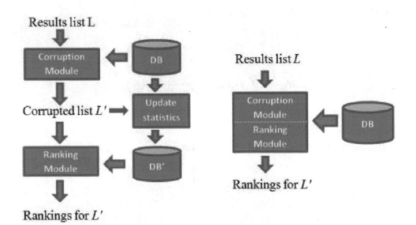

Fig. 2 Ranking schema

A few terms show up in two reports, some seem just in one archive. The aggregate number of records is $N = 3$. Consequently, the idf values for the terms are:

"cameroon $\log_2 (3/1) = 1.584$"
"diaz $\log_2 (3/1) = 1.584$"
"tom $\log_2 (3/2) = 0.584$"
"future $\log_2 (3/1) = 1.584$"
"MIB $\log_2 (3/2) = 0.584$"
"cruise $\log_2 (3/1) = 1.584$"
"hunk $\log_2 (3/1) = 1.584$"

In above document, we calculate the values of documents weight according to the term frequency in each document based on $\log_2$ of the ratio of document terms and whole document.

Presently, we reproduce the *tf* scores by the *idf* estimations of every term, acquiring the accompanying grid of reports by terms: (All the terms seemed just once in every report in our little accumulation, so the greatest quality for standardization is 1.)

For the all above document set, we execute query "tom cruise MIB", and we compute the *tf–idf* vector for the query and store the value for further calculation to compute the final ranking list of the result (Tables 2 and 3).

Given the going with inquiry: "tom tom MIB", we figure the *tf–idf* vector for the query and calculate the term frequency to get the value get similarity score which is helpful to get ranking of result. These query terms are now matched with document set, and distance between query and document set is calculated.

For "q" 0 (2/2) * 0.584 = 0.584 0 (1/2) * 0.584 = 0.292 0 0

We compute the length of every report and of the inquiry (Table 4):

At that point the likeness qualities are:

As per the similarity values, the last request in which the reports are exhibited as result of the inquiry will be: d_1, d_2, d_3 (Table 5).

Table 2 Value for keyword in documents

	Tom	Cruise	MIB	Hunk	Future	Cameroon	Diaz
d_1	1	1	1	0	0	0	0
d_2	1	0	0	1	1	0	0
d_3	0	0	1	0	0	1	1

Table 3 Value for further calculation

	Tom	Cruise	MIB	Hunk	Future	Cameroon	Diaz
d_1	0.584	1.584	0.584	0	0	0	0
d_2	0.584	0	0	1.584	1.584	0	0
d_3	0	0	0.584	0	0	1.584	1.584

Table 4 Calculation of length of documents and query

Length of d_1 = "sqrt$((0.584)^2 + (1.584)^2 + (0.584)^2)$ = 1.786"
Length of d_2 = "sqrt$((0.584)^2 + (1.584)^2 + (1.584)^2)$ = 2.316"
Length of d_3 = "sqrt$((1.584)^2 + (1.584)^2 + (0.584)^2)$ = 2.316"
Length of q = "sqrt$((0.584)^2 + (0.292)^2)$ = 0.652"

Table 5 Final ranking

cosSim(d_1, q) = (0 * 0 + 0 * 0 + 0.584 * 0.584 + 0 * 0 + 0.584 * 0.292 + 0.584 * 0 + 0 * 0/(1.011 * 0.652) = 0.776
cosSim$(d_2,$ q) = (0 * 0 + 0 * 0 + 0.584 * 0.584 + 1.584 * 0 + 0 * 0.292 + 0.84 * 0 + 0 * 0)/(1.786 * 0.652) = 0.292
cosSim$(d_3,$ q) = (1.584 * 0 + 1.584 * 0 + 0 * 0.584 + 0 * 0 + 0.584 * 0.292 + 0 * 0 + 0 * 0)/(2.316 * 0.652) = 0.112

4 Implementation and Discussion

The framework is implementing with the help of java, and query raking is efficiently calculated by this implementation. We use the database MySQL to store the data. We use two table name movie and actor. We access the data with the help of java programming language. For example, we store data in actor table

insert into actor values ('tom cruise', 'titanic', '2000');
insert into actor values('tom cruise', 'mission impossible', '2002');

After the execution of the queries, we can get ranking of the queries based on the result (Fig. 3).

The method is performing very well, and precision is considerable (Fig. 4).

From this figure, we can conclude that our proposed scenario produces maximum precision values rather than our existing scenario. By using our method proposed system achieves high precision values compared than base paper method in existing system. For number of data values, it generates the higher precision values in current scenario. Thus, we achieve the higher precision value for proposed system rather than the existing system.

If we follow the keyword query suggestions, then we can get efficient result with precision values near 0.8–0.9.

Fig. 3 Software for predicting performance of keyword queries over databases

Fig. 4 Similarity score calculation based on model

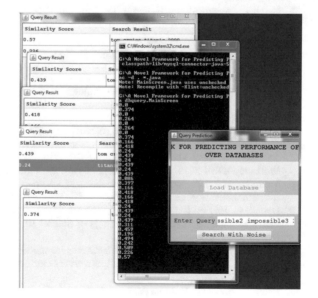

5 Conclusion

In our work, we try to find the efficient result for the given keyword query based on the ranking of the result calculated with our suggested mathematical model which gives high precision value result as according to user needs. They are: Seeking quality is lower than the other framework, and dependability rate of the framework is most minimal. Keeping in mind the end goal to defeat these downsides, we are proposing the enhanced ranking calculation which is utilized to improve the exactness rate of the framework. Moreover, we proposed the idea of philosophy-based algebraic model apparatus for enhancing the top k efficient results productivity. It is utilized for giving comparable words as well as semantic importance for the given keyword query. From the efficient result, we are acquiring the proposed framework is well powerful than the current framework by method for exactness rated, nature of result, and effectiveness of our model. This model tries to predict the effectiveness of the query on the database.

References

1. Kurland, O., Shtok, A., Carmel, D., Hummel, S.: A unified framework for post-retrieval query-performance prediction. In: Proceedings of 3rd International ICTIR, Bertinoro, Italy, pp. 15–26 (2011)
2. Lam, K.-Y., Ulusoy, O., Lee, T.S.H., Chan, E., Li, G.: An efficient method for generating location updates for processing of location-dependent continuous queries. 0-7695-0996-7/01, IEEE (2001)
3. Hauff, C., Azzopardi, L., Hiemstra, D., Jong, F.: Query performance prediction: evaluation contrasted with effectiveness. In: Proceedings of 32nd ECIR, Milton Keynes, U.K., pp. 204–216 (2010)
4. Kurland, O., Shtok, A., Hummel, S., Raiber, F., Carmel, D., Rom, O.: Back to the roots: a probabilistic framework for query performance prediction. In: Proceedings of 21st International CIKM, Maui, HI, USA, pp. 823–832 (2012)
5. Hristidis, V., Gravano, L., Papakonstantinou, Y.: Efficient IR style keyword search over relational databases. In: Proceedings of 29th VLDB Conference, Berlin, Germany, pp. 850–861 (2003)
6. Luo, Y., Lin, X., Wang, W., Zhou, X.: SPARK: top-k keyword query in relational databases. In: Proceedings of 2007 ACM SIGMOD, Beijing, China, pp. 115–126 (2007)
7. Trotman, A., Wang, Q.: Overview of the INEX 2010 data centric track. In: 9th International Workshop INEX 2010, Vugh, The Netherlands, pp. 1–32 (2010)
8. Tran, T., Mika, P., Wang, H., Grobelnik, M.: Semsearch 'S10. In: Proceedings of 3rd International WWW Conference, Raleigh, NC, USA (2010)
9. Demidova, E., Fankhauser, P., Zhou, X., Nejdl, W.: DivQ: diversification for keyword search over structured databases. In: Proceedings of SIGIR' 10, Geneva, Switzerland, pp. 331–338 (2010)
10. Salton, G., Wong, A., Yang, C.S.: A vector space model for automatic indexing. Commun. ACM **18**(11), 613–620 (1975). http://www.cs.uiuc.edu/class/fa05/cs511/Spring05/other_papers/p613-salton.pdf
11. Finin, T., Mayfield, J., Joshi, A., Cost, R.S., Fink, C.: Information retrieval and the semantic web. In: Proceedings of 11th International Conference on Information and Knowledge Management, pp. 461–468, ACM (2002)
12. Ganti, V., He, Y., Xin, D.: Keyword++: a framework to improve keyword search over entity databases. Proc. VLDB Endow. **3**(1), 711–722 (2010)
13. Manning, C., Raghavan, P., Schütze, H.: An Introduction to Information Retrieval. Cambridge University Press, New York (2008)

Predicting and Accessing Security Features into Component-Based Software Development: A Critical Survey

Shambhu Kr. Jha and R. K. Mishra

Abstract Software development communities have made the true venture to software development through the concept of component-based software approach and commercial off-the-shelf (COTS). Majority of the present software applications have software components as the basic elements, and component-based software development (CBSD) has been successful in building applications and systems. However, the security of CBS for the software component is still not properly noticed. Developing secure software is the accountability of all the stakeholders involved with component-based software development model. The main challenge is to access how much security we have achieved or how can we predict and evaluate the security at the early stage of software development? Software security has a very constructive impact on software productivity, maintainability, cost, and quality. Therefore, more early we introduce and evaluate security into component-based software more productivity and quality we can achieve. In this paper, efforts are done to provide some suitable guiding principle to the software engineers in the development of secure component-based software products. This paper also discusses the overview of requirement specification and analyzes the software architectures and design for developing secure component-based software products.

Keywords Commercial off-the-shelf (COTS) · Component-based software development (CBSD) · Component integrator · Intrusion detection
System resilience

S. Kr. Jha (✉)
Mewar University, Chittorgarh, India
e-mail: skjha2@amity.edu

R. K. Mishra
National Informatics Centre, New Delhi, India
e-mail: r.k.mishra@nic.in

© Springer Nature Singapore Pte Ltd. 2019
M. N. Hoda et al. (eds.), *Software Engineering*, Advances in Intelligent Systems and Computing 731, https://doi.org/10.1007/978-981-10-8848-3_28

1 Introduction

Components-based software is considered as a significant justification to many of the challenges among software community [1]. It is accredited with improving the efficiency, maintainability and reducing the development time and cost. Majority of software development organizations have claimed significant benefits from it. Some of the software developing organizations have implemented systematic reuse programs which have resulted in-house libraries of reusable components off-the-shelf (COTS) [2, 3]. Other software developing organizations have supported their reuse with component-based technologies and tools. Explosive popularity of the Internet has resulted in a new situation for reusable software components. Consequently, many organizations are spending much time in reusable component selection and its retrieval since the choice of the appropriate components has a major impact on the software project and finally the resulting products. Despite its never-ending potential, both in terms of cost and in terms of quality of the product, the technology of software reuse has not become as popular as expected. Regular survey has been conducted on the component-based software development, and it was found that more than more than 50% software companies around the world are using component-based approach in its development. Current literature for CBSD approach mainly concerns on integrating and reusability by acquiring existing component from the repository with unknown security properties [3–5]. In most of the component-based development approach, security is given the last priority, whereas functionality is given as top priority. Therefore, the current component-based development process is miserably lacking to develop secure software systems. The main reason behind security lapses is due to lack of trusted software components and producing software in a secure manner. It is very important because individuals and organizations mostly depend on software. Despite huge popularity of CBSD in the industry and the large number of research publications about it in academia, CBSD still lacks fundamental formal foundations for the requirement, composition, and verification of security requirements [6]. Current CBSD practices do not provide the essential requirements for developing secure systems [7, 8]. Various surveys have been conducted, and it was reported about various hurdles involved in the use of CBSD. Since the component-based development approach is mainly based on interdependencies among reusable software components which create troubles at the time of integrating it, therefore, security characteristics of software components must be measured and evaluated earlier in the CBSD life cycle.

2 Security Specification for Software Component

Software security requirements must be considered as basic fundamental steps for the development of secure system [9]. It must be integrated into the development process at very early requirement phase. Unfortunately, in most of the software

Table 1 General software security requirements

I	Totally ignored about security goals due to various other project constraints like development time, budget, and complexity in business process
II	Specify vague security goals at early development phase of the software as they are unclear about it
III	Functional manager gives least priority to the security issues as he is more concern about it
IV	Specify commonly used security mechanisms as architectural constraints
V	Many of the users who are playing major role with the software are not contacted about security goals

development process including component-based approach, security features are always given as a second choice. Functional manager of the software is always concern about meeting the functional goals and objectives considering the complexity, time, and budget constraints of the software projects. People from software community including academicians, researchers, software developers specifically component integrators, and other practitioners working in domain of component-based development were contacted to express their views on security requirements of component-based software [10]. Most of them have said that security goals which are specified at the early development phase are unclear and given least priority. During the early requirement specification of software development, only very few selected component users are contacted and rest are simply ignored. We can conclude the above observations as follow (Table 1).

Early requirement plans are most likely to change as the development process proceeds, but early planning must help to ensure that major security requirements are not ignored. If we can estimate and quantify the security requirement at the early stage of development, we can have better control in managing and implementing it at its highest level. The reason behind the difficulty in security requirement specification at the time of development of component-based software is the specific security need of different component-based applications and the complex nature of different operating environment under which same software components operate. In component-based approach where same component has different level of security requirement as it is used under different operating environment, component integrators or users have to implement security requirements while designing application program interface (API) at the time of integrating different software component in different ways as component, in its entire lifetime, may go underuse of different applications running in many types of environments and perform different task (Fig. 1).

Software component vendors are also playing major role in fulfilling the security requirements of component-based software development. Component vendors should apply various security mechanisms such as component certification, user verification, access control, component encryption, and intrusion detection systems. Each software component should thoroughly document before its actual use. A software component might authenticate various security measures in particular

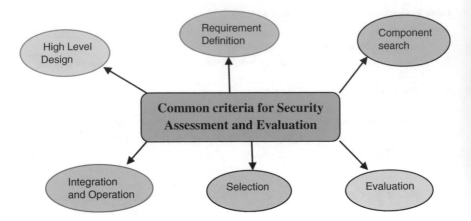

Fig. 1 Requirement centric security attributes

application in a specific operating environment, but that same component security might not give the same performance in a completely different operating environment. The ability to produce highly secure and quality software applications within the fixed time and budget remains a big challenge to most software development companies. Any faults in the software or delay in its delivery will cause problems for many stakeholders involved.

3 Architecture and Design for Secure Software Component

Embedment of security attributes in component-based development is remaining a huge challenge at the architectural design level. In the process of exploring the architecture and early design aspects of software components to obtain awareness of the embedding of security features in the CBSD process, we have met with various experts from different industry and academia. An online survey was also conducted through e-mail and other social media like LinkedIn, Twitter, Whatsapp, and Facebook in form of questionnaires to all potential candidates. The potential candidates involved in the survey mainly included experts from industry including software component vendors, component integrators, project managers of component-based projects, academician from computer science and applications, and Ph.D. research scholars who are conducting research in software quality assessments. The questionnaires contain questions on the basis of component-based software design processes and its software security features. Participants were needed to share their professional view on the specified statements in the form of question. Questionnaires were mainly of following types as presented in Table 2.

Table 2 Category of questionnaires

Category	Description
A	Life cycle models used during development of software component repository and component-based software
B	Selection criteria used by CBS developer for selecting individual software component
C	Desired attributes of functional and non-functional security requirements by the various stakeholders at application level
D	Security feature incorporated by component integrator during design of application program interface required to integrate various software component

After spending lots of time for compilation of data, it was observed that security assessment for component-based software development must occur at the three different levels as shown in Fig. 2.

Once all the functional or non-functional security requirements are precisely identified and estimated, available COTS components must be evaluated to determine their suitability for use in the application being developed. Accessibility of a component repository is advantageous for component integrator to select most suitable component for development of specific application. While interpreting the respondent's feedback for **category A** questionnaires, it was observed that the majority of the component integrators do not use a proper CBSD process for developing software application. For **category B**, component documentation and vendor reputation play more important role than any other factors. For **category C**, majority of the participants have the same opinion on the concept of embedding security activities at the component level rather than system level. High-risk factors were associated with use of external component while developing in house application. For **category D**, access control and applying encryption technique were preferred by majority of the respondent.

Fig. 2 Level of security
needed in CBSD

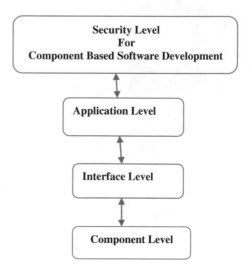

4   Proposed Framework for Security of Component-Based Software

Development of secure and trustworthy component-based systems needs to address the problem of security evaluation and prediction at the individual component level and application level too. This research paper proposes a component security framework for development of secure and trustworthy component-based applications. In the proposed framework, CBSD security criteria are broadly classified into two categories which are named as

(i) **functional security criteria**, (ii) **non-functional security criteria**.

Functional security criteria evaluate and predict security mechanisms by confirming all valid user of the component before its actual use. Controlled navigation of the component by the component user plays very important role, whereas encryption of data at the time of intercomponent communication adds extra security at application level. It also ensures data integrity at component level as well as application level (Fig. 3).

The goal of these mechanisms is to help in estimating and predicting security level of the proposed component-based software application to fulfill high-level system's non-functional security requirements. Similarly, non-functional security criteria identify a system's resilience and level of immunity to attack from outside

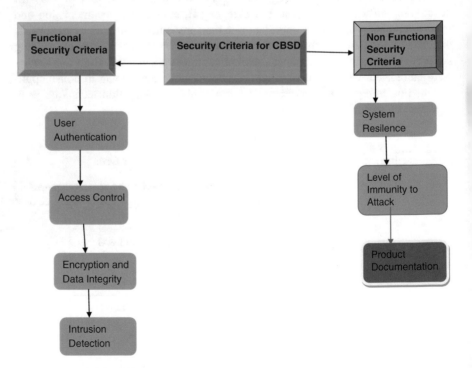

Fig. 3 Security framework for CBSD

agency. Outside agency may be hackers, crackers, or any so-called cyber terrorist intending to perform some fraud or manipulation. We are considering majority of the component as black box in nature; however, software components may be white box and gray box in nature also. Encryption mechanism of the proposed framework is more suitable for components which are white box in nature at the component level, whereas same encryption mechanism can be applied at the level of inter-component communication for the component which is black box in nature at the application level. Access control methods provide guidelines to the component integrators while selecting most suitable software components which can produce high-quality component-based application. Component certification and documentation also play major role while establishing various security issues. While proposing this framework, a survey was also conducted among the various component user working at different level about component certification and documentation. It was observed that very few component vendors are properly working on the issue of component documentation. Even the component certification issue is unexplored. Out of 150 components selected as sample, less than 5% of components were found thoroughly documented.

5 Conclusion and Future Scope

This paper is mainly discussing about challenges faced by software component integrator while implementing various functional and non-functional security issues at the time of component-based software development. It also talks about impact of early security requirements specification during the development process of component-based application. This paper certainly provides some guidelines to component-based software developer about incorporating various security mechanisms through prescribed security framework. It also discusses about security issues at three different levels which include component level security, application level security, and security applied at time of intercomponent communications.

Improvement of component documentation and standardization of component certification is area of concern which can be considered as future scope for predicting and accessing security for component-based software development. More accurate validation of proposed framework can also improve both functional and non-functional security of component-based software development.

References

1. Agrawal, J.R.D.V.K.: Study of perfective maintainability for component-based software systems using aspect-oriented-programming techniques. In: Proceedings of the International Conference on Intelligent Computational Systems, Dubai, 7–8 Jan 2012
2. Jha, S.K., Mishra, R.K.: Accessing software quality for component based software through trustworthiness and dependability analysis. Int. J. Develop. Res. 5(4) (2015)

3. Gill, N.S.: Importance of software component characterization for better software reusability. ACM SIGSOFT SEN **31** (2000)
4. Sharma, A., Grover, P.S., Kumar, R.: Investigation of reusability, complexity and customizability for component based systems. ICFAI J. IT **2** (2006)
5. Mir, I.A., Quadri, S.M.: Analysis and evaluating security of component-based software development: a security metrics framework. Int. J. Comput. Netw. Inf. Secur. (2012)
6. Kahtan, H., Bakar, N.A., Nordin, R.: Dependability attributes for increased security in CBSD. J. Comput. Sci. **8**(10) (2014)
7. Alberts, C., Allenm, J., Stoddard, R.: Risk-based measurement and analysis: application to software security. Software Engineering Institute, Carnegie Mellon University (2012)
8. Soni, N., Jha, S.K.: Component based software development: a new paradigm. Int. J. Sci. Res. Educ. **2**(6) (2014)
9. Zurich, E.T.H.: A common criteria based approach for COTS component selection. Chair of software engineering ©JOT, 2005 special issue: 6th GPCE Young Researchers Workshop (2004)
10. Bertoa, M.F., Vallecillo, A.: Quality attributes for COTS components. In: Proceeding of the 6th ECOOP Workshop on Quantitative Approaches in Object-Oriented Software Engineering (QAOOSE 2002). Malaga, Spain (2002)

Traditional Software Reliability Models Are Based on Brute Force and Reject Hoare's Rule

Ritika Wason, A. K. Soni and M. Qasim Rafiq

Abstract This research analyses the causes for the inaccurate estimations and ineffective assessments of the varied traditional software reliability growth models. It attempts to expand the logical foundations of software reliability by amalgamating techniques first applied in geometry, other branches of mathematics and later in computer programming. The paper further proposes a framework for a generic reliability growth model that can be applied during all phases of software development for accurate runtime control of self-learning, intelligent, service-oriented software systems. We propose a new technique to employing runtime code specifications for software reliability. The paper aims at establishing the fact that traditional models fail to ensure reliable software operation as they employ brute force mechanisms. Instead, we should work on embedding reliability into software operation by using a mechanism based on formal models like Hoare's rule.

Keywords Learning automata · Software reliability · Formal methods
Automata-based software reliability model · Finite state automata

R. Wason (✉)
Department of MCA, Bharati Vidyapeeth's Institute of Computer Applications
and Management, New Delhi, India
e-mail: rit_2282@yahoo.co.in

A. K. Soni
School of Engineering and Technology, Sharda University, Greater Noida, India
e-mail: ak.soni@sharda.ac.in

M. Qasim Rafiq
Department of Computer Science and Engineering, Aligarh Muslim University,
Aligarh, India
e-mail: mqrafiq@hotmail.com

© Springer Nature Singapore Pte Ltd. 2019
M. N. Hoda et al. (eds.), *Software Engineering*, Advances in Intelligent Systems
and Computing 731, https://doi.org/10.1007/978-981-10-8848-3_29

1 Introduction

Ensuring correct operation by implementing dependable software is the most important challenge of software production today [1]. Accurate reliability assessment not only optimizes the overall software life cycle costs but also allows for efficient scheduling of resources for software [2]. It makes way for able performance appraisal of operational software. Reliability assessments form the basis of various activities like software project management, software feasibility and software modification decision. Hecht [3] describes software reliability functions into three major categories of measurement, estimation and prediction. Software reliability "measurement" relies upon failure interval data obtained by executing the software in its real operational environment [4]. Software reliability "estimation" refers to determining software reliability based upon operation in some test environment. Reliability "prediction" implies the practice of computing software reliability measures from program data which does not include failure intervals and takes into account factors like size and program complexity [5]. Diverse applications and importance of software reliability metrics can be strongly coupled to the functions described above. For example, system engineering relies upon prediction; project management upon estimation; and operational software management upon measurement [6].

To ensure the above characteristics, many varied software reliability models have been proposed since early 1970s [7]. A careful analysis of these models reveals that they actually try to provide a mechanism for describing a random process called failure either as a function of the number of failures experienced of next time to failure [8]. For the past four decades, all these models have estimated software reliability combining failure history data with their individual assumptions as depicted in Table 1.

An analysis of the different classes of software reliability models as depicted in Table 1 reveals that all the traditional reliability models suffer from what we may call the "conditional applicability syndrome". None of the existing software reliability models are capable of maintaining and controlling software reliability throughout the software life cycle. Though these models may be successful for a particular software system under one operational environment, they may fail or yield inaccurate estimates for the same software under different settings.

A major lacuna of all software dependability and reliability research is the absence of a generic, intelligent, self-learning reliability estimation model. Despite huge effort and volumes of work, we are still looking for a formal reliability assessment model that can identify possible states the software may assume during its life cycle to ensure accurate reliability "prediction", precise reliability "estimation" and correct reliability "measurement" once the software is operational [9, 10].

All **the conventional models treat software as a black box and estimate software reliability using complex statistical or mathematical functions** which have been borrowed from hardware reliability models [11]. Detailed analysis of the history of software reliability estimation parameters reveals that all the common

Table 1 Applicability of traditional reliability models in different software development phases

S. No.	Software development phase	Features	Usable reliability models	Drawbacks
1	Design phase	Faults are detected by other formal and informal methods	None	Absence of test cases and failure data makes all existing software reliability models unsuitable
2	Unit testing phase	Test cases generated module-wise from input domain in deterministic fashion. In most cases, programmer himself is the tester	Fault seeding models or input domain-based models	Test cases are not a representative sample of the actual operational usage; hence, estimates obtained may not be of much use
3	Integration testing phase	Test cases generated to verify the correctness of the partial or whole system in either a random or deterministic fashion	Time between failures, fault seeding, failure count and input domain-based models	Different reliability estimation models applicable under diverse assumptions. Choice of model should be based on operational environment
4	Acceptance testing phase	Inputs for operational usage are generated to verify software acceptability	Fault count and input domain-based models	Reliability model based on operational environment
5	Operational phase	Allied, deterministic user inputs instead of random	Fault count models	Reliability model based on operational environment

software reliability estimation parameters such as failure rate (λ), hazard function ($\lambda(t)$), MTBF, MTTR, MTTF were initially suggested for the reliability prediction of hardware products [12] and were simply fitted to the software process over-looking the different nature of software versus hardware as well as their reliability.

Hence, it has been observed that the shortcomings of the existing software reliability models have been the major cause of the unreliability of modern software.

Major challenges of software reliability can be defined as the ability to achieve the following [13]:

(i) Encompass heterogeneous runtime execution and operation mechanisms for software components.

(ii) Provide abstractions that can identify, isolate and control runtime software errors.

(iii) Ensure robustness of software systems.

Hence, it is time that the software engineering community learns from mistakes of conventional reliability models and utilizes post-testing failure data to control software operation at run-time [14, 15].

The above discussion implies that what is required is a more holistic approach, integrating formal methods like Hoare's logic and automata [16]. The key feature of this approach shall be a shift of emphasis from probabilistic assumptions about the reliable execution of software to actual runtime operation control [8, 12, 17, 18]. This paper proposes a general framework for a reliability model based on finite state machines.

The remainder of this paper is designed as follows. Section 2 reviews some popular software reliability models. Section 3 establishes the brute force nature of all traditional SRGMs as the major cause of their inaccurate estimates. Section 4 discusses the viability of modelling reliability metrics using formal methods like Hoare's logic. Section 5 discusses the basic framework for a generic, intelligent, self-learning reliability estimation model. Section 6 discusses the conclusion and future enhancements for this study.

2 Software Reliability Measurement

Chow [7] was the first to suggest a software reliability estimation model. Since then hundreds of models were applied for calculating reliability of different software systems. However, with every model, the search for another model that overcomes the limitations of its ancestors intensifies. Actually, none of the traditional reliability models offer silver bullet for accurate reliability measurement for software. It is observed that traditional reliability models are only trying to mathematically represent the interaction between the software and its operational environment. As such most of these models are hence brute force as they are probabilistically trying to estimate software reliability by fitting some mathematical model [7] onto the software reliability estimation process. The limitation of traditional models along with the growing size and complexity of modern software makes accurate reliability prediction all the more hazardous.

As observed from Table 1, most of the software reliability models calculate reliability based on failure history data obtained from either the testing or debugging phase of software development [12]. However, difficulty lies in the quantification of this measure. Most of the existing reliability models assess reliability growth based on failure modes surfaced during testing and combine them with different assumptions to estimate reliability [1, 2, 10]. Some of the well-known traditional software reliability models can be classified according to their main features as detailed in Table 2.

Tables 1 and 2 establish that all the existing reliability models have limited applicability during software testing, validation or operational phases of the software life cycle. However, the basic foundation of most software reliability growth

Table 2 Feature classification of traditional reliability models

S. No.	Class	Example	Assumptions
1	Time between failure/ deterministic models	Jelinski–Moranda de-eutrophication model; Goel–Okumoto imperfect debugging model; Littlewood–Verrall Bayesian model	(i) Independent times between failures (ii) Equal probability of each fault exposure (iii) Embedded faults independent of each other (iv) Debugging and perfect fault removal after each occurrence
2	Fault count models	Goel–Okumoto NHPP model; Musa's execution time model; Shooman exponential model;	(i) Independent testing intervals (ii) Homogeneous testing during intervals (iii) Number of faults detected per interval independent of each other
3	Fault seeding models	Mills hypergeometric model	(i) Seeded faults are randomly distributed in the software with equal probability of being detected with native faults
4	Input domain-based model	Nelson model; Ramamoorthy and Bastani model	(i) Known input profile distribution (ii) Random testing used (iii) Input domain can also be partitioned into equivalence classes

models is often viewed doubtfully due to the unrealistic assumptions they are based on, hence being the underlying cause of the reliability challenge of this century.

3 Brute Force Nature of Traditional Models

Despite decades of continual research and progress, software reliability remains a term of aspiration. As the human society comes to rely heavily on powerful systems that keep shrinking in size and growing in complexity, software systems have come under harsh tectonic stresses due to the growing demand for reliable, distributed systems. Despite more than half-a-century of advancement, the software industry continues to strive for a mature engineering discipline to meet the reliability demands of an information-age society [13]. The fundamental cause of this failure is the fact that our basic approach to software construction is flawed. All traditional software reliability estimation models demand more information about the software than is actually known like failure rate. As a result, this produces dubious assumptions about software resulting in misleading results. Having understood the root cause of all our software quality problems, we now need to identify and debug the mistakes of traditional reliability models in order to enable a befitting solution to our software reliability crisis.

At this point, it would be logical to first understand the nature of computing. A computer program in reality can be termed as a behaving machine (BM) or an automaton that can detect modifications in its environment and effect alterations in it just like our biological nervous system [13]. Such a universal behaving machine (UBM) may be composed of a couple of elementary behaving entities called nodes and an environment that can bring a change in the state of these nodes. The above description maps to what we know of mathematically as a finite state machine (FSM) [8, 17–19]. Hence, from the above discussion, we may conclude that at its core all software behave as a finite state machine.

Unfortunately for the software world, traditional reliability models do not treat the software as a tightly integrated collection of communicating entities that can switch states upon environmental stimuli [20, 21]. The cause for this can be attributed either to sheer ignorance or vested interest of ensuring oneself a lifetime career as reliability engineer. All traditional models present a time-variant reliability analysis of existing software by calculating reliability using brute force efforts for generating assumptions and parameter values to be fitted onto a mathematical model [1, 7]. However, the accuracy of the model assumptions and parameter values is questionable.

From the long legacy of software failures, the software community has cultivated a belief that large, complex software are less reliable [9]. The belief strikingly contrasts the human brain, the most dependable and complex system in the world, with reliability scores of magnitude greater than that of any composite existing software [13]. Hence, the human brain is a living proof of the fact that the reliability of a behaving system does not have to be inversely proportional to its complexity. The problem with the traditional reliability models lies in their way of quantifying reliability. Most existing reliability models use either of the alternative way to quantify reliability: failure intensity (expected number of failures per unit time) or mean time to failure (MTTF, expected value of the failure interval) [1]. However, both the estimates involve estimation of software reliability from failure data obtained during testing and validation phases of software which may significantly differ from the actual operational environment where the system may be actually implemented.

The primary purpose of any software reliability model is to anticipate failure behaviour that will be observed from the program at run-time [22]. This runtime behaviour, however, changes rapidly with the implementation environment under which a program operates and cannot be completely tracked during program testing. Developer alliance can further diminish secure coding practices.

4 Perceiving Reliability with Hoare's Logic

Uncertainty will continue to disrupt reliability of all our software systems, unless we transition to some metric rooted firmly in science and mathematics [4, 9, 23]. Engineers have always relied on mathematical analysis to predict how their designs will behave in the real world [2]. Unfortunately, the mathematics that describes physical hardware systems does not apply within the artificial binary universe of software systems [2]. However, computer scientists have contrived ways to translate software specifications and programs into equivalent mathematical expressions which can be analysed using theoretical tools called formal methods [5, 15]. In the current decade when reliable software is no longer just a negotiable option but a firm requirement for many real-time, critical software systems, we need to become smarter about how we design, analyse and test software systems.

Hoare's logic/Floyd–Hoare logic is an axiomatic means of proving program correctness which has been the formal basis to formally verify the correctness of software [16]. However, it is rarely applied in actual practice. We propose development of a reliability model that can control the traversed program path using an underlying automata-based software representation and apply Hoare's logic as the basis to ensure correct runtime program execution [11]. Our approach performs dynamic checking of software transition and instead of halting the program upon failure state transition; we allow the program to continue execution through an alternate path. Formal, Hoare's logic-based software verification provides strong possibility to establish program correctness [16]. However, practical use of this logic is limited due to difficulties like determining invariants for iterations and side effects of invoking subroutines (methods/functions/procedures) in different programming languages.

Hoare's logic based on predicate logic [16] defines a set of axioms to classify the semantics of programming languages. It describes an axiom for each program construct. These axioms are further applied to establish program correctness for programs written in different programming languages.

We propose applying axioms of Hoare's logic for ensuring reliable software operation [16]. To clarify the same, we discuss the Hoare axiom for assignment:

Let $x: = E$ be an assignment, then

$$\overline{\{Q(E|x)\}x := E\{Q\}} \tag{1}$$

Equation 1 states that $x: = E$ is acceptable with respect to the particular post-assertion Q and the derived pre-assertion $Q(E|x)$.

Taking, Hoare's axiom of assignment as basis, we propose an *axiom of reliability* to be followed by each software transition.

$x := \sum$ is acceptable with respect to the given post-state $q_i \in Q$ and the previous pre-state $q_j \in Q(\sum |\delta)$. This implies that a given user input x is correct only if it transforms the state of software under study to an acceptable post-state.

5 Proposed Model Framework

Systems crash when they fail to expect the unexpected [2]. The unreliability of software stems from the problem of listing and/or identifying all the possible states of the program [13]. To conquer this limitation, we propose development of an automata-based software reliability model [11, 24]. The proposed model is based on the conventional idea of a Markov model [25, 26]. This model divides the possible software configurations into distinct states, each connected to the others through a transition rate. In this framework, the software at run-time would be controlled by an underlying automata representation of the software. Each software state change and/or transition shall be allowed by the compiler and/or interpreter only after validating if it takes the software to an acceptable automata node. The basic flow of this automata-based reliability model is depicted in Fig. 1.

As depicted in Fig. 1 above, the proposed model framework utilizes the equivalent assembly code of the software under study to extract the underlying opcodes. Utilizing these opcode instructions, a next state transition table is obtained which is used as the basis for designing the underlying finite state automata (FSM). Each node of the obtained FSM can be assigned a probability value. Initially, each node of the FSM can be assigned an equivalent probability. With each software execution, the node probability can be incremented and/or decremented depending upon the software path of execution. The proposed framework shall help ensure reliable software execution by monitoring each software transition. In case, the framework detects that in the next transition the software may transit to a failure node, it may halt the system immediately and work on finding an alternate route.

Fig. 1 Basic flow diagram of proposed automata-based software reliability model

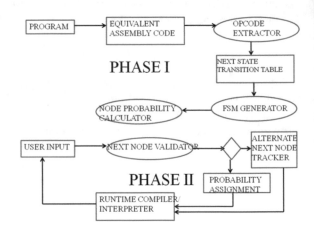

6 Conclusion

The ultimate objective of this study is to embrace the software community with the fact that existing software reliability models are all brute force as they do not capture the actual nature of software execution [27]. With this work, we also have built upon a novel software reliability model that uses the formal model of an automaton to control runtime software operation. The utmost importance of this framework is that the framework can be built into the software execution engine (compiler and/or interpreter) to ensure similar automata-based execution for all software sharing similar execution semantics. However, this remains a tall objective to achieve in the near future.

This research may be considered as generic model for ensuring reliable software operation of modern agent-based, cloud-based, distributed or service-oriented software. This research could also be classified as a generic one which could instantiate numerous other studies. Possible extensions to this research can be training of the FSM framework into learning automata to identify and register faulty nodes as well as incorrect user input types leading to the same. Further, the model can also be applied to improve runtime performance of software. This study is a step forward towards overcoming all software reliability issues and ensuring robust software systems.

References

1. Vyatkin, V., Hanisch, H.M., Pang, C., Yang, C.H.: Closed-loop modeling in future automation system engineering and validation. IEEE Trans. Syst. Man Cybern. Part C: Appl. Rev. **39**(1), 17–28 (2009)
2. Yindun, S., Shiyi, Xu: A new method for measurement and reduction of software complexity. Tsinghua Sci. Technol. **12**(S1), 212–216 (2007)
3. Hecht H.: Measurement, estimation and prediction of software reliability, in software engineering technology, vol. 2, pp. 209–224. Maidenhead, Berkshire, England, Infotech International (1977)
4. Samimi, H., Darli, A.E., Millstein, T.: Falling back on executable specifications. In: Proceedings of the 24th European Conference on Object-Oriented Programming (ECOOP'10), pp. 552–576 (2010)
5. Wahls, T., Leavens, G.T., Baker, A.L.: Executing formal specifications with concurrent constraint programming. Autom. Softw. Eng. **7**(4), 315–343 (2000)
6. Leuschen, M.L., Walker, I.D., Cavallaro, J.R.: Robot reliability through fuzzy markov models. In: Proceedings of Reliability and Maintainability Symposium, pp. 209–214 (1998)
7. Beckert, B., Hoare, T., Hanhle, R., Smith, D.R., et al.: Intelligent systems and formal methods in software engineering. IEEE Intell. Syst. **21**(6), 71–81 (2006)
8. Musa, J.D., Okumoto. A logarithmic poisson execution time model for software reliability measurement. In: Proceedings of the 7th International Conference on Software Engineering, pp. 230–237. Orlando (1984)
9. Meyer, B., Woodcock, J.: Verified software: theories, tools, experiments. In: IFIP TC 2/WG 2.3 Conference VSTTE 2005, Springer-Verlag (2005)

10. Hsu, C.J., Huang, C. Y.: A study on the applicability of modified genetic algorithms for the parameter estimation of software reliability modeling. In: Proceedings of the 34th Annual IEEE Computer Software and Applications Conference, pp. 531–540 (2010)
11. Jelinski, Z., Moranda, P.B.: Software reliability research. In: Statistical Computer performance Evaluation, pp. 465–484. Academic Press, New York (1972)
12. Benett, A.A.: Theory of probability. Electr. Eng. **52**, 752–757 (1933)
13. Hoare, C.A.R.: How did software get so reliable without proof. In: Proceedings of The Third International Symposium of Formal Methods Europe on Industrial Benefits and Advances in Formal Methods, pp. 1–17 (1996)
14. Zee, K., Kuncak, V., Rinard, M.C.: Full functional verification of linked data structures. In: Proceedings of the 2008 ACM SIGPLAN Conference on Programming Language Design and Implementation PLDI '08, pp. 349–361. ACM, New York (2008)
15. Flanagan, C., Leino, K.R.M., Lillibridge, M., Nelson, G., Saxe, J.B., Stata, R.: Extended static checking for java. In: Proceedings of the ACM SIGPLAN 2002 Conference on Programming language design and implementation PLDI '02, pp. 234–245. ACM, New York (2002)
16. Zee, K., Kuncak, V., Rinard, M.C.: An integrated proof language for imperative programs. In: Proceedings of the 2009 ACM SIGPLAN Conference on Programming Language Design and Implementation PLDI '09, pp. 338–351. ACM, New York (2009)
17. Wason, R., Ahmed, P., Rafiq, M.Q.: Automata-based software reliability model: the key to reliable software. Int. J. Softw. Eng. Its Appl. **7**(6), 111–126 (2013)
18. Benes, N., Buhnova, B., Cerna, I., Oslejsek, R.: Reliability analysis in component-based development via probabilistic model checking. In: Proceedings of the 15th ACM SIGSOFT Symposium on Component-Based Software Engineering (CBSE'12), pp. 83–92 (2012)
19. Sharygina, N., Browne, J.C., Kurshan, R.P.: A formal object-oriented analysis for software reliability: design for verification. In: Proceedings of the 4th International Conference on Fundamental Approaches to Software Engineering (FASE'01), pp. 318–322. Springer-Verlag (2001)
20. Afshar, H.P., Shojai, H., Navabi, Z.: A new method for checking FSM correctness (Simulation Replacement). In: Proceedings of International Symposium on Telecommunications, pp. 219–222. Isfahan–Iran (2003)
21. Alur, R., Dill, D.L.: A theory of timed automata. Theoret. Comput. Sci. **126**(2), 183–235 (1994)
22. Chow, T.S.: Testing software design modeled by finite state machines. IEEE Trans. Softw. Eng. **SE-4**(3), 178–187 (1978)
23. Hoare, C.A.R.: An axiomatic basis for computer programming. ACM Commun. **12**(10), 576–580 (1969)
24. Crochemore, M., Gabbay, D.M.: Reactive automata. Inf. Comput. **209**(4), 692–704 (2011)
25. Goseva-Popstojanova, K., Kamavaram, S.: Assessing uncertainty in reliability of component-based software systems. In: 14th International Symposium on Software Reliability Engineering (ISSRE 2003), pp. 307–320 (2003)
26. Goel, A.L.: Software reliability models: assumptions, limitations and applicability. IEEE Trans. Softw. Eng. **11**(12), 1411–1414 (1983)
27. Ramamoorthy, C.V., Bastani, F.B.: Software reliability—status and perspectives. IEEE Trans. Softw. Eng. **SE-8**(4), 354–371 (1982)

Object-Oriented Metrics for Defect Prediction

Satwinder Singh and Rozy Singla

Abstract Today, defect prediction is an important part of software industry to meet deadlines for their products. Defect prediction techniques help the organizations to use their resources effectively which results in lower cost and time requirements. Various metrics are used for defect prediction in within company (WC) and cross-company (CC) projects. In this paper, we used object-oriented metrics to build a defect prediction model for within company and cross-company projects. In this paper, feed-forward neural network (FFNN) model is used to build a defect prediction model. The proposed model was tested over four datasets against within company defect prediction (WCDP) and cross-company defect prediction (CCDP). The proposed model gives good results for WCDP and CCDP as compared to previous studies.

Keywords Object-oriented metrics · Defect prediction
Artificial neural network (ANN)

1 Introduction

Defect prediction is a technique to find defects in software before its delivery. It is an important part of software engineering to control the schedule and cost of a software system. There are various models that can be used for defect prediction. Defect prediction models help the engineer to check the reliability of the software against time and cost factor. These models are developed using various metrics. But today, object-oriented metrics are more popular. So in this paper, object-oriented metrics are used for defect prediction.

S. Singh · R. Singla (✉)
BBSBEC, Fatehgarh Sahib, Punjab, India
e-mail: rozysingla92@gmail.com

S. Singh
e-mail: satwinder.singh@bbsbec.ac.in

© Springer Nature Singapore Pte Ltd. 2019   305
M. N. Hoda et al. (eds.), *Software Engineering*, Advances in Intelligent Systems
and Computing 731, https://doi.org/10.1007/978-981-10-8848-3_30

Software metrics are collected with the help of automated tools which are used by defect prediction models to predict the defects in the system. There is generally a dependent variable, and various independent variables are present in any fault prediction model. Dependent variable defines that the software modules are faulty or not. Various metrics such as process metrics, product metrics, etc., can be used as independent variables. For example, cyclomatic complexity and lines of code which are method-level product metrics [1].

Cross-company defect prediction (CCDP) is a mechanism that builds defect predictors which use data from various other companies, and the data may be heterogeneous in nature. Cross-project defect prediction uses data from within company projects or cross-company projects. CC (cross-company) data involve knowledge from many different projects and are diversified as compared to within company (WC) data [2].

Previous works mostly focus on defect prediction within company projects. Very few studies were based on cross-company and cross-projects defect prediction but did not produce satisfactory results.

Defect prediction from static code can be used to improve the quality of software. Here in this paper, to cover the above gap focus is on to predict the parts of the code which is defective. Further, efforts will be made to create the general framework or model for defect prediction in cross-company and cross-project software to improve the quality of software.

Zimmermann et al. observed that many companies do not have local data which can be used in defect prediction as they may be too small. The system which has to be tested might be released for first time, and so there is no past data [3].

Mainly, the focus of various defect prediction studies is to build prediction models using the available local data (i.e., within company predictors). For this purpose, companies have to maintain a data repository where data of their past projects can be stored. This stored data are useful in defect prediction. However, many companies do not follow this practice.

In this research, the focus is on binary defect prediction and examines if there is any conclusion or not. This research presents the assets of cross-company (CC) versus within company (WC) data for defect prediction.

2 Literature Survey

As per the title of the paper, efforts over here will be made to design a defect prediction model that can be used for with-in and cross-company projects. To design a defect prediction model, it is required to study the previous work done by the research community so far. The same is done as follow.

Zimmermann et al. [3] calculated the performance of defect prediction for cross-projects by using data from 12 projects (622 combinations). Among of these combinations, only 21 pairs resulted in efficient prediction performance. Data distributions of the initial and final projects are different which result in low prediction performance. It is expected that training and test data have the same distribution of data. This assumption is good for within-project prediction and may be not suited for cross-project prediction. Cross-project prediction can be indicted in two dimensions: the domain dimension and the company dimension. They noticed that many software companies may or may not have local data for defect prediction as they are small or they do not have any past data. Zimmermann et al. [3] observed the datasets from Firefox and Internet Explorer (IE). They experimented on these Web browsers and found that Firefox data could predict for defects in IE very well, but vice versa was not true. They come up with the result that "building a model from a small population to predict a larger one is likely more difficult than the reverse direction."

Peters et al. [4] described one way to find the datasets for training and testing which would help in cross-company defect prediction and within company defect prediction. The authors divided the datasets as labeled or unlabeled data. Unlabeled datasets can be used for predicting the defects in cross-company projects. They introduce a new filter "Peters filter" which generates the training datasets. The performance of Peters filter is compared with the Burak filter which uses k-nearest neighbor method for calculating the training dataset. These filters are used with various prediction models to calculate their performance. They used random forest (RF), Naïve Byes (NB), linear regression (LR), and k-nearest neighbor (k-NN) prediction models for calculating the performance of filters. The performance measurement parameters are accuracy, recall, precision, f-measure, and g-measure. After this experiment, they come with ideas that the cross-company defect prediction is needed for predicting results over small datasets.

Zhang et al. [5] proposed a universal model for defect prediction that can be used in within company and cross-company projects. One issue in building a cross-company defect prediction is the variations in data distribution. To overcome this, the authors first suggested collecting data and then transforming the training and testing data to make more similar in their data distribution. They proposed a context-aware rank transformation for limiting the variations in the distribution of data before applying them to the universal defect prediction model. The six context factors are used by authors which are programming language, issue tracking, the total lines of code, the total number of files, the total number of commits, and the total number of developers for prediction. They used 21 code metrics and 5 process metrics in their research. Their experimental results show higher AUC values and higher recall than with-in project models and have better AUC for cross-projects.

Zimmerman et al. [3] proposed a novel transfer learning algorithm called Transfer Naive Bayes (TNB) for cross-company defect prediction. The advantage of transfer learning is that it allows that training and testing data to be heterogeneous. They have used instance-transfer approach in their research which assigns weights to source instances according to their contribution in the prediction model. They use four performance metrics, probability of detection (PD), probability of false alarms (PF), F-measure, and AUC to measure the performance of defect predictor. They show that the TNB gives good performance.

Kitchenham et al. [2] analyzed a cross-company dataset of Web projects. The Web projects may be Web hypermedia or Web software application. They developed a cost estimation model based on these datasets. They used STATA^{TM} tool for the experiment, which uses regression. Their experiment results show that a cross-company effort estimation model can be constructed [6].

3 Methodology

Feed-forward neural networks (FFNNs) are the most popular neural networks which are trained with a back-propagation learning algorithm. It is used to solve a wide variety of problems. A FFNN consists of neurons, which are organized into layers. The first layer is called the input layer, the last layer is called the output layer, and the layers between are hidden layers. The used FFNN model is shown in Fig. 1. Each neuron in a particular layer is connected with all neurons in the next layer.

The connection between the ith and jth neuron is characterized by the weight coefficient w_{ij}. The weight coefficient has an impact on the degree of importance of the given connection in the neural network. The output of a layer can be determined by equations

$$a = x_1 w_1 + x_2 w_2 + x_3 w_3 \cdots + x_n w_n \tag{1}$$

In this research, seven neurons are used at input layer and three neurons are used at hidden layer. The seven inputs are object-oriented metrics which are: NOC[4], RFC[4], DIT[4], WMC[4], CBO[4], LCOM[4], and LCOM5[9].

In this research, following activation functions are used:

1. Hyperbolic tangent sigmoid function (tansig)
2. Linear transfer function (purelin)

Fig. 1 A multi-layer feed-forward neural network

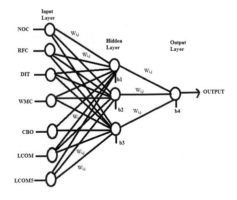

tansig is used as activation function for hidden layer, and purelin is used as activation function for the output layer.

1. **Hyperbolic Tangent Sigmoid Function (tansig)**

It takes two real-valued arguments and transforms them to a range $(-1, 1)$. The equation used for tansig is

$$a = \text{tansig}\,(n) = \frac{2}{(1 + e^{-2*n})} - 1 \tag{2}$$

2. **Linear Transfer Function (purelin)**

Purelin (n) takes one input and returns value n.
The equation for purelin is

$$a = \text{purelin}\,(n) = n + b \tag{3}$$

where b is bias value.

3.1 Performance Evaluation Parameters

Performance evaluation parameters are needed to calculate or validate the performance of the proposed model. If these parameters are not considered, then the performance of the proposed model cannot be evaluated.

Table 1 shows the confusion matrix for fault prediction. The confusion matrix is divided into four subparts which are as following:

  i. True positives (TP): number of modules correctly classified as faulty modules.
 ii. False positives (FP): number of not-faulty classes predicted as faulty classes.
iii. True negatives (TN): number of non-faulty modules correctly predicted as non-faulty.
 iv. Finally, false negatives (FN): number of faulty classes incorrectly predicted as not-faulty classes. According to the confusion matrix, following performance parameter is used to measures the performance of the proposed model:

Specificity: It is also known as true negative rate (TNR). It defines how the faulty classes are classified as faulty by the predictor. It is defined as:

Table 1 Fault detection confusion matrix		Non-faulty	Faulty
	Non-faulty	True negative (TN)	False positive (FP)
	Faulty	False negative (FN)	True positive (TP)

$$\text{Specificity} = \frac{\text{TN}}{\text{FP} + \text{TN}} \qquad (4)$$

ROC (Receiver Operating Characteristics): The performance of a binary classifier is shown by ROC curve. It is in graphical form. The curve is created by plotting the true positive rate (TPR) against the false positive rate (FPR) at various threshold settings.

The true positive rate is calculated as:

$$\text{TPR} = \frac{\text{TP}}{(\text{TP} + \text{FN})} \qquad (5)$$

The false positive rate is calculated as:

$$\text{FPR} = \frac{\text{FP}}{(\text{FP} + \text{TN})} \qquad (6)$$

ROC graphs are two-dimensional graphs in which TP rate is plotted on the Y-axis and FP rate is plotted on the X-axis. The area under ROC curve (AUC) is often calculated to compare different ROC curves. Higher AUC values indicate the classifier is, on average, more to the upper left region of the graph [7]. The ROC curve ranges between 0 and 1. It measures the perceptiveness of the proposed model. The general values of ROC to evaluate perceptiveness of the model are as follow:

If $0.5 \leq \text{ROC} \leq 0.6$: no perceptiveness, i.e., not better than guessing.
If $0.6 \leq \text{ROC} \leq 0.7$: poor perceptiveness.
If $0.7 \leq \text{ROC} \leq 0.8$: good perceptiveness.
If $0.8 \leq \text{ROC} \leq 0.9$: excellent perceptiveness.
If $0.9 \leq \text{ROC} \leq 1.0$: outstanding perceptiveness.

4 Collection of Data

In order to perform this research, data was collected from the Bugzilla[1] database for two versions of Mozilla Firefox (MF) 2.0 and 3.0 and for one version of Mozilla Seamonkey (SM) in which the number of bugs found and corrected in each class of the system. The Bugzilla database contains all errors (bugs) that have been found in projects with detailed information that includes the release number, error severity, and summary of errors. As this study is focused on object-oriented metrics, so only those bugs were considered which were affecting these classes.

---

[1]www.bugzila.org.

Table 2 Dataset details

Name	Number of classes	Number of defect classes	% Defected classes
Licq	280	126	45
Firefox Version 2.0	4524	81	1.79
Firefox Version 3.0	4971	59	1.186
SM Version 1.0.1	4103	47	1.145

Table 3 Descriptive statistical analysis of Licq dataset

		NOC	RFC	DIT	WMC	CBO	LCOM	LCOM5
Mean		0.7071	16.5964	1.5929	24.2571	4.6071	452.721	1.5821
Median		0.0000	7.0000	1.0000	4.0000	3.0000	1.0000	1.0000
Std. deviation		4.16074	52.5919	1.39326	126.54807	12.0081	3936.03	1.31997
Variance		17.312	2765.91	1.941	16014.414	144.196	1.549E7	1.742
Minimum		0.00	0.00	0.00	0.00	0.00	0.00	0.00
Maximum		57.00	720.00	5.00	1920.00	195.00	45002.00	11.00
Percentiles	25%	0.0000	3.0000	0.0000	2.0000	1.0000	0.0000	1.0000
	50%	0.0000	7.0000	1.0000	4.0000	3.0000	1.0000	1.0000
	75%	0.0000	14.7500	3.0000	12.7500	6.0000	8.0000	2.0000

Table 4 Descriptive statistical analysis of Firefox MF Ver. 2.0 dataset

		NOC	RFC	DIT	WMC	CBO	LCOM	LCOM5
Mean		1.0654	27.0009	1.9931	202.1603	10.5524	40.2962	4.3035
Median		0.0000	12.0000	2.0000	4.0000	5.0000	9.0000	2.0000
Std. deviation		16.24396	47.3012	1.8057	1298.32154	14.03634	112.744	8.33282
Variance		263.866	2237.409	3.261	1685638.82	197.019	12711.4	69.436
Minimum		0.00	0.00	0.00	0.00	0.00	0.00	0.00
Maximum		1074.00	764.00	10.00	54619.00	182.00	3233.00	101.00
Percentiles	25%	0.0000	4.0000	1.0000	0.0000	3.0000	1.0000	1.0000
	50%	0.0000	12.0000	2.0000	4.0000	5.0000	9.0000	2.0000
	75%	1.0000	29.0000	3.0000	44.0000	13.0000	36.0000	5.0000

Two MF Versions, i.e., 2.0 and 3.0 and SM Version 1.0.1 open source systems were used for analysis in this study. Another system chosen for cross-company and cross-domain analysis is Licq (an instant messaging or communication client for the UNIX). The database for bugs is obtained from social community known as GitHub[2] community. Licq is smaller system with 280 classes (Tables 2, 3, 4, 5, and 6).

From the descriptive statistics, it was noticed that the maximum DIT level is 11 for Firefox Version 3.0 dataset and almost 75% classes were having three levels of

[2]www.github.com.

Table 5 Descriptive statistical analysis of Firefox MF Ver. 3.0 dataset

		NOC	RFC	DIT	WMC	CBO	LCOM	LCOM5
Mean		1.0758	26.9111	2.1362	40.0406	10.3750	225.845	4.6966
Median		0.0000	11.0000	2.0000	8.0000	5.0000	3.0000	2.0000
Std. deviation		16.4041	48.9986	2.02096	116.30474	14.2038	1451.15	10.0614
Variance		269.096	2400.86	4.084	13526.793	201.750	2105844.9	101.233
Minimum		0.00	0.00	0.00	0.00	0.00	0.00	0.00
Maximum		1132.00	769.00	11.00	3294.00	194.00	55612.00	104.00
Percentiles	25%	0.0000	4.0000	1.0000	1.0000	3.0000	0.0000	1.0000
	50%	0.0000	11.0000	2.0000	8.0000	5.0000	3.0000	2.0000
	75%	1.0000	27.0000	3.0000	34.0000	12.0000	41.0000	4.0000

Table 6 Descriptive statistical analysis of Seamonkey 1.0.1 dataset

		NOC	RFC	DIT	WMC	CBO	LCOM	LCOM5
Mean		1.0846	29.7714	2.0041	245.1311	11.0943	44.4619	4.3215
Median		0.0000	12.0000	2.0000	3.0000	5.0000	7.0000	1.0000
Std. deviation		17.0505	53.7139	1.79840	1523.63884	14.7759	127.550	8.65779
Variance		290.720	2885.18	3.234	2321475.30	218.328	16269	74.957
Minimum		0.00	0.00	0.00	0.00	0.00	0.00	0.00
Maximum		1078.00	770.00	10.00	54950.00	174.00	3250.00	101.00
Percentiles	25%	0.0000	4.0000	1.0000	0.0000	3.0000	1.0000	1.0000
	50%	0.0000	12.0000	2.0000	3.0000	5.0000	7.0000	1.0000
	75%	1.0000	31.0000	3.0000	48.0000	14.0000	37.0000	5.0000

inheritance. Descriptive dataset value of Firefox Versions over Seamonkey Version shows the differentiate data which are expected also. This is only because of the cross-project selection. This selection will help the study to analyze the results in better way for cross-projects. Following object-oriented metrics are used in this research: number of children (NOC), response for a class (RFC), depth of the inheritance tree (DIT), weighted methods per class (WMC), coupling between object classes (CBO), lack of cohesion in methods (LCOM) [8], lack of cohesion in methods (LCOM5) [3].

5 Results

In this section, results are shown which were captured during the experiment conducted for 500, 1000, and 2000 epochs. The experiment was performed on all the datasets to test if the proposed model works for within company, cross-projects, and cross-company defect prediction.

From Table 7, it was analyzed that the Licq dataset gives the highest TNR which is 1 when tested using other datasets. MF Ver. 3.0 shows lowest TNR rate when tested using Licq dataset that represents poor cross-company defect prediction. Further, it was analyzed that when proposed model is applied over the cross-projects (MF Ver. 3.0) or over the cross-company projects (Licq), the results shown in Table 7 were not as favorable as compared to the within company projects.

Table 8 shows the results of proposed fault prediction model for 1000 epochs. The datasets were trained using 1000 iterations.

When TNR rate was analyzed, it shows highest value when Licq tested using other datasets, i.e., the model is favorable for cross-company defect prediction if only TNR is considered. MF Ver. 3.0 gives lowest TNR rate when the model was trained using Licq dataset. Further, it was analyzed that when proposed model was executed on the cross-projects, then the model was favorable for cross-projects as compared to the within company projects and is shown in Table 10.

Table 7 Results for model validation for 500 epochs

Training on	Testing on	% TNR	AUC
MF Ver. 2.0	MF Ver. 2.0	99.91	0.500
	MF Ver. 3.0	99.90	0.619
	SM Version 1.0.1	99.80	0.619
	Licq	100	0.576
MF Ver. 3.0	MF Ver. 2.0	99.91	0.309
	MF Ver. 3.0	99.90	0.662
	SM Version 1.0.1	99.83	0.662
	Licq	100	0.575
SM Version 1.0.1	MF Ver. 2.0	99.62	0.303
	MF Ver. 3.0	99.57	0.646
	SM Version 1.0.1	99.36	0.646
	Licq	100	0.576
Licq	MF Ver. 2.0	33.78	0.685
	MF Ver. 3.0	32.96	0.699
	SM Version 1.0.1	35.20	0.734
	Licq	61.03	0.600
MF Ver. 2.0 with low severity level	MF Ver. 2.0	99.91	0.305
	MF Ver. 3.0	99.90	0.651
	SM Version 1.01	99.83	0.651
	Licq	100	0.571
MF Ver. 2.0 with medium severity level	MF Ver. 2.0	99.93	0.303
	MF Ver. 3.0	99.90	0.650
	SM Version 1.01	99.83	0.650
	Licq	100	0.577

(continued)

Table 7 (continued)

Training on	Testing on	% TNR	AUC
MF Ver. 2.0 with high severity level	MF Ver. 2.0	99.93	0.303
	MF Ver. 3.0	99.90	0.649
	SM Version 1.01	99.83	0.649
	Licq	100	0.576
MF Ver. 3.0 with low severity level	MF Ver. 2.0	99.91	0.310
	MF Ver. 3.0	99.90	0.662
	SM Version 1.01	99.83	0.662
	Licq	100	0.570
MF Ver. 3.0 with medium severity level	MF Ver. 2.0	99.93	0.311
	MF Ver. 3.0	99.90	0.663
	SM Version 1.01	99.83	0.663
	Licq	100	0.576
MF Ver. 3.0 with high severity level	MF Ver. 2.0	99.93	0.308
	MF Ver. 3.0	99.90	0.661
	SM Version 1.01	99.83	0.661
	Licq	100	0.573

Table 8 Results for 1000 epochs

Training on	Testing on	% TNR	AUC
MF Ver. 2.0	MF Ver. 2.0	99.93	0.307
	MF Ver. 3.0	99.90	0.656
	SM Version 1.0.1	99.83	0.656
	Licq	100	0.574
MF Ver. 3.0	MF Ver. 2.0	99.93	0.310
	MF Ver. 3.0	99.90	0.665
	SM Version 1.0.1	99.83	0.665
	Licq	100	0.575
SM Version 1.0.1	MF Ver. 2.0	99.84	0.298
	MF Ver. 3.0	99.76	0.638
	SM Version 1.0.1	99.63	0.638
	Licq	100	0.580
Licq	MF Ver. 2.0	31.87	0.320
	MF Ver. 3.0	31.57	0.233
	SM Version 1.0.1	33.94	0.235
	Licq	72.05	0.461
MF Ver. 2.0 with low severity level	MF Ver. 2.0	99.93	0.305
	MF Ver. 3.0	99.90	0.652
	SM Version 1.0.1	99.83	0.652
	Licq	100	0.573

(continued)

Table 8 (continued)

Training on	Testing on	% TNR	AUC
MF Ver. 2.0 with medium severity level	MF Ver. 2.0	99.95	0.304
	MF Ver. 3.0	99.90	0.650
	SM Version 1.0.1	99.83	0.650
	Licq	100	0.577
MF Ver. 2.0 with high severity level	MF Ver. 2.0	99.95	0.303
	MF Ver. 3.0	99.90	0.650
	SM Version 1.0.1	99.85	0.650
	Licq	100	0.577
MF Ver. 3.0 with low severity level	MF Ver. 2.0	99.93	0.310
	MF Ver. 3.0	99.90	0.664
	SM Version 1.0.1	99.83	0.664
	Licq	100	0.572
MF Ver. 3.0 with medium severity level	MF Ver. 2.0	99.95	0.311
	MF Ver. 3.0	99.90	0.663
	SM Version 1.0.1	99.85	0.663
	Licq	100	0.570
MF Ver. 3.0 with high severity level	MF Ver. 2.0	99.95	0.308
	MF Ver. 3.0	99.90	0.663
	SM Version 1.0.1	99.85	0.663
	Licq	100	0.573

In Table 9, the results of proposed fault prediction model are shown for 2000 epochs; i.e., the training was performed over the selected datasets using 2000 iterations.

Table 9 Results for 2000 epochs

Training on	Testing on	% TNR	AUC
MF Ver. 2.0	MF Ver. 2.0	99.95	0.309
	MF Ver. 3.0	99.90	0.663
	SM Version 1.0.1	99.85	0.663
	Licq	100	0.578
MF Ver. 3.0	MF Ver. 2.0	99.95	0.311
	MF Ver. 3.0	99.90	0.668
	SM Version 1.0.1	99.85	0.668
	Licq	100	0.575
SM Version 1.0.1	MF Ver. 2.0	99.91	0.296
	MF Ver. 3.0	99.88	0.627
	SM Version 1.0.1	99.80	0.627
	Licq	100	0.579

(continued)

Table 9 (continued)

Training on	Testing on	% TNR	AUC
Licq	MF Ver. 2.0	90.23	0.709
	MF Ver. 3.0	43.97	0.726
	SM Version 1.0.1	45.38	0.772
	Licq	67.19	0.629
MF Ver. 2.0 with low severity level	MF Ver. 2.0	99.95	0.307
	MF Ver. 3.0	99.90	0.660
	SM Version 1.0.1	99.85	0.660
	Licq	100	0.574
MF Ver. 2.0 with medium severity level	MF Ver. 2.0	99.95	0.304
	MF Ver. 3.0	99.90	0.652
	SM Version 1.0.1	99.85	0.652
	Licq	100	0.575
MF Ver. 2.0 with high severity level	MF Ver. 2.0	99.95	0.304
	MF Ver. 3.0	99.90	0.650
	SM Version 1.0.1	99.85	0.650
	Licq	100	0.577
MF Ver. 3.0 with low severity level	MF Ver. 2.0	99.95	0.309
	MF Ver. 3.0	0.999	0.666
	SM Version 1.0.1	0.9985	0.666
	Licq	1	0.573
MF Ver. 3.0 with medium severity level	MF Ver. 2.0	99.95	0.310
	MF Ver. 3.0	99.90	0.663
	SM Version 1.0.1	99.88	0.663
	Licq	100	0.568
MF Ver. 3.0 with high severity level	MF Ver. 2.0	99.95	0.311
	MF Ver. 3.0	99.90	0.664
	SM Version 1.0.1	99.90	0.664
	Licq	100	0.576

TNR rate is more than 90% in most of the cases except for the Licq dataset which gives lowest results when the proposed model was trained with it.

6   Conclusion

After studying these results, it is concluded that good prediction system is required for predicting the software defects at an early stage of software development. Neural network is based on a machine learning approach. The proposed neural network model has identified the relationship between errors and metrics. The

Table 10 Comparison with previous work

	Proposed model	Zhang et al. [5]	Ma et al. [9]
AUC for within company projects	0.821	0.70	0.76
AUC cross-projects	0.815	0.79	0.78
AUC cross-company projects	0.772	0.79	0.78

proposed model is also used for cross-company projects also, but the results are not up to the mark. The proposed model has provided better accuracy, AUC, and MSE values (Table 10).

As compared to previous work, these results are better. The proposed model gives AUC value 0.821 using Firefox MF Ver. 3.0 on Firefox MF Ver. 3.0, 0.815 for SM Version 1.0.1 when the model is trained with Firefox MF Ver. 2.0. The model proposed by Zhang et al. [5] is tested on few datasets, so it may not applicable to other datasets. The model proposed by Ma et al. [9] helps to transfer the results of one dataset to others to predict defects in the dataset. It does not provide any defined model for cross-project and cross-company projects [10, 11]. After analyzing these results, it is analyzed that model is well suited for predicting defects in both within company projects and as well as in within company cross-projects but for cross-company projects, and results are not favorable as compared to within company projects. It gives better AUC values for cross-project defect prediction [12–14].

The proposed model predicts defects under different severity levels; as the proposed model was tested under different severity levels, it performs better.

The prediction model is not capable of predicting defects in the cross-company projects [15, 16]. Licq cannot predict defects in MF Ver. 2.0, MF Ver. 3.0, and SM Version 1.0.1 effectively [17, 18]. MF Ver. 2.0, MF Ver. 3.0, and SM Version 1.0.1 cannot predict defect in Licq efficiently.

In future, these models can be used for inter languages software. These models can be further modified for cross-company projects for the better results.

References

1. Pan, S.J., Yang, Q.: A survey on transfer learning. IEEE Trans. Knowl. Data Eng. **22**(10), 1345–1359 (2010)
2. Kitchenham, B.A., Mendes, E., Travassos, G.H.: Cross versus within-company cost estimation studies: a systematic review. IEEE Trans. Softw. Eng. **33**(5), 316–329 (2007)
3. Zimmermann, T., Nagappan, N., Gall, H., Giger, E., Murphy, B.: Cross-project defect prediction: a large scale experiment on data vs. domain vs. process. In: Proceedings of ESEC/ FSE 2009 7th Joint Meeting of the European Software Engineering Conference and the ACM SIGSOFT Symposium on the Foundations of Software Engineering, New York, NY, USA, pp. 91–100 (2009)
4. Peters, F., Menzies, T., Gong, L., Zhang, H.: Balancing privacy and utility in cross-company defect prediction. IEEE Trans. Softw. Eng. **39**(8), 1054–1068 (2013)

5. Zhang, F., Mockus, A., Keivanloo, I., Zou, Y.: Towards building a universal defect prediction model. In: MSR 2014 Proceedings of 11th Working Conference on Mining Software Repositories, pp. 182–191
6. Hitz, M., Montazeri, B.: Chidamber & Kemerer's metrics suite: a measurement theory perspective. IEEE Trans. Softw. Eng. **22**(4), 267–271 (1996)
7. Fawcett, T.: ROC graphs: notes and practical considerations for data mining researchers. Intelligent Enterprise Technologies Laboratory, HP Laboratories Palo Alto, HPL-2003-4, 7 Jan 2003
8. Jamali, S.M.: Object Oriented Metrics (A Survey Approach) (Jan 2006)
9. Ma., Y., Zang, G.L.X., Chen, A.: Transfer learning for cross-company software defect prediction. Inf. Softw. Technol. **54**(3), 248–256 (2012)
10. Chidamber, S.R., Kemerer, C.F.: A metrics suite for object oriented design. IEEE Trans. Softw. Eng. **20**(6), 476–493 (1994)
11. Henderson-Sellers, B.: Software Metrics. Prentice Hall, Hemel Hempstaed, U.K. (1996)
12. Kaur, T., Kaur, R.: Comparison of various lacks of cohesion metrics. Int. J. Eng. Adv. Technol. (IJEAT) **2**(3), 252–254 (2013). ISSN: 2249–8958
13. Mitchell, T.M.: Machine Learning, 1st edn. McGrawHill (1997)
14. Hagan, M.T., Menhaj, M.B.: Training feedforward networks with the Marquardt algorithm. IEEE Trans. Softw. Eng. **5**(6), 989–993 (1994)
15. Aggarwal, K.K., Singh, Y., Kaur, A., Malhotra, R.: Investigating effect of design metrics on fault proneness in object-oriented systems. J. Object Technol. **6**(10), 127–141 (2007)
16. Canfora, G., Lucia, A.D., Penta, M.D., Oliveto, R., Panichella, A., Panichella, S.: Multi-objective cross-project defect prediction. In: Proceedings of the 6th IEEE International Conference on Software Testing, Verification and Validation, 18–22 Mar 2013, pp. 252–261. IEEE, Luxembourg
17. Gayathri, M., Sudha, A.: Software defect prediction system using multilayer perceptron neural network with data mining. Int. J. Recent Technol. Eng. (IJRTE) **3**(2), 54–59 (2014)
18. Jamali, S.M.: Object Oriented Metrics (A Survey Approach) (January 2006)

A Comparative Analysis of Static and Dynamic Java Bytecode Watermarking Algorithms

Krishan Kumar and Prabhpreet Kaur

Abstract Software piracy is one of the most serious issues confronted by software industry creating a huge number of dollars misfortune consistently to the product creating organizations. The worldwide income misfortune was assessed to be more than $62.7 billion in the year 2013 because of the product theft. Software watermarking demoralizes theft, as a proof of procurement or origin, and likewise helps in following the wellspring of unlawful redistribution of duplicates of programming. In this paper, we have compared and analyzed the static and dynamic Java bytecode watermarking algorithms. Firstly, each Java jar file is watermarked using the watermarking algorithms, and after this, distortive attacks are applied to each watermarked program by applying obfuscation and optimizing. After studying the results obtained, we found that dynamic watermarking algorithms are slightly better than static watermarking algorithms.

Keywords Software piracy · Watermarking · Java bytecode · Obfuscation

1 Introduction

From the last decade, code of the software is distributed in an architecturally neutral format which has increased the ability to reverse engineer source code from the executable. With the availability of large amount of reversing tools on the Internet, it had become easy for crackers and/or reverse engineer to copy, decompile, and disassemble of software especially which are made from Java and Microsoft's common intermediate language as they are mostly distributed through Internet.

K. Kumar (✉)
Faculty of Science and Technology, ICFAI University, Baddi, HP, India
e-mail: Krishankumar@iuhimachal.edu.in

P. Kaur
Department of Computer Science and Technology, Guru Nanak Dev University,
Amritsar, India
e-mail: prabhsince1985@yahoo.co.in

© Springer Nature Singapore Pte Ltd. 2019
M. N. Hoda et al. (eds.), *Software Engineering*, Advances in Intelligent Systems
and Computing 731, https://doi.org/10.1007/978-981-10-8848-3_31

319

Many of the software protection techniques can be reversed using the model described in [1].

As per Business Software Alliance (BSA) report [2], the commercial value of pirated software is $62.7 billion in the year 2013. The rate of pirated software had been increased from 42% in 2011 to 43% in 2013, and in most of the emerging economies this rate is high. So, software protection has become an important issue in current computer industry and become a hot topic for research [3, 4].

Numbers of techniques are being developed and employed to control the software piracy [5–12]. One of the techniques to prevent the software piracy is software watermarking. *Software watermarking* is a technique [13] used for embedding a unique identifier into an executable of a program. A watermark is similar to copyright notice; it asserts that you can claim certain rights to the program. The presence of watermark in program would not prevent any attacker from reverse engineering it or pirating it. However, the presence of watermark in every pirated copy later will help you to claim the program is ours.

The embedded watermark is hidden in such a way that it can be recognized at later by using the *recognizer* to prove the ownership on pirated software [14]. The embedded watermark should be *robust* that it should be resilient to semantics-preserving transformations. But in some cases it is necessary that watermark should be *fragile* such that it becomes invalid if the semantics-preserving transformation is applied. This type of watermark is mostly suitable for the software licensing schemes, where if any change is made to the software which could disable the program. Obfuscation and encryption are used for the purpose either preventing the decompilation or decreasing the program understanding, while fingerprinting and watermarking techniques are used to uniquely identify software to prove ownership.

In this paper, we present a comparative analysis of existing static and dynamic Java bytecode watermarking algorithms implemented in Sandmark [15] framework. A total of 12 static and 2 dynamic watermarking algorithms are tested and results are compared.

First section represents the details regarding the watermarking system, types, techniques, etc. In second section, evaluation of testing procedure is presented. In third section, we will present the results of our research work, and finally, fourth section contains the results and future work.

2   Background

Watermarking algorithms are utilized widely in the multimedia industry to recognize the multimedia files such as video and audio files, and similar idea has extended to software industry. The motivation behind watermarking is not to make program harder as in case of obfuscation, but it discourages the software thieves from illegal distributing copies of software as they know they could be identified.

2.1 Difficulties Faced by Software Watermarking

There are several problems related to implementation of software watermarks, and some of the watermarking techniques are vulnerable to various attacks such as distortive attacks. Watermarking software must meet the following set of constraints:

1. Program size: Embedded watermarks should not increase the size of program significantly.
2. Program efficiency: Effectiveness of watermarked system or software must be like unique program and need not be diminished essentially.
3. Robust watermarks: Embedded watermarks must be sufficiently solid to distortive or semantics saving changes.
4. Embedded watermarks must be well hidden, to avoid removal of watermark by the attacker.
5. Watermarks extraction process must be unique such that only software owner can extract the watermark.

One of the troublesome issues which have to unravel is keeping the watermark avoided enemies, while in the meantime permitting the product proprietor to proficiently extricate the implanted watermark when required. In the event that is sufficiently simple then a foe would have the capacity to concentrate watermark as well. In the event that the watermark is concealed well then programming proprietor may have an issue in separating the watermark.

2.2 Watermarking Techniques

Software watermarks can be classified into two classifications: static and dynamic [16]. Static watermark strategies embed the watermark in the information and/or code of the project while dynamic watermarking systems insert the watermark in an information structure assembled at runtime.

Static watermarks are embedded in the information and/or code of a system. For instance, insert a copyright notice into the strings. If there should be an occurrence of Java projects, watermarks could be embedded inside of their consistent pool or system groups of Java class records.

As before the scholastic exploration in the field of software watermarking began, some of pioneer static software watermarking systems were displayed in patents [16, 17]. The principle issue with embedding a string watermark in software is that pointless variables could likewise be effectively uprooted by performing dead code examination, and the majority of the times when obfuscation or optimization of code is applied numerous useless method or variable names are either lost or renamed.

2.3   Classification of Watermark

Nagra et al. classified the watermark into four types [13, 18]:

Authorship Marks are utilized to recognizing a product creator, or creators. These watermarks are mostly visible and robust to the attacks.

Fingerprinting Marks are utilized to serialize the spread article by implanting an alternate watermark in each circulated duplicate. It is utilized to discover the system or channel of dissemination, i.e., the individual who has unlawfully circulated the duplicates of software. The watermarks are for the most part strong, undetectable and comprise of a one of a kind identifier, e.g., client reference number.

Validation Marks are utilized by basically end clients to confirm that product item is authentic, real, and unaltered, for instance, if there should arise an occurrence of Java, digitally marked Java Applets. A typical system is to process the summary of programming item and implants into programming as a watermark. An overview is registered by utilizing the MD5 or SHA-1. An acceptance imprint ought to be delicate and obvious.

Licensing Marks are utilized to guarantee the product is valid against a permit key. One property of these watermarks is that they are fragile. The key ought to wind up futile if the watermark is harmed.

2.4   Types of Attacks to Watermarks [13]

   I. Distortive attacks: These kinds of attacks include applying the semantics-preserving changes to a product, for example, optimizations and obfuscations in this way uprooting any watermark which depend on system language structure.
  II. Additive attack: In these attacks, another watermark is added by an adversary to the effectively watermarked system so as to provide reason to feel ambiguous about which watermark was included first [19].
 III. Subtractive attacks: In these attacks, an aggressor decompiled or dismantled the code keeping in mind the end goal to expel the watermark from the program.

3   The Empirical Evaluation

Static and dynamic software watermarking algorithms are assessed and examined by watermarking the 35 [20] jar files with the available watermarking algorithms implemented in Sandmark and afterward applying distortive attacks to each watermarked jar program file by utilizing obfuscation techniques. After all the jar files have been obfuscated, we attempt to find the inserted watermarks from the obfuscated jar files. It is conceivable that numerous watermarks will be lost due to the obfuscation. We attempt to embed and recognize the watermark **GNDU-Asr** from the jar files.

3.1　The Watermarker

We are going to assess and investigate the 12 out of 14 static watermarking calculations and 2 dynamic watermarking calculations executed in Sandmark [15].

3.1.1　Static Watermarking Algorithms Are as

1. **Add Expression**: A bogus expression containing the watermark is added to class file by this algorithm.
2. **Add Initialization**: This algorithm adds the fake local variable to the distinctive methods as a string into the constant pool of a class file.
3. **Add Method and Field**: Inserts the watermark by partitioning a watermark into two sections: First section is stored in the field's name, and second section is stored in method's name.
4. **Add Switch**: A watermark is embedded as case values of switch statement by this algorithm.
5. **Davidson/Myhrvold** [21]: Watermark is inserted by reordering the fundamental block present in software.
6. **Graph Theoretic Watermark** [22]: Watermark is inserted in a CFG of software, further added to the original software.
7. **Monden**: Watermark is installed by supplanting op-codes in dummy method, produced by Sandmark.
8. **Qu/Potkonjak** [23]: Watermark is embedded in neighborhood variable assignments by adding requirements to the impedance diagrams.
9. **Register Types**: Watermark is embedded by presenting neighborhood variables of certain Java standard library sorts.
10. **Static Arboit** [24]: It is a watermarking calculation that installs the watermark through murky predicates. A watermark is encoded in a misty predicate and after that adding the predicate to a chose branch.
11. **Stern**: Watermark is inserted as a factual item by making a recurrence vector representation of the code.
12. **String Constant**: Embeds the watermark in a string of an arbitrary class.

3.1.2 Dynamic Watermarking Algorithms

1. **Arboit Algorithm** [24]: In this, a trace of the program is used to select the branches. The watermark can be encoded in the opaque predicate by ranking the predicates in the library and then assigning each predicate a value or by using constants in the predicated to encode. It is also possible to embed the watermark through the use of opaque methods. In this case, a method call is appended to the branch and this method evaluates the opaque predicate. If the watermark is encoded using the rank of the predicate, then it is possible to reuse the opaque methods to further distinguish the watermark.
2. **The Collberg-Thomson Algorithms** [15]: This algorithm is a dynamic software watermarking method that embeds the watermark in the topology of a graph structure built at runtime. Watermarking a Java jar file using the CT algorithm and recognizing that watermark requires several phases. First, the source program has to be **annotated**. This means that calls to sandmark.watermark.trace.Annotator.mark() are added to the source program in locations where it is OK to insert watermarking code. Next, the source program is compiled and packaged into a jar file. Then the program is **traced**, i.e., run with a special (secret) input sequence. This constructs a trace file, a sequence of mark ()-calls that were encountered during the tracing run. The next step is embedding which is where the watermark is actually added to the program, using the data from the tracing run.

3.2 The Transformation Attacks

We are using distortive attacks to evaluate the watermarking algorithms. Sandmark research framework contains variety of semantics-preserving obfuscation techniques which will be applied to watermarked jar files. We also use ProGuard [25] to apply optimizations to test case programs.

3.3 The Test Case Jar Files

Test jar files used are plug-ins of jEdit [20] downloaded by installing jEdit [26].

4 Results

Obtained results are represented in Sects. 4.1 and 4.2 regarding static and dynamic algorithms.

4.1 Static Watermarking Algorithms

4.1.1 Watermarking

After embedding watermark GNDU-ASR [27, 28], we have obtained 336 water-marked jar files. Few algorithms failed to insert the predetermined watermark, which may be because of incompatible program or error. For instance, Add expression, String constant, and Allatori successfully embedded watermarks in every one of the 35 test jar program [29–30]. After examining the obtained jar files, we have obtained about 80% of the watermarked jar files (Fig. 1; Table 1).

After examining the 336 obtained watermarked jar files, only 294 watermarked jar files have watermarks which were successfully recognized. That implies success rate of recognizing the watermark is 87.5% (Fig. 2; Table 2).

4.1.2 Obfuscation

We obfuscated 336 jar programs with 36 obfuscation algorithms and 1 optimization, which should have produced 12432 obfuscated watermarked jars files. There are few algorithms failed to produce jars files. So after applying obfuscation to watermarked jar files, we have got 11223 obfuscated watermarked jars utilizing the 37 transformations. This means that only 90.28% attacked watermarked jar files were actually produced (Fig. 3; Table 3).

Fig. 1 Depicts that around ~80% watermarks embeds and 20% gets failed due to some error or incompatible jar file

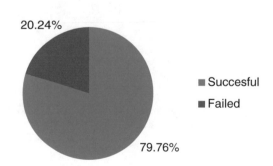

Watermarks embeds

20.24%

■ Succesful

■ Failed

79.76%

Table 1 Percentage of watermarks are embedded and failed

	Total	Successful	Failed
Watermarks embeds	420	336	84
% age		79.76	20.24

Fig. 2 Depicts that 87.5%
watermarks are recognized
while 12.5% got failed before
the transformative attacks are
applied

Watermarks Recognitions

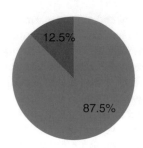

Table 2 Percentage of
watermark recognition before
the transformative attack
applied

	Total	Successful	Failed
Watermarks recognition	336	294	42
% age		87.5	12.5

Fig. 3 Depicts that we have
obtained around 90% jar files
after successfully applying the
obfuscation to the
watermarked jar files

Obfuscations

Table 3 Percentage of jar
file obtained after obfuscation
is applied

	Total	Successful	Failed
Obfuscation	12432	11223	1209
% age		90.28	9.72

4.1.3   Recognition

Result of recognizing the watermark, embedded by different watermarking algorithms after applying the transformative attack i.e. after applying obfuscation, the
resulting obtained watermarked jar files are shown by line graph [31]. The

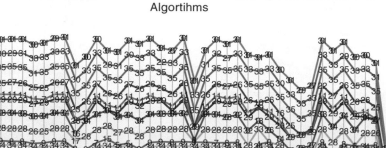

Fig. 4 Depicts the number of successful watermarks recognized embedded by static software watermarking algorithms

horizontal bar line is marked with numbers indicating the number of successful recognition of watermarks with respect to particular obfuscation algorithm (Fig. 4).

4.2 Dynamic Watermarking Algorithms

4.2.1 Watermarking

After embedding watermark, we have obtained 65 out of an expected 70 water-marked jars. Five watermarked jar files failed to embed the specified watermarks, due to error or incompatible program jar (Fig. 5; Table 4).

After examining the 65 watermarked jar files, only 62 jar files having water-marks were successfully recognized. That implies success rate of recognizing the watermark is 95.85% (Fig. 6; Table 5).

Fig. 5 Depicts that around
93% successfully
watermarked jar files are
obtained after watermarking

Watermarks Embeds

■ Successful ■ Failed

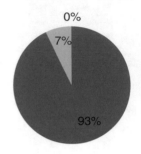

Table 4 Percentage of
successful embedding of
dynamic watermark

	Total	Successful	Failed
Watermarks embeds	70	65	5
% age		92.85	7.15

Fig. 6 Depicts that more
than 95% embedded
watermarks are recognized
before applying obfuscation

Watermarks recognized

■ Successful ■ Failded

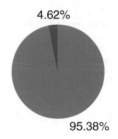

Table 5 Percentage of
watermarks recognized after
watermarking

	Total	Successful	Failed
Watermarks embeds	65	62	3
% age		95.38	4.62

4.2.2 Obfuscation

We obfuscated the 65 jar files with 36 obfuscation techniques, which should have
produced 2340 obfuscated watermarked jars files. There are few algorithms that
failed to produce some jars files. So after applying obfuscation to watermarked jar
files, we have got 2253 obfuscated watermarked jars utilizing 36 transformations
(Fig. 7; Table 6).

In case of Dynamic Arboit algorithm, results are shown (Fig. 8; Table 7).

obfuscation

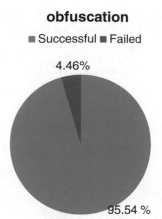

Fig. 7 Depicts that more than 95% obfuscated jar files are obtained after applying obfuscation in case of CT algorithm

Table 6 Percentage of obfuscated jar files after applying transformation with 36 obfuscations algorithms watermarked by CT algorithm

	Total	Successful	Failed
CT Algorithm	1188	1135	53
% age		95.54	4.46

Obfuscation

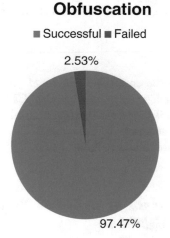

Fig. 8 Depicts that more than 97% obfuscated jar files are obtained after applying obfuscation in case of dynamic Arboit algorithm

Table 7 Percentage of obfuscated jar files obtained after applying transformation with 36 obfuscations algorithms watermarked by dynamic Arboit algorithm

	Total	Successful	Failed
Dynamic Arboit	1147	1118	29
% age		97.47	2.53

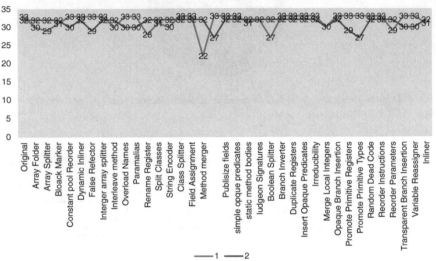

Fig. 9 Depicts the number of successful watermarks gets recognized, embedded by CT and Arboit watermarking algorithms against the obfuscation algorithms

4.2.3 Recognition

The result of recognizing the embedded watermark in the obfuscated jar files is demonstrated by line graph in case of Dynamic CT and Arboit watermarking algorithm [32, 33]. Figure 9 shows the bar line marked with numbers which show the number of jar files successfully recognized the watermark obfuscated by respective obfuscation algorithms shown on x-axis.

4.3 Comparative Analysis of Static and Dynamic Software Watermarking Algorithms

Software watermarking techniques should be resilient against the determined attempts at disclosure and removal of watermark with a specific end goal to stay compelling against the copyright infringement and software piracy. Very little work has been done in this field on assessing the quality of software watermarking algorithms. Our investigation of software watermarking algorithms utilizing the Sandmark had tested the 12 static and 2 dynamic software watermarking algorithms. Test results are indicated in Fig. 10. The algorithms are tested against the distortive attacks. The attacks comprise of arrangement of semantics-safeguarding transformations which are applied to the product or system trying to make the watermark unrecoverable while keeping up the product execution and usefulness like the first.

Figure 10 demonstrates the comparative analysis of static and dynamic software watermarking algorithms. Different algorithms are represented by distinctive shades of bar line checked with number as demonstrated in figure. Each software watermarking algorithm undergone for 37 obfuscation transformations and result of recognizing the watermark after obfuscation are shown below in Fig. 10.

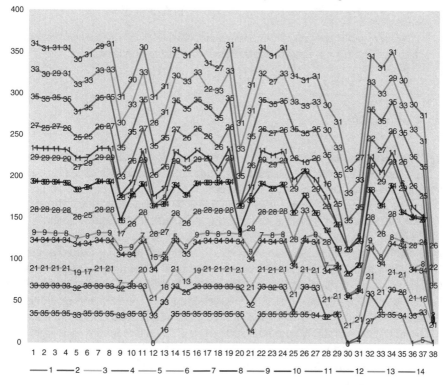

Fig. 10 Comparative analysis of static and dynamic watermarking algorithms. From the above graph, it can be seen that dynamic watermarking algorithms CT and dynamic Arboit are slightly better than static watermarking algorithms

4.4 Analysis of Results

We have tested both the static and dynamic watermarking algorithms within Sandmark with respect to *distortive attacks*. Distortive attacks are any semantics-preserving code transformations, such as code obfuscation or optimization algorithms.

By examining the above figure, it is found that many watermarks got lost due to obfuscations techniques applied.

Important observations of **comparative analysis** are as:

  i. Number of watermarks gets lost because of change applied by obfuscation algorithms.
 ii. String constant watermarking algorithms create the best result and strongest to the distortive attacks, yet it can be effectively evacuated.
iii. Qu/Potkonjak static watermarking algorithm is the weakest algorithms, while it does not effectively installed any watermark.
 iv. Dynamic watermark is marginally superior to anything static against the distortive attacks.
  v. ProGuard analyzer makes the best results with a lower number of watermark affirmations for all watermarkers, beside the string constant.

5 Conclusion

Software piracy is one of most serious issues for software industry, creating loss of a large number of dollars consistently to the product business. Software watermarking is a system which had demonstrated adequate to fight against the product theft. The strategy not ensures but rather helps in discovering the wellspring of unlawful dispersion of software and making legitimate move against them.

We have depicted an examination of the static and dynamic Java bytecode watermarking algorithms implemented inside Sandmark utilizing distortive attacks and affirmed that most watermarks inserted by static watermarking algorithms are very little strong to the distortive attacks applied by obfuscation techniques. From the above results, we can observe that string constant watermarking algorithm delivers best results yet it can be effortlessly uprooted. In the case of dynamic watermarking algorithm, watermarks inserted by CT and dynamic Arboit algorithm are strong to the distortive attacks applied by obfuscation techniques.

From the above results, this is clear that dynamic WM algorithms are somewhat stronger than static WM algorithms when distortive attacks are applied.

Software watermarking must be incorporated with other form of protection such as obfuscation or tamper-proofing techniques in order to better protect software from copyright infringement and decompilation.

References

1. Krishan, K., Kaur, P.: A generalized process of reverse engineering in software protection & security. Int. J. Comput. Sci. Mob. Comput. **4**(5), 534–544 (2015). ISSN 2320–088X
2. http://globalstudy.bsa.org/2013/index.html. Last accessed 20 May 2015
3. Ertaul, L., Venkatesh, S.: Novel obfuscation algorithms for software security. In: 2005 International Conference on Software Engineering Research and Practice, SERP'05, pp. 209–215 (June 2005)
4. Ertaul, L., Venkatesh, S.: Jhide—a tool kit for code obfuscation. In: 8th IASTED International Conference on Software Engineering and Applications (SEA 2004), pp. 133–138 (Nov 2004)
5. Nehra, A., Meena, R., Sohu, D., Rishi, O.P.: A robust approach to prevent software piracy. In: Proceedings of Students Conference on Engineering and Systems, pp. 1–3. IEEE (March 2012)
6. Mumtaz, S., Iqbal, S., Hameed, I.: Development of a methodology for piracy protection of software installations. In: Proceedings of 9th International Multitopic Conference, pp. 1–7. IEEE (Dec 2005)
7. Jian-qi, Z., Yan-heng, L., Ke, Y., Ke-xin, Y.: A robust dynamic watermarking scheme based on STBDW. In: Proceedings of World Congress on Computer Science and Engineering, vol. 7, pp. 602–606. IEEE (2009)
8. Zhu, J., Xiao, J., Wang, Y.: A fragile software watermarking algorithm for software configuration management. In: Proceedings of International Conference on Multimedia Information Networking and Security, vol. 2, pp. 75–78. IEEE (Nov 2009)
9. Shengbing, C., Shuai, J., Guowei, L.: Software watermark research based on portable execute file. In: Proceedings of 5th International Conference on Computer Science and Education, pp. 1367–1372. IEEE (Aug 2010)
10. Donglai, F., Gouxi, C., Qiuxiang, Y.: A robust software watermarking for jMonkey engine programs. In: Proceedings of International Forum on Information Technology and Applications, vol. 1, pp. 421–424. IEEE (July 2010)
11. Shao-Bo, Z., Geng-Ming, Z., Ying, W.: A strategy of software protection based on multi-watermarking embedding. In: Proceedings of 2nd International Conference on Control, Instrumentation and Automation, pp. 444–447. IEEE (2011)
12. Zhang, Y., Jin, L., Ye, X., Chen, D.: Software piracy prevention: splitting on client. In Proceedings of International Conference on Security Technology, pp. 62–65. IEEE (2008)
13. Collberg, C., Nagra, J.: Surreptitious Software: Obfuscation, Watermarking, and Tamper proofing for Software Protection. Addison Wesley Professional (2009)
14. Myles, G.: Using software watermarking to discourage piracy. Crossroads—The ACM Student Magazine (2004) [Online]. Available: http://www.acm.org/crossroads/xrds10-3/watermarking.html
15. Collberg, C.: Sandmark Algorithms. Technical Report, Department of Computer Science, University of Arizona, July 2002
16. Collberg, C., Thomborson, C.: Software watermarking: models and dynamic embeddings. In: Proceedings of Symposium on Principles of Programming Languages, POPL'99, pp. 311–324 (1999)
17. Collberg, C., Thomborson, C., Low, D.: On the limits of software watermarking. Technical Report #164, Department of Computer Science, The University of Auckland (1998)
18. Zhu, W., Thomborson, C., Wang, F.-Y.: A survey of software watermarking. In: IEEE ISI 2005, LNCS, vol. 3495, pp. 454–458 (May 2005)
19. Myles, G., Collberg, C.: Software watermarking via opaque predicates: implementation, analysis, and attacks. In: ICECR-7 (2004)
20. World-Wide Developer Team.: jEdit—programmer's text editor (2015) [Online]. Available: http://www.jedit.org/
21. Nagra, J., Thomborson, C.: Threading software watermarks. In: IH'04 (2004)

22. Nagra, J., Thomborson, C., Collberg, C.: A functional taxonomy for software watermarking. In: Oudshoorn, M.J. (ed.) Australian Computer Science Communication, pp. 177–186. ACS, Melbourne, Australia (2002)
23. Qu, G., Potkonjak, M.: Analysis of watermarking techniques for graph coloring problem. In: Proceeding of 1998 IEEE/ACM International Conference on Computer Aided Design, pp. 190–193. ACM Press (1998)
24. Arboit, G.: A method for watermarking java programs via opaque predicates. In: The Fifth International Conference on Electronic Commerce Research (ICECR-5) (2002) [Online]. Available: http://citeseer.nj.nec.com/arboit02method.html
25. http://proguard.sourceforge.net/
26. Sogiros, J.: Is Protection Software Needed Watermarking Versus Software Security. http://bb-articles.com/watermarkingversus-software-security (March, 2010) [Online]. Available: http://bb-articles.com/watermarking-versus-software-security
27. Weiser, M.: Program slicing. In ICSE'81: Proceedings of the 5th International Conference on Software Engineering, p. 439449. IEEE Press, Piscataway, NJ, USA (1981)
28. Kumar, K., Kaur, P.: A thorough investigation of code obfuscation techniques for software protection. Int. J. Comput. Sci. Eng. 3(5), 158–164 (2015)
29. Collberg, C.S., Thombor-son, C.: Watermarking, tamper-proofing, and obfuscation—tools for software protection. In: IEEE Transactions on Software Engineering, vol. 28, pp. 735–746 (Aug 2002)
30. Stytz, M.R., Whittaker, J.A.: Software protection-security's last stand. IEEE Secur. Priv. 95–98 (2003)
31. Qu, G., Potkonjak, M.: Hiding signatures in graph coloring solutions. In: Information Hiding, pp. 348–367 (1999). citeseer.nj.nec.com/308178.html
32. Collberg, C., Sahoo, T.R.: Software watermarking in the frequency domain: implementation, analysis, and attacks. J. Comput. Secur. 13(5), 721–755 (2005)
33. Hamilton, J., Danicic, S.: An evaluation of the resilience of static java bytecode watermarks against distortive attacks. Int. J. Comput. Sci. (International Association of Engineers (IAENG), HongCong), 38(1), 1–15 (2011)

Software Architecture Evaluation in Agile Environment

Chandni Ahuja, Parminder Kaur and Hardeep Singh

Abstract The function and significance of mission-critical software-intensive systems have got substantial recognition. Software architecture has become a new field since system software is all the time more intricate. Agile software development counters the advancement in requirement, besides to attend to the fixed plan. In this paper, the effort has been made to find parameters for software architecture evaluation and then evaluate software architecture under agile environment based on the determined parameters.

Keywords Software architecture · Agile · Parameters · Metrics

1 Introduction

Present civilization cannot do without the mission-critical software-intensive systems. Software systems are difficult and costly to build and devise. The success of software systems depends on its software architecture as it grows in complexity as well as cost. The analysis of software architecture and designing of major activities is the part of software development. Software engineering has its majority of activities based on software architecture engineering. The function and significance of software architecture have got substantial recognition in past two decades, though it is not a new activity, but has become a new field since system software is all the time more intricate. Now, it is taken into consideration at the time of the

C. Ahuja (✉) · P. Kaur · H. Singh
Department of Computer Science and Engineering, Guru Nanak Dev University,
Amritsar 143005, Punjab, India
e-mail: ahujachandni2@gmail.com

P. Kaur
e-mail: parminder.dcse@gndu.ac.in

H. Singh
e-mail: hardeep.dcse@gndu.ac.in

© Springer Nature Singapore Pte Ltd. 2019
M. N. Hoda et al. (eds.), *Software Engineering*, Advances in Intelligent Systems
and Computing 731, https://doi.org/10.1007/978-981-10-8848-3_32

software development process. Software architecture has number of alternatives to its specification and explanation.

1.1 Definition of Software Architecture

Besides all the denotation of architectonics of software in the published work till now; no such explanation is there that can define software architecture completely in every aspect. The definitions by their commonality define the framework or framework of the system that encompasses software gears, the superficially evident properties of those gears, and the associations amid them [1]. That an architectonics is related with two of all framework and behavior and is related to important decisions, it may abide to styles of architecture, is affected by customers and its surroundings, and takes decision rationally [2].

1.2 Software Architectonics and Software Architect

The vicinity of software architecture has great importance amid software formation and evolvement. The success of a software project depends on the proper use of software architecture, which affects the explanation, implementation, and evaluation aspects of software.

For an outstanding software architect or a team of software architects, it is essential to maintain thin line between the external and internal requirements of software development. Activities, duties, and roles of architects must be attuned to its software development process. Every software developer, without bypassing, has to pass through the activities: requirement, analysis, design, and implementation, and testing cycles, during software development. The accepted Software Development Life cycles (SDLC) in various form of current exercise are (1) waterfall, (2) iterative, (3) iterative and incremental, (4) evolutionary prototyping, and (5) ad-hoc or code-and-fix SDLC [4]. A SDLC provides the idea of how a problem is solved in various stages of software development by an engineer. These activities depict that architects are involved throughout the life cycle of the project's development.

1.3 Agile Software Development

Although in plan-driven methodologies, architectural activities are only limited to the first stage of project development life cycle; almost all stages of agile software development life cycle involve architectural activities. Agile methods have made its base on the Agile Manifesto (http://agilemanifesto.org) that proposes values that uncover the enhanced ways of embryonic software and aids rest to do the similar:

- "Individuals and interactions over processes and tools;
- Working software over comprehensive documentation;
- Customer collaboration over contract negotiation;
- Responding to change over following a plan" [4].

The agenda of agile software development is to counter the advancement in requirement besides to attend to the fixed plan. This leads to the alterations in the results required, which is managed by development process. Such a trend of advancement in work makes it necessary for software architecture to adapt to agile evolution. Apart from various life cycles, the chief principle of agile software maturity is refactoring. Refactoring is alteration of source code and design of the software without changing the functionality or exterior performance of software. The key is to make sure of the attributes of product quality [5]. The capability of an association en route for creation and response to alter in bid to yield in a tumultuous commerce atmosphere is defined as agility [6].

Agile software development is a way to advance the software incrementally and iteratively by reducing waste and only performing actions that directly add value. Agile methods like extreme programming, scrum, agile programming emphasize on rapid and pliable development and reveal the inborn vitality of up-to-date software design. The brimming boon of expeditive iterations is elucidation of constraints that are incorrectly defined earlier, recuperating the dialog amid the project owner and developer and clearing things that cannot work. Secondary benefits involve revision of code that was incorrectly written, which is difficult to clarify in pre-planned projects, and partial cost optimization.

1.4 Agile Architecture Is a Paradox

On one hand, traditional models take account of a number of issues and suffer from the delay due to time and effort invested in designing and implementing components of software as per a good software architecture design in order to cover all requirements, which perhaps may not be utilized in the end. On the other hand, agile models lay emphasis on less documentation, with hardly any planning ahead, and redesigning the software from scratch if it no longer serves the latest demands. On the whole, "it means that architecture and business do not evolve in the same way and same speed" [7]. Agile models manage to adapt to new changes very quickly, whereas software architecture aims at superiority attributes for the system software. Architecture has become potent part of huge and compound projects irrespective of the methods applied. Software architecture is found related in the situation of agile expansion; though, novel methodology and extraordinary preparation are necessary to put together architectural practices in agile expansion [8].

So, using software architectonics skills in agile methodology can get better toward producing system software which has a suitable arrangement as well a satisfactory quality rank [9] and ensuring rapid response change to market needs [10].

2 Literature Survey

The relevant research papers covered for defining problem are given below.

Kruchten [3] presents "what do software architects really do?" Software architect or a team must manage the delicate balance between external and internal forces, to be successful. Teams that go beyond the equilibrium fall into traps which are described as the architectural anti-patterns.

Kunz et al. [5] state agile software development methodologies are widely accepted. Not all metrics and methods from traditional life cycle model are used without adaptation for software evaluation. Different and new techniques are required in the field of software measurement.

Abrahamsson et al. [6] proposed guidelines as to how design and deploy agile processes engrained with sound architectural principles and practices, by presenting the contrasts in both the approaches to the development of software.

Mordinyi et al. (2010) [7] proposed an architectural framework for agile software development, to which on separating the computational and coordination and computational models can offer a great deal of pliability in regard with the architectural and design changes introduced by agile business processes.

Falessi et al. [8] presented a study, to separate the fact from the myths about the potential coexistence of agile development and software architecture, at the IBM Software Laboratory in Rome.

Breivold et al. [10] surveyed the research literature about the relationship between agile development and software architecture. The main findings were that there was no scientific support for the claims made about agile and software development and that more empirical studies are needed in same area to reveal benefits and shortcomings of agile software development methods.

Gardazi et al. [1] describe software architecture as an old activity that has gained recent popularity as a separate activity the during development process. A survey of description, evolution, evaluation, and usage of software architecture in software industry is done and arrived at a conclusion.

Hadar et al. [2] presented a study to understand activities related to software architecture as seen by software architect with or without the knowledge of agile methodologies, to find that software architecture activities are not confined to first phase of software development instead to most or all of the phases of software development life cycle.

Aitken et al. [4] presented a comparative analysis of the presently used agile and traditional methodologies, methods, and techniques and proposed, since the two approaches are not found to be incompatible, which leads to future possibility of Agile Software Engineering.

Akbari et al. [9] present the review to the usage of concepts of software architecture in agile methods, that combine software architecture and agile methods to improve software developments. By using software architecture skills in agile methods can improve the structure of software systems, thus providing quality attributes for software systems. Table 1 shows the comparative analysis of research papers surveyed.

Table 1 Comparative analysis

Reference No.	Advantages	Disadvantages
[1]	Most of the people prefer scenario-based methods software evaluation approach. When a project results in deliverables that are designed to meet a thoroughly architected project, then there is greater likely hood of success	In software industry, most of the projects are offshore projects and are done by purely technical teams. Its success is greatly affected by the use of selection of software architecture
[2]	Strengths of agile methodologies, where the agile architects perceive that their activities are spread throughout the development life cycle. One contributing reason is agile architects reduce their effort in up-front architecture decisions, and so they have much time to devote to every other phase which needs their attention	Quantitative research is needed to validate and verify the hypothesis with willing participation of architects from different methodologies and domains, i.e., how architects with experience in both agile and non-agile methodologies directly perceive the differences between the two methodologies
[3]	A way to track the productive time of architects, by sorting it in three categories, consisting of internal architectural design, external (inward and outward communication), and keeping them in the ratio, is suggested	Implementation reviews are missing, and whether the presented method conforms to the results, is not known
[4]	Agile software development methodologies and traditional software development methodologies are very similar and can be put together to improve efficiency and effectiveness of overall software development	Possibility to merge the two approaches, known as Agile Software Engineering, is left on future researches
[5]	An approach to support agile software development and refactoring using software measurement is presented	Different types of software metrics have not been implemented, and tool only supports Java as a programming language
[6]	Steps for those who are interested in designing and deploying agile processes architectural principles and practices are presented	Empirical study and researchers results in the same field are missing

(continued)

Table 1 (continued)

Reference No.	Advantages	Disadvantages
[7]	Architecture framework for agile processes (AFA) to allow the proficient understanding of new business needs with fewer effects on other gears in the architecture is described	The framework does not have benchmark. A clear evaluation with respect to testing and development time is not available
[8]	Agile developers are found to agree on the values of architectural design patterns for merging agile methods into architectural practices	Non-agile developers seem to be negative about the concept of merging the two approaches
[9]	Several ways to merge and embed software architecture and agile methods are proposed	
[10]	Insight about what researchers all over the globe say about agile and architecture is known	Results of large-scale industrial studies in order to understand how agile and architecture interrelate, i.e., wide range of empirical data is missing

3 Problem Definition

Software architecture, a novel field of software engineering, is a structure of program or a system, which gives correct and well-formed information about its components, and relationship between them. Software architecture is a basis to explain and study the software system.

Agile environment is a conceptual framework, consisting of group of techniques and methods that follow incremental way of development for constant evolution, in order to respond to the changing requirements of the client by delivering small increments of running software.

Many have considered plan-driven software development and agile software development as polar opposites, and software architecture still plays a great role in case of large systems. Real conflict lies in the heavy documentation of software architecture and need of minimalism in agile software development methodologies, whereas many believe amalgam of two can provide software developers with expansive range of tools and options.

4 Objectives

1. To find parameters for software architecture evaluation under agile environment.
2. To evaluate the change in architecture under agile environment based on the determined parameters.

5 Experimental Design

Software is intrinsically ethereal. Systems may be made up of a large number of software elements connected collectively with the help of dissimilar type of need. Creator of software avail oneself of kit to envisage being fit to raise the level of speculation and lessen the amount of facts required. Such category of software kit allows the person to have an access to various windows and themes. Such a subject toggle poses an issue of downloading, installing, and then using tools or system external in a code editor, which is the time-intensive process. Building and implementing such open source software (OSS) visualization plug-in is a substantial initiative in involving the visualization tools in the forward engineering process.

This section presents various software architecture metrics for evaluating software and various agile software metrics to evaluate software in agile environment. Following each is a table listing the metrics with their descriptions.

5.1 Software Architecture Metrics

Design and architectural metrics issues have gained much attention in current years owing to growing size and intricacy of industrial software. These metrics affect four important quality attributes of software architecture that are reusability, interoperability, reliability, and maintainability. The data and the changing software qualities of a software product are measured on the evolution. Metrics are used to find out the quality of the software product during its evolution [11]. Table 2 lists the software architecture metrics.

5.2 Agile Software Metrics

Growth in agile software development methodologies such as extreme programming or agile programming reveals the inborn vitality of up-to-date software design. The pliability of software, the rapid advancement of consumer and technology-driven needs, the complexity of in scripting accurate specifications given all the unknowns, and the intricacy of the software ecosystem itself makes the ancient development waterfall from specification through execution and QA to release a perilous and predominantly futile concern [12]. At the top level, the aim of a software development project is to convey value to patrons with high quality, in time, and in competence. Then is the need of rolling forecast for the overall financial plan and timeline against the business value desired. These are all aspects of situations of the output of a software development process, but not all of them can be simple or measured in a straight line [12]. Table 3 lists the Agile Software Metrics.

Table 2 Software architecture metrics

Abbreviation	Full name of metric	Description
No3C	Number of third-party components	This metric consists of the number of components taken from the outside vendors and reflects the ingenuousness of architecture of the software [11]
NoC	List of components	This metric consists of the total number of architectural units of a particular system which is the highest level of abstraction. It indicates the size of the system. Components can be composite objects, clients, and servers, machines that are virtual in nature
NoCC	Number of control components	This metric indicates those components that give valid output for a given set of valid input. Control components can be also called active units and are like processes, machine at a particular state, knowledge providers. This metric comes under the number of component metric
NoDC	Number of data components	This metric consists of the components that are not actively present at the front, which is passive in nature, like data storage units
TNEI	Total number of external interfaces	This metric consists of the connecting units that make the communication between the internal and external components of the system. This even indicates the level of coupling exhibited by the system. The measure of this metric varies depending upon the level of clustering
TNII	Total number of internal interfaces	This metric consists of the connecting units that make the communication among the internal components of the system. Its measure again varies with the intra-grouping of components
NoSC	Number of specialized components	This metrical tells the list of components which are system specific by nature. These parts are of specific service and do not serve other fields. Its measure depends on the subjectivity of architects and designers
LPSC	List of purpose significant components	The metrical shows the list of major parts whose breakdown badly affects the performance of the system. This is also subjective in nature and measure depends on the designers
LMMP	List of mutual memory parts	The metrical is an essential part which is universal in nature. Due to the global nature of shared memory, it is not a suitable non-functional quality attribute but is still very important from performance point of view
LoAR	List of architectural revisions	The metrical indicates the list of variations that architecture of software was before the present architecture. As the number of architectural revision increases, the architectural quality improves. One should note the architectural revisions can be more than the number of releases of the software architecture

(continued)

Table 2 (continued)

Abbreviation	Full name of metric	Description
NoIT	Number of interface types	This metric is meant to count the various interaction methods available in the system to support the several interactions. The complexity of the system increases with the increase in the number of interface types
NoV	Number of versions	This metric indicates the development of the system, which is the list of product releases so far
LoGC	List of generic components	The metrical is used to number the components which are generic in their usability and functionality
NoRC	Number of redundant components	Components can fail during their working. To recover the system from these failures, the system consists of a list of software and hardware parts which are replication of other components in functionality. Redundant components are maintained to be useful during failures
NoSS	Number of subsystems	The metric indicates the logical or physical components clusters. The number of subsystems indicates the abstraction level of the system, which should be low in coupling and high in cohesion
LoS	List of services	The metrical indicates the list of telecommunication facilities that are provided to the system. As the services increase so does the service interactions, which further increases the complexity
LCP	List of concurrent parts	The metrical indicates the list of parts that are working together at a real time. The measure of this metric affects the quality of the system

In this section, the Eclipse framework and its structure are described; plug-in: X-Ray [15] is introduced, followed by metrical applied in the plug-in with its polymeric outlook; JArchitect features are described; and open source software particularly JFreeCharts is discussed.

5.3 Eclipse

Eclipse has been an open source; a Java-based software structure that is autonomous of platform. The structure is operated to fabricate an Integrated Development Environment (IDE) as well as a compiler which is a portion of Eclipse. It lays stress on putting up off the latch development plan of action that is constructed by extendable structure, tools, and estimated time for constructing, changing, and handling the system. With an enormous sightseer, Eclipse is being used and supported by many universities, known researchers and volunteer individuals.

Table 3 Agile software metrics

Metric	Description	Needs to be
Software size	In agile methodologies, the size of the software is depicted in story points. This is done by breaking down the functionality in user's view to the stories of user [13]	Minimized
Estimate of effort Estimate of staffing	For the proper knowledge of the cost drivers, effort and staffing are at the pinnacle. Agile methodologies do not alter the basic information; also, it does not alter the method for monitoring the growth. It is expected to ought the required skills in the agile teams. It is difficult to do staffing at the early stages. Systems are tested by test teams appointed by the organization outside the scene of the development team	Varies at different stages of development process
Schedule	Speed of performing the work leads to schedule. Agile development has the goal of fixing the schedule variable and it works by maximizing the performance of teams within fixed time frame. This emphasizes stakeholders to properly discuss the needs and take part in prioritizing the work	Maximized
Quality check and customer complacency	Agile methods provide much opportunity for insight in quality check and customer complacency. This makes the customer look into the product itself on frequent delivery of working software, besides the immediate products of work like need of specifications and design documentation. A consistent check on the required functionality and features of the product is very important for the customer content	Maximized
Price and funds	Cost and funding frameworks can be altered by influencing the repetitive feature of agile methodologies. Non-obligatory agreement funding lines frameworks work by adding pliability to managing development and planning organization work	Minimized
Requirements	Requirements are thorough and whole requirements specification document that is not a precondition to the initiation of activities for development in agile methodologies. But, it is advantageous to have the pliability to elucidate, describe extensively and arrange requirements as per the need, which has been presented by user stories, or wide range of programs. The cost of altering the need is noticed at later stages. The rapid incremental approach to agile development reduces the rework	Average

(continued)

Table 3 (continued)

Metric	Description	Needs to be
Delivery and progress	In delivery and progress monitoring, the regular delivery of operational software products provides a clear view of progress. Showing up of system features allows early chances to filter the ultimate product and by making sure that the team of development focuses on the required technological performance	Maximized
High quality	The overall quality of the system can be evaluated by tracking the partial defect rate. • New bug reporting rate The bug rate of complex features is higher than normal, which on iterations decline as the product improves. On the completion of project, it should go down the normal bug rate • Average bug longevity. The quality of the software architecture and team depends on the length of time bugs remain open. The small bug can be fixed in near real-time. Bugs will remain open for longer time or can take an iteration to close in case of serious design flaws	Maximized
Timeliness	The timeliness metric makes sure of feature completion over time. In order to maintain trust between business owners and developers, there is need of transparency of delivered software on a standard schedule. For this features are not released to make sure the schedule is on	Minimized
Efficiency/ Adaptability	The iteration is efficient if it provides evidence as to the estimated total time and cost of the project. Adaptability is a check of how easily an organization is able to adapt to the expected development of a specification, customer feedback, and internal learning that happens as a project proceeds. Adaptability is close to efficiency as the right suitable time to make changes is when the work is being done on the feature. Longer the wait alter a feature, the higher is the cost	
Defects	Agile approaches help development teams to minimize defects over the iterations. Tracking defect metrics tells how well it helps in preventing issues and when to refine its processes [14]	Minimized

(1) *Eclipse Description*

Eclipse is being managed by the Eclipse Foundation and was actually developed by IBM. The company, Eclipse, is not dividend oriented. It lays trustworthy plan of action, free of royalty with right to allot it to all over the world. Open source engagements' rules are its ground rules, which have clean metrical-oriented creation. Everyone has the chance to supply and take part by availing oneself of the plug-in. The Eclipse structure which is the implementation of presenter has its direct interaction with the plug-in. New facilities can be appended or alterations in previously provided facilities can be done. Also, the facilities can be shared among other plug-ins. Eclipse has been created by a huge group of developers around the globe.

(2) *Eclipse Infrastructure*

Hundreds of plug-ins surround a small kernel, making Eclipse a non-single monolithic program. X-Ray is one of the hundred plug-ins. Every plug-in depends on the core services of Eclipse, or which are provided by other plug-ins or combination of both. Hence, code from dissimilar applications and various plug-in is shared and run.

(3) *Eclipse Platform Overview*

Pinnacle projects are there in the workspace, which are further linked to directories specified by the user in the systems. The user is allowed to have access to the structure of system. This is known as the workbench.

5.4 X-Ray

A plug-in called X-Ray operates for the structure of Eclipse. Software visualization significantly assists in software and reverse engineering. Software visualization provides ways to decrease the complex nature of the system in use, rendering it straightforward and simpler perspectives and abstraction properly and fully understand any system. X-Ray plug-in is used to study mini and major projects, which gives the user the chance to understand the system without using stand-alone applications or tools or analyzing the source code.

In this plug-in, the user is allowed to envisage the project while operating it, without using any other tool in order to envisage it, at one place in Eclipse framework irrespective of the stand-alone nature of visualization tools, as shown in Fig. 1. The user can head on to any system, studying its shapes, detecting errors, and collecting favorable information, given various views and using various metrics.

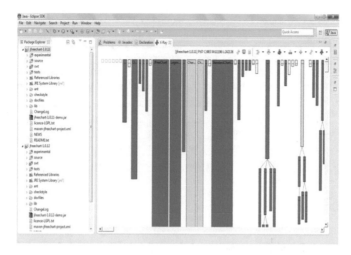

Fig. 1 X-Ray plug-in providing the system complexity view in Eclipse IDE

(1) *Metrics*

Metrical provides a concise version of significant facts. A metrical, which is the consequence of matching a distinctive quality to a mathematical value of an element, is a number. Metrical aids in providing a numerical value of what is not a number in reality. It helps to abridge the unique aspect of the element, to be able to have a significant representation of that aspect in the overall graphical depiction [15]. A polymetric visual image overworks on various metrics to depict them as group of entities.

(2) *X-Ray Metrical*

A variety of metrical X-Ray plug-in is used in for its views, in order to model classes and entities like packages in the form of nodes according to the view where it is shown. It is used to model number of methods, number of lines of a particular code, class of the type, along with weights of its dependency.

(3) *Metrical View of System Complexity*

In X-Ray plug-in view of system complexity, the position of the class is depicted by the position of each and every node of the system which is under consideration. In order to represent the class, hierarchy nodes are placed in a tree structure. Nodes are the visual images of the classes in Java which have different color. White color visualizes interfaces, light blue visualizes abstract classes, blue visualizes concrete classes, and green nodes depict the classes that are external to the system under study. By knowing the kind of representation of various entities, it helps in detecting the design flaws. Table 4 abridges the various metrics used on node in the system complexity view.

Table 4 Various metrics used in the system complexity view

Metrics	Features
Place	Calculated on the basis of the tree arrangement that is in the top-down fashion
Color	White color visualizes interfaces, light blue visualize abstract classes, blue visualize concrete classes and green nodes depicts the classes that are external to the system under study
Width	Number of used methods
Height	Number of lines of a code
Border	Red for stand-alone class; orange for inner class
Edges	It depicts hierarchy of nodes, thus inheritance between classes

5.5 JArchitect

JArchitect is a static analyzer that simplifies complex Java code base. JArchitect has following features:

- Rules and code analysis through CQLinq queries;
- Powerful way to combine many Java tools;
- Interactive tooling;
- Meaningful reporting.

JArchitect makes it easy to manage a complex Java code base. One can analyze code structure; specify design rules, do effective code reviews and master evolution by comparing different versions of the code. JArchitect makes it possible to achieve high Code Quality. With JArchitect, software quality can be measured using Code Metrics, visualized using Graphs and Treemaps, and enforced using standard and custom rules [16].

5.6 JFreeChart

The JFreeChart project was established by David Gilbert in February 2000. JFreeChart is the most commonly used chart library for Java, with 2.2 million downloads till date. JFreeChart is a 100% free Java chart library that makes it simple for developers to produce professional quality charts inside their applications. JFreeChart is meant to be used by developers. JFreeChart has wide range of aspects that include:

- a regular and well-documented API, supporting a wide selection of chart types;
- a pliable blueprint that can easily be extended and is meant to target both client-side and server-side application;
- support for several types of output, including Swing and JavaFX components, image files (including PNG and JPEG), and vector graphics file formats (including PDF, EPS, and SVG);

- JFreeChart is open source free software. It is available beneath the terms of the GNU Lesser General Public License (LGPL), which allows use in proprietary applications.

(1) *Requirements*

- Java 2 platform (JDK version 1.6.0 or later);
- JavaFX requires JDK 1.8

(2) *Funding*

Object Refinery Limited is a private limited liability company that is based in UK and provides funds for the project. It trades documentation for:

- JFreeChart
- Orson Charts (a 3D chart library for Java)
- Orson PDF (a PDF generator for Jave 2D)

6 Results and Discussion

On selecting a project as a target for X-Ray, a default polymeric view opens to the user which tells about the system complexity. Forty-seven versions of JFreeChart are analyzed to acquire general information of respective project which is drawn inside the X-Ray plug-in, as shown in Fig. 2 and Fig. 3.

On placing the cursor on the body of the node, the *tooltip* gives facts about node and reason of its due size. Details of entropy provided by the tooltip are class and its

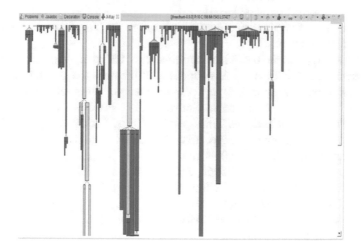

Fig. 2 X-Ray analysis of JFreeChart-0.9.0

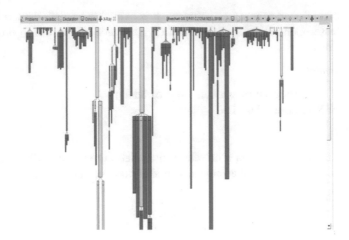

Fig. 3 X-Ray analysis of JFreeChart-0.9.1

name, methods, number of lines of a code, with the Java file which has the source code, a few more classes that are operated by current classes.

The general information for version 1 implementing JFreeChart-0.9.0 is— [X-Ray] P:10 C:196M:1545 L:37427, as shown in Fig. 2. This tells about metrical envisaged by plug-in X-Ray and number of entities, respectively.

The general information for version 2 implementing JFreeChart-0.9.1 is— [X-Ray] P:11 C:212M:1623 L:39196, as shown in Fig. 3. This tells about metrical envisaged by plug-in X-Ray and number of entities, respectively. The X-Ray visualization shows the change from version1 JfreeChart-0.9.0 to version2 JFreeChart-0.9.1, in terms of size, i.e., length and width, and color of nodes. Similarly, rest 45 versions implementing JFreeChart in X-Ray are analyzed and their general information is collected.

Same number of versions of JFreeChart is run in the Visualjarchitect.exe UI, as shown in Figs. 4 and 5.

The result appears in the Visualjarchitect.exe UI when various versions of JfreeChart are run for the analysis of metrics. It provides the general information about each version analyzed, ByteCode Instruction, Lines of Code, Lines of Comment, Percentage Comments, Source Files, Projects, Packages, Types, Methods, Fields, and it analyzes Third-party Projects, Packages, Types, Methods, and Fields used along with the respective JFreeChart version.

In version 1, JFreeChart-0.9.0 is run, as shown in Fig. 4, to give results as follows, ByteCode Instruction: 75966, Lines of Code: 11762, Lines of Comment: 10531, Percentage Comments: 47, Source Files: 192, Projects: 1, Packages: 10, Types: 210, Methods: 1711, Fields: 912, and it analyses Third-party Projects: 2, Packages: 40, Types: 343, Methods: 640, and Fields: 35, that are used along with the respective JFreeChart version.

Fig. 4 Metric evaluation of JFreeChart-0.9.0

Fig. 5 Metric evaluation of JFreeChart-0.9.1

In version 2, JFreeChart-0.9.1 is run, as shown in Fig. 5, to give results as follows, ByteCode Instruction: 79273, Lines of Code: 12185, Lines of Comment: 11222, Percentage Comments: 47, Source Files: 207, Projects: 1, Packages: 11, Types: 233, Methods: 1840, Fields: 932, and it analyses Third-party Projects: 2, Packages: 41, Types: 347, Methods: 650 and Fields: 35, that are used along with the respective JFreeChart version. It provides the general information about JFreeChart versions in Visualjarchitect.exe UI.

In order to find the effect on metrics due to the development of next version for each existing version of JFreeChart, the value of all versions for few metrics is taken, and the difference between two consecutive versions is found. This difference in values of respective metrics is graphically represented in Figs. 6, 7, 8, and 9. It is evident that rate of change is greater from 2nd to 10th version, then sudden rise and

C. Ahuja et al.

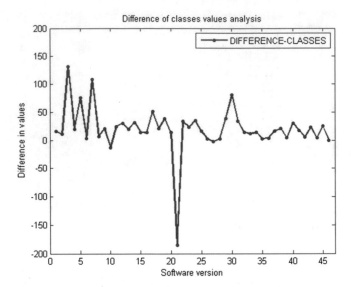

Fig. 6 Difference of classes values analysis

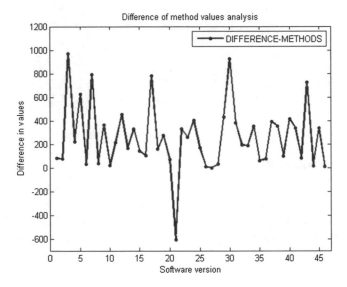

Fig. 7 Difference of method values analysis

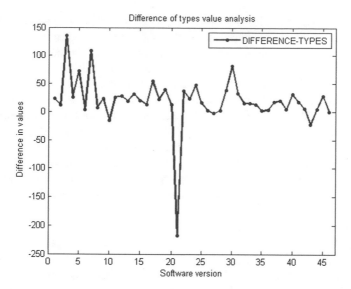

Fig. 8 Difference of types values analysis

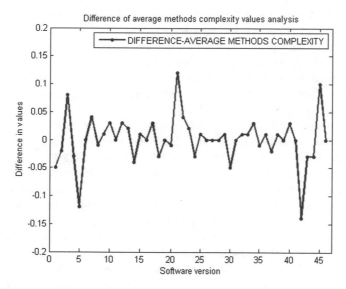

Fig. 9 Difference of average method complexity values analysis

fall at 16th to 18th, then fall and rise at 20th to 22nd version, rise and fall at 28th to 32nd version, again a visible rise and fall at 42nd to 44 version.

In Fig. 6, the value of differences among consecutive values of versions has drastic variations. Versions 2nd to 10th have sudden peaks and valleys. Tenth version onwards highs and lows are even. At versions 20th to 22nd, there is a low valley depicting the sudden decrease in the number of classes. With a sudden increase in the value at versions 28th to 32nd, the highs and lows are again even till last version.

In Fig. 7, the value of differences among consecutive values of versions has drastic variations. Versions 2nd to 10th have sudden peaks and valleys. Tenth version onwards highs and lows are even. At versions 20th to 22nd, there is a low valley depicting the sudden decrease in the number of classes used. With a sudden increase in the value at versions 28th to 32nd and at 42nd to 44th, the rest highs and lows are again even till last version.

In Fig. 8, the value of differences among consecutive values of versions has drastic variations. Versions 2nd to 10th have sudden peaks and valleys. Tenth version onwards small highs and lows are visible. At versions 20th to 22nd, there is a low valley depicting the sudden decrease in the number of types used. With a sudden increase in the value at versions 28th to 32nd, the highs and lows are again even till last version.

In Fig. 9, the value of differences among consecutive values of versions has drastic variations. Versions 2nd to 10th have sudden peaks and valleys. Tenth version onwards considerable valleys can be seen. At versions 20th to 22nd, there is a high peak depicting the sudden increase in the average method complexity. Versions ahead of this witness valleys again, with a sudden decrease in average methods complexity at version 42nd to 44th and sudden increase in the value at versions 44th to 47nd.

In Figs. 6 and 7, the rate of change in classes is proportional to the rate of change in methods used in version, mainly at 2nd to 10th version, and 28th to 32nd version, respectively. This aims to fulfil the expected requirement of newer versions, as the requirements increase so does that classes, and hence the number of methods to implement them. However, the rate of change in methods continues to be high for the version groups from 16th to 18th, and 42nd to 44th version. This usually happens in two cases, firstly, if the number of classes remains same as compared to number of methods which increase in the next version; and secondly, if same number of classes is discarded as the number of new classes added to match the increasing functionality of methods in the next version. Also, the rate of change in rest of the classes and methods remains even and proportional. So far, this observation is very natural, but a striking feature noticed in the two graphs was the sudden decrease in the value at version 21, indicating less number of classes and methods in use and again a sudden rise at version 22, indicating rise in the value of classes and methods in use. The behavior is common in both the cases of classes and methods.

In Figs. 8 and 9, it is clearly visible that the rate of change of types is inversely proportional to rate of change of method complexity from version 20th to 22nd.

Like the striking feature noticed in case of classes and methods, type values used behave similarly, thus increasing the average method complexity. The portion comprising of versions 4th to 6th, 23rd to 25th, 28th to 32nd, and 34th to 36th depicts the increase in the rate of change of types and decrease in the rate of change of methods complexity, which tells about the cohesiveness of the methods. At versions 2nd to 4th, 6th to 8th, 16th to 18th, and 45th to 47th, the increment in the rate of change of types is proportional to the rate of change of methods complexity, i.e., as the number of types increases, so does the method complexity; and vice versa for the versions 28th to 32nd, and 42nd to 44th, i.e., as the number of types decreases, so does the method complexity.

7   Conclusion

Agile software development is a popular way to advance the software incrementally and iteratively by reducing waste and only performing actions that add value. In order to evaluate the change in architecture under agile environment, software with its iterations is analyzed for basic parameters. The change in the parameters like classes, methods, and types is proportional to the user requirement, and with the increase in the methods used to fulfil the user requirements, the average complexity with newer iterations decreases, depicting the cohesiveness of methods.

8   Future Scope

In the near future, the work can be extended by

- Using other software, like system software, application software and then test for results of the tools used to analyze and evaluate software architecture under agile environment.
- Also by broadening the base by increasing number of metrics used in evaluation for significant improvement of the work.

References

1. Gardazi, S.U., Shahid, A.A.: Survey of software architecture description and usage in software industry of Pakistan. In: International Conference on Emerging Technologies, 2009 (ICET 2009), pp. 395–402. IEEE (2009)
2. Hadar, I., Sherman, S.: Agile vs. plan-driven perceptions of software architecture. In: 2012 5th International Workshop on Cooperative and Human Aspects of Software Engineering (CHASE), pp. 50–55. IEEE (2012)
3. Kruchten, P.: What do software architects really do? J. Syst. Softw. **81**(12), 2413–2416 (2008)

4. Aitken, A., Ilango, V.: A comparative analysis of traditional software engineering and agile software development. In: 2013 46th Hawaii International Conference on System Sciences (HICSS), pp. 4751–4760. IEEE (2013)
5. Kunz, M., Dumke, R.R., Zenker, N.: Software metrics for agile software development. In: 19th Australian Conference on Software Engineering, 2008 (ASWEC 2008), pp. 673–678. IEEE (2008)
6. Abrahamsson, P., Babar, M.A., Kruchten, P.: Agility and architecture: can they coexist? Softw. IEEE **27**(2), 16–22 (2010)
7. Mordinyi, R., Kuhn, E., Schatten, A.: Towards an architectural framework for agile software development. In: 2010 17th IEEE International Conference and Workshops on Engineering of Computer Based Systems (ECBS), pp. 276–280. IEEE (2010)
8. Falessi, D., Cantone, G., Sarcia, S.A., Calavaro, G., Subiaco, P., D'Amore, C.: Peaceful coexistence: agile developer perspectives on software architecture. IEEE Softw. **2**, 23–25 (2010)
9. Akbari, F., Sharafi, S.M.: A review to the usage of concepts of software architecture in agile methods. In: 2012 International Symposium on Instrumentation and Measurement, Sensor Network and Automation (IMSNA), vol. 2, pp. 389–392. IEEE (2012)
10. Breivold, H.P., Sundmark, D., Wallin, P., Larsson, S.: What does research say about agile and architecture? In: 2010 Fifth International Conference on Software Engineering Advances (ICSEA), pp. 32–37. IEEE (2010)
11. Kalyanasundaram, S., Ponnambalam, K., Singh, A., Stacey, B.J., Munikoti, R.: Metrics for software architecture: a case study in the telecommunication domain. IEEE Can. Conf. Electr. Comput. Eng. **2**, 715–718 (1998)
12. http://ianeslick.com/2013/05/06/agile-software-metrics/
13. http://blog.sei.cmu.edu/post.cfm/agile-metrics-seven-categories-264
14. http://www.dummies.com/how-to/content/ten-key-metrics-for-agile-project-management.html
15. Jacopo Malnati. http://xray.inf.usi.ch/xray.php (2008)
16. http://www.jarchitect.com/

Mutation Testing-Based Test Suite Reduction Inspired from Warshall's Algorithm

Nishtha Jatana, Bharti Suri and Prateek Kumar

Abstract This paper presents an approach that provides a polynomial time solution for the problem of test suite reduction or test case selection. The proposed algorithm implements dynamic programming as an optimisation technique that uses memorisation which is conceptually similar to the technique used in Floyd–Warshall's algorithm for all pair shortest path problem. The approach presents encouraging results on TCAS code in C language from Software-artifact Infrastructure Repository (SIR).

Keywords Test case reduction · Test case optimisation · Floyd–Warshall's algorithm

1 Introduction

Reduction of test cases is an important and a tedious task, and there have been many attempts by numerous researchers to automate its process. Test suite minimisation is, in general, an NP complete problem [1]. Several algorithms have been proposed to generate reduced test suites that are approximately minimal [2].

Mutation testing was originally proposed by DeMillo [3] and Hamlet [4]. It is a technique that was initially proposed to measure the quality of the test cases. It is a fault-based approach that uses 'mutation score' as the adequacy score for the test suite that needs to be evaluated. Later, the researchers started using it as a technique for generation of test data [5]. The concept of mutation testing is to deliberately

---

N. Jatana (✉) · P. Kumar
Department of Computer Science and Engineering, MSIT, New Delhi, India
e-mail: nishtha.jatana@gmail.com

P. Kumar
e-mail: prateek061093@gmail.com

B. Suri
USICT, GGS Indraprastha University, New Delhi, India
e-mail: bhartisuri@gmail.com

© Springer Nature Singapore Pte Ltd. 2019
M. N. Hoda et al. (eds.), *Software Engineering*, Advances in Intelligent Systems and Computing 731, https://doi.org/10.1007/978-981-10-8848-3_33

357

introduce faults into the source code, thereby generating 'mutants'. The underlying principle that makes mutation testing effective as a testing criterion is that the introduced faults may be very much similar to the faults that a skilled programmer may make. The mutants which are caught by the test cases are said to be killed, and the rest are said to be live mutants. Jia and Harman [5] comprehensively surveyed the overall analysis and development in the field of mutation testing.

Floyd–Warshall's algorithm [6] for finding solution to all pair shortest path problem has been mapped to the test suite reduction problem in this paper. The time complexity of the dynamic programming approach to solve the all pair shortest path problem using Floyd–Warshall turns out to be polynomial, given as $O(n^3)$ [7]. It was originally proposed by Robert Floyd and is popular till date by his name. The 'three nested loop algorithm' that is used today was formulated in the same year by Ingerman [8].

In this paper, we strive to trail the principal of KISS that is an acronym for 'Keep it simple, stupid' [9] that advocates the use of simple techniques rather than complicated ones in design of a solution to a problem. We, therefore, hereby propose a straightforward technique for test case reduction for which many complicated techniques already exist.

The contributions of this paper include

- Demonstrating the problem of selection of test suite reduction as a polynomial time-solvable problem.
- Proposing a method that uses similar concept as used by Floyd–Warshall's algorithm along with the process of mutation testing.
- Empirically stating the results of executing the proposed technique on TCAS code from SIR and triangle problem.

The remainder of this paper is organised as follows: Sect. 2 presents the related work. Section 3 explains the proposed technique. Section 4 illustrates the results, while Sect. 5 gives the conclusion and intended future work.

2 Related Work

Minimising the test suite is an NP-complete problem, so heuristic approaches have been significantly considered to deal with it [1]. Greedy approaches have been applied to obtain minimised test suite [1, 10, 11]. Agrawal [12, 13] minimised the test suite using a delayed greedy approach and the notion of dominators, super-blocks and mega-blocks in order to derive coverage implications amongst the basic blocks for the coverage of statements and branches in the reduced suite. To overcome the limitations of single-criteria test minimisation, multi-criteria test suite minimisation techniques were developed [14, 15]. Yoo and Harman [16] used a genetic algorithm and Pareto-efficient approach for multi-objective minimisation of test suite.

3 Methodology

The proposed approach for test suite reduction uses a concept which is analogous to Floyd–Warshall's algorithm. Research questions address the aim of the study. The experimental design includes the subject programs and tool used in the study. The procedure used to conduct the experiment gives the steps followed for the technique proposed.

3.1 Research Questions

As an evidence for showing that proposed solution is capable of solving test case selection problem, the study addresses the following research questions:

RQ1: Can traditional concepts like dynamic programming be applied for selection of test cases that can run in polynomial time?
RQ2: Is the proposed approach capable of killing significant number of mutants and hence in detecting large number of faults?

3.2 Experimental Design

Subject Programs: Two programs have been used as test benches in our experiment. These programs have been used by numerous researchers in the field of mutation testing [17, 18]. Triangle program is used for the determination of the type of triangle using its dimensions. It takes three variables as input. The code is as used by Jia and Harman [17], and the test cases were randomly generated by specifying the range of input variable from [−10 to 101]. Traffic collision avoidance system (TCAS) is a program designed to avoid or reduce collisions between aircraft. It takes 12 variables as input. The source code and the test cases for TCAS have been downloaded from Software-artifact Infrastructure Repository (SIR) for assessing our technique under controlled experimentation [19]. Table 1 gives description of the subject programs used.

Table 1 Description of subject programs

S. No.	Name of subject program	Size (LOC)	Description	Number of mutants created
1.	Triangle	50	Determines type of triangle from the given length of the sides	121
2.	TCAS	173	Traffic collision avoidance system	79

Tool used: Milu [20] is a mutation testing tool for C language that is efficiently designed for generation of both first-order and higher-order mutation testing. Milu provides easy generation of mutants and provides flexible environment for general purpose mutation testing. This tool was used in this study to generate first-order mutants for the subject programs as mentioned in Table 1. These mutants were used in further evaluation of the proposed approach to measure its effectiveness.

3.3 Procedure

The procedure for the proposed approach is as follows:

1. The mutants of the two subject programs are generated using Milu [20].
2. Test cases are executed against each of the generated mutants, and the corresponding results are to be stored in output files.
3. Test cases are considered to be vertices of a weighted graph, and the weight assigned to each edge is the union of the mutants killed by the two test cases that are assigned to the vertices that are the end points of this particular edge. The aim of the approach is to maximise the mutants killed by a dynamic programming approach on the adjacency matrix of the fully connected graph.
4. The output of the proposed approach is a 2-D matrix W[1...n][1...n], where W [i][j] denotes the maximum mutants killed in going from vertex i to vertex j. The second output is another 2-D matrix P[1...n][1...n], where P[i][j] is a list of all the test cases that were traversed in going from vertex i to vertex j. This path matrix is significant in terms of providing a solution to test case selection problem as the paths specified in the path matrix give us the test cases that can be used for testing the program to detect errors.

3.3.1 Algorithm of Proposed Approach

Variables used:

N: number of test cases
T: a set containing N test cases (initially randomly generated)
S[1...N]: list, where S[i] = Set containing mutants killed by ith test case
P: total number of distinct mutants killed by all test cases combined
PUT: program under test
Sets: total number of test cases.
arr[i][j]: arr[i][j] is the adjacency matrix of the completely connected graph. Initially, it contains the mutants killed by the test case (i) and (j) combined. Finally, it will store the maximum mutants that can be killed if we go from test case (i) to test case (j) in the completely connected graph of the test cases as the nodes.

path[i][j]: total nodes in the path from ith node to jth node in the graph.

p[i][j]: a list to store the node numbers used in the path from test case (i) to test case (j).

Modules used:

Gen_Init_Pop(N): generates initial random test cases

FindMutantsKilled(j): finds the list of mutants (denoted by mutant numbers) killed by the jth test case in T

GetDistinctMutantsKilled(S[], TOTAL): returns the count of the distinct mutants killed by all test files in T

find_union(i,j): finds union of mutants killed by ith and jth test cases

find_union_count(i,j,k): finds count of the mutants killed by kth test case combined with ith and jth test case

find_union(i,j,k): finds union of mutants killed by test case combined with ith and jth test case

enqueue(p[i][j],k): inserts k at the end of p[i][j]

print(k,sets): used to print the status of p[][] and the path[][] matrix at the kth iteration.

Steps followed:

```
1. Begin
2. Generate Mutants of PUT using an automated tool (MILU)
3. T={}
4. T =Gen_Init_Pop(N)
5. Run T on mutants and PUT. This step generates an output for each mutant and PUT in a separate
file.
6. j=0
7. While j<N do
8.      S[j]=FindMutantsKilled(j)
9. end
10. P=GetDistinctMutantsKilled(S[], N)
11. SET sets=N
12. for i=0 to sets do {
13.      for j=0 to sets do {
14.           if(i==j)
15.                arr[i][j].clear();
16.           else
17.                find_union(i,j); } }
18. for k=0 to sets  do {
19.    for  i=0 to sets  do {
20.       for  j=0 to sets  do {
21.          int kill=find_union_count(i,j,k);
22.             if(arr[i][j].size()<kill) {
23.                  find_union(i,j,k)
24.                  path[i][j]++;
25.                  enqueue( p[i][j], k) } } }
26. print(k,sets);  }
```

3.3.2 Time Complexity of the Proposed Approach

The time complexity of the original Warshall's algorithm for all pair shortest path $T1(n) = O(n^3)$ where n is the number of nodes in the graph. Our presented approach for test suite reduction that is conceptually similar to Floyd—Warshall's algorithm has worst-case time complexity, $T2(n) = O(M*n^3)$ where M is the number of mutants and n is the number of test cases. This provides and answers to RQ1, that the proposed technique that implements dynamic approach can provide a polynomial time solution for test case reduction problem.

4   Results

Figure 1 depicts the result of the approach applied to the subject programs. As an answer to RQ2, it can be stated that the proposed technique is able to kill significant number of mutants and thus can be used for test case reduction. It can be seen from the figure that 69% mutants are killed for TCAS code and 89% mutants are killed for triangle code. Therefore, we can conclude that the proposed technique is capable of finding a minimised test suite that is able to detect faults in the program under test. The minimised test suite shown in case of TCAS consists of 14 test cases from the 1608 test cases downloaded from SIR repository and 14 test cases in case of triangle problem also from the 1000 test cases that were randomly generated.

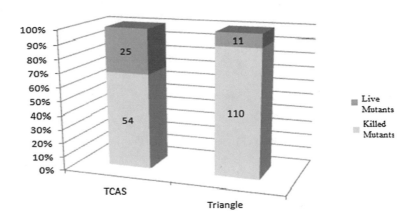

Fig. 1 Result of executing the proposed approach on the test benches ('killed mutants' represent the mutants killed using the proposed approach, and 'live mutants' represent the mutants which were not killed)

5 Conclusion and Future Work

This study proposed a technique for test suite reduction using a dynamic programming approach conceptually similar to that used by Floyd–Warshall's algorithm and its evaluation on TCAS code and triangle problem. The proposed technique runs in polynomial time. The results depict that the proposed technique is capable of finding a minimised test suite that can find faults in the program under test.

As a part of future work, we intend to further verify the proposed approach on larger programs and also apply more traditional algorithms like Kruskal's algorithm, Prim's algorithm, Dijkstra's algorithm and other approaches that employ greedy approach or dynamic programming approach that can be applied with mutation testing for test case generation/optimisation/selection.

References

1. Tallam, S., Gupta, N.: A concept analysis inspired greedy algorithm for test suite minimization. SIGSOFT Softw. Eng. Notes **31**(1), 35–42 (2006)
2. Zhang, L., Marinov, D., Zhang, L., Khurshid, S.: An empirical study of JUnit test-suite reduction. In: 2011 IEEE 22nd International Symposium on Software Reliability Engineering (ISSRE), pp. 170–179 (2011)
3. DeMillo, R.A., Lipton, R.J., Sayward, F.G.: Hints on test data selection: help for the practicing programmer. Computer **11**, 34–41 (1978)
4. Hamlet, R.G.: Testing programs with the aid of a compiler. IEEE Trans. Softw. Eng. **3**(4), 279–290 (1977)
5. Jia, Y., Harman, M.: An analysis and survey of the development of mutation testing. IEEE Trans. Softw. Eng. **37**(5), 649–678 (2010)
6. Floyd, R.: Algorithm 97: shortest path. Commun. ACM **5**(6) (1962)
7. Cormen, T.H., Leiserson, C.E., Rivest, R.L.: The Floyd-Warshall algorithm. In: Introduction to Algorithms, pp. 558–565. MIT Press and McGraw-Hill (1990)
8. Ingerman, P.: Algorithm 141: path matrix. Commun. ACM **5**(11) (1962)
9. Partridge, E., Dalzell, T., Victor, T.: The Concise New Partridge Dictionary of Slang. Psychology Press (2007)
10. Offutt, A.J., Pan, J., Voas, J.M.: Procedures for reducing the size of coverage-based test sets. In: Twelfth International Conference on Testing Computer Software, Washington, D.C., pp. 111–123 (1995)
11. Hsu, H.Y., Orso, A.: MINTS: a general framework and tool for supporting test-suite minimization. In: IEEE Computer Society, pp. 419–429 (2009)
12. Agrawal, H.: Dominators, super blocks, and program coverage principles of programming languages. In: Symposium on 21st ACM SIGPLAN-SIGACT, Portland, Oregon (1994)
13. Agrawal, H.: Efficient coverage testing using global dominator graphs. In: ACM Sigplan-sigsoft Workshop on Program Analysis for Software Tools and Engineering, Toulouse, France (1999)
14. Black, J., Melachrinoudis, E., Kaeli, D.: Bi-criteria models for all-uses test suite reduction. In: 26th International Conference on Software Engineering(ICSE'04), Washington, D.C., USA, pp. 106–115 (2004)

15. Yoo, S., Harman, S.U.M.: Highly scalable multi objective test suite minimisation using graphics cards. In: Search Based Software Engineering, pp. 219–236. SpringerLink (2011)
16. Yoo, S., Harman, M.: Using hybrid algorithm for Pareto efficient multi-objective test suite minimisation. J. Syst. Softw. **83**(4), 689–701 (2010)
17. Jia, Y., Harman, M.: Constructing subtle faults using higher order mutation testing. In: 8th International Working Conference on Source code Analysis and Manipulation (SCAM 2008), pp. 249–258 (2008)
18. Papadakis, M., Malevris, N.: Automatic mutation test case generation via dynamic symbolic execution. In: 21st International Symposium on Reliability Software Engineering, pp. 121–130 (2010)
19. Do, H., Elbaum, S.G., Rothermel, G.: Supporting controlled experimentation with testing techniques: an infrastructure and its potential impact. Empirical Softw. Eng. Int. J. **10**(4), 405–435 (2005)
20. Jia, Y., Harman, M.: MILU: a customizable, runtime-optimized higher order mutation testing tool for the full C language. In: Practice and Research Techniques, 2008. TAIC PART'08. Testing: Academic & Industrial Conference, Windsor, 29–31 Aug 2008, pp. 94–98 (Online). http://ieeexplore.ieee.org/xpl/articleDetails.jsp?arnumber=4670308, http://ieeexplore.ieee.org/xpl/articleDetails.jsp?arnumber=4670308

Software Component Retrieval Using Rough Sets

Salman Abdul Moiz

Abstract Software reusability is one of the important mechanisms needed to maintain its quality and productivity. Even though the candidate components are available in the repository to be reused, software engineers prefer to develop the system from scratch. There exists fear of reuse because the developers are not sure whether candidate component will work. In this paper, first the focus is on retrieving the desired components based on rule generation using rough sets. If the component is not found, then it can be developed and stored in repository. Secondly, uncertainty in identifying the desired component is addressed and an approach to model such uncertainty is proposed. Rough set exploration system (RSES) tool is used to simulate the results on certain behaviors of banking domain.

Keywords Uncertainty · Component extraction · Use case · Rough sets
Decision rules · RSES

1 Introduction

Software reuse is the process of implementing or updating software systems using existing software assets [1]. Software reuse has become a topic of much interest in the software community due to its potential benefits, which include increased product quality, decreased product cost, and schedule. The idea is to maintain a repository of developed components, which forms the basis of reusing them. Reusable components are increasingly replacing the use of monolithic and proprietary technologies [2]. Several approaches are presented in the literature for retrieving reusable components, but a methodology is needed to maintain a repository which helps in retrieving the components effectively.

In this paper, an approach to maintain the component repository is proposed. It is assumed that the repository includes the action states of each of the functionalities

S. A. Moiz (✉)
School of Computer & Information Sciences, University of Hyderabad, Hyderabad, India
e-mail: salman.abdul.moiz@gmail.com

© Springer Nature Singapore Pte Ltd. 2019
M. N. Hoda et al. (eds.), *Software Engineering*, Advances in Intelligent Systems and Computing 731, https://doi.org/10.1007/978-981-10-8848-3_34

so that the appropriate functionality could be retrieved effectively. For a particular domain, there could be several functionalities and corresponding action states. The huge set of action states will be a barrier to retrieve the components. It is proposed to retrieve the components by generating rules using rough sets. Given the requirements realized using actions, the rough set approach can help in retrieving the desired functionalities effectively. Further, there could be a possibility that a different component is retrieved when the same set of action states are given at various instances of time. This leads to a chaos in selecting a particular component. Rough sets are used to address the issues with uncertainty.

The remaining part of this paper is organized as follows. Section 2 specifies the various approaches for component retrieval; Sect. 3 illustrates the mechanism of retrieving components using rough set and later describes the proposed approach in retrieving components using rule generation. Section 4 describes the mechanism to retrieve components for ATM application using RSES tool, and Sect. 5 concludes the paper.

2 Related Work

In most of the reuse-driven development, software assets can be reused when the organizations have significant amount of applications; there exist culture of thinking in terms of reuse, and the development team understands the value of the artifacts when made reusable. Techniques for software component retrieval usually have a problem with maintenance of consistent component repositories. Several approaches for component retrieval are proposed in the literature. In [3], an experiment is proposed in which several components can be retrieved using full-text indexing. However, the issue is to maintain the index structure because as the repository grows the index structure also grows. In [4], an approach for selection of component is proposed using genetic algorithms. But the overlap of functionalities causes confusion, thereby leading to uncertainty. In [5], a mechanism is adopted to compare the components with respect to the structure, behavior, and granularity, and a metric called "direct replace ability similarity" is proposed. As the granularity increases, the performance of component retrieval goes down. In [6], a metamodel is used to retrieve interconnected components by incorporating ontology and taxonomies characteristics. The retrieval approach is based on the given architecture. The retrieval of the component differs from the architecture selected. This may require a huge component repository, and there may be issues in retrieving the component, and the throughput of the system decreases as the repository increases. In [7], cluster of related components forms a subset of libraries. This approach uses text mining approach and clusters the related components. Since the component search starts at word level, the component retrieval may be difficult when the repository grows.

In the proposed approach, the given requirements are modeled using use cases. The action states generated using the use case specifications act as input for component retrieval. The decision rules are generated which helps in selecting a component from the repository.

3 Decision Making Using Rough Sets

Rough sets theory is used in varied applications. It can be used to model and measure uncertainty in applications. Its purpose is to arrive at a proper decision in presence of uncertainty. The approach can be used in many activities of software engineering as the developer is not certain about the artifacts throughout the software development life cycle.

3.1 Rough Sets

A classical set theory for handling of incomplete information call rough set theory was introduced by Pawlak [8]. Rough sets can be introduced informally in software engineering as follows:

Let S be the satisfaction set which specifies the satisfaction of customer from the given set of requirements R (R is a requirements set). The conformance of the end product with respect to given set of requirements can be as follows:

$C1$: All the functionalities (realized for given set of requirements) are up to the satisfaction level of customer

$C2$: All the functionalities are not up to the satisfaction of customer

$C3$: The functionalities are possibly satisfied by the customer

In the rough sets, terminology $C1$ is the lower approximation, $C1$ U $C3$ is upper approximation, and the difference between the lower and upper approximation is the boundary region B. The boundary region specifies the functionalities where customer's satisfaction criterion is unknown. Those functionalities are uncertain with respect to the customer's satisfaction. Rough set is one of the mathematical models to deal with uncertainties [9]. The challenge is to model the uncertainties using approximation in a way that leads to rule generation.

3.2 Methodology for Component Extraction

The goal of the proposed approach is to extract components when the requirements captured using use cases are realized such that it lists the action states. Given the action states, a component may be successfully retrieved or it may not exist or there could be uncertainty in retrieving the components. The uncertainty may arise when

Table 1 Component repository

Requirements	Conditional attributes	Decision attribute

same action state is given at different instances, but the desired outcome differs in each instance. The structure of proposed component repository motivated by Khoo et al. [10] is specified in Table 1.

The requirements set is a universal set (U), and the objects of universal set represent instance of requirements of a domain. For each object, there exists conditional attributes and decision attribute. The decision and conditional attributes together form a set P. As each use case is set of sequence of activities, all the action states are realized as conditional attributes. Few of the action states are selected for implementation of particular functionality. Use case realizes the functionalities of the system. The decision attribute specifies the respective function, component or module available to implement the use case. The decision attributes constitute the functionalities of the system.

In general, whenever there is a request for retrieval of a component or a module, required action states are extracted from use case specification. Given the action states decision, rules are generated using rough sets. These rules help in selecting a component. This would be effective even if the repository grows. In real-time applications, there can be numerous action states as such it will be difficult to identify whether a component for the given functionality is available to be reused.

Consider the following component repository with seven objects which specifies several requests for component retrieval. Two conditional attributes specify the action states, and one decision attribute specifies the functionality selected. To demonstrate the application of rough set theory in component retrieval, one component is assumed to be available in the repository. The decision attributes increases as the number of reusable components increase. In Sect. 4, the results are simulated for few scenarios of ATM applications.

Table 2 specifies a component repository log that specifies the different instances of requirements as a function of action sates and a decision attribute specifying whether a component is available in repository to be retrieved.

The confusion is caused due to uncertainty. Confusion or chaos arises when the retrieved component is same for different action states. The *atoms* and *concepts* are derived from the information given in Table 2.

From Table 2, the $\{a_1\}$—elementary sets are $B_1 = \{r_2, r_6, r_7\}$ and $B_2 = \{r_1, r_3, r_4, r_5\}$. The $\{a_2\}$—elementary sets are $B_3 = \{r_3, r_4, r_6\}$ and $B_4 = \{r_1, r_2, r_5, r_7\}$.

The elementary sets formed by action states are known as atoms [10].

$C = f$ (action states). (r_1, r_4) and (r_2, r_7) are identical as they retrieve the similar components for the identical action states. The atoms are $A_1 = \{r_1, r_5\}$, $A_2 = \{r_2, r_7\}$, $A_3 = \{r_3\}$, $A_4 = \{r_4\}$, and $A_5 = \{r_6\}$. The elementary sets formed by decisions are called concepts [10].

For the decision attribute 1, $C_1 = \{r_3, r_6\}$, and for the decision attribute 0, $C_2 = \{r_1, r_2, r_4, r_5, r_7\}$. r_3, r_4 lead to confusion as it is not certain that whether the component retrieval is possible for the same set of action states (conditional

Table 2 Component repository log

Requirement request	conditional attributes (action states)		Decision attribute (component)
	$a1$	$a2$	
r_1	0	0	0
r_2	1	0	0
r_3	0	1	1
r_4	0	1	0
r_5	0	0	0
r_6	1	1	1
r_7	1	0	0 .

attributes). Rough set theory is used to address these uncertainties. The lower and upper approximation of the selected component (decision attribute = 1) is evaluated as follows:

Only $A_5 = \{r_6\}$ is distinguishable from other atom(s) in C_1 which is r_3. Therefore, lower approximation of C_1 is $\underline{R}(C_1) = \{r_6\}$. The upper approximation is the union of $\underline{R}(C_1)$, and those atoms which are indistinguishable. $\{r_3, r_4\}$ are indistinguishable in C_1. Therefore, upper approximation of C_1 is $\overline{R}(C_1) = \{r_3, r_4, r_6\}$. The boundary region of C_1 is defined as $\overline{R}(C_1) - \underline{R}(C_1)$. Though the boundary region can be computed manually, but when repository grows, it is difficult to compute the uncertainty in uncertainty in retrieving components. As such decision rules can be directly generated when the action states are given. The decision rules are generated using various available mechanisms, viz. exhaustive algorithm, LEM2 algorithm, genetic and covering algorithm. Learning for Example Module, Version 2 (LEM2) [11] is a rule induction algorithm which uses the idea of multiple attribute–value pairs. LEM2 is used in this paper to generate the rules which map the action states to the respective components available in the repository.

The above example only illustrates retrieval of a single component. In the repository, there will be numerous components available and each instance of action state may or may not retrieve a component. If there does not exist uncertainty and the decision variable is 0 for a given set of action state, then the component does not exist and it has to be developed and again stored in repository. There may be a possibility that the existing component may be configured. Hence, there could be several versions of the same components available in the repository.

The steps in the component retrieval are shown in Fig. 1. Given the requirements, the goal is to identify whether there exist any reusable component available in component repository to realize the given requirement. The given requirements are modeled using use cases, and action states are identified. The action states act as input for rule generation, and the decision attribute is analyzed. If the decision attribute is 1 for a particular component, it can be reused. Otherwise, the desired functionality needs to be developed and the repository is to be updated. If the

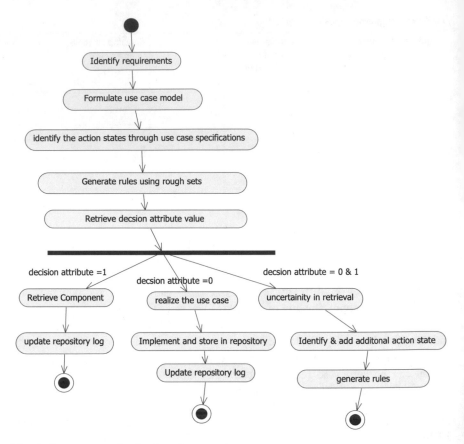

Fig. 1 Component retrieval using rule generation

decision attribute value is 0 at one instance and one at another, then there exists uncertainty. The uncertainty can be modeled by introducing additional attributes, and the rules are generated again by introducing the derived attributes. The derived attribute values help in resolving uncertainty to an extent. In this paper, LEM2 algorithm is used to generate the rules.

4   Results and Analysis

In the proposed approach, an attempt is made to model the component retrieval using rough sets. Consider the transactions of an ATM machine which has several functionalities. Three operations are considered in this paper, viz. withdraw cash, query account, and transfer funds. Each of these functionalities is a use case which includes several action states derived from use case specification. All the action states are maintained in the component repository log relation. The action states form the decision attributes, viz. Boolean. If the action state is selected, then it is high (1), otherwise it is low (0). The problem of choosing an appropriate functionality depends on the action state selected. The action states which are modeled as conditional attributes are used for rule generation. The criterion for selection of the candidate component differs from one domain to the other. Table 3 specifies the component repository log of ATM operations.

The components for the withdraw cash, query account, and transfer funds are represented by F1, F2, and F3, respectively. The total number of conditional attributes, i.e., the action states for these three operations, is represented as A1 to A12. The action states A1 to A12 are captured from use case specification. It was observed from the specification documents of the three functionalities that some of the action states are common between several functionalities of the ATM application. The action states specified by A1, A10, A11, and A12 are common for functionalities for F1 and F2, respectively.

The common action states help in knowing the commonality of various functionalities with respect to action states of a particular domain. If there is a change in few of the action states, then the existing functionality can easily be modified and stored in repository. Several versions of same functionality can be stored in the repository. There may be a possibility that for a given set of action states, no existing functionality exists to be used. This is denoted as F0 in the component repository log of ATM transactions. These functionalities are designed and implemented; then, the component repository is updated with new set of action states and respective functionalities realized.

Table 3 Component repository Log for ATM

A1	A2	A3	A4	A5	A6	A7	A8	A9	A10	A11	A12	Function
1	1	1	1	1	1	1	1	0	0	0	0	F1
1	0	0	0	0	0	0	0	1	0	0	0	F2
1	0	0	0	0	0	0	0	0	1	1	1	F3
1	0	0	0	0	0	0	0	0	1	1	0	F0
1	0	0	0	0	0	0	0	0	1	0	1	F0
1	0	0	0	0	0	0	0	0	1	0	0	F0
1	1	1	1	1	1	1	1	0	0	0	1	F0
1	1	1	1	1	1	1	1	0	0	1	0	F0
1	1	1	1	1	1	1	1	0	0	1	1	F0
1	1	1	1	1	1	1	1	0	1	0	0	F0
1	0	0	0	0	0	0	0	0	1	1	1	F3
1	0	0	0	0	0	0	0	0	1	1	1	F0
1	1	1	1	1	1	1	1	0	0	0	0	F1
1	1	1	1	1	1	1	1	0	0	0	0	F1
1	1	1	1	1	1	1	1	0	0	0	0	F1

Given the component repository log relation as input, rough set exploration system (RSES) tool is used to generate rules using LEM 2 algorithm. The rules generated for Table 3 using LEM2 algorithm on RSES tool are as follows:

(a) $(A1 = 1)$ & $(A2 = 1)$ & $(A3 = 1)$ & $(A4 = 1)$ & $(A5 = 1)$ & $(A6 = 1)$ & $(A7 = 1)$ & $(A8 = 1)$ & $(A9 = 0)$ & $(A10 = 0)$ & $(A11 = 0)$ & $(A12 = 0)$ => (Function = F1[4]) 4

(b) $(A1 = 1)$ & $(A2 = 0)$ & $(A3 = 0)$ & $(A4 = 0)$ & $(A5 = 0)$ & $(A6 = 0)$ & $(A7 = 0)$ & $(A8 = 0)$ & $(A9 = 0)$ & $(A10 = 1)$ & $(A11 = 1)$ & $(A12 = 1)$ => (Function = F3[2]) 2

(c) $(A1 = 1)$ & $(A9 = 0)$ & $(A2 = 1)$ & $(A3 = 1)$ & $(A4 = 1)$ & $(A5 = 1)$ & $(A6 = 1)$ & $(A7 = 1)$ & $(A8 = 1)$ & $(A10 = 0)$ & $(A11 = 1)$ => (Function = F0[2]) 2

(d) $(A1 = 1)$ & $(A9 = 0)$ & $(A10 = 1)$ & $(A2 = 0)$ & $(A3 = 0)$ & $(A4 = 0)$ & $(A5 = 0)$ & $(A6 = 0)$ & $(A7 = 0)$ & $(A8 = 0)$ & $(A11 = 0)$ => (Function = F0 [2]) 2

(e) $(A1 = 1)$ & $(A9 = 0)$ & $(A10 = 1)$ & $(A2 = 0)$ & $(A3 = 0)$ & $(A4 = 0)$ & $(A5 = 0)$ & $(A6 = 0)$ & $(A7 = 0)$ & $(A8 = 0)$ & $(A11 = 1)$ & $(A12 = 0)$ => (Function = F0[1]) 1

(f) $(A1 = 1)$ & $(A9 = 0)$ & $(A2 = 1)$ & $(A3 = 1)$ & $(A4 = 1)$ & $(A5 = 1)$ & $(A6 = 1)$ & $(A7 = 1)$ & $(A8 = 1)$ & $(A11 = 0)$ & $(A10 = 0)$ & $(A12 = 1)$ => (Function = F0[1]) 1

(g) $(A1 = 1)$ & $(A9 = 0)$ & $(A10 = 1)$ & $(A2 = 1)$ => (Function = F0[1]) 1

Description of the rule:

$(A1 = 1)$ & $(A2 = 1)$ & $(A3 = 1)$ & $(A4 = 1)$ & $(A5 = 1)$ & $(A6 = 1)$ & $(A7 = 1)$ & $(A8 = 1)$ & $(A9 = 0)$ & $(A10 = 0)$ & $(A11 = 0)$ & $(A12 = 0)$ => (Function = F1[4]). If A1 = 1 and A2 = 1 and A3 = 1 and A4 = 1 and A5 = 1 and A6 = 1 and A7 = 1 and A8 = 1 and A9 = 0 and A10 = 0 and A11 = 0 and A12 = 0, then function F1 will be selected. The log specifies that this retrieval was done four times.

For a given set of requirements captured using use case, the use case specification is used to capture the action states. If the action states A1 to A8 are only selected, the functionality F1 can be retrieved. Similarly,

$(A1 = 1)$ & $(A9 = 0)$ & $(A10 = 1)$ & $(A2 = 1)$ => (Function = F0[1]). If A1 = 1, A2 = 1, A9 = 0, A10 = 1, function F0 is selected. This means there does not exist any function or component which satisfies these conditional attributes or action states. Hence, the new functionality is to be realized and mapping of action states and new functionality is again stored in repository so that it can be reused in future. This is true for functional requirements. The proposed approach can be implemented by mapping the use case specification to action states. Once the requirements are given, use case is to be modeled, the action states are to be captured, and the same is to be used to generate rules. These rules may help in identifying whether a functionality satisfying these requirements is available for reuse. If it is available, it can be reused directly or can be developed or existing functionality can be modified. For the real-time applications, the quality attributes form a candidate for decision attribute. In some of the applications, the performance, time for execution form important elements in selecting a required component. In such applications though the action states may be same, it may not retrieve the desired component. In such cases, additional attributes are realized for action states such that uncertainty of selecting a proper functionality can be realized.

5 Conclusion

Software reusability is one of the important building blocks which are used to develop a highly productive software within time and budget. In this paper, an approach is presented to retrieve the components by mapping each component with its action states. The decision rules help in mapping the action states to the functionalities available for reuse. Rough sets approach using LEM2 is used to generate the rules. The result shows that given action states, it is possible to select an existing component or identify a functionality which is not available for reuse. The uncertainty can be resolved by introducing additional attributes. The additional attribute may include other action states or a composition of few of other action states. In future, there is a need to model uncertainty but the challenge is to decide upon the additional attribute. Later a domain-specific component repository with rule generation can be maintained so that the component retrieval will be faster.

References

1. Mahmood, S., Lai, R., Kim, Y.S.: Survey of component-based software development. IET Softw. **1**(2) (2007)
2. Kim, H.K., Chung, Y.K.: Transforming a legacy system into components. Springer, Berlin, Heidelberg (2006)
3. Mili, H., Ah-ki, E., Godin, R., Mcheick, H.: An experiment in software retrieval. Inf. Softw. Technol. **45**(10), 663–669 (2003)
4. Dixit, A.: Software component retrieval using genetic algorithms. In: International Conference on Computer & Automation Engineering, pp. 151–155 (2009)
5. Washizaki, H., Fukazawa, Y.: A retrieval technique for software component using directed replace ability similarity. Object Oriented Inf. Syst. LNCS **2425**, 298–310 (2002)
6. Singh, S.: An experiment in software component retrieval based on metadata & ontology repository. Int. J. Comput. Appl. **61**(14), 33–40 (2013)
7. Srinivas, C., Radhakrishna, V., Gurur Rao, C.V.: Clustering & classification of software components for efficient component retrieval & building component reuse libraries. In: 2nd International Conference on Information Technology & Quantitative Management, ITQM, Procedia CS 31, pp. 1044–1050 (2014)
8. Pawlak, Z.: Rough sets. Int. J. Comput. Inform. Sci. **11**(5), 341–356 (1982)
9. Laplante, P.A., Neil, C.J.: Modeling uncertainty in software engineering using rough sets. Innov. Syst. Softw. Eng. **1**, 71–78 (2005)

10. Khoo, L.P., Tor, S.B., Zhai, L.Y.: A rough-set-based approach for classification and rule induction. Int. J. Adv. Manuf. Techol. **15**(7), 438–444 (1999)
11. Grazymala–Busse, J.W.: A new version of the rule induction system Lers. Fundam. Informatica **31**(1), 27–39 (1997)

Search-Based Secure Software Testing: A Survey

Manju Khari, Vaishali and Manoj Kumar

Abstract In today's era, each software developer is developing enormous products consisting non-functional requirements but fails to provide security. Metaheuristic search is used to estimate the test cases with the help of fitness functions, search-based secure software testing (SBST) Security is not possible without the vulnerabilities in the software. The overall objective is to study various vulnerabilities and various metaheuristic techniques. The results of the survey highlighted the numerous fitness functions that could lead to security, further tools were mentioned for various vulnerability scans. The research questions and corresponding solutions to enlighten the scenario are provided in this survey.

Keywords Security · Non-functional requirements · Metaheuristic
Vulnerability scan · Search-based testing

1 Introduction

To ensure good quality software, non-functional requirements (NFRs) must be included along with the functional requirements (FRs). NFR specifies essential need of the system that evaluates operations rather than its significant performance. SBST can be used as an extension to metaheuristic search techniques which generates software tests. Search-based software engineering (SBSE) converts software engineering problem into computational search problem that can be handled with metaheuristic techniques. This involves defining search space or set of possible solutions. SBSE helps as an optimization technique in solving software engineering

M. Khari · Vaishali (✉) · M. Kumar
Department of Computer Science, AIACTR, Geeta Colony, New Delhi 110031, India
e-mail: vaishalig1012@gmail.com

M. Khari
e-mail: manju.khari@yahoo.co.in

M. Kumar
e-mail: mnj_gpt@rediffmail.com

© Springer Nature Singapore Pte Ltd. 2019
M. N. Hoda et al. (eds.), *Software Engineering*, Advances in Intelligent Systems
and Computing 731, https://doi.org/10.1007/978-981-10-8848-3_35

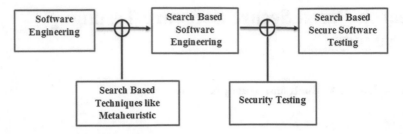

Fig. 1 Evolution of search based secure software testing

problems. In this paper, after identifying the non-functional requirements and the various metaheuristic search algorithms, the focus will be on the fitness functions used for different kinds of algorithms [1]. While using the software, there could be the case when various kinds of vulnerabilities can attack the system. There are different categories of the vulnerabilities, defined in this paper. Security aspects are enlightened with different kinds of solutions in the Web applications as well as in the local system. Various metaheuristic techniques are shown in coming sections along with the susceptibilities, for example buffer overflows, SQL Injection. Their tools and the fitness function are well complemented to provide the security aspects.

In Fig. 1, it is shown that evolution of search-based secure software testing (SBSST) which comprises of various individual stand-alone phases. At the earliest, software engineering (SE) was evolved but that could not provide efficient approach to provide an efficient search within software. So, SE combined with search-based techniques like metaheuristic and search-based software engineering is generated. But SBSE failed to provide security in software. To fulfil those needs, if SBSE is integrated with the security testing (ST) module, then it can be said that SBSST can be successfully formed.

Distribution of the rest of the paper is as follows: Sect. 2 highlights some of the key concepts which will be highly used during the entire paper, explaining the meaning of the keywords used. Section 3 focuses on the most appropriate research questions focuses on this survey and their solutions based on depth research literature. Threats, conclusions are represented in Sects. 4 and 5, respectively.

2 Key Points

- **Metaheuristic**: Metaheuristic is an advanced problem which is standa-lone framework in algorithm. It offers norms, rules, or course of action to formulate algorithms for optimization.
- **SBSE**: SBSE was proved as an efficient technique in development of software ranging from requirements analysis phase to testing of software. It contains particular procedures for testing known as SBST, and test cases generated is

referred as search-based data generation (SBDG). The motive is to formulate a testing requirement in prototype model which could generalize optimization problem for various distinct fitness functions with heuristic.

- **ST**: The objective of it is to expose enormous vulnerabilities and flaws which could be possible in any system. The process can be done through different techniques.
- **Vulnerability Scan**: This is the phenomenon used to match conditions with the existing security issues with the help of automated tools. The upcoming risk is set automatically with no manual verification or interpretation by the test vendor.

3 Strategies of Research

The survey is a process of study and analysis of all available researches done previously by great researchers. It can be interpreted by the means of creating a short summary that can explain the previous work done. With the help of the work done, the survey is being summarized in the form of different research questions and their answers.

3.1 Research Questions

To scrutinize the verification of analysing the non-functional properties which is security whether in local system or in Web-systems, it should have the ability to detect any possible vulnerability by doing vulnerability scan. We have the following research questions:

RQ1: What is metaheuristic and its techniques?
RQ2: Why SBST is used to tackle security vulnerabilities?
RQ3: What is meant by software security testing?

4 Elucidation for Research Questions

4.1 RQ1: What Is Metaheuristic and Its Techniques?

Metaheuristic is an advanced method which is used to discover, create, or pick a heuristic that generates an efficient solution to solve an optimization problem, even with partial collection of knowledge or capacity [2].

Fig. 2 Taxonomy for
"metaheuristic"

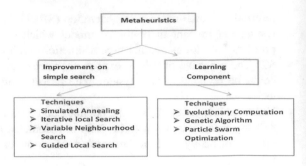

- Properties of Metaheuristic:

  - Metaheuristic is the technique that directs the searching procedure.
  - The aim is to find strengthful solutions, so efficient dealing with search space has been applied.
  - Movement of complex procedure from simple search.
  - In general, metaheuristic is uncertain and non-deterministic.
  - Metaheuristic does not obey problem of explicit domain.

- Classifications on the basis of "type of Strategy" as shown in Fig. 2:

  - **Single versus population-based searches**: Single solution approach concentrates on altering and updating a single solution. It consists of various techniques which are specific and constant in nature whereas, population-based approach updates and modifies compound solutions. It includes evolutionary computation, genetic algorithm (GA), and particle swarm optimization (PSO).
  - **Swarm intelligence**: It is considered as combined or group behaviour of decentralised, self-coordinated mediators in a population or swarm. Examples are: ant colony optimization, PSO, artificial bee colony.
  - **Hybrids and parallel metaheuristic**: Hybrid metaheuristic is the one which integrates present techniques with the other optimization approaches, like mathematical programming, constraint programming, and machine learning. Whereas, parallel approach employs the techniques of parallel programming to run the various metaheuristic searches simultaneously.

4.2 RQ2: Why SBST Is Used to Tackle Security Vulnerabilities?

- SBST attempts to solve two aspects of cost vulnerability problem as follows:

  - Firstly, it is less economical, because as compared to traditional system it is very much less labour concentrated.

Table 1 Analysis of various vulnerabilities

Article	Vulnerability	Fitness function (if any)	Tools used
Antoniol [3]	Buffer overflow	Dynamic weight fitness function (DWF)	RatScan, CodeSonar
Grosso [1]	SQL Injection	–	AMNESIA
Avancini [5]	Cross-site scripting	Subset of population is selected to produce more population and gives final solution	Txl, Yices

- Secondly, SBST techniques are specifically used to tackle subsets of all already familiar vulnerabilities which are accountable for general security threats.

- Search-based security [3] is used to uncover the vulnerabilities and applies different methods to improve its security functionalities as shown in Table 1.

Table 1 summarizes all the vulnerabilities, their corresponding fitness function, and the tools which are helpful in providing security to them. Buffer overflow, SQL Injection, and XSS are the vulnerabilities which mostly occur while working on the software, so their tools are also mentioned in order to provide enough security.

4.3 RQ3: What Is Meant by Software Security Testing?

With the wide use of computers in the era of new technologies, software has become more complicated and implemented in a larger scale resulting in more software security problems. Software security testing is one of the vital means to ensure the security of a software trustiness and reliability.

It can be divided into

- Security functional testing: it states either security functions deployed correctly and in consistent form or not with their specific security requirements or not.
- Security vulnerability testing: it states and discovers security vulnerabilities from the viewpoint of attacker [4].

5 Threats

Whenever any software is prone to any of the vulnerability, we say that particular vulnerability is considered as a threat to the system. Software, prone to threat, can be categorized into

- Progression stage (internal threats): Any software can be interjected at any time by the software engineer in its life cycle of the requirements specification phase and in the SRS document.
- Computation stage (both internal and external threats): This threat is detected when the particular software runs on systems which are connected by the network and when vulnerability is openly shown during the working stage [6]. This stage can be misused by the attackers in the form of leaked script they can login into the system through remote systems, and resulting in the attacks like buffer overflow.

6 Conclusion

This survey showcased the usage of various search techniques for testing security in the running software present in local as well as web system. In ST, GA, LGP, PSO techniques have been applied in order to detect the possible vulnerabilities. It focused on the type of vulnerabilities which could be possible and may cause an attack. There is extensive acceptance of automatic computer systems, and the responsibility played by many of software, and their motive is to provide very high security when it comes to connecting the software applications with the user through networking.

Various tools and their corresponding fitness functions were mentioned in order to protect and detect any upcoming vulnerability in the system. When compared to similar research efforts previously done, this paper concentrates to only the security as the primary parameter to work on. This paper concludes the most important vulnerabilities ever attacked in any system.

Finally, it is clearly felt that the system needs more efficient algorithms and those methods in the software engineering, which can provide secure environment, so that the user can access freely. In the near future, the system will be focussing on the situation where the vulnerabilities should not enter the system without the permission.

References

1. Grosso, C.D., Antoniol, G., Penta, M.D., Galinier, P., Merlo, E.: Improving network applications security: a new heuristic to generate stress testing data. In: GECCO. Proceedings of the Seventh Annual Conference on Genetic and Evolutionary Computation, pp. 1037–1043. ACM (2005)
2. Blum, C., Roli, A.: Metaheuristics in combinatorial optimization: overview and conceptual comparison. ACM Comput. Surv. 35, 263–308 (2003)
3. Antoniol, G.: Search Based Software Testing for Software Security: Breaking Code to Make it Safer, pp. 87–100. IEEE (2009)

4. Gu, T., Shi, Y.-S., Fang, Y.: Research on software security testing. World Acad. Sci. Eng. Technol. **70**, 647–651 (2010)
5. Avancini, A., Ceccato, M.: Security testing of web applications: a search based approach for cross-site scripting vulnerabilities. In: 11th IEEE International Working Conference on Source Code Analysis and Manipulation, pp. 85–94 (2011)
6. Hamishagi, V.S.: Software security: a vulnerability activity revisit. In: Third International Conference on Availability, Reliability and Security, pp. 866–872. IEEE (2008)

Limitations of Function Point Analysis in Multimedia Software/Application Estimation

Sushil Kumar, Ravi Rastogi and Rajiv Nag

Abstract Till date the Function Point Analysis (FPA) was and it is mostly accepted size estimation method for the software sizing community and it is still in use. In developing the software system, software projects cost plays very important role before it is developed in the context of size and effort. Allan J. Albrecht in 1979 developed the FPA, which, with some variations has been well accepted by the academicians and practitioner (Gencel and Demirors in ACM Trans Softw Eng Methodol 17(3):15.1–15.36, 2008) [1]. For any software development project, estimation of its size, completion time, effort required, and finally the cost estimation are critically important. Estimation assists in fixing exact targets for project completion. In software industry, the main concern for the software developers is the size estimation and its measurement. The old estimation technique—line of code—cannot solve the purpose of size estimating requirements for multilanguage programming skill capabilities and its ongoing size growing in the application development process. However, by introducing the FP, we can resolve these difficulties to some degree. Gencel and Demirors proposed an estimation method to analyze software effort based on function point in order to obtain effort required in completion of the software project. They concluded that the proposed estimation method helps to estimate software effort more precisely without bearing in mind the languages or developing environment. Project manager can have the track on the project progress, control the cost, and ensure the quality accurately using given function point (Zheng et al. in estimation of software projects effort based on function point, IEEE, 2009) [2]. But, the use of multimedia technology has provided a different path for delivering instruction. A two-way multimedia training is a process, rather than a technology, because of that interested users are being benefited and have new learning capabilities. Multimedia software developer should use

S. Kumar (✉)
Sharda University, Greater Noida, India
e-mail: sushilkumar_2002@yahoo.com

R. Rastogi
Department of CS & E, Sharda University, Greater Noida, India

R. Nag
B I T Mesra Extention Centre, Noida, India

© Springer Nature Singapore Pte Ltd. 2019
M. N. Hoda et al. (eds.), *Software Engineering*, Advances in Intelligent Systems and Computing 731, https://doi.org/10.1007/978-981-10-8848-3_36

383

suitable methods for designing the package which will not only enhance its capabilities but will also be user-friendly. However, FPA has its own limitations, and it may not estimate the size of multimedia software projects. The characteristics and specifications of multimedia software applications do not fall under FPA specifications. The use of FPA for multimedia software estimation may lead to wrong estimates and incomplete tasks which will end up into annoying all the stakeholders of the project. This research paper is an attempt to find out the constraint of function point analysis based on highlighting the critical issues (Ferchichi et al. in design system engineering of software products implementation of a software estimation model, IMACS-2006, Beijing, China, 2006) [3].

Keywords FPA—function point analysis · CAF—complexity adjustment factor UFPs—unadjusted function points · External outputs (EOs) · External inputs (EIs) External inquiries (EQs) · External logical files (ELFs) · Internal logical files (ILFs)

1   Introduction

In recent times, multimedia software has the potential to be used to share numerous information in lively and interesting ways by merging hypermedia systems with instruction in every walk of life. The end users could be motivated to learn the subjects of their interest through a systematic representation and combination of predictors like multimedia files, scripts, Web building blocks, and hyperlinks.

Designers/developers of multimedia software must decide in advance with the help of clients and end users regarding positioning and locations of textual and graphical elements in the screen or console. While designing the software, it is desirable to have congruence between the functional location and the tools used for designing. Thus, the end user can adequately focus and have experience on the multimedia elements flow instead of having known to internal architecture of multimedia software.

The interactive multimedia instructional packages should be lucid and attractive for the end user. Generally, the developers have the tendency to use lots of audio and video in a single program which is neither cost-effective nor efficient.

So, the judicious mix of audio and video with the instructional material is essential for designing the cost-effective multimedia software. The software industry/developer should not be swayed away by the capacity and capability of voluminous space; otherwise, it will result in wastage of time and effort.

2 Function Point Analysis (FPA)

Allan J. Albrecht, in the middle of 1970, was first one to devise the function point analysis method. Previously, the lines of code were used to calculate the software size to overcome difficulties associated with it, and then, FPA was introduced to help in developing a method to forecast endeavor related with the software development process. The function point analysis was first introduced in 1979; then, later in 1983, he came up with the next edition.

According to Albrecht, the functionality from user's perspective is measured from FPA on the basis of what information the user sends and gets back in return from the system.

The function point formula for calculation of FP is as follows:

$$FP = UFP * CAF$$

where UFP stands for unadjusted function points and CAF is complexity adjustment factor.

The UFP and CAF calculation are shown below.

UFP Calculation:

Based on the counts, five functional factors, the unadjusted function points can be calculated as follows:

(1) External Inputs (EIs),
(2) External Outputs (EOs),
(3) External Inquiries (EQs),
(4) Internal Logical Files (ILFs), and
(5) External Interface Files (EIFs).

2.1 External Inputs (EIs)

EIs are a simple process where the control data or business data cross the borderline from outside of the system to inside of the system. The data can be received from a data input source or a different function. Few internal logical files may be maintained by the data.

2.2 External Outputs (EOs)

A simple process by which processed data cross the borderline from inside of the system to outside of the system is termed as EOs. Additionally, an internal logical file (ILF) is updated by EO. The processed data produce reports or output files with the help of ILFs which are sent to other applications.

2.3 External Inquiries (EQs)

EQ is a simple process of retrieving data form ILFs and external interface files (EIFs). It has both input and output components. Internal logical files are not updated by the input process, and the output side does not contain processed data.

2.4 Internal Logical Files (ILFs)

ILF is a unique collection of logically related data which can be identified by the user. It exists entirely within the applications boundary and is preserved through external inputs.

2.5 External Interface Files (EIFs)

EIF is a collection of logically connected data which are only for referencing purpose. The existence of EIF is outside the application and is taken care of by another application. The EIF is an internal logical file for that application.

2.6 Rating of Components

All the components are put under one of the five major components, i.e., functional units (EIs, EOs, EQs, ILFs, or EIFs), and then, the ranking is done as low, average, or high (weighting factors). Table 1 shows the distribution of components in terms of functional units, weighting factors, and the rate of weights.

Table 1 Functional units and weighting factors

Functional units	Weighting factors		
	Low	Average	High
EIs	3	4	6
EOs	4	5	7
EQs	3	4	6
ILFs	7	10	15
ELFs	5	7	10

Table 2 Table used for calculating UFP

Type of components	Complexity levels			
	Low	Average	High	Total
EI	_x3=_	_x4=_	_x6=_	
EO	_x4=_	_x5=_	_x7=_	
EQ	_x3=_	_x4=_	_x6=_	
ILF	_x7=_	_x10=_	_x15=_	
ELF	_x5=_	_x7=_	_x10=_	
Total number of unadjusted function points				

Table 2 shows the complexity levels of the components. The counts for each and every component can be put as shown in Table 2. For getting the rated value, each count it is multiplied by the numerical value as shown in Table 1. The rated values on every row are added across the table, giving a total value for each type of component. These totals are then again added down to get the final total number of unadjusted function points.

2.7 Calculation of Complexity Adjustment Factor (CAF)

The complexity adjustment factor calculation in FPA is done on the basis of 14 general characteristics (GSCs) for rating of general functionality of the application being counted. These characteristics have allied details which assist in deciding the weights of the characteristics. A scale of zero to five is used to signify no influence to strong influence.

Table 3 describes the GSC briefly.

After getting all the inputs from 14 GSCs, they should be combined and placed in a tabular manner using complexity adjustment equation (CAE). Rate of factors varies from 0 to 5. The factors not useful for the system are rated as 0; the other relevant factors are rated by their influence (importance) as given below:

0—no influence, 1—incidental, 2—moderate, 3—average, 4—significant, 5—essential

$$CAF = 0.65 + 0.01 \left(\sum Fi \right)$$

Here i range from 1 to 14 represents each general system characteristic one by one, and

Fi is the degree of influence of each GSC. Lastly, all 14 GSCs are summed up.

Numerous works have been accomplished in the field of software size and effort estimation in software engineering, and still, a lot many improvements may be required in future.

In software engineering, effort estimation for software projects has been found to be costly and challenging problem. Stakeholders expect a precise estimate for the

Table 3 Description of complexity adjustment factors

S. No.	GSC (general system characteristic)	Description
a	Data communications	Assists in information movement that facilitates the no. of communications with the application
b	Distributed data processing	Handling process of distributed data and its functions
c	Performance	The reply time required by the user
d	Heavily used configuration	Load on the hardware platform where the application is executed
e	Transaction rate	Frequency of transactions: daily, weekly, or monthly
f	Online data entry	Percentage of the information entered online
g	End-user efficiency	The application was designed for end-user efficiency
h	Online update	No. of ILFs updated by online transaction
i	Complex processing	Applications having extensive logical/mathematical processing
j	Reusability	The application developed to meet user/s needs
k	Installation ease	Ease/difficulty is conversion and installation
l	Operational ease	Effective and/or automated; start-up, backup, and retrieval process
m	Multiple sites	Specifically designed, developed, and supported applications to be installed at a no. of sites in many organizations
n	Facilitate change	Application designed, developed, and supported for facilitating change

projects in the early stages, and coming up with those numbers is not only difficult but also at times not technically feasible. Boehm et al. report that estimating a project in its first stages yields estimates that may be off by as much as a factor of 4. Even at the point when detailed specifications are produced, professional estimates are expected to be wrong by ±50% [4].

The author suggested a number of metrics are suggested in the literature by different researchers like—line of code (LOC), feature point, use case point (UCP), object points, and function points for accurate calculation of software size [5].

According to the author, in LOC method, the calculation of software size is done with the help of counting the number of instructions/lines in a given software program. Methods based on LOC are very simple but not very effective in terms of large size software projects [6].

The accurate software size estimation of a software project is really a difficult task, if the code of the software is large enough. The exact sizing of software is very essential component for the software development phase, since it ultimately decides the cost of the given software project. The author also proposed a method for the purpose of accurate software size estimation by proposing a new general system property [7].

The number of end-user programmers will expand exponentially, so end-user programming environments will definitely have impact on software size and effort estimation for software projects. Sizing is a key estimating activity. However, the author anticipates that more precise estimates and characterizations of end-user practices will help researchers target further work in developing languages and tools to assist end users in programming tasks [8].

This paper highlights the point on the software evaluation methods which are already available. According to the author, no model can evaluate the multimedia software cost accurately. Conventional estimation techniques highlight only on the actual development efforts; this paper tries to describe test effort estimation. In fact, testing activities make up 40% of total software development effort. Hence, test effort estimation is a crucial part of evaluation process [9].

3 Multimedia Systems Features Against FPA

The multimedia component such as graphics, menus, audio, video, hyperlinks, scripts that contributes to the representation on the screen cannot be ascertained by using FPA. The developer must focus on three points while developing multimedia software, first getting the user's attention, and then helping the user to find and organize pertinent information, and in the last to integrate all those information into the user's knowledge structure.

Designers/developers should ascertain the positioning of navigational buttons, content display control buttons, status, and progress indicators, and the areas should be separated from each other. For getting the best results, the consistency between screens should be maintained. The location of functional areas should not change, and the devices used in the design should remain the same throughout as defined at the beginning of the program.

To make multimedia software interactive, motivating, and relevant, a framework has to be developed. The successful development of multimedia modules must grab attention; inform about its objectives to the end user and motivate the user, create awareness of prior learning, present the stimulus material to intended, provide learning guidance, elicit performance, provide feedback to the user, assess performance, and enhance retention for maintaining the quality. If these things are taken care of in the software package, then it will effectively lead to easy learning.

For achieving the above, the following multimedia components are required:

Screen Design: The designing of screen is very important for multimedia developers as it is the area of various contents. The screen design should include the textual and graphic elements for presenting the content in a sequential manner to highlight the learning specifics. The content will vary as per the requirements of the package being developed. Each instructional screen or input field should not only be designed aesthetically but also provide appropriate navigation tools and effective instruction to the user.

Navigation/Animation: The navigation/animation features make the multimedia modules interactive which enhances learning and also makes easy for the user to handle it. Navigational elements not only compose a program and perform housekeeping tasks but also provide the user some control over the events. The navigation process should be clearly defined within the system for the user and should remain consistent throughout the program.

Graphics Capabilities: In multimedia software, the information can be provided in either text mode or graphics mode, or, both (if required). Users unable to read the information given in text may easily understand it, if the same is presented or supplemented by use of various visuals. Generally, it has been seen that complex and difficult topics could be understood easily if appropriate graphics are used for explaining them.

Audio: Many multimedia programs use texts as a critical instructional component which is difficult for the beginners to understand. Text type of information is easy and inexpensive to develop, so at times, developers use it extensively as it also used minimal computer memory. The text should be supported by audio.

Video: The multimedia software is incomplete without motion video, like home videos, commercial tapes, and movies, but the video display needs more storage space in the computer than simple animations. This requires special hardware and/or software.

All these multimedia files audio, video, and images required effort to incorporate.

Scripts: To generate reports automatically, it requires an effort to link HTML/XML data.

Web Building Blocks: It required effort to use standard Web components.

Links: To link applications to databases and other applications, it required effort.

Domain of multimedia system is increasing year by year. Because of underestimation or overestimation of multimedia software, an estimation tool has to be evolved. FPA also may not be taken as an accurate tool which lacks the necessary attribute to estimate multimedia software.

Table 4 indicates the features of multimedia software system and FPA.

3.1 Limitations of FPA

1. Calculated function points are not suitable for most of the programming languages.
2. FPA can be successfully used for size estimation of scientific programs, system programs, and networking programming modules.
3. Animations, the simulations size and effects of additional document used in multimedia software are not considered in FPA perspective.
4. Multimedia software holds huge volume of data. FPA occupies less data storage.

Table 4 Significant features required for multimedia software estimation

S. No.	Features	Multimedia software	FPA
1	Technology	Knowledge/expertise in MM	Parametric/proxy-based/algorithmic method
2	Past project experience	Necessary for effective estimation	For producing useful variables for estimation in the case of FPA
3	Time	More time	Time reduced
4	Accuracy	Web/GUI-based applications	Accurate according to the specifications of FPA
5	Dependency		Language dependent
6	Cost	More cost for estimation	Cost is less for estimation
7	Reusability	More considered	Less considered
8	GUI support	Supported	Not supported
9	Database	More considered	Less considered
10	Networking	More considered	Less considered
11	Storage	More considered	Less considered
12	Distribution	More considered	Less considered
13	Multimedia specialization	Must be specialist	Not required
14	Effort in special effects	Required	Not required
15	Consideration of animation	Required	Not required
16	Simulation	Required	Not required

5. Multimedia software requires high level of synchronized service networking, but this kind of data transfer facilities is not available in case of FPA.
6. Multimedia software is extensively used for transmitting the secured data, so to achieve this, high-level security codes are required. Each line in the program, related to security codes, has much weight. FPA does not provide any attention to such codes.

4 Conclusion

The software industry has many models developed by various researchers for estimation of size in terms of time and effort required in developing software packages. The commonly used models are expert estimation, Function Point and its derivatives like use case point, object points, and COCOMO. All the models are available for size and effort estimation.

However, in this modern era with the introduction of new technologies like Java- and Android-based applications, the analysis stated above illustrates that FPA is not fully compatible for estimation of multimedia software system. So, for multimedia software industry, one has to come up with a better software size estimation model which will consider the special requirements of the industry.

References

1. Gencel, C., Demirors, O.: Functional size measurement revisited. ACM Trans. Softw. Eng. Methodol. **17**(3), 15.1–15.36 (2008)
2. Zheng, Y., Wang, B., Zheng, Y., Shi, l.: Estimation of Software Projects Effort Based on Function Point. IEEE (2009)
3. Ferchichi, A., Bourey, J.P., Bigand, M., Barron, M.: Design System Engineering of Software Products Implementation of a Software Estimation Model. IMACS-2006. Beijing, China (2006)
4. Boehm, B., Clark, B., Horowitz, E., Westland, C., Madachy, R., Selby, R.: Cost models for future software life cycle processes: COCOMO 2.0. Ann. Softw. Eng. Softw. Process Product Meas (1995)
5. Diwaker, C., Dhiman, A.: Size and effort estimation techniques for software development. Int. J. Soft. Web Sci. (IJSWS) (2013)
6. Choursiya, N., Yadav, R.: A survey on software size and effort estimation techniques. Cogn. Tech. Res. J. **2**(2) (2014)
7. Nilesh, C., Rashmi, Y.: An enhanced function point analysis (FPA) method for software size estimation. Int. J. Comput. Sci. Inf. Technol. **6**(3), 2797–2799 (2015)
8. Archana, S., Qamar, A.S., Singh, S.K.: Enhancement in function point analysis. Int. J. Softw. Eng. Appl. (IJSEA) **3**(6) (2012)
9. Borade, J.G., Khalkar, V.R.: Software project effort and cost estimation techniques. Int. J. Adv. Res. Comput. Sci. Softw. Eng. **3**(8) (2013). ISSN: 2277 128X

Maintainability Analysis of Component-Based Software Architecture

Nitin Upadhyay

Abstract The analysis of the maintainability of a component-based software system (*CBSS*) architecture is a critical issue as it majorly contributes to the overall quality, risks, and economics of the software product life cycle. Architectural styles' features of *CBSS*, which characterize maintainability, are identified and represented as architecture-style-maintainability digraph. The maintainability scenarios are represented by the digraph nodes. The edges of the digraph represent the degree of influence among the scenarios. A detailed procedure for the maintainability analysis of *CBSS* is suggested through a maintainability function. The scenario maintainability index *SMI* measures the maintainability of a system. A lower value of the *SMI* implies better maintainability of the system. The maintainability analysis procedure mentioned in the paper helps the key stakeholders of the *CBSS* in managing, controlling, and improvising the maintainability of a system by appropriately incorporating maintainability scenarios in heterogeneous architectural styles.

Keywords Maintainability · Software architecture · Software component
Architecture analysis · Maintainability index

1 Introduction

The maintenance analysis and execution in software product life cycle are considered to be the critical issue as it contributes to 60–80% of the total life costs [1–3] no matter whether the software is built from custom or commercial-off-the-shelf (COTS). As maintenance process majorly contributes to the overall quality, risks, and economics of the software product life cycle, some organizations are looking at their maintenance process life cycle as an area for competitive age [4]. Software

N. Upadhyay (✉)
Information Technology and Production & Operations Management,
Goa Institute of Management, Sattari, India
e-mail: nitin@gim.ac.in

© Springer Nature Singapore Pte Ltd. 2019   393
M. N. Hoda et al. (eds.), *Software Engineering*, Advances in Intelligent Systems
and Computing 731, https://doi.org/10.1007/978-981-10-8848-3_37

organizations nowadays prefer the usage of component technology to get just-in-time software product. Building a software system from COTS does not change the importance nor the expense associated with the maintenance, evolution, and management [5]. Software maintenance as per IEEE Standard 1219 is defined as:

> Modification of a software product after delivery to correct faults, to improve performance or other attributes, or to adapt the product to a modified environment [6].

Software architecture design phase is considered as a major and critical phase as most of the decisions taken at this stage a have major impact on overall software product life cycle. Maintainability is considered to be a design attribute of a system and thus plays a significant role during system operation. The inputs to the design stage are the requirements which include all desired system features and specifications as per system stakeholders. The quality of the product is driven by its architectural design decisions. A software architectural design would be completely successful if it fulfills all/maximum system's functional and non-functional requirements. Authors in their work [7, 8] have mentioned that the quality of a component-based software system is influenced by the composition and complexity of the components in the system. Software architecture encompasses set of components, connectors, and configurations describe the software structure at an abstract level [9]. An architectural style represents the software architecture repeatable pattern that characterizes its configurations of components and connectors [10]. Researches have come with many effective architectural styles and many new styles continuously emerging as the consequence of technological advancements [11–13]. The maintainability scenarios required to address the maintainability requirement will have a great impact on the architectural style. Thus, a practitioner needs to understand *how to analyze maintainability scenario and associated architecture as a whole to get the desired quality*? A method or model that supports analysis of the maintainability of a CBSS considering architectural style(s) and scenarios can certainly provide benefit to practitioners, maintainers, and designers to configure, control, and manage the overall product life cycle that best fits their maintainability quality demands. In the paper [8], the authors have utilized system graph to represent complete CBSS in terms of its subsystems. The system graph models CBSS structure as system structural graphs considering subsystems and interactions between them. In the current paper, aforementioned problem is addressed and correlation of the maintainability of the CBSS with its architecture and maintainability scenarios is accomplished.

Most techniques in the research in the maintainability assessment and evaluation relate to the number of lines of code and generally based on linear regression. The rest of the paper is structured as follows: Sect. 2 describes the development of maintainability scenario and graph. In Sect. 3, maintainability analysis and scenario evaluation is discussed. Finally, in Sect. 4 concluding remarks are presented by providing the benefits of the developed method.

2 Maintainability Scenario and Graph

According to the authors [10], to understand the software architecture, during the requirement elicitation phase the scenarios must be used and documented throughout, considering operator's viewpoint of the system [14]. To understand system's maintainability, it is to be noted that the scenarios of change to the software product can be used as a method of comparing design alternatives [15, 16]. By analyzing the scenarios associated with the quality attribute for the architectural style, one can figure out how to satisfy the quality attribute of the architecture. In this paper, three scenarios are considered for the analysis—addition of a component, deletion of a component, and edition of a component. The organization can take up more or altogether different scenarios as per their requirements. The necessary scenarios for analyzing the maintainability quality attribute in heterogeneous architecture style(s) are sown in Table 1.

Architecture style and scenarios need to be represented in an analytical framework to get more precise results from analyzing scenarios in architectural styles. A system represents configurations of components and connectors. These configurations include description of ports and roles. Ports are the interfaces of components, therefore define the point of interaction among component and environment and roles define the interfaces of the connectors. An overview of a system can be depicted in Fig. 1.

The structure of software systems in the style is related to the structural feature of an architectural style. These features include: constituent parts, control topology, data topology, control/data interaction topology, and control/data interaction indirection. As Table 2 shows, different styles have different features/elements. However, all of them have component, connector, port, and role. Thus, in order to get numerical index for maintainability, suitable weights or experimental values can be assigned to each element and for their interactions. Cost for performing each scenario is different, thus suitable weights can be assigned to each scenario for the analysis. It is to be noted that while applying scenario on architecture, if there exists more than one state, then the average values of the states as the result value will be considered for the analysis. By putting values obtained for all the scenarios and their interactions in the system maintainability function, a numerical index (SMI) can be calculated. By having variations in the architectural styles, different indexes can be obtained. This will provide the facility to set up the benchmarks and also helps in evaluating and selecting the particular or combination of architecture style(s).

Table 1 Maintainability scenarios

Scenario name	Scenario description
Addition	Addition of a new component to the architecture
Deletion	Deletion of an existing component from the architecture
Edition	Edition of an existing component. Two cases – Change in ports – No change in ports

Fig. 1 Component-based
system overview

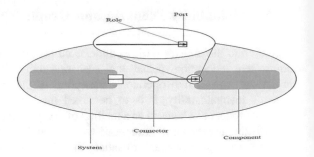

A maintainability scenario graph (MSG) models the maintainability scenarios and their influence. This digraph comprises of a set of nodes $V = \{v_i\}$, where $i = 1$, 2, 3...n scenarios; and a set of directed edges $E = \{e_i\}$, where $i = 1, 2, 3...$ m influences/interactions among set of scenarios (nodes). A node v_i represents the ith maintainability scenario and edges represent the influence of one scenario over another scenario. The number of nodes "n," in a maintainability scenario graph, considered is equal to the number of maintainability scenario considered for the given CBSS. If scenario s_i, represented by node v_i, upon completion has influence on other scenario s_j, represented by node v_j, then an edge (directed) from v_i to v_j is considered. If both the scenarios are influencing each other, then bidirectional edge is considered (from v_i to v_j and from v_j to v_i).

It can be inferred that applying one scenario on architecture style may have ripple effect in executing other or all scenarios. Thus, the MSG for the typical case for the three scenarios (edition, addition, deletion) is shown in Fig. 2.

Table 3 shows the degree of influence among the scenarios. Various possibilities and cases can come in relation to degree of influence. For example, the degree of influence/interaction for addition scenario and among other two scenarios is shown in first row. The degree of influence/interaction is strong for edition scenario (i.e., S. No. C and edge (e13)) and weak for deletion scenario (i.e., S. No. B and edge (e12)). Similarly, the degree of influence/interaction among other scenarios is shown in Table 3. It is advised to get the experts opinion in formulating the influence/interaction value among the scenarios.

For the easy analysis, the cost/weight of different elements of the architecture in different styles is considered to be same. The scenario cost/weight are based on person-day and shown in Table 4.

The MSG provides a visual representation of the CBSS scenarios and their influence. The digraph becomes more complex if the number of nodes (scenarios) and edges increases. In such situation, visual analysis becomes complex. To overcome the complexity, the MSG digraph is converted and represented in the form of a matrix. The matrix is further utilized to generate an expression of the maintainability. The matrix proposed for the same is called a system maintainability scenario matrix (SMSM), one-to-one representation of MSG. This is represented as matrix, expression (1)

Table 2 Style, elements, and topology

Style	Elements				Topology
	Component	Connector	Port	Role	
Data flow	Processing elements	Data flows	Processing elements	Data flows	Arbitrary
Pipe and filter	Filters/Transducers	Pipes/Data streams	Transducers	Data streams	Directed graphs
Batch sequential processing	Phase stand-alone programs	Batch data	Stand-alone programs	Batch data	Linear
Independent component	Process; modules	Communication protocol	Process; modules	Communication protocol	Arbitrary
Event-based implicit invocation	Processes; event handler	Events; message protocol	Processes; event handler	Message protocol	Arbitrary
Communicating process	Processes; event handler	Events; message protocol	Processes; event handler	Events; message protocol	Arbitrary
Call and return	Procedures; data stores	Procedure calls; data access	Procedures; data stores	Procedure calls; data access	Arbitrary
Layered system	Layer set of procedures	Procedure calls	Set of procedures	Procedure calls	Hierarchical
Abstract data type	Managers	Procedure calls	Managers	Procedure calls	Arbitrary
Event-based implicit invocation	Processes; event handler	Events; message protocol	Processes; event handler	Message protocol	Arbitrary
Object-oriented	Managers object/classes	Procedure calls	Managers object/classes	Procedure calls	Arbitrary
Data centered	Data store; computation clients	Data access; data queries	Data store; computation clients	Data access; data queries	Star
Virtual machines	Data memory; state memory; program memory	Data paths	Data memory; state memory; program memory; interpretation engine	Data paths	Fixed

Fig. 2 Maintainability
scenario graph

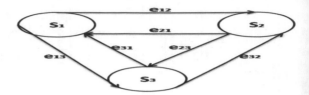

Table 3 Scenario and degree of influence

S. No.	Scenario	Degree of influence			
		Strong = 3	Medium = 2	Weak = 1	None = 0
A	Addition	C (e13)		B (e12)	
B	Deletion		C (e23)	A (e21)	
C	Edition		A (e31)	B (e32)	

Table 4 Scenario action and elements cost/weight description

Actions	Cost/Weight (Person-day)	Elements	Cost/Weight (Person-day)
Leading to add component	3	Component	1
Leading to delete component	1	Connector	0.5
Leading to edit component	2	Port	0.75
		Role	0.25

$$\text{SMSM} = \begin{matrix} & 1 & 2 & 3 & \text{Scenarios} \\ & \begin{bmatrix} S_1 & e_{12} & e_{13} \\ e_{21} & S_2 & e_{23} \\ e_{31} & e_{32} & S_3 \end{bmatrix} & & & \begin{matrix} 1 \\ 2 \\ 3 \end{matrix} \end{matrix} \qquad (1)$$

Diagonal element S_i, where $i = \{1, 2, 3\}$, represents value of ith maintainability scenario as scenario cost and off-diagonal elements e_{ij} the degree of influence/ interaction of ith maintainability scenario over jth maintainability scenario. To generate a meaningful information for the SMSM, a resultant characteristic expression is generated based on the permanent of the matrix that contains number of terms which are invariants.

Permanent of a matrix is a standard matrix function and is used in combinatorial matrix. Utilizing such concept will help in considering maintainability scenario structural information from combinatorial point of view. This facilities in associ- ating proper meaning to structural features and their combinations. Moreover, no information will be lost as the expression does not contain any negative sign. Permanent of this matrix is called as system maintainability scenario function, abbreviated as SMS-f. The characteristics of the CBSS based on heterogeneous architecture style upon performing scenarios are represented by SMS-f.

The SMS-f (Permanent) of matrix, expression (1), is mentioned as below as expression (2).

$$
\begin{aligned}
\text{SMS-}f = & [[S_1 * S_2 * S_3]] + [e_{23} * e_{32} * S_1 + e_{12} * e_{21} * S_3 + e_{13} * e_{31} * S_2] \\
& + [e_{13} * e_{32} * e_{21} + e_{12} * e_{23} * e_{31}]]
\end{aligned}
\tag{2}
$$

The expression 2 can easily be written by simply visually inspecting CBSS system of Fig. 1. For easy analysis, the expression 2 is rearranged as groups $(N + 1)$. In general, the permanent of a $N * N$ matrix, A where entries $a_{i,j}$ is defined in [17], is written as in expression (3):

$$
\text{Per}(A) = \sum_{P} \prod_{i=1}^{N} a_i, P(i),
\tag{3}
$$

where the sum is overall permutations P. The expression 3, in general, shows the SMS-f of complete CBSS.

3 Maintainability Analysis and Scenario Evaluation

The CBSS system maintainability scenario characteristic is represented in Eq. (1) where diagonals' elements correspond to the different scenarios as considered and off-diagonal elements correspond to influences/interactions between scenarios. The values of diagonal elements S_1, S_1, and S_1 are calculated as:

$$
S_1 = \text{SMSM } (S_1) \quad S_2 = \text{SMSM } (S_2) \quad S_3 = \text{SMSM } (S_3)
\tag{4}
$$

SMSM (S_1), SMSM (S_2), and SMSM (S_3) are the system maintainability scenario matrices for three scenarios and can be calculated by generating respective SMSMs. This can be generated by considering the sub-scenario of respective scenarios. The whole procedure is repeated recursively until terminal node appears (last node: no further decomposition). In short, procedure to do so is mentioned below:

1. Determine the sub-scenario considering their various sub-sub-scenarios.
2. Determine the degree of interactions/influences, etc., between different sub-scenarios.
3. Repeat step 1 and 2 until terminal node appears.

For an exhaustive analysis, a MSG digraph (like Fig. 1) of different scenarios for a CBSS under study can be formulated considering their respective SMSMs and SMS-fs. Technical experts help can be taken in order to finalize the exact degree of influence between scenarios or sub-scenarios. Maintainability of the CBSS architecture considering scenarios early in the software development life cycle can be assessed through an index. The numerical value of SMS-f is called scenario maintainability index (SMI). The SMI can be utilized to perform comparison of two or more competing alternative CBSS architectural designs considering maintainability aspect. The lower the value of the maintainability index, the better is the CBSS software product from a maintainability consideration.

4 Conclusion

In the current research work, a systematic analytical model based on graph theory is developed to analyze the maintainability of the CBSS architectural designs considering architectural styles and maintainability scenarios. The proposed maintainability analysis method provides benefits to designers, architects, quality analyst, and other key stakeholders to face the global competition and challenges by controlling maintainability of a set of CBSS. The proposed method is capable of considering the complete CBSS system from point of view of maintainability scenarios and possible interactions among them. The proposed method considers prominent maintainability scenarios—edition, addition, deletion, of all CBSS architectural design. The method encompasses the development of maintainability scenario graph, system scenario maintainability matrix, and system maintainability index for CBSS architectural design. The method can handle all possible combinatorial formulation of interrelations of the scenarios/sub-scenarios of CBSS under study. System maintainability index provides a quantitative measure of maintainability of CBSS that can be used to benchmark the alternative designs from the maintainability point of view. Future work will carry out the applicability of the proposed method in considering different architectural styles for analyzing CBSS.

References

1. Lientz, B.P., Swanson, E.B.: Characteristics of application software maintenance. Comm. ACM 21(6), 466–471 (1978)
2. Parikh, G.: The Guide to Software Maintenance. Winthrop Publishers, Cambridge, Mass (1982)
3. Pigoski, T.M.: Practical Software Maintenance, pp. 29–31. Wiley, New York, NY (1997)
4. Moad, J.: Maintaining the competitive edge. Datamation 36(4), 61–66 (1990)
5. Szyperski, C.: Component Software: Beyond Object-Oriented Programming. Addison-Wesley (2002)
6. IEEE.: Standard for Software Maintenance, IEEE Std 1219, IEEE Computer Society, Los Alamitos, CA (1993)
7. Woit, D.: Specify component interactions for modular reliability estimation. In: Proceedings of First International Software Quality Week (1997)

8. Upadhyay, N., Deshpande, B.M., Agrawal, V.P.: MACBSS: modeling and analysis of component based software system. IEEE World Congr. Comput. Sci. Inf. Eng. 595–601 (2009)
9. Pen, H., He, F.: Software trustworthiness modelling based on interactive Markov chains. Inf. Technol. Eng. 219–224 (2014) (Liu, Sung and Yao, editors)
10. Bass, L., Clements, P., Kazman, R.: Software Architecture in Practice, SEI Series. Pearson Education (2013)
11. Perry, D.E., Wolf, A.L.: Foundation for the study of software architecture. Softw. Eng. Notes **17**(4), 40–52 (1992)
12. Shaw, M., Garlan, D.: Software Architecture: Perspectives on an Emerging Discipline. Prentice Hall (1996)
13. Hofmeister, C., Nord, R., Soni, D.: Applied Software Architecture, Notes in Computer Science. Addison Wesley (1998)
14. Niu, N., Starkville, M.S, Xu, D.L., Cheng, J.R.C., Zhendong, N.: Analysis of architecturally significant requirements for enterprise systems. IEEE Syst. J. **8**(3) (2014)
15. Bernard, K.F., Yvan, M.: Software architecture knowledge for intelligent light maintenance. Adv. Eng. Softw. **67**, 125–135 (2014)
16. Knodel, J., Naab, M.: Software architecture evaluation in practice: retrospective on more than 50 architecture evaluations in industry. In: Proceedings of Software Architecture (WICSA), pp. 115–124 (2014)
17. Forbert, H., Marx, D.: Calculation of the permanent of a sparse positive matrix. Comput. Phys. Commun. **150**(3), 267–273 (2003)

An Assessment of Vulnerable Detection Source Code Tools

Anoop Kumar Verma and Aman Kumar Sharma

Abstract The commonly used programming language includes C and C++ for the software development and even introduced as a course contents in computer applications in number of institutions. As software development proceeds through various phases of system development life cycle, the design phase and coding phase have the greatest impact of the rest of phases, so every software development should have a good user interface and database design including writing a source code in order to make user interface active.

Keywords Vulnerabilities · Software development · Source code
Static source code analysis · Software tools

1 Introduction

When detecting C/C++ program vulnerabilities, static source code analysis can be used. This paper makes a comparative analysis of three open-source static source code analysis tools for C/C++ programming languages. Threats and vulnerabilities are responsible for creating challenges in security of information [1], so there arise a need to make source code good enough to prevent flaws and therefore reduce testing efforts. To make source code effective, errors or vulnerabilities in code need to be identified as soon as possible. Initially, a programmer writes a program in a particular programming language. This form of the program is called the source program, or more generically, source code. Secure software development should be engineered in such a way that the software functions smoothly and handles security threats effectively during malicious attack [2].

A. K. Verma (✉) · A. K. Sharma
Department of Computer Science, Himachal Pradesh University, Shimla, India
e-mail: anoopthakur14@gmail.com

A. K. Sharma
e-mail: sharmaas1@gmail.com

© Springer Nature Singapore Pte Ltd. 2019
M. N. Hoda et al. (eds.), *Software Engineering*, Advances in Intelligent Systems
and Computing 731, https://doi.org/10.1007/978-981-10-8848-3_38

A bug may be defined as error that causes undesirable behavior of the source code. A bug is classified into three types: syntax, data, and logical [3]. Syntax error occurs due to the violation of rules of a programming language, if these kinds of errors are not removed program will not run. With data errors, the program gets compiled successfully but the data values that were passed into the program were created. With logic errors, program runs and data values accepted, but the result is not the desired one as expected. Program vulnerability is a property of the program that allows a user to disturb confidentiality, integrity, and/or availability of the software [4]. Vulnerability detection methods can be classified into static and dynamic methods [5]. These methods can be applied in order to detect the various types of errors in a source code. When detecting vulnerabilities statically, the source code need not be executed while in case of dynamic detection of vulnerabilities, the source code needs to be executed. To detect vulnerabilities in a C or C++ programs, some static code analyzer tools are being used in this study.

Programs with errors either will not be executed or will give incorrect results; this may be due to the syntax errors or the semantic errors or may be due to data errors. Software with syntax errors are reported by the compiler. The developer rectifies the syntax based on the error message. These errors are identified at initial stage; such errors are least deadly as they were detected and rectified at the initial stage. Programs having semantic errors are not identified at earlier stages, and their life is long with deadly impact on the program as they affect the efficiency of the program. With data errors, results are not valid as expected. If vulnerabilities in the program are decreased to minimum possible extent, the efficiency, compilation time, execution time improves considerably.

The following are some common source code vulnerabilities.

1. **Divide Error**: This error occurs during the division of a number by zero.
2. **Out of Bounds**: This error occurs during the accessing of an array element out of the given range.
3. **Memory Leaks**: A memory leak occurs in programming languages that do not support garbage collector mechanism. It is basically a situation where the allocated memory to pointer-type variables is not freed while program is in execution [6].
4. **Uninitialized Variable**: This type of error occurs while using an uninitialized variable.

If vulnerabilities are detected manually during the testing phase of the software development, it may consume more time and all the errors may not be identified thus include more human labor. Instead of manual testing, automated testing of source code can be performed using some source code analysis tools.

2   Tools

This section describes the following open-source static source code analysis tools.

1. Cppcheck 1.68
2. Flawfinder
3. Visual Code Grepper (VCG)

2.1   Cppcheck 1.68 [7]

As its name suggests, it analyzes C/C++ source code developed by Daniel Marjamaki and Cppcheck team during the period 2007–2010. This tool does not detect syntax errors, but detect the errors that compilers fails to detect.

Features:
1. Runs on both Windows and Ubuntu operating systems.
2. Can be run through GUI or through command prompt.
3. Out of bounds checking.
4. Generates output in XML and HTML formats also.
5. Checks for uninitialized variables.
6. Memory leaks checking.

Benefits:
The following are the some of the benefits that can be analyzed while running this tool.

1. Provides checking of a single file or all file within the same directory.
2. Displays various severities as errors, warning, style, performance, portability, and information.
3. Allows setting through command prompt with the available switches.
4. Cppcheck can be integrated to Microsoft Visual Studio.
5. It is possible to write Cppcheck extension using dump files in python. For example, the cppcheckdata.py module allows loading such dump files.

Source of Availability:

Cppcheck is freely available at http://cppcheck.sourceforge.net.

2.2   Flawfinder [8]

Flawfinder is developed by David A. It scans through C/C++ source code and looks for the potential security flaws. After complete scanning of source code, it produces a list of hits sorted by the riskiest hits displayed firstly. The level of risk is shown inside square brackets that may vary from 0, very little risk, to 5, great risk. The risk level also dependent on the arguments passed to the functions. Flawfinder works on Unix platform and on Windows platform.

Features:
1. Flawfinder works by performing simple lexical tokenization (skipping comments and correctly tokenizing strings), looking for token matches to the database (particularly to find function calls).
2. File name given to analysis on command line is examined for the extension.
3. After analysis is completed, summary of the results is displayed that reports number of hits, number of line analyzed including total number of lines analyzed source line of code (SLOC).
4. It reports hit density means number of hits per thousand lines of source code.

Benefits:
Following are the some of the benefits that can be analyzed while running this tool.

1. It produces physical SLOC analyzed excluding blank and commented lines.
2. It displays information about line analyzed in the source code per second.
3. It can display the output in HTML format.

Source of Availability:

Flawfinder is freely available at http://www.dwheeler.com/flawfinder.

2.3 Visual Code Grepper (VCG) [9]

VCG is freely available code analysis tool written by Jonathan Murray and Nick Dunn that quickly identifies bad/insecure code. It also have a configuration file for all languages that user can customize accordingly as per his needs and requirements. This security scanner also breaks down the vulnerabilities to six pre-defined levels of severity. The results can also be exported to XML.

Features:
1. Configuration file for each language allows user to add bad functions that programmer wants to search for.
2. It can also find some common phases within comments like "ToDo", "FixMe", etc.
3. It generates a pie chart displaying proportions of the code including overall code, overall whitespace, overall comment, and potentially dangerous code.

Benefits:

The following are some of the benefits that can be analyzed while running this tool.

1. It provides support for multiple languages source code scanning.
2. It has configuration files for different languages that have setting for potentially dangerous function, such files are modifiable.
3. Results can be exported to XML format.
4. It has options to scan the code (excluding comments) and scanning of complete code.
5. The results can be filtered based on the levels (low, medium, high, critical, potentially unsafe, etc.).

Source of Availability:

VCG is freely available at http://sourceforge.net/projects/visualcodegrepp/.

3 Comparison/Analysis of Tools

The approach that parses the source code to look for vulnerabilities thoroughly is known as static code analysis [10]. The source code analysis tools were compared based on the features supported by each of them. The tools considered for analysis are as follows:

1. Cppcheck
2. Flawfinder
3. Visual Code Grepper

3.1 Conceptual Comparison

Table 1 shows the comparative analysis of the tools.

From Table 1, the following observations can be revealed:

1. All the tools considered are open-source software and are freely available.
2. Cppcheck and Visual Code Grepper are GUI whereas the flawfinder tool is not a GUI it is a command line interface.
3. Among the tools, Cppcheck can be run in both the modes of GUI as well as through command line.
4. Cppcheck and Visual Code Grepper are supported only on Windows platform, whereas the flawfinder is supported on Ubuntu platform.
5. Only VCG provides multiple language support.
6. Calculations of line of code are available in both flawfinder and VCG.

Table 1 Comparative analysis of tools on various parameters

Tool/ parameters	OSS	GUI	Command line	Windows platform supported	Ubuntu platform supported	Multiple language support	Calculate KLOC/ sec
Cppcheck	✓	✓	✓	✓	✕	✕	✕
Flawfinder	✓	✕	✓	✕	✓	✕	✓
Visual Code Grepper	✓	✓	✕	✓	✕	✓	✓

Where ✓ denotes that the tool supports the concerned feature
✕ denotes that the tool does not support the concerned feature

3.2 Empirical Comparison

For the empirical evaluation of the software tools, a source code to find the sum and average of numbers in the array is written in C language which is given in Table 2 "Program for finding sum and average of numbers in the array". The program is given as input; the all the above described tools and following results are revealed along with their screen shots. The given C source code will take an array of n number as input, and their sum is calculated inside a loop; after the sum of values in array is obtained its average is calculated, and the sum and average is displayed and

Table 2 Program for finding sum and average of numbers in the array

```
//todo
//Program to find sum and average of numbers in the array.
int main()
{
unsigned short n, a[10];
int i,sum = 0;
float avg;
printf("Enter the number of elements to be stored");
scanf("%d",&n);
for (i = 0; i < n; i++)
{
scanf("%d",&a[i]);
}
for (i = 0; i < n; i++)
{
sum = sum + a[i];
}
avg = sum/n;
printf("Sum = :%d",sum);
printf("Average = %f",avg);
system("pause");
}
```

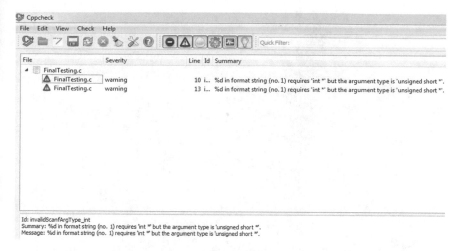

Fig. 1 Showing results on Cppcheck

system will be paused for a while after execution. The physical SLOC is 21. The mentioned code is passed as parameter to the tools, namely Cppcheck, Flawfinder, and Visual Code Grepper.

Results:

The results obtained from the tools are presented.

1. Cppcheck

Figure 1 shows the results as given by Cppcheck tool. The source code mentioned in Table 2 is given a file name "FinalTesting.c" and is added to the tool through file menu of the tool. The tool reports the severity as warning at line number 10 and 13 for format String, at the bottom a summary detail with the error messages "requires 'int *' but the argument type is 'unsigned short *'." is displayed.

2. Flawfinder

Figure 2 shows the results as given by flawfinder tool. The source code as given in Table 2 is given a file name "FinalTesting.c". Flawfinder produces a list of "hits" as shown in the figure sorted by risk; the riskiest hits are shown first. The level of risk is shown inside square brackets that may vary from 0, very little risk, to 5, great for example "[0+] 12" indicated that at level 0 or higher there were 12 hits. After the list of hits is displayed, a summary is shown including number of hits, lines analyzed, and the physical source lines of code (SLOC) analyzed. A physical SLOC is exclusion of blank, commented lines in this case SLOC = 21.

3. Visual Code Grepper

Figure 3 shows the results obtained from Visual Code Grepper corresponding to the given source code. The results given by the tool for the potentially unsafe codes

```
😕⬤⊖   anu@anu-Satellite-C850: ~
anu@anu-Satellite-C850:~$ falwafinder
falwafinder: command not found
anu@anu-Satellite-C850:~$ flawfinder
Flawfinder version 1.27, (C) 2001-2004 David A. Wheeler.
Number of dangerous functions in C/C++ ruleset: 160
*** No input files
anu@anu-Satellite-C850:~$ flawfinder '/home/anu/Desktop/FinalTesting.c'
Flawfinder version 1.27, (C) 2001-2004 David A. Wheeler.
Number of dangerous functions in C/C++ ruleset: 160
Examining /home/anu/Desktop/FinalTesting.c
/home/anu/Desktop/FinalTesting.c:22:  [4] (shell) system:
  This causes a new program to execute and is difficult to use safely.
  try using a library call that implements the same functionality if
  available.

Hits = 1
Lines analyzed = 22 in 0.51 seconds (2751 lines/second)
Physical Source Lines of Code (SLOC) = 21
Hits@level = [0]   0 [1]   0 [2]   0 [3]   0 [4]   1 [5]   0
Hits@level+ = [0+]   1 [1+]   1 [2+]   1 [3+]   1 [4+]   1 [5+]   0
Hits/KSLOC@level+ = [0+] 47.619 [1+] 47.619 [2+] 47.619 [3+] 47.619 [4+] 47.619
[5+]   0
Minimum risk level = 1
Not every hit is necessarily a security vulnerability.
```

Fig. 2 Showing results on flawfinder

along with line number in which they occurs. This tool also generates a pie chart as depicted in Fig. 4 after analyzing the source code as shown in Fig. 3, depicting overall line of code, overall comment, and potentially dangerous code.

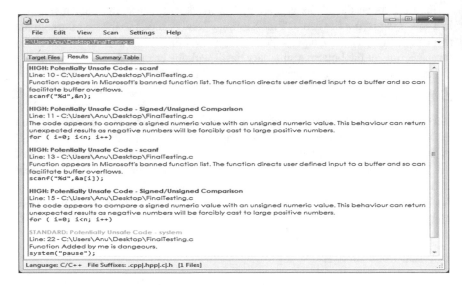

Fig. 3 Showing results on VCG

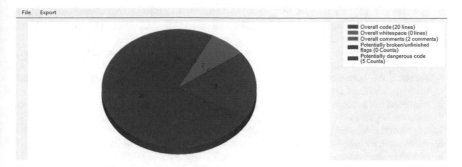

Fig. 4 Showing graphical results on VCG

4 Conclusion and Future Scope

The major focus of this study is the use of static source code analysis tool during the development phase in order to avoid programming bugs that may lead to vulnerabilities and if occurred can be found easily at earliest using static source code analysis tools so that testing time of the application can be reduced and programming bugs can be handled to improve the coding practices used by the programmer. The tools considered in this study provide the support for the C and C++ but the tool VCG (support multiple languages, such as C, Java, C#, VB, PHP) among them illustrated tool VCG is to be good enough as it also depicts the results in the form of pie chart that also depicts the summary including overall code (including comment appended code), overall comments, overall whitespaces, potentially dangerous functions, and potentially broken/unfinished flags. But in order to avoid vulnerabilities in the source code, organizations may not rely completely only on the static code analysis tools, instead the security must be considered as a functional aspect of the software development life cycle and should be considered at every stage. Furthermore, some kind of security framework should be developed for the secure software development and in designing such a framework secure design patterns and secure coding practices must be used. The proposed framework should be verified by organizations and IT professionals, and its output needs to be evaluated in order to measure its effectiveness. Some security models should be built and synchronized with the traditional software engineering models to consider security at every stage of SDLC.

References

1. Bakshi, S.: Security in software development. In: CSI Communication (2014)
2. Daud, M.I.: Secure software development model: a guide for secure software life cycle. In: International MultiConference of Engineers and Computer Scientist, vol. 1, 17–19 Mar, Hong Kong (2010)

3. Delwiche, L.D., Slaughter, S.J.: Errors, warnings and notes (oh my) a practical guide to debugging SAS programs. In: Proceedings of the 2003 SAS Users Group International (SUGI) Conference (2003)
4. Ermakov, A., Kushik, N.: Detecting C program vulnerabilities. In: Proceedings of the Spring/Summer Young Researches Colloquium on Software Engineering (2011)
5. Jimenez, W., Mammar, A., Cavalli, A.R.: Software vulnerabilities, prevention and detection methods a review. In: SECMDA Workshop—Enschede (2009)
6. Vipindeep, V., Jalote, P.: List of common bugs and programming practices to avoid them. Electronic (2005)
7. http://sourceforge.net/projects/visualcodegrepp/. Accessed on 8 June 2015 at 0800 hrs
8. http://www.dwheeler.com/flawfinder/. Accessed on 20 July 2015 at 0600 hrs
9. http://cppcheck.sourceforge.net/. Accessed on 29 July 2015 at 0900 hrs
10. Godbole, S.: Developing secure software. In: CSI Communication (2014)

Devising a New Method for Economic Dispatch Solution and Making Use of Soft Computing Techniques to Calculate Loss Function

Ravindra Kumar Chahar and Aasha Chuahan

Abstract This paper has a description of a new method which is designed for the economic dispatch problem of power system. This method demonstrates a new technique for calculating loss in the economic dispatch problem. This technique can be utilized for online generation of solution by using soft computing methods to find out loss function in the solution. A new method to find out the loss function using two new parameters is described here. Fuzzy sets and genetic algorithm are used to find a penalty term based on the values of these two parameters. Thus, all the calculations required to accommodate loss function in the solution of economic dispatch are presented here. The algorithm for the new proposed system is presented in this paper.

Keywords Economic dispatch problem · Loss function · Soft computing methods
Fuzzy sets · New parameters for calculating loss function · Genetic algorithm

1 Introduction

The economic dispatch problem of power system is solved by using deterministic approach [1]. In the deterministic approach, the input parameters are known with certainty and the solution is found using mathematical equations [2]. However, there are various inaccuracies, and uncertainties are present in the solution. These inaccuracies could be due to fuel cost variations, inaccuracies in measurements, wear and tear of equipment, and other calibration errors [3].

Due to these inaccuracies, the deterministic solution may not give an optimal solution. Thus, there is a need to account for these inaccuracies and uncertainties in the solution. This paper presents a new technique employing fuzzy sets and genetic algorithm that uses risk management in the solution of economic dispatch problem.

R. K. Chahar (✉) · A. Chuahan
EEE Department, Lingaya's University, Faridabad, India
e-mail: far56nb@gmail.com

A. Chuahan
e-mail: aashachuahan07@gmail.com

© Springer Nature Singapore Pte Ltd. 2019   413
M. N. Hoda et al. (eds.), *Software Engineering*, Advances in Intelligent Systems
and Computing 731, https://doi.org/10.1007/978-981-10-8848-3_39

Firstly, the algorithm for deterministic approach is described. The design of the solution employing fuzzy sets is described. The usage of genetic algorithm with the fuzzy sets is also described. Thus, a novel method is formulated based on risk management for the solution of economic dispatch problem.

2 New Approach for the Solution of Economic Dispatch Problem

2.1 Steps of the Deterministic Approach

The various steps of the deterministic approach are listed below:

Step 1 Declare various parameters:
$a[i]$, $b[i]$, $c[i]$, P_d, optimal_total_cost, Pg, alpha, ep, Lagr, Lagr$_{new}$, it, It$_{max}$, in, In$_{max}$, pg$_{min}$, pg$_{max}$, and B_{ij}.
$a[i]$, $b[i]$, and $c[i]$ are cost coefficients. P_d is the load demand (MW). Optimal fuel cost is represented by optimal_total_cost, pg is output of a generator, and alpha and ep are parameters used in Lagrangian technique.
it and in indicate iteration counters. Lagr and Lagr$_{new}$ are Lagrangian multipliers. It$_{max}$ and In$_{max}$ are maximum number of iterations.
pg$_{max}$ and pg$_{min}$ are maximum and minimum limits of a generator.
B_{ij} is transmission line coefficients [4].

Step 2 Read the values of input parameters:
$a[i]$, $b[i]$, $c[i]$, B_{ij}, pg$_{min}$, and pg$_{max}$.

Step 3 Assign the values of parameters used:
$P_d = 220$
alpha = 0.005
ep = 0.0001 and ep$_2$ = 0.001
ep$_2$ is used for inner loop.

Step 4 Guess the value of Lagr.

Step 5 Initialize the values of generator outputs P_1, P_2, and P_3.
Let $P_1 = P_2 = P_3 = 0.0$
Initialize it = 1.
It$_{max}$ = In$_{max}$ = 100.

Step 6 Test whether it < It$_{max}$?
If yes, then go to Step 7 else display the message 'solution not converging in 100 iterations' and stop.

Step 7 Initialize in = 1.
$P_1[\text{it} - 1] = P_2[\text{it} - 1] = P_3[\text{it} - 1] = 0.0$

Step 8 Test whether in $<$ In$_{max}$?

If yes, then go to Step 9 else go to Step 13.

Step 9 Calculate the value of pg[i][it] for $i = 1$ to 3 using the following equation:

pg[i][it] = Term$_1$/Term$_2$.

Term$_1$ = Lagr $\times$ $(1 -$ Term$_3) -$ b[i]

Term$_2$ = 2 $\times$ (Term$_4$ + Term$_5$ + Term$_6$)

Term$_3$ = $\sum_{j \neq i} (2 \times B_{ij} \times P_j[\text{it} - 1])$

Term$_4$ = a[i] + (a[i] $\times$ cvp$_i^2$)

The parameter cvp$_i$ is the coefficient of variation for ith generator.

Term$_5$ = $p \times$ cvp$_i^2$

The parameter p is a penalty term that represents risk.

Term$_6$ = Lagr $\times$ $B_{ii} \times (1 +$ cvp$_i^2$)

Step 10 Check for upper and lower limits of pg[i][it].

If pg[i][it] $<$ pg$_{min}$, then pg[i][it] = pg$_{min}$.

If pg[i][it] $>$ pg$_{max}$, then pg[i][it] = pg$_{max}$.

Step 11 Find the value of Delta$_i$.

Delta$_i$ = |pg[i][it] $-$ pg[i][it-1]|

max = max (Delta$_1$, Delta$_2$, Delta$_3$)

Step 12 Test whether max $\leq$ ep$_2$?

If yes, then go to Step 13 else increment the value of in and pg[i][it $-$ 1] = pg[i][it], go to Step 8.

Step 13 Calculate transmission losses (P_L):

P_L = Term$_7$ + Term$_8$

Term$_7$ = $\sum_{i=1 \text{to} 3}(B_{ii} \times P_i)$

Term$_8$ = $\sum_{i=1 \text{to} 3}\sum_{j=1 \text{to} 3}, {}_{j \neq i}(P_i \times B_{ij} \times P_j)$

Step 14 Calculate Delta$_p$.

Delta$_p$ = |Pd + P_L $- \sum_{i=1 \text{to} 3} (P_i)$|

Step 15 Test whether Delta$_p$ $\leq$ ep?

If yes, then calculate the optimal_total_cost, display the value, and stop else go to Step 16.

F_T = a[i] $\times$ Pg[i]^2 + b[i] $\times$ pg[i] + c[i]

The parameter F_T is the optimal_total_cost and is calculated using the equation given above [4].

Step 16 Calculate Lagr$_{new}$.

Lagr$_{new}$ = Lagr + (alpha $\times$ Delta$_p$)

Lagr = Lagr$_{new}$

Step 17 Increment the value of counter it by 1 and go to Step 6.

2.2   Description of Fuzzy Sets Used in the New Approach

The deterministic approach finds the solution of economic dispatch problem by taking the values of risk factor p and cvp_i as zero. As there is a need to account for risk in the solution, the fuzzy sets are used to determine the value of risk.

The fuzzy set uses a triangular membership function [5] to find the membership values of p_i.

Let $u(p_1) = t_1$

The value of $u(p_2) = t_2$

Here, p_1 and p_2 are penalty term for Generator1 and Generator2.

To find out the values of p_1 and p_2, two new parameters are defined:

Parameter A represents the value of loss function.

Parameter B shows the deviation of value from mean value of the generator output.

The parameter B is chosen by taking $\text{Pg}_{\max}$ and multiplying by cvp_i.

For example, if $\text{Pg}_{\max} = 1000$ MW and $\text{cvp}_2 = 0.04$, then parameter B is calculated as:

$$\text{Parameter } B = 1000 \times 0.04 = 40$$

Parameter A is selected by assigning penalty term equal to approximately 1% of Lagrangian multiplier (which is calculated in deterministic schedule).

For example, let Lagrangian multiplier = 27.2.

$$\text{Penalty term} = (1/100) \times 27.2 = 0.272$$

The penalty term is given as follows:

The penalty term p_i is defined as:

Parameter $A/(\text{parameter } B)^2$

Thus, parameter $A = 0.272 * (\text{parameter } B)^2 = (435.2)$. An appropriate value equal to 435 may be assigned to parameter A.

Here, u is used for membership value.

$$\text{Factor}_1 = \sum (t_1 + t_2)$$

This factor is used by genetic algorithm to find out the value of risk based on the values of cvp_i.

2.3 Usage of Genetic Algorithm in the Method

The value of $factor_1$, that is being calculated using fuzzy set described above, is used in the genetic algorithm.

Let $y_1 = factor_1 \times a[1]$
$\quad y_2 = factor_1 \times a[2]$
$\quad y_3 = factor_1 \times a[3]$

$\quad fa_1 = \alpha_1 \times y_1^2 + \beta_1 \times y_1$
$\quad fa_2 = \alpha_2 \times y_2^2 + \beta_2 \times y_2$
$\quad fa_3 = \alpha_3 \times y_3^2 + \beta_3 \times y_3$
$\quad \alpha_1 = cvp_1$
$\quad \alpha_2 = cvp_2$
$\quad \alpha_3 = cvp_3$
$\quad \beta_i = 10 \times \alpha_i$

The genetic algorithm is used to find optimal solution of fa_i.
The risk factor is found using the following equation:

$$p = \min(\ fa_i)$$

This value of p is used in the algorithm described for deterministic approach.

Thus a method, which is capable to include risk factor, is being devised. The genetic algorithm uses crossover and mutation operators for each generation and then uses wheel selection algorithm to select next generation according to fitness values. Initially, genetic algorithm finds random numbers and calculates fitness values.

3   Illustrations and Result

3.1   Sample System Consisting of Two Generators

A sample system having two generators is chosen. The various input parameters are listed below (Table 1):

Table 1 Output of the method using fuzzy sets

P_D (MW)	F_T ($/h)	Lagrangian multiplier ($/MW-h)
500	5806.16	12.21
600	7137.41	14.45
700	8693.866	16.65
800	10,376.68	17.89
900	12,178.016	19.169

$$A_1 = 0.008 \quad b_1 = 10.0 \quad c_1 = 0.0$$
$$A_2 = 0.009 \quad b_2 = 8.0 \quad c_2 = 0.0$$

$$B[1][1] = 0.00015 \quad B[1][2] = 0.000010 \quad B[2][2] = 0.000030$$

Fuzzy sets are used for a_1, a_2, b_1, b_2, and cvp_2.

$$Cvp_1 = 0.0 \quad Cvp_2 = 0.04$$

Computed membership of $a_1 = 0.4$
Computed membership of $a_2 = 0.45$
Computed membership of $b_1 = 0.4$
Computed membership of $b_2 = 0.32$
Computed membership of $cvp_2 = 0.08$
Sum of membership values $= 1.65$
Computed membership using sum $= 0.55$
Value of parameter $B = 40.0$
Value of parameter $A = 880.0$

3.2   Conclusions

A method is presented that is capable of including risk analysis in the solution of economic dispatch problem. The need for including uncertainty in economic dispatch problem is described and discussed [6]. A new method for unit commitment is presented [7]. The solution for nonconvex economic dispatch is given in [8]. A method using particle swarm optimization for nonconvex economic dispatch is given in [9].

The method described in this paper uses fuzzy sets and genetic algorithm to formulate a novel technique for risk analysis. The deterministic approach for solving economic dispatch problem is described. The penalty term calculated using the new method is used with the deterministic approach to solve the economic dispatch problem. Thus, a method that is capable of generating solution in situations of uncertainties has been formulated. This can be utilized for online solution of the economic dispatch problem. The method described above is capable of generating an optimal solution [5] under situations of uncertainties and inaccuracies. It takes into considerations fuel cost, transmission losses, and cost of risk to find an optimal solution of the economic dispatch problem.

References

1. Kusic, G.L.: Computer Aided Power Systems Analysis. Prentice-Hall of India, New Delhi (1986)
2. Kirchmayer, L.K.: Economic Operation of Power Systems. Wiley Eastern, New Delhi (1958)
3. Parti, S.C.: Stochastic Optimal Power Generation Scheduling. Ph.D. (Thesis), TIET, Patiala (1987)
4. Kothari, D.P., Dhillon, J.S.: Power Optimization, 2nd edn, pp. 135–200. PHI Learning Private Limited, Delhi (2013)
5. Klir, G.J., Folger, T.A.: Fuzzy Sets, Uncertainty and Information. Prentice-Hall India, New Delhi (1997)
6. Overholt, P.: Accommodating Uncertainty in Planning and Operations. Department of Energy (DOE), CERTS (1999)
7. Ongsakul, W., Petcharaks, N.: Unit commitment by enhanced adaptive Lagrangian relaxation. IEEE Trans. Power Syst. **19**(1) (2004)
8. Binetti, G., Davoudi, A., Naso, D., Turchiano, B., Lewis, F.L.: A distributed auction-based algorithm for the nonconvex economic dispatch problem. IEEE Trans. Ind. Inf. **10**(2) (2014)
9. Park, J.-B., Jeong, Y.-W., Shin, J.-R., Lee, K.Y.: An improved particle swarm optimization for nonconvex economic dispatch problems. IEEE Trans. Power Syst. **25**(1) (2010)

Trusted Operating System-Based Model-Driven Development of Secure Web Applications

Nitish Pathak, Girish Sharma and B. M. Singh

Abstract This paper adds security engineering into an object-oriented model-driven software development for real-life Web applications. In this paper, we use mining patterns in Web applications. This research paper proposes a unified modeling language-based secure software maintenance procedure. The proposed method is applied for maintaining a large-scale software product and real-life product-line products. After modeling, we can implement and run this Web application, on SPF-based trusted operating systems. As we know, reverse engineering of old software is focused on the understanding of legacy program code without having proper software documentation. The extracted design information was used to implement a new version of the software program written in C++. For secure designing of Web applications, this paper proposes system security performance model for trusted operating system. For re-engineering and re-implementation process of Web applications, this paper proposes the model-driven round-trip engineering approach.

Keywords Design patterns · Design recovery · Reverse engineering structured design · Re-implementation and re-engineering language translation Temporal patterns · Navigation patterns

N. Pathak (✉)
UTU, Dehradun, India
e-mail: nitish_pathak2004@yahoo.com

G. Sharma
Department of Computer Science, BPIBS, Government of NCT of Delhi, New Delhi, India
e-mail: gkps123@gmail.com

B. M. Singh
Department of Computer Science and Engineering, College of Engineering, Roorkee, India
e-mail: bmsingh1981@gmail.com

© Springer Nature Singapore Pte Ltd. 2019
M. N. Hoda et al. (eds.), *Software Engineering*, Advances in Intelligent Systems and Computing 731, https://doi.org/10.1007/978-981-10-8848-3_40

1   Introduction

When long-established structured programming model could not manage with large-scale business application development, object-oriented programming was introduced to resolve such problems in programming. Object-oriented programming is a latest way of study on programming. In OOP, a software program is separated into a group of objects, which concurrently hold information (attributes or data members) and member function (methods) [1]. Software application is developed throughout combining objects in a similar way as structuring a house with bricks [2]. Lots of pleasant words may have been used by software developers to express their valuation on OOP. Approximately, every modern software applications are constructed based on object-oriented analysis and designing [3].

The object-oriented model offers a number of features that are intended to help the development of large and flexible software, if employed properly. By flexibility, it is meant that the principles of encapsulation, information and data hiding, data abstraction, inheritance, and polymorphism should be properly applied so as to remove any odors of weakness and rigidity [4]. Basically, the addition of new functionality in an object-oriented system should have as partial impact on obtainable code as probable. We use Web usage mining to understand user's activities when computer user interacts with the Web sites. After understanding user activities, the Web site and security performance flexibility model can be reorganized according to the user requirement [5]. To accomplish this, design information was extracted from the old C++ source code and entered into an object-oriented software development process.

There are several Web log resources such as Web server log, Web proxy log, user browsers history files, cookies files of browser etc. Web server log is used which records user request of server sites. In 1994, UML arose from the unification of three object-oriented design methods: the Booch Method, the Object Modeling Technique (OMT), and the Objectory Method [6, 7]. The unified modeling language standard was set and is managed by the Object Management Group. UML offers a structure to incorporate several diagrams. "Only class diagrams are being used regularly by over half the respondents, with sequence and use case diagrams used by about half." In software industry, collaboration/communication diagrams were the least popular and accepted and not widely used by software designer [8]. Exponential expansion of the Web makes it a fashionable and rich place for latest research. The vibrant and amorphous environment of the Web applications for automatic tools for analyzing Web application data and their patterns [9, 10]. Web mining has been described as the analysis of appealing and helpful patterns from the Web. It requires analysis of diverse aspects of a business software application: the platform on which software runs, the interaction of a software system with other applications, the libraries and the components of the programming language that the business application uses etc. As we know, Much of the previous work on reverse engineering in software engineering has focused on the source code analysis [11, 12].

Object-oriented design information is improved from the source code and some obtainable design documentation. The procedure of improving a program's design is known as design recovery [13]. A design is improved by piecing equally information from the source code, obtainable documents, software developer's experienced with the software system knowledge. As we know, the software round-trip engineering, i.e., forward engineering and backward engineering, plays a vital role in software development life cycle [14, 15]. Figure 1 indicates the reverse engineering and re-implementation process for software development process.

If there is no software requirement specification, i.e., SRS for a software system, reverse engineering will become more and more complex. The object-oriented design should be represented at an abstraction level that eliminates implementation language dependence [16]. This makes it potential to re-implement the software system in a new language. There are various business object-oriented tools that provide the reverse engineering abilities.

Object-oriented design and software engineering focus on the object-oriented design and completion of a software product without considering the lifetime of a software product [17]. As we know, the major attempt in software engineering organizations is exhausted after development, and on maintaining the software systems to eliminate accessible errors, bugs and to acclimatize them to changed software requirements. For recently developed software systems, the complexity can be reduced by carefully documenting the software system. The information can furthermore be used to develop and preserve other software systems; i.e., we achieve supplementary information that can be used by a forward engineer for the purpose of forward engineering.

This paper discusses a unified modeling language-based software maintenance process [18]. In this paper there are two major points, one trusted operating system base secure reverse engineering and second is model analysis. Still, the construction of UML models from the source code is far from simple, even if an object-oriented programming language has been used [19]. Because of the differences in concepts

Fig. 1 Reverse engineering and re-implementation process for Web applications

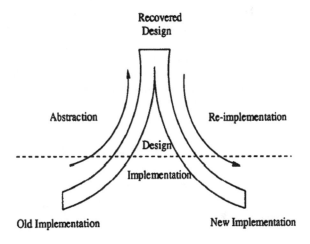

Fig. 2 General model for
software re-engineering

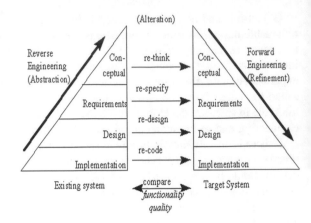

at the design and implementation levels, interpretations are essential even for the
extraction of class diagrams from the source code. Figure 2 is related to general
model for software re-engineering process for software development.

To attain high quality throughout the secure Web application development,
requirement discovery and analysis play an essential role. This research paper
presents an empirical study carried out to assess the object-related metrics from
Web applications. The objective of this research work is related to the under-
standability worth perceived by the user through code, i.e., also known as forward
engineering process [20, 21]. If a software solution is being designed for the first
time, our purpose is to be capable to properly model that software solution and to
make as much of implementation/code from the object-oriented model. This will
serve our motivation to enable IT services' companies to maintain object-oriented
software development on several platforms. Our purpose is to reprocess as much of
that software solution as possible in making that software solution accessible on
several platforms.

Models are the foremost artifacts in software development process. These
models can be used to signify a variety of things in the software design and
software development life cycle. These object-oriented models are at the core of
forward engineering and reverse engineering [22]. In forward engineering, normally
platform-independent object-oriented models are developed by software designers
as part of software design document. In reverse engineering, these object-oriented
models are usually derived automatically using model-driven transformations.

2 Secure Web Application Modeling

In this paper, we are suggesting the security performance flexibility model for
trusted operating system. And we implemented this SPF model to retain balance
among security and performance issue in Web applications. In this paper, we are

proposing mining-based system SPF for trusted operating system. As we know, only a small amount of parts of the operating system security are actually necessary [23]. According to Fig. 3, SPF allows computer system administrators to selectively stop some unnecessary parts of the security for secure Web applications; with the help of this contribution, we can maintain high-performance security for any Web application. Whenever we avoid some useless security checks at system and kernel level, the performance of software system will be improved in all respect [24].

For such designing and development of Web applications, first of all, we have to recognize which part can be disabled to get the highest performance, in particular Web application.

As we identify that each and every security check and security constraints are not noteworthy in all software systems. For improving the performance, speed, efficiency for particular system, this paper proposes that we should use secure operating systems for better security performance in Web applications. The consideration behind the SPF configuration is explained in Fig. 3. With this approach, the Web server's efficiency, speed effectiveness, security aspect, and all can be improved.

Web applications can be described in unified modeling language with diverse object-oriented diagrams: Class diagram is used for application components; object diagram is used for object components; use case diagram is used for functional requirement and interactions with external systems. As we know, during software development process, it is very much common for software requirements to change and for faults to be corrected and removed. Each and every change in software may require that the UML object-oriented model be changed and a small change may lead to several other related changes.

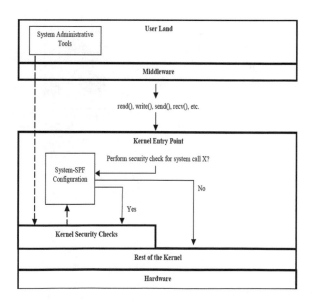

Fig. 3 System-SPF structural design for stock control Web application

3   Axes of Change in Round-trip Engineering

In order to highlight the interference between the classes of a computer system, the proposed object-oriented model defines numerous axes of change through which a change in a class can influence other classes enforcing them to be modified, i.e., ripple effect. By change, we signify that given a change in one of the affecting classes, the affected classes should be updated, in order for the software system to function properly. For example, the change in the signature of a member function in a class will need the update of all classes that use this member function. Each class can change because of its participation in one or more axes of change. Consider a software system for supporting a public library. Figure 4 indicates the object-oriented class diagram.

C++ source code for secure forward and reverse engineering:

```
#include "Admin.h"
//##ModelId = 4F7A74800186
Admin::Manages Library()
{
}
//##ModelId = 4F7A747201D4
class Admin
{
  public:
    //##ModelId = 4F7A74800186
    Manages Library();
```

Fig. 4 Generic object-oriented class diagram for round-trip engineering

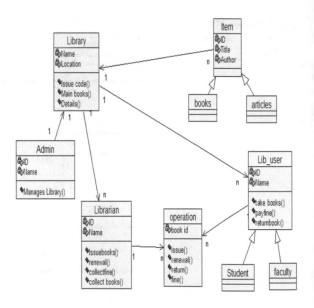

```
 private:
   //##ModelId = 4F7A7477002E
   ID;
   //##ModelId = 4F7A747A0280
   Name;
};
//##ModelId = 4F7A75040119
class articles : public Item
{
};
#endif /* ARTICLES_H_HEADER_INCLUDED_B085108E */
//##ModelId = 4F7A74FF0242
class books : public Item
{
};




//##ModelId = 4F7A7583037A
class faculty : public Lib_user
{
};
#endif /* FACULTY_H_HEADER_INCLUDED_B0851E4D */
//##ModelId = 4F7A74E400FA
class Item
{
   //##ModelId = 4F7A74E90203
   ID;
   //##ModelId = 4F7A74F00222
   Title;
   //##ModelId = 4F7A74F40280
   Author;
};
#endif /* ITEM_H_HEADER_INCLUDED_B0851A6E */
#include "Lib_user.h"
//##ModelId = 4F7A7534009C
Lib_user::take books()
{
}
//##ModelId = 4F7A753A0167
Lib_user::payfine()
{
}
//##ModelId = 4F7A753D001F
Lib_user::returnbook()
```

```
{
}
//##ModelId = 4F7A750D032C
class Lib_user
{
 public:
   //##ModelId = 4F7A7534009C
   take books();
   //##ModelId = 4F7A753A0167
   payfine();



   //##ModelId = 4F7A753D001F
   returnbook();
 private:
   //##ModelId = 4F7A7526005D
   ID;
   //##ModelId = 4F7A75290128
   Name;
};
#endif /* LIB_USER_H_HEADER_INCLUDED_B0856AD8 */
#include "Librarian.h"
//##ModelId = 4F7A74C003A9
Librarian::Issuebooks()
{
}
//##ModelId = 4F7A74C9037A
Librarian::renewal()
{
}



//##ModelId = 4F7A74CF0167
Librarian::collectfine()
{
}
//##ModelId = 4F7A74D9003E
Librarian::collect books()
{
}
//##ModelId = 4F7A749100EA
class Librarian
{
```

```
public:
  //##ModelId = 4F7A74C003A9
  Issuebooks();
  //##ModelId = 4F7A74C9037A
  renewal();
  //##ModelId = 4F7A74CF0167
  collectfine();
  //##ModelId = 4F7A74D9003E
  collect books();
 private:
  //##ModelId = 4F7A74AD00AB
  ID;
  //##ModelId = 4F7A74B1004E
  Name;
};
#endif /* LIBRARIAN_H_HEADER_INCLUDED_B0855943 */
#include "Library.h"
//##ModelId = 4F7A745500DA
Library::Issue code()
{
}
//##ModelId = 4F7A7459037A
Library::Main books()
{
}
//##ModelId = 4F7A746203B9
Library::Details()
{
}
class Library
{
 public:
  //##ModelId = 4F7A745500DA
  Issue code();
  //##ModelId = 4F7A7459037A
  Main books();
  //##ModelId = 4F7A746203B9
  Details();
 private:
  //##ModelId = 4F7A743D033C
  Name;
  //##ModelId = 4F7A744602EE
  Location;
};
operation::issue()
```

```
{
}
//##ModelId = 4F7A756600FA
operation::renewal()
{
}
//##ModelId = 4F7A756A00BB
operation::return()
{
}
//##ModelId = 4F7A756C004E
operation::fine()
{
}
class operation
{
 public:
   //##ModelId = 4F7A756400EA
   issue();
   //##ModelId = 4F7A756600FA
   renewal();
   //##ModelId = 4F7A756A00BB
   return();
   //##ModelId = 4F7A756C004E
   fine();
 private:
   //##ModelId = 4F7A755A03D8
   book id;
};
#endif /*
#include "Lib_user.h"
//##ModelId = 4F7A75C40109
class Student : public Lib_user
{
};
#endif /* STUDENT_H_HEADER_INCLUDED_B0851C73 */
```

Unified modeling language has been widely used for designing software models for software development. Reverse engineering for Web applications has to be focused on object-oriented design recovery.

4   Conclusion

This research paper has presented a process for redesigning of an existing software system, with the help of reverse engineering. This paper focuses on security performance flexibility model of trusted operating system for maintaining the security in various Web applications. As we know, it is very easier to modify an object-oriented design than source code. The recovered design of old software describes the existing software system, after that we can design and develop the new system. After reverse engineering and round-trip engineering of any old Web application, we will get a new software system that is improved structured, proper documented, and extra easily maintained than the old and previous software version. Therefore, object-oriented reverse engineering is a part of re-engineering of software systems.

In this research paper, we proposed a novel method to software design and to software maintenance and showed how it has been used for maintaining large-scale software. In this paper, we also proposed the model-driven development of secure operating system for secure Web applications.

References

1. Briand, L.C., Di Penta, M., Labiche, Y.: An experimental investigation of formality in UML-based development. IEEE Trans. Softw. Eng. **31**(10) (2005)
2. Xing, Z., Stroulia, E.: Analyzing the evolutionary history of the logical design of object-oriented software. IEEE Trans. Softw. Eng. **31**(10) (2005)
3. Brambilla, M., Ceri, S., Fraternali, P.: Process modeling in web applications. ACM Trans. Softw. Eng. Methodol. **15**(4) (2006)
4. Simons, C.L., Parmee, I.C., Gwynllyw, R.: Interactive, evolutionary search in upstream object-oriented class design. IEEE Trans. Softw. Eng. **36**(6) (2010)
5. Fonseca, J., Vieira, M., Madeira, H.: Evaluation of web security mechanisms using vulnerability & attack injection. IEEE Trans. Dependable Secure Comput. **11**(5) (2014)
6. De Lucia, A., Gravino, C., Oliveto, R., Tortora, G: An experimental comparison of ER and UML class diagrams for data modeling. Empirical Softw. Eng. **15**, 455–492 (2010). https://doi.org/10.1007/s10664-009-9127-7. © Springer Science + Business Media, LLC 2009
7. Bernardi, S., Merseguer, J., Petriu, D.C.: Dependability modeling and analysis of software systems specified with UML. ACM Comput. Surv. **45**(1), Article 2 (2012)
8. Wu, O., Hu, W.: Measuring the visual complexities of web pages. ACM Trans. Web **7**(1), Article 1 (2013)
9. Desnoyers, P., Wood, T., Shenoy, P.: Modellus: automated modeling of complex internet data center applications. ACM Trans. Web **6**(2), Article 8 (2012)
10. Marcus, A., Poshyvanyk, D.: Using the conceptual cohesion of classes for fault prediction in object-oriented systems. IEEE Trans. Softw. Eng. **34**(2) (2008)
11. Pathak, N., Sharma, G., Singh, B.M.: Forward engineering based implementation of TOS in social networking. Int. J. Comput. Appl. USA **102**(11), 33–38 (2014). ISSN: 0975–8887
12. http://link.springer.com/article/10.1007/s13198-015-0338-6
13. Pathak, N., Sharma, G., Singh, B.M.: Designing of SPF based secure web application using forward engineering. In: IEEE International Conference on IndiaCom2014, pp 464–469. IEEE Xplore (2015). ISBN: 978-9-3805-4415-1

14. Runeson, P., Höst, M.: Guidelines for conducting and reporting case study research in software engineering. Empirical Softw. Eng. **14**, 131–164 (2009). https://doi.org/10.1007/s10664-008-102-8. Open access at Springerlink.com, Dec 2008
15. Pathak, N., Sharma, G., Singh, B.M.: Experimental analysis of SPF based secure web application. Int. J. Mod. Educ. Comput. Sci., 48–55 (2015). ISSN: 2075-0161
16. Kosiuczenko, P.: Redesign of UML class diagrams: a formal approach. Softw. Syst. Model. **8**, 165–183 (2009). https://doi.org/10.1007/s10270-007-0068-6. (Nov 2007 © Springer 2007)
17. Barna, P., Frasincar, F.: A workflow-driven design of web information systems. In: ICWE'06, 11–14 July 2006, Palo Alto, California, USA. ACM 1-59593-352-2/06/0007
18. Davis, J.P.: Propositional logic constraint patterns and their use in UML-based conceptual modeling and analysis. IEEE Trans. Knowl. Data Eng. **19**(3) (2007)
19. Barrett, R., Pahl, C., Patcas, L.M., Murphy, J.: Model driven distribution pattern design for dynamic web service compositions. In: ICWE'06, 11–14 July 2006, Palo Alto, California, USA. ACM 1-59593-352-2/06/0007
20. Cooley, R.: The use of web structure and content to identify subjectively interesting web usage patterns. ACM Trans. Internet Technol. **3**(2), 93–116 (2003)
21. Trujillo, J.: A report on the first international workshop on best practices of UML (BP-UML'05). In: SIGMOD Record, vol. 35, no. 3, Sept 2006
22. Ricci, L.A., Schwabe, D.: An authoring environment for model-driven web applications. In: WebMedia'06, 19–22 Nov 2006, Natal, RN, Brazil. Copyright 2006 ACM 85-7669-100-0/06/0011
23. Jiang, D., Pei, J., Li, H.: Mining search and browse logs for web search: a survey. ACM Trans. Intell. Syst. Technol. **4**(4), Article 57 (2013)
24. Valderas, P., Pelechano, V.: A survey of requirements specification in model-driven development of web applications. ACM Trans. Web **5**(2), Article 10 (2011)

Navigational Complexity Metrics of a Website

Divyam Pandey, Renuka Nagpal and Deepti Mehrotra

Abstract Navigation is the ease with which user traverses through a website while searching for information. The smooth is the navigation, the better are the chances of finding our concerned piece of information. Hence, it can be considered as an important parameter that contributes to the usability of the website. There are several factors that enhance the complexity of navigation of website. The important ones are website structural complexity, broken links, path length, maximum depth, etc. In this study, navigational complexity of seven websites is evaluated and compared on these parameters.

Keywords Navigation · Complexity · Usability · Broken links
Sitemap

1 Introduction

Designing a website that satisfies the visitor by providing the desired information effectively and quickly is a challenging task. Navigation and search are the two main parameters considered for finding any information on the website. The usage of the website depends upon many parameters [1, 2], and navigation [3] is crucial among them. Website is a collection of different pages which are connected through each other via hyperlinks, and information can reside in any of the pages. Navigating through the structure of the hyperlink greatly affects the user experience and satisfaction, and too much of traversing may lead to dissatisfaction. The breadth versus depth issue in website design for optimal performance is widely studied.

D. Pandey (✉) · R. Nagpal · D. Mehrotra
Amity School of Engineering and Technology, Amity University, Noida, Uttar Pradesh, India
e-mail: divyampandey@hotmail.com

R. Nagpal
e-mail: rnagpal1@amity.edu

D. Mehrotra
e-mail: mehdeepti@gmail.com

© Springer Nature Singapore Pte Ltd. 2019
M. N. Hoda et al. (eds.), *Software Engineering*, Advances in Intelligent Systems and Computing 731, https://doi.org/10.1007/978-981-10-8848-3_41

Zaphris [4] found that for a website having 64 links, a two-level website design with 8 links per page had provided the fastest response time and lowest navigational effort. With the increasing size of websites and diverse applications, the complexity of the website grows, and looking for some information in a website, the user tends to get lost. Instead of finding the correct information, the user either ends at the wrong place or finds incorrect, incomplete or inappropriate information which decreases the usability of the website. Zhang et al. [5] proposed metrics for website navigability based on the structural complexity of the website which depends on the connectivity of the links. More the Web pages are interlinked together, more is the structural complexity of the website and more is the difficulty in navigation of the website. Jung et al. [6] have given entropy-based structural complexity measures WCOXIN (in-link complexity) and WCOXOUT (out-link complexity) for Web applications to measure the structural changes. The ease of navigation primarily depends on website design and user using the website. With respect to website design its size, complexity, possible paths, defects, search tool effect navigational dimension and the user input can be measured by using user feedback (perceptual view of the target people), analysing the server log files from which Web usage is measured with respect to visitor per page, pages per visitor (questionnaire) or Web log analysis (Web mining) by considering the will definitely improve. It is important to construct a good navigational website and for that one need to study navigation of a website, so that users are able to find the information they are looking for. In this paper, a metrics is proposed to measure the navigability of the website w.r.t. its design aspects. The major factors that will affect the ease of navigational complexity of the website are hyperlink structure, possible path defects, path length and path density in the website.

2 Factors Affecting Navigational Complexity of the Website

Different factors affecting the navigational complexity of the website are discussed in the following section.

2.1 Website Structural Complexity

Website structural complexity is relationship between the various pages of a website. A website is linked to other pages of the website through various hyperlinks. These hyperlinks are generally the path through which users browse the Web page to navigate various parts of the website, in order to get the information they want. The greater the complexity, the more are the chances of the user getting lost in the website and not being able to find the information that they required. Apart from structural complexity, there are other factors on which navigational complexity depends.

2.2 Other Factors

2.2.1 Website Defects

Website may have many defects such as broken links and orphan pages which affect the navigation of the website adversely. Broken links are Web pages which no longer exist on the Web either because they are deleted accidentally or URL is renamed. Broken links affect navigation as the user cannot find the piece of information that might be earlier available on the broken link. Orphan links are created when we create a page but forget to link it or mistype the link. The visitors may feel upset by incorrect links. These are depicted in the sitemap of the website as shown in Fig. 1 by 'cross-sign'.

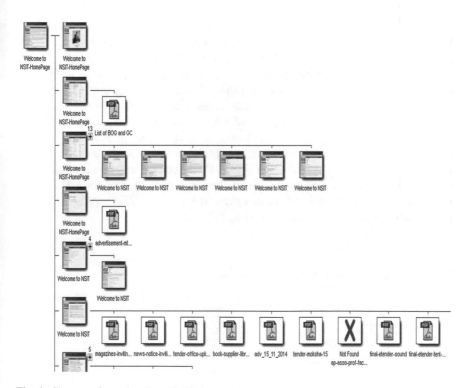

Fig. 1 Sitemap of an educational institute

2.2.2 Maximum Depth

Maximum depth is the deepest level to which we can go in the hierarchical structure of the website. A broader hierarchical Web structure is preferable in comparison with deeper hierarchical Web structure as it enables the user to find the complete yet concise information and also does not let the user get lost in the deeper levels.

2.2.3 Path Density

Path density or the average connected distance is the number of clicks that are required to move from one Web page to another Web page where our desired information is present. The lesser the number of clicks between the two Web pages, the better it is. Impacts of different factors on the website are given in Table 1. This implies if any of the above mentioned factors increases, it shall increase the navigational complexity of the website. However for better designing, it is required to have less navigational complexity.

3   Methodology

To compute the navigational complexity of the website, sitemap is established. Sitemap with the help of a POWER MAPPER TOOL which selects the URL of the website and depending on the design it may be organized into different levels. The sitemap of the university, U1, is shown in Fig. 1. The sitemap is used to create the tree structure using the hyperlinks in the website. In the tree structure, the Web pages at each level link to Web pages at other level and the node which are not linked to other Web pages are treated as leaf node. In the current study, seven websites of educational institutes are taken, and consequently, the tree structure is created using sitemap and is shown in Fig. 2. Once full tree structure is created, the total number of links ($'e'$), various nodes in the graph ($'n'$), the leaf nodes ($'d'$), etc., are evaluated. With the help of these values, the value of WSC_1, WSC_2, WSC_3, WSC_4, WSC_5 using Fig. 2 is evaluated as follows:

Table 1 Impact of factors on navigability of the website

Factors	How do they impact the navigation of a website?
1. Structural complexity	Positively
2. Broken link, orphan pages (website defects)	Positively
3. Maximum depth	Positively
4. Path density	Positively

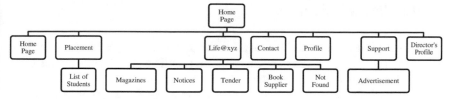

Fig. 2 Tree structure of website

Total no. of pages: 15
Total no. of out links = 14
$e = 14$ (Total no. of links in the graph)
$n = 15$ (Total no. of nodes in the graph)
$d = 11$ (Total leaf nodes)

$$\text{WSC}_1 = \sum_{i=1}^{n} \text{outlink}(i) = \sum_{i=1}^{n} \text{inlink}(i) = \text{total number of links} = 14 \quad (1)$$

$$\text{WSC}_2 = \frac{\text{WSC}_1}{n} = \frac{\sum_{i=1}^{n} \text{outlink}(i)}{n} = \frac{14}{15} = 0.933333 \quad (2)$$

$$\text{WSC}_3 = \text{NOIP}(G) = e - n + d + 1 = 14 - 15 + 11 + 1 = 11 \quad (3)$$

$$\text{WSC}_4 = \frac{\text{WSC}_3}{n} = \frac{e - n + d + 1}{n} = \frac{11}{15} = 0.733333 \quad (4)$$

$$\text{WSC}_5 = \sum_{i=1}^{n} \text{out\_link}^2(n) = \frac{76}{15} = 5.066667 \quad (5)$$

Broken links and orphan pages can be easily identified. We have a page not found node in the sitemap which is indicative of a broken link and orphan pages.

As shown in Fig. 2, the maximum depth is 2. The average connected distance or path density is two (2). To have the same range of values for all the inputs, normalization of the input parameters is done. Normalized data was calculated by the formula

$$v' = \left(v - \min_{A}\right) / \left(\max_{A} - \min_{A}\right) \quad (6)$$

4   Results and Discussion

Using Eqs. (1)–(5), the website structural complexity (WSC$_1$-WSC$_5$) is calculated for seven educational websites and given in Table 2. The complexities for the entire website are calculated by taking the average of WSC$_4$ and WSC$_5$.

Using the sitemap and creating the tree structure of the websites under study, other parameters on which the complexity of the website depends are computed as given in Table 3.

To have the same range of values for all the inputs, normalization of the input parameters is done using Eq. (6). The normalized data for all the input variables is given in Table 4. Navigational complexity is evaluated by taking the average of all the input parameters, i.e.

$$\text{Navigational Complexity} = \frac{(\text{Structural Complexity} + \text{Website Defects} + \text{Path Length} + \text{Path Density})}{4}$$

(7)

Using Eq. (7), navigational complexity metrics is evaluated and given in Table 4.

As per the results obtained from Table 4, the highest navigational complexity is of site U1 and the least navigational complexity is of site U6. It is clear from the above results that structural complexity and Website defects of U5 were the highest,

Table 2 Structural complexity

Website	WSC$_1$	WSC$_2$	WSC$_3$	WSC$_4$	WSC$_5$	Complexity
U1	999	0.999	678	0.678	18.757	9.7175
U2	87	0.988636	79	0.897727	15.55682	8.227273
U3	70	0.985915	61	0.859155	15.49296	8.176056
U4	280	0.996441	217	0.772242	15.51601	8.144128
U5	154	0.993548	116	0.748387	24.59355	12.67097
U6	97	0.989796	80	0.816327	1.265306	1.040816
U7	100	0.990196	87	0.852941	23.08824	11.97059

Table 3 Other parameters affecting complexity of website

Website	Website defects, broken link, orphan pages	Path length (maximum depth)	Path density
U1	3	Level 7	2
U2	2	Level 3	1
U3	10	Level 3	1
U4	13	Level 6	1
U5	21	Level 5	1
U6	7	Level 3	1
U7	3	Level 4	1

Table 4 Normalized data

Website	Structural complexity	Website defects	Maximum depth	Path density	Navigational complexity
U1	0.746051	0.052632	1	1	0.699671
U2	0.617916	0	0	0	0.154479
U3	0.613512	0.421053	0	0	0.258641
U4	0.610767	0.578947	0.75	0	0.484929
U5	1	1	0.5	0	0.625
U6	0	0.263158	0	0	0.065789
U7	0.939779	0.052632	0.25	0	0.310603

but when other parameters, i.e. maximum depth and path lengths, were included, the site U1 was found to have maximum navigational complexity as all the factors contribute equally in calculating the navigational complexity of the website.

5 Conclusions

Navigational complexity plays a vital role in evaluating the usability of the website. Hence, it is desired to have minimum navigational complexity for an effective website. The website having the minimum value of navigational complexity is the one in which user faces less problems; it facilitates easy navigation to find our concerned information and thereby is the best website design. The website having the maximum value of navigational complexity is the one in which a user faces the most difficulty in navigation and consequently the user is not able to find its share of information rendering the website as the worst website. U6 has been concluded to be the best navigable website as its navigational complexity is the minimum.

References

1. Sreedhar, G., Vidyapeetha, R.S., Centre, N.I.: Measuring quality of web site navigation 1 1. Science (**80**-), 80–86 (2010)
2. Nagpal, R., Mehrotra, D., Kumar Bhatia, P., Sharma, A.: Rank university websites using fuzzy AHP and fuzzy TOPSIS approach on usability. Int. J. Inf. Eng. Electron. Bus. **7**, 29–36 (2015). https://doi.org/10.5815/ijieeb.2015.01.04
3. Chhabra, S.: A survey of metrics for assessing the navigational quality of a website based on the structure of website. 167–173 (1989)
4. Zaphiris, P.G.: Depth vs breath in the arrangement of web links. Proc. Hum. Factors Ergon. Soc. Annu. Meet. **44**, 453–456 (2000). https://doi.org/10.1177/154193120004400414

5. Zhang, Y.Z.Y., Zhu, H.Z.H., Greenwood, S.: Web site complexity metrics for measuring navigability. In: Fourth International Conference on Quality Software, 2004 QSIC 2004 Proceedings (2004). https://doi.org/10.1109/qsic.2004.1357958
6. Jung, W., Lee, E., Kim, K.: An entropy-based complexity measure for web applications using structural information. J. Inf. Sci. **619**, 595–619 (2011)

Evaluation and Comparison of Security Mechanisms In-Place in Various Web Server Systems

Syed Mutahar Aaqib and Lalitsen Sharma

Abstract This paper presents a novel approach to study, identify, and evaluate the security mechanisms in-place across various Web server platforms. These security mechanisms are collected and compiled from various sources. A set of security checks are framed to identify the implementation of these security mechanisms in diverse Web server platforms. The paper is concluded with a case study which implements this approach.

Keywords Web server · Web server security · Information security

1 Introduction

Security in computer science literature is considered to be the maintenance the confidentiality, integrity, and availability of information [1–3]. Security is a primary concern for World Wide Web researchers as the frequency of Distributed Denial of Service (DDoS) attacks, probability of exposure, or compromise of sensitive information, data manipulation and spoofing have increased [1]. Initially, the architecture of Web server was conceived to serve only static Web pages, which was later extended into dynamic content [2, 4, 5]. Although this functionality delivers more customized content, it also implies that there is an increasing growth of security problems which needs to be mitigated while migrating to new supportive architectures. Web servers are therefore considered to be a vital backbone for Web applications, from simple file transfer applications to delivery of confidential data for e-commerce applications. The security compromises of any type can thus cause heavy damage of data including economic and financial losses. The security of the Web server is also characterized by the operating system interfaces, communication and security protocols, network configuration and its environment. The implementation of security features like Secure Socket Layer (SSL) within Web servers is

S. M. Aaqib (✉) · L. Sharma
Department of Computer Science & IT, University of Jammu, Jammu Tawi, J&K, India
e-mail: syed.auqib@gmail.com

© Springer Nature Singapore Pte Ltd. 2019
M. N. Hoda et al. (eds.), *Software Engineering*, Advances in Intelligent Systems and Computing 731, https://doi.org/10.1007/978-981-10-8848-3_42

therefore mandatory for all contemporary Web servers. However, some of the Web servers who have been claimed to be developed in adherence to various security guidelines still contain known and unknown vulnerabilities [6]. The source of these vulnerabilities is sometimes the misconfiguration of the networking infrastructure such as intrusion detection system and firewalls.

Thus, there is need to evaluate the security of a Web server system by taking into consideration the holistic view of the system which includes the security features provided by the Web server software, the operating system, the configuration of the networking infrastructure and its environment. Such an approach should allow the evaluation and comparison of the security mechanism in-place in Web server systems. A standardized procedure should be adopted where tests can be applied and reapplied across various Web server systems. These tests may also be repeated for reproducibility and validation. Comparing security of two Web servers is a complicated issue. One obvious way to measure security of a Web server is by checking the chances of violation of the confidentiality, integrity, and availability of information.

2 Background and Related Work

A lot of work has focused to study the security of a computer system in general and security of Web server in particular [6]. Bishop [1] in his work stressed about the three dimensions of security which viz, security requirements, security policy, and security mechanisms. A number of methodologies elaborating Web security characteristics have been presented by numerous organizations [7]. These methodologies have gained international acceptance and are used as security policy standard in the development of Web servers. The first security evaluation methods based on Common Criteria standard [7] was proposed by the United States Department of Defense [8]. This standard emphasized a set of security requirements that must be present in a Web server system. Centre for Internet Security (CIS) presented a benchmark [9] which evaluates the security configuration settings for commonly used Apache and IIS Web servers. The Department of Information Technology (DIT), Govt. of India, has also published a set of security recommendation for securing a Web server [10]. National Informatics Centre (NIC), Govt. of India, has published a manual [11] for enhancing the security of government Web sites. Such security recommendations have been found effective in preventing security hacks of government Web sites [11]. Researchers [6] have made vertical comparison between various generic servers based on the number of security flaws and severity and have also studied the vulnerabilities in operating systems [12, 13]. Others have used quantitative empirical models for the comparison of security vulnerabilities in Apache and IIS Web servers [13]. Another technique reported in the literature is to characterize and count potential vulnerabilities that exist in a product [14]. In this paper, a different approach to evaluate the security of Web servers across different Web server platforms is presented.

3 Methodology

A comprehensive survey of technical security manuscripts published by various security organizations was done and a total of 390 best security mechanisms were compiled. The security mechanisms of Web servers were evaluated by performing a test to verify whether a set of security mechanisms have been implemented on the target system. A security comparison was then performed between various Web servers to identify which Web server implements most of the security mechanisms. The number of steps involved in this process is listed below:

- Survey for identification of best security mechanisms for Web servers;
- Categorization of security mechanisms in various classes;
- Execution of a number to tests to verify the implementation of security mechanisms in Web servers;
- Case Study: Comparison of the security mechanisms implemented in various Web servers.

A detailed study of the technical security manuscripts published by various organizations like CIS [9], NIST [8], Common Criteria [7], Web server security guidelines (DIT, Govt. of India) [10], and Web site security recommendation published by National Informatics Centre [11] was performed and a total of 390 best security mechanisms were identified. These security mechanisms were then divided into various classes for ease in the evaluation of security tests. A set of tests were then designed to identify whether these security mechanisms are implemented with a particular Web server system. For the comparison of security of Web servers, a case study of eight Web server system installations was taken to implement this approach. Finally, a number of tests were performed for each Web server, and these tests verify whether the system implements the security mechanisms compiled.

3.1 Metrics

A simple metric employed in this approach is the count of the number of best security mechanism implemented in a particular Web server. The final security score is thus the weighted percentage of the total security practices implemented, which implies the security level of the system. Till date, no consensus has been drawn about the set of best security mechanisms that should be applied to Web server systems. The huge amount of diverse technical manuscripts in the form of books, manuals, reports, and papers are available on the subject of Web server security, but researchers have found no common ground for any agreement on the best standard mechanisms.

List of the technical documents included in this study is:

- Apache Benchmark document;
- IIS benchmark document;

Table 1 Characterization of security mechanisms into classes

Categories of security mechanisms	Class assigned
Security policy	Class A
Access control	Class B
Communication and operations management	Class C
Human resource security	Class D
Information system acquisition development	Class E
Physical environment security	Class F

- Web server Common Criteria;
- Web server NIST document;
- DIT Web Server Guidelines;
- NIC Web site Security Guidelines.

After the end of the thorough study of all this literature and technical manuscripts, 390 security mechanisms were complied. Out of these 146 came from CIS documentation (Apache Web server: 101, IIS Web server: 45), 38 from DIT document, 11 from NIC, 39 from Common Criteria, and 156 from NIST. Out of all the mechanisms compiled, it was found that most of them are similar (equivalent) and deal with same security problems. The categorization of such similar security mechanisms was done, and they were grouped together under a unique directive. After applying this method, the numbers of unique security mechanisms were counted and a total of 78 best security mechanisms were identified.

This set of 78 best security mechanisms were characterized into six categories based on an internationally valid standard for information security [15]. The characterization of security mechanisms into these six classes was done for ease in using them in evaluation. Table 1 lists the categories of security mechanisms grouped under six categories and the class assigned to each category.

3.2   Web Server Tests

A set of tests were designed to identify whether or not this set of 78 of security mechanisms are implemented in a particular Web server system. Based on the nature of the security mechanisms, a set of tests were defined. These tests comprise of a set of questions with optional procedure to verify presence of each security mechanisms within the system. The output of the test, yes/no, would occur only after the execution of the optional procedure.

4 Case Study—Results and Discussion

To validate the approach used, a case study for the comparison of security of five different Web servers was taken. Table 2 presents details about each Web server tested, its version, the operating system, and the number of applications running on the server. The results of these tests for Web server are presented in the following tables (Table 3). "Test OK" in Table 3 refers to the successful execution of tests which implies presence of a set particular security mechanism in the Web server under study. "Test Fail" refers to the number of tests failed and unknown refers to unknown test, for each set of best mechanisms presented in Table 3. This case study was used to check the number of best security mechanism in-place in these Web server systems. A number of significant insights were gained from this study. One of the interesting observations was that the two Web servers of different version from a same vendor, showed different results in this study. Such different results were obtained for a same Web server while comparing their installations on different platforms.

The reason being the security of a Web server is not dependent only on the Web server software only but it is also characterized by the underlying operating system architecture, the network management, and its configuration.

For example, while comparing the same Apache HTTPd server on Scientific Linux CERN and Windows XP 2000, it was found that Apache on SLC CERN system passed more tests and thus was more secure [16]. Another aspect used in this study was the comparison of diverse Web server systems, of different underlying operating systems. While comparing the security mechanism in Apache Tomcat 6.0.13 and Apache Tomcat 6.0.16 on Windows Server 2003 platform, it was revealed that Apache Tomcat 6.0.16 passed more tests and hence was more secure. Here also, the explanation is the support provided by the underlying operating system platform and its security configuration. Among all the Web servers under study, it was found that Microsoft IIS passed more number of tests than any other Web server and thus implements higher number of security mechanisms. The only limitation of this approach is that the execution of these tests requires

Table 2 Web servers examined in the case study

S. No.	Web server	Operating system	Applications running
1	*Apache HTTPd* 2	Windows XP	6
2	*Apache* Tomcat 6.0.13	Windows Server 2003	3
3	Microsoft *IIS* 6.0	Windows XP	2
4	*Apache* Tomcat 6.0.16	Windows Server 2003	2
5	*Apache HTTPd* 2	Scientific Linux SLC *CERN*	3
6	Microsoft *IIS* 7.0	Windows Server 2003	3
7	Nginx Web Server	Scientific Linux SLC *CERN*	2
8	Nginx Web Server	Windows Server 2003	2

Table 3 Results of case study for eight different Web server system installations

Case 1, Apache HTTPd 2	Test OK	Test fail	Unknown
Class A	0	7	0
Class B	17	8	1
Class C	18	15	0
Class D	1	1	0
Class E	4	4	0
Class F	1	1	0
Total	41	36	1

Case 2, Apache Tomcat 6.0.13	Test OK	Test fail	Unknown
Class A	0	7	0
Class B	14	12	0
Class C	16	16	1
Class D	1	1	0
Class E	4	4	0
Class F	2	0	0
Total	37	40	1

Case 3, Microsoft IIS 6.0	Test OK	Test fail	Unknown
Class A	03	04	0
Class B	10	16	1
Class C	18	14	0
Class D	02	00	0
Class E	05	03	0
Class F	02	00	0
Total	40	37	1

Case 4, Tomcat 6.0.16	Test OK	Test fail	Unknown
Class A	0	7	0
Class B	13	13	0
Class C	21	12	1
Class D	2	0	0
Class E	4	4	0
Class F	2	0	0
Total	42	36	0

Case 5, Apache HTTPd	Test OK	Test fail	Unknown
Class A	7	0	0
Class B	9	17	0
Class C	15	18	1
Class D	2	0	0
Class E	2	6	0
Class F	0	2	0
Total	35	43	0

Case 6, Microsoft IIS 7.0	Test OK	Test fail	Unknown
Class A	7	0	0
Class B	9	17	0
Class C	15	18	0
Class D	2	0	0
Class E	2	6	0
Class F	0	2	0
Total	35	43	0

Case 7, Nginx Server SLC	Test OK	Test fail	Unknown
Class A	02	03	2
Class B	07	15	4
Class C	11	18	4
Class D	02	00	0
Class E	02	05	1
Class F	01	01	0
Total	25	42	11

Case 8, Nginx Server Windows	Test OK	Test fail	Unknown
Class A	02	03	2
Class B	07	16	3
Class C	11	16	6
Class D	02	00	0
Class E	02	04	2
Class F	01	01	0
Total	25	40	13

immense computer proficiency as this approach requires verification of mechanisms in-place for different Web servers systems.

References

1. Bishop, M.: What is computer security. IEEE Secur. Priv. (2003)
2. Laprie, J.C.: Dependability of computer systems: concepts, limits, improvements. In: Proceedings of the 6th International Symposium on Software Reliability Engineering (1995)
3. Lin, P.: So You Want High Performance (Tomcat Performance). Jakarta Tomcat (2003)
4. Aaqib S.M., Sharma L.: Analysis of delivery of web contents for kernel-mode and user–mode web servers. Int. J. Comput. Appl. **12**(9), 37–42 (Foundation of Computer Science, New York, USA) (2011)
5. Arlitt, M., Williamson, C.: Understanding web server configuration issues. Softw. Pract. Experience **34**(2), 163–186 (2004)
6. Ford, R., Thompson, H., Casteran, F.: Role Comparison Report-Web Server Role. Technical Report, Security Innovation (2005)
7. Common Criteria: US Government Protection Profile. Web Server for Basic Robustness Environments, Version 1.1 (2007)
8. NIST.: National Institute of Standards and Technology, Guidelines on Securing Public Web Servers, Special Publication, 800-44 Version 2 (2007)
9. CIS. Centre for Internet Security 2008. Retrieved from CIS http://www.cisecurity.org/as accessed on June 2015
10. CERT-In.: Web Server Guidelines 2004. Department of IT, Government of India (2004)
11. NIC Guidelines for Indian Government Websites.: National Informatics Centre (2013). Retrieved from: http://darpg.gov.in as accessed on June 2015
12. Alhazmi, O.H., Malaiya, Y.K., Ray, I.: Security vulnerabilities in software systems: a quantitative perspective. In: Proceedings of the Annual IFIP WG11.3 Working Conference on Data and Information Security, pp. 281–294 (2005)
13. Rescorla, E.: Is finding security holes a good idea? IEEE Secur. Priv. **03**(1), 14–19 (2003)
14. Neto, A.A., Mendes, N., Duraes, J., M., Madeira, H.: Assessing and comparing security of web servers. In: 14th IEEE Pacific Rim International on Dependable Computing (2008)
15. IEC-ISO. 17799:2005: Information Technology-Security Technique—Code of Practice for Information Security Management. Retrieved from http://www.iso.org/iso/ as on Oct 2012
16. Web Server Protection Profile. Retrieved from http://llniap.nist.govIcc-scheme (2001). Woo, S., Alhazmi, O.H., Malaiya, Y.K.: Assessing Vulnerabilities in Apache and IIS HTTP Servers. Colorado State University, Fort Collins (2008).

Component-Based Quality Prediction via Component Reliability Using Optimal Fuzzy Classifier and Evolutionary Algorithm

Kavita Sheoran and Om Prakash Sangwan

Abstract Sequentially to meet the rising necessities, software system has become more complex for software support from profuse varied areas. In software reliability engineering, many techniques are available to ensure the reliability and quality. In design models, prediction techniques play an important role. In case of component-based software systems, accessible reliability prediction approaches experience the following drawbacks and hence restricted in their applicability and accuracy. Here, we compute the application reliability which is estimated depend upon the reliability of the individual components and their interconnection mechanisms. In our method, the quality of the software can be predicted in terms of reliability metrics. After that the component-based feature extraction, the reliability is calculated by optimal fuzzy classifier (OFC). Here, the fuzzy rules can be optimized by evolutionary algorithms. The implementation is done via JAVA and the performance is analyzed with various metrics.

Keywords Quality prediction · Component-based system · Reliability
Fuzzy classifier · Evolutionary algorithm

1 Introduction

In software development life cycle, software architecture is estimated of higher significance. It is utilized to symbolize and converse the system structure and performance to all of its stakeholders through a variety of concerns. In addition, SA smooths the progress of stakeholders in accepting design decisions and rationale, more promoting reprocess and competent development. Recently, in software systems, development one of the foremost concerns is systematic SA reorganizing

K. Sheoran (✉)
Department of Computer Science, MSIT, Delhi, India
e-mail: kavitasheoran0780@gmail.com

O. P. Sangwan
Department of Computer Engineering, Guru Jambeshwar University, Hissar, India

© Springer Nature Singapore Pte Ltd. 2019
M. N. Hoda et al. (eds.), *Software Engineering*, Advances in Intelligent Systems and Computing 731, https://doi.org/10.1007/978-981-10-8848-3_43

to accommodate novel necessities because of the new market opportunities, technologies, platforms, and frameworks [1–3].

In this proposed method, we compute the application reliability which is estimated depending on individual components reliability values and their interconnection mechanisms. In our proposed method, the quality of the software can be predicted in terms of reliability metrics. Subsequent to the component-based feature extraction, the reliability is calculated by optimal fuzzy classifier (OFC). Here, the fuzzy rules can be optimized by using evolutionary algorithms. The paper is well organized in the below sections as follows. The literature that are associated with our proposed method are mentioned in Sect. 2. The proposed method of software quality prediction is explained in Sect. 3. Section 4 explains the result of the proposed methodology and finally our proposed method is concluded with suggestions for future works in Sect. 5.

2 Related Work

Numerous researches have been performed in the field of software quality as it has gained more significance with the advance in computer technologies. Some of the recent researches are as mentioned below.

Brosch et al. [4] by unequivocally modeling the system procedure outline and execution environment. The technique has offered a UML-like modeling notation, where these models are mechanically changed into a proper analytical model. Utilizing methods of data propagation and reliability assessment their work has created upon the Palladio Component Model (PCM), In general with the employment of reliability-improving architecture methods the case studies recognized effectual hold up of practice profile analysis and architectural configuration ranking.

Ahmed and Jamimi [5] have anticipated a route for developing fuzzy logic-based transparent quality forecasting models, in which they have used the procedure to a case study to forecast software maintainability where Mamdani fuzzy inference engine was utilized.

Brosig et al. [6], e.g., Queueing Petri Nets and Layered Queueing Networks, have managed an in-depth assessment and quantitative assessment of demonstrating model transformations.

3 Proposed Methodology for Software Quality Prediction

The process of predicting the quality to be required to develop a software system is software quality prediction [7]. The evaluation of quality in software is more demanding task and frequent researches were approved out. For software quality prediction in our proposed method, we craft the use of soft computing-based software quality prediction where fuzzy logic incorporated with the evolutionary algorithm is used [8].

3.1 Steps Involved in the Software Quality Prediction

Here, we calculate the application reliability which is predictable based on the reliability of the individual components and their interconnection mechanisms. In our proposed method, the quality of the software can be predicted in terms of reliability metrics. After the component-based feature extraction, the reliability is calculated by optimal fuzzy classifier (OFC). Here, the fuzzy rules can be optimized by using evolutionary algorithms (Fig. 1).

3.2 Software Cost and Reliability Measure to Estimate the Quality

3.2.1 Software Reliability Measure

The reliability can be measured by estimating the testing effort of the particular software. The failure rate with respect to the time of execution can be calculated and this gives the reliability of that particular software at the execution time. The reliability of the software can be measured while computing the expression given below,

Fig. 1 Proposed software quality prediction model

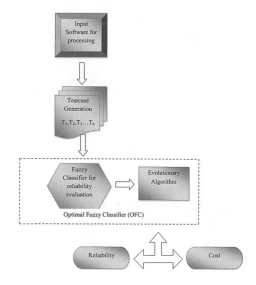

$$r(t) = f(t)/e_t \tag{1}$$

where, $f(t)$ = Failure rate at time (t) and e_t = execution time.

Fuzzy Logic

Fuzzy logic is a technique that decides issues too intricate and to be understood quantitatively.

(i) *Fuzzy Triangular Membership Function*

By means of the triangular membership function, the attributes having mathematical values in the XML database is changed into the fuzzy. The triangular membership function is selected herein which p, q, and r stand for the x coordinates of the three vertices of $f(x)$ in a fuzzy set where r is the higher boundary and p is the lower boundary where the membership degree is zero, q is the center where membership degree is 1. To compute the membership values, the formula used is depicted as below,

$$f(x) = \begin{cases} 0 & \text{if } x \le p \\ \frac{(x-p)}{(q-p)} & \text{if } p \le x \le q \\ \frac{(r-x)}{(r-q)} & \text{if } q \le x \le r \\ 0 & \text{if } x \ge r \end{cases} \tag{2}$$

(ii) *Fuzzy Rules*

A set of rules have been described for a fuzzy arbiter where it outputs the software efforts in reference to the attributes fuzzy value. The software efforts are grouped into different rules based on the parameters, and in our method we utilize optimization procedure so as to optimize the fuzzy rules. We have utilized evolutionary programming for optimizing the rules.

Fuzzy Rule Optimization Using Evolutionary Programming (EP)

(i) *Generation of Random Chromosomes*

Originally each chromosome has N_d gene values and N_p numbers of random chromosomes are produced, where chromosomes symbolize the values. At this time, the process makes use of the measures that have relevant indices and the gene values specify the indices of the reliability measure. Hence the chromosome created can be represented as given below,

$$D_l^{(j)} = \left\{ d_0^{(j)}, d_2^{(j)}, d_3^{(j)}, \ldots, d_{N_d-1}^{(j)} \right\} \quad 0 \le j \le N_p - 1 \, 0 \le l \le N_d - 1 \quad (3)$$

Here $D_l^{(j)}$ signifies the lth gene of the jth chromosome and here d symbolize the measures.

$$\left\{ \hat{F}_l^{(j)} \right\} = \left(\frac{\left| F_l'^{(j)} \right|}{\sum_{q=0}^{\left| F_l'^{(j)} \right| - 1} \left(F_l'^{(j)}(q) \right)^2} \right)^{1/2} F_l'^{(j)}(q) \quad (4)$$

where,

$$F_l'^{(j)}(q) = F_l^{(j)}(q) \left| F_l^{(j)} \right| - \sum_{q=0}^{\left| F_l^{(j)} \right| - 1} F_l^{(j)}(q) \quad (5)$$

The normalized feature set $\left\{ \hat{F}_l^{(j)} \right\}$ acquired from Eq. (4) is the ultimate feature set extracted for an exacting reliability measure.

(ii) **Fitness Function**

To examine the similarity among the reliability measures that are being designed the fitness value predicted for the EP is SED which is the distance measure developed.

$$F^{(j)} = \frac{\sum_{l=0}^{N_d-1} \delta_l^{(j)}}{\left| \delta_l^{(j)} \right|} \quad (6)$$

where,

$$\delta_l^{(j)} = \sum_{r=0}^{\left| F\hat{S}_k^{(j)} \right| - 1} \left(\hat{F}_l^{(j)}(r) - \hat{F}_q(q) \right)^2 \quad (7)$$

In Eq. (7), $\hat{F}_q$ is the value of selected measure, $\delta_l^{(j)}$ symbolizes the SED among each $D_l^{(j)}$ of the jth chromosome and the respective measure. Consequently, the $F^{(j)}$ is arranged in the ascending order and $N_p/2$ number of mean distances are selected from $f^{(j)}$. Then the equivalent $D_l^{(j)}$ of the selected $F^{(j)}$ is acquired and then the chosen chromosomes are subjected to the genetic operator, mutation.

(iii) *Mutation*

t number of values are chosen from the mean of chromosomes which are already in sorted form. The selected means are known as $D_{newl}^{(j)}$. The genes which are having least SED values are replaced by the new ones.

(iv) *Selection of Optimal Solution*

The chromosome having maximum fitness is selected and the iteration repeated I_{max} times. It denotes that the reliability value recovered in an effective way. So, we compute the reliability measure value based on these features that is used for quality measurement of the specified application software.

3.2.2 Software Cost Measure

To speedup the testing process, automated testing tools are used. It does not only hurry up the testing process but it increases the efficiency of the testing by certain extent. The total cost of software is given as;

$$C_t = C_{0t} + C_1(1+k)f(t) + C_2\left[f(t_j) - (1+k)f(t)\right] + C_3\left(\int_0^t x(t)dt\right) \quad (8)$$

where P is described as fractions of extra errors found during the software testing phase and is the number of additional faults during the testing time. C_{0t} is cost of adopting new automated testing tools into testing phase. k is directly proportional to cost as k increases cost also increases.

4 Results and Discussion

Software quality prediction using optimal fuzzy classifier (OFC) with the aid of evolutionary algorithm is implemented in the working platform of JAVA. Table 1 shows the fitness value of our proposed improved particle swarm optimization method using different iterations.

Table 1 Fitness value for different iteration	No. of iterations	Fitness value using IPSO	Proposed method
	5	12.658	15.2
	10	10.354	14.6
	15	10.354	12.8
	20	10.123	11.32
	25	9.654	10.5

Fig. 2 Comparison of the
fitness value for the existing
work using IPSO and our
proposed method

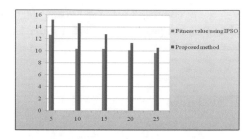

Table 2 Reliability and cost
value of our proposed method

Time	Reliability	Cost
0.001	0.00932	985.25
0.003	0.01134	993.32
0.004	0.01243	1012.42
0.005	0.01623	1025.21
0.007	0.02315	1078.68
0.008	0.02512	1100.35

Table 3 Comparison of
software quality measures for
our proposed and existing
method

Methods	Reliability	Cost
Existing method using IPSO	0.0294	1150.76
Proposed method	0.03242	1118.26

Figure 2 shows the compared fitness value for the existing work using IPSO and
our method where optimal fuzzy classifier is used. The graph shows that our
proposed method has delivered better fitness value which aids in improving the
quality of the software.

Table 2 illustrates the reliability and the cost value that is obtained using our
proposed method of quality prediction. For various time intervals, the corresponding reliability and the cost values are estimated (Table 3).

5 Conclusion

Software quality prediction is measured as a main aspect while designing software.
The proposed system is developed to forecast improved software quality by means
of soft computing method. Initially, test cases are generated from the input and then
extract the component-based software metrics from the test cases. Subsequently, the
component-based feature extraction the reliability is computed by optimal fuzzy
classifier (OFC). Here, the fuzzy rules can be optimized by using evolutionary
algorithms. The reliability and cost of the software are then evaluated, and these

values are compared with the existing method. From the comparative analysis, it is clear that our proposed method achieved better outcome when compared to other existing methods.

References

1. Dobrica, L., Ioniţa, A.D., Pietraru, R., Olteanu, A.: Automatic transformation of software architecture models. U.P.B. Sci. Bull Series C **73**(3), 3–16 (2011)
2. Seiffert, C., Khoshgoftaar, T.M., Van Hulse, J.: Improving software-quality predictions with data sampling and boosting. IEEE Trans. Syst. Man Cybern. Part A Syst. Hum. **39**(6) (2009)
3. (Cathy) Liu, Y., Khoshgoftaar, T.M., Seliya, N.: Evolutionary optimization of software quality modeling with multiple repositories. IEEE Trans. Softw. Eng. **36**(6) (2010)
4. Brosch, F., Koziolek, H., Buhnova, B., Reussner, R.: Architecture-based reliability prediction with the palladio component model. IEEE Trans. Softw. Eng. **38**(6) (2012)
5. Ahmed, M.A., Al-Jamimi, H.A.: Machine learning approaches for predicting software maintainability: a fuzzy-based transparent model. IET Softw. (2013)
6. Brosig, F., Meier, P., Becker, S., Koziolek, A., Koziolek, H., Kounev, S.: Quantitative evaluation of model-driven performance analysis and simulation of component-based architectures. IEEE Trans. Softw. Eng. (2013)
7. Hsu, C.-J., Huang, C.-Y.: Optimal weighted combinational models for software reliability estimation and analysis. IEEE Trans. Reliab. **63**(3) (2014)
8. Shepperd, M., Bowes, D., Hall, T.: Researcher bias: The use of machine learning in software defect prediction. IEEE Trans. Softw. Eng. **40**(6) (2014)

Applying Statistical Usage Testing Along with White Box Testing Techniques

Sunil Kumar Khatri, Kamaldeep Kaur and Rattan Datta

Abstract Cleanroom software engineering (CSE) reference model is a rigorous incremental model that focuses on defect prevention using sound mathematical principles combined with statistical usage testing (Linger, Trammell, in cleanroom software engineering reference model, 1996, [1]). Similar to the concept of hardware cleanrooms, this model is also used for the development of zero defect and extremely reliable software (Mills, Poore, in Quality Progress, 1988, [2]). Statistical usage testing (SUT) is a technique defined for testing as a part of CSE model [1]. The technique works by performing usage modelling and assigning usage probabilities (Runeson, Wohlin in IEEE Trans Softw Eng 20(6): 494–499, 1994, [3]). Next statistical tests are carried out on the usage models [3]. CSE relies on SUT for testing, and unit testing is not defined in the CSE process (Hausler et al. in IBM Syst J 33(1): 89, 109, 1994, [4]). However, additional testing can be carried out along with SUT depending on the need (Prowell et al. in cleanroom software engineering technology and process, 1999, [5]). The paper presents the usefulness and advantages of applying SUT along with various white box testing techniques. The white box testing techniques used in the paper are data flow testing, control flow testing and mutation testing.

Keywords Statistical usage testing · White box testing · Data flow testing
Control flow testing · Mutation testing

S. K. Khatri (✉)
Amity Institute of Information Technology, Amity University, Noida, India
e-mail: skkhatri@amity.edu; sunilkkhatri@gmail.com

K. Kaur
Department of Computer Science, New Delhi Institution of Management, New Delhi, India
e-mail: kamaldeepkaurkalsi@yahoo.co.in

R. Datta
Mohyal Educational and Research Institute of Technology, New Delhi, Delhi, India
e-mail: rkdatta_in@yahoo.com

© Springer Nature Singapore Pte Ltd. 2019
M. N. Hoda et al. (eds.), *Software Engineering*, Advances in Intelligent Systems
and Computing 731, https://doi.org/10.1007/978-981-10-8848-3_44

1   Introduction

Cleanroom software engineering (CSE) reference model is a rigorous model that focuses on defect prevention using sound mathematical principles combined with statistical usage testing [1]. Similar to the concept of hardware cleanrooms, this model is also used for the development of zero defect and high-reliability software [2, 3]. Cleanroom software engineering has three very important and prominent characteristics: developing the software incrementally, function-oriented specification and statistical usage testing [5]. Cleanroom certification process includes two vital steps:

- Converting the software usage into usage models and test planning [5]
- Statistical usage testing and also the certification of the software [5].

Authors have already shown the benefits of using SUT with black box testing techniques [6]. This paper illustrates the usage of SUT in conjunction with one of the unit testing technique, i.e. white box testing. This section of the paper gives an introduction to the SUT process. Section 2 defines various white box testing techniques used in the paper in conjunction with SUT. The software that is used in the paper is an 'HTML to Text utility' that changes HTML documents into easy text files, by eliminating various HTML tags. Section 3 defines the process of performing SUT on HTML to TEXT utility. Section 4 demonstrates the application of combined testing techniques on the software under consideration, while the last section deals with results obtained after the study.

Statistical Usage Testing

Statistical usage testing (SUT) technique is a technique described for testing as a part of CSE model [1], and it forms the certification part of this model [3]. SUT is based on the point of view of the user and is simply related with the interfaces to the users [7]. The intent of SUT is not in testing the software implementation, but its ability to satisfy the anticipated function from the user's point of view [7]. SUT is therefore a black box testing technique [7] where the internal details of the programming structures are not checked.

Statistical usage testing is performed as a formal experiment that is statistical in nature [5]. The technique works by performing usage modelling and assigning usage probabilities [3]. Next statistical tests are carried out on the usage models [3]. All the feasible executions of the software usage are sampled by the generation of random test cases [8]. Next the test cases are executed, and the outcomes are comprehended using a defined level of confidence [5]. Finally, the failure data is collected, and the results are reported [5].

Statistical usage testing can be performed with the aid of Markov chains [8]. The process begins with the development of the usage Markov chain, which models all possible software usages [8]. When the sequences from the usage Markov chain are performed as test cases on the software, the testing Markov chain is permitted to

Fig. 1 Steps of SUT using
Markov chain model [5]

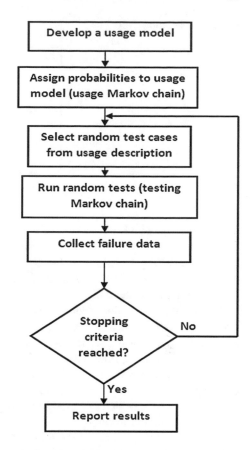

progress according to the results of the tests [8]. The process continues by running test cases and reporting failures [8]. The process of cleanroom certification is depicted in Fig. 1.

SUT has many applications, and moreover, SUT using Markov chains can be efficiently applied to uncover failures in the simple customized software [9].

2 White Box Testing Techniques (WBTT)

2.1 Use of White Box Testing Techniques (WBTTs) with SUT

CSE relies on SUT for testing, and unit testing is not defined in the CSE process [4]. However, additional testing can be carried out along with SUT depending on the need [5]. The application of other testing techniques in conjunction with SUT can be elemental to exhibit precise scenario of usage or to accomplish complete usage

Fig. 2 Gap in testing [12]

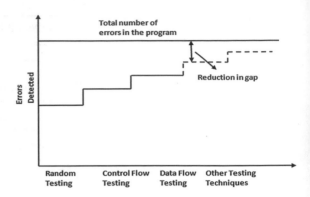

model coverage with lesser number of test cases [5]. It is normally desirable to carry out any non-statistical tests before performing statistical testing [5]. The usage of appropriate testing technique at the correct level can aid in the development of high-quality software [10]. In fact, SUT can be more effectual if incorporated with other testing techniques [11].

Unit testing is a testing technique which checks the internal details of the code. But it is not defined in CSE model [4]. Not permitting the programmer admittance to the code can be less productive. Figure 2 shows the gap in testing [12], which can be filled by using other testing techniques. The paper highlights the usage of SUT in juxtaposition with one of the unit testing technique, i.e. white box testing. The paper presents the usefulness and advantages of applying SUT along with various WBTTs. The WBTTs used in the paper are data flow testing, control flow testing and mutation testing.

In WBTTs, the testers need the information regarding the internal structure [13] and working of the software [14]. It is related with testing the implementation of the software [15]. The principal purpose of this testing technique is to implement various programming structures like decisions, loops, variables and also various data structures used in the program [15]. Since WBTT starts working at most basic level of the software development process, it offers advantages like forcing the test developer to rationale circumspectly concerning the implementation, illuminating errors in the code [16] and compelling the desired coverage of loops, decisions, variables, etc. [15].

2.2 Types of White Box Testing Techniques

Various white box testing techniques are as follows:

1. *Control Flow Testing*

Control flow testing (CFT) is a technique that makes use of the control structures of the program to generate the test cases for the program [17]. The test cases are

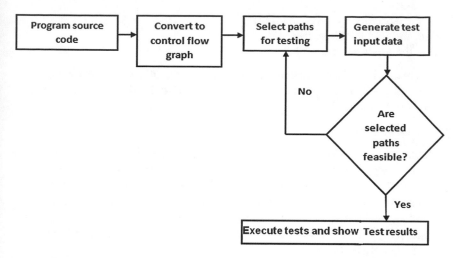

Fig. 3 Process of CFT [19]

generated to sufficiently cover the entire control structure of the program [17]. A control flow graph (CFG) which is a pictorial representation [18] is used to represent the control structure of a program [17]. The control flow graph can be represented as $G = (N, E)$ where N denotes the set of nodes and E indicates the set of edges [17]. Each node corresponds to a set of program statements [17]. The process of CFT is shown in Fig. 3. The process begins with converting the program into a control flow graph [19]. Next various paths are selected, and test input data is generated [19]. The test cases are executed, and results are reported [19]. Control flow testing includes statement, branch and path coverage.

- Statement coverage entails that every statement of the program should be executed at least once during testing [15].
- Branch coverage necessitates the traversal of every edge in the CFG at least once [15].
- Path coverage entails the execution of all the feasible paths in the CFG [15].

2. *Data Flow Testing*

In data flow testing (DFT), information regarding the location of variables definition and also the location of the usage of definitions is used to indicate the test cases [15]. The fundamental intent of data flow testing is to test the various definitions of variables and their successive uses [15]. For DFT, a definition-use graph is initially developed from the control flow of the program [15]. A variable appearance in the program can be one of the below given types:

Def: the definition of a variable [15]
C-use: the computational use [15]
P-use: the predicate use [15].

There can be different criteria like all-defs criteria, all c-uses criteria, all p-uses criteria, all c-uses/some p-uses criteria, all, all-uses criteria, all-paths criteria, p-uses/some c-uses criteria. [15].

3. Mutation Testing

Mutation testing (MT) is a white box structural testing method in which a small fault or change (known as mutants) is introduced in the original software [15]. Unlike DFT or CFT, it does not consider any paths for testing; instead it creates 'mutants' [15]. The elemental concept of mutation testing is to ensure that during the testing, every mutant results into a dissimilar output than the output of the original program [15]. If the test case is capable of differentiating and locating the change, then mutant is said to be killed [20].

The basic concept of mutation testing is shown in Fig. 4. As depicted in the diagram, a fault is introduced in the original code to generate a mutant code [21]. Next the test cases are applied to both the original code and the mutant code, and then the output of both is compared [21]. If the selected test data distinguishes the original program from the mutant program, then the mutant is killed [15]. If no, then the mutant is alive and more test cases are required [15]. Mutation testing has further subtypes like operator mutation, value mutations, decision mutation.

Fig. 4 Mutation testing process [21]

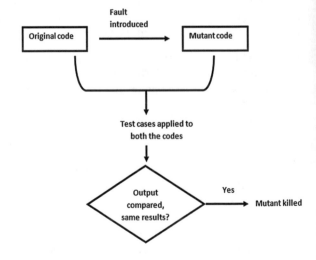

3 Testing 'HTML to Text Converter Utility' Using SUT

3.1 HTML to TEXT Utility

HTML to Text utility changes HTML documents into easy text files, by eliminating all HTML tags. The converter takes as input the HTML file and produces the text version by removing tags. Figure 5 shows the graphical user interface of the utility.

3.2 SUT for HTML to TEXT Converter

SUT is the technique used for testing given in the CSE model [1], and it forms the certification part of this model [3]. The process of SUT begins by the development of usage models [8]. A usage model is usually depicted as a graph as a Markov chain. A Markov chain is a directed graph in which the nodes depict events and the arcs correspond to transitions amid the states. There are two types of Markov chains used in SUT process: the usage chain and the testing chain. The usage Markov chain starts by setting up the states and arcs of the chain [8]. Once all the states and arcs are complete, all the arcs are assigned transition probabilities [8]. In the second phase, the testing Markov chain is constructed [8]. The testing chain is permitted to progress with respect to the result of the test, when the sequences from the usage chain are applied to the software [8]. To begin with, the testing chain has the similar nodes and transition arcs as the usage chain with every arc assigned with a

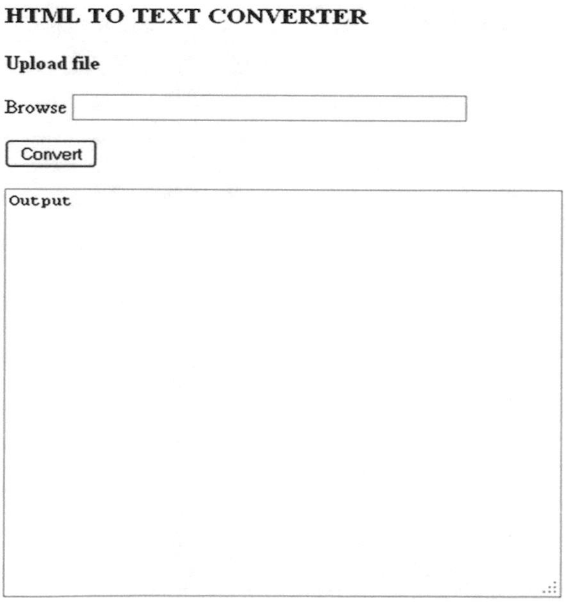

Fig. 5 HTML to text converter GUI

HTML TO TEXT CONVERTER

Upload file

Browse [   ]

[Convert]

Output

frequency count of 0 [8]. The frequency counts specified on the arcs are incremented as the sequences are produced from the usage chain [8]. All the feasible executions of the software usage are sampled by the generation of random test cases [8]. Next the execution of various randomly generated test cases is carried out [5]. Finally, the failure data is collected and the results are reported [5].

Figure 6 shows initial Markov chain. After invocation, the user browses the source file, converts it into text form, views the output, and finally terminates the application.

Table 1 enumerates various transition probabilities from one state to the other state, and Table 2 depicts the transition matrix. In the table, the captions 'From state' means the starting state, and 'to state' refers to the destination state. For example, the transition from 'invocation' to 'browse source file' has the transition probability of 1, as this is the only transition from the invocation state. The entry 0 depicts there no transition is possible in these states.

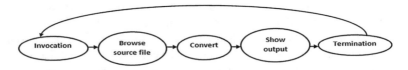

Fig. 6 Initial Markov chain

Table 1 Transition probabilities for usage model

Sequences used:		
From state	To state	Probability
<Invocation><browse source file><convert><show output><termination>		
Invocation	Browse source file	1
Browse source file	Convert	1
Convert	Show output	1
Show output	Termination	1
Termination	Invocation	1

Table 2 Transition matrix

To state						
	States	Invocation	Browse source file	Convert	Show output	Termination
From state	Invocation	0	1	0	0	0
	Browse source file	0	0	1	0	0
	Convert	0	0	0	1	0
	Show output	0	0	0	0	1
	termination	1	0	0	0	0

The usage chain serves as the basis of statistical test cases for any software [8]. A test case in SUT is actually any connected sequence of states in the usage chain that starts with the initial state and finishes with the termination state. In other words, a test case is a random walk through the transition matrix [22]. Thus, once usage model has been developed, any number of test cases can be attained from the model [8]. For example, random numbers <84, 31, 10, 25> serve as a test case and lead to the following sequence of events [22].

<Invocation><Browse Source File><Convert><Show Output><Termination>

Random number 84 generates the move from 'invocation' to 'browse source file' as the probability is 100% [22]. In fact, any random number would produce the same sequence. It can be noted that the Markov chain permits adequate statistical assessment [8]. Many important statistical results can be obtained using Markov chains which can be highly beneficial to the testers [8]. Various significant statistical results include:

π (stationary distribution) of the Markov chain which can be computed as:

$$\pi = \pi T$$

where T is the transition matrix, πi is the time the usage chain expends in state in the long run. With respect to the test case, it is the projected appearance rate of state i in long run [8]. This information permits the testing team to find out various parts of software will get the maximum concentration from the test cases [8]. For the problem under consideration T and π are given below:

$$T = \begin{matrix} 0 & 1 & 0 & 0 & 0 \\ 0 & 0 & 1 & 0 & 0 \\ 0 & 0 & 0 & 1 & 0 \\ 0 & 0 & 0 & 0 & 1 \\ 1 & 0 & 0 & 0 & 0 \end{matrix}$$

Here

$$\pi = \begin{bmatrix} \pi_1, \pi_2, \pi_3, \pi_4, \pi_5 \end{bmatrix}$$
$$\pi = \pi T$$

$$\pi = \begin{bmatrix} \pi_1, \pi_2, \pi_3, \pi_4, \pi_5 \end{bmatrix} \begin{pmatrix} 0 & 1 & 0 & 0 & 0 \\ 0 & 0 & 1 & 0 & 0 \\ 0 & 0 & 0 & 1 & 0 \\ 0 & 0 & 0 & 0 & 1 \\ 1 & 0 & 0 & 0 & 0 \end{pmatrix}$$

$$\pi_1 = 0\pi_1 + \pi_2 + 0\pi_3 + 0\pi_4 + 0\pi_5$$

$$\text{i.e. } \pi_1 = \pi_2 \tag{1}$$

$$\text{Similarly } \pi_2 = \pi_3, \pi_3 = \pi_4, \pi_5 = \pi_1 \tag{2}$$

$$\text{As } \pi_1 + \pi_2 + \pi_3 + \pi_4 + \pi_5 = 1 \tag{3}$$

Putting 1 and 2 in 3
We get $5\pi_1 = 1$
$\pi_1 = 1/5$
Similarly, other values of π can be computed, i.e.
$\pi_2 = 1/5, \pi_3 = 1/5, \pi_4 = 1/5, \pi_5 = 1/5$
Another important statistic is
$n_i = 1/\pi_i$

When the value of n_i is calculated for i equal to final terminating state, the output is projected number of states till the final or last state of the software [8]. This refers to the anticipated test case length for usage model [8]. For the problem under consideration n_i, i.e. $n_1, n_2, n_3, n_4, n_5 = 1/0.2 = 5$.

4 Applying SUT Along with WBTT

The above section performed SUT on the case under consideration. But no unit testing was performed on the code. For the problem under consideration, it is seen that even after performing SUT, some errors are left uncovered. Figures 7 and 8 show the output window for a sample HTML page and Google HTML page, respectively. It was found that the output was not correct for the Google page as many tags and script codes were seen in the output window. Therefore, other testing techniques related to the code scrutiny must be performed in this case.

The below section performs various WBTTs (CFT, DFT and MT) on the problem in conjunction with SUT. The comparative analysis of applying SUT alone and SUT along with other WBTT is also shown. The software had many modules which were tested, but since it was not feasible to demonstrate all the modules, the paper uses 'take_tag' and 'convert' module to demonstrate control flow graphs.

4.1 Control Flow Testing (CFT)

A control flow graph is a pictorial representation of all possible control flow of a program while taking into account the label of every statement [15]. A node in the graph refers to a statement with its label in the program and edges correspond to the likely transfer of control flow between statements [15]. Figures 9 and 10 show the control flow graph for take_tag() and convert() modules, respectively. As shown in

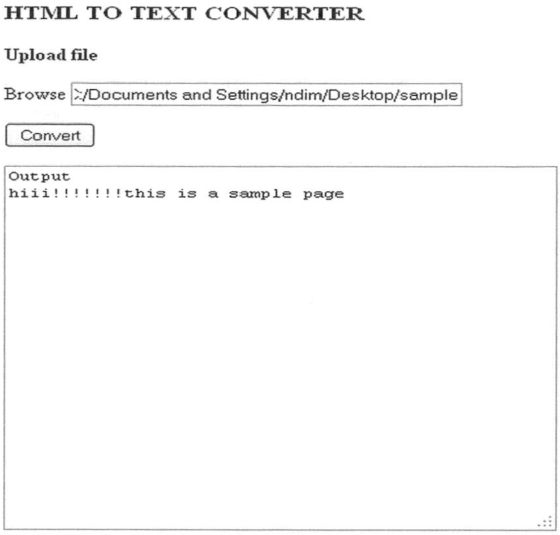

Fig. 7 HTML to text converter output window for a sample page

HTML TO TEXT CONVERTER

Upload file

Browse `:/Documents and Settings/ndim/Desktop/sample`

Convert

```
Output
hiii!!!!!!!this is a sample page
```

Fig. 8 Output window for Google page

HTML TO TEXT CONVERTER

Upload file

Browse `cuments and Settings/ndim/Desktop/Google.html`

Convert

```
Output
Google(function(){window.google=
{kEI:'WV_PVOWsEoia8QXFwoCoCg',kEXPI:'3700337,40115
50,4011552,4011556,4011559,4013605,4017578,4020346
,4020562,4021073,4021587,4021598,4021965,4022542,4
023678,4023709,4024681,4025090,4025124,4025128,402
6108,4026330,4027922,4028063,4028128,4028134,40283
35,4028508,4028586,8300095,8300111,8500394,8501081
,8501083,10200083,10200095,10200904',authuser:0,j:
{en:1,bv:21,pm:'p',u:'a66a5f1e',qbp:0,rre:false},k
SID:'WV_PVOWsEoia8QXFwoCoCg'};google.kHL='en-
IN';})();(function(){google.lc=[];google.li=0;
google.getEI=function(a){for(var
b;a&&(!a.getAttribute
(b=a.getAttribute("eid")));)a=a.parentNode;return
b||google.kEI};google.https=function()
{return"https:"==window.location.protocol};
google.ml=function(){};google.time=function()
{return(new
Date).getTime()};google.log=function(a,b,d,e,k){va
r c=new
```

the control flow graphs, labels on the arcs indicate the transition from one statement to another. For simplicity, alphabets have been used.

a. *Test Cases for Path Coverage for Program* [15]

Since it is unfeasible to show all the modules, we use take_tag() module to demonstrate our testing. The module takes as its input HTML code. There are numerous HTML files that could be input to program making it unfeasible to test all possible inputs.

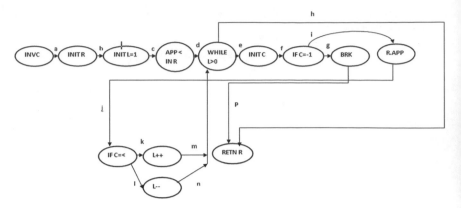

Fig. 9 Markov chain for take_tag module

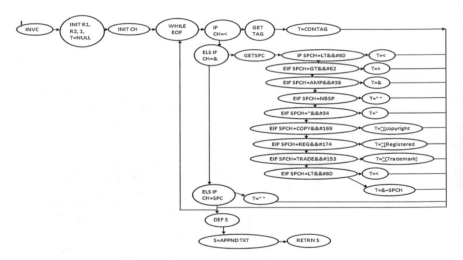

Fig. 10 Markov chain for convert module

b. *Test Cases for Statement and branch Testing Coverage*

Consider the control flow graph already constructed (as in Fig. 9). (In Fig. 9 INV refers to invocation, INIT R-initialize R, INIT L-initialize R, APP<IN R append '<' in result, WHILE L>0, INIT C is initialize C, IF is for condition, BRK-break, R.APP is append in R, IF C=< is for condition, L++ increment L, L−− decrement L, RETN R is return R.).

Table 3 depicts the test cases to satisfy statement testing coverage. For example, if path is 'abcdefgp', then EOF is reached, and if path is 'abcdefijkmh', then its L is incremented.

Table 3 Test cases to satisfy statement testing coverage

P	Process links															Test cases	
	a	b	c	d	e	f	g	h	i	j	k	l	m	n	p	I	O
abcdefgp	✓	✓	✓	✓	✓	✓	✓								✓	HTML code	EOF reached
abcdefijkmh	✓	✓	✓	✓✓	✓	✓		✓	✓	✓	✓		✓			HTML code	Output string
abcdefijlnh	✓	✓	✓	✓	✓	✓		✓	✓	✓		✓		✓		HTML code	Output string

P paths, *I* input, *O* output

Table 4 Test cases to satisfy branch testing coverage for program

Paths	Decisions	Test cases	
		Input	Output
abcdefgp	EOF	HTML code	EOF reached
abcdefijkmh	T	HTML code	Output string
abcdefijlnh	F	HTML code	Output string

Table 4 shows the test cases to satisfy branch testing coverage for program. For example, if path is 'abcdefgp', then the file reaches the end of file.

Table 5 enumerates the summary and comparison of applying SUT and SUT together with control flow testing. It is found during testing that additional errors are uncovered when both the techniques are applied in conjunction. It is seen that there is no change in the size of transition matrix or number of states in Markov chain. But there was an increase in number of errors detected as indicated in Table 5.

4.2 Data Flow Testing (DFT)

DFT is performed by locating the definition computation use (DCU) and definition predicate use (DPU) of different variables used in the program [15]. The predicate use and computational use for various variables are given in Table 6. For example, the variable R is defined in node named INIT R. The c-use of the variable R occurs in nodes APP in R and R.APP, while its p-use does not occur in any of the nodes.

DFT uses a number of criteria for testing like all-defs, all c-uses, all p-uses, all-edges, all p-uses and some c-uses [15]. To generate the test cases for this program using various criteria of DFT, the problem is divided into two parts [15]. Initially, those paths are selected that satisfy the chosen criteria. In the next step, the

Table 5 Comparison: SUT and SUT along with CFT

Parameter	SUT	SUT with CFT
Markov chain states	5	5
Total transitions	5	5
Transition matrix size	5×5	5×5
Entries in transition matrix	25	25
Errors detected	3	6

Table 6 DCU and DPU data flow testing criteria

(Node, variable)	DCU	DPU
(INIT R, R)	{APP in R, R. APP}	ø
(INIT L, L)	{L++, L−}	{WHILE}
(INIT C, C)	ø	{IF C=−1, IF C=<}

selection of the test cases that will implement those paths takes place [15]. For the problem, following criteria have been used.

a. *All-edges*

All-edges criteria is same as 100% branch coverage [15]. Considering all-edges criteria, if the paths executed by the test cases consist of the paths given below, then it is seen that all-edges are covered:

(INVC, INIT R, INIT L, APPL IN R, WHILE, INT R, IF C=−1, BRK, RETN R)
(INVC, INIT R, INIT L, APPL IN R, WHILE, INT R, IF C=−1, R APP, IF C=<, C++, WHILE, RETN R)
(INVC, INIT R, INIT L, APPL IN R, WHILE, INT R, IF C=−1, R APP, IF C=<, C−−, WHILE, RETN R)

b. *All-defs*

All-defs criterion necessitates that for all the definitions of all the variables, at least one use which can either computation or predicate use, ought to be exercised during testing. The below given set of paths will assure the all-defs criteria is satisfied.

(INVC, INIT R, INIT L, APPL IN R, WHILE, INT R, IF C=−1, BRK, RETN R)
(INVC, INIT R, INIT L, APPL IN R, WHILE, INT R, IF C=−1, R APP, IF C=<, C++, WHILE, RETN R)
(INVC, INIT R, INIT L, APPL IN R, WHILE, INT R, IF C=−1, R APP, IF C=<, C−−, WHILE, RETN R)

C. *All-Uses, All P-Uses and All C-Uses*

The same paths as specified above can be used to satisfy all-uses criteria, which require that all p-uses and all c-uses of all variable definitions.

Table 7 enumerates the summary and comparison of applying SUT and SUT together with DFT. It is found during testing that additional errors are uncovered when both the techniques are applied in conjunction. It is seen that there is no change in the size of transition matrix or number of states in Markov chain. But there was an increase in number of errors detected as indicated in Table 7.

Table 7 Comparison: SUT and SUT along with DFT

Parameter	SUT	SUT with DFT
Markov chain states	5	5
Total transitions	5	5
Transition matrix size	5×5	5×5
Entries in transition matrix	25	25
Errors detected	3	5

4.3   Mutation Testing

Mutation testing is used to choose test data which has the capability of finding errors. The elemental concept of mutation testing is to ensure that during the testing process, each mutant produces a dissimilar result than the outcome of the original code [15]. If the test case is capable of differentiating and locating the change, then mutant is said to be killed [20]. For the same program, we consider following mutants as indicated in Table 8.

During testing process of this software utility, various strings and tags were given as input and the three test mutants specified about in Table 8 were killed.

Table 9 enumerates the summary and comparison of applying SUT and SUT along with DFT. It is found that combination of both the techniques found more errors.

Table 8 Mutants used for testing

ORIGINAL CODE	MUTANT 1	MUTANT 2	MUTANT 3

String take_tag(Reader r) {
String R = new String();
int L,c;
L= 1;
R.append(' < ');
while (L > 0) {
c = r.read();
    if (c == -1)
break;
R.append((char)c);
        if (c == '<') L++;
else
  if (c == '>') L--;
    }
return R.toString();
      }
	String take_tag(Reader r) {
	String R = new String();
	int L,c;
	L= 0;
	R.append(' < ');
	while (L > 0) {
	c = r.read();
	if (c == -1) break;
	R.append((char)c);
	if (c == '<') L++;
	else
	  if (c == '>') L--;
	}
	return R.toString();
	}
		String take_tag(Reader r) {
		String R = new String();
		int L,c;
		L= 1;
		R.append(' < ');
		while (L < 0)
		{
		  c = r.read();
		if (c == -1) break;
		R.append((char)c);
		if (c == '<') L++;
		else
		  if (c == '>') L--;
		}
		return R.toString();
		}
			String take_tag(Reader r) {
			String R = new String();
			int L,c;
			L = 1;
			R.append(' < ');
			while (L > 0) {
			  c = r.read();
			if (c == 1)
			  break;
			R.append((char)c);
			if (c == '<') L++;
			  else
			  if (c == '>') L--;
			}
			return R.toString();
			}

Parameter	SUT	SUT with MT
Errors detected	3	4

Table 9 Comparison: SUT and SUT along with MT

5 Findings and Conclusion

For the software under consideration, it was found that even after performing SUT, some errors were left uncovered, as the software did not produce the correct output for some of the web pages. Therefore, white box techniques were highly essential. The use of WBTT in combination with SUT was found beneficial in the following ways:

(1) In some cases when errors are not uncovered using SUT alone and code scrutiny is required, then white box techniques must be used.
(2) Using SUT with data flow testing aids to validate the correctness of variables defined and used. Using DFT along with SUT helps to find more errors related to the usage and definition of data in the code.
(3) Control flow testing can be used along with statistical usage testing for code inspection so as to make certain that every control structure like statement, branch and loop has been exercised least once. It also facilitates to test an adequate number of paths to attain coverage. Therefore, all the control structures including all the statements, conditions and loops can be tested.
(4) Mutation testing can also be used with SUT for fault identification and to eliminate code ambiguity.
(5) All the above techniques along with SUT enable code inspection which aids in detecting internal code errors.

6 Limitations and Future Work

The paper has used only one software for testing. For more general results, the combined testing techniques can be applied to various other software also.

In future, the authors intend to find new application areas where SUT can be applied.

Acknowledgements Authors express their deep sense of gratitude to the founder president of Amity University Dr. Ashok K. Chauhan for his keen interest in promoting research in Amity University and have always been an inspiration for achieving great heights.

References

1. Linger, R.C., Trammell, C.J.: Cleanroom Software Engineering Reference Model. Nov 1996. [Online] Available: http://leansoftwareengineering.com/wp-content/uploads/2009/02/cleanroomsei.pdf
2. Mills, H.D., Poore, J.H.: Bringing software under statistical quality control. In: Quality Progress, Nov 1988
3. Runeson, P., Wohlin, C.: Certification of software components. IEEE Trans. Softw. Eng. **20** (6), 494–499 (1994)
4. Hausler, P.A., Linger, R.C., Trammell, C.J.: Adopting Cleanroom software engineering with a phased approach. IBM Syst. J. **33**(1), 89, 109 (1994). https://doi.org/10.1147/sj.331.0089. URL: http://ieeexplore.ieee.org/stamp/stamp.jsp?tp=&arnumber=5387350&isnumber=5387343
5. Prowell, S.J., Trammell, C.J., Linger, R.C., Poore, J.H.: Cleanroom Software Engineering Technology and Process, 14. Addison-Wesley. ISBN 0-201-85480-5 (1999)
6. Khatri, S.K., Kaur, K., Datta, R.: Using statistical usage testing in conjunction with other black box testing techniques. Int. J. Reliab. Qual. Saf. Eng. **22**(1), 1550004 (23 p) c World Scientific Publishing Company (2015). https://doi.org/10.1142/s0218539315500047
7. Runeson, P., Wohlin, C.: Statistical Usage Testing for Software Reliability Certification and Control (1993)
8. Whittaker, J.A., Poore, J.H.: Statistical testing for Cleanroom software engineering. In: Proceedings of the Twenty-Fifth Hawaii International Conference, System Sciences, vol. 2, pp. 428–436. ISBN: 0-8186-2420-5 (1992)
9. Kaur, K., Khatri, S.K., Datta, R.: Analysis of statistical usage testing technique with Markov chain model. In: ICRITO (2013)
10. Kaur, K., Khatri, S.K., Datta, R.: Analysis of various testing techniques. Int. J. Syst. Assur. Eng. Manag. (2013). ISSN 0975-6809. https://doi.org/10.1007/s13198-013-0157-6
11. Chugh, N.: Framework for Improvement in Cleanroom Software Engineering Thesis. Thapar University Patiala (2009)
12. https://ece.uwaterloo.ca/~snaik/MYBOOK1/Ch5-DataFlowTesting.ppt
13. BCS SIGIST.: Standard for Software Component Testing by British Computer Society Specialist Interest Group in Software Testing (2001). http://www.testingstandards.co.uk/Component%20Testing.pdf
14. http://istqbexamcertification.com/what-is-white-box-or-structure-based-or-structural-testing-techniques/
15. Jalota, P.: An Integrated Approach to Software Engineering, 3rd edn. Narosa Publication, New Delhi (2005)
16. http://www.tutorialspoint.com/software_testing_dictionary/white_box_testing.htm
17. http://www.cs.ccu.edu.tw/~naiwei/cs5812/st4.pdf
18. Beizer, B.: Software Testing Techniques, 2nd edn. (1990)
19. https://ece.uwaterloo.ca/~snaik/MYBOOK1/Ch4-ControlFlowTesting.ppt
20. http://www.softwaretestinggenius.com/mutation-testing
21. http://www.guru99.com/mutation-testing.html
22. Trammell, C.: Quantifying the reliability of software: statistical testing based on a usage model. In: Software Engineering Standards Symposium, 1995. (ISESS'95) 'Experience and Practice', Proceedings, Second IEEE International, pp. 208, 218, 21–25 Aug 1995. https://doi.org/10.1109/sess.1995.525966

Sunil Kumar Khatri Prof. Sunil Kumar Khatri (Ph.D. in Comp. Science, MCA and B.Sc. in Computer Science) is working as Director in Amity Institute of Information Technology, Amity University, Noida, India. He has been conferred 'IT Innovation and Excellence Award for Contribution in the field of IT and Computer Science Education' in 2012 and 'Exceptional

Leadership and Dedication in Research' in the year 2009. He has edited four books, six special issues of international journals and published several papers in international and national journals and proceedings of repute. His areas of research are software reliability, data mining and network security.

Kamaldeep Kaur Ms. Kamaldeep Kaur did her BCA and MCA from GNDU with top merit positions. She worked as a lecturer in Lovely Professional University for three years. At present, she is working as an Assistant Professor at New Delhi Institution of Management, New Delhi. She is also doing her Ph.D. in software testing from Amity University.

Rattan K. Datta Prof. (Dr.) Rattan K. Datta is first-class M.Sc. from Punjab University and Ph.D. from IIT-D. He has been associated with IT and its applications for the last over three decades heading main frames, mini and supercomputers. He is Fellow of Computer Society of India, IETE, India Met Society, Telematic Forum and member of Indian Science Congress Association (ISCA). He was also National President of Computer Society of India (CSI), Indian Meteorological Society and IT section of ISCA. He has guided a number of students for Ph.D. (IIT, BITs Pilani, PTU and other universities). Currently he is Honorary C.E.O. and Director, MERIT, New Delhi.

A Review on Application Security Management Using Web Application Security Standards

A. Rakesh Phanindra, V. B. Narasimha and Ch. V. PhaniKrishna

Abstract Software influences almost every aspect of modern society. Development of quality software systems has always been a great experiment for software developers. By and by, it happens that non-practical elements are frequently disregarded while concentrating on the usefulness of the framework. A few frameworks have fizzled due to the carelessness of non-utilitarian necessities. As of late, Web application security has turned into the essential talk for security specialists, as application assaults are always on rise and posturing new dangers for associations. A few patterns have risen recently in the assaults propelled against Web application. The execution of international security standard is to minimize the security disappointments and to moderate their results. Applications have been helpless for whatever length of time that they have existed. To ponder the effect of non-utilitarian prerequisites on necessities development, we are proposing a very important non-functional requirement Application Security Management is to define the requirements for security in all applications that use the web application security standards (WASS).

Keywords Non-functional requirements · Software quality · Application security management · Web application security standards

A. Rakesh Phanindra (✉) · Ch. V. PhaniKrishna
Department of CSE, KL University, Guntur, India
e-mail: rakeshmtech2011@gmail.com

Ch. V. PhaniKrishna
e-mail: phanik16@kluniversity.in

V. B. Narasimha
Department of CSE, UCE, Osmania University, Hyderabad, India
e-mail: vbnarasimha@gmail.com

© Springer Nature Singapore Pte Ltd. 2019
M. N. Hoda et al. (eds.), *Software Engineering*, Advances in Intelligent Systems and Computing 731, https://doi.org/10.1007/978-981-10-8848-3_45

1 Introduction

When people speak about really great value software, they usually reflect in terms of its usefulness, easiness or aesthetics. But there is more to it than that. A really great piece of software will exploit quality completely like a piece of Brighton Rock [1].

Web applications have become the main targets for several reasons:
1. The web-based applications are unprotected to the Internet with standard boundaries. Attackers can simply determine applications and look for vulnerabilities.
2. Regular intelligence manages that Web sites should be revived always keeping in mind the end goal to draw in and hold clients. This frequently prompts shortcutting arrangement administration and control techniques, bringing about untested and misconfigured Web applications being uncovered.
3. Web applications regularly comprise of blends of off-the-rack programming, business- or foreman-created applications and open-source parts. A significant part of the helplessness in these segments goes disregarded until broken or a patch notice comes to. What's more, the instability and multifaceted nature of these parts can lessen programming advancement and testing procedures unsuccessful. Web applications convey assailants with a decent start point to enter into the association, for example, a joined database, or to misuse the Web page keeping in mind the end goal to download malware onto the PC of customers going to the site.

2 Objective

The purpose of proposing a very important non-functional requirement application security management is to define the requirements for security in all applications that use the Web application security standards (WASSs) [2]. Security rules safeguard applications, and the underlying information, by preventing unauthorised alteration, destruction or loss of use.

3 Scope

The intended audience for this management practice is all users with responsibility for the development, implementation, and management of security in applications.

4 Types of Vulnerabilities

Some of the top issues associated with Web applications that must be addressed are shown in the following diagram (Fig. 1).

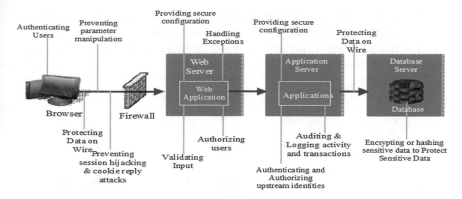

Fig. 1 Issues associated with Web applications

Estimation units and learning of security properties are not really known. This procedure causes the intricate frameworks deterioration into less complex and littler frameworks in this way permitting the estimative of properties that will help the comprehension and estimation of programming frameworks security properties [3].

A bad design can cause potential problems for different types of security vulnerabilities. Table 1 lists the vulnerabilities, category wise and the potential problems that can be caused due to bad design.

Table 1 Vulnerabilities category-wise problems that can be caused due to bad design

Rule category	Vulnerability type
Authentication rules	Lacking authentication
	Weak password and password recuperation validation
Authorization rules	Insufficient authorization
	Parameter manipulation
	Insecure direct object reference
Session management rules	Session hijacking
	Session fixation
	Insufficient session expiry
Input validation rules	SQL injection (injection flaws)
	Cross-site scripting (XSS)
	Malicious file execution
Error handling rules	Improper error handling
Information security rules	Information leakage
Cryptography rules	Insufficient cryptographic storage
Environment and application server rules	Directory indexing
	Transport layer security
	Database security
Logging rules	Auditing and logging

The rules for securing a site's applications can be sorted out in a various leveled structure keeping in mind the end goal to address security at every level. The principal level, the single exchange, is the littlest bit of rationale in a Web application [1]. The following level is the complete session and is comprised of various exchanges. The highest level is the complete application including countless sessions. Examination of the security prerequisites for every level is essential.

5   Methodology

The logical activities for software development life cycle for a Web Application development project phases are given below:

1. Design
2. Coding
3. Security Testing
4. Delivery and Deployment.

5.1   Design

The applicable rules to be considered while designing secure Web applications are as follows:

- Authentication Rules
- Authorization Rules
- Session Management Rules
- Input Validation Rules
- Error Handling Rules
- Information Security Rules
- Cryptography Rules
- Environment and Application Server Rules
- Logging Rules (Table 2).

Table 2 Applicable rules to be considered while design secure Web applications

Entry	Application design phase
Inputs	Baselines software requirement specification Security requirements Classification of information stored in application under design
Tasks	Ensure compliance to applicable rules, refer: Web application security standards (WASSs) document for details
Verification/validation	Design review
Outputs	Updated traceability matrix, review reports
Exit	Reviewed detailed modeling elements

5.2 *Coding*

All rules in WASS document are applicable during the coding phase depending on the type of application (Level 1, Level 2, Level 3); however, for unit testing and code review, verification matrix in this document can be referred [4].

Entry	Coding phase
Inputs	Baselines design document Security requirements, classification of information stored in application under design
Tasks	Code according to the coding standards and method specifications, checklist for code review
Verification/ validation	Unit testing, code review
Outputs	Code review, reports updated, traceability matrix review reports
Exit	Baselined source code

5.3 *Security Testing*

All rules in WASS document are applicable during the security testing phase depending on the type of application (Level 1, Level 2, Level 3); however, verification matrix in this document can be referred for any details.

Entry	Completion of one round of functional testing
Inputs	Functionally stable application, security requirements, classification of information stored in application under design
Tasks	Perform automated and manual security testing
Verification/ validation	Reviewed and approved security test reports
Outputs	Security test reports against WASS review reports
Exit	Baselined and tested application

5.4 *Delivery and Deployment*

- Authentication Rules
- Authorization Rules
- Session Management Rules
- Input Validation Rules

- Error Handling Rules
- Information Security Rules
- Cryptography Rules
- Environment and Application Server Rules
- Logging Rules

Entry	User acceptance test (UAT) sign-off by the customer
Inputs	Tested deliverables Acceptance criteria as defined in project plan Contract for information on deliverables agreed with the customer Project plan for any specific replication, delivery and onsite installation requirements
Tasks	Develop deployment plan, document delivery checklist, conduct pre-delivery checks, deliver the work products
Verification/ validation	Deployment plan
Outputs	Deployment plan, product delivery checklist, review reports
Exit	Sign-off from customer on delivered and accepted application

6 Management Practices

6.1 Requirements, Design, and Development

- Before an application is developed, acquired, or enhanced, security requirements must be formally documented to address all relevant security rules as defined in WASS [1, 5].
- Each project must establish mechanisms to certify the completeness of security requirements of each high-risk application within formally documented project review processes.
- Application design specifications must be formally documented to address all security requirements.
- Applications should rely on approved IT services (e.g., strategic enterprise directory, single sign-on, Microsoft NTLM) for security processes (e.g., authentication, authorization).
- A formal plan (either separate plan or integrated with the project plan) must be documented for Level 1 applications and approved by the business owner.

6.2 Testing

- New or significantly enhanced version releases of applications (including legacy applications) must be fully tested against applicable security rules prior to production deployment [6].
- Confidential information should not be used for the purpose of application development and testing. The use of confidential information for development and testing must be authorized by the business owner of the application.
- Successful testing of an application's security rules must be recorded in accordance with formal change control processes.
- Personally identifiable information (PII) must not be used in application development or testing, unless otherwise permitted under applicable data protection laws, rules, or regulations (e.g., healthcare information portability and accountability, EU data protection directive).
- Where the use of confidential information is required for test purposes, access controls must be applied to applications and underlying systems in the test environment. Confidential information must be deleted from the test environment as soon as feasible following the test execution.

6.3 Audience

- The standards must be shared with the customer, customized (if required), and approved before putting it to use. This must happen before the application design starts.
- Project teams are accountable for ensuring that Web applications within their scope are compliance with this standard.
- Project architects are accountable for ensuring that this standard is appropriately complied with on projects where they are the named architect.
- Project managers should ensure that compliance with this standard is included in system requirements.
- Developers are responsible for developing code that complies with this standard.
- Web security testers must ensure that the application is not vulnerable to vulnerabilities described in this document.

6.4 Verification Matrix

Compliance to WASS can be verified in several ways. The following gives an indication on complying with each rule.

Each rule maybe verified in two ways. Manual testing is a series of security-related tests available that may be used to verify most rules [7, 8]. Rules which cannot be verified by manual testing will require code review. Code review requires access to the source code of the application [9, 10].

The verification matrix is provided as an aid to navigate the various rule statements. A 1 indicates that the rule statement is verifiable via the corresponding verification technique. Multiple check marks mean the rule statement is verified by a combination of techniques. Specific guidance on how to verify each rule is available in Table 3.

Table 3 Application security management design, development and testing guidelines

Rule ID	Rule description	Verification responsibility	
		Code review	Manual testing
1	Try not to permit the login procedure to begin from a unencrypted page		☒
2	Secret key quality ought to be upheld to utilize upper- and lower-case letters, numbers, and images		☒
3	Secret key maturing ought to be implemented to guarantee that passwords do not stay unaltered for drawn-out stretches of time	☒	
4	Validate authorization on every request		☒
5	Employ access control in the business layer, not only the presentation layer	☒	☒
6	Do not pass any credentials or parameters that can be used to bypass authentication or authorization rules within a URL		☒
7	Ensure that all URLs and business functions are protected by an effective access control mechanism that verifies the user's role and entitlements	☒	☒
8	Only use the inbuilt session management mechanism within the development framework	☒	☒
9	Ensure that a new session is regenerated upon successful authentication	☒	☒
10	Ensure that every page has a logout link		☒
11	Use an appropriate timeout period that automatically logs out an inactive session		☒
12	Try not to acknowledge new, preset or invalid session identifiers from the URL or in the solicitation		☒
13	Utilize a standard info approval system to validate all input data for length, type, syntax, and business rules before tolerating the information to be shown or put away		☒

(continued)

Table 3 (continued)

Rule ID	Rule description	Verification responsibility	
		Code review	Manual testing
14	Ensure that all user-supplied data is HTML/URL/URI information is HTML/UR/URI encoded before rendering	☒	☒
15	Use strongly typed parameterized queries or stored procedures	☒	
16	Validate any application critical information passed as variables in cookies		☒
17	Check any user-supplied documents or filenames taken from the client for genuine purposes	☒	
18	Avoid point by point slip messages that are helpful to an aggressor		☒
19	Utilize custom error pages in order to guarantee that the application will never leak error messages to an attacker	☒	☒
20	In the case of any system failure, the application must "fail closed" the resource		☒
21	Do not store any confidential information in cookies		☒
22	Prevent sensitive data from being cached on client side		☒
23	Ensure that confidential information is transmitted by using HTTP POST method		☒
24	Do not write/store any sensitive information in HTML source		☒
25	Ensure proper masking techniques are used while displaying sensitive personally identifiable information to users	☒	☒
26	Do not use hidden fields for sensitive data		☒
27	Abstain from uncovering private item references to user at whatever point conceivable, for example essential keys or filenames		☒
28	Do not save passwords within cookies to allow users to be remembered	☒	☒
29	Do not store any confidential information including passwords in log entries unless encrypted	☒	
30	Do not use weak cryptographic algorithms or create cryptographic algorithms for the generation of random numbers used in security-related processes	☒	☒
31	Employ one-way hash routines (SHA-1) to encrypt passwords in storage	☒	
32	Use cryptographically secure algorithms to generate the unique IDs being used in the URLs, hence securing the URLs from being rewritten	☒	☒
33	Guarantee that infrastructure credentials, for example database qualifications or message queue access points of interest, are legitimately secured	☒	

(continued)

Table 3 (continued)

Rule ID	Rule description	Verification responsibility	
		Code review	Manual testing
34	Employ the principle of least privilege while assigning rights to execute queries	☒	
35	Encrypt confidential information in transit across public networks		☒
36	Provide an appropriate logging mechanism to detect unauthorized access attempts	☒	

7 Conclusion

Before an application is developed, acquired, or enhanced, security requirements must be formally documented to address all relevant security rules as defined in WASS. On providing security of Web application, development will be improved by relating security checkpoints and procedures at right on time phases of advancement and in addition all through the product improvement lifecycle. Distinct importance should be applied to the coding phase of development. Security mechanisms that should be used include threat modeling, risk analysis, static analysis, digital signature, among others.

References

1. http://eyefodder.com/2011/06/quality-software-non-functional-requirements.html
2. Khatter, K., Kalia, A.: Impact of non-functional requirements on requirements evolution. In: 6th International Conference on Emerging Trends in Engineering and Technology (ICETET), pp. 61–68. IEEE (2013)
3. https://en.wikipedia.org/wiki/Web_application_security
4. Shuaibu, B.M., Norwawi, N.M., Selamat, M.H., Al-Alwani, A.: Systematic review of web application security development model, Artif. Intell. Rev. **43**(2), pp. 259–276 (2015)
5. Aydal, E.G., Paige, R.F., Chivers, H., Brooke, P.J.: Security planning and refactoring in extreme programming. Lecture Notes in Computer Science, vol. 4044 (2006)
6. Web and mobile security best practices. http://www.faresweb.net/e-books/web-mobile-security-best-practices/download
7. Alalfi, M.H., Cordy, J.R., Dean, T.R.: A verification framework for access control in dynamic web applications. Paper presented at the proceedings of the 2nd Canadian conference on computer science and software engineering, Montreal, Quebec, Canada 2009
8. http://csrc.nist.gov/publications/nistpubs/800-50/NIST-SP800-50.pdf
9. https://www.owasp.org/images/4/4e/OWASP_ASVS_2009_Web_App_Std_Release.pdf
10. http://www.sans.org/reading-room/whitepapers/analyst/application-security-tools-management-support-funding-34985

A Review of Software Testing Approaches in Object-Oriented and Aspect-Oriented Systems

Vasundhara Bhatia, Abhishek Singhal, Abhay Bansal and Neha Prabhakar

Abstract Software testing is considered to be a very important phase in the development of any software. It becomes crucial to inculcate appropriate software testing techniques in every software development life cycle. Object-oriented software development has been in use for a while now. Aspect-oriented approach which is comparatively new and works on the basics of object-oriented approach. But aspect-oriented approach also aims to provide modularity, higher cohesion, and separation of concerns. In this paper, we have reviewed the various testing techniques that are developed for both object-oriented and aspect-oriented systems.

Keywords Object-oriented · Object-oriented testing · Aspect-oriented
Aspect-oriented testing · Software testing

1 Introduction

Software testing is considered to be a very important phase in the development of any software. It tries to ensure that the software produced is of high quality and reliable [1]. The testing activity requires about 30–40% of the total effort that is put in the development of software [2]. This amount of effort is put so that end product produced must not contain any errors or minimum errors. It is said that if a bug

V. Bhatia (✉) · A. Singhal · A. Bansal · N. Prabhakar
Department of CSE, ASET, Amity University, Noida, Uttar Pradesh, India
e-mail: vasundhara.bhatia9@gmail.com

A. Singhal
e-mail: asinghal1@amity.edu

A. Bansal
e-mail: abansal1@amity.edu

N. Prabhakar
e-mail: nehaprabhakar91@gmail.com

© Springer Nature Singapore Pte Ltd. 2019
M. N. Hoda et al. (eds.), *Software Engineering*, Advances in Intelligent Systems and Computing 731, https://doi.org/10.1007/978-981-10-8848-3_46

487

or an error is found out after the software has been released; the cost for fixing it is 4 times as compared to the cost incurred if an error is found at the testing phase [3].

Object-oriented approach aims to map the real-life objects into software objects [4]. This approach uses the concepts of classes and objects where class tries to support information hiding and object tries to support reusability. This approach includes a number of features such as encapsulation, inheritance, abstraction, polymorphism, and reusability [5]. But, as these features are included, the complexity also increases [6]. Thus, it becomes very important to test the entire object-oriented system in a well-defined way.

Aspect-oriented approach is built on the basics of object-oriented approach. In the object-oriented approach, the cross-cutting concerns are present in the core classes. The aim of aspect-oriented programming is to separate cross-cutting concerns by modularizing these concerns into a single unit, which is known as an aspect [7]. These cross-cutting concerns could be security, exception handling, logging, etc. This separation helps to increase modularity in a system, and the system also becomes more cohesive [8].

This paper is divided into five sections. Section 2 presents evaluation criteria on which various papers are analyzed. Section 3 analyzes papers on object-oriented testing. Section 4 analyzes various papers on aspect-oriented testing. Section 5 presents a conclusion and limitation of the paper. Finally, the acknowledgment is provided.

2 Evaluation Criteria

To perform the review of object-oriented and aspect-oriented papers, certain criteria have to be considered for evaluation. A number of research questions are proposed here, and each paper is evaluated according to this research criteria. These research questions are adapted from [8] and [9]. The research questions are as follows:

R1: Is the objective of the study clearly specified?

An analysis has to be done on the condition if the paper clearly specifies the objective of the search and the objective is fulfilled.

R2: Does the paper propose a new technique?

This specifies that if a paper has proposed a new method or technique. The paper should contribute some new work and point out certain results.

R3: Is a new tool developed?

Certain researchers develop new tool which supports the objective of their search. Our aim is to find if a new tool exists. In certain conditions, an existing tool is used.

Table 1 Fields used for analysis

Field	Meaning
Testing level	The level of testing here could be: unit testing: testing the smallest part/unit in an application. Integration testing: testing a number of units in collaboration with each other
Model used	They are used for representation of design of an application. They could be sequence diagram, class diagram, collaboration diagram, state chart diagram, object relation diagram
Tool used	A tool is used to support the approach being proposed. It defines the name of the tool which is used. The tool could be developed the researcher, or an existing tool can be used
Source code domain	This specifies the language of the code on which the analysis is done. Also, if certain further details about the code are given, then it is specified

R4: Is the system fully/partially automated?

The research work might be done either manually or through an automated system. We have to find if the technique proposed automates the system either fully or partially.

R5: Is the data/system used for analysis sufficient for search?

It has to be considered that the data or the system, which is used for the analysis of the research, is sufficient to give accurate results to the proposed technique.

R6: Does the paper specify what benefits will search provide?

The benefits that an approach might offer might not be clear in certain cases. We have to analyze if the researcher specifies what benefits the approach will provide in a clear and precise manner.

R7: Are any limitations of the study defined?

We have to identify if the researcher has identified what limitations does the proposed approach provides. The limitations or the future possible work must be clearly defined.

R8: Can the technique be used in real-world applications?

It has to be found out if the technique is capable of being used the real-world applications. Some approaches might work well in a certain environment, but it has to be seen that if it might work well in real-world applications (Table 1).

In addition, some other criteria are identified through which the basic characteristics of the research work can be identified which are adapted from [10] and defined in Table 2. They are as follows:

Table 2 A review of characteristics of object-oriented and aspect-oriented testing literature

Paper	Testing level	Model used	Tool used	Source code domain	Research questions R1, R2, R3, R4, R5, R6, R7, R8
Object-oriented testing					
[11]	Integration testing	Sequence diagram, use case diagram	Integration testing coverage analysis tool	Java	R1, R2, R3, R4, R6
[12]	Unit testing	Automatic test generation	Palus	Java	R1, R2, R3, R4, R5, R6, R8
[13]	Unit testing	–	EATOOS	Java	R1, R2, R3, R4, R6, R7
[14]	Unit testing	Automatic test generation	MATLAB	Java	R1, R2, R4, R6, R7
[15]	Unit testing	State chart diagram	–	Object-oriented	R1, R2, R6, R7
[16]	Unit testing	State chart diagram	JUnit	Object-oriented	R1, R2, R4, R5, R6, R7, R8
[17]	Unit testing	Automatic test generation	–	Java	R1, R2, R4, R5, R6, R7
[18]	Unit testing	–	–	Java	R1, R2, R6, R7
[19]	Unit testing	State chart diagram	–	Object-oriented	R1, R2, R6, R7
[20]	Integration testing	Class diagram, sequence diagram, state chart diagram	–	Object-oriented	R1, R2, R4, R5, R6, R7
[21]	Unit testing	–	Diffut	Java	R1, R2, R3, R4, R5, R6
Aspect-oriented testing					
[22]	Integration testing	Class diagram, object relation diagram	AJMetrics, Eclipse, EMF	AspectJ	R1, R2, R4, R6, R7
[23]	Unit testing	State chart diagram	–	Aspect-oriented	R1, R2, R6, R7
[25]	Unit testing	–	APTE, AJTE	AspectJ	R1, R2, R3, R4, R6
[26]	Integration testing	–	–	AspectJ	R1, R2, R6, R7
[27]	Unit testing	State chart diagram	AJUnit	AspectJ	R1, R2, R3, R4, R6, R7, R8
[28]	Integration testing	–	JaBUTi/AJ	AspectJ	R1, R2, R4, R5, R6, R7, R8

(continued)

Table 2 (continued)

Paper	Testing level	Model used	Tool used	Source code domain	Research questions R1, R2, R3, R4, R5, R6, R7, R8
[29]	Unit testing	–	Parasoft JTest 4.5, Raspect	AspectJ	R1,R2,R3,R4, R6
[30]	Integration testing	Collaboration diagram	–	AspectJ	R1, R2, R4, R6, R7
[31]	Integration testing	Object relation diagram	AJATO	AspectJ	R1, R2, R3, R4, R6, R7, R8
[32]	Unit testing	State chart diagram	–	AspectJ	R1, R2, R6, R7, R8
[33]	Integration testing	Class diagram	Eclipse	AspectJ	R1, R2, R4, R6
[34]	Integration testing	Collaboration diagram	Sequence generator	AspectJ	R1, R2, R3, R4, R6, R7
[35]	Unit testing	Class diagram	JUnit, JamlUnit, JAML	AspectJ	R1, R2, R3, R4, R6, R7, R8

3 Object-Oriented Testing

Object-oriented testing aims to test the various features offered in the object-oriented programming. The features are encapsulation, inheritance, abstraction, polymorphism, and reusability. With the introduction of these features, the complexity also increases and thus the need to test the system. In this section, we have analyzed a number of papers which are based on testing object-oriented systems.

The tool, which is proposed by Augsornsri and Suwannasart [11], performs integration testing for object-oriented software. It presents the total coverage of the class and the method and generates test cases for uncovered methods.

Zhang et al. [12] presented a static and dynamic automated approach for test generation, addressing the problem of creating tests, which are legal and behaviorially diverse.

Mallika [13] proposed a tool, which could provide automation in unit testing of object-oriented classes. A choice is given to the tester to choose which methods should be tested.

Suresh et al. [14] provide test data generation to perform testing in object-oriented programs. Extended control flow graph is used to achieve it. It utilizes artificial bee colony and binary particle swarm optimization algorithm to generate the optimized test cases.

Swain et al. [15] propose an optimization approach for test data generation. State chart diagram is used here. The state chart diagram provides information through which test cases are thus created and minimized.

A model-based testing approach has been proposed by Shirole et al. [16]. In this approach, test cases are generated from state chart diagrams which are represented as extended finite state machine and genetic algorithm.

An approach proposed by Gupta and Rohil [17] automates the generation of both feasible and unfeasible test cases which leads to higher coverage. This is done using evolutionary algorithms.

The work by Mallika [18] presents a modified approach for unit testing in object-oriented systems where an analysis has been made to identify the method with the highest priority using a DU pair algorithm.

Shen et al. [19] proposed a technique, which is novel for the testing of object-oriented systems. It aims to divide the classes available into an integrated value, which measures the frequency and the significance of each class. The class, which has the highest value, is utilized to generate test cases. It helps to find the faults which are often not easily found and reduces the cost of testing.

A test model has been proposed by Wu et al. [20]. It is generated from class, sequence, and state chart diagrams. It focuses on the issues encountered when integration testing takes place and defines coverage criteria where interaction among classes is enhanced.

A framework, which is known as Diffut given by Xie et al. [21] is proposed to perform differential unit testing. The aim is to compare the output from two versions of a method and ensure that the system performs correctly with both the versions.

4 Aspect-Oriented Testing

Aspect-oriented testing is done to ensure that both classes and aspects work correctly in integration with each other. Aspects introduce modularity in aspect-oriented programming by separating cross-cutting concerns from the core concerns. So, it becomes very essential to test both classes and aspects, and thus, the concept of aspect-oriented testing comes into effect. In this section, we consider a number of papers which are based on aspect-oriented testing.

An approach was proposed by Delamare and Kraft [22], where the test order of class integration is based on the amount of impact the aspects have on the classes. It is modeled using genetic algorithm.

A state-based approach has been proposed by Xu et al. [23] for testing of aspect-oriented programs. Aspectual state model is used. It is based on an existing model, which is known as flattened regular expression (FREE) state model [24].

A framework known as Automated Pointcut Testing for AspectJ Programs (APTE) given by Anbalagan and Xie [25] tests the pointcuts present in an AspectJ program. APTE uses an existing framework, which performs unit testing without weaving.

The approach proposed by Xu et al. [26] presents a hybrid testing model. The class state model and scope state model are merged forming aspect scope state model (ASSM). It combines state models and flow graph to produce test suites.

An approach was given by Badri et al. [27] who proposed a state-based automated unit testing approach. It also proposes a tool AJUnit which is based on JUnit. It tries to ensure that the integration of the aspects and classes is done in such a way that the behavior of the class independently is not affected.

Cafeo and Masiero [28] proposed a model, based on the integration of object-oriented and aspect-oriented programs contextually. A model which is known as Contextual Def-Use (CoDu) graph is used to represent the control flow and data flow units.

Xie et al. [29] proposed a framework known as Raspect. It is used to remove the test cases, which are redundant present in the aspect-oriented programs. To automate the test case generation the tools, which are used to generate test cases in Java, are used.

A technique is proposed by Massicotte et al. [30] in which test sequences are generated based on the interactions that take place between classes and aspects dynamically. The integration of a number of aspects is done with collaborating objects. This approach follows an iterative process.

An approach has been proposed by Colanzi et al. [31]. This approach deals with determining the appropriate order, which is used to integrate the classes and aspects and also the correct order to test them.

A technique was proposed by Xu et al. [32] to test what is the behavior of an aspect and the aspect's corresponding base class. A state-based strategy was proposed, which could also consider what impact the aspects have on the classes.

A model proposed by Wang and Zhao [33] is proposed to test aspect-oriented programs, and algorithm is implemented which generates the relevant test cases. A tool is developed so that the test case generation is automated.

An approach proposed by Massicotte et al. [34] develops a strategy for integration of class and aspects. It performs a static and a dynamic analysis in which testing sequences are generated and verified.

A tool known as JamlUnit [35] was proposed by Lopes and Ngo [35] as a framework, which performed unit testing. This testing was done for the aspects, which were written in Java Aspect Markup Language (JAML). This tool enabled the testing of aspects as independent units.

5 Conclusion and Limitations

In this paper, the number of papers of object-oriented and aspect-oriented testing was reviewed. This is done on the basis of several research questions according to which each paper is evaluated. It provides a guideline to a researcher for further research in the areas related to object-oriented and aspect-oriented testing. It also gives a roadmap to a researcher to go through few researches done over the past few years. Further, the limitation of this paper is that the review is given for the papers of only unit and integration testing levels. Also, evaluation criteria are limited to eight research questions. A number of other factors and questions can be considered to refine the search in future.

Acknowledgements We are thankful to the researchers of the papers we have covered, who have given their contribution to provide some valuable work in the area of object-oriented and aspect-oriented testing. We have carried out this review only because of the work done by these researchers.

References

1. Gong, H., Li, J.: Generating test cases of object-oriented software based on EDPN and its mutant. In: The 9th International Conference for Young Computer Scientists, pp. 1112–1119. Hunan (2008)
2. Pressman, R.S.: Software Engineering—A Practitioner's Approach, 3rd edn. McGraw-Hill, New York (1992)
3. Watanabe, H., Tokuoka, H., Wu, W., Saeki, M.: A technique for analysing and testing object-oriented software using coloured petri nets. In: Software Engineering Conference, Asia Pacific (1998). https://doi.org/10.1109/apsec.1998.733718
4. Kartal, Y.B., Schmidt, E.G.: An evaluation of aspect oriented programming for embedded real-time systems. In: 22nd International Symposium on Computer and Information Sciences. IEEE, Ankara (2007). https://doi.org/10.1109/iscis.2007.4456890
5. Gulia, P., Chugh, J.: Comparative analysis of traditional and object oriented software testing. ACM SIGSOFT Softw. Eng. Notes **4**(2), 1–4 (2015)
6. Gordan, J.S., Roggio, R.F.: A comparison of software testing using the object-oriented paradigm and traditional testing. In: Proceedings of the Conference for Information Systems Applied Research, 6(2813). USA (2013)
7. Laddad, R.: AspectJ in Action, 2nd edn. Manning Publications co. (2009)
8. Singhal, A., Bansal, A., Kumar, A.: A critical review of various testing techniques in aspect-oriented software systems. ACM SIGSOFT Softw. Eng. Notes **38**(4), 1–9 (2013)
9. Ali, M.S., Babar, M.A., Chen, L., Stol, K.-J.: A systematic review of comparative evidence of aspect-oriented programming. Inf. Softw. Technol. **52**, 871–887 (2010)
10. Neto, A.C.D., Subramanyan, R., Vieira, M., Travassos, G.H.: A survey on model-based testing approaches: a systematic review. In: Proceedings of the 1st ACM International Workshop on Empirical Assessment of Software Engineering Languages and Technologies: held in conjunction with the 22nd IEEE/ACM International Conference on Automated Software Engineering (ASE), pp. 31–36 (2007)
11. Augsornsri, P., Suwannasart, T.: An integration testing coverage tool for object-oriented software. In: International Conference on Information Science and Applications. IEEE, Seoul (2014). https://doi.org/10.1109/icisa.2014.6847360
12. Zhang, S., Saff, D., Bu, Y., Ernst, M.D.: Combined static and dynamic automated test generation. In: Proceedings of the 2011 International Symposium on Software Testing and Analysis, pp. 353–363 (2011)
13. Mallika, S.S.: EATOOS-testing tool for unit testing of object oriented software. Int. J. Comput. Appl. (0975–8887) **80**(4), 6–10 (2013)

14. Suresh, Y., Rath, S.K.: Evolutionary algorithms for object-oriented test data generation. ACM SIGSOFT Softw. Eng. Notes **39**(4), 1–6 (2014)
15. Swain, R.K., Behera, P.K., Mohapatra, D.P.: Generation and optimization of test cases for object-oriented software using state chart diagram. In: Proceedings of International Journal CSIT-CSCP-2012, pp. 407–424 (2012)
16. Shirole, M., Suthar, A., Kumar, R.: Generation of improved test cases from UML state diagram using genetic algorithm. In: Proceedings of the 4th India Software Engineering Conference, pp. 125–134 (2011)
17. Gupta, N.K., Rohil, N.K.: Improving GA based automated test data generation technique for object oriented software. In: 3rd IEEE International Advance Computing Conference, pp. 249–253. Ghaziabad (2013)
18. Mallika, S.S.: Improvised DU pairs algorithm for unit testing of object oriented software. Int. J. Adv. Res. Comput. Sci. Softw. Eng. **3**(7), 853–857 (2013)
19. Shen, X., Wang, Q., Wang, P., Zhou, B.: A novel technique proposed for testing of object oriented software systems. In: IEEE International Conference on Granular Computing. IEEE, Nanchang (2009). https://doi.org/10.1109/grc.2009.5255073
20. Wu, C.S., Huang, C.H., Lee, Y.T.: The test path generation from state-based polymorphic interaction graph for object-oriented software. In: 10th International Conference on Information Technology: New Generations, pp. 323–330. Las Vegas (2013)
21. Xie, T., Taneja, K., Kale, S., Marinov, D.: Towards a framework for differential unit testing of object-oriented programs. In: Second International Workshop on Automation of Software Test. Minneapolis (2007). https://doi.org/10.1109/ast.2007.15
22. Delamare, R., Kraft, N.A.: A genetic algorithm for computing class integration test orders for aspect-oriented systems. In: IEEE Fifth International Conference on Software Testing, Verification and Validation, pp. 804–813. Montreal (2012)
23. Xu, D., Xu, W., Nyagard, K.: A state-based approach to testing aspect-oriented programs. In: The Proceedings of the 17th International Conference on Software Engineering and Knowledge Engineering (SEKE'05). Taiwan (2005)
24. Binder, R.V.: Testing Object Oriented Systems: Models, Patterns and Tools. Addision Wesley, New York (2000)
25. Anbalagan, P., Xie, T.: APTE: automated pointcut testing for aspectj programs. In: Proceedings of the 2nd Workshop on Testing Aspect-Oriented Programs, pp. 27–32 (2006)
26. Xu, W., Xu, D., Goel, V., Nygard, K.: Aspect flow graph for testing aspect-oriented programs. In: the Proceedings of the IASTED International Conference on Software Engineering and Applications. Oranjestad, Aruba (2005)
27. Badri, M., Badri, L., Fortin, M.B.: Automated state based unit testing for aspect-oriented programs: a supporting framework. J. Object Technol. **8**(3), 121–126 (2009)
28. Cafeo, B.B.P., Masiero, P.C.: Contextual integration testing of object-oriented and aspect - oriented programs: a structural approach for Java and AspectJ. In: 25th Brazilian Symposium on Software Engineering, pp. 214–223 (2011)
29. Xie, T., Zhao, J., Marinov, D., Notkin, D.: Detecting redundant unit tests for AspectJ programs. In: 17th International Symposium on Software Reliability Engineering, pp. 179–190. Raleigh (2006)
30. Massicotte, P., Badri, M., Badri, L.: Generating aspects-classes integration testing sequences: a collaboration diagram based strategy. In: Proceedings of the 2005 Third ACIS International Conference on Software Engineering Research, Management and Applications (SERA'05), pp. 30–37 (2005)
31. Colanzi, T., Assuncao, W.K.G., Vergilio, S.R., Pozo, A.T.R.: Generating integration test orders for aspect-oriented software with multi-objective algorithms. In: the Proceedings of 5th Latin-American Workshop on Aspect-Oriented Software Development (2011)
32. Xu, D., Xu, W.: State-based incremental testing of aspect-oriented programs. In: Proceedings of the 5th International Conference on Aspect-Oriented Software Development (AOSD'06), pp. 180–189 (2006)

33. Wang, P., Zhao, X.: The research of automated select test cases for aspect oriented software. In: The Proceedings of International Conference on Mechanical, Industrial and Manufacturing Engineering (2012). https://doi.org/10.1016/j.ieri.2012.06.002
34. Massicotte, P., Badri, L., Badri, M.: Towards a tool supporting integration testing of aspect-oriented programs. J. Object Technol. **6**(1), 67–89 (2007)
35. Lopes, C.V., Ngo,T.C.: Unit testing aspectual behavior. In WTAOP: Proceedings of the 1st Workshop on Testing Aspect-Oriented programs held in conjunction with 4th International Conference on Aspect-Oriented Software Development (AOSD'05) (2005)

A Literature Survey of Applications of Meta-heuristic Techniques in Software Testing

Neha Prabhakar, Abhishek Singhal, Abhay Bansal
and Vasundhara Bhatia

Abstract Software testing is a phenomenon of testing the entire software with the objective of finding defects in the software and to judge the quality of the developed system. The performance of the system is degraded if bugs are present in the system. Various meta-heuristic techniques are used in the software testing for its automation and optimization of testing data. This survey paper demonstrates the review of various studies, which used the concept of meta-heuristic techniques in software testing.

Keywords Software testing · Ant colony optimization (ACO) · Genetic algorithm (GA) · Bugs · Test cases · Optimization

1 Introduction

Software testing is the stage of software development life cycle (SDLC), which is about testing the functionality and behavior of the developed system with the intention of finding errors in the system. Software testing is generally considered as an important phase of SDLC because it ensures the quality of the system [1]. The acceptance/rejection of the developed system depends upon the quality of the system, which ensures that the system is free from defects. The essential task of the software testing is creation of test suite on which the testing methodologies are applied [2].

N. Prabhakar (✉) · A. Singhal · A. Bansal · V. Bhatia
Department of CSE, ASET, Amity University, Noida, Uttar Pradesh, India
e-mail: nehaprabhakar91@gmail.com

A. Singhal
e-mail: asinghal1@amity.edu

A. Bansal
e-mail: abansal1@amity.edu

V. Bhatia
e-mail: vasundhara.bhatia9@gmail.com

© Springer Nature Singapore Pte Ltd. 2019
M. N. Hoda et al. (eds.), *Software Engineering*, Advances in Intelligent Systems and Computing 731, https://doi.org/10.1007/978-981-10-8848-3_47

Software testing is considered as a basic technique to acquire customer's belief in the software. Testing is a lengthy as well as an expensive task [3]. However, modern approaches for software testing would result in comparatively lesser cost [4].

The goal of testing is not just to catch bugs and defects in the system; it could be done for the purposes [5] such as assurance of the quality of the software, verification and validation and checking the functionality of the software.

Once the testing is done, there arises a need to address the defects/bugs that occurred during testing. The significance of the bugs relies upon factors like frequency, correction cost, consequential cost, and application cost.

This paper is segregated into five sections. Section 2 consists of brief introduction about the meta-heuristic techniques such as ant colony optimization (ACO) and genetic algorithm (GA). Section 3 describes the method adopted for carrying out the literature review and proposes the criteria for evaluating research papers. Section 4 presents the analysis of some relevant papers of GA and ACO along with the results of our observations in those papers. Finally, the conclusion of survey is portrayed in Sect. 5.

2 Meta-heuristic Techniques

Perfectly created test suites not only reveal the bugs in the software, but also it minimizes the cost associated with software testing. If the test sequence could be generated automatically, then the load on the tester can be minimized and required test coverage could be achieved. For the purpose of optimization of software testing, two meta-heuristic techniques such as ant colony optimization and genetic algorithm are used.

2.1 Ant Colony Optimization

The basic concept behind ACO is to mimic the actions of actual ants to resolve various optimization difficulties. The capability of ants like searching for the nearest food source, reaching a destination could become possible due to a chemical called pheromone. As more ants traverse the same path, the measure of pheromone dropped by the ants on particular path increases [6].

2.2 Genetic Algorithm

Genetic algorithm is a biologically inspired technique. It is a searching mechanism, which gives the optimized results of problems. The concept of GA depends on the fact that only the fittest generations can survive. Initially, many random solutions are picked, which acts like population. Recombination, selection, and mutation are the main phases of the genetic algorithm [7].

3 Benchmark for Evaluation

A well-defined approach for software testing consists of the series of processes that could be implemented in software to reveal the defects in the software. A meticulous literature review has been performed to analyze the gaps in the existing technologies. Various databases were referred for gathering research papers for the review purpose like IEEE Xplore, ACM digital library, other online sources like Google scholar and open access journal (Table 1).

Following keywords were used for searching relevant research papers:

We have considered various benchmarks in the form of research questions to analyze the application of ACO and GA in software testing and finally evaluating all the testing techniques based on the number of factors satisfied by the research papers [, 2, 5, 6, 8–18]. The final result of the survey is shown in Table 2. The research questions for the evaluation are as follows:

Table 1 Keywords used in searching papers

Serial number	Keywords used
1	Software testing using meta-heuristic techniques
2	Software testing using genetic algorithm
3	Software testing using ACO
4	Software testing using ACO and genetic algorithm

Table 2 Analysis of numerous research papers

Factors	[2]	[2]	[10]	[8]	[11]	[12]	[13]	[6]	[14]	[15]	[16]	[17]	[18]	[21]
R1				✓							✓	✓		
R2	✓	✓	✓	✓			✓	✓	✓	✓	✓	✓	✓	
R3			✓	✓	✓			✓	✓	✓	✓			
R4	✓			✓	✓	✓							✓	✓
R5			✓		✓				✓	✓		✓		
R6	✓	✓		✓		✓	✓		✓	✓	✓		✓	✓
R7													✓	✓
R8	✓	✓			✓	✓					✓	✓	✓	✓
R9											✓			
R10		✓	✓		✓		✓	✓	✓	✓	✓			
Total number of factors satisfied	4	4	4	5	5	3	3	3	5	5	7	4	5	4

R1: Does the system reduce efforts required for software testing and test case generation?

Software testing is considered as a complicated task. The generation of test cases is a time-consuming process since whole testing depends on test data suite? Rathore et al. [9] explained that 50% of the effort of software development project is absorbed by software testing and generation of test data. So according to the above-mentioned research question, the system should minimize the efforts required for testing and test case generation.

R2: Does the system generate optimum set of data?

A good system generates an optimum set of data, which means it has to generate such set of data, which gives best result of testing; generation of unnecessary data set should be avoided by the system.

R3: Does the system reduce the testing time?

As testing is considered as time-consuming process and it actually takes months to test a complete software, so testers always need a system or a technique that could minimize the testing time.

R4: Does the proposed system generate test data automatically?

Generation of test data automatically or automation testing is a demand of every tester. Automatic generation of test data reduces the time of the tester as tester does not have to create the test data manually, everything is done by a tool itself, and testers just have to check the results given by the testing tool.

R5: Does the proposed system minimize the size of test suite?

Test suite reduction helps in reduction of load on tester. Large test suite with redundant test data or unnecessary data increases the complexity of the testing, and burden on tester is also increased.

R6: Is the system efficient enough?

A system is said to be efficient if it achieves higher work rate with less efforts of tester and negligible wastage of expenses. An efficient system saves the resources of organizations like manpower, money, energy consumption, various machines.

R7: Does the system focus on finding global optimum solution?

Global optimum solution is the one, which finds the best solution among all the possible solutions of a problem. Rather than converging to a local optimum solution, i.e., finding solution within the neighborhood, system should explore all the possible solutions and then choose the appropriate one.

R8: Does the system choose optimal path and that path leads to maximum coverage for fault detection?

Path testing is done by selecting a path that assures that every code linked to that path of a program is executed at least once. In case of path testing, the selection of path should be an optimal one, and it should expand its root to the maximum portion of the program so that maximal code of the program gets executed and helps to detect the maximum faults in one go.

R9: Does the system reduce redundant paths?

Sometimes system includes already existing path in the data set and attempts to execute already executed path again, which leads to the wastage of time. So to avoid this situation, system should detect the presence of already existing data set in the test suite.

R10: Does the system focus on the minimization of cost on the testing?

Minimization of expenses is an ultimate goal of every task, and same goes for software testing also. Prakash et al. [10] explained that close to 45% of the software development cost is spent on software testing. Minimization of resources, manpower, time, etc., leads to minimized cost of the system.

4 Analysis of ACO and GA

ACO and GA both are the techniques for the optimization of software testing. The results produced by these techniques are far better than traditional techniques. These techniques are considered as biologically inspired techniques, which gives solutions to most of the real-life problems that arise in industries.

We have analyzed available papers to study the application of these techniques in software testing and explained crux of each paper scrutinized by us.

4.1 Genetic Algorithm

Mahajan et al. [2] proposed a model that examines the performance of the GA when applied for automatic creation of test suite using data flow testing technique. An incremental coverage method is adopted to enhance the convergence.

Rathore et al. [9] proposed a method for automatic creation of test data in software testing. The proposed technique applies the concept of tabu search and GA and merges the power of the two techniques to produce more useful results in lesser time.

Rao et al. [5] proposed an approach that worked on those paths which were more fault finding and resulted in the enhancement of the testing performance.

Prakash et al. [10] proposed that the faults eliminating ability is directly proportional to the accuracy of the software testing and test cycles. Important factor is to minimize the testing time and cost but without compromising with the quality of the software. For this, it is required to follow a technique and reduce the test data by recommending N test cases based on some heuristics.

Srivastava et al. [8] proposed a model which generates the practical testing data suite using GA. Various experiments have been performed to automatically create the test data suite. Present systems do not assure to produce test information only in achievable path.

Manual test data generation is a complex task and accomplished by intelligence of neurons to observe the patterns [11]. Automated test data generators generally do not possess the capability to create effective test data as they do not mimic the natural mechanism.

Khor and Grogono [12] proposed an automatic test generator called GENET using formal concept analysis and GA, to automatically attain the branch coverage test data.

Gulia and Chillar [19] recommended a tactic in which optimized test data could be generated. They are generated using state chart diagram of the UML. Using the genetic algorithm, test cases can be optimized easily. Genetic algorithm works best when the input is large.

Varshney et al. [20] have provided a study of meta-heuristic techniques and the hybrid approaches which have been proposed to carry the test data generation. In their study, they provided various areas which can be explored, issues that arise and the future directions in the area of test cases creation for structural testing.

4.2 Aco

Srivastava et al. [13] worked on the creation of test cases by means of meta-heuristic techniques like GA and ACO. In this paper, GA is used to produce the test suite for an algorithm requesting for resources. Numerous test cases were generated and also estimated the amount of usable and worthless test cases among those test data. Srivastava et al. [13] also performed the analysis for the success ratio of both of these techniques and found that the success ratio of GA is 45–46%, whereas the success ratio of ACO is 53–55% and proved that ACO has better success rate.

An approach is proposed by Mala and Mohan [6] which take the decision of optimized test sequence called intelligent search agent (ISA). Software which is under test is symbolized by graph, in that graph every vertex is represented by a heuristic value, and every edge is assigned a weight called edge weight. Intelligent agent takes decision of finest arrangement by observing those vertices which meets fitness benchmark and then produces the optimized test data by using all the paths of software.

Mala and Mohan [6] have also proved that the performance of the ISA is better than ACO in terms of the generation of optimized data and time.

An algorithm is proposed by Cui Donghua and Yin Winjie. [14] Based on ACO, which focused on the problem of test suite reduction, this reduces the pressure on the tester since exhaustive testing becomes difficult. Two criteria are considered for the test suite reduction such as test cost criteria and test coverage criteria.

Based on these criteria, a comparison is performed between this algorithm and other classical algorithm and proved that this algorithm reduced the budget and size of test data and attained effectiveness.

Singh et al. [15] proposed an algorithm which implements a technique called regression test prioritization technique which rearranges the test data in a time constraint environment. Since time is always a constraint for a tester, so there arises a need for prioritizing the available test cases. ACO has been used to implement this problem.

Srivatava [16] presented an algorithm which automates the generation of the paths in control flow graph in structural testing using cyclomatic complexity. The basic fundamental behind this algorithm is pheromone releasing behavior of ants which determines the optimal paths in the testing.

Suri et al. [17] analyzed the technique proposed in [15] and concluded that ant colony optimization discovers improved arrangements at different conditions of time constraint. The accuracy of this method is proved to be nearly optimal.

Yi [18] proposed an algorithm which is a mixture of ant colony system algorithm and genetic algorithm (ACSGA) to achieve path specific software testing data. The result of this algorithm shows that the creation capability of target path has been improved seemingly.

Li et al. [21] have proposed a model which can generate test data. This is done using ant colony optimization which is improved. The coverage criteria considered here are path testing.

Noguchi et al. [22] suggested a framework for prioritizing test data. The researchers suggest that often the testers may not have the access to the source code. In that case, black box testing is used where the testing is done only on the input and the output provided. They also suggest that a lot of previous work has been done on white box testing. In the proposed framework, the researchers use a test execution history which they have collected from another product. This is done using ant colony optimization. Two products are used here to show the accuracy of the results.

Srivastava and Baby [23] proposed an approach which helps to generate test sequences to get full coverage of the code. They try to do it by automating the system. Ant colony optimization technique is applied to automate the system.

Table 2 represents the set of research question in the form of R1–R10 along with the papers form which those questions were assumed [24–28]. The tick mark shows the listed factor is satisfied by that corresponding research paper.

5 Conclusion

This review paper presents a detailed survey of the study of the outcomes and application of ant colony optimization and genetic algorithm in software testing. It is found that ACO and GA both can be used for distinct software testing areas like generation of test data, optimization of test suite, minimization of test suite, automatically generation of test cases, prioritization of test cases. On the other hand, few limitations of GA and ACO were also observed. In this paper, analysis of papers based on research questions will provide future guidance to researchers.

References

1. Mayan, J.A., Ravi, T.: Test case optimization using hybrid search. In: International Conference on Interdisciplinary Advances in Applied Computing. New York, NY, USA (2014)
2. Mahajan, M., Kumar, S., Porwal, R.: Applying genetic algorithm to increase the efficiency of a data flow-based test data generation approach. ACM SIGSOFT Softw. Eng. Notes (2012) (New York, NY, USA)
3. Binder, R.V.: Testing Object-Oriented Systems: Models, Patterns, and Tools, 1st edn. Addison-Wesley Professional (1999)
4. Li, H., Lam, C.P.: An ant colony optimization approach to test sequence generation for statebased software testing. In: Proceedings of Fifth International Conference on Quality Software. Melbourne, pp. 255–262 (2005)
5. Rao, K.K., Raju, G.S.V.P., Nagaraj, S.: Optimizing the software testing efficiency by using a genetic algorithm—a design methodology. ACM SIGSOFT Softw. Eng. Notes **38**, 10 (2013). New York, NY, USA
6. Mala, J.D., Mohan, V.: IntelligenTester-software test sequence optimization using graph based intelligent search agent. In: Computational Intelligence and Multimedia Applications. Sivakasi, Tamil Nadu (2007)
7. Roper, M., Maclean, I., Brooks, A., Miller, J., Wood, M.: Genetic Algorithms and the Automatic Generation of Test Data (1995)
8. Srivastava, P.R., Gupta, P., Arrawatia, Y., Yadav, S.: Use of genetic algorithm in generation of feasible test data. ACM SIGSOFT Softw. Eng. Notes **34** (2009)
9. Rathore, A., Bohara, A., Gupta, P.R., Lakshmi, P.T.S., Srivastava, P.R.: Application of genetic algorithm and tabu search in software testing. In: Fourth Annual ACM Bangalore Conference (2011)
10. Prakash, S.S.K., Dhanyamraju Prasad, S.U.M., Gopi Krishna, D.: Recommendation and regression test suite optimization using heuristic algorithms. In: 8th India Software Engineering Conference (2015)
11. Bhasin, H.: Artificial life and cellular automata based automated test case generator. ACM SIGSOFT Softw. Eng. Notes **39** (2014)
12. Khor, S., Grogono, P.: Using a genetic algorithm and formal concept analysis to generate branch coverage test data automatically. In: 19th IEEE International Conference on Automated Software Engineering (2004)
13. Srivastava, P.R., Ramachandran, V., Kumar, M., Talukder, G., Tiwari, V., Sharma, P.: Generation of test data using meta-heuristic approach. In: TENCON 2008 IEEE Region 10 Conference. Hyderabad (2008)
14. Donghua, C., Wenjie, Y.: The research of test-suite reduction technique. In: Consumer Electronics, Communications and Networks (CECNet). XianNing (2011)
15. Singh, Y., Kaur, A., Suri, B.: Test case prioritization using ant colony optimization. ACM SIGSOFT Softw. Eng. Notes **35** (2010)
16. Srivastava, P.R.: Structured testing using Ant colony optimization. In: First International Conference on Intelligent Interactive Technologies and Multimedia (2010)
17. Suri, B., Singhal, S.: Analyzing test case selection & prioritization using ACO. ACM SIGSOFT Softw. Eng. Notes **36** (2011)
18. Yi, M.: The research of path oriented test data generation based on a mixed Ant colony system algorithm and genetic algorithm. In: Wireless Communications, Networking, and Mobile Computing (WiCOM). Shanghai (2012)
19. Gulia, P., Chillar, R.S.: A new approach to generate and optimize test cases for uml state diagram using genetic algorithm. ACM SIGSOFT Softw. Eng. Notes **37** (2012)
20. Varshney, S., Mehrotra, M.: Search based software test data generation for structural testing: a perspective. ACM SIGSOFT Softw. Eng. Notes **38** (2013)

21. Li, K., Zhang, Z., Liu, W.: Automatic test data generation based on ant colony optimization, vol. 6. Tianjin (2009)
22. Noguchi, T., Washizaki, H., Fukazawa, Y., Sato, A., Ota, K.: History-based test case prioritization for black box testing using ant colony optimization. Graz (2015)
23. Srivastava, P.R., Baby, K.: Automated software testing using meta-heuristic technique based on an Ant colony optimization. In: Electronic System Design (ISED). Bhubaneswar (2010)
24. Talbi, E.G.: Meta Heuristic from Design to Implementation. Wiley, Hoboken, New Jersey (2009)
25. Goldberg, D.E.: Genetic Algorithms in Search, Optimization and Machine Learning. Addison-Wesley Longman Publishing Co. Inc., Boston, MA, USA (1989)
26. Bueno, P.M.S. Jino, M.: Identification of potentially infeasible program paths by monitoring the search for test data. In: Automated Software Engineering, Grenoble (2000)
27. Ayari, K., Bouktif, S., Antoniol, G.: Automatic mutation test input data generation via Ant colony. In: GECCO'07 Proceedings of the 9th Annual Conference on Genetic and Evolutionary Computation (2007)
28. Wong, W.E., Horgan, J.R., London, S.: Effect of test set minimization on fault detection effectiveness. In: Proceedings of the 17th International Conference on Software Engineering (1995)

A Review of Test Case Prioritization and Optimization Techniques

Pavi Saraswat, Abhishek Singhal and Abhay Bansal

Abstract Software testing is a very important and crucial phase of software development life cycle. In order to develop good quality software, the effectiveness of the software has been tested. Test cases and test suites are prepared for testing, and it should be done in minimum time for which test case prioritization and optimization techniques are required. The main aim of test case prioritization is to test software in minimum time and with maximum efficiency, so for this there are many techniques, and to develop a new or better technique, existing techniques should be known. This paper presents a review on the techniques of test case prioritization and optimization. This paper also provides analysis of the literature available for the same.

Keywords Software testing · Regression testing · Test case prioritization
Test case optimization

1 Introduction

Software testing is an important phase of software development life cycle (SDLC), and it consumes substantial amount of time. A proper strategy is required for its effectiveness to carry out the testing activities [1, 3].

So software testing is the testing of the software product for its effectiveness and accuracy [1], and testing is done with objectives that testing process should be able to detect the errors in the software in minimum amount of time and effort. It should detect that the product is developed as per the specification. It should demonstrate that the

P. Saraswat (✉) · A. Singhal · A. Bansal
Department of CSE, ASET, Amity University, Noida, Uttar Pradesh, India
e-mail: pavisaraswat@gmail.com

A. Singhal
e-mail: asinghal1@amity.edu

A. Bansal
e-mail: abansal1@amity.edu

© Springer Nature Singapore Pte Ltd. 2019   507
M. N. Hoda et al. (eds.), *Software Engineering*, Advances in Intelligent Systems
and Computing 731, https://doi.org/10.1007/978-981-10-8848-3_48

product has a good quality, and it should be able to test cases that cover yet undetected errors. Testing is facing a big dilemma, as on the one hand thinking is that the software should be made with zero errors but on the other hand, the main aim of the testing team is to find out maximum errors in minimum time, and in testing the product's output is been tested to every possible input that means it may be valid or invalid [2]. We have mainly two types of testing, such as static testing and dynamic testing. The two main approaches of testing are functional approach and structural approach.

1.1   Regression Testing

Regression testing is the process of retesting the modified and affected parts of the software and ensuring that no new errors have been introduced into the previously tested code [4]. So after adding some functionalities or doing some changes in the software, the product is modified which is fault of commission, and then regression testing is needed. In regression testing, existing test suites and test plans are also useful. Here testing is done only on modified or the affected components, not the whole software. There are no such limitations on performing regression testing it is performed as many times as it is needed [1, 4]. But schedule gives no time for the regression testing that is why it is performed under larger time constraints.

1.2   Test Case Prioritization

Test case prioritization is scheduling of test cases in some order that they detect the faults very fast and easily in that particular order rather than some random order [1, 3, 5]. As it is well known that there is no such specified budget and time for regression testing, so the aim is to find maximum faults in minimum time; for that arrangement of test cases or test suites is done in some confined order. This even defines some criteria like fault detection and code coverage according to which test cases are prioritized.

1.3   Techniques of Test Case Prioritization and Optimization

Test case prioritization is a very beneficial process and much needed process as in this, we arrange test cases in some priority-based order, which gives us an efficient testing output or results [1]. We have approaches for test case prioritization, and one of them is greedy approach in which some criterion is fixed on which the maximum weighted element is chosen. The major drawback of greedy approach is that it gives the local optimal solution not the global optimal of the problem considered. Other than this there is one more, which is additional genetic algorithm or two optimal algorithms; it is same as greedy but uses different strategies. Even meta-heuristic search techniques are used in finding a solution to a particular problem with a reasonable computational cost. So some techniques are prioritization in parallel scenario for multiple queues (PSMQ) [3], multi-objective particle swarm optimizer for test case optimization, ant colony optimization (ACO) algorithm for fault coverage is used, and regression test case prioritization [7], genetic Algorithm and greedy algorithm, multi-objective test case prioritization (MOTCP) [11], multi-objective regression test optimization (MORTO) [15], testing importance of module approach (TIM). Metrics are used in test case prioritization techniques to calculate the efficiency; some of them are average percentage block coverage (APBC), average percentage decision coverage (APDC), average percentage of faults detected (APFD), average percentage statement coverage (APSC), and average percentage-fault-affected module cleared per test case (APMC).

This paper is divided into four sections; Sect. 2 describes the literature survey on Test Case Prioritization Techniques and the research questions. Section 3 describes analysis of the literature work in tabular form, and Sect. 4 presents conclusion on the work study done.

2 Literature Survey

In order to analyze various techniques available for test case prioritization and optimization technique, we broadly divided those into mainly two paradigms like procedural paradigm and object-oriented paradigm.

We studied and analyzed available papers that what are its contents that mean that what technology is being used in it and what are the algorithms used in the paper for the test case prioritization and optimization. Then we defined that what are the metrics used in the papers for their efficiency calculation and what are all coverage focused in the paper. And after getting all the information from the paper, we can get the information that in which area which all techniques are more useful as compared to the others. And the same procedure is followed for the object-oriented paradigm.

2.1 Research Questions

Few research questions that are formed and also been answered below are as follows:

RQ1: Are there metrics used in the paper?
RQ2: Is fault coverage considered?
RQ3: Is code coverage considered?
RQ4: Is APFD or its some version is used?
RQ5: Is genetic approach used?

3 Analysis of Papers

In this phase, we present the review study in tabular form as given in Tables 1, 2, and 3.

Table 1 Analysis of techniques in the procedural paradigm

Reference ID	Technique and algorithm	Metric used	Coverage	Implementation	Reference ID	Technique and algorithm	Metric used	Coverage	Implementation
[1]	Prioritization in parallel scenario	APFD (parallel scenarios)		Microsoft PowerPoint 2003	[11]	MOTCP, a software tool	APFD	Code and application requirement coverage	Four Java applications: AveCalc, LaTazza, iTrust, ArgoUml
[2]	Particle swarm optimization		(1) Statement (2) Function (3) Branch (4) Code	20 test cases from JUnit test suite	[12]	Genetic algorithm is used	Information flow metric (IF)	Code coverage is used	It is implemented on two sample C codes
[3]	Multi-objective particle swarm optimization (MOPSO)		Fault coverage and execution time	PC with Intel core 15 and 4 GB memory and MATLAB R2009b	[13]	Test planner and test manager		Code coverage is used	It is implemented on triangle problem
[4]	Failure pursuit sampling and adaptive failure pursuit sampling	APFD	Fault coverage	Programs available in the Siemens suite at SIR initiative	[14]	MORTO approach		Code-based coverage	On costs and values that incorporated into such a MORTO approach
[5]	Meta-heuristic (a) Genetic algorithm (b) PSO		Fault coverage	It is implemented on JAVA	[15]	Ant colony optimization	APFD	Fault coverage	Medical software and financial software
[6]	Test suite refinement on basis of risk and specification		Functionality coverage	It is implemented on multiple test cases present	[16]	TIM approach EIS algorithm	APFD and APMC metrics are used	Program structure coverage	On two Java programs with JUnit and jtopas from SIR

(continued)

Table 1 (continued)

Reference ID	Technique and algorithm	Metric used	Coverage	Implementation
[7]	ACO parallelized and non-parallelized environment		Fault coverage	It is implemented on Hadoop framework where time is reduced for really well extend
[8]	Genetic algorithm greedy algorithm	APFD, APSC, APDC	Fault coverage, statement coverage, and decision coverage	It compares all the techniques and their approaches and the metric used
[9]	Prioritized pairwise combination and prioritized pairwise sorting algorithm	Weight coverage (WC)	Pairwise coverage	Both the PPC and PPS are compared and implemented in the classification tree editor
[10]	Analytical approach	Area selector indicator	Defect coverage	TETRA system release
[17]	Similarity-based TCP using the ordered sequence of program elements	APFD	Code coverage and ordered sequence are used	On the simple code and some of the research questions are answered on that basis
[18]	Modular-based technique and greedy algorithm are used	APFD	Fault coverage is used	On university student monitoring system, hospital management system, and industrial process operation system
[19]	Particle swarm optimization			It is demonstrated by the test system of six-generation units

Table 2 Analysis of techniques in the object-oriented paradigm

Reference Id	Technique and algorithm	Metric used	Coverage	Implementation
[20]	Hierarchical test case prioritization is used	APFD	Fault coverage	On four classes, study, lec_time, sports time, and use time
[2]	Particle swarm optimization technique is used		Statement, function, branch, and code coverage	Implemented by executing 20 test cases from the JUnit test suite
[21]	Bacteriological adaptation technique is used		Specification, implementation, and test consistency is checked	on component written in C# in the .NET framework
[22]	Genetic algorithm	$APBC_m$, APFD, APBC	Additional modified lines of code coverage AMLOC	Experimented on the two database using genetic algorithm
[23]	Tabu search and GA		Fault coverage	On prototype of sample voters id
[24]	ART	F measure P measure		Aspects and java codes
[27]	Bacteriological algorithm	Memorization, filtering, and mutation function		It is implemented on a .NET components
[28]	Genetic algorithm and mutation testing	Mutation score and fitness function		On a .NET component
[29]	Event flow technique		Data flow coverage	On Java programs
[30]	Genetic algorithm		Prime path coverage	On ATM system
[31]	Genetic algorithm	Key assessment metric	Code coverage	On the Java decoding technique
[32]	Genetic algorithm	Pareto frontier no. of non-dominated solutions	Fault coverage	On 11 open-source programs

(continued)

Table 2 (continued)

Reference Id	Technique and algorithm	Metric used	Coverage	Implementation	Reference Id	Technique and algorithm	Metric used	Coverage	Implementation
[25]	VART			Regression fault in the function available products	[33]	Genetic algorithm and particle swarm optimization		Code and fault coverage	On MATLAB programming
[26]	RTS			Implemented on tool and compared with manual RTS	[34]	Bee colony optimization		Fault coverage	On Java programming application

Table 3 Analysis of papers based on research questions

ID	RQ1	RQ2	RQ3	RQ4	RQ5	ID	RQ1	RQ2	RQ3	RQ4	RQ5
[1]	X			X		[19]					X
[2]			X			[20]	X	X		X	
[3]		X				[2]			X		
[4]	X	X		X		[21]					X
[5]		X			X	[22]	X	X		X	X
[6]						[23]		X			X
[7]		X				[24]	X				
[8]	X	X		X	X	[25]					
[9]	X					[26]					
[10]	X					[27]	X				X
[11]	X		X	X		[28]	X				X
[12]	X		X		X	[29]					
[13]			X			[30]					X
[14]			X			[31]	X		X		X
[15]	X	X		X		[32]	X	X			X
[16]	X			X		[33]		X	X		X
[17]	X		X	X		[34]		X			
[18]	X	X		X							

4 Conclusion

In this paper, an empirical review has been performed on the techniques used in test case prioritization and optimization in procedural paradigm and object-oriented paradigm. All the available related papers of the research have been taken from the literature. They are reviewed deeply, and each paper has been analyzed on the basis of techniques or algorithm used, metrics used for efficiency, coverage that has been taken and implementation basis of that paper. After reading this present paper, researchers can get a quick review of the papers and get the relevant information like coverage, metrics used and much more. They can also know the depth of the papers and their research work.

References

1. Qu, B., Nie, C., Xu, B.: Test case prioritization for multiple processing queues. In: ISISE'08 International Symposium on Information Science and Engineering, vol. 2, pp. 646–649. IEEE (2008)
2. Hla, K.H.S., Choi, Y. Park, J.S. Applying particle swarm optimization to prioritizing test cases for embedded real time software retesting. In: 8th International Conference on Computer and Information Technology Workshops, pp. 527–532. IEEE (2008)

3. Tyagi, M., Malhotra, S.: Test case prioritization using multi objective particle swarm optimizer. In: International Conference on Signal Propagation and Computer Technology (ICSPCT), pp. 390–395. IEEE (2014)
4. Simons, C., Paraiso, E.C.: Regression test cases prioritization using failure pursuit sampling. In: 10th International Conference on Intelligent Systems Design and Applications (ISDA), pp. 923–928. IEEE (2010)
5. Nagar, R., Kumar, A., Kumar, S., Baghel, A.S.: Implementing test case selection and reduction techniques using meta-heuristics. In: Confluence The Next Generation Information Technology Summit (Confluence), 2014 5th International Conference, pp. 837–842. IEEE (2014)
6. Ansari, A.S., Devadkar, K.K., Gharpure, P.: Optimization of test suite-test case in regression test. In: IEEE International Conference on Computational Intelligence and Computing Research (ICCIC), pp. 1–4. IEEE (2013)
7. Elanthiraiyan, N., Arumugam, C.: Parallelized ACO algorithm for regression testing prioritization in hadoop framework. In: International Conference on Advanced Communication Control and Computing Technologies (ICACCCT), pp. 1568–1571. IEEE (2014)
8. Sharma, N., Purohit, G.N.: Test case prioritization techniques-an empirical study. In: International Conference on High Performance Computing and Applications (ICHPCA), vol. 28(2), pp. 159–182. IEEE (2014)
9. Kruse, P.M., Schieferdecker, I. Comparison of approaches to prioritized test generation for combinatorial interaction testing. In: Federated Conference on Computer Science and Information Systems (FedCSIS), pp. 1357–1364. IEEE (2012)
10. Stochel, M.G., Sztando, R.: Testing optimization for mission-critical, complex, distributed systems. In: 32nd Annual IEEE International Conference on Computer Software and Applications, 2008. COMPSAC'08, pp. 847–852. IEEE (2008)
11. Islam, M.M., Scanniello, G.: MOTCP: a tool for the prioritization of test cases based on a sorting genetic algorithm and latent semantic indexing. In: 28th IEEE International Conference on Software Maintenance (ICSM), pp. 654–657. IEEE (2012)
12. Sabharwal, S., Sibal, R., Sharma, C.: A genetic algorithm based approach for prioritization of test case scenarios in static testing. In: 2nd International Conference on Computer and Communication Technology (ICCCT), pp. 304–309. IEEE (2011)
13. Khan, S.U.R., Parizi, R.M., Elahi, M.: A code coverage-based test suite reduction and prioritization framework.In: Fourth World Congress on Information and Communication Technologies (WICT), pp. 229–234. IEEE (2014)
14. Harman, M.: Making the case for MORTO: multi objective regression test optimization. In: Fourth International Conference on Software Testing, Verification and Validation Workshops, pp. 111–114. IEEE (2011)
15. Noguchi, T., Sato, A.: History-based test case prioritization for black box testing using ant colony optimization. In: IEEE 8th International Conference on Software Testing, Verification and Validation (ICST), pp. 1–2. IEEE (2015)
16. Ma, Z., Zhao, J.: Test case prioritization based on analysis of program structure. In: Software Engineering Conference, 2008. APSEC'08. 15th Asia-Pacific, pp. 471–478. IEEE (2008)
17. Wu, K., Fang, C., Chen, Z., Zhao, Z.: Test case prioritization incorporating ordered sequence of program elements. In: Proceedings of the 7th International Workshop on Automation of Software Test, pp. 124–130. IEEE Press (2012)
18. Prakash, N., Rangaswamy, T.R.: Modular based multiple test case prioritization. In: IEEE International Conference on Computational Intelligence and Computing Research (ICCIC), pp. 1–7. IEEE (2012)
19. Rugthaicharoencheep, N., Thongkeaw, S., Auchariyamet, S.: Economic load dispatch with daily load patterns using particle swarm optimization. In: Proceedings of 46th International Universities Power Engineering Conference (UPEC), pp. 1–5. VDE (2011)

20. Chauhan, N., Kumar, H.: A hierarchical test case prioritization technique for object oriented software. In: International Conference on Contemporary Computing and Informatics (IC3I), pp. 249–254. IEEE (2014)
21. Baudry, B., Fleurey, F., Jezequel, J.M., Le Traon, Y.: Automatic test case optimization using a bacteriological adaptation model: application to. net components. In: Proceedings of the ASE 2002. 17th IEEE International Conference on Automated Software Engineering, pp. 253–256. IEEE (2002)
22. Malhotra, R., Tiwari, D.: Development of a framework for test case prioritization using genetic algorithm. ACM SIGSOFT Softw. Eng. Notes **38**(3), 1–6 (2013)
23. Mayan, J.A., Ravi, T.: Test case optimization using hybrid search technique. In: Proceedings of the 2014 International Conference on Interdisciplinary Advances in Applied Computing. ACM (2014)
24. Arcuri, A., Briand, L.: Adaptive random testing: an illusion of effectiveness? In: Proceedings of the 2011 International Symposium on Software Testing and Analysis, pp. 265–275. ACM (2011)
25. Pastore, F., Mariani, L., Hyvärinen, A.E.J., Fedyukovich, G., Sharygina, N., Sehestedt, S., Muhammad, A.: Verification-aided regression testing. In: Proceedings of the 2014 International Symposium on Software Testing and Analysis, pp. 37–48. ACM (2014)
26. Gligoric, M., Negara, S. Legunsen, O., Marinov, D.: An empirical evaluation and comparison of manual and automated test selection. In: Proceedings of the 29th ACM/IEEE International Conference on Automated Software Engineering, pp. 361–372. ACM (2014)
27. Baudry, B., Fleurey, F., Jézéquel, J.M., Le Traon, Y.: Automatic test case optimization: a bacteriologic algorithm. IEEE Softw. **22**(2), 76–82 (2005)
28. Baudry, B., Fleurey, F., Jézéquel, J.M., Le Traon, Y.: Genes and bacteria for automatic test cases optimization in the. net environment. In: Proceedings of the 13th International Symposium on Software Reliability Engineering, ISSR, pp. 195–206. IEEE (2002)
29. Liu, W., Dasiewicz, P.: The event-flow technique for selecting test cases for object-oriented programs. In: Canadian Conference on Engineering Innovation: Voyage of Discovery, vol. 1, pp. 257–260. IEEE (1997)
30. Hoseini, B., Jalili, S.: Automatic test path generation from sequence diagram using genetic algorithm. In: 7th International Symposium on Telecommunications (IST), pp. 106–111. IEEE (2014)
31. Mahajan, S., Joshi, S.D., Khanaa, V.: Component-based software system test case prioritization with genetic algorithm decoding technique using java platform. In: International Conference on Computing Communication Control and Automation, pp. 847–851. IEEE (2015)
32. Panichella, A., Oliveto, R., Di Penta, M., De Lucia, A.: Improving multi-objective test case selection by injecting diversity in genetic algorithms. IEEE Trans. Softw. Eng. **41**(4), 358–383 (2015)
33. Valdez, F., Melin, P., Mendoza, O.: A new evolutionary method with fuzzy logic for combining particle swarm optimization and genetic algorithms: the case of neural networks optimization. In: International Joint Conference on Neural Networks, IJCNN, (IEEE World Congress on Computational Intelligence), pp. 1536–1543. IEEE (2008)
34. Karnavel, K., Santhosh Kumar, J.: Automated software testing for application maintenance by using bee colony optimization algorithms (BCO). In: International Conference on Information Communication and Embedded Systems (ICICES), pp. 327–330. IEEE (2013)

Software Development Activities Metric to Improve Maintainability of Application Software

Adesh Kumar pandey and C. P. Agrawal

Abstract The maintenance is very important activity of the software development life cycle. The maximum percentage of design and development cost of software system is going into maintenance to incorporate the change into functional requirement. The increased functional requirements lead towards system configuration changes, which may further increase the cost of development. Every software company want to design and develop the software which is easy to maintain at lower costs. It is better to design and develop more maintainable software to meet this objective; this paper proposed software development activities metric, which will help software developers to develop the easy-to-maintain application software.

Keywords Application software · Metric · Software development life cycle

1 Introduction

The maintenance activities consume a large portion of the total life cycle cost and time. Software maintenance activities may account almost 70% of total development cost. If we analyse the distribution of efforts during design and development of a software system, 60% of the maintenance budget goes in enhancement activities, and 20% each for adaptation and correction [1].

Maintenance activities consume lot of time and cost of software development life cycle; it motivates us to design and develop software, which are easy to maintain and cost effective. Any new functional requirement by user or client reinitiates development in the analysis phase. Fixing of a software problem may require working in the analysis phase, the design phase or the implementation

A. K. pandey (✉)
Department of Information Technology, KIET Group of Institutions, Ghaziabad, India
e-mail: adeshpandey.kiet@gmail.com

C. P. Agrawal
Department of Computer Applications, M.C.N.U.J.C., Bhopal, India
e-mail: agrawalcp@yahoo.com

© Springer Nature Singapore Pte Ltd. 2019
M. N. Hoda et al. (eds.), *Software Engineering*, Advances in Intelligent Systems and Computing 731, https://doi.org/10.1007/978-981-10-8848-3_49

phase. It is clear that software maintenance may require almost all tools and techniques of software development life cycle. It is very important to understand the scope of desired change and do the analysis accordingly during software maintenance. Design during maintenance involves redesigning the product to incorporate the desired changes by users or clients. It is essential to update all internal documents, and whenever the changes take place in the code of the software system, new test cases must be designed and implemented. It is important to update the all supporting documents like software requirements specification, design specifications, test plan, user's manual, cross-reference directories and test suites to reflect the changes suggested by the user or client. Updated versions of the software and all related updated documents must be released to various users and clients. Configuration control and version control must be updated and maintained [1].

It is clear from above discussion that there is urgent need to identify and apply the maintainability factors to in initial phase of software design and development life cycle to increase the system availability and decrease overall development cost.

2 Software Development Activities Metric to Improve the Maintainability

Yang and Ward say that "Possibly the most important factor that affects maintainability is planning for maintainability" [2]. This means that maintainability has to be built inside a project during the development phase or it will be very difficult if not impossible to add afterwards. Therefore, estimation and improvements need to be done continuously starting from the beginning of the project.

There are number of activities in software development life cycle which may directly or indirectly affects the maintainability of application software.

The developers should identify the expected changes and prioritize theses changes as per their importance, so that their considerations can result in correct architecture design to accommodate the changes. The analysis phase of software development is concerned with determining customer requirements and constraints and establishing feasibility of the product [1]. From the maintenance viewpoint, the most important activities that occur during analysis are develop standards and guidelines, set milestones for the supporting documents, specify quality assurance procedures, identify likely product enhancements, determine resources required for maintenance and estimate maintenance costs [1].

Different types of standards and guidelines for design, coding and documentation can be developed to enhance the maintainability of software. Architectural design is concerned with developing the functional components, conceptual data structures and interconnections in a software system. The most important activity for enhancing maintainability during architectural design is to emphasize clarity, modularity and ease of modification as the primary design criteria [3].

Configuration management of software is probably the single most important management and maintainability concept [1].

Refactoring is a disciplined technique for restructuring an existing body of code, changing its internal structure without changing its external behaviour. Its heart is a series of small behaviour preserving transformations [4].

The complexity is another issue in maintainability. One issue affecting complexity is the coupling of modules. It has been proposed that the complexity of a component-based system could be computed with a coupling measurement. The complexity of a program depends upon its magnitude, its control structure and its data flows. Some of the factors, which may affect the complexity, are system stability, team stability, program age and changing requirement [4].

Software implementation activities should be aligned with the goal of producing software that is easy to understand, easy to modify and cost effective. Single-entry, single-exit coding constructs should be used, standard indentation of constructs should be observed, and a straightforward coding style should be adopted. Ease of maintenance is enhanced by use of symbolic constants to parameterize the software, by data encapsulation techniques and by adequate margins on resources such as table sizes and overflow tracks on disks [1].

Testing is part of maintainability. In the "IEEE Standards for a Software Quality Metrics Methodology", maintainability is defined as consisting of three factors: correctability, expandability and testability. Testability is defined by IEEE as "the effort required to test software" [5].

The personal interests of developers also affect software's maintainability. It is often schedule, budget or fear of breaking something that lead developers to write bad code [6].

The importance of software development activities to develop maintainable application software clearly signifies from the above deliberation in literature survey [7–12].

Researchers have chosen different software development activities in their research work, which are critical to develop maintainable application software. We summarize all these critical software development activities (SDA) metric in the form of SDA matrix, as shown in Table 1.

3 Analysis of SDA Metric

We have discussed the attributes of SDA metric and their subfactors with software developers and experts of software engineering from academics. We finally conclude the following about the SDA metric:

1. The early planning and analysis activities are part of requirement analysis phase of software life cycle development process.
2. Refactoring and design activities are part of design phase of software development.

Table 1 Development activities metric

Early planning	Analysis activities	Standards and guidelines	Design activities	Configuration management	Refactoring	Complexity	Implementation activities	Conceptual integrity
Expected changes	Standards and guidelines	Uniform conventions	Clarity and modularity	Maintenance guide	Refactoring opportunity and time	Program size (total statement)	Technical debt	Architectural design
Prioritization of changes	Set milestones	Naming conventions	Ease to enhancements	Develop a test suite	Refactoring techniques	Subprogram size (statement per module)	Clean code	Common conventions
Decomposition of functionalities	Quality assurance procedures	Coding standards, comments and style	Functions, structure and interconnection	Management of the SCM process	Preserving the behaviour	Branch density (per statement)	Normalized code	Uniform guidelines
	Expected enhancements	Defencing programming	Principles of information hiding	Software configuration identification	Consistency between refactoring code and other software artefacts	Decision density (per statement)	Dead code	Communication between team members
	Resources for the maintenance		Data abstraction and top-down hierarchical decomposition	Software configuration identification	Software development methodology	System stability (SS)	Dependencies	
	Estimated maintenance costs		Standardized notations for algorithms	Software configuration status accounting	Features of programming languages	Team stability (TS)	Patched code	

(continued)

Table 1 (continued)

Early planning	Analysis activities	Standards and guidelines	Design activities	Configuration management	Refactoring	Complexity	Implementation activities	Conceptual integrity
			Data Structures and procedure interface specifications	Software configuration auditing	Style of programming	Program age (PA)	Duplicated code	
			Specific effects and exception handling	Software release management and delivery		Requirement stability		
			Cross-reference directories					

3. It is clear from the deliberation of standard and guidelines and conceptual integrity that we can merge subfactors of these two into one. Finally, we consider refined version of standard and guidelines attribute only.
4. Software development methodologies depend on the type of software and the environment of development, so we can ignore this attribute.

The subfactors of SDA metric are analysed as follows:

1. Two subfactors of analysis activities, standard and guidelines and set milestone are part of standard and guidelines metric. The resource for the maintenance is already covered under estimation of maintenance cost.
2. The subfactors of design like clarity and modularity, ease to enhancement and function interconnection are similar so we can call them modularity and enhancement as one unit. The subfactor information hiding and specific effects and exception handling are part of programming style so we can remove them from design activities.
3. Refactoring opportunities and time, software development methodologies, features of programming languages and style of programming are standard parameters, which cannot be controlled during software development life cycle.
4. In case of complexity, program size and subprogram size are covered under the subfactors module size. The team stability is the part of human factor metric.

On the basis of above deliberations, we are proposing the optimized software development activities metrics to develop maintainable application software, as shown in Fig. 1.

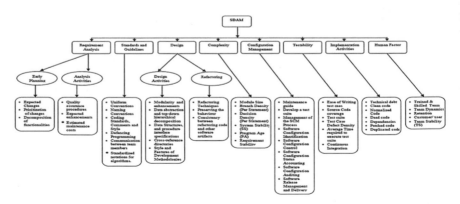

Fig. 1 Optimized SDA metric to developing maintainable application software

4 Conclusion

Maintainability is about the ease of change in software system as and when required.

Maintainability cannot be built into software after it has been implemented and delivered. The ease of maintenance has to be considered from the very beginning during the design and development of software. We are proposing the factors, which are critical to design and development of maintainable application software. These factors will help to increase system availability and decrease overall design, development and operating cost of application software.

References

1. Fairley, R.: Software maintenance. In: Software Engineering Concepts. Tata McGraw-Hill, pp. 311–329 (1997)
2. Yang, H., Ward, M.: Successful Evolution of Software Systems. Artech House Publishers (2003)
3. Software Design for Maintainability. http://engineer.jpl.nasa.gov/practices/dfe6.pdf
4. Washizaki, H., Nakagawa, T., Saito, Y., Fukazawa, Y.: A coupling based complexity metric for remote component based software systems toward maintainability estimation. In: Software Engineering Conference, APSEC 2006. 13th Asia Pacific, pp. 79–86 (Dec 2006)
5. IEEE Standard for a Software Quality Metrics Methodology. In: IEEE Std 1061–1992, vol., no., p 1 (1993). doi: 10.1109/IEEESTD.1993.115124.
6. Martin, R.: Clean Code: A Handbook of Agile Software Craftsmanship. Prentice Hall (2008)
7. Singh, R., Yadav, V.: Predicting design quality of object-oriented software using UML diagrams. In: 3rd IEEE International Advance Computing Conference (IACC), pp. 1662–1667 (2013)
8. Kleinschmager, S., Robbes, R., Stefik, A.: Do static type systems improve the maintainability of software systems? An empirical study. In: IEEE 20th International Conference on Software Engineering, 153–162 (June 2012)
9. Dubey, S.K., Rana, A., Dash, Y.: Maintainability prediction of object-oriented software system by multilayer perceptron model. ACM SIGSOFT Softw. Eng. Notes 1–4 (2012)
10. Ren, Y., Xing, T., Chen, X., Chai, X.: Research on software maintenance cost of influence factor analysis and estimation method. In: Intelligent Systems and Applications (ISA), 3rd International Workshop, pp. 1–4 (May 2011)
11. Sharma, A., Kumar, R., Grover, P.S.: Estimation of quality for software components: an empirical approach. ACM SIGSOFT Softw. Eng. Notes 33(6) (2008)
12. Grover, P.S., Kumar, R., Sharma, A.: Few useful considerations for maintaining software components and component-based systems. ACM SIGSOFT Softw. Eng. Notes 32(5), 1–5 (2007)

Label Count Algorithm for Web Crawler-Label Count

Laxmi Ahuja

Abstract Web crawler is a searching tool or a program that glance the World Wide Web in an automated style. Through GUI of the crawler, user can specify the URL and all the links related are retrieved and annexed to the crawl frontier, which is a tally to visit. The links are then checked and retrieved from the crawl frontier. The algorithms for crawling the Web are vital when it comes to select any page which meets the requirement of any user. The present paper analyzes the analysis on the Web crawler and its working. It proposes a new algorithm, named as label count algorithm by hybridization of existing algorithms. Algorithm labels the frequently visited site and selects the best searches depending on the highest occurrence of keywords present in a Web page.

Keywords Web crawler · Breadth-first search · Depth-first search
Page rank algorithm · Genetic algorithm

1 Introduction

There are about 1.7 billion of Web pagess [1, 2], the various search engines like Google, Yahoo, and Bing hinge on the crawlers to intensify, and lot of pages are maintained for the expeditious piercing. The data search is when performed, thousands of results are appeared. The users do not have the tenacity to brook each and every page. Therefore, to sort out the best result, the search engine has a bigger job to perform. Web crawler is needed to maintain the mirror site for all the well-liked Web sites. Many sites in a particular search engines use crawling to have up-to-date data and are mainly used to create a copy of all the visited Web pages which are frequently or often used for later processing [3]. This will provide the fast searches for a search engine to index the downloaded pages. The HTML code and the hyperlinks can be endorsed by the help of the crawler. Web crawlers are also

L. Ahuja (✉)
Amity Institute of Information Technology, Amity University, Noida, India
e-mail: lahuja@amity.edu

© Springer Nature Singapore Pte Ltd. 2019
M. N. Hoda et al. (eds.), *Software Engineering*, Advances in Intelligent Systems
and Computing 731, https://doi.org/10.1007/978-981-10-8848-3_50

known as automatic indexers [4]. The aptness for a computer to sweep documents of large volumes in anticipation of a supervised vocabulary, taxonomy, synonym, or ontology and use these terms to catalog large document cache more quickly and effectively is called automatic indexing [5]. As the documents' number rapidly enlarges with the built up of the Internet, the aptness to be maintained to find applicable information in a marine of no applicable information, the automatic indexing will grow useful. It is also useful for the data-driven programming which is also called the scraping of Web [5].

2 Preliminaries

The crawler persistently substantiates the loop for replication. This is done to evade the replicas which will take a levy on the coherence of the crawling process. Theoretical wise, this process of retrieving all the connection is continued till completely the links are reposed but practical wise, the crawler searches only the levels of depth of 5 and after this it concludes that no need to go further under a compulsion. The reason why it goes till depths of 5 is (a) 5 depths or levels are ample to assemble majority of information. (b) The safeguard to avoid 'spider traps'. Spider trap occurs when Web pages contain infinite loop within them [6]. Crawler is pin down in the page or can even wreck. It can be done intentional or unintentional. As the page bandwidth is eaten up, so it is intentionally done to trap the crawler. An ability of a crawler to circumvent spider traps is known as robustness. The first thing a crawler is supposed to do when it visits a Web site is to look for a 'robots.txt' file. The file contains instructions to which part of the Web site is to be indexed and which part is to be ignored. Using a robots.txt file is the only way to control what a crawler can see on your site [7, 8].

2.1 Crawling Strategy

There are various strategies which are being followed by the crawler:

- Politeness strategy: It defines that the overloading of the Web sites should be avoided.
- Selection strategy: This type of strategy defines that what pages should be downloaded. In arrangement with restricting the followed links, an HTTP HEAD request is made by the crawler to determine a MIME type's Web resource before a request to the entire resource is made with a GET request. URL is then examined with the crawler, and if the URL ends with .html, .htm, . asp, php, .jsp, etc., then only a resource is requested. To avoid the crawling more than once for the same resource, URL normalization is performed by the crawlers.

- Revisit strategy: This strategy states that for changes of the page when is to be checked. Often cost functions which are used: freshness and age.
- FRESHNESS: Freshness indicates that the local copy is accurate or not in terms of a binary measure [9].
- AGE: Age is measure in terms of how the local copy is outdated. The uniform policy necessitates revisiting all pages with the same frequency in the collection nevertheless of their change of rates. Whereas on the other hand proportional strategy necessitates revisiting the pages more often which changes more frequently, where the change in frequency is directly proportional to the frequency visited (estimated one).
- Parallelization strategy: It defines that coordination between the Web crawlers which are distributed is done.

2.2 Architecture

A crawler should have an optimized structure and a well strategy to crawl. They are a focal point for any engine of search, and the information related to these is kept secret [10, 11].

Figure 1 describes the general structure of the Web crawler, and the working details are given below:

- Fetch: To fetch the URL, it generally uses the http protocol.
- Duplicate URL Eliminates: In this, the URL is checked for duplicate or redundant data which is to be eliminated.
- URL Frontier: It contains the URLs which are to be yield in the current crawl. Firstly, in URL Frontier a set of seed is stored and from that set of seed crawler is arise.
- Parse: Texts, videos, images, etc., are obtained while parsing the page.

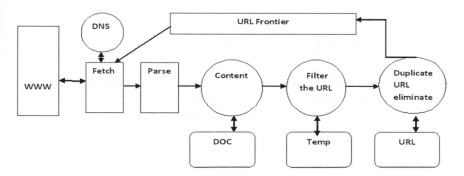

Fig. 1 General architecture of a crawler

- DNS: It looks up an IP address for domain names. It is a domain name service resolution.
- URL Filter: It filters the URL deciding that the extracted URL from the frontier (robots.txt) should be excluded or the URL would be normalized, i.e., relative encoding.
- Content: It tests whether a Web page having the same content has already been perceived at another URL or not, and develops a method to quantify the impression of a Web page.

3 Schemes for Web Crawling

The crawling algorithm regulates the applicable and sanctions from a consigned origin of powerful accurate information form of elements such as keyword location and frequency [12]. And not all information constitutes is useful as some hostile user, attempting to allure extra traffic into their site by lodging the frequently used keywords. Thus, this becomes the challenge for the Web crawler, the capacity to download huge relevant and robustness number of pages.

3.1 Genetic Algorithm

This is the best type of algorithm which is useful when the user does not have time or have less time to search a huge database. It also performs efficient results in case of multimedia. In a confined still point, the risk of becoming trapped is reduced [13]. It always operates on a whole population. Solution is taken from the population which in turn will be used for the new population. This algorithm also produces result to search and optimization issues. It starts with result set known as population. There is a hope that new population will be better than the old population.

3.2 Breadth-First Search Algorithm

This type of algorithm starts the search from the main node which is the root node and then proceeds to the other child nodes [13–15]. But it goes level by level. If the node is found, i.e., the data which is to be searched is found then it will be denoted as victory but in case not it continues with the search by performing in the next level unless the final goal is met. And if all the nodes are traversed and no data is found, then it is termed as aborted.

3.3 Page Rank Algorithm

On counting back links for a given page, the importance of Web pages is determined. It does not determine the page rank of the whole Web site but is individually determined for each page [13–15].

3.4 Depth-First Search Algorithm

In depth-first search algorithm, the traversing is done. The searching is always started from the main node which is the root node and then follows with the other child nodes. If the child nodes are found more than two, then the priority is in favor of the child node which is at the left side. It is then cross profound unless there is not a single child is left. It goes back to the node which is not visited and continues in a same manner. It always makes sure that at least once all the nodes are visited. There is a chance of an infinite loop if the branches are too large (Table 1).

Label count Searching Algorithm

This particular algorithm will search the keyword depending on the two possible criteria [16]. Firstly, it will label all the Web sites or Web pages which are being frequently visited which in turn will depend on the highest number of hit counters, let us say the number of hits above 40% will be considered [17, 18]. If it fulfills the above-mentioned criteria, we move on to the next step of the level search. A level-by-level search is performed on the selected (labeled) pages and on basis of the pages having the highest occurrence of the keyword will be added to the crawl frontier [19]. And through the crawl frontier, user can have a check on the links. And on the basis of his requirement, he can visit the Web pages.

Pseudocode

1. Start
2. Procedure LCS (graph, source)
3. Create a queue Q
4. Let there are 4 Web pages A, B, C, D
5. If the hit.counter ()>=40% and out of 4 Web pages 3 falls under the criteria. Then labels are appended to the pages.
6. A<-label.1
7. B<-label.2
8. D<-label.3
9. If the keyword.occurence () > 6. Then
10. Enqueue source onto Q
11. End

Figure 2 describes the percentage of the sites visited frequently.

Table 1 Comparative study on various Web crawling algorithms

Criteria	BFS	DFS	Page Rank	Genetic
Concept	It is a cautious search where you uniformly advance in each and every feasible way, if the objective is somewhere out there we may find it	It is a more hostile and chance-taking search where we select only one path and all the other paths are ignored until the end of the selected path is reached	It is considerable direction applying communal intelligence to regulate the significance of a Web page	It is a heuristic search which emulates the selecting the natural process
Memory	It will use a lot of memory but will find the first best search	If search graph is shallow then low memory	Efficient usage of memory takes place	Efficient usage of memory takes place
Robustness	Robust	Less robust	Robust	More robust
Time	Takes time	Takes really long time	Less time	Less time
Solution	Always shallowest solution	May not find the shallowest solution. If the graph has infinite depth, then it fails to decide	We can use only single-precision or double-precision value for source and destination arrays. The use of single-precision rank vector will not lead to numerical error	It gives solution to search and optimization issues. They do not break easily even if the inputs changed slightly
Time complexity	$O(|V| + |E|)$	$O(|E|)$	$O(n * m)$	$O(gens * n * m)$
Space complexity	$O(|V|^2)$	$O(|V|)$	$O(n * m)$	$O(gens * n * m)$

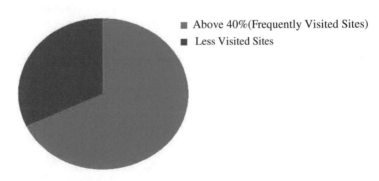

■ Above 40%(Frequently Visited Sites)
■ Less Visited Sites

Fig. 2 Percentage of visited sites

4 Conclusion and Future Work

The exponential growth of Web is raising many challenges for the Web crawler. The main intent of this paper was to shed light on the Web crawler and its working. It also considered the best suitable algorithms which are used for the Web crawling and made a comparative study on these algorithms depending on their advantages and disadvantages. We created a new algorithm which can be useful for future development of a Web crawler. As the amount of available data continues to grow, Web crawling algorithms will become an increasingly improvement area of research. The label count searching algorithm we created will provide a relevant data from the authorized Web sites in a timely manner.

References

1. http://en.wikipedia.org/wiki/Breadth-first_search
2. Russel, S., Norvigin, P.: The Artificial Intelligence: A Modern Approach (2003)
3. Kurant, M., Markopoulou, A., Thiran, P.: The International Teletraffic Congress (ITC 22) (2010)
4. Abiteboul, S., Preda, M., Cobena, G.: An adaptive on-line page importance computation. In: The Proceedings of the 12th International Conference on the World Wide Web, pp. 280–290. ACM Press (2003)
5. Najork, M., Wiener, J.L.: Breadth-first search crawling leads to high-quality pages. In: Proceedings of the 10th International Conference on World Wide Web (2001)
6. McCallum, A., Nigam, K., Rennie, J., Seymore, K.: An approach for machine learning to build domain-specific search engines. In: Proceedings of the 16th International Joint Conference on Artificial Intelligence. Morgan Kaufmann, San Francisco, CA, 662–667 (1999)
7. Beamer, S., Asanović, K., Patterson, D.: Direction optimizing breadth-first search algorithm in the international conference. In: Networking (SC '12), Article No. 12 (2012)
8. Page, L., Brin, S., Motwani, R., Winograd, T.: The PageRank citation ranking algorithm which Brought order to the web. A Technical Report by Stanford University (1998)
9. Internet Archive, from the http://archive.org/
10. Internet Archive, Heritrix home page, from http://crawler.archive.org/
11. Brin, S., Page, L.: The anatomy of a large-scale hypertextual web search engine. In: Seventh World Wide Web Conference International Proceedings (1998)
12. Qin, Y., Xu, D.: A Balanced rank algorithm based on the PageRank and the Page Belief recommendation (2010)
13. Coppin, B.: An Artificial Intelligence, p. 77. Jones and the Barlett Publishers (2004)
14. de kunder, M.: The size of world wide web. Retrieved from http://www.worldwidewebsize.com/8/8/11
15. Signorini, A.: A survey of the ranking algorithms. Retrieved from http://www.divms.uiowa.edu/~asignori/phd/report/asurvey-of-ranking-algorithms.pdf, 29/9/2011
16. www.wikipedia.org/wiki/Automatic_indexing
17. Boldi, P., Codenotti, B., Santini, M., Vigna, S.: UbiCrawler: a fully distributed scalable web crawler. Softw Pract. Exp. 34(8), 711–726 (2004)
18. Papapetrou, O., Samaras, G.: A distributed location aware web crawling. In: Proceedings of the 13th International World Wide Web Conference on Alternate Track Papers & Posters. ACM, New York (2004)
19. Wolf, J.L., Squillante, M.S., Yu, P.S., Sethuraman, J., Ozsen, L.: The optimal crawling strategies for web search engines. In: Proceedings of the 11th International Conference on World Wide Web, pp. 136–147. ACM, New York USA (2002)

Vulnerability Discovery in Open- and Closed-Source Software: A New Paradigm

Ruchi Sharma and R. K. Singh

Abstract For assisting the developers in process of software development, vulnerability discovery models were developed by researchers which helped in discovering the vulnerabilities with time. These models facilitate the developers in patch management while providing assistance in optimal resource allocation and assessing associated security risks. Among the existing models for vulnerability discovery, Alhazmi–Malaiya logistic model is considered the best-fitted model on all kinds of datasets owing to its ability to capture s-shaped nature of the curves. But, it has the limitation of dependence on shape of dataset. We have proposed a new model that is shape-independent accounting for better goodness of fit as compared to the earlier VDM. The proposed model and Alhazmi–Malaiya logistic model for vulnerability discovery has been evaluated on three real-life datasets each for open- and closed- source software, and the results are presented toward the end of the paper.

Keywords Vulnerability discovery · Open source · Closed source
Gamma · Alhazmi–Malaiya logistic model

1 Introduction

The high-order connectivity of computing systems has raised the concerns for already existing software security. These concerns marked the outset of quantitative modeling of the process of vulnerability discovery. Vulnerability discovery models assist the developers in patch management, optimal resource allocation and assessment of associated security risks. In this paper, we have proposed a new

R. Sharma · R. K. Singh (✉)
Department of Information Technology, Indira Gandhi Delhi Technical University
for Women, Delhi, India
e-mail: rksingh988@gmail.com

R. Sharma
e-mail: rs.sharma184@gmail.com

© Springer Nature Singapore Pte Ltd. 2019
M. N. Hoda et al. (eds.), *Software Engineering*, Advances in Intelligent Systems
and Computing 731, https://doi.org/10.1007/978-981-10-8848-3_51

VDM to find the number of vulnerabilities and their distribution with time in a software system by using analytical modeling techniques while enumerating the difference in vulnerability detection patterns for open- and closed-source software. The vulnerability detection rate in open- and closed-source software shows some significant differences owing to the differences in strategies followed during their development and testing [1–3]. In the literature, work on quantitative characterization of vulnerabilities has been done based on two approaches. Some researchers used distribution functions to model the vulnerability discovery process while others used functions [4]. Distribution function approach proceeds with a presumption that the trend of vulnerability discovery will follow a specific shape like exponential, logarithmic or linear [5–7]. The best-fitted model proposed by Alhazmi and Malaiya uses a logistic function which follows an S-shaped curve [8]. The first vulnerability discovery model was proposed by Ross Anderson and is known as Anderson Thermodynamic (AT) model [5, 9]. AT model for cumulative number of vulnerabilities with time by function $N(t)$. [5, 10]

$$N(t) = \frac{k}{\gamma t} \ln(ct) \tag{1}$$

where C is the constant of integration. This VDM is not defined at $t = 0$. Also, some of the values obtained initially were negative which is not viable. Another model termed as AML model was proposed by Alhazmi and Malaiya. It states that in the initial phases of a software's operational phase, the cumulative number of vulnerabilities follows an upward trend as the system attracts more users followed by a linear curve which later declines due to reduced number of remaining vulnerabilities and decreasing attention [8, 10]. Cumulative number of vulnerabilities is given by:

$$N(t) = \frac{a}{ace^{-abt} + 1} \tag{2}$$

where $N(t)$ is the total number of vulnerabilities in the system at time t. a is the total number of vulnerabilities in the system, b and c are the regression coefficients. The well-established models in software reliability growth modeling say that at $t = 0$, the number of bugs discovered should be equal to zero [11]. But, according to this model, there are $\frac{a}{ac+1}$ number of vulnerabilities discovered at $t = 0$. Further, following the concept of AML, vulnerability discovery process follows a sigmoid shape which is always not the case. Two VDM, namely quadratic model and exponential model, were proposed by Rescorla. They used function distribution and proceeded with a pre-assumed shape of the vulnerability discovery curve [6]. Rescorla quadratic model proposed that the cumulative number of vulnerabilities follows a quadratic relationship with time and can be obtained by the following equation:

$$N(t) = \frac{Bt^2}{2} + kt \tag{3}$$

where k and B are coefficients of regression. B is the curve slope and k is a constant obtained with the datasets used. Rescorla proposed another model based on Goel–Okumoto SRGM [12]. This exponential model can be given as follows:

$$N(t) = a(1 - e^{-\lambda t}) \tag{4}$$

where "a" and λ denotes the total vulnerabilities and rate constant, respectively. Some other models present in the literature include the logarithmic Poisson model by Musa and Okumoto [7]. This model was developed as a software reliability growth model and later applied to discover vulnerability trends in the software.

$$N(t) = k \ln(1 + bt) \tag{5}$$

where k and b are regression coefficients. Alhazmi et al. also worked on vulnerability discovery in multiple upgradations of software [13]. They also used Weibull distribution in their VDM in [4]. But, the existing models for vulnerability discovery do not capture all kinds of data shapes efficiently due to which they cannot be used for a variety of datasets.

2 Proposed Approach

The approach used in this work follows from non-homogenous Poisson process (NHPP)-based software reliability growth models [11]. NHPP-based models have following assumptions [11].

(i) The vulnerability detection/fixation is modeled by NHPP.
(ii) Software system may suffer failure during execution due to remaining vulnerabilities in the system.
(iii) All the vulnerabilities remaining in the software equally influence the rate of failure of the software.
(iv) The no. of vulnerabilities found at any time instant is in direct proportion to the no. of vulnerabilities remaining.
(v) When a failure is encountered, vulnerability causing the failure is detected and removed with certainty.
(vi) From detection and correction point of view, all vulnerabilities are mutually independent.

The various functions/distribution functions used in existing models for the process of vulnerability discovery are dependent on the shape of dataset used, and therefore, decision makers are required to select the model after analyzing the dataset of software under consideration. To eliminate this limitation, we have used gamma distribution function in our proposed VDM which is a shape-independent distribution and fits all kind of datasets with a better goodness of fit. The gamma distribution is a two-parameter continuous probability distribution. It can be convex or concave both upward and downward facing depending on the value of its scale and shape parameters. Due to these properties, it fits a wider range of datasets as compared to fixed shape models. The failure density function for gamma distribution is given as follows:

$$f(t) = \frac{1}{\Gamma(\alpha)\beta} \left(\frac{t}{\beta}\right)^{\alpha-1} e^{-\left(\frac{t}{\beta}\right)}; \qquad t \geq 0, \qquad \alpha, \beta > 0 \tag{6}$$

where α, β denote the shape and scale parameters, respectively. α controls the shape of distribution. When $\alpha < 1$, the gamma distribution is exponentially shaped and asymptotic to both the horizontal and vertical axes. While stretching or compressing, the range of distribution is governed by the scale parameter β. When β is taken as an integer value, the distribution represents the sum of β exponentially distributed random variables that are independent of each other and each variable has a mean of α (which is equivalent to a rate parameter of α^{-1}). For $\alpha = 1$, gamma distribution is the same as the exponential distribution of scale parameter β. When α is greater than one, the gamma distribution assumes a unimodal and skewed shape. As the value of α increases, the skewness of curve decreases.

Gamma distribution is used to describe the distribution until the nth occurrence of an event in a Poisson process [11]. We have used the cumulative distribution function for gamma to perform vulnerability prediction in this study which is given by

$$cdf(\text{Gamma}) = F(t; \alpha, \beta) = \int_0^t f(u; \alpha, \beta)du = \frac{\gamma(\alpha, \beta t)}{\Gamma(\alpha)} \tag{7}$$

$$\text{So, } N(t) = a * F(t, \alpha, \beta) \tag{8}$$

where "a" is the total number of vulnerabilities in the software and $N(t)$ is the number of vulnerabilities at a time instant "t". When "t" tends to ∞, $N(t)$ tends to α. Equation (7) gives the cumulative distribution function of gamma distribution, and Eq. (8) gives the final model for vulnerability discovery which is referred as gamma vulnerability discovery model (GVDM). Equation (8) is applied on various datasets from closed and open-source software to find out the values of parameters a, α and β. The parameters used in the proposed and existing VDM are estimated by applying nonlinear regression technique using Statistical Package for the Social Sciences (SPSS).

3 Parameter Estimations

Vulnerability discovery models are estimated on six datasets using Statistical Package for Social Sciences (SPSS). The datasets used in this study are collected from National Vulnerability Database [14]. The closed-source software datasets used in this study includes: Zonealarm (C1), Google Chrome (C2), and Windows 7 (C3). O1 and C1 are antivirus datasets, O2 and C2 are browser datasets, and O3 and C3 denote the datasets for operating system. Table 1 presents the estimated value of parameters in AML and GVDM.

4 Prediction Capabilities of Models

The prediction capabilities of models described above are evaluated based on bias, variance, root mean square prediction error (RMSPE), mean square error (MSE), and coefficient of multiple determination (R^2). The results for comparison based on the criteria described above are tabulated in Table 2.

For various studies in the literature, goodness of fit for vulnerability discovery models has been evaluated using chi-square test and Akaike information criteria (AIC) [8, 10, 15]. In these studies, the AML model showed best results for all the systems. We applied AML model and GVDM to datasets described in the previous sections and observed the following results:

- The proposed model, GVDM, gave better results for datasets of open-source community as observed from Table 2.
- AML model performed well for the datasets belonging to closed-source community of software as seen from Tables 2 [16–18].

Table 1 Parameter estimates for Alhazmi–Malaiya logistic model (AML) and gamma vulnerability discovery model (GVDM)

Datasets	Models					
	AML			GVDM		
	Parameters					
	a	b	c	a	α	β
(O1)	72.087	0.015	1.244	77.685	5.686	1.251
(O2)	1324.3	0	0.028	2130.142	2.555	0.189
(O3)	346.553	0.001	0.028	1047.686	1.086	0.025
(C1)	32.764	0.014	0.517	134.309	1.388	0.047
(C2)	1072	0.001	0.106	1122.852	6.745	1.455
(C3)	388.873	0.002	0.069	423.276	3.134	0.798

Table 2 Results for comparison criteria

Parameters	VDM	AML	GVDM	VDM	AML	GVDM	VDM	AML	GVDM
Bias	O1	0.175	−0.15	O2	4.507	0.42	O3	1.695	0.959
	C1	0.015	−0.11	C2	5.592	0.045	C3	1.4872	0.075
Variance	O1	1.635	1.689	O2	30.74	23.41	O3	28.99	24.27
	C1	0.722	0.877	C2	23.6	5.327	C3	16.1	12.9
RMSPE	O1	1.644	1.696	O2	31.066	23.415	O3	29.05	24.29
	C1	0.722	0.884	C2	24.253	5.327	C3	16.111	12.91
MSE	O1	6.156	7.012	O2	899.11	509.16	O3	783.69	547.8
	C1	0.447	0.672	C2	518.62	24.837	C3	222.81	142.88
R^2	O1	0.991	0.989	O2	0.994	0.997	O3	0.892	0.924
	C1	0.987	0.981	C2	0.997	1	C3	0.987	0.992

5 Conclusion

This work presented a new vulnerability discovery model based on gamma distribution. The AML model and the proposed GVDM were evaluated for their prediction capabilities based on five different comparison criteria. The results obtained are presented in Table 2 that show the gamma vulnerability discovery model (GVDM) is best suited for open-source software and AML model is best suited for closed-source software. The parallel and evolutionary development of open source is captured effectively by GVDM, whereas a relatively planned approach of closed source development follows the logistic behavior as suggested by AML. Closed-source software goes through planned phases, and therefore in the initial phases, the cumulative number of vulnerabilities follows an upward trend as the system attracts more users after which it follows a linear curve. Later, the rate of vulnerability discovery declines owing to decreased number of remaining vulnerabilities and decreasing attention. Therefore, the logistic function of AML model captures this data effectively, whereas for open-source software, the development is generally parallel or evolutionary and follows no specific trend and therefore the GVDM captures vulnerabilities among the open datasets efficiently.

References

1. Llanos, J.W.C., Castillo, S.T.A.: Differences between traditional and open source development activities. In: Product-Focused Software Process Improvement, pp. 131–144. Springer, Berlin (2012)
2. De Groot, A., et al.: Call for quality: open source software quality observation. In: Open Source Systems, pp. 57–62. Springer, US (2006)
3. Potdar, V., Chang, E.: Open source and closed source software development methodologies. In: 26th International Conference on Software Engineering, pp. 105–109 (2004)

4. Joh, H.C., Kim, J., Malaiya, Y.K.: Vulnerability discovery modeling using Weibull distribution. In: 19th International Symposium on Software Reliability Engineering. https://doi.org/10.1109/issre.2008.32

5. Anderson, R.J.: Security in opens versus closed systems—the dance of Boltzmann, Coase and Moore. In: Open Source Software: Economics, Law and Policy, Toulouse, France, 20–21 June 2002

6. Rescola, E.: Is finding security holes a good idea? IEEE Secur. Priv. 3(1), 14–19 (2005)

7. Musa, J.D., Okumoto, K.: A Logarithmic Poisson Execution Time Model for Software Reliability Measurement. 0270-5257/84/0000/0230/ IEEE (1984)

8. Alhazmi, O.H., Malaiya, Y.K.: Quantitative vulnerability assessment of systems software. In: Proceedings of Annual Reliability and Maintainability Symposium, pp. 615–620, Jan 2005

9. Brady, R.M., Anderson, R.J., Ball, R.C.: Murphy's Law, the Fitness of Evolving Species, and the Limits of Software Reliability. Cambridge University Computer Laboratory Technical Report No. 471 (September 1999)

10. Alhazmi, O.H., Malaiya, Y.K.: Modeling the vulnerability discovery process. In: Proceedings of 16th IEEE International Symposium on Software Reliability Engineering (ISSRE'05), pp. 129–138 (2005)

11. Kapur, P.K., Pham, H., Gupta, A., Jha, P.C.: Software Reliability Assessment with OR Applications. Springer, UK (2011)

12. Goel, A.L., Okumoto, K.: Time-dependent error detection rate model for software and other performance measures. IEEE Trans. Reliab. 28(3), 206–211 (1979)

13. Kim, J., Malaiya, Y.K., Ray, I.: Vulnerability discovery in multi-version software systems. In: 10th IEEE High Assurance Systems Engineering Symposium (2007)

14. https://nvd.nist.gov/, 10 Mar 2015

15. Alhazmi, O.H., Malaiya, Y.K.: Application of vulnerability discovery models to major operating systems. IEEE Trans. Reliab. 57(1), 14–22 (2008)

16. Browne, H.K., Arbaugh, W.A., McHugh, J., Fithen, W.L.: A trend analysis of exploitations. University of Maryland and CMU Technical Reports (2000)

17. Schneier, B.: Full disclosure and the window of vulnerability. Crypto-Gram, 15 Sept 2000. www.counterpane.com/cryptogram-0009.html#1

18. Pham, H.: A software reliability model with vtub-shaped fault detection rate subject to operating environments. In: Proceeding of the 19th ISSAT International Conference on Reliability and Quality in Design, Hawaii (2013)

Complexity Assessment for Autonomic Systems by Using Neuro-Fuzzy Approach

Pooja Dehraj and Arun Sharma

Abstract IT companies want to reach the highest level in the development of best product within a balance cost. But with this development, systems and network complexity are increasing thus leading toward unmanageable systems. Therefore, there is a strong need for the development of self-managed systems which will manage its internal activities without or with minimum human intervention. This type of systems is called as autonomic systems and is enabled with self-abilities. However, there are both the sides of the autonomic systems. Due to the implementation of autonomic capabilities in the system, overall complexity is also increased. In the present paper, authors extended their approach by using the neuro-fuzzy-based technique to predict the complexity of systems with autonomic features. Results obtained are comparatively better than previous work where authors applied fuzzy logic-based approach to predict the same. The proposed work may be used to assess the maintenance level required for autonomic systems, as higher complexity index due to autonomic features will lead toward low maintenance cost.

Keywords Modified maintenance assessment model (MAM) · Computation index
Fuzzy logic · Neuro-fuzzy

1 Introduction

Today, it is the world of demand where IT companies want to reach the highest level in the development of best product within a balance cost. Computation Science is the branch which develop mathematical model based on the analysis techniques for computer to solve problems. But with the increase in the code

P. Dehraj (✉) · A. Sharma
Department of Information Technology, Indira Gandhi Delhi Technical
University for Women, Delhi, India
e-mail: poojadehraj2000@gmail.com

A. Sharma
e-mail: arunsharma2303@gmail.com

© Springer Nature Singapore Pte Ltd. 2019
M. N. Hoda et al. (eds.), *Software Engineering*, Advances in Intelligent Systems
and Computing 731, https://doi.org/10.1007/978-981-10-8848-3_52

complexity, maintenance is also increasing. To provide solutions back to the managed system in real-time need continuous monitoring by expertise which has thorough knowledge of all kinds of system errors and security failures. But this is the worst case scenario. Practically, this is not possible all the time so there is need to develop intelligent system that itself handles its internal activities like configuration, optimization of system's resources, securing system from the attacks. In 2001, IBM [1] proposed this idea in the Harvard University and relates this concept with human body. Like our body handles its internal temperature, heals minor injuries and take intelligent actions when it identifies some malfunctions within the body. Similarly, the systems can also be designed with all such kind of abilities require for computation purpose so that they handle system's activities at some level which in result reduces maintenance of overall autonomic systems. Some IT-based companies have worked on this idea and developed some autonomic applications [2, 3]. Also, there are few systems that support some level of auto-nomicity [4]. But how the maintenance level of autonomic system is evaluated?

In this paper, maintenance assessment of self-features enabled system is eval-uated using Neuro-Fuzzy Technique (NFT) [5]. This is an attempt to improve the results which were evaluated using fuzzy approach on the previously proposed Maintenance Assessment Model (MAM). In our previous paper, the evaluation was done on the small dataset values due to unavailability of the autonomic applica-tion's data. Neuro-fuzzy is the combination of neural network and fuzzy system. It uses a learning algorithm for training the dataset so that results will come out to be more accurate and interpretable [6]. The paper is divided into few sections. The introduction of autonomic computing technique is explained in the second section followed with brief detail of autonomic systems. In the third section, literature review is mentioned. The modified maintenance assessment model with the implementation part is continued in the fourth section. In the fifth section, con-clusion and future work are mentioned.

2 Autonomic Computing-Enabled Systems

Autonomic computing is the computation technique that shifts the management activity of the system to the system [7]. The work of administrator is to design high-level terms and policies on which system works. This concept is there in the hardware part of the computation network but not in the software or application. To make system's software intelligent to handle its activities, there is need to enable the system with some autonomic functionality like self-adjusted, self-optimized, self-protected, self-healed, self-awareness, self-configured. IBM categories all features into four major attributes that an autonomic system requires. Figure 1 shows four major attributes of the autonomic system. The attributes are abbreviated as CHOP.

Fig. 1 Features of autonomic system (AS) [7]

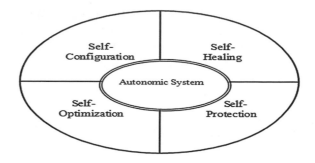

The working of these attributes performs a management task using MAPE-K loop which was designed by IBM [8]. That architecture is considered as reference architecture of the autonomic system. That architecture is explained below.

2.1 Architecture of Autonomic System

The architecture of autonomic system is based on policies and rules provided with some repository database; e.g., if there is need to increase a system's resource utilization, then an autonomic system must be aware of all its resources, resource specification, and their connectivity with different systems. On the basis of this knowledge, system will analyze and then plan for the execution of the response onto the managed element for the optimization of its resources. Similarly, healing, protection, and configuration can also be performed using a generalized MAPE-K loop that work for all kind of system's activities. For this purpose, IBM defined few policies. The conclusion of those policies and rules is [9]:

"System must be aware of its environmental activities and capable of handling the problems using some defined solution provided as the knowledge database". Figure 2 presents the MAPE-K loop which works as a self-control loop during the process.

Autonomic system consists of autonomic agent or manager and managed element. In MAPE-K loop, M performs monitoring of the system's activities. If agent identifies any unwanted activity in the managed element, then A will do analysis of that unwanted activity using *K* which is a knowledge data. Knowledge data

Fig. 2 Architecture of AS [8]

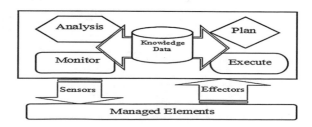

is a kind of repository of the solutions that is structured or designed on basis of previous problems of same kind. After that, P does the overall planning for execution of the solution back to the managed entity using effectors [8]. The gathering of information and execution of solutions is done by the sensors and effectors, respectively.

3 Literature Review

The development of computer systems started in 1939 called first generation computers [10]. These computers are extremely large in size and with the development, and the size of the computers was reduced and management also became easy. Initially, the connectivity was done by wired and then wireless networks came into existence. With this fast development in computer-based communication world, systems become more complex and their management also. Now, the developers wanted to design applications that can handle basic level of configuration, optimization of system's resources, and security using user's intervention. But it was found that, the complexity has reached at an extent where it was not possible to provide management methods in real time. So, the need of designing autonomic system became an emerging task for the developers of IT industries. This term was coined by IBM in 2001 [1] but Kephert [7] provided a detailed description of autonomic system's attributes. These attributes are based on the management process of the system. Many IT companies tried to approach this concept in their computer network [3]. IBM also highlighted high-level policies for such systems provided with reference architecture for autonomic system [9]. The basic attributes of autonomic system and its architecture have already been introduced. Table 1 [4] shows some autonomic applications with the autonomic capabilities which are implemented on them.

These are the few applications developed by IBM, HP, and by some universities [11]. No application out of six has all the features incorporated in them. A. Sharma et al. [12] proposed generic approach for the SDLC of the autonomic system. According to them, the autonomic system required different approach because

Table 1 Autonomic application

Properties	Application					
	SMART	Optimal grid	Auto Admin	ROC	Autonomia	Software rejuvenation
Self-configuration	✓	✓	–	–	✓	–
Self-healing	–	–	–	✓	✓	✓
Self-optimization	✓	✓	✓	–	✓	–
Self-protection	–	–	–	✓	✓	✓
Self-awareness	✓	–	–	✓	–	✓
Anticipatory	✓	✓	–	–	–	–

requirements of autonomic applications differ based on its domain specification. Chauhan et al. [13] further extended the development of autonomic systems and found that Agile Modeling Approach (AMA) will be best suited to the autonomic system. To provide standardization to the autonomic approach, few authors have described the attributes affecting its quality and fewer have attempted to assess it. Quality here does not mean conventional quality measures; it means the factors determine how much autonomic any system is. Nami and Sharifi [14] worked to find the relationship between autonomic attributes and factors which effect system's quality in case of autonomic system.

The maintenance of such systems will definitely be low but not 0%. In our previous work, a Maintenance Assessment Model (MAM) has been proposed and complexity phase of that model was evaluated using fuzzy logic approach [8]. In that work, the author first identified maintenance-based factors considering functionality of an autonomic system and then selects only those factors which have direct relationship with the CHOP and maintenance [15]. The factors are listed below:

1. Complexity
2. Reusability
3. Performance
4. Security

After this, minor factors under each factor are identified based on software engineering concepts and autonomic computing technique. One phase of that model has been implemented using fuzzy logic [16, 17]. They used the dataset values of some autonomic applications which are not completely autonomic. Figure 3 is the one phase of MAM. The fuzzy inferences rules were designed and minor factors under complexity were taken as input variables which gave overall application's complexity as output [8]. The actual value of complexity is compared with experimental values and it was found that complexity of the autonomic applications falls under low category with 21% error. The interpretation of the result shows that fully autonomic applications have not been developed yet.

Fig. 3 Complexity phase of MAM

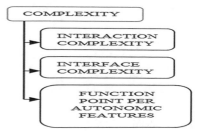

4 Proposed Model

Autonomic concept not remains a hypothetical concept but it still required the development to reach fully autonomic communication system. The implementation of fully autonomic system needs to approach different domain-specific requirements because this concept will reduce the management complexity of any IT area. However, such systems can never be considered as maintenance free. Their development and deployment still require some maintenance. Maintenance of such system will definitely be low after developing self-managed systems. To identify their level of maintenance, some factors which have direct dependency with the CHOP are taken into consideration. During our further study, the author analyzed that there are other factors which follow the properties of autonomic computing. To design more generalized form of MAM, some changes have been done that are shown in the paper. For this purpose, the three conditions are taken before modifying MAM. These conditions are:

- There should exist bidirectional dependency between CHOP level and major factors.
- The major factors should incorporate autonomicity concept.
- The factors should be affected if there is a change after recovery-oriented measurements (Fig. 4).

This model is now modified and complexity is replaced with computation index because complexity is not considered as a better term for autonomic system. Computation index will be more relevant attribute that fulfills autonomicity concept and also the system's adaptability can be considered as a part of availability; i.e., if complete system is available for different platform or domain for use, then it is also adaptable to those respective domain specifications. So, availability term is more relevant in autonomic system context.

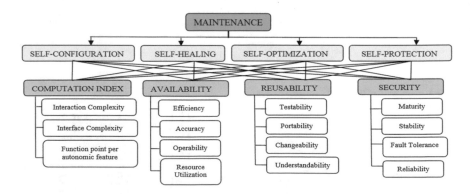

Fig. 4 Modified MAM [8]

4.1 Implementation of the Proposed Approach

There are other soft computing techniques also like neural network, neuro-fuzzy, genetic algorithm. The previous paper limitations have been overcome in the present paper by using hybrid neuro-fuzzy approach which gives the better result than fuzzy. Neuro-fuzzy technique is the combination of fuzzy and derived algorithm of neural network. The result of the neuro-fuzzy is the hybrid intelligent system, combination of fuzzy system which is capable of doing human-like reasoning and the learning algorithm derived from neural network. For using fuzzy logic, neuro-fuzzy is applied on two contradictory attributes: accuracy and interpretability. Linguistic fuzzy modeling and precise fuzzy modeling are used for interpretability and accuracy, respectively. Neuro-fuzzy system includes parameter's adaptation recursively, dynamic evolution and components pruning for handling system behaviors and to keep system updates.

Kumari and Sunita [18] performed a survey analysis of few soft computing techniques and concluded that neuro-fuzzy is better among all in case of diagnosis. This approach is better because it works on data which is trained by the neural network-based learning algorithm. But preparation of trained data will only be done on local information and performs modifications only on that available data. Neural network can be viewed as three-layer procedure. First layer is the input variables; fuzzy rules work as second layer in the structure, and third layer is the output. Neuro-fuzzy involves feedback and then forwards the response again to the system.

4.2 Empirical Evaluation

The training data and testing data files are created and simulated by using same fuzzy rules that were designed in previous work [8]. For neuro-fuzzy, Sugeno style is used for simulation. The experiment is performed for the same autonomic

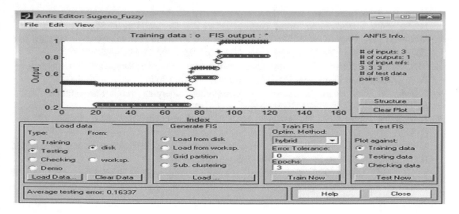

Fig. 5 Simulation results of the proposed approach

applications as in [8]. The results were compared with the previous work [8]. The root mean square value is improved from 21% to 16% in case of neuro-fuzzy-based approach. The screen shot given here shows the experimentation of the proposed approach (Fig. 5).

5 Conclusion and Future Work

Autonomic system's maintenance activities are found to be different from the non-autonomic system because an autonomic system is capable of doing many activities automatically which requires human intervention in case of non-autonomic system and also complexity of autonomic system is due to the implementation of self-features. In our empirical study, we have found that the computation index value of autonomic application lies in low range which may require high level of maintenance. The previous work limitation is overcome by using neuro-fuzzy approach and result has been verified with the experimental values, which is calculated based on fuzzy inferences rules designed using dataset values. All self-features have not been implemented in those applications. So, the computation index is still low. As computation index increases with the implementation of autonomic features, it means the application's dataset values which are used for experiment are not fully autonomic. Secondly, in MAM, the overall maintenance is determined from the evaluation of CARS factors. So after determining CARS impact then only correct level of maintenance which an autonomic application still requires will be evaluated. Future work includes estimating the remaining part of the MAM model based on some more dataset information and study.

References

1. Horn, P.: Autonomic computing: IBM's perspective on the state of information technology. In: Technical Report, International Business Machines Corporation (IBM), USA (2001)
2. McCann, J.A., Huebscher, M.C.: Evaluation issues in autonomic computing. In: Grid and Cooperative Computing Workshops, pp. 597–608. Springer, Berlin (2004)
3. Parashar, M., Hariri, S.: Autonomic computing: an overview. In: Unconventional Programming Paradigms, pp. 257–269. Springer, Berlin (2005
4. Salehie, M., Tahvildari, L.: Autonomic computing: emerging trends and open problems. ACM SIGSOFT Softw. Eng. Notes 30(4), 1–7 (2005)
5. Jang, J.S.R., Sun, C.T.: Neuro-fuzzy modeling and control. Proc. IEEE 83(3), 378–406 (1995)
6. Mitra, S., Hayashi, Y.: Neuro-fuzzy rule generation: survey in soft computing framework. IEEE Trans. Neural Netw. 11(3), 748–768 (2000)
7. Kephart, J.O., Chess, D.M.: The vision of autonomic computing. IEEE Comput. 36(1), 41–50 (2003)

8. Dehraj, P., Sharma, A.: Complexity based maintenance assessment for autonomic agent. In: Advances in Computer Science, pp. 221–231 (2015)
9. Lohman, G.M., Lightstone, S.S.: SMART: making DB2 (More) autonomic. In: Proceedings of the 28th International Conference on Very Large Data Bases. VLDB Endowment (2002)
10. Schoenherr, S.E.: Computer evolution. Available at http://www.aes.org/aeshc/docs/recording. technology.history/computer1.html
11. Menon, J., Pease, D.A., Reese, R., Duyanovich, L., Hillsberg, B.: IBM storage tank—a heterogeneous scalable SAN file system. IBM Syst. J. 42(2), 250 (2003)
12. Sharma, A., Chauhan, S., Grover, P.: Autonomic computing: paradigm shift for software development. CSI Commun. 35 (2011
13. Chauhan, S., Sharma, A., Grover, P.: Developing self managing software systems using agile modeling. ACM SIGSOFT Softw. Eng. Notes 38(6), 1–3 (2013)
14. Nami, M.R., Sharifi, M.: Autonomic computing: a new approach. In: First Asia International Conference on Modelling & Simulation (AMS'07), pp. 352–357. IEEE (2007)
15. Chess, D.M., Palmer, C.C., White, S.R.: Security in an autonomic computing environment. IBM Syst. J. 42(1), 107–118 (2003)
16. Zadeh, L.A.: Fuzzy logic. Computer 21(4), 83–93 (1988)
17. Takahagi, E.: Fuzzy measure-Choquet integral calculation system. Available: http://www.isc. senshu-u.ac.jp/~thc0456/Efuzzyweb/fm11.html
18. Kumari, N., Sunita, S.: Comparison of ANNs, fuzzy logic and neuro-fuzzy integrated approach for diagnosis of coronary heart disease: a survey. Int. J. Comput. Sci. Mobile Comput. 2(6), 216–224 (2013)

Proposal for Measurement of Agent-Based Systems

Sangeeta Arora and P. Sasikala

Abstract The software industry is always striving for new technologies to improve the productivity of software and meet the requirement of improving the quality, flexibility, and scalability of systems. In the field of software engineering, the software development paradigm is shifting towards ever-increasing flexibility and quality of software products. A measure of the quality of software is therefore essential. Measurement methods must be changed to accommodate the new paradigm as traditional measurement methods are no longer suitable. This paper discusses the significant measurement factors as they relate to agent-based systems, and proposes some metrics suitable for use in agent-based systems.

Keywords Agent-based system · Measurement · Metrics

1 Introduction

Artificial intelligence is acclimatising agents current principles in addition to playing an important role in global network connection, with search engines being a particularly relevant example of this importance. Technology is accumulating intricacy of software hence agents are becoming familiar with it as a paradigm in software engineering. Agents are centered on societal opinion of computations and assistance by the sensors those are the reason after their continuous environment sensing.

Franklin and Grasser [1] discussed agents as intelligent organisms placed in the environment and capable of taking autonomous actions to fulfil their design objectives within a long-lived computational system, with sensors and effectors. Agents are smart enough to decide on self-directed actions in order to capitalize and make progress towards their goals.

S. Arora (✉) · P. Sasikala
Makhanlal Chaturvedi National University of Journalism and Communication,
Bhopal, India
e-mail: ar.sangeeta@gmail.com

© Springer Nature Singapore Pte Ltd. 2019
M. N. Hoda et al. (eds.), *Software Engineering*, Advances in Intelligent Systems
and Computing 731, https://doi.org/10.1007/978-981-10-8848-3_53

Categories of agents are outlined based on their functionality, i.e. simple agents with predefined processing rules that are self-activated as a result of arising conditions. Agents are self-governed and experienced, no external intervention from resource (users). For example, when a telephone call is made, a bell rings, and after a defined period of time the call is transferred automatically to an answering machine.

A dynamic environment is the best suited to intelligent agents constructed with an ability to learn from their environment as well as train from predefined situations.

Jennings [2, 3] detailed how agent-based computing is moving toward multifaceted and distributed systems, which leads in turn to the maximization of complex systems towards the mainstream software engineering paradigm.

Software development is continually improving in a fashion and is helping to increase and enrich productivity. In recent decades, the software development paradigm has changed from being procedural to being object oriented and currently we succeeded to component and aspect, now moving to agent [4].

The agent-oriented paradigm is an emerging one in software engineering, agent in active form unlike in object and component oriented paradigm. This is diverse concept from object paradigm like classes to role, variable to belief/knowledge and method to message. Being a component, an agent has its own interface through which to communicate with other agents without residing components in memory.

A system is situated within an environment and senses that environment and acts on it, over time, in pursuit of its own agenda, thereby effecting what it senses in the future [5].

Agents follow a goal-oriented approach sensing the environment constantly. They autonomously perform their own controllable actions if any changes are detected, and with the help of other agents interact to complete the task without the need for any human intervention. The characteristics of agents are discussed below (Fig. 1).

(i) Situated: Agents stay in the memory and monitor the environment for activation.

(ii) Autonomous: Agents are activated as they detect a change in the environment. They do not need to operate explicitly.

Fig. 1 Characteristics of an agent

(iii) Proactive: Each agent has its own goal. As they sense for the requirement of the environment, they will be active to achieve the goal.

(iv) Reactive: Agents continuously monitor the environment. They react when changes occur in the environment.

(v) Social Ability: One agent cannot perform all tasks. An agent has to communicate with other agents to complete required tasks.

On top of the distinctiveness it has been attested that an agent is a component, which activates itself by sensing the environment.

Software development has allowed the adoption of new techniques with increasing complexity that allow improvement in the quality and adaptability of systems in different environments and on multiple platforms.

The measurement of software quality should be of a high quality, and not be evaluated by old defined method due to legacy tricks for new technology-driven systems. The new paradigm requires a new methodology to improve the quality of systems through the enhancement of the quality of measurement of systems.

This paper is presented in five sections. Section 2 provides some guidelines regarding existing metrics. Section 3 discusses the necessity for new metrics. Section 4 proposes some metrics for agent-based systems and discusses the relationship between metrics and dependent factors. The paper concludes in Sect. 5.

2 Existing Metrics

Quantitative evaluation is the best means of measurement as it is numerically based and this is a requirement for the evaluation of systems. Despite this, its use to assess the system quality will still result in subjective evaluation. Metrics are employed by software to maintain the quality of a system and serve as a means of comparison, cost estimation, fault prediction, and forecasting. Software metrics play a vital role in measuring the quality of software development but new metrics are required for agents. New generation technology requires different segments to measure the quality of software, which leads to metrics growth.

Software metrics were familiarized in the late 1960s to support management decisions taken at the time of development. They were used to calculate effort, time, and other predictions, such as LOC (lines of code) or similar size counts, function points, defect counts, and effort figures by Etzkorn et al. [6] and Sedigh Ali et al. [7].

Here in a test by a top metrics emphasizes on the functionality of the system.

Several metrics are available for the measurement of computer software and its processes, which can deliberate to enrich its Query continuously too. Measurement radiate the estimation, quality control, productive assessment, and project control used by software engineers to help assess the quality of technical products and to assist in the tactical decision making of a project.

Metrics of the software process and products are quantitative evaluations that enable the software industry to gain insights into the efficacy of the process and any projects that are conducted using it as a framework. Basic quality and productivity data can be analyzed and means of the data can be compared with those of the past to better identify how future progress can be made. Metrics can be used to identify and isolate problems in order to facilitate remedies and improve the process of software development. If a quantitative evaluation is not made then judgment can be based only on subjective evaluation. With a quantitative evaluation, trends (either good or bad) can be better identified and used to make true improvements over time. The first step is to define a limited set of process, project, and product measures that are easy to collect and which can be normalized using either size or function-oriented metrics. The results are analyzed and compared to past means for similar projects performed within the organization. Trends are assessed and conclusions are generated.

Abreu and Carapuca [8] discussed metrics relating to design, size, complexity, reuse, productivity, quality, class, and method basically for object-oriented systems. In a similar fashion, Binder [9] put forward the measurement of encapsulation, inheritance, polymorphism, and complexity. Dumke et al. [10] proposed for all phases of object-oriented development. Lee et al. [11] clarified metrics for class coupling and cohesion. A metrics suite was also proposed for object-oriented design by Chidamber and Kemerer [12]. These metrics were purely for key concepts of object-oriented programming, such as object, class, and inheritance etc. [13]. These metrics evaluated reusability and the coupling factor between classes.

Measurement methods were proposed for components and focused on the complexity of interaction (Narasimhan and Hendradjaya [14], Mahmood and Lai [15], Salman [16], Kharb and Singh [17], Gill and Balkishan [18]). Similarly, metrics based on (Boxall and Araban [19], Washizaki et al. [20], Rotaru and Dobre [21]) reusability and component size, probability, integration, reliability, resource utilization, etc., were proposed by Gill and Grover [22].

3   The Necessity for New Metrics

The agent is relatively related to object and component, which is based on system, and follows the concept of object-oriented development. The agent is an active object in contrast to an object acting passively in an object-oriented paradigm. An agent with autonomous and reactive properties provides a diverse potency applicable in different environments. Consequently, the metrics proposed for object-based and component-based systems are inadequate.

Accordingly, additional software metrics are needed to ensure the quality of agent-based systems through the measurement of the quality of those systems.

Hitch in an established metrics aimed at a number of deduces:

- An agent has an individual thread of control due to its autonomous nature.
- On account of its autonomous nature an agent will decide on an action by itself. It perceives any changes to its environment.
- Agents are social in nature. A single agent cannot perform all necessary activities. An agent needs the cooperation of other agents to complete its task.
- Adaptability is one of the important features of an agent. When an agent moves from one environment to another, adaptability to the new environment is required.
- Agents communicate with other agents via the help of their own interface. Each agent has an independent interface through which it can communicate with other agents.
- Agents are reactive by nature. How much time is taken by an agent after it has identified its aim? This means that agent action time is also important.
- When an agent is moving in different environments, resources are acquired by that agent. Resource accessibility is therefore important in achieving the goal.
- An agent stays in memory to sense the environment. An agent senses the environment for activation.
- Agents are proactive in achieving their goal. They set their goals and wait for them to be achieved.
- Agents have to communicate with different environments and with different types of agents. This is why they need to have a dynamic nature.
- Agents are active objects unlike the passive objects in object-oriented systems.
- Each agent communicates with other agents through an interface without knowing the details of the other agents.
- Agents have to trust other agents to fulfil their goal.

4 Advancement in Metrics

Agent-based systems are constituted of one or more agents. Different agents have the aforementioned identifiable roles and interact and cooperate with other agents in different environments as required by their tasks. Various significant issues regarding complexity have an effect on the nature of the agent:

- Agent communication
- Process time
- Receptiveness of resources for an agent in its surroundings
- Time to grasp surroundings
- Switching time from one environment to another
- Action taken by agents
- Number of unpredictable changes in an environment
- Interoperability among agents
- Belief and reputation

In the way of agents, metrics have accomplished many upright endeavours. Klugal [23] discussed metrics for various aspects of agent-based systems. Mala and Cil et al. [24] proposed complexity dimensions in terms of system size, intelligence, and agent interaction. Sarkar and Debnath [25] introduced a new framework and metrics based on collaboration. Sterling [26] discussed quality goals based on adaptivity. Magarino et al. [27] proposed a metrics suite for measuring agent-oriented architectures. The respective quality attributes are getting on with metrics: extensibility, modularity and complexity.

Sivakumar et al. [28] presented a metric to measure the quality of software for an agent-oriented system, proposing a tool to measure the quality. Dam and Winikoff [29] worked on the maintenance phase with the help of agents detailing the repair of inconsistencies using event-triggered plans.

Bitonto et al. [30] proposed competency factors in terms of rationality, autonomy, reactivity, and environment adaptability. The measures were also represented with perspective of different points. These factors lie on many other various lines. Closed intervals were used for calculating the different factors. We have used some aspects of this work in the preparation of this paper.

Bakar et al. [31] proposed a framework to assess the quality of interaction among agents. In this paper, both availability and trustability metrics are addressed. Marir et al. [32] discussed metrics used to measure the complexity of multi-agent systems. Stocker et al. [33] provided a solution that enables the measurement of workload in the early stages of a design. Their work is founded on multi-agent systems based on the belief-desire-intention (BDI) model.

Atop altogether all have been accomplishing their work towards agent-based metrics. Metrics are proposed in various dimensions like in direction of traditional metrics and perspective of agent. The factors to be considered for our proposed metrics are as follows:

(i) **Resource Availability**

This refers to available resources in different environments. It is only possible when an agent has complete, accurate, and current state information of an environment.

$$\{r|r \in R, \ r \text{ is number of resources required for process}\}$$

(ii) **Process Time**

This refers to the length of time required to perform any task by single or multiple agents.

$$\text{process time} = \text{activation time of agents} + \text{execution time}$$

(iii) **Agent Type (Static or Dynamic)**
A static agent works in a deterministic environment where any action has a single effect, whereas a dynamic agent works in a non-deterministic environment where the same action in identical situations may have entirely different effects. Dynamic agents are also capable of learning.

(iv) **Pathway Transit (Interrupted or Uninterrupted)**
When one agent is shifting to another environment, then it is either interrupted or uninterrupted.

(v) **Pathway Type (Static or Dynamic)**
A static passage means that the environment is not changing at the time of action, whereas a dynamic passage means the environment is changing at the time of action.

(vi) **Number of Agents**
This specifies how many agents should participate in achieving the goal. AG represents the agents present in an environment while ag represents the number of active agents for the particular task.

$$ag \subseteq AG$$

(vii) **Number of Actions**
How many actions should be taken in order to achieve the goal?
AC represents the total number of actions assigned to the agent and ac is number of actions taken by the agent to fulfil the particular task.

$$ac \subseteq AC$$

(viii) **Learning Ability**
A dynamic agent is able to learn from experience.

(ix) **Agent Success Rate**
The agent success rate depends on the task being successfully completed by the agent.

$$\text{Success Rate} = \frac{t}{T} * 100$$

T represents the total tasks undertaken by the agent and t represents the number of successful tasks completed by the agent.

(x) **Leadership**
Is the agent able to initiate the task or not?

(xi) **Agent Action**
What type of action is taken by the agent? This applies to dynamic agents only.

  (xii) **Expected Action**
        The action specified at the time of development of the system.
  (xiii) **Diplomacy**
        Is the agent able to undertake negotiations in the case of actions?
  (xiv) **Instrumentation**
        Is the agent actually able to diagnose the error while taking action? This
        factor depends upon the proactive ability of the agent.
  (xv) **Generality**
        This is when any agent does the task of another agent (deactivated agent).

In addition to these factors are the foundations of the following projected metrics:

Agent Competence Metric (ACM): This measures the effectiveness of an agent.

Agent Support Metric (ASM): This provides a measurement of the number of agents communicating to complete the task.

Resource Receptive Metric (RRM): This helps to calculate the resources accessible in other environments.

Agent Versatility Metric (AVM): This measures the adaptability of an agent to different environments.

Agent Skill Metric (ASKM): This metric calculates how an agent performs in different situations.

Agent Shift Metric (ASHM): This provides a measure of the switching time taken by an agent moving from one environment to another.

Agent Environment Shift Metric (ASSM): In achieving its goal, an agent will move from one environment to another. As a result an environment transition measurement is required.

Agent Achievement Metric (AACM): As well as agent participation, success rate depth is also important.

Cooperation Agent Metric (CAM): This relates to communication among agents and the help given by one agent to another.

Trust Metric (TM): This helps to calculate the trust factor of an agent and its environment.

The relationships between metrics and factors are shown in Table 1.

The table shows the proposed metrics based on the behavior of an agent in the system. It shows the relationship among the proposed metrics and their dependency factors. For example, to measure agent competency, we must be aware of the type of agent, process time, and surroundings. These parameters differ with respect to surrounding, process, and communication time. Through the use of these parameters we can see that the success of the metrics depends on several factors. It is essential to regard these parameters as the parameters on which metrics depends.

Table 1 Relationships between metrics and factors

Metric	Factor															
	Unreachable	Process time	Agent type (static or dynamic)	Pathway transient (interrupted or uninterrupted)	Pathway type (static or dynamic)	Number of agents	Number of actions	Knowledge aptitude	Reliability	Generality	Agent ection	Expected ection	Negotiation	Failure analysis	Deputation	Effort estimation
Agent competence metric	Y	Y	Y		Y		Y	Y	Y	Y			Y	Y	Y	
Agent support metric	Y		Y			Y	Y	Y		Y						
Agent achievement metric			Y					Y	Y	Y			Y	Y		
Resource receptive metric	Y		Y					Y							Y	
Agent versatility metric	Y	Y	Y				Y	Y	Y				Y	Y	Y	Y
Agent skill metric									Y		Y	Y		Y		
Agent shift metric		Y	Y												Y	
Agent environment shift metric	Y	Y	Y	Y							Y	Y	Y	Y	Y	Y
Agent achievement metric								Y					Y	Y	Y	Y
Cooperation agent metric			Y			Y		Y					Y	Y	Y	Y
Trust metric									Y	Y			Y	Y	Y	
Autonomy degree								Y							Y	Y

5   Conclusion

Agents-based development is promising technique for the development of complex and distributed systems. Technology is accumulative intricacy of software hence Agents are acquainting with as a paradigm in software engineering. Agents are centered on societal opinion of computations and assistance by the sensors that are the reason for their continuous environment sensing.

In this paper we have discussed agents and conclude that measurement requires a quantification of quality and provides an inexperienced glance en-route for measurement of an agent-based system. Popular existing metrics are inadequate and new metrics are required to measure the quality of agent-based systems. In this light upon essentiality of metrics for various type of paradigm towards agent-based systems, we have considered some significant issues as well as some issues relating to complexity.

As a result of these complexity issues certain new metrics are proposed in this paper. These metrics depends various factors, e.g., process time, knowledge, and aptitude etc. The values of these metrics are not precise and vary from system to system, having vague values. Soft computing may be better approach for addressing these types of factors. Future work should look to address the effectiveness of these factors for metrics using soft computing techniques.

References

1. Franklin, S., Graesser, A.: Is it an agent, or just a program? A taxonomy for autonomous agents. In: Proceedings of the Third International Workshop on Agent Theories, Architectures, and Languages. Springer, Berlin (1996)
2. Jennings, N.R.: On Agent-Based Software Engineering, pp. 277–296. Elsevier, New York (2000)
3. Jennings, N.R.: An agent-based approach for building complex software systems. Commun. ACM **44**(4), 35–41 (2001)
4. Arora, S., Sasikala, P., Agarwal, C.P., Sharma, A.: Developmental approaches for agent oriented system—a critical review. In: CONSEG 2012 (2012)
5. Maes, P.: The agent network architecture (ANA). SIGART Bull. **2**(4), 115–120
6. Etzkorn, L.H., Hughes Jr., W.E., Davis, C.G.: Automated reusability quality analysis of OO legacy software. Inf. Soft. Technol. J. **43**(2001), 295–308 (2001)
7. Sedigh-Ali, S., Ghafoor, A., Paul, R.A.: Software engineering metrics for COTS-based systems. IEEE Comput. J. 44–50 (2001)
8. Abreu, F.B., Carapuca, R.: Candidate metrics for object-oriented software within a taxonomy framework. J. Syst. Softw. **26**, 87–96 (1994)
9. Binder, R.V.: Design for testability in object-oriented systems. Commun. ACM **37**(9), 87–101 (1994)
10. Dumke, R., Foltin, E., Koeppe, R., Winkler, A.: Measurement-Based Object-Oriented Software Development of the Software Project. Software Measurement Laboratory. Preprint Nr. 6, 1996, University of Magdeburg (40 p.)

11. Lee, Y., Liang, B., Wu, S., Wang, F.: Measuring the coupling and cohesion of an object-oriented program based on information flow. In: Proceedings of the ICSQ'95, Slovenia, pp. 81–90 (1995)
12. Chidamber, S.R., Kemerer, C.F.: A metrics suite for object oriented design. J. IEEE Trans. Softw. Eng. **20**, 476–493 (1994)
13. Jang, K.S., Nam, T.E., Wadhwa, B.: On measurement of objects and agents. http://www.comp.nus.edu.sg/~bimlesh/ametrics/index.htm
14. Narasimhan, L., Hendradjaya, B.: Some theoretical considerations for a suite of metrics for the integration of software components. Inf. Sci. **177**, 844–864 (2007)
15. Mahmood, S., Lai, R.: A complexity measure for UML component-based system specification. Softw. Practice Exp. **38**, 117–34 (2008)
16. Salman, N.: Complexity metrics AS predictors of maintainability and integrability of software components. J. Arts Sci. (2006)
17. Kharb, L., Singh, R.: Complexity metrics for component-oriented software systems. SIGSOFT Softw. Eng. Notes **33**, 1–3 (2008). http://doi.acm.org/10.1145/1350802.1350811
18. Gill, N.S., Balkishan: Dependency and interaction oriented complexity metrics of component-based systems. SIGSOFT Softw. Eng. Notes, **33**, 1–5 (2008). http://doi.acm.org/10.1145/1350802.1350810
19. Boxall, M.A.S., Araban, S.: Interface metrics for reusability analysis of components. In: Proceedings of the 2004 Australian Software Engineering Conference, IEEE Computer Society, p. 40 (2004)
20. Washizaki, H., Yamamoto, H., Fukazawa, Y.: A metrics suite for measuring reusability of software components. In: Proceedings of the 9th International Symposium on Software Metrics, IEEE Computer Society, p. 211 (2003)
21. Rotaru, O.P., Dobre, M.: Reusability metrics for software components. In: Proceedings of the ACS/IEEE 2005 International Conference on Computer Systems and Applications, IEEE Computer Society, p. 24-I (2005)
22. Gill, N.S., Grover, P.S.: Component-based measurement: few useful guidelines. ACM SIGSOFT Softw. Eng. Notes **28**(6), 4 (2003)
23. Klügl, F.: Measuring complexity of multi-agent simulations—an attempt using metrics. In: Dastani, M.M., El Fallah Seghrouchni, A., Leite, J., Torroni, P. (eds.) LADS 2007. LNCS (LNAI), vol. 5118, pp. 123–138. Springer, Heidelberg (2008)
24. Mala, M., Çil, İ.: A taxonomy for measuring complexity in agent-based systems. In: IEEE 2nd International Conference on Software Engineering and Service Science (ICSESS'11), pp. 851–854 (2011)
25. Sarkar, A., Debnath, N.C.: Measuring complexity of multi-agent system architecture. IEEE (2012)
26. Sterling, L.: Adaptivity: a quality goal for agent-oriented models? In: Preprints of the 18th IFAC World Congress, pp. 38–42 (2011)
27. García-Magariño, I., Cossentino, M., Seidita, V.: A metrics suite for evaluating agent-oriented architectures. In: Proceedings of the 2010 ACM Symposium on Applied Computing SAC 10 (2010). ACM Press, pp. 912–919 (2010)
28. Sivakumar, K. Vivekanandan, Sandhya, S.: Testing agent-oriented software by measuring agent's property attributes. In: ACC 2011. Springer, Berlin, pp. 88–98 (2011)
29. Dam, H.K., Winikoff, M.: An agent-oriented approach to change propagation in software maintenance. Auton. Agents Multi-Agent Syst. **23**(3), 384–452 (2011)
30. Di Bitonto, P., Laterza, M., Roselli, T., Rossano, V.: Evaluation of multi-agent systems: proposal and validation of a metric plan. In: Transactions on Computational Collective Intelligence VII, vol. 7270, pp. 198–221. Springer, Berlin (2012)
31. Bakar, N.A., Selamat, A.: Assessing agent interaction quality via multi-agent runtime verification. In: Proceeding ICCCI 2013, pp. 175–184. Springer, New York (2013)

32. Marir, T., Mokhati, F., Bouchelaghem-Seridi, H., Tamrabet, Z.: Complexity measurement of multi-agent systems. In: Proceeding MATES 2014, vol 8732. Springer, New York, pp. 188–201 (2014)
33. Stocker, R., Rungta, N., Mercer, E., Raimondi, F., Holbrook, J., Cardoza, C., Goodrich, M.: An approach to quantify workload in a system of agents. In: Proceeding AAMAS'15 International Foundation for Autonomous Agents and Multiagent Systems Richland, SC ©2015, ISBN: 978–1-4503-3413-6, pp. 1041–1050 (2015)

Optimal Software Warranty Under Fuzzy Environment

A. K. Shrivastava and Ruchi Sharma

Abstract Prolonged testing ensures a higher reliability level of the software, but at the same time, it adds to the cost of production. Moreover, due to stiff contention in the market, developers cannot spend too much time on testing. So, they offer a warranty with the software to attract customers and to gain their faith in the product. But servicing under warranty period incurs high costs at the developer end. Due to this, determining optimal warranty period at the time of software release is an imperative concern for a software firm. Determination of optimal warranty is a trade-off between providing maximum warranty at minimum cost. One of the prime assumptions in the existing cost models in software reliability is that the cost coefficients are static and deterministic. But in reality, these constants are dependent on various non-deterministic factors thus leading to uncertainty in their exact computation. Using fuzzy approach in the cost model overcomes the uncertainty in obtaining the optimal cost value. In this paper, we addressed this issue and proposed a generalized approach to determine the optimal software warranty period of a software under fuzzy environment, where testing and operational phase are governed by different distribution functions. Validation of the proposed model is done by providing a numerical example.

Keywords Optimal warranty · Fuzzy environment · Software reliability
Generalized framework · Testing

A. K. Shrivastava (✉)
Research Development Center, Asia Pacific Institute of Management, New Delhi, India
e-mail: kavinash1987@gmail.com

R. Sharma
Department of Computer Engineering, Netaji Subhash Institute of Technology, Delhi, India
e-mail: rs.sharma184@gmail.com

© Springer Nature Singapore Pte Ltd. 2019
M. N. Hoda et al. (eds.), *Software Engineering*, Advances in Intelligent Systems
and Computing 731, https://doi.org/10.1007/978-981-10-8848-3_54

1   Introduction

Nowadays, providing warranty with software at the time of purchase is a fairly common phenomenon. Warranty is an attribute that helps the firms in establishing reliability of their product to the customers. It acts as an add-on which attracts customers to buy their product with a greater faith. But providing warranty on the software costs a lot to the firm; therefore, it is important to find the optimal warranty period of the software so as to bear minimum cost for fixing bugs or replacing the software during warranty period. In past, many researchers have worked on the problem release time problems of software [1]. Researchers also incorporated the role of software warranty in the cost models [2]. Pham and Zhang [3] revised the traditional cost model and proposed a cost model incorporating the effect of warranty and risk in the cost modeling. Dohi et al. [4] worked toward minimizing the total cost involved during software development by finding the optimal software warranty period assuming that the process of debugging follows NHPP. Rinsaka and Dohi [5] proposed cost model to determine the optimal software warranty period under discrete and continuous operational circumstances using environment factor to differentiate between testing and operational phase. Generally, operational environment is different from testing phase due to various factors like skill, usage resources. Several methods to assess reliability during operational phase have been suggested [6]. Yang and Xie [7] proposed different reliabilities for operational and testing phase in software reliability modeling and differentiated the testing and operational phase depending on the number of faults. From the above literature review, we find that two common and strong assumptions were made in all the cost models. Firstly, the testing and operational phases are governed by same distribution functions. Secondly, release time studies for several existing SRGM have been carried out, but they have been formulated under the assumption of clearly defined constraints and goals and precisely computed value of constants. But, these attributes depend on various aspects that are non-deterministic and hence cannot be computed accurately. So, defining this problem in a fuzzy environment is a more realistic approach. Fuzzy set theory [8] quantitatively deals with uncertainty by permitting imprecision in the conventional set theory. Kapur et al. [9] developed a cost model for optimal release time of a software under fuzzy environment. Pachauri et al. [10] extended the work of Kapur et al. [9] by incorporating imperfect debugging and proposed a cost model for optimal release time of SRGM with testing effort. In this paper, we have formulated a generalized cost model to determine optimal software warranty with reliability constraints under fuzzy environment. The paper organization is as follows. Section 2 describes the notations and assumptions of the proposed cost model. In Sect. 3, we have formulated the cost model, its formulation, and solution based on fuzzy approach. Section 4 provides the numerical illustration and results of the proposed model. Finally, conclusion has been drawn in Sect. 5.

2 The Cost Model

A. *Notations*

a	Number of expected faults in the software	c_1	Testing cost per unit testing time
b	Rate of fault removal per remaining fault	c_2	Cost of fixing a fault during testing phase
t_{lc}	Software life cycle length	c_3	Testing cost during warranty period
w	Warranty period	c_4	Cost of fixing a fault during warranty phase
$m(t)$	Expected number of faults removed in time interval (0, t]	c_5	Penalty cost of debugging a fault after warranty period

B. *Assumptions of the proposed model:*

(1) The fault that led to software failure is detected and removed as soon as the failure takes place.

(2) The time of detecting each error is independent of other faults and is a nonnegative random variable which is distributed identically with the probability density function $f(t)$.

(3) t_o is the time of software release into the market.

(4) t_{lc} is the length of the software life cycle that is known in advance, and it is believed to be sufficiently large in comparison to t_o.

(5) The warranty period is measured from the release time t_o.

(6) After the end of warranty period, whenever a failure is encountered by the user, a penalty cost is incurred by the software developer.

The basic cost model proposed by Okumoto and Goel [11] included a cost function for the total cost of debugging in testing phase and operational phase and is given as

$$C(t) = c_1 t + c_2 m(t) + c_3 (a - m(t)) \qquad (1)$$

In the cost model given above, it was assumed that the rate of detecting the fault in testing and operational phase remains the same. But in reality, it may differ. By unified scheme, we know that

$$m(t) = a \cdot F(t) \qquad (2)$$

Software warranty plays an imperative role for product in the market. Therefore, researchers extended the basic cost model to include warranty period and proposed cost function as

$$C(t) = c_1 t + c_2 m(t) + c_3 (m(t+w) - m(t)) \tag{3}$$

Software life cycle is divided into three phases, namely testing phase, warranty phase, and after warranty phase, i.e., $[0, t_0]$, $[t_0, t_0 + w]$ and $[t_0 + w, t_{lc}]$. The generalized cost function using different distribution function for different phases is given by

$$
\begin{aligned}
C(w) = & c_1 t_0 + c_2 a F_1(t_0) + c_3 w + c_4 a (1 - F_1(t_0)) F_2(t_0 + w - t_0) \\
& + c_5 a (1 - F_1(t_0))(1 - F_2(t_0 + w - t_0)).F_3(t_{lc} - (t_0 + w))
\end{aligned} \tag{4}
$$

In the cost model given by Eq. (4), first term denotes the cost of testing, second term denotes the cost of debugging the faults encountered during testing phase, third term denotes the testing cost in warranty period, fourth term denotes the cost of debugging in warranty phase, and last term is for cost of debugging after warranty period. Fuzzified form of the cost function is given as:

$$
\begin{aligned}
\widetilde{C}(w) = & \tilde{c}_1 t_0 + \tilde{c}_2 a F_1(t_0) + \tilde{c}_3 w + \tilde{c}_4 a (1 - F_1(t_0)) F_2(t_0 + w - t_0) \\
& + \tilde{c}_5 a (1 - F_1(t_0))(1 - F_2(t_0 + w - t_0)).F_4(t_{lc} - (t_0 + w))
\end{aligned} \tag{5}
$$

3   Problem Formulation

Here, we consider an optimization problem with constraints on desired reliability level by the end of warranty period. The problem addressed in our study can be given as

$$
\begin{aligned}
& \text{Minimize } \widetilde{C}(w) \\
& \text{Subject to } R(w) = \frac{m(w)}{a^*} \gtrsim R_0
\end{aligned} \tag{P1}
$$

where R_0 represents the aspiration level of number of faults detected in warranty phase and a^* represents the remaining number of faults after release. The symbol $\gtrsim$ ($\lesssim$) denotes "fuzzy greater (less) than or equal to" and has linguistic interpretation "essentially greater (less) than or equal to." In the next section, we discuss the fuzzy mathematical programming approach to solve the above problem (P1).

A. *Problem solution*

The algorithm to solve the above said fuzzy optimization problem based on the fuzzy mathematical programming approach is described below.

Algorithm

1. Find the crisp equivalent of the fuzzy parameters using a defuzzification function. Here, we use the defuzzification function of type $F_2(A) = (a_1 + 2a + a_u)/4$
2. Fix the aspiration (restriction) level of objective function of the fuzzifier min (max).
3. Define suitable membership functions for fuzzy inequalities. The membership function for the fuzzy less than or equal to and greater than or equal to is given as

$$\mu_1(t) = \begin{cases} 1; & G(T) \leq G_0 \\ \frac{G^* - G(t)}{G^* - G_0}; & G_0 < G(T) \\ 0; & G(T) > G^* \end{cases} \quad \mu_2(t) = \begin{cases} 1; & H(T) > H_0 \\ \frac{H(t) - H^*}{H_0 - H^*}; & H^* \leq H(T) \\ 0; & H(T) < H^* \end{cases}$$

respectively, where G_0 and H_0 are the restriction and aspiration levels, respectively, and G^* and Q^* are the corresponding tolerance levels. The membership functions can be a linear or piecewise linear function that is concave or quasiconcave.

4. Use the extension principle to identify fuzzy decision, which gives a mathematical programming problem for a crisp environment as follows

$$\begin{aligned} &\text{Maximize} \quad \alpha \\ &\text{Subject to} \quad \mu_i(w) \geq \alpha, \quad 0 \leq \alpha \leq 1, \quad w \geq 0, \quad i = 1, 2, \ldots n; \end{aligned} \quad \text{(P2)}$$

We can arrive at the solution of the problem (P2) using the standard crisp mathematical programming algorithms where α is the degree of aspiration of the management goals. Closer the value of α to 1, greater is the level of satisfaction.

4 Numerical Example

This section presents a numerical illustration of fuzzy optimization method discussed above. Based on the model assumptions, we obtain an exponential distribution model proposed by Goel and Okumuto [12]. We estimated the unknown parameters of GO model on a software failure data set [13]. Parameter estimation is done using least square method of the nonlinear regression function of SPSS software. Parameters estimates and residual sum of square (R^2) are obtained as $a = 130.201, b = 0.083, R^2 = 0.986$. The fuzzy cost coefficient constants $\widetilde{C}_i, i = 1, 2, 3, 4, 5$ and $\widetilde{R}_0$ are specified as triangular fuzzy number (TFN) represented as $A = (a_1, a, a_u)$ which are given in Table 1.

The problem (P1) is restated using the defuzzification function $F(P)$ as

Table 1 Defuzzified values of the cost (in $) coefficients and reliability aspiration level

Fuzzy (P) parameter	$\tilde{C}_1$	$\tilde{C}_2$	$\tilde{C}_3$	$\tilde{C}_4'$	$\tilde{C}_5$	$\tilde{R}_0$	$\tilde{C}_B$
a_l	35	8	75	10	145	0.65	4000
a	40	10	80	15	150	0.70	5000
a_u	50	12	85	20	155	0.75	6000
Defuzzified value $F(P)$	60	10	80	15	150	0.70	5000

$$\text{Minimize} \quad F\big(\tilde{C}(w)\big) = F(\tilde{c}_1)t_0 + F(\tilde{c}_2)aF_1(t_o) + F(\tilde{c}_3)t_w$$
$$+ F(\tilde{c}_4)a(1 - F_1(t_0))F_2(t_0 + w - t_0)$$
$$+ F(\tilde{c}_5)a(1 - F_1(t_0))(1 - F_2(t_0 + w - t_0)) \cdot F_4(t_{lc} - (t_0 + w))$$

$$\text{Subject to} \quad F(\tilde{R})(t) \gtrsim F(\widetilde{R_0}) \text{ and } w \geq 0$$

$$(P3)$$

Now with imprecise definition of the available budget, the cost objective function is introduced as a constraint. Membership function corresponding to the above problem (P3) is defined as

$$\mu_1(w) = \begin{cases} 1; & C(w) \leq 4000 \\ \frac{5000 - C(w)}{5000 - 4000}; & 4000 < C(w) < 5000 \\ 0; & C(w) > 5000 \end{cases}$$

$$\mu_2(w) = \begin{cases} 1; & R(w) > 0.90 \\ \frac{R(w) - 0.70}{0.90 - 0.70}; & 0.70 \leq R(w) \leq 0.90 \\ 0; & R(w) < 0.70 \end{cases}$$

Now the objective function is defined as

$$\text{Max } \alpha$$
$$\text{s.t. } \mu_1(w) \geq \alpha, \quad \mu_2(w) \geq \alpha, \quad \alpha \geq 0, \quad \alpha \leq 1$$

$$(P4)$$

Now on taking $F(t) = 1 - e^{-bt}$ and release time of the software $t_0 = 20$ in problem (P4), we get a nonlinear constrained problem. On solving this problem using MAPLE software, we obtain that firm can provide warranty period $w^* = 20.12$ weeks on the software which is released after 20 weeks of testing. Also, the level of satisfaction $\alpha = 0.613$ is achieved from firms point.

5 Conclusion

Ambiguity in defining the management goals can be handled by considering fuzzy approach. Two important objectives of cost minimization and reliability maximization from developer's point of view are taken in the problem definition. We have considered TFN to define fuzzy numbers which can be compared with other type of fuzzy numbers for the possible variations that could result. We can use different methods for defuzzification. In future, we can extend our model to incorporate testing effort in the cost model. We are working on the cost model to incorporate imperfect debugging in the above cost model to make it more realistic.

References

1. Kapur, P.K., Pham, H., Gupta, A., Jha, P.C.: Software reliability assessment with or applications. Springer, UK (2011)
2. Yamada, S.: Optimal release problems with warranty period based on a software maintenance cost model. Trans. IPS Jpn. **35**(9), 2197–2202 (1994)
3. Pham, H., Zhang, X.: A software cost model with warranty and risk costs. IEEE Trans. Comput. **48**(1), 71–75 (1999)
4. Dohi, T., Okamura, H., Kaio, N., Osaki, S.: The age-dependent optimal warranty policy and its application to software maintenance contract. In: Kondo, S., Furuta, K. (eds.) Proceedings of the 5th International Conference on Probability Safety Assessment and Management, vol. 4, pp. 2547–52. Academy Press, New York (2000)
5. Rinsaka, K., Dohi, T.: Determining the optimal software warranty period under various operational circumstances. Int. J. Qual. Reliab. Manag. **22**(7), 715–730 (2005)
6. Okamura, H., Dohi, T., Osaki, S.: A reliability assessment method for software products in operational phase—proposal of an accelerated life testing model. Electron. Commun. Jpn. Part 3 **84**, 25–33 (2001)
7. Yang, B., Xie, M.: A study of operational and testing reliability in software reliability analysis. Reliab. Eng. Syst. Safety **70**, 323–329 (2000)
8. Zimmermann, H.J.: Fuzzy Set Theory and Its Applications. Kluwer Academic Publisher (1991)
9. Kapur, P.K., Pham, H., Gupta, A., Jha, P.C.: Optimal release policy under fuzzy environment. Int. J. Syst. Assur. Eng. Manag. **2**(1), 48–58 (2011)
10. Pachauri, B., Kumar, A., Dhar, J.: Modeling optimal release policy under fuzzy paradigm in imperfect debugging environment. Inf. Softw. Technol. **55**, 1974–1980 (2013)
11. Okumoto, K., Goel, A.L.: Optimum release time for software systems based on reliability and cost criteria. J. Syst. Softw. **1**, 315–318 (1980)
12. Goel, A.L., Okumoto, K.: Time dependent error detection rate model for software reliability and other performance measures. IEEE Trans. Reliab. **28**(3), 206–211 (1979)
13. Wood, A.: Predicting software reliability. IEEE Comput. **9**, 69–77 (1996)

Automation Framework for Test Script Generation for Android Mobile

R. Anbunathan and Anirban Basu

Abstract System testing involves activities such as requirement analysis, test case design, test case writing, test script development, test execution, and test report preparation. Automating all these activities involves many challenges such as understanding scenarios, achieving test coverage, determining pass/fail criteria, scheduling tests, documenting result. In this paper, a method is proposed to automate both test case and test script generation from sequence diagram-based scenarios. A tool called Virtual Test Engineer is developed to convert UML sequence diagram into Android APK to test Android mobile applications. A case study is done to illustrate this method. The effectiveness of this method is studied and compared with other methods through detailed experimentation.

Keywords Android test · Test framework · Test automation · Menu tree navigation · Test case generation · Test script generation · APK generation Model-based testing

1 Introduction

System testing involves major activities such as test case generation and test execution. Usually, test Engineer needs to understand scenarios from requirement document, and then design test cases. Test case includes a set of inputs, execution conditions, and expected results [IEEE Standard 829-1998]. While designing test cases, test coverage needs to be ensured. Test coverage includes normal functional scenarios, alternative scenarios, and non-functional aspects. Test execution can be manual or automated [1]. To automate these test cases, test script has to be

R. Anbunathan (✉)
Bharathiar University, Coimbatore, India
e-mail: anbunathan.r@gmail.com

A. Basu
Department of CSE, APS College of Engineering, Bengaluru, India
e-mail: abasu@anirbanbasu.in

© Springer Nature Singapore Pte Ltd. 2019
M. N. Hoda et al. (eds.), *Software Engineering*, Advances in Intelligent Systems and Computing 731, https://doi.org/10.1007/978-981-10-8848-3_55

developed. Test Engineer needs to learn scripting language supported by commercial-off-the-shelf tool or in-house built tool.

In this paper, a method is proposed to automate the above system testing activities and a tool was developed based on this methodology. Scenarios in the form of UML sequence diagrams [2] are considered as input. XMI file of sequence diagram is parsed by using method proposed in [3]. From the XMI file, messages along with method name and arguments, nodes, edges, conditions are extracted. Using this information, a CFG is generated. From CFG, test cases are generated for all basis paths. These test cases are converted to XML file.

Also menu tree database generated from the target device (mobile) [4] is taken as another input. An APK is generated which takes the generated XML file and menu tree database as inputs and generates events in order to execute test cases. In this paper, the design issues faced while realizing this architecture are discussed. Also the advantages of this method, comparing with other methods, are explained. A case study is done as a proof of concept.

2   Related Work

This section discusses various methods that have been proposed for test automation. Several test automation frameworks [5] are available in literatures.

In [3], Kundu et al. proposed a method to parse sequence diagram-based XMI file and then generate Control Flow Graph (CFG). Different sequence diagram components such as messages, operands, combined fragments, guards are considered. From XMI file, nodes, edges, guards are extracted and then a graph is created. A defined set of rules are applied, which are based on the program structures such as loop, alt, break, and then, CFG is arrived.

Sawant and Sawant [6] proposed a method to convert UML diagrams such as Use Case Diagram, Class Diagram, and Sequence Diagram into test cases. A graph called Sequence Diagram Graph (SDG) is generated from these diagrams and then test cases are generated from this graph. The UML diagrams are exported to XML file using MagicDraw tool. This XML file is edited, based on test case requirement. A Java program is developed to read this XML and then generate all nodes, edges from start to end. Scenarios are generated by scanning these nodes using breadth first algorithm.

Sarma et al. [7] transformed a UML Use Case Diagram into a graph called Use Case Diagram Graph (UDG), and Sequence Diagram into a graph called the Sequence Diagram Graph (SDG) and then integrated UDG and SDG to form the System Testing Graph (STG). The STG is then traversed to generate test cases for system testing. In this approach, state-based transition path coverage criteria for test case generation. Also, complex scenarios are considered which include negative scenarios and multiple conditions.

In [8], Fraikin et al. proposed a tool called SeDiTeC, to generate test stubs from testable sequence diagram. This approach involves together to control center tool for creating sequence diagram and then export into XML file. An extension program is developed to create test stubs from this XML file. In early development phase, these stubs help to test other completed sequence diagrams. SeDiTeC tool also allows to instrument source code of associated classes, which behaves like test stub.

In [9], Swain et al. proposed a method to generate test cases from Use Case Dependency Graph (UDG) derived from Use Case Activity Diagram and Concurrent Control Flow Graph (CCFG) derived from sequence diagram. Also, it implements full predicate coverage criteria. From UDG, paths are determined using depth first algorithm. Sequence diagram is converted into corresponding Activity diagram using defined set of rules. From Activity diagram, sequences are obtained, and then decision table is constructed to generate test cases. A semi-automated tool called ComTest is built to parse XML, which is exported from sequence diagram, and then test cases are generated.

3 Architecture of Proposed Framework

In this section, architecture and design constraints of proposed framework are discussed.

3.1 Overview of the proposed framework

The proposed framework is based on Model-Based Testing (MBT). In this approach, sequence diagrams are created to capture input scenarios. XMI file obtained from this sequence diagram is parsed to extract model information such as messages. From these messages, a sequence of executable commands is extracted and stored in a XML file as nodes. This XML file is parsed by an Android application (APK), and the commands are executed to produce events in Android mobile.

3.2 Architecture of the Virtual Test Engineer

Figure 1 illustrates proposed framework to generate test script for Android mobile. The framework includes two major tools known as Virtual Test Engineer (VTE) and a menu tree generator. VTE is a Java-based application, consists of a User Interface (UI) having controls and buttons to select input files. It has major modules such as XMI parser, test case generator, and APK generator. XMI parser is exactly same as mentioned in [3], generates CFG from sequence diagram. Test case generator converts this CFG into basis path test cases in the form of XML file. APK

Fig. 1 Architecture of
automation framework

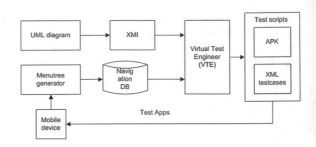

generator takes this XML file and menu tree database file and then creates a new
APK file, which can be installed in Android mobile. This APK invokes Android
service, which in turn parses XML test cases and then generates events. These
events are passed to an UI Automator [10]-based jar file, which is nothing but
library of functions such as Click button, Click menu, Navigate, Wait,
VerifyUIText. These functions perform Android button/menu clicks to simulate
user actions, and then reading UI texts to verify expected results.

(1) *XMI parser module*

UML sequence diagram as shown in Fig. 2 is converted to XMI [11] using
Papyrus tool [12]. This XMI file is parsed using SAX parser and then different
sequence diagram components such as synchronous messages, asynchronous
messages, reply messages, combined fragments, interaction operands, and
constraints are extracted. Combined fragment includes different interaction
operators such as alternatives, option, break, and loop. The precedence relations
of messages and combined fragments are found recursively. Using precedence

Fig. 2 Sequence diagram
and corresponding CFG

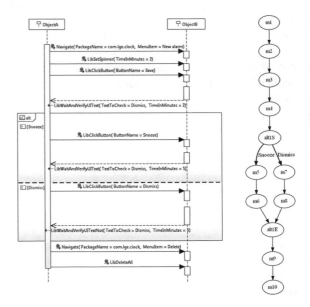

Fig. 3 UI of generated APK

relations, edges are identified. From edges list, a Control Flow Graph (CFG) is generated. Figure 3 illustrates a sequence diagram and the corresponding CFG for alarm test case.

(2) *Test case generator module*

Basis paths are identified from CFG. Each basis path constitutes one test case. One test case contains several test steps. One or more test cases are grouped under a test suite. From edges in each basis path, method name, arguments are extracted and then XML file is generated using simple tool [13]. Simple tool uses XML annotations to generate XML nodes such as TestSuite, TestCase, TestStep. For example, the following XML content shows how nodes are nested:

```
<TestSuite>
  <TestCase>
   <TestStep>
     <methodname>Navigate</methodname>
      <argument key="PackageName">com.lge.clock</argument>
     <argument key="MenuItem">New alarm</argument>
   </TestStep>
   <TestStep>
     <methodname>LibSetSpinner</methodname>
     <argument key="TimeInMinutes">2</argument>
   </TestStep>
        .
```

```
         .
    <TestCase>
    <TestCase>
         .

         .
    <TestCase>
    <TestSuite>
```

(3) *APK generator module*

An APK is generated by using a template APK. The template APK includes Activity (Java) file, Android manifest.xml, String.xml file, layout file. These files are copied to target APK and then modified as given in following steps:

1. Create Android project using "Android create project" command
2. Copy Activity (Java) file, AndroidManifest.xml, Strings.xml file, layout file etc to new project
3. Build using "ant release" command. This will create unsigned APK in bin folder of new project.
4. Sign this unsigned APK using "jarsigner" command.
5. Generate signed APK using "zipalign" command.
6. Copy signed APK to destination folder.

3.3 Mobile side architecture

Mobile side architecture is as shown in Fig. 4. The purpose of generated APK is to pass file names of generated XML file and menu tree Sqlite db file to VTE service. VTE service parses XML file and generates events such as Navigate, ClickButton, VerifyUIText. These events are sent to UI Automator-based jar. This jar includes library functions such as Navigate, ClickButton, VerifyUIText. For example, ClickButton library function contains UI Automator-based commands to simulate button click as given below:

```
            UiObject Button = new UiObject(new UiSelector().text
(ButtonName));
            if(Button.exists() && Button.isEnabled())
            {
                    Button.clickAndWaitForNewWindow(10000);
                    sleep(1000);
                    clickwidgetstatus=true;
            }
```

Fig. 4 Mobile side architecture

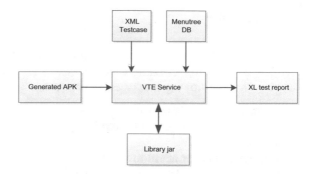

This UI Automator commands are actually simulating touch events in mobile device. For example, if ButtonName is "Save," then UI Automator searches for "Save" button in current screen and then clicks over the text "Save." Navigate command searches the target menu item in menu tree DB and finds corresponding navigation path as shown in Fig. 5. By using this path, it navigates through menu tree to reach this menu item. Library functions send the result of each operation to VTE service. VTE service saves these results in Excel test report.

	rowno	colno	caption	widtype	widname	rootpath	absolutepath
58	58	2	Alarm/Set alarm	TextView	Puzzle lock	com.lge.clock#$*#$appname#$$#Clock#$*#$TextView#$$#Alarms#$*#$Tabtext#$$#Alarm#$*#$TextView	com.lge.clock#$*...
59	59	2	Alarm/Set alarm	TextView	Memo	com.lge.clock#$*#$appname#$$#Clock#$*#$TextView#$$#Alarms#$*#$Tabtext#$$#Alarm#$*#$TextView	com.lge.clock#$*...
60	60	2	Alarm/Set alarm	Button	Cancel	com.lge.clock#$*#$appname#$$#Clock#$*#$TextView#$$#Alarms#$*#$Tabtext#$$#Alarm#$*#$TextView	com.lge.clock#$*...
61	61	2	Alarm/Set alarm	TextView	Alarm	com.lge.clock#$*#$appname#$$#Clock#$*#$TextView#$$#Alarms#$*#$Tabtext#$$#Alarm#$*#$TextView	com.lge.clock#$*...
62	62	2	Alarm/Set alarm	Button	Save	com.lge.clock#$*#$appname#$$#Clock#$*#$TextView#$$#Alarms#$*#$Tabtext#$$#Alarm#$*#$TextView	com.lge.clock#$*...
63	63	2	Alarm/Set alarm	TextView	Alarm	com.lge.clock#$*#$appname#$$#Clock#$*#$TextView#$$#Alarms#$*#$Tabtext#$$#Alarm#$*#$TextView	com.lge.clock#$*...
64	64	2	Alarm/Set alarm	System	BACK	com.lge.clock#$*#$appname#$$#Clock#$*#$TextView#$$#Alarms#$*#$Tabtext#$$#Alarm#$*#$TextView	com.lge.clock#$*...
65	65	1	Alarms/Clock	ButtonDesc	New alarm	com.lge.clock#$*#$appname#$$#Clock#$*#$TextView#$$#Alarms#$*#$Tabtext	com.lge.clock#$*...
66	66	1	Alarms/Clock	System	BACK	com.lge.clock#$*#$appname#$$#Clock#$*#$TextView#$$#Alarms#$*#$Tabtext	com.lge.clock#$*...
67	67	1	Alarms/Clock	ButtonDesc	Delete	com.lge.clock#$*#$appname#$$#Clock#$*#$TextView#$$#Alarms#$*#$Tabtext	com.lge.clock#$*...
68	68	1	Alarms/Clock	System	BACK	com.lge.clock#$*#$appname#$$#Clock#$*#$TextView#$$#Alarms#$*#$Tabtext	com.lge.clock#$*...
69	69	0	Clock	Tabtext	Timer	com.lge.clock#$*#$appname#$$#Clock#$*#$TextView	com.lge.clock#$*...
70	70	1	Timer/Clock	TextView	00	com.lge.clock#$*#$appname#$$#Clock#$*#$TextView#$$#Timer#$*#$Tabtext	com.lge.clock#$*...

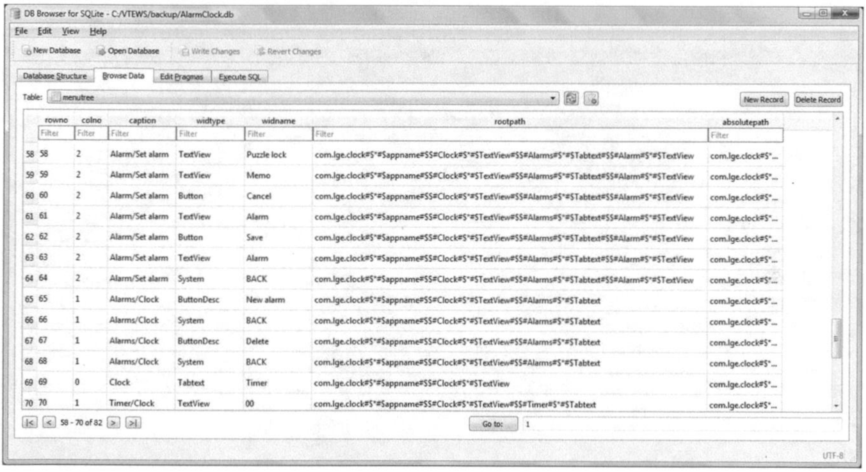

Fig. 5 Menu tree database

4   Case Study

In this section, the application of the tool is explained with a case study. The case study involves setting an alarm, which snoozes after 5 min. A sequence diagram is drawn with the following messages, as shown in Fig. 2:

1. Navigate to new alarm widget
2. Set spinner value to current time+2 min
3. Save alarm
4. Wait for 2 min for alarm to invoke
5. Verify "Dismiss" text in current screen
6. Select Snooze option
7. Wait for 5 min for snoozing
8. Verify again "Dismiss" text in current screen
9. Delete the alarm

One of the combined fragment construct, "Alt," is used to draw messages 6, 7, and 8. Alt has both if and else constructs. Else part contains "Dismiss" alarm message, so that two test cases are generated for one sequence diagram by VTE. Figure 6 shows two basis path test cases generated for alarm scenarios. VTE uses "Dot" tool [14] to display basis path graphs. At the same time, XML-based test cases are generated by VTE as shown in Fig. 7.

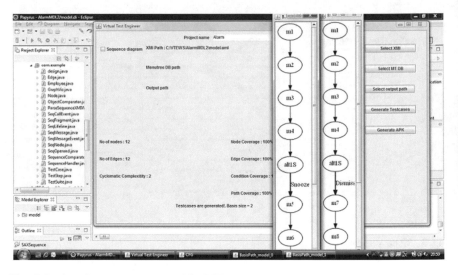

Fig. 6 Basis path test cases generated by VTE

Fig. 7 Generated
XML-based test cases

By clicking "Generate APK" button in VTE, an APK with project name, in this case "Alarm.apk" is generated. This APK sends XML name, menu tree DB name to VTE service. VTE service parses XML test case and triggers the following command to invoke library function in "Library.jar" file:

$$proc = java.lang.Runtime.getRuntime().exec("uiautomator runtest Library.jar$$
$$- c com.uia.example.my.Library" + " - e command"$$
$$+ commandstr + " - eargument1name" + argument1name + "$$
$$- eargument2name" + argument2name + " - eargument1value"$$
$$+ argument1value + " - eargument2value" + argument2value + "$$
$$- edatabase" + databasestr);$$

Library function in Library.jar file generates events in Android mobile to simulate user actions such as clicking menu items, buttons in order to execute these test cases. When "Execute" button of Alarm.apk as shown in Fig. 3 is clicked, test cases are executed sequentially and an Excel-based test report is generated automatically as shown in Fig. 8.

Testcase number	Command	Argument1	Argument2	Test Result
1	Navigate	MenuItem = New alarm	PackageName = com.I	Pass
1	LibSetSpinner	TimeInMinutes = 2	NotApplicable = NotAp	Pass
1	LibClickButton	ButtonName = Save	NotApplicable = NotAp	Pass
1	LibWaitAndVerifyUIText	TimeInMinutes = 2	TextToCheck = Dismiss	Pass
1	LibClickButton	ButtonName = Dismiss	NotApplicable = NotAp	Pass
1	LibWaitAndVerifyUIText	TimeInMinutes = 5	TextToCheck = Dismiss	Pass
1	Navigate	MenuItem = Delete	PackageName = com.I	Pass
1	LibDeleteAll	NotApplicable = NotAp	NotApplicable = NotAp	Pass
2	Navigate	MenuItem = New alarm	PackageName = com.I	Pass
2	LibSetSpinner	TimeInMinutes = 2	NotApplicable = NotAp	Pass
2	LibClickButton	ButtonName = Save	NotApplicable = NotAp	Pass
2	LibWaitAndVerifyUIText	TimeInMinutes = 2	TextToCheck = Dismiss	Pass
2	LibClickButton	ButtonName = Snooze	NotApplicable = NotAp	Pass
2	LibWaitAndVerifyUIText	TimeInMinutes = 5	TextToCheck = Dismiss	Pass
2	Navigate	MenuItem = Delete	PackageName = com.I	Pass
2	LibDeleteAll	NotApplicable = NotAp	NotApplicable = NotAp	Pass

Fig. 8 Test report for alarm scenarios

5 Experimental Results

The tool was applied to verify whether system testing is feasible with this approach to satisfy the following test conditions:

a. Different Android applications
b. Different Android OS versions (e.g., Kitkat and Lollypop)
c. Devices with different form factors (e.g., QVGA(240 × 320) and WVGA (480 × 800)]
d. Different UI versions
e. Program structures coverage (e.g., loop, alternative, option, and break)
f. Structural coverage (e.g., path coverage, node coverage, edge coverage, guard coverage)
g. Different verification methods (e.g., UIText verification, log verification)
h. Test case type (e.g., normal flow and alternative flow)
   Alarm application is taken for experiment to generate test cases and test scripts automatically to meet all above coverage criteria.

5.1 Horizontal deployment

In this experiment, different applications such as alarm, messaging, and calculator are considered. Different coverage criteria as listed above are considered. Total 19 test cases are automated using this method. This has to be elaborated to cover all applications in future. Table 1 shows deployment data captured for different Android applications. The coverage achieved is showed using a $\sqrt{}$ symbol.

In this experiment, different applications such as alarm, messaging, and calculator are considered. Different coverage criteria as listed above are considered. Total

Table 1 Deployment data for android applications

Application name	No of test cases	Android OS		Form factor		UI version		Program structure				Test coverage			
		Kitkat	Lollipop	QVGA	WVGA	4	4.1	Loop	Alt	Opt	Break	Path	Node	Edge	Guard
Alarm	5	✓	✓	✓	✓	✓	✓	✓	✓	✓	X	✓	✓	✓	✓
Stop watch	5	✓	✓	✓	✓	✓	✓	X	X	X	X	X	✓	✓	X
Timer	4	✓	✓	✓	✓	✓	✓	X	X	X	X	X	✓	✓	X
world clock	3	✓	✓	✓	✓	✓	✓	X	X	X	X	X	✓	✓	X
Settings	4	✓	✓	✓	✓	✓	✓	X	X	X	X	X	✓	✓	X
Calculator	4	✓	✓	✓	✓	✓	✓	X	X	X	X	X	✓	✓	X
Message	4	✓	✓	✓	✓	✓	✓	✓	✓	✓	X	✓	✓	✓	✓

19 test cases are automated using this method. This has to be elaborated to cover all applications in future. Table 1 shows deployment data captured for different Android applications. The coverage achieved is showed using a $\sqrt{}$ symbol.

5.2 Bug fixing/Enhancement

During experimentation, the following bugs are fixed:

1. When input model is using combined fragments such as "loop," "alt," the generated XML test cases are not carrying related information. For example, in case of "loop," loop count has to be passed as attribute within a test step.
2. When different testers are making test cases for same package, more than one *. uml files are resulted. For example, model.uml and model1.uml are resulted from two testers for "Alarm" package. VTE supports this feature allowing more than one input (*.uml) files and generates one single output XML file, containing all test cases.

6   Comparison with Other Methods

In [3], a method to parse XMI exported from sequence diagram is illustrated. And then a Control Flow Graph (CFG) is constructed from nodes, edges, and guards. In our approach, basis path-based test cases in the form of XML file are generated from CFG. Also, test scripts in the form of APKs are generated, which simulate user interface events in Android phones.

In [6], after parsing XML file exported from sequence diagram, scenarios are generated by traversing through all paths. But the algorithm to traverse the paths is not clearly given. In our approach, a recursive algorithm is made to generate basis path-based test cases, to ensure coverage criteria such as path coverage, node coverage, edge coverage, and guard coverage are achieved.

In [7], test cases are generated from sequence diagram. Object Constraint Language (OCL) is used to define messages, guards, etc. In our approach, library functions with method names and arguments are defined. All messages need to use these pre-defined library functions, so that XML-based test cases are generated with these method names and arguments used as XML tags.

In [8], test stubs are generated to perform integration testing. Code instrumentation is required for executing test cases. In our case, test cases and test scripts are generated for performing system testing. It is a block box approach.

In [9], ComTest tool is proposed, which is generating test scripts. But test script format is not explained. In our approach, Virtual Test Engineer (VTE) is developed. It takes menu tree database and XML-based test cases as inputs. Menu tree database helps to navigate through menu tree path and reach any menu item in phone. An UI Automator-based jar file is used to simulate user interface events such as click menu item, click button to navigate.

7 Conclusions

In this paper, an automation framework for generating system test scripts for Android mobile is proposed. A tool called "Virtual Test Engineer" is built to realize this approach. Testing activities such as requirement analysis, test case design, test case generation, test script generation, and test execution are automated. The scenarios are captured in the form of sequence diagram. XMI file exported from sequence diagram is parsed to get CFG. Basis path test cases are generated from CFG in the form of XML file. An APK is generated to handle this XML and simulate user interface events such as click menu item, click button. Also, this APK takes menu tree database as input and facilitates navigation through menu tree of Android phone. To execute multiple APKs in sequence, a test scheduler is involved. The objective is to reduce the test effort by automating test engineering activities throughout the test cycle.

Currently, few applications of Android mobile are testable with this method. In future, this method will be elaborated to cover all Android applications.

In future, a suitable algorithm will be developed using genetic algorithm and Artificial Intelligence (AI) planning, to generate test data.

This method will be more generalized, so that this method will be adaptable for other embedded systems, Windows, or Linux-based applications.

References

1. Anbunathan R., Basu, A.: An event based test automation framework for android mobiles. In: IEEE First International Conference on Contemporary Computing and Informatics (IC3I) (2014)
2. Binder, R.V.: Testing object-oriented systems: models, patterns, and tools, Addison-Wesley (1999)
3. Kundu, D., Samanta, D., Mall, R.: An approach to convert XMI representation of UML 2.x interaction diagram into control flow graph. Int. Sch. Res. Netw. (ISRN) Softw. Eng. (2012)
4. Anbunathan R., Basu, A.: A recursive crawler algorithm to detect crash in android application. In: IEEE International Conference on Computational Intelligence and Computing Research (ICCIC) (2014)
5. Basu, A.: Software quality assurance, testing and metrics, PHI Learning (2015)
6. Sawant, V., Shah, K.: Automatic generation of test cases from UML models. In: Proceedings of International Conference on Technology Systems and Management (ICTSM) published by International Journal of Computer Applications (IJCA) (2011)
7. Sarma, M., Kundu, D., Mall, R.: Automatic test case generation from UML sequence diagram. In: Proceedings of the 15th International Conference on Advanced Computing and

Communications (ADCOM, '07), pp. 60–67, IEEE Computer Society, Washington, DC, USA (2007)

8. Fraikin, F., Leonhardt, T.; SeDiTeC—testing based on sequence diagrams. In: Proceedings of the IEEE International Conference on Automated Software Engineering, (ASE '02), pp. 261–266 (2002)

9. Swain, S.K., Mohapatra, D.P., Mall, R.: Test case generation based on use case and sequence diagram. Int. J. Softw. Eng. 3(2), 21–52 (2010)

10. Android Developers. UI automator. Available at: http://developer.android.com/tools/help/uiautomator/index.html. Last accessed 29 Nov 2014

11. OMG, XML metadata interchange (XMI), v2.1 (2004)

12. https://eclipse.org/papyrus/

13. http://simple.sourceforge.net/

14. http://www.graphviz.org/Documentation/dotguide.pdf

Optimizing the Defect Prioritization in Enterprise Application Integration

Viral Gupta, Deepak Kumar and P. K. Kapur

Abstract Defect prioritization is one of the key decisions that impacts the quality, cost, and schedule of any software development project. There are multiple attributes of defects that drive the decision of defect prioritization. Generally in practice, the defects are prioritized subjectively based on few attributes of defects like severity or business priority. This assignment of defect priority does not consider other critical attributes of the defect. There is a need of a framework that collectively takes into consideration critical attributes of defects and generates the most optimum defect prioritization strategy. In this paper, critical attributes of defects are considered and a new framework based on genetic algorithm for generating optimized defect prioritization is proposed. The results from the experimental execution of the algorithm show the effectiveness of the proposed framework and improvement by 40% in the overall quality of these projects.

Keywords Defect prioritization · Triage · Genetic algorithm · Enterprise application · Quality · Testing · And optimization

1 Introduction

Software testing is the process of executing the program under test with the intent of finding defects. The process of analysis, prioritization, and assignment of defects is known as defect triaging [1]. Defect triaging is a complex process that brings

V. Gupta (✉) · D. Kumar
Amity Institute of Information Technology, Amity University, Noida 110025,
Uttar Pradesh, India
e-mail: viralgupta@hotmail.com

D. Kumar
e-mail: deepakgupta_du@rediffmail.com

P. K. Kapur
Centre for Interdisciplinary Research, Amity University, Noida 110025,
Uttar Pradesh, India
e-mail: pkkapur1@gmail.com

© Springer Nature Singapore Pte Ltd. 2019
M. N. Hoda et al. (eds.), *Software Engineering*, Advances in Intelligent Systems
and Computing 731, https://doi.org/10.1007/978-981-10-8848-3_56

585

stakeholders from multiple teams like test, business, and development together. Test team raises the defect with basic attributes in the defect tracking system and assigns the value of severity to the defect. Severity of the defect signifies the impact on the system. The business team verifies the defect and updates the priority of the defect. Priority of the defect signifies the order in which the defect needs to be fixed. Development manager analyses various attributes of the defects like severity, priority, estimate to fix, next release date, skills required to fix, availability of resources and prioritizes and assigns the defects to the developers. The prioritization of defects is the very important factor in the defect management process that impacts the quality, cost, and schedule of the project releases. Defect prioritization should ideally consider multiple attributes of the defects [2]. In the present scenario, defect prioritization is being done subjectively and manually by the business team leader or the development manager based on very few attributes like severity and priority. In a large enterprise application integration project where the daily defect incoming rate is 80–100, team accumulates more than 1000 defects to be fixed. Considering five days of release drop cycle, development team faces the challenge to decide which defects to fix for the next code drop cycle to get optimized results. In order to make this decision, the development team requires a framework that takes into account multiple attributes of the defects and can generate the optimized defect prioritization for these defects, so that the development team will focus on the resolution of the prioritized defects only. This effective defect prioritization can improve the total number of defects fixed for the next release, customer satisfaction, and faster time to market. In a large enterprise application integration project, the complexity of defect management and release management increases due to heterogeneous systems involved in the integration and additional attributes of the defects comes into action [3]. In this paper, a new framework using genetic algorithm is proposed that considers multiple attributes of the defects and generates the optimized defect prioritization that overall results in the process improvements by more than 40%. This paper begins by providing the brief overview of the past work conducted in this area, followed by details of genetic algorithm, proposed methodology. An experiment is conducted on an enterprise application development project. Finally, the paper is concluded with the discussions of the results of the experiment.

2 Literature Review

Kaushik et al. [1] in their study surveyed defect triages engaged in the software product development company and identified various challenges faced by practitioners during the defect prioritization and assignments. These challenges are ambiguity in understanding requirements, defect duplication, conflicting objectives of defects, and incomplete supporting knowledge. The study emphasized the issue of subjective assignment of severity and priority to the defects and underlines the ignorance of various critical factors like cost to fix defects, technical risks, and exposure in defect prioritization. The study proposed adoption of research directions like multiobjective defect prioritization, utilization of software artefacts traceability matrix for resolving the issue of defect prioritization.

Cubranic et al. [4] proposed the adoption of supervised machine learning using Bayesian learning approach to automatically assign bug reports to the developers. The study conducted an experiment to analyse the group of more than 15,000 bug reports from the large project and assigned these defects automatically to the developers based on text categorization techniques. The six-step heuristic was proposed to conduct the experiment. Except 180 bugs, all bugs were assigned to 162 developers. The results showed overall 30% accuracy in prediction of the defect assignment. The results were evaluated by the project.

Ahmed et al. [5] in their study discussed various ways to optimize the manual analysis of the incoming defects and categorization of these defects. The study highlights the amount of efforts and cost spent in manually analysing deluge of defects and categorizing them into various categories. An experiment was conducted on the group of more than 4000 defects from telecom projects. The study used k-nearest classification and Naïve Bayes algorithms to categorize the incoming defects into functional, logical, standard, and GUI-related categories. The results show the highest accuracy achieved using Bayes algorithm was 79%.

Alenezi et al. [6] presented an approach for predicting the priority of the defect based on the algorithms, namely Naïve Bayes, decision trees, and random forest. These algorithms are based on the machine learning techniques. An experimental evaluation has been conducted on the software projects. The element of subjectivity in manually assigning the priority of the defects has been highlighted in the study. Two feature sets are used in order to execute the proposed algorithms. These feature sets are textual contents of the bug report and the metadata information of the bug report. More than 8000 defects from two projects were categorized in the priority classes of high priority, medium, average, and low priority. The results show that the feature set of metadata information outperforms the other feature set. The results from random forest and decision trees outperform the Naïve Bayes results.

Malhotra et al. [7] in their paper proposed text classification techniques to predict and assess the severity of defects. The report of defects was taken from the software projects, and support vector machine algorithm is used to predict the severity of defects. The study advocates the prediction and automatic allocation of the severity of defects using the text classification techniques. The study executed the algorithm based on 5, 25, 50, and 100 feature set. The results were evaluated using the precision and recall metrics to find out the effectiveness of the algorithms.

Chen et al. [8] conducted an experiment to achieve test case prioritization for the functional testing. This experiment is conducted to prioritize the functional test cases that were derived from the functional specifications. The study assumes that the primary factors for the evaluation of test case prioritization are requirement severity score and the interdependency between the test cases. The requirements are categorized into four categories, and the scores are assigned to each category, while test case dependency was also categorized under six categories, and the scores are assigned. The researchers executed genetic algorithm (GA) and ant colony optimization (ACO) algorithms on the five sets of test suites. It was concluded that the

GA and ACO algorithms provided similar efficiency in achieving the test case prioritization.

Xuan et al. [9] in their study analysed the developer's priorities to improve three aspects of defect management, namely defect triage, defect severity identification and assignment and the prediction of the reopened defects. The results show that the average prediction accuracy has been approved by 13% after considering the developer's priority. The main premise of the study is that developers have different capability of fixing these defects [10, 11]. These developers are ranked and prioritized, and this developer prioritization is used for improving the defect triaging process.

There has been a very little research work done in the literature for achieving defect prioritization [12–15]. Most of the past work is focussed on the utilizing machine language algorithms and text categorization techniques for defect categorization [16, 17]. There has been slight evidence of work done for utilizing genetic algorithm for test case prioritization, but there has not been any concrete experimental work done in the past showing usage of genetic algorithm in defect prioritization.

3 Genetic Algorithm

Usage of evolutionary algorithms in the software testing is an emerging trend that helps in the automatic generation of the test cases, test data, and also helps in sequencing these test cases to achieve the optimization in test execution phase [18–20]. Genetic algorithm is an optimization technique and the search method that is based on the concept of evolution of species using natural selection of the fittest individuals [1]. The genetic algorithm works on the population which consists of possible solutions of a given problem for which an optimized solution is sought. The possible solutions from the population are represented by chromosome which is denoted by a string of binary digits known as genes. Genetic algorithm uses three main operators, namely selection, crossover, and mutation. As a part of selection process, all chromosomes are evaluated based on the fitness value. Fitness function defines the capability of an individual to qualify as best among others. The best chromosomes are selected for crossover [21]. In the crossover process, the genes of the selected chromosomes are swapped in order to produce more capable next-generation chromosomes or the offsprings [22, 23]. The process is repeated until next generation has sufficient chromosomes. The last step is mutation which alters a part of the chromosomes to produce good results.

4 Proposed Approach and Experimental Set-up

In the past, defect prioritization has been done based on few attributes like priority or severity. It has been identified that defect prioritization is a multiattribute problem. From the survey of the literature, authors found four attributes that drive the defect prioritization. These attributes are severity, priority, time to fix, and blocked test cases. Authors identified ten experts from the software industry. These experts are working as delivery head, delivery manager, test manager, and business consultants in software companies that execute enterprise application integration projects. Each of these experts has more than 15 years of experience in the industry. A questionnaire was sent to these experts to seek their opinion about the importance of these attributes and to find out if there is any additional attribute that impacts the defect prioritization and has not been mentioned in the past work. Each expert $(E_1, E_2, E_3, E_4 \ldots E_{10})$ was required to provide response on a five-point scale, namely very strong impact (VSI), strong impact (SI), medium impact (MI), low impact (LI), VLI (no impact). These responses were assigned numerical scores as VSI is assigned as 5, SI is assigned score as 4, MI is assigned score as 3, LI is assigned score as 2, and VLI is assigned score as 1. Overall scores for each attribute is calculated from the responses of all experts. A software development project that implements the enterprise application integration is chosen, and an experiment is conducted by executing genetic algorithm to prioritize the defects and evaluate the effectiveness of outcomes. This software project, namely "Banking Payments Platform (BPP)", is a very large integration project of 30 applications that are operational in bank for many years. The software development team is working on the major upcoming release to integrate these applications. Total line of code for these applications is 10 Million, and the total software development and testing team size is 50. At the time of the study, the project is in system testing phase. Total 1000 defects have been identified till date, and 600 defects have been closed. Daily defect arrival rate is 25–30. Daily closure rate from the development team is 15–20, which is resulting in increase in backlog defects. In the system testing phase, there are 40 developers in the team and on an average ten defects are assigned to each developer. The release code drop cycle is 5 days, and authors have found this project to be the most relevant project to conduct the experiment. Each developer has ten backlogs of defects, and the next release code drop is 5 days away. Each developer is faced with the decision to prioritize the defects assigned to him. This study proposes usage of genetic algorithm. For the purpose of this experiment, chromosomes consist of the set of defects to be fixed by the developers (Table 1).

Fitness function in the experiment is a function of multiple attributes of the defects. These attributes were identified from the literature and ranked based on the expert's interview. The fitness function is derived from rankings of the attributes achieved by the expert's interview. EAI score (ES) is derived by assigning numerical scores to the EAI values for each defect. 7 is assigned to orchestration defects, 5 is assigned to maps/schema defects, 3 is assigned to pipeline defect, and 1 is assigned to adaptors defects. Severity score (SS) is derived by assigning numerical scores to the severity values for each defect. 7 is assigned for critical defect, 5 is assigned for high, 3 is assigned for medium defect, and 1 is assigned for low defect. Similarly, priority score (PS) is derived by assigning numerical scores to the priority values for each defect. 7 is assigned for very high priority defect, score of 5 is assigned for high priority defect, score of 3 is assigned for medium priority

Table 1 Initial chromosomes

D1	D2	D8	D3	D5	D4	D9	D6	D7	D10
Chromosome 1									
D9	D1	D2	D3	D8	D4	D7	D5	D6	D10
Chromosome 3									

D5	D8	D1	D6	D2	D4	D10	D3	D7	D9
Chromosome 2									
D1	D5	D8	D2	D4	D6	D10	D3	D7	D9
Chromosome 4									

defect, and score of 1 is assigned for low priority defect. Total SevPriority Score (PS) is calculated as (1).

$$PS_n = SS_n * PS_n \tag{1}$$

$$TBTC_n = \frac{(BTC_n)}{\sum_{k=0}^{n} BTC_k} \tag{2}$$

The number of blocked test cases for each defect is represented by $(BTC_1, BTC_2, BTC_3, BTC_4 \ldots BTC_{10})$. The total blocked test case score $TBTC_n$ for a defect would be calculated as (2). The time required to fix a defect is represented as by $(TF, TF_2, TF_3, TF_4 \ldots TF_{10})$, and the proposed rank to fix the nth defect is represented as by $(R, R_2, R_3, R_4 \ldots R_{10})$. The total time score (TS) would be calculated as follows:

$$TS_n = \frac{11 - (R_n)}{TF_n} \tag{3}$$

Fitness score (FS_n) for each defect given by following equation:

$$FS_n = (SS_n * PS_n) + \frac{(BTC_n)}{\sum_{k=0}^{n} BTC_k} + \frac{11 - (R_n)}{TF_n} + EAI_n \tag{4}$$

Total fitness score (FS_{tot}) for the entire chromosome is given by following equation, where m is the rank of the defect where time to fix the defects stretches beyond the next release code drop date.

$$FS_{tot} = \sum_{n=1}^{m} \left((SS_n * PS_n) + \frac{(BTC_n)}{\sum_{k=0}^{n} BTC_k} + \frac{11 - (R_n)}{TF_n} + EAI_n \right) \tag{5}$$

Initial number of chromosomes taken was 4. The encoding used for chromosome is alphanumeric [24–26]. The crossover rate (C.R.) is 0.8, and mutation rate is 0.3. Section technique is used as fitness function that is based on five attributes of the defects. The crossover method was hybrid, namely single point and double point. Mutation method was random.

5   Outcomes and Discussions

Based on the responses received from the experts, it has been identified that the top five attributes of the defects that must be considered during the defect prioritization activity were severity, priority, time to fix, blocked test cases, and EAI factor. Authors found that EAI factor is the new factor that has not been identified in any of the past work. The values for EAI factors are orchestration, maps/schema, pipeline,

Table 2 Defect attributes ranked by experts

Defects attributes	VSI	SI	MI	LI	VLI	VSI score (VSIs$_1$)	SI score (SIs$_1$)	MI score (MIs$_1$)	LI score (LIs$_1$)	VLI score (VLIs$_1$)	Total score (TSIs$_1$)
Severity	4	3	3	0	0	20	12	9	0	0	41
Priority	3	4	2	1	0	15	16	6	2	0	39
Time to fix	3	2	2	3	0	15	8	6	6	0	35
Blocked test cases	6	3	1	0	0	30	12	3	0	0	45
EAI factor	5	2	1	1	1	25	8	3	2	1	39

and adaptor-related defects. The highest impacting factor is the number of blocked test cases. Attributes identified from the survey questionnaire and the expert's interview were incorporated in the calculation of the fitness function for the selection operator of the genetic algorithm. Multiple cycles of genetic algorithm were executed. The first cycle of genetic algorithm had four chromosomes, and the highest fitness score was 194.516 (Tables 2, 3, 4, 5, 6, 7, 8, and 9).

Table 3 lists four initial chromosomes that represent initial defect priorities that a developer has considered. The maximum fitness score of 194.516 is for the third chromosome. Using the total fitness scores, average fitness score, and the cumulative fitness score, three chromosomes are selected for the next operation of the

Table 3 Genetic algorithm cycle 1: selection—fitness scores

#	Chromosome	FS	FA	FC	RN	DF	PF	TCU
1	1, 2, 8, 3, 5, 4, 9, 6, 7, 10	164.175	0.255	0.255	0.275	3	3	22
2	5, 8, 1, 6, 2, 4, 10, 3, 7, 9	142.008	0.221	0.476	0.832	3	2	64
3	9, 1, 2, 3, 8, 4, 7, 5, 6, 10	194.516	0.302	0.778	0.166	4	4	23
4	1, 5, 8, 2, 4, 6, 10, 3, 7, 9	143.008	0.222	1.000	0.547	3	2	64

Table 4 Genetic algorithm cycle 1: crossover and mutation

#	Parent	Child	Mutation
3	9, 1, 2, 3, 8, 4, 7, 5, 6, 10	1, 5, 8, 2, 4, 4, 7, 5, 6, 10	1, 9, 8, 2, 3, 4, 7, 5, 6, 10
4	1, 5, 8, 2, 4, 6, 10, 3, 7, 9	9, 1, 2, 3, 8, 6, 10, 3, 7, 9	5, 1, 2, 4, 8, 6, 10, 3, 7, 9
1	1, 2, 8, 3, 5, 4, 9, 6, 7, 10	9, 1, 2, 3, 8, 4, 9, 6, 7, 10	9, 1, 2, 3, 8, 4, 5, 6, 7, 10
3	9, 1, 2, 3, 8, 4, 7, 5, 6, 10	1, 2, 8, 3, 5, 4, 7, 5, 6, 10	1, 2, 8, 3, 5, 4, 7, 9, 6, 10

Table 5 Genetic algorithm cycle 2: selection—fitness scores

#	Chromosome	FS	FA	FC	RN	DF	PF	TCU
5	1, 9, 8, 2, 3, 4, 7, 5, 6, 10	205.508	0.275	0.277	0.123	4	4	22
6	5, 1, 2, 4, 8, 6, 10, 3, 7, 9	184.270	0.246	0.523	0.658	4	3	76
7	9, 1, 2, 3, 8, 4, 5, 6, 7, 10	194.516	0.260	0.783	0.267	4	4	63
8	1, 2, 8, 3, 5, 4, 7, 9, 6, 10	164.175	0.219	1.000	0.581	3	3	22

Table 6 Genetic algorithm cycle 2: crossover and mutation

#	Parent	Child	Mutation
7	9, 1, 2, 3, 8, 4, 5, 6, 7, 10	9, 1, 2, 4, 8, 6, 10, 6, 7, 10	9, 1, 2, 4, 8, 5, 3, 6, 7, 10
6	5, 1, 2, 4, 8, 6, 10, 3, 7, 9	5, 1, 2, 3, 8, 4, 5, 3, 7, 9	6, 1, 2, 10, 8, 4, 5, 3, 7, 9
7	9, 1, 2, 3, 8, 4, 5, 6, 7, 10	9, 1, 8, 2, 3, 4, 7, 6, 7, 10	9, 1, 8, 2, 3, 4, 5, 6, 7, 10
5	1, 9, 8, 2, 3, 4, 7, 5, 6, 10	1, 9, 2, 3, 8, 4, 5, 5, 6, 10	1, 9, 2, 3, 8, 4, 7, 5, 6, 10

Table 7 Genetic algorithm cycle 3: selection—fitness scores

#	Chromosome	FS	FA	FC	RN	DF	PF	TCU
9	9, 1, 2, 4, 8, 5, 3, 6, 7, 10	243.905	0.309	0.309	0.250	5	5	30
10	6, 1, 2, 10, 8, 4, 5, 3, 7, 9	160.937	0.204	0.513	0.640	4	2	26
11	9, 1, 8, 2, 3, 4, 5, 6, 7, 10	192.516	0.244	0.757	0.301	4	4	34
12	1, 9, 2, 3, 8, 4, 7, 5, 6, 10	191.516	0.243	1.000	0.024	4	4	30

Table 8 Genetic algorithm cycle 3: crossover and mutation

#	Parent	Child	Mutation
9	9, 1, 2, 4, 8, 5, 3, 6, 7, 10	9, 1, 2, 4, 3, 4, 5, 6, 7, 10	9, 1, 2, 4, 3, 7, 5, 6, 8, 10
11	9, 1, 8, 2, 3, 4, 5, 6, 7, 10	9, 1, 8, 2, 3, 5, 3, 6, 7, 10	9, 1, 8, 2, 3, 5, 4, 6, 7, 10

genetic algorithm. Crossover method was single point, and first five genes were crossed over between two chromosomes. After the crossover and mutation operations, four child chromosomes are generated for the second cycle of the genetic algorithm. In the next cycle, the maximum fitness score of 205.508 is for the first chromosome. Using the total fitness scores, average fitness score, and the cumulative fitness score, three chromosomes are selected for the next cycle. Crossover method was hybrid, and five elements from the fourth element were crossed over between two chromosomes. After the crossover and mutation operations, four child chromosomes are generated for the third cycle of the genetic algorithm. In the next cycle, the maximum fitness score of 243.905 is for the first chromosome. Using the total fitness scores, average fitness score, and the cumulative fitness score, two chromosomes are selected for the next operation of the genetic algorithm. Two child chromosomes are generated for the third cycle of the genetic algorithm. In the next cycle, the maximum fitness score of 270.111 is for the first chromosome. This defect sequence can fix defect 6 defects for the next code drop. All of these six defects are from top two severities. These six defects are responsible for total 56 blocked test cases. From the outcomes of the experiment, it has been proved that the fitness scores for the chromosomes have improved over multiple cycles of the executed genetic algorithm. In the first cycle, the developer was able to fix four defects and unblock 22 test cases, while after the application of the genetic algorithm, developer can fix six defects and unblock 56 test cases. There has been 46% improvement in the defects closed, 54% improvement in the closure of the top two severities/priorities of defects, and 21% reduction in the test case blockage.

Table 9 Final genetic algorithm cycle 4: selection—fitness scores

Chromo #	Chromosome	Fitness score	Fitness average	Fitness cumulative	Random number	Defects fixed	Top two priority defects fixed	Test cases unblocked
13	9, 1, 2, 4, 3, 7, 5, 6, 8, 10	270.111	0.568	0.568	0.450	6	6	56
14	9, 1, 8, 2, 3, 5, 4, 6, 7, 10	208.508	0.432	1.000	0.360	1	4	22

6 Conclusions

Defect prioritization involves the decision-making process to prioritize defects based on various attributes of the defects. In the past, there has been very less work done that empirically demonstrates defect prioritization resulting in improvements. This study proposed a framework to utilize genetic algorithm for defect prioritization that results in quality improvements. Authors of this study ranked the defect attributes required by the genetic algorithm for defect prioritization problem. Totally five attributes were identified and ranked; a new attribute, namely EAI factor has been identified, which was not mentioned in the past work. The experiment result demonstrated overall 46% improvement in the number of defects closed by a developer for the next code drop, 54% improvement in the closure of the top two severities/priorities of defects, and 21% reduction in the blockage of test cases. The outcome of the experiment has been found very useful by the development, business, and testing teams.

References

1. Kaushik, N., Amoui, M., Tahvildari, L, Liu, W, Li, S.: Defect prioritization in the software industry: challenges and opportunities. In: IEEE Sixth International Conference on Software Testing, Verification and Validation, pp. 70–73 (2013). https://doi.org/10.1109/icst.2013.40
2. Somerville, I.: Software engineering, 6th edn. Addison-Wesley, Boston (2001)
3. Themistocleous, M.G.: Evaluating the adoption of enterprise application integration in multinational organizations (Doctoral dissertation) (2002)
4. Cubranic, D., Murphy, G.C.: Automatic bug triage using text categorization. Online (n.d.). Retrieved from https://www.cs.ubc.ca/labs/spl/papers/2004/seke04-bugzilla.pdf
5. Ahmed, M.M., Hedar, A.R.M., Ibrahim, H.M.: Predicting bug category based on analysis of software repositories. In: 2nd International Conference on Research in Science, Engineering and Technology, pp. 44–53 (2014). http://dx.doi.org/10.15242/IIE.E0314580
6. Alenezi, M., Banitaan, S.: Bug report prioritization: which features and classifier to use? In: 12th International Conference on Machine Learning and Applications, pp. 112–116 (2013). https://doi.org/10.1109/icmla.2013.114
7. Malhotra, R., Kapoor, N., Jain, R., Biyani, S.: Severity assessment of software defect reports using text categorization. Int. J. Comput. Appl. **83**(11), 13–16 (2013)
8. Chen, G.Y.H., Wang, P.Q.: Test case prioritization in a specification based testing environment. J. Softw. **9**(4), 2056–2064 (2014)
9. Xuan, J., Jiang, H., Ren, Z., Zou, W.: Developer prioritization in bug repositories. In: International Conference of Software Engineering, 2012, pp. 25–35, Zurich, Switzerland, (2012)
10. Bhattacharya, P., Iliofotou, M., Neamtiu, I., Faloutsos, M.: Graph-based analysis and prediction for software evolution, [Online] (n.d.). Retrieved from http://www.cs.ucr.edu/~neamtiu/pubs/icse12bhattacharya.pdf
11. Cohen, J., Ferguson, R., Hayes, W.: A defect prioritization method based on the risk priority number, [Online] (n.d.). Retrieved from http://resources.sei.cmu.edu/asset_files/whitepaper/2013_019_001_70276.pdf
12. Goldberg, D.E.: Genetic algorithms: in search, optimization and machine learning, p. 1989. Addison Wesley, M.A. (1989)

13. Guo, P.J., Zimmermann, T., Nagappan, N., Murphy, B.: Characterizing and predicting which bugs get fixed: an empirical study of microsoft windows. In: International Conference on Software Engineering, ACM (2010)
14. Gupta, N.M., Rohil, M.K.: Using genetic algorithm for unit testing of object oriented software. Int. J. Simul. Syst. Sci. Technol. **10**(3), 99–104 (2008)
15. Jeong, G., Kim, S., Zimmermann, T.: Improving bug triage with bug tossing graphs. In: European Software Engineering Conference, ESEC-FSE'09 (2009)
16. Keshavarz, S., Javidan, R.: Software quality control based on genetic algorithm. Int. J. Comput. Theor. Eng. **3**(4), 579–584 (2011)
17. Kim, D., Tao, Y., Kim, S., Zeller, A.: Where should we fix this bug? A two-phase recommendation model. IEEE Trans. Softw. Eng. **39**(11), 1597–1610 (2013)
18. Krishnamoorthi, R., Sahaaya, S.A., Mary, A.: Regression test suite prioritization using genetic algorithms. Int. J. Hybrid Inf. Technol. **2**(3), 35–52 (2009)
19. Majid, H.A., Kasim, N.H., Samah. A. A.: Optimization of warranty cost using genetic algorithm: a case study in fleet vehicle. Int. J. Soft Comput. Eng. (IJSCE), **3**(4), 199–202 (Sept 2013)
20. Mala, D.J., Ruby, E., Mohan, V.: A Hybrid test optimization framework—coupling genetic algorithm with local search technique. Comput. Inform. **29**, 133–164 (2010)
21. Pargas, R.P., Harrold, M. J., Peck, R. R.: Test data generation using genetic algorithm. J. Softw. Test. Verific. Reliab. 1–19 (1999)
22. Patel, K., Sawant, P., Tajane, M., Shankarmani, R.: Bug tracking and prediction. Int. J. Innov. Emerg. Res. Eng. **2**(3), 174–179 (2015)
23. Sharma, Chayanika, Sabharwal, Sangeeta, Sibal, Ritu: A survey on software testing techniques using genetic algorithm. Int. J. Comput. Sci. Issues **10**(1), 381–393 (2013)
24. Srivastava, P.R., Kim, Tai-hoon: Application of genetic algorithm in software testing. Int. J. Softw. Eng. Its Appl. **3**(4), 87–96 (2009)
25. Sthamer, H.H.: The automatic generation of software test data using genetic algorithms (Doctoral dissertation) (1995). Retrieved from profs.info.uaic.ro
26. Tian, Y., Lo, D., Sun, C.: DRONE: predicting priority of reported bugs by multi-factor analysis. IEEE Int. Conf. Softw. Mainten. **2013**, 199–209 (2013)

Desktop Virtualization—Desktop as a Service and Formulation of TCO with Return on Investment

Nitin Chawla and Deepak Kumar

Abstract Cloud computing provides multiple deployment options to organizations such as Software as a Service (SaaS), Platform as a Service (PaaS), Infrastructure as a Service (IaaS). Desktop as a Service is upcoming deployment model which has a multi-tenancy architecture, and the service is available on a subscription basis. Desktop as a Service (DaaS) authorizes users to access the applications anytime using virtualized desktop. Virtualized desktops hosted on cloud provided flexibility to use any device. With no software for IT to maintain, Desktop as a Service is straightforward to buy and easy to manage. This paper describes the needs of Desktop as a Service, benefits of DaaS, barriers to widespread DaaS adoption, comparison of industry DaaS leaders, and describes its application in real. A general model and framework have also been developed to calculate the total cost of ownership and return on investment to help the organization to take decisions and have relevant discussions to adopt DaaS.

Keywords Cloud computing · Desktop virtualization · Desktop as a Service Deployment model · Cloud security

1 Introduction

The principle of cloud desktops has been around for many years, but it has only just begun to gain a foothold in terms of adoption. That could be because IT shops are interested in VDI [1] but cannot front the money for it, or because the cloud is just a hot-button topic these days. Either way, many people do not know the details of DaaS [1] technology or how it compares to VDI. Start here for the basics on how it works, how it is different from VDI, and why the comparisons are not necessarily

N. Chawla (✉) · D. Kumar
Amity University, Noida 110025, Uttar Pradesh, India
e-mail: nitin1203@gmail.com

D. Kumar
e-mail: deepakgupta_du@rediffmail.com

M. N. Hoda et al. (eds.), *Software Engineering*, Advances in Intelligent Systems and Computing 731, https://doi.org/10.1007/978-981-10-8848-3_57

fair. VDI has seen pretty slow adoption—some experts think it will never crack 20%—so what does that say about how quickly organizations will adopt cloud desktops? There are tons of options out there now, and they'll just improve over time. Many companies try to get VDI off the ground but find that it is too expensive or that users reject it. Especially in small companies where VDI is often cost prohibitive, DaaS can be a great option because you're taking advantage of infrastructure someone else already built and has pledged to maintain. It might seem like DaaS and VDI are dissimilar, but the two share a lot of the same benefits, including easier desktop management, more flexibility and mobility, and less hardware. They also both come with licensing complexity. But of the two, only DaaS brings cloud security concerns.

For many VDI projects, costs can balloon down the line, and the infrastructure is hard to scale up and down on your own. But with a subscription-based, cloud-centric model, costs are predictable over the long term, and you can scale quickly in either direction if you need to. And with DaaS, it can be easier to set up a pilot program. The DaaS cost models that vendors such as Amazon push are flawed. When you compare the highest-priced VDI software with all the bells and whistles to the lowest-priced DaaS setup based on server images, of course, DaaS is going to look cheaper. But you can't compare Windows 7 to Windows Server. They're just not the same thing. DaaS can be confusing. For example, did you know that some application delivery techniques are technically DaaS? And there is a big difference between hosting Windows Server images in the cloud and hosting desktops. Don't forget about the potential licensing costs and complexity that can come with DaaS—they mean that sometimes cloud desktops won't save money over VDI. Depending on which provider and platform you settle on, deploying cloud desktops may not save money over VDI in the long run. Management costs—because you still need to maintain and update images, applications, security, and the network—subscription fees, and hardware requirements all play into how much cash stays in the company kitty. With hosted desktops, you have to license the Windows OSes, the desktop virtualization software, and the endpoint devices.

Additionally, every DaaS vendor and service provider handles licensing in its own way. Some providers need you to bring your own Virtual Desktop Access licenses. Windows desktop OS licensing restrictions make it really hard for companies to do "real" DaaS. Instead, DaaS vendors such as Amazon and VMware skin Windows Server 2008 R2 images to look like Windows. It works and customers want it, but it is not a true desktop. Just like some rectangles are squares, some DaaS providers are platforms—but not all platforms are providers, and not all providers are platforms. If that's got your head spinning, don't fret. There are ways to find the right provider and platform for you, but you'll have to take charge. Make sure you ask the right questions and negotiate a service-level agreement (SLA) that sways in your favor. In the DaaS market, there are many providers, but not as many platforms. The platform is what cloud desktops run on, and providers are the companies you buy that service from.

For example, VMware [2] has a platform and is a provider, but if you want to host desktops on to cloud infrastructure, you'll need to talk to a provider that has a relationship with that platform. Not all DaaS providers are created equal. Some vendors and platforms might not support the clients, operating systems, or applications you need. Management consoles and capabilities also differ from one product to the next. The provider you choose should have an SLA that outlines how the company will handle security breaches and outages.

In this paper, we state multiple factors to calculate the TCO. Factors which can affect the TCO are divided into two parts: tangible benefits and intangible benefits. A general ROI model has also been developed to help the organizations in adopting the new technology like DaaS.

2 Components of DaaS

Virtualization has become the new leading edge, and Desktop as a Service (DaaS) is gaining ground in this space. Due to increasing constraints on IT budgets, Desktop as a Service provides secure, flexible, and manageable solution to economically satisfy organization's needs. Desktop as a Service is well-suited environment as it provides agility and reduction in up-front capital investment as compared to the on-premise environment consisting of physical and decentralized desktop environment with high cost. Desktop as a Service platform solution provides organizations the flexibility of cloud services in a secure enterprise-class cloud (Figs. 1 and 2).

DaaS solution provides facility to the user to connect via RDP to a client OS such as Windows XP or Linux as a VM on a server. For this infrastructure to function, a DaaS solution must have the following components.

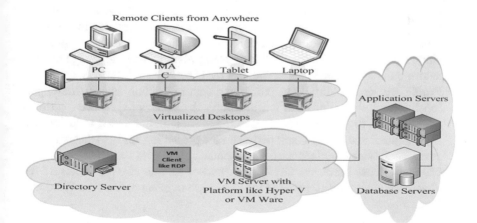

Fig. 1 Desktop virtualization architecture

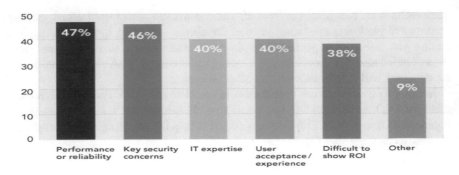

Fig. 2 Inhibitors to DaaS and VDI adoption

- **A virtualization platform**. A platform can run client operating systems like Linux, Windows. The platform should be able to host multiple VMs to support concurrency. Some of the virtual platforms are VMware, Hyper-V [3].
- **A protocol for the users to connect to the virtualized OS**. Most of the users use Windows, and RDP , part of windows, is used. Using RDP, once can use its features such as device and printer redirection. Multiple options such as thin client or remote client under full OS are available to take a decision for the protocol.
- **A virtual management platform**. This platform offers the creation and configuration of VM on the servers. A physical server can be divided into multiple VMs using the virtual management platform. Virtual platform transforms static desktops into secure, virtual workspaces that can be delivered on demand. Virtual platform can provision virtual or remote desktops and applications to streamline management and easily entitle end users.
- **A connection broker**. A session is created the very first time user logs in. This connection broker ensures that users log into their existing sessions.
- **Application virtualization**. Virtualization is done at multiple levels such as hardware virtualization and software virtualization. For software virtualization, application virtualization and database virtualization are done. Application virtualization ensures the distribution of evenly distribution of logged-in users to reduce the load on single application server [4].
- **Profile and data redirection**. Profile and data redirection enables users' personalization to be maintained. It also ensures that data stored by users is stored on the server. Profiles and data redirection is what allows a user to logon onto any computer and have all their personal files and setting apply to that computer as it was the last time they used a computer.
- **Client devices**. Users use any device, known as thin clients, to access the virtualized environment. Some of the OSes used in client devices are Windows, Linux.

3 Comparison of DaaS Providers

While evaluating a DaaS solution, one needs to observe multiple areas. First is the hypervisor [5], which is a platform for configuring and running virtual machines. Hypervisors differ in their capabilities; cloud providers contrast in their solutions offering. How to appropriately choose hypervisor for the desired server/desktop virtualization is really challenging, because a trade-off between virtualization performance and cost is a hard decision to make in the cloud. Others components are processor speed and cores, RAM, type of storage.

Below is the comparison of various service providers which offer technical components along with the commercials (Table 1).

Table 1 Comparison of various service providers

Desktop model	Horizon air desktops and horizon air apps (standard) [10]	Amazon workspaces (value) [11]	desktopasservice.com [12]	Microsoft Azure (basic tier) [13]
Price per month	$35/desktop/month MSRP (minimum order quantity of 50)	$27 (no up-front commitment and you can delete workspaces at anytime)	$30 (7 or more users)	INR 782
Processor	1 vCPU	1 vCPU		1 core
Memory	2 GB VRAM	2 GB VRAM	4 GB RAM	1.75 GB
Hard disk	30 GB	10 GB	20 GB + 20 GB (operating system)	40 GB
Access device	Horizon view clients, browser, PCoIP zero clients	Laptop computer (Mac OS or Windows), iPad, Kindle fire, or Android tablet, PCoIP zero clients	Android, iPhone, an iPad, Windows mobile/computer PC, Mac, Linux, thin clients, etc.	Android. iPhone and iPad, Windows mobile/computer PC, Mac, Linux, thin clients, etc.
Desktop device	Persistent and nonpersistent VDI	Persistent	Persistent	Persistent
Available OS	Windows XP, 7, 8 × 64 Windows Server 2008 R2 Windows Server 2012 R2	Windows 7 experience to users (provided by Windows Server 2008 R2 with RDS)	Windows and Linux based	Windows and Linux based
Technology	VMware	Amazon workspaces and Amazon workspaces application manager	Microsoft remote desktop services (RDP)-based Windows desktops Citrix XenApp or XenDesktop can also be offered on request and is priced $15 extra per month per desktop	Microsoft's remote desktop service (RDS)

4   Obstacles in Adoption of DaaS

Despite the benefits, there are multiple obstacles to the adoption of DaaS. Trust is one of the major obstacles for many institutions/organizations because of low control of IT departments over the data entered through DaaS. Doubt related to the security of data maintained by services providers is always a distrust factor. Connectivity is another obstacle as outages are planned by the service providers because of handling of multiple customers in the same data centers as well as the application of patches to remove the bugs or issues resolved by OEMs apart from upgrading to the higher version of the technologies.

User customization is also one of the difficulties in DaaS. As virtualized desktop is hosted on cloud and cloud is managed by provider so it is difficult to tailor the end user environment because the same environment is available to the users of multiple companies/organizations. Some of the customizations can be done by admin using VDI but that is also up to an extent.

As far as data is concerned, clarity on data ownership and its compliance has to be decided. Incase DaaS provider controls one's data but archiving or purging-related activities shall be governed by data owners so that regulatory compliance related to data can be maintained. Another major area to focus on is licensing regulations; DaaS should be compliant with licensing types and security roles provided to multiple users. An expert should be available in a company adopting for DaaS to oversee these kinds of issues as licensing noncompliance might cause in spending more money.

There are multiple service providers available in the market to offer DaaS to the organizations. The adoption of DaaS is more in urban areas than in nonurban areas because of multiple major issues such as latency, availability of local resources, conservation in putting the data in cloud due to security. With the continuous advancement in technologies available with service providers, high-speed Internet has resolved latency issues. Service providers are also providing services, using multiple technologies, which require low bandwidth needs.

Data migration is also very important factor as companies while migrating from on-premise deployed applications to cloud-based applications do think about the history of the data. In data migration cases, the size of data also matters and need to create a data migration strategy [6] arises. The challenge is to perform the data migration within reasonable performance parameters. Stretching out a migration over days or even weeks becomes a data center dilemma. The migration solution, has to increase its efficiency to allow for business change and for agility to decrease the likelihood of errors in the process of confining precious IT administrative resources.

Availability of critical application is required by all businesses. For applications, hosted on cloud, availability is backed by stringent SLAs provided by cloud service providers. There are important applications which require scheduled downtime. To achieve application availability, virtualization is done at hardware as well as software levels.

DaaS has huge potential in the market especially for the organizations which want high security and do not want users to store any company-related data in their devices like PC, laptop, but these are early years for DaaS with a limited number of organizations as buyers due to main challenge of consistent or unavailable bandwidth

The human factor presents challenges in adoption as well: IT skill sets and user acceptance/experience were both cited as inhibitors by 40% of respondents.

5 Formulation of TCO/ROI

This aim of this section is to provide the parameters to be used to calculate the TCO [7] and then the ROI to adopt DaaS. TCO is total costs included to set up and adopt DaaS. The view given below can used to give the short-term view instead of long-term view and also not able to provide the hidden investments that might minimize the ROI. TCO is unlike ROI as it defines the costs related to purchase of new things. Multiple vendors provide TCO calculation such as TCO/ROI evaluated at VMware TCO/ROI calculator [8, 9].

1. DaaS Benefits

DaaS promises a major value add of shifting cost from CAPEX to OPEX, lowering the up-front investments, generating standardization of processes, higher agility to enable organization users. Some of the benefits are tangible, and some are intangible.

Table 2 shows the benefits, challenges, and cost components to be considered to calculate the TCO.

ROI calculation is significant for the organization which is looking to do any transformation. DaaS adoption is also a kind of transformation which involves change management across all the employees as users will be connected to centralized servers to access their desktop instances. It is vital to answer few questions: "Is it right time to shift to DaaS?" and "Are we doing it with right consultants or vendors?" ROI not only includes up-front investments but also includes resources effort, time, and organizational maturity to adopt DaaS.

Although the applicability of ROI cannot be generalized and depends upon one organization to another, a base model can help any organization to validate the initial levels and then can customize as per the needs. These organizations have structured way of calculating ROI; nevertheless, it is important to pursue cloud-specific ROI models. Below are the formulas used.

$$\text{TCO} = \text{Upfront Investments} + \text{Recurring Expenditure} + \text{Termination Expenditure}$$

$$\text{ROI} = \frac{\text{DaaS Benefits(Tangible Benefits} + \text{Intangible Benefits} - \text{Business Challenges Impact)} - \text{TCO}}{\text{TCO}}$$

Table 2 Tangible (quantifiable) and intangible (strategic) benefits, challenges, and cost

Tangible benefits	Description
Reduction of high-end PC	PC cost for employees is shifted from CAPEX to OPEX as users will be moved to DaaS (cloud)
Reduction of operating systems	Licenses purchase cost is shifted from CAPEX to OPEX
Reduction of antivirus licenses	Licenses purchase cost is shifted from CAPEX to OPEX
Reduction of workstation security tools	Licenses purchase cost is shifted from CAPEX to OPEX
Reduction of upgrades/updates cost	Maintenance (upgrades, updates, patches, etc.) are required to be done at server instead of PC
Increased productivity	User mobility and ubiquitous access can increase productivity. Collaborative applications increase productivity and reduce rework
Improved data security and privacy	As the data is stored in server so theft of laptop shall not affect any organization data privacy
Disaster recovery	As the data is stored in server which is linked to disaster recovery site
No data loss in case of PC crash	As the data is stored in server so loss or crash of PC shall not affect
Improved performance due to less SLA to configure	Configuration of new user can be done in very less time
Intangible benefits	Description
Focus on core business	Relocation of IT resources to support core business functions.
Risk transfer like data loss	Make sure the cloud service provider is providing the facility of disaster recovery so that data loss risk can be covered in case of any mishap
Challenges to consider	Description
Bandwidth issues	Bandwidth issues at user end can refrain connecting to DaaS at cloud
Up-front cost	Description
Infrastructure readiness	Some investment in bandwidth may be necessary to accommodate the new demand for network/Internet access. Other infrastructure components may need to be upgraded
Implementation	Contracting to perform consulting and implementation activities to migrate to cloud
Change management	Implementation of new process and then execution of processes to support users
Integration	Services required to integrate other internal applications or cloud-based applications
Recurring cost	Description
Subscription fee	These will comprise agreed-on periodic fees (monthly, quarterly, yearly) for the use of cloud services
Professional implementation fee	In case of DaaS, server integration is required with the existing organization servers

(continued)

Table 2 (continued)

Tangible benefits	Description
Subscriber management	Management of subscriber to keep track of maintenance activities, contract scope of work and SLA adherence
Data migration from cloud	Data migration from the cloud to internal raw database and then transform the data into new form according to the new application database.
Readiness of internal hardware and its related infrastructure	Procurement and configuration of internal hardware including processing power and storage
Termination charges	Charges for early termination
IT resources	Resources to support the new applications and infrastructure

6 Conclusion

This paper introduces the comparison of various service providers. Desktop virtualization technologies offer many advantages, but attention must be paid what is the main goal and accordingly which technology to implement—to follow the trends, to reduce costs, to make administration easier, to achieve user flexibility or something else. The way organizations are moving from private infrastructure, those days are not far away when all the services on cloud will be available and used. Almost every organization is thinking of moving servers on cloud, and desktops connect with these servers so the movement of desktops on cloud is the next to be available on cloud.

It is very difficult to create an ROI model which can provide result straightaway to the organizations. There are cases where savings are obvious due to the reduction of costly hardware and other mandatory software licenses for the PC/laptop/mobile/ tablets. However, there are hidden costs in the long term and most evident one is bandwidth required to use DaaS. ROI should also factor the view of time duration such as short term, medium term, or long term. Weightage of the factors is also dependent on the organization; for example, security is a major factor for some organizations like call center whereas IT resources want to have their machines for the development purpose

References

1. https://en.wikipedia.org/wiki/Desktop_virtualization
2. http://www.vmware.com/
3. Haga, Y., Imaeda, K., Jibu, M.: Windows server 2008 R2 hyper-V server virtualization. Fujitsu Sci. Tech. J. **47**(3), 349–355 (2011)
4. http://www.webopedia.com/TERM/A/application_virtualization.html

5. Hardy, J., Liu, L., Lei, C., Li, J.X.: Internet-based virtual computing infrastructure for cloud computing. In: Principles, Methodologies, and Service-Oriented Approaches For Cloud Computing, Chap. 16, pp. 371–389. IGI Global, Hershey, Pa, USA (2013)
6. Kushwah, V.S., Saxena, A.: Security approach for data migration in cloud computing. Int. J. Sci. Res. Publ. **3**(5), 1 (2013)
7. Kornevs, M., Minkevica, V., Holm, M.: Cloud computing evaluation based on financial metrics. Inf. Technol. Manag. Sci. **15**(1), 87–92 (2013)
8. VMware TCO/ROI Calculator, VMware, http://roitco.vmware.com/vmw/
9. Frequently Asked Questions, Report of VMware ROI TCO Calculator, Version 2.0, VMware (2013)
10. http://www.vmware.com/cloud-services/desktop/horizon-air-desktop/compare.html
11. http://aws.amazon.com/workspaces/pricing/
12. http://www.desktopasservice.com/desktop-as-a-service-pricing/
13. http://azure.microsoft.com/en-us/pricing/details/virtual-machines/
14. https://en.wikipedia.org/wiki/Bring_your_own_device
15. http://investors.citrix.com/releasedetail.cfm?ReleaseID=867202
16. http://blogs.gartner.com/chris-wolf/2012/12/10/desktop-virtualization-trends-at-gartner-data-center/
17. http://custom.crn.com/cloudlive/intelisys/assets/pdf/DaaS-Gaining-Ground-2014-Research-Survey-FINAL.PDF

An Assessment of Some Entropy Measures in Predicting Bugs of Open-Source Software

Vijay Kumar, H. D. Arora and Ramita Sahni

Abstract In software, source code changes are expected to occur. In order to meet the enormous requirements of the users, source codes are frequently modified. The maintenance task is highly complicated if the changes due to bug repair, enhancement, and addition of new features are not reported carefully. In this paper, concurrent versions system (CVS) repository (http://bugzilla.mozilla.org) is taken into consideration for recording bugs. These observed bugs are collected from some subcomponents of Mozilla open-source software. As entropy is helpful in studying the code change process, and various entropies, namely Shannon, Renyi, and Tsallis entropies, have been evaluated using these observed bugs. By applying simple linear regression (SLR) technique, the bugs which are yet to come in future are predicted based on current year entropy measures and the observed bugs. Performance has been measured using various R^2 statistics. In addition to this, ANOVA and Tukey test have been applied to statistically validate various entropy measures.

Keywords Bug prediction · Entropy · Coding · Software repositories
Open-source software

V. Kumar
Department of Mathematics, Amity School of Engineering and Technology,
New Delhi 110061, India
e-mail: vijay_parashar@yahoo.com

H. D. Arora · R. Sahni (✉)
Department of Applied Mathematics, Amity Institute of Applied Sciences,
Amity University, Sector-125, Noida, Uttar Pradesh, India
e-mail: smiles_ramita@yahoo.co.in

H. D. Arora
e-mail: hdarora@amity.edu

© Springer Nature Singapore Pte Ltd. 2019
M. N. Hoda et al. (eds.), *Software Engineering*, Advances in Intelligent Systems
and Computing 731, https://doi.org/10.1007/978-981-10-8848-3_58

1   Introduction

The software industry people are gaining a lot of attention due to the success and development of open-source software community. Open-source software is the software whose source code is available for modification by everyone with no central control. Due to factors like fewer bugs, better reliability, no vendor dependence, educational support, shorter development cycles, open-source software system gives an aggressive competition to the closed-source software. Due to increasing popularity of open-source software, changes in source code are unavoidable. It is a necessity to record changes properly in storage locations, viz. source code repositories. There is a direct correlation between the number of changes and faults or bugs in the software system. Bugs may be introduced at any phase of the software development life cycle, and by lying dormant in the software, bugs affect the quality and reliability of the software system, thereby making the system complex. Measuring complexity is an essential task which starts from development of code to maintenance. Entropy, a central concept of information theory, is defined as measure of randomness/uncertainty/complexity of code change. It tells us how much information is present in an event. Information theory is a probabilistic approach dealing with assessing and defining the amount of information contained in a message. While dealing with real-world problems, we cannot avoid uncertainty. The paramount goal of information theory is to capture or reduce this uncertainty.

In this paper, the data has been collected for 12 subcomponents of Mozilla open-source system, namely Doctor, Elmo, AUS, DMD, Bonsai, Bouncer, String, Layout Images, Toolbars and Toolbar Customization, Identity, Graph Server, and Telemetry Server. Initially, the number of bugs/faults present in each component is reported for 7 years from 2008 to 2014. Thereafter, for the data extracted from these subcomponents, Shannon entropy [1], Renyi entropy [2], and Tsallis entropy [3] have been evaluated for each time period, i.e., from 2008 to 2014. Simple linear regression (SLR) using Statistical Package for Social Sciences (SPSS) has been applied between the entropy calculated and observed bugs for each time period to obtain the regression coefficients. These regression coefficients have been used to calculate the predicted bugs for the coming year based on the entropy of the current year. Performance has been measured using goodness of fit curve and other R^2 statistics. In addition to this, ANOVA and Tukey test have been applied to statistically validate various entropy measures. There are many measures of entropy, but only these three entropies are considered for this study to compile and conclude results based on these measures, other measures may also be taken for further study and analysis, and comparative study is another area of research. The paper is further divided into the following sections. Section 2 contains the literature review of the work previously been done. Section 3 provides the basics of entropy measures and the code change process. Section 4 discusses the methodology adopted in this paper with data collection and preprocessing and calculation of entropy measures. In Sect. 5, the bug prediction modeling approach is described. In Sect. 6, the assessment of entropy measures has been discussed. Finally, the paper is concluded with limitations and future scope in Sect. 7.

2 Literature Review

Researchers have proposed and implemented a huge number of approaches for prediction of dormant bugs lying in the software and for measuring the reliability growth of the software (Goel and Okumoto [4]; Huang et al. [5]; Kapur and Garg [6]; Kapur et al. [7]; Kapur et al. [8]; etc.). Hassan [9] proposed information theory to measure the amount of uncertainty or entropy of the distribution to quantify the code change process in terms of entropy and used entropy-based measures to predict the bugs based on past defects. Ambros and Robbes [10] provided an extensive comparison of well-known bug prediction approaches. Singh and Chaturvedi [11] developed a theoretical agenda for developing bug tracking and reliability assessment (BTRAS) based on different classification criteria. Khatri et al. [12] presented a generalized model to find out the proportion of bug complexity present in the software for providing better software production. Singh and Chaturvedi [13] collected the source code change data of Mozilla components to validate the proposed method and to predict the bugs yet to come in future based on the current year entropy by applying simple linear regression and support vector regression techniques. Chaturvedi et al. [14] presented a novel approach to predict the potential complexity of code changes using entropy-based measures. These predicted changes help in determining the remaining code changes yet to be diffused in the software. The diffusion of change complexity has been validated using some subcomponents of Mozilla project. Singh et al. [15] proposed three approaches, namely software reliability growth models, potential complexity of code change-based models, and code change complexity-based models to determine the presence of potential bugs in the software. Sharma et al. [16] developed prediction models for determining severity level of a reported bug based on attributes, namely priority, number of comments, number of dependents, number of duplicates, complexity, summary weight, and CC list (a list of people who get mail when the bug changes) in cross-project context. They also considered bug reports of some products of Mozilla open-source project for empirical validation.

3 Entropy Measures and Code Change Process

The concept of entropy in information theory was developed by Shannon [1]. He defined a formal measure of entropy, called Shannon entropy:

$$S = -\sum_{i=1}^{n} p_i \log_2 p_i \tag{1}$$

where p_i is the probability of occurrence of an event.

A systematic approach to develop a generalization of Shannon entropy [1] was made by Renyi [2] who characterized entropy of order α defined as follows:

$$R = \frac{1}{1-\alpha} \log\left(\sum_{i=1}^{n} p_i^{\alpha}\right), \qquad \alpha \neq 1, \alpha > 0 \tag{2}$$

where α is a real parameter.

Tsallis [3] proposed another generalization of Shannon entropy [13] defined as:

$$T = \frac{1}{\alpha - 1}\left(1 - \sum_{i=1}^{n} p_i^{\alpha}\right), \qquad \alpha \neq 1, \alpha > 0 \tag{3}$$

Renyi entropy [2] and Tsallis entropy [3] reduce to Shannon entropy [1] when $\alpha \to 1$.

For Renyi [2] and Tsallis entropies [3], any value of $\alpha > 0$ can be taken, other than 1 to study the variation and effect of varying alpha on entropies. So here, five values of parameter α i.e., 0.1, 0.3, 0.5, 0.7, and 0.9 are taken into consideration.

The code change process refers to study the patterns of source code changes/modifications. Bug repair, feature enhancement, and the addition of new features cause these changes/modifications. The entropy-based estimation plays a vital role in studying the code change process. Entropy is determined based on the number of changes in a file for a particular time period with respect to total number of changes in all files. Keeping in mind the frequency of changes in the code, we can decide the specific duration to be day, month, year, etc. For example, consider that there are 13 changes occurred for four files and three periods. Let P1, P2, P3, and P4 be the four files and S1, S2, and S3 be the three periods. In S1, files P1, P2, and P4 have one change each and P3 has two changes. Table 1 depicts the total number of changes occurring in each file in respective time periods S1, S2, and S3.

Table 1 Number of changes (denoted by *) in files with respect to a specific period of time where P1, P2, P3, and P4 represent the files and S1, S2, and S3 represent the time periods

File/time	S1	S2	S3
P1	*	*	*
P2	*		*
P3	**	**	
P4	*	**	*

Total files in S1 = 5. Thus, probability of P1 for S1 = 1/5 = 0.2; probability of P2 for S1 = 1/5 = 0.2; probability of P3 for S1 = 2/5 = 0.4; and probability of P4 for S1 = 1/5 = 0.2. Similarly, we can find out the probabilities of the time periods S2 and S3. Based upon the above probabilities, we have calculated Shannon entropy [13], Renyi entropy [11], and Tsallis entropy.

4 Methodology

In this paper, first the data is collected and preprocessed and then entropy measures have been calculated.

4.1 Data Collection and Preprocessing

Mozilla is open-source software that offers choice to the users and drives innovation on the Web. It is a free software community which produces a large number of projects like Thunderbird, the bug tracking system Bugzilla, etc. In this paper, we have selected few components of Mozilla software with respective bugs from the CVS repository: http://bugzilla.mozilla.org [17]. Steps for data collection, extraction, and prediction of bugs are as follows:

1. Choose the project, select the subsystems, and browse CVS logs.
2. Collect bug reports of all subsystems, extract bugs from these reports, and arrange bugs on yearly basis for each subsystem.
3. Calculate Shannon entropy, Renyi entropy, and Tsallis entropy for each time period using these bugs reported for each subsystem.
4. Use SLR model to predict bugs for the coming year based on each entropy calculated for each time period.

In our study, we have taken a fixed period as 1 year taken from 2008 to 2014. We have considered 12 subsystems with number of bugs as 6 bugs in Doctor, 32 bugs in Elmo, 72 bugs in Graph Server, 43 bugs in Bonsai, 45 bugs in Bouncer, 33 bugs in String, 12 bugs in DMD, 90 bugs in Layout Images, 23 bugs in AUS, 39 bugs in Identity, 12 bugs in Telemetry Server, and 36 bugs in Toolbars and Toolbar Customization.

4.2 Evaluation of Shannon, Renyi, and Tsallis Entropies

This data information has been used to calculate the probability of each component for the seven time periods from 2008 to 2014 as discussed in Sect. 3. Using these probabilities Shannon [1], Renyi [2] and Tsallis entropies [3] are calculated using

Eq. (1)–(3), respectively, for each time period. For Renyi [2] and Tsallis entropies [3], five values of α, i.e., 0.1, 0.3, 0.5, 0.7, and 0.9 are considered. Table 2 shown below depicts the Shannon entropy [1], Renyi entropy [2], and Tsallis entropy [3] for each year.

From this analysis, it has been observed that Shannon entropy [1] lies between 2 and 4. It is maximum in the year 2014 and minimum in the year 2009. Renyi entropy [2] and Tsallis entropy [3] decrease as the value of α increases. At $\alpha = 0.1$, Renyi entropy [2] is maximum for each time period, and at $\alpha = 0.9$, Renyi entropy [11] is minimum for each time period. Similarly, at $\alpha = 0.1$, Tsallis entropy [3] is maximum for each time period, and at $\alpha = 0.9$, Tsallis entropy [3] is minimum for each time period.

5 Bug Prediction Modeling

Simple linear regression (SLR) [18] model is the most elementary model involving two variables in which one variable is predicted by another variable. The variable to be predicted is called the dependent variable, and the predictor is called the independent variable The SLR has been widely used to repress the dependent variable Y using independent variable X with the following equation

$$Y = A + BX \tag{4}$$

where A and B are regression coefficients.

The regression coefficients can be obtained using the simple linear regression technique using Statistical Package for Social Sciences (SPSS). After estimating the regression coefficients using different measures of entropy and historical data of observed bugs, a system is constructed with which we can predict bugs likely to occur in the next year. In this study, X, i.e., entropy measure, is considered to be an independent variable and Y, i.e., predicted bugs likely to occur next year, is considered to be a dependent variable. Here X, i.e., entropy measure, is different in each case, i.e., as Shannon entropy [1], Renyi entropy [2], and Tsallis entropy [3]. For Renyi [2] and Tsallis entropies [3], five parameter values are considered, viz. 0.1, 0.3, 0.5, 0.7, and 0.9. The following notations are used for simplicity:

X: entropy measures; Y_o: observed bugs; Y: predicted bugs for Shannon entropy. YR_α represents the predicted bugs for Renyi entropy with α varying as 0.1, 0.3, 0.5, 0.7, and 0.9, respectively. YT_α represents the predicted bugs for Tsallis entropy with α varying as 0.1, 0.3, 0.5, 0.7, and 0.9, respectively. Table 3 depicts the predicted bugs along with Shannon entropy [13], Renyi entropy [11], and Tsallis entropy [19].

Table 2 Shannon entropy, Renyi entropy, and Tsallis entropy for each time period with different values of α

Year	S	R(0.1)	R(0.3)	R(0.5)	R(0.7)	R(0.9)	T(0.1)	T(0.3)	T(0.5)	T(0.7)	T(0.9)
2008	2.4909	0.8342	0.8131	0.7935	0.7799	0.7578	5.1493	3.8698	2.9865	2.3599	1.9065
2009	2.4761	0.7745	0.7673	0.7609	0.7544	0.7484	4.4203	3.4929	2.8026	2.2798	1.8805
2010	2.7319	0.8928	0.8735	0.8568	0.8416	0.8284	5.9567	4.4119	3.3632	2.6284	2.1016
2011	2.7281	0.8955	0.8798	0.8639	0.8471	0.8299	5.9973	4.4714	3.4075	2.6509	2.1058
2012	2.9942	0.9873	0.9638	0.9435	0.9251	0.9088	7.4868	5.3278	3.9264	2.9821	2.3277
2013	3.0171	1.0599	1.0222	0.9870	0.9535	0.9227	8.8831	5.9949	4.2305	3.1073	2.3671
2014	3.1596	1.0309	1.0108	0.9924	0.9749	0.9588	8.3007	5.8589	4.2697	3.2032	2.4702

Table 3 Predicted bugs using entropy measures

Year	Y_o	Y	$YR_{\alpha=0.1}$	$YR_{\alpha=0.3}$	$YR_{\alpha=0.5}$	$YR_{\alpha=0.7}$	$YR_{\alpha=0.9}$	$YT_{\alpha=0.1}$	$YT_{\alpha=0.3}$	$YT_{\alpha=0.5}$	$YT_{\alpha=0.7}$	$YT_{\alpha=0.9}$
2008	45	29	40	38	35	33	30	40	38	35	32	30
2009	27	27	25	25	25	25	26	29	27	26	26	26
2010	41	56	55	55	54	54	55	53	53	53	54	55
2011	53	55	56	56	57	56	56	54	55	55	56	56
2012	80	85	79	80	81	83	84	77	79	81	82	84
2013	68	88	98	96	95	92	89	100	98	95	93	89
2014	129	104	90	93	96	100	102	90	94	97	100	103

6　Assessment of Entropy Measures

The statistical performance and regression coefficients using SPSS for the considered data sets are shown in Table 4.

From Table 4, it is concluded that for Shannon entropy [1], R^2 is maximum, i.e., 0.775, and adjusted R^2 is maximum, i.e., 0.730. For Renyi entropy [2], it is observed that on increasing α from 0.1 to 0.9, the value of R^2 increases from 0.620 to 0.763 and adjusted R^2 also increases from 0.544 to 0.716. For example, $R^2 = 0.775$ implies that 77.5% of the variance in dependent variable is predictable from independent variables, and adjusted $R^2 - 0.730$ implies that there is 73.0% variation in the dependent variable. Similar conclusion can be drawn for Tsallis entropy [3].

Further, we have performed the analysis of variance (ANOVA) test and Tukey test to validate the entropy measure results considered in this paper. The one-way ANOVA is used to only determine whether there are any significant differences between the means of three or more independent (unrelated) groups. To determine which specific groups differed from each other, multiple comparison test, i.e., Tukey's HSD test, is used. It takes into consideration the number of treatment levels, the value of mean square error and the sample size and the statistic q that we look up in a table (studentized range statistic table). Once the HSD is computed, we compare each possible difference between means to the value of the HSD. The difference between two means must equal or exceed the HSD in order to be significant. The formula to compute a Tukey's HSD test is as follows:

Table 4 Statistical performance parameters for entropy measures using simple linear regression

Entropy measures	Parameter (α)	R	R^2	Adjusted R^2	Std. error of the estimate	Regression coefficients	
						A	B
Shannon entropy	–	0.881	0.775	0.730	17.57127	−250.486	112.073
Renyi entropy	0.1	0.787	0.620	0.544	22.86081	−171.528	253.845
	0.3	0.812	0.659	0.590	21.65929	−190.628	280.770
	0.5	0.835	0.697	0.637	20.39309	−209.866	308.490
	0.7	0.860	0.739	0.687	18.93128	−232.461	340.699
	0.9	0.874	0.763	0.716	18.03841	−243.825	361.012
Tsallis entropy	0.1	0.782	0.611	0.534	23.11530	−41.947	15.946
	0.3	0.814	0.663	0.595	21.53316	−72.233	28.378
	0.5	0.841	0.707	0.648	20.06774	−110.451	48.672
	0.7	0.862	0.742	0.691	18.82165	−158.038	80.642
	0.9	0.876	0.767	0.721	17.89233	−216.574	129.226

$$HSD = q\sqrt{\frac{MSE}{n}} \tag{5}$$

where MSE: mean square error, n: sample size, and q: critical value of the studentized range distribution

6.1 One-Way ANOVA

We have applied one-way ANOVA for Shannon [1], Renyi [2], and Tsallis entropies [3]. The ANOVA test has been applied to five cases. In case 1, Shannon entropy, Renyi entropy for $\alpha = 0.1$, Tsallis entropy for $\alpha = 0.1$ are considered, and in case 2, Shannon entropy, Renyi entropy for $\alpha = 0.3$, Tsallis entropy for $\alpha = 0.3$ are considered. Other cases are defined similarly taking α as 0.5, 0.7, and 0.9 respectively. In all the cases, Shannon entropy values remain the same as this entropy is independent of α. We set null and alternate hypothesis as

H_o : There is no significant difference between the three means. H_1 : There is a significant difference between the three means. Level of confidence is chosen as 0.05 for ANOVA test. Table 5 depicts the results obtained from ANOVA.

It is observed from Table 5 that the calculated value of F in all the five cases is greater than the critical value of F at 0.05. Thus, the null hypothesis is rejected, and alternate hypothesis is accepted. Thus, there is a significant difference in the means of three different measures of entropy, viz. Shannon's [1], Renyi's [2], and Tsallis's [3] entropies. In order to find out which groups show a significant difference, Tukey's HSD test is applied.

6.2 Tukey's HSD Test

We find 'q' from studentized range statistic table using degree of freedom (within) (ANOVA results) and number of conditions 'c.' Here, in all the cases, degree of freedom (within) is 18, and number of conditions is 3, and sample size 'n' is 7. Thus, 'q' from the table for 0.05 level of confidence is 3.61. HSD is computed using Eq. (5), and MSE (mean square error) values are observed from ANOVA

Table 5 Variability of Shannon, Renyi, and Tsallis entropies using ANOVA

Cases	F(calculated)	p value	F critical
Case 1	61.8925	8.57E-09	3.554557
Case 2	76.91664	1.52E-09	3.554557
Case 3	95.27835	2.66E-10	3.554557
Case 4	121.6313	3.5E-11	3.554557
Case 5	159.5823	3.52E-12	3.554557

Table 6 Results of Tukey test

Cases	MSE	HSD	Shannon entropy (mean)	Renyi entropy (mean)	Tsallis entropy (mean)	Shannon versus Renyi entropy (difference of means)	Renyi versus Tsallis entropy (difference of means)	Tsallis versus Shannon entropy (difference of means)
Case 1	0.945251	1.326574	2.799714	0.925029	6.599174	1.874685	5.674145	3.79946
Case 2	0.34099	0.796762	2.799714	0.904346	4.775417	1.895368	3.871071	1.975703
Case 3	0.140342	0.511154	2.799714	0.885448	3.569534	1.914266	2.684086	0.76982
Case 4	0.069593	0.359948	2.799714	0.868061	2.744516	1.931653	1.876455	0.055198
Case 5	0.043352	0.284094	2.799714	0.850694	2.165657	1.94902	1.314963	0.634057

results. The mean of Shannon entropy is same for all cases as it is independent of α. Using these values, the difference between each pair of means is evaluated. The pairs are defined as follows: Shannon entropy versus Renyi entropy, Renyi entropy versus Tsallis entropy, and Tsallis entropy versus Shannon entropy. Table 6 depicts the values of HSD, MSE, means of the entropies, and difference of means for all the cases.

In case 1, case 2, case 3, and case 5 for all the three pairs, i.e., Shannon versus Renyi, Renyi versus Tsallis, and Tsallis versus Shannon, the HSD value is less than their respective difference of means. Thus, according to Tukey test, the difference between Shannon entropy and Renyi entropy, Renyi entropy and Tsallis entropy, and Tsallis entropy and Shannon entropy are statistically significant. But in case 4, the difference of means of the pair Tsallis versus Shannon is less than the HSD value. Thus, for this case, the difference between Tsallis entropy and Shannon entropy is not statistically significant, whereas the difference between Shannon entropy and Renyi entropy and Renyi entropy and Tsallis entropy are statistically significant.

7 Conclusion and Future Scope

The quality and reliability of the software are highly affected by the bugs lying dormant in the software. After collecting bug reports of each subcomponent from the CVS repository, the number of bugs present in each of them is recorded on yearly basis taken from 2008 to 2014. Using these data sets, the Shannon entropy, Renyi entropy, and Tsallis entropy are calculated. Renyi entropy and Tsallis entropy for five different values of α are considered, i.e., $\alpha = 0.1, 0.3, 0.5, 0.7, 0.9$. It is observed that for this data set obtained, Shannon entropy lies between 2 and 4. Renyi and Tsallis entropies decrease as α value increases. Simple linear regression technique is applied to calculate the predicted bugs using the calculated entropy and observed bugs in SPSS software. These predicted bugs help in maintaining the quality of the software and reducing the testing efforts. We have compared the performance of different measures of entropy considered on the basis of different comparison criteria, namely R^2, adjusted R^2, and standard error of estimate. It is also observed that among Shannon entropy, Renyi entropy, and Tsallis entropy, R^2 is maximum in the case of Shannon entropy, i.e., $R^2 = 0.775$. In the case of Renyi entropy, R^2 is maximum when $\alpha = 0.9$, i.e., $R^2 = 0.763$. Similarly, for Tsallis entropy also, R^2 is maximum when $\alpha = 0.9$, i.e., $R^2 = 0.767$. By applying ANOVA and Tukey test, the different measures of entropy are validated. In this paper, only open-source Mozilla products are considered. The study may be extended to other open-source and closed-source software systems with different subcomponents. Entropy measures, namely, Shannon entropy, Renyi entropy, and Tsallis entropy, are considered for evaluation of predicted bugs, and the parameter value for Renyi entropy and Tsallis entropy is limited to few values. The study may be extended for other measures of entropy with different parameter values. This study can further be extended to analyze the code change process using other entropy measures in other projects which can be further used in predicting the future bugs in a project.

References

1. Shannon, C.E.: A mathematical theory of communication. Bell Syst. Tech. J. **27**(3), 379–423 (1948). 623–656
2. Renyi, A.: On measures of entropy and information. In: Proceedings 4th Berkeley Symposium on Mathematical Statistics and Probability, vol. 1, pp. 547–561 (1961)
3. Tsallis, C., Mendes, R, Plastino, A. The role constraints within generalised non extensive statistics. Physica 261A, pp. 534–554 (1998)
4. Goel, A.L., Okumoto, K.: Time dependent error detection rate model for software reliability and other performance measures. IEEE Trans. Reliab. **28**(3), 206–211 (1979)
5. Huang, C.Y., Kuo, S.Y., Chen, J.Y.: Analysis of a software reliability growth model with logistic testing effort function. In: Proceedings of Eighth International Symposium on Software Reliability Engineering, pp. 378–388 (1997)
6. Kapur, P.K., Garg, R.B.: A software reliability growth model for an error removal phenomenon. Softw. Eng. J. **7**, 291–294 (1992)
7. Kapur, P.K., Pham, H., Chanda, U., Kumar, V.: Optimal allocation of testing effort during testing and debugging phases: a control theoretic approach. Int. J. Syst. Sci. **44**(9), 1639–1650 (2013)
8. Kapur, P.K., Chanda, Udayan, Kumar, Vijay: Dynamic allocation of testing effort when testing and debugging are done concurrently communication in dependability and quality management. Int. J. Serbia **13**(3), 14–28 (2010)
9. Hassan, A.E.: Predicting faults based on complexity of code change. In: The proceedings of 31st International Conference On Software Engineering, pp. 78–88 (2009)
10. Ambros, M.D., Robbes, R.: An extensive comparison of bug prediction approaches. In: MSR'10: Proceedings of the 7th International Working Conference on Mining Software Repositories, pp. 31–41 (2010)
11. Singh, V.B., Chaturvedi, K.K.: Bug tracking and reliability assessment system (BTRAS). Int. J. Softw. Eng. Appl. **5**(4), 1–14 (2011)
12. Khatri, S., Chillar, R.S., Singh, V.B.: Improving the testability of object oriented software during testing and debugging process. Int. J. Comput. Appl. **35**(11), 24–35 (2011)
13. Singh, V.B., Chaturvedi, K.K.: Improving the quality of software by quantifying the code change metric and predicting the bugs. In: Murgante, B., et al. (eds.) ICCSA 2013, Part II, LNCS 7972, pp. 408–426. Springer, Berlin (2013)
14. Chaturvedi, K.K., Kapur, P.K., Anand, S., Singh, V.B.: Predicting the complexity of code changes using entropy based measures. Int. J. Syst. Assur. Eng. Manag. **5**(2), 155–164 (2014)
15. Singh, V.B., Chaturvedi, K.K., Khatri, S.K., Kumar, V.: Bug prediction modelling using complexity of code changes. Int. J. Syst. Assur. Eng. Manag. **6**(1), 44–60 (2014)
16. Sharma, M., Kumari, M., Singh, R.K., Singh, V.B.: Multiattribute based machine learning models for severity prediction in cross project context. In: Murgante, B., et al. (eds.) ICCSA 2014, Part V, LNCS 8583, pp. 227–241 (2014)
17. http://bugzilla.mozilla.org
18. Weisberg, S.: Applied linear regression. Wiley, New York (1980)

A Path Coverage-Based Reduction of Test Cases and Execution Time Using Parallel Execution

Leena Singh and Shailendra Narayan Singh

Abstract A novel method for ameliorating the effectiveness of software testing is proposed, which focuses the reduction of number of test cases using prevailing techniques. The domains of each input variable are reduced by using ReduceDomains algorithm. Then, the method allocates fixed values to variables using algebraic conditions for the reduction of number of test cases by using prevailing method. By performing this, the values of the variables would be restricted in a fixed range, subsequently making lesser number of potential test cases to process. The projected method is based on the parallel execution in which all the independent paths are executed parallelly in spite of sequential execution and reduces the number of test cases and execution time.

Keywords Software testing · Test case generation · Test suite reduction

1 Introduction

Software testing is used for enhancing the quality and reliability of the software. It promotes assurance of the actual software that it sticks to its specification appropriately. "It is a time-consuming job that accounts for around 50% of the cost of development of a software system due to high intricacy and large pool of labor." "Software testing is based on execution of the software on a fixed set of inputs and an evaluation of the expected output with the actual output from the software" [1]. The set of inputs and expected outputs corresponding to each other is known as a test case. A group of test cases is known as a test suite. Software testers maintain a diversity of test sets to be used for software testing [2]. "As test suites rise in size, they may develop so big that it becomes necessary to decrease the sizes of the test sets.

L. Singh (✉) · S. N. Singh
ASET, AMITY University, Noida, India
e-mail: leenasingh25@gmail.com

S. N. Singh
e-mail: sns2033@gmail.com

© Springer Nature Singapore Pte Ltd. 2019
M. N. Hoda et al. (eds.), *Software Engineering*, Advances in Intelligent Systems and Computing 731, https://doi.org/10.1007/978-981-10-8848-3_59

Reduction of test cases is most thought-provoking than creating a test case. The goal of software testing is to identify faults in the program and provide more robustness for the program in test." "One serious task in software testing is to create test data to satisfy given sufficiency criteria, among which white box testing is one of the most extensively recognized. Given a coverage criterion, the problem of creating test data is to search for a set of data that lead to the maximum coverage when given as input to the software under test." So any methods which could reduce the cost, achieve high testing coverage and number of test cases will have boundless potential. An approach of reducing testing work, while confirming its efficiency, is to create minimum test cases automatically from artifacts required in the initial stages of software development [3]. Test-data creation is the procedure of recognizing an input data set that suites a specified testing condition. Test generation technique and application of a test-data sufficiency criterion are the two main aspects [4]. A test generation technique is an algorithm to create test sets, whereas a sufficiency criterion is a condition that finds out whether the testing process is complete or not. Generation of test-data techniques, which automatically generate test data for satisfying a given test coverage criterion, has been developed. The common test-data creation techniques are random test-data generation techniques, symbolic test-data generation technique, dynamic test-data generation techniques, and, recently, test-data generation techniques based on optimization techniques [5, 6]. Different studies have been conducted to propose a reduced test suite from the original suite that covers a given set of test requirements. Several new strategies of test suite reduction have been reported. Most strategies have been proposed for code-based suites, but the results cannot be generalized and sometimes they are divergent [7, 8]. A. Pravin et al. developed an algorithm for improving the testing process by covering all possible faults in minimum execution time [9]. B. Subashini et al. proposed a mining approach which is used for the reduction of test cases and execution time using clustering technique [10]. A practical based influencing regression testing process has been developed by T. Muthusamy et al. for quick fault detection to test case prioritization [11]. For reducing test cases, there are many techniques in the literature such as dynamic domain reduction (DDR), Coverall algorithm, each having their own advantages and disadvantages. DDR [12] is based upon an execution of specific path and statement coverage, which covers all the statement from header files till the end of the source code. In this case, a number of test cases obtained were 384 for a particular example of calculation of mid-value of three integers. "Coverall algorithm is used to reduce test cases by using algebraic conditions to allot static values to variables (maximum, minimum, constant variables). In this algorithm, numbers of test cases are reduced to 21 for a single assumed path" [13].

In this paper, a set of tests is generated that each one traverses a specified path. The purpose is to assure none of the paths in the code is uncovered. For these paths, generation of a large set of test data is very tedious task. As a result, certain strategy should be applied to reduce the number of large amount of test cases which is redundant, i.e., same set of test cases repeating. By applying strategy to avoid

conflicts, test path generation will be exceeded up to reduce redundancy and produce effective test cases to cover all paths in a control flow graph.

2 Problem Description

To execute all test cases it takes more time because all test cases are executing
sequentially. As the time being constraint parameter, it is always preferred to reduce
the execution time. As test cases and time are directly related, more the test cases
more will be the execution time. The proposed method is based on the parallel
execution for the reduction of the number of test cases and time of execution. The
advantage of the proposed approach is that in this technique, all the independent
paths are executed parallelly in spite of sequential execution.

3 Proposed Technique

It is based on the parallel execution of all independent paths parallelly which
reduces the quantity (in number) of test cases and execution time. A potential
drawback of existing reduction techniques is that they have covered only one single
path. The goal of the proposed approach is to cover all independent paths which are
executing parallelly in spite of sequential execution.

3.1 Algorithm

A brief outline of the steps involved in the generation of test case and reduction is
as follows:

1. Using the source code (for a program which determines the middle value of
   three given integers f, s and t [12]), draw the corresponding control flow graph
   of the problem.
2. Then, the cyclomatic complexity is determined from the graph (flow graph).
3. After that, the basis set of linearly independent paths is determined.
4. Then, the domains of each input variable are reduced by using ReduceDomains
   algorithm.
5. After that generation of test suites by using algebraic conditions to allot specific
   values to variables and check the coverage criteria, if satisfied.
6. Apply parallel test case executer for reduction of large amount of test cases
   which is redundant.

The first step is to construct the control flow graph for a program which finds out the mid-value of the given three integers f, s and t. The corresponding control flow graph is constructed as shown in Fig. 1.

A control flow graph illustration of a program is a directed graph comprising of nodes and edges, where each statement is symbolized by a node and each possible transfer of control from one statement to another is symbolized by an edge. The next step is to calculate the cyclomatic complexity which is used to determine the quantity (in number) of linearly independent paths from flow graph. Each new path presents a new edge. It is a sign of the total number of test sets that are required to attain maximum coverage of code. The subsequent test sets offer more in-depth testing than statement and branch coverage. "It is defined by the equation $V(G) = e - n + 2p$ where "e" and "n" are the total number of edges and total number of nodes in a control flow graph and p is number of linked components. The value of $V(G)$ is a sign of all the probable execution paths in the program and denotes a lower bound on the number of test cases necessary to test the method completely." From Fig. 1, cyclomatic complexity is $V(G) = 14 - 0 + 2 = 6$.

Therefore, numbers of independent paths are **6**, i.e.,

Path1   1 —6   —7 — 10
Path2   1 — 6 — 8 — 9 — 10
Path3   1 — 2 — 3 —10
Path4   1 — 2 — 4 — 10
Path5   1 — 6 —8 — 10
Path6   1 —2 —3 — 5 — 10

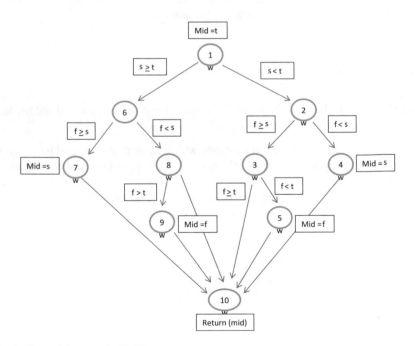

Fig. 1 Control flow graph (CFG)

Table 1 All test cases for all paths

Test cases	Path	Variable f	Variable s	Variable t
T1	Path 1	10	−10 to −5	−10
T2	Path 2	−5 to 5	5	−10
T3	Path 3	5	−10	0–5
T4	Path 4	−5	−10 to −5	10
T5	Path 5	−10	5	0–5
T6	Path 6	−5 to 2	−5	10

After this, constraints on each separate path are used to reduce the domain and then test cases are generated by using algebraic conditions to allot specific values to variables. All test cases for all paths receive from are shown in Table 1.

From Table 1, range values for variables "f" are used in path 2 and path 6, "s" used in path 1 and path 4, "t" used in path 3 and path 5, respectively.

Therefore, range values for variables f, s and t are defined as follows:

$$f_1 = -5 \text{ to } 5$$
$$s_1 = -10 \text{ to } -5$$
$$t_1 = 0 \text{ to } 5$$

Here, f_1, s_1 t_1 are range identifiers.

Individual path test case identifier as shown in Table 2 creates some exclusive value to every interval on an independent path.

4 Parallel Test Case Executor

The last step is parallel test case executor. The proposed algorithm was executed on a PC with a 2.10 GHz Intel Core i3-2310 M Processor and 2 GB RAM running on the Windows 7 operating system. For parallel execution of all paths, Eclipse Parallel Tools Platform in C is used. As each independent path is executed parallelly by using thread, it contains all combinations of test cases. Figure 2 shows a part of the source code of parallel execution of all test cases. The screenshot for parallel execution of all test cases with execution time is presented in Fig. 3.

Table 2 Individual path test case identifier

Test cases	f	s	t
T_1	10	s_1	−10
T_2	f_1	5	−10
T_3	5	−10	t_1
T_4	−5	s_1	10
T_5	−10	5	t_1
T_6	f_1	−5	10

Fig. 2 Part of source code of parallel execution of all test cases

Fig. 3 Parallel test case execution result of all independent paths

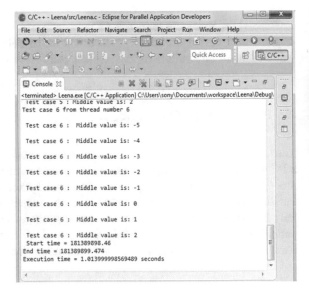

5 Result and Analysis

In this paper, the test suites have been developed for a particular example of calculation of mid-value of three integers. The total number of test cases for the proposed method is 55,566 for all paths, whereas in Coverall algorithm and Get Split algorithm, the total numbers of test cases are 9261 for a single assumed path.

Table 3 Comparison of proposed method with other existing algorithms

Methods area	Proposed method	Coverall algorithm	GetSplit algorithm
Program	Mid-value	Mid-value	Mid-value
Over all test cases	55,566	9261	9261
Reduced test cases	6	21	384
Path coverage criteria	All path (multiple)	Specific path	Specific path
Saving (%)	99.99	99.77	95.85
Execution time (s)	0.0139999	10.5	192

The technique which is proposed covers all the possible independent paths, numbers of test cases are reduced to 6 with execution time 0.0139999 s as compared to Coverall and Get Split algorithm where number of test cases obtained were 21 and 384 with execution time 10.5 and 192 s, respectively. The comparison of the proposed method with other existing algorithms is shown in Table 3.

6 Conclusion

The proposed method is based on the parallel execution to cover all independent paths which are executing parallelly in spite of sequential execution for the reduction of the number of test cases and time of execution. From Table 3, the proposed method achieves greater percentage in reduction of test cases in comparison with other existing techniques and improves the efficiency of software. This method has also achieved lower execution time using parallelism as well as reducing test cases. The technique which is proposed, the test cases for all the paths are obtained to be 6 with execution time 0.0139999 s that are lesser than the existing algorithm even with all possible independent path coverage.

References

1. Beizer, B.: Software testing techniques. Van Nostrand Reinhold, 2nd edn (1990)
2. Jeffrey, D.B.: Test suite reduction with selective redundancy. MS thesis, University of Arizona (2005)
3. Gong, D., Zhang, W., Zhang, Y.: Evolutionary generation of test data for multiple paths. Chin. J. Electron. **19**(2), 233–237 (2011)
4. Ghiduk, A.S., Girgis, M.R.: Using gentic algorithms and dominance concepts for generating reduced test data. Informatics (Solvenia) **34**(3), 377–385 (2010)
5. Korel, B.: Automated software test data-generation. Conf. Softw. Eng. **10**(8), 870–879 (1990)
6. Clarke, L.A.: A system to generate test data and symbolically execute programs. IEEE Trans. Softw. Eng. **SE-2**(3), 215–222 (1976)
7. Gallagher, M.J., Narsimhan, V.L.: ADTEST: A test data generation suite for ada software systems. IEEE Trans. Softw. Eng. **23**(8), 473–484 (1997)

8. Gupta, N., Mathur, A.P., Soffa, M.L.: Automated test data generation using an iterative relaxation method. In: ACM SIGSOFT Sixth International Symposium on Foundations of Software Engineering (FSE-6), pp. 231–244. Orlando, Florida (1998)
9. Pravin A., Srinivasan, S.: An efficient algorithm for reducing the test cases which is used for performing regression testing. In: 2nd International Conference on Computational Techniques and Artificial Intelligence (ICCTAI'2013), pp. 194–197, 17–18 March 2013
10. Subashini, B., JeyaMala, D.: Reduction of test cases using clustering technique. Int. J. Innov. Res. Eng. Technol. 3(3), 1992–1996 (2014)
11. Muthusamy, T., Seetharaman, K.: Effectiveness of test case prioritization techniques based on regression testing. Int. J. Softw. Eng. Appl. (IJSEA) 5(6), 113–123 (2014)
12. Jefferson, A., Jin, Z., Pan, J.: Dynamic domain reduction procedure for test data generations design and algorithm. J. Softw. Pract. Experience 29(2), 167–193 (1999)
13. Pringsulaka, P., Daengdej, J.: Coverall algorithm for test case reduction. In: IEEE Aerospace Conference, pp. 1–8 (2006). https://doi.org/10.1109/aero.2006.1656028

iCop: A System for Mitigation of Felonious Encroachment Using GCM Push Notification

Saurabh Mishra, Madhurima Hooda, Saru Dhir and Alisha Sharma

Abstract A mobile application can enable a user to get control on an infrared or IR sensor device, remotely and also along with detecting and notifying of any movement that should happen around the sensor via GPRS. To further improve this thought, we interfaced the mobile technology with hardware. The focus is placed on getting the control of the secured zones, by monitoring the human movement IR sensors alongside some other movement that might happen in the fringe of the sensor. The use of this thought can be extremely very much expected in the circumstances that are exceedingly secure and in which, not withstanding manual security, electronic and mobile security efforts to establish safety are likewise needed. These spots could be banking sector, money midsections, criminal prisons, atomic establishments, confidential and very secret exploration zones, and so forth. The paper implements an intrusion detection system iCop and also presents the testing results showing expected output and actual output. Also, the risk factors and their corresponding mitigation plan are discussed.

Keywords Arduino · IR sensor · GPRS · Google C2DM

S. Mishra · M. Hooda (✉) · S. Dhir
Amity University, Noida 110025, Uttar Pradesh, India
e-mail: mhooda@amity.edu

S. Mishra
e-mail: mishrasaurabh95@gmail.com

S. Dhir
e-mail: sdhir@amity.edu

A. Sharma
NIIT Technologies Ltd., Noida, India
e-mail: alishasharma361@gmail.com

M. N. Hoda et al. (eds.), *Software Engineering*, Advances in Intelligent Systems and Computing 731, https://doi.org/10.1007/978-981-10-8848-3_60

1 Introduction

An intrusion detection system (IDS) protects felonious admittance to user system or network software. A wireless IDS can easily perform this chore through sensors at different work stations via Internet. These systems supervise traffic on the network and have the authority to look at all the individuals who are logging in and may threat the private data of the company and can also put forth the request of alerting the personnel to respond. The wireless networking system no way requires wired intrusion detection. The reason is that the wireless communication medium itself needs to be secured apart from protecting it from other attacks associated with a wired system [1]. Because of this unpredictable arrangement of the system, it is moderately perplexing to prevent the Trojan assault despite of suitable software programs and hardware equipments (utilized as a part of request to ensure the Trojans assault on the system, in the same route there are considerably more tools designed which are intended to crush them) [2]. So keeping in mind the end goal to anticipate such issue, developing and implementing the wireless intrusion detection system are the need of great importance [3]. The sensor nodes of a remote sensor system are freely distributed so as to perform an application-oriented global errand. The sensors are not just invaluable in measuring climate conditions, for example, stickiness, temperature and weight however, when these gadgets are used inside a system, they are keen, reasonable and assumes an imperative part in observing the remote system.

The archaic of this paper includes feasibility study in Sect. 2 followed by Sect. 3, which presents an overview of Arduino architecture followed by Sect. 4, which discusses the methodology adopted for implementing iCop intrusion detection system. Section 5 describes detailed description of the iCop system, testing results and risk analyses, finally leading to the conclusion.

2 Feasibility Study

To select the best system, that can meet the performance requirements, a feasibility study must be carried out [4]. It is the determination of whether or not a project is worth doing. Our iCop system is financially plausible in the light of the fact that the hardware part will be utilized in project, which is effortlessly accessible in the business sector at an extremely ostensible expense. The iCop is profoundly versatile which can be for all intents and purposes actualized at whatever time anyplace. It is actually possible as it can assimilate modifications. In manual processing, there is more risk of blunders, which thus makes bunches of muddling, and is less specialized or logical. Through the proffered system, we can without much of a stretch set this procedure into an exceptionally deliberate example, which will be more specialized, imbecile evidence, bona fide, safe and solid. Notwithstanding it, the proffered system is exceedingly adaptable in the light of the fact that when the interruption is identified, the individual can get the notice ready message on their android advanced mobile phones, which demonstrates its proficiency and viability, smart phones, which proves its efficiency and effectiveness.

3 A Brief About Arduino Platform

We make use of Arduino open-source platform which is based on I/O board, and furthermore, an advancement domain for coding of microcontroller in C dialect. Arduino uses an integrated development environment and can be deployed in many computing projects. Also, Arduino can very easily communicate with software running on your computer, for example with softwares such as NetBeans and Eclipse. It is very helpful in controlling sensors for sensing stuff such as push buttons, touch pads, tilt switches, photo resistors etc. and actuators to do stuff such as motors, speakers, lights (LEDS), LCD (display). It is very adaptable and offers a wide mixed bag of digital and analog inputs, for example serial peripheral interface (SPI) and pulse width modulation (PWM) outputs. It is quite amiable and can be tack on with a computer system by means of universal serial bus (USB). It delineates via a standard serial protocol and runs on a stand-alone mode. It is likewise truly cheap, generally dollar thirty per board furthermore accompanies with free authoring software. Also, being an open-source undertaking, programming and equipment are to a great degree available, and exceptionally adaptable for being redone and amplified.

Sensors are devices which are basically used to detect the presence of any object, intrusion or sound. The sensor that we have used in our iCop system is basically used to detect the presence of humans. In order to switch on the sensor, set the pin with output high and to switch off the sensor, the pin is set to output low. The code snippet shown below set the pin to high and low.

```
strPosition=readString.indexOf("codes");
switchChar=readString.charAt(strPosition+5);
switch (switchChar)
{
    case '1':
    clientUser.println("HTTP/1.1 200 OK");
    digitalWrite(outPin1, HIGH);
    break;
    case '2':
    clientUser.println("HTTP/1.1 201 OK");
    digitalWrite(outPin1, LOW);
    break;
    default:
    clientUser.print("Default Status");
}
break;
```

4 Methodology

Different techniques are used for modifying the data on a device such as pushing, polling and Cloud to Device Messaging (C2DM). In the polling technique, the application contacts the server and modifies the latest data on the device. In this method, a background service is built, which will uphold a thread that would go and drag something (data) from the Web and will be on hold for the allotted time and then again endeavoured to drag something from the Web. This cycle will work in a repetitive way. In opposite of it, in the pushing technique, the server contacts the installed application and shows the availability of updated application with the latest data, on the device. This can be implemented by pushing a message to the device and the application can hold the message service directly. For this updation, we require a permission "android permission. Receive_SMS", to obtain the message (SMS) during the server [5]. On the other hand, C2DM has multi-layered parties implicated in it like an application server which will push the message to the android application. When the message is pushed from application server to the android application, then it routes the message towards the C2DM server. C2DM sends the message to the respective device and suppose the device is not available at that time, then the text will be forwarded once it will be online. As soon as the message is received, the broadcast target will be generated. The mobile application will authorize an intended receiver for this broadcast by registering the application.

There is a necessity taking the permission to perform Google C2DM along with numerous implementation steps, such as invoking a registration identification number from the Google C2DM, registering as a receiver for the C2DM messaging along with an authentication of the application with C2DM server.

5 iCop System

The intrusion detection system is a cyclic process. There will be several components which will be deployed in order to detect the intrusion. The components will be server, mobile and embedded components, etc.

Figure 1 shows the block diagram of the iCop system described in this paper. The embedded part is written in C and is mainly responsible for sending high/low input to the sensor. It will receive the enable and disable command through the Web server via a USB cable which will be eventually turned on/off. Moreover, it is also responsible for detecting any movement that happens around the IR sensor with the help of a circuit, which will route it to the Web server and further route it to the Android device via the Web and the alert will be displayed in the form of notification message with the help of Google Cloud Messaging (GCM) service of Google, along with the beep sound which emphatically alerts the user [6].

The android part will be written in Java Platform, Micro Edition (J2ME) and will be installed in the android device with version above 2.2. The device will be

Fig. 1 Block diagram of
iCop system

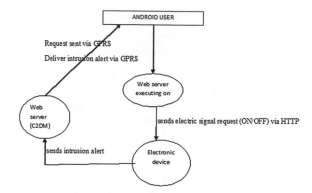

connected to the computer via general packet radio service (GPRS) and will send
the on/off command for enabling and disabling the sensor. The Web server running
on the computer will further route the request to the electrical circuit in which
embedded code to enable and disable the sensor is stored. The Web server part will
be deployed in this component and will mainly responsible for receiving the request
from the android device and transfer it to the Arduino circuit. The PC on which the
Web server will be running will be connected to the Internet and its IP address will
be used by the mobile application for connection.

Keeping in mind the end goal to make an application for cell phones, Google
C2DM administration is a valuable option, which will approve to associate the IR
sensor gadget consistently. The mobile application which when joined with the
e-chip and IR sensors using the GPRS mode [7], with two important parts: the
mobile part and the electronic part. The mobile part may have an interface, through
which one can control the infrared sensor (IR). This notification framework for
intrusion caution for cell phones and different gadgets is the greatest point of
preference of the iCop system as it permits the client to get caution messages about
the interruption identification at whatever point they utilize their cell phone, from
the cloud. An automatic message is sent to every enlisted gadget when an assault on
a system is identified.

5.1 Testing Results

The testing is applied on Web part and mobile part of the iCop system. Table 1
shows the input, expected output and actual output of the system. The results show
that all the output is OK for mobile as well as Web part of the system.

Table 1 Test results showing expected output and actual output

Module	Input	Expected output	Actual output	Result
Mobile part	Incorrect username and password	The J2ME application should inform the user with an appropriate message	The application should display the message	OK
Mobile part	Correct username and password	The J2ME should load the appropriate contacts from the remote server via GPRS	Contacts are getting loaded	OK
Mobile part	Correct username and password	If the GPRS feature is not enabled or not working, the application should display the message	Message is getting displayed about GPRS feature not working	OK
Mobile part	Correct username and password	After contacts are loaded from the database, the application should give the option to add, edit, delete, synchronize and logout	The mobile application gives these options, and when the user adds new contacts they are transferred to the remote server via GPRS. When a contact is being added or deleted, it is committed to the database via GPRS. The synchronization features fetch any new contact which are added at the remote server and display on the handset	Ok
Web part	Sign up details	The user's category registration detail should be successfully inserted in the database, and he should be able to delete, add and edit the contacts in that category	Details are getting added in the database, and the user is able to manage the records from the Web pan	OK
Web part	Login username and password	Correct contact should be fetched from the database. If there is any new contact added from the mobile device	Addition, editing and deletion are correctly getting synchronized from the mobile device to the remote server via GPRS	OK

5.2 Risk Analysis

Table 2 shows the risk identified in the implementation phase of the iCop system. It is identified that the risk area is coded when connectivity is between mobile clients and cloud server. The mitigation plan is to handle this is, for establishing the connection, static IP address is taken using a data card and wireless connection is created to connect the mobile client with the server. Also, it is identified that the risk

Table 2 Risk analysis with mitigation plan

Risk ID	Classification	Description	Risk area	Probability	Impact	Mitigation plan
R1	Implementation	Connectivity between mobile client and cloud server	Coding	High	High	In order to establish the connectivity, we took the static IP address using a data card and created a wireless network through which the mobile client could connect to the server
R2	Implementation	Connectivity between mobile and hardware device	Coding	High	High	In order to mitigate this connectivity risk, we took the help of Google's cloud service called C2DM which would help us keep a track of notification events

area is coded when connectivity is between mobile and hardware devices. In order to diminish this connectivity risk, Google's cloud service called C2DM was used to keep a track of notification events.

6 Conclusion

Application permits the client to manage the intrusion sensors remotely through GPRS, so that the remote detecting is not needed. This will help the clients to screen the crucial and sensitive establishments remotely from an unapproved access. It can be killed without human intermeddling. Also, the client might secure access Google's dependable cloud administrations keeping in mind the end goal to secure the sensitive areas. We can further extend this application in order to detect the intrusion of a larger area by connecting large intrusion sensors. Furthermore, we can integrate several other sensors to our application which will not only detect human intrusion, but also detect smoke and fire alarms. This application has the scope of scalability in which we can measure the parameters of different premises at the same time.

References

1. Maiti, A., Sivanesan, S.: Cloud controlled intrusion detection and burglary prevention stratagems in home automation systems. In: 2nd Baltic Congress on Future Internet Communications, pp. 182–185 (2012)
2. Galadima, A.A.: Arduino as a learning tool. In: 11th International Conference on Electronics, Computer and Computation (ICECCO) (2014)
3. Hakdee, N., Benjamas, N., Saiyod, S.: Improving intrusion detection system based on snort rules for network probe attack detection. In: 2nd International Conference on Information and Communication Technology, pp. 70–72 (2014)
4. Yilmaz, S.Y., Aydin, B.I., Demirbas, M.: Google cloud messaging (GCM): an evaluation. In: Symposium on Selected Areas in Communications, pp. 2808–2810 (2014)
5. Ryan, J.L.: Home automation. Electron. Commun. Eng. J. 1(4), 185–190 (1989)
6. Google cloud messaging: http://www.androidhive.info/2012/10/android-push-notifications-using-google-cloud-messaging-gcm-php-and-mysql/
7. Kumar, P., Kumar, P.: Arduino based wireless intrusion detection using IR sensor and GSM. IJCSMC 2(5), 417–424 (2013)

Clustering the Patent Data Using *K*-Means Approach

Anuranjana, Nisha Mittas and Deepti Mehrotra

Abstract Today patent database is growing in size and companies want to explore this dataset to have an edge for its competitor. Retrieving a suitable patent from this large dataset is a complex task. This process can be simplified if one can divide the dataset into clusters. Clustering is the task of grouping datasets either physical or abstract objects into classes of similar objects. *K*-means is a simple clustering technique which groups the similar items in the same cluster and dissimilar items in different cluster. In this study, the metadata associated with database is used as attribute for clustering. The dataset is evaluated using average distance centroid method. The performance is validated via Davies–Bouldin index.

Keywords Patents · *K*-means · Davies–Bouldin index · International patent classification · Cooperative patent classification

1 Introduction

A patent is an invention for which the originator is granted the intellectual rights for which he is developing something new and beneficial for the society [1, 2]. The patentee has the right to partially or wholly sell the patent. Patent analysis helps enterprises and researchers with the analysis of present status of technology, growth of economy, national technological capacity, competitiveness, market value, R&D capability, and strategic planning to avoid unnecessary R&D expenditure [2, 3]. Patents contain a lot of unknown and useful information that is considered essential

Anuranjana (✉) · N. Mittas · D. Mehrotra
Amity School of Engineering and Technology, Amity University,
Noida, Uttar Pradesh, India
e-mail: aranjana@amity.edu

N. Mittas
e-mail: nsh.mtts@gmail.com

D. Mehrotra
e-mail: mehdeepti@gmail.com

© Springer Nature Singapore Pte Ltd. 2019
M. N. Hoda et al. (eds.), *Software Engineering*, Advances in Intelligent Systems and Computing 731, https://doi.org/10.1007/978-981-10-8848-3_61

from R&D and advancement of technology point of view. Large amount of patent data from various sources become difficult and time-consuming for the analysis of the relevant dataset.

Patent data analysis is been done for efficient patent management. There are various patent analysis tools and techniques for solving the problem. The basic approaches include data mining, text mining, and visualization techniques. Classification and clustering are popular methods of patent analysis. Unstructured data uses the text mining approach for datasets like images, tables, figures. Natural Language Processing (NLP) technique is widely used for patent documents which are highly unstructured in nature [4, 5]. The second commonly used approach is visualization technique which works on citation mechanism in relation to patents. These approaches find application in statistical analysis of results in terms of graphs, histograms, scatter plots, etc. [6].

The work proposed is to demonstrate patent mining capability through K-means clustering on RapidMiner tool [7]. With K-means clustering technique, objects with similar characteristics make one cluster and dissimilar objects make another cluster based on distance between the two.

2 Background Study

A patent document has information related to one's claim, the abstract, the full text description of the invention, its bibliography, etc. [8, 9]. The information found on the front page of a patent document is called patent metadata. Patent mining uses classification and clustering techniques for patent analysis. Supervised classification is used to group patents by a preexisting classification. Clustering the unsupervised classification technique helps the patents to be divided into groups based on similarities of the internal features or attributes [10]. Presently, the clustering algorithm used in text clustering is the K-means clustering algorithm. The patent analysis technique needs suitable dataset obtained from stored information repositories. The task is performed on selection of suitable attributes, the dataset, mining technique, etc.

K-means is an important unsupervised learning algorithm. At every step, the centroid point of each cluster is observed and the remaining points are allocated to the cluster whose centroid is closest to it, hence called the centroid method. The process continues till there is no significant reduction in the squared error, and also it enables to group abstract patent objects into classes of similar group of patent objects, called as "clusters." Clustering helps the search to get reduced from huge amount of patents repository to a cluster comprising patents of same nature. Hence, it is widely adopted for narrowing down the search for fast execution of query.

2.1 Processing of Algorithm

The *K*-means clustering algorithm is a popular partition clustering algorithm that works to bring similar objects in a cluster. The steps involved are:

1. The given dataset points are classified into certain number of clusters (*K*). The initial choice of *K* is random.
2. These points are considered as a centroid point for each cluster and are placed as far as possible.
3. Now, take each point of a given dataset and associate it with the nearest centroid point.
4. Once all elements of dataset are distributed, the new centroid is calculated based on the clusters obtained from previous step.
5. Once again all elements are redistributed in the clusters with the closest centroid.
6. The steps are repeated until the centroid do not change.

The Davies–Bouldin index "is a similarity measure between the clusters and is defined as a measure of dispersion of a cluster and a dissimilarity measure between two different clusters." The following conditions were stated to satisfy the X_{ij} index:

1. $X_{ij} \geq 0$
2. $X_{ij} = X_{ji}$
3. If $m_i = 0$ and $m_j = 0$ then $X_{ij} = 0$
4. If $m_j > m_k$ and $b_{ij} = b_{ik}$ then $X_{ij} > X_{ik}$
5. If $m_j = m_k$ and $b_{ij} < b_{ik}$ then $X_{ij} < X_{ik}$

The above given conditions state that X_{ij} is a positive and symmetric value. Davies–Bouldin index satisfies the above said conditions for X_{ij} as:

$$X_{ij} = (m_i + m_j)/b_{ij}$$

Hence, the DB index was given the following definition as

$$DB\, nc = 1/nc \sum_{i=1}^{nc} X_i$$

$$X_i = \max$$
$$i = 1, \ldots, nc, \quad i\_ = jX_{ij}, \quad i = 1, \ldots, nc$$

The clusters should have minimum possible similarity between each other. The result with minimum value of DB gets up with better cluster formation. The performance level is plotted graphically.

3   Methodology

The analysis of the patent dataset is done through data mining tool called RapidMiner [11, 12]. The tool can easily handle numeric and categorical data together. The RapidMiner tool provides a broad range of various machine learning algorithms and data preprocessing tools for researchers and practitioners so that analysis can be done and optimum result be obtained [13]. This tool contains different number of algorithms for performing clustering operation. Here, the K-means operator in RapidMiner is used to generate a cluster model.

4   Experiments and Results

Data dataset: The data dataset contains five attributes: appln_id, cpc, cpc_maingroup_symbol, publn_auth, and publn_kind. Last three attributes contain categorical values. To process it through K-means algorithm, these attributes are converted into numerical values for accuracy of results. Through RapidMiner, this can be easily achieved using nominal to numeric conversion operator. The K-means clustering technique is applied on patent dataset which is obtained from Patent Statistical Database (PATSTAT) [14].

Data acquisition process: The raw datasets have been obtained from EPO Worldwide Patent Statistical Database, also known as "PATSTAT" where the data is available as public. The patent dataset contains attributes such as appln_id, cpc_maingroup_symbol, publn_auth, publn_nr, publn_kind.

- appln_id refers to application id of the PATSAT application.
- publn_nr refers to the unique number given by the Patent Authority issuing the publication of application.
- publn_auth refers to a code indicating the Patent Authority that issued the publication of the application.
- cpc_maingroup_symbol refers to the code for specific field of technology. The field of technology chosen here for experimentation and validation is ELECTRICITY and its code starts with H.
- publn_kind is specific to each publication authority (Fig. 1).

The validation process includes the following steps.

Patent dataset $\rightarrow$ Preprocessing $\rightarrow$ Attribute selection $\rightarrow$ modeling through K-means clustering $\rightarrow$ Evaluation through cluster distance performance.

The process is repeated for different clusters till we get optimum DB value (Figs. 2, 3 and 4).

The process is performed for various values of k. The result shows that for $k = 4$, the cluster assignment is best. The intraspace within cluster is maximum and interspace between clusters is minimum; it minimizes the sum of squared distances to the cluster centers [15].

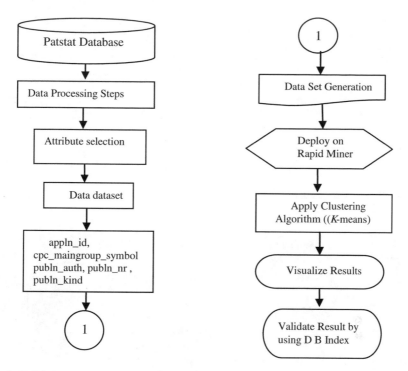

Fig. 1 Validation process for *K*-means clustering

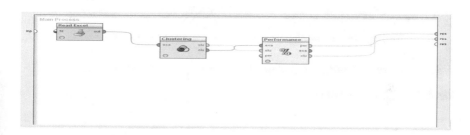

Fig. 2 Clustering using RapidMiner

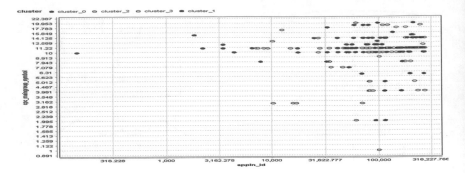

Fig. 3 Cluster plot for $k = 4$

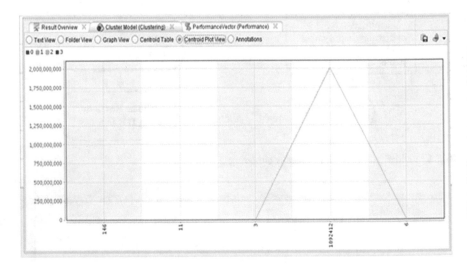

Fig. 4 Validation using DB index

5 Conclusion

In this paper, K-means cluster approach is used for clustering the patent dataset based on the metadata attributes like appln_id, cpc_maingroup_symbol, publn_auth, publn_nr, publn_kind. The experimental results show that optimal clustering in this case study is obtained for $k = 4$. This is evaluated using DB index for k values ranging from 2 to 7. In future, the study can be extended using fuzzy approach as it gives an idea of overlapping members and topics which are interrelated.

References

1. Hartigan, J., Wong, M.: Algorithm AS136: a k-means clustering algorithm. Appl. Stat. 100–108 (1979)
2. Alsabti, K., Ranka, S., Singh, V.: An efficient K-means clustering algorithm. http://www.cise.ufl.edu/ranka/ (1997)
3. Modha, D., Spangler, S.W.: Feature weighting in k-means clustering. Mach. Learn. 52(3) (2003)
4. Kovács, F., Legány, C., Babos, A.: Cluster validity measurement techniques. In: Proceedings of the 6th International Symposium of Hungarian Researchers on Computational Intelligence, Budapest, Nov 2005, pp. 18–19 (2005)
5. WIPO-Guide to Using Patent Information: WIPO Publication No. L434/3 (E) (2010). ISBN 978-92-805-2012-5
6. Shih, M.J., Liu, D.R., Hsu, M.L.: Discovering competitive intelligence by mining changes in patent trends. Expert Syst. Appl. 37(4), 2882–2890 (2010)
7. Vlase, M., Muntaeanu, D., Istrate, A.: Improvement of K-means clustering using patents metadata. In: Perner, P. (ed.) MLDM 2012, LNAI 7376, pp. 293–305 (2012)
8. Candelin-Palmqvist, H., Sandberg, B., Mylly, U.-M.: Intellectual property rights in innovation management research: a review. Technovation 32(9–10), 502–512 (2012)
9. Abbas, A., Zhang, L., Khan, S.U.: A literature review on the state-of-the-art in patent analysis. World Patent Inf. **37**, 3–13 (2014)
10. Sunghae, J.: A clustering method of highly dimensional patent data using Bayesian approach. IJCSI. ISSN (online): 1694-0814
11. Mattas, N., Samrika, Mehrotra, D.: Comparing data mining techniques for mining patents. In: 2015 Fifth International Conference on Advanced Computing & Communication Technologies, 22–23 Feb 2015, pp. 217–221
12. The United States Patent and Trademark Office: http://www.uspto.gov
13. European Patent Office: http://www.epo.org
14. Davies, D.L., Bouldin, D.W.: A cluster and separation measure. IEEE Trans. Pattern Anal. Mach. Intell. **1**(2), 224–227 (1979)
15. Halkidi, M., Batiktakis, Y., Vazirgiannis, M.: On clustering validation techniques. Intell. Inf. Syst. (2001)

Success and Failure Factors that Impact on Project Implementation Using Agile Software Development Methodology

Saru Dhir, Deepak Kumar and V. B. Singh

Abstract In the agile software development, there are different factors behind the success and failure of projects. Paper represents the success, failure, and mitigation factors in agile development. A case study is presented depending on all of these factors after the completion of small projects. Each team grouped into 10 team members and developed the project with different approaches. Each group maintained the documentation from initial user stories and factors employed on the projects. Final outcomes are observed based on the analysis of efficiency, accuracy, time management, risk analysis, and product quality of the project. Final outcomes are identified using the different approaches.

Keywords Agile development process · Scrum · Factors

1 Introduction

Software development is the process whose success and failure depends upon the team, organization, and technical environment. Software project development is a teamwork where the delivery of the project depends upon different factors or circumstances. In the traditional development, the customer got the final product after the completion of development and testing that final product sometimes satisfied or unsatisfied the customer. According to the agile development, customer has the continuous involvement in the project through the daily meetings. Agile methodology has four agile manifesto and twelve principles [1].

S. Dhir (✉) · D. Kumar
Amity University, Noida 110025, Uttar Pradesh, India
e-mail: sdhir@amity.edu

D. Kumar
e-mail: deepakgupta_du@rediffmail.com

V. B. Singh
University of Delhi, New Delhi, India
e-mail: singh_vb@rediffmail.com

© Springer Nature Singapore Pte Ltd. 2019
M. N. Hoda et al. (eds.), *Software Engineering*, Advances in Intelligent Systems and Computing 731, https://doi.org/10.1007/978-981-10-8848-3_62

Different methods such as scrum, XP, FDD, DSDM, lean are coming with agile development. Agile methodology overcomes the problems of the traditional development. Agile approach is driven by self-organizing teams that coordinate their tasks on their own. This enables the employee innovate, team work and increases the productivity and quality of the product. While different steps have been taken to understand the barriers occurred in software teams, and all these issues may be addressed by taking into the concerns of involved customer and stakeholders. In fact, due to various roles and their expectations, the software team may have perceptual differences on issues such as delivery time of software, risk factors, success and failure of the project [2]. Due to lack of knowledge and understanding about the project, it may directly affect the performance and delivery of the project. In the agile team, knowledge sharing is a challenging task to enlarge user's motivation to share their knowledge with the developers and other team members; to handle the diversity of social identities and cross-functionally involved in the software development [3].

2 Literature Review

The software development process depends upon the interest of the project team and the other resources. One of the major problems with software development is causing during the change of project development technology and business environment [4]. During the survey of agile projects in government and private sectors in Brazil and UK, five sociological (such as experience of team members, domain expertise and specialization) and five projects (team size, estimation of project, delivery of the product, etc.) related factors were added [5].

Tore Dyba signifies a major departure from traditional approaches to agile software development by identifying the 1996 studies, out of which 36 were the empirical studies. The studies fell into four groups: introduction and adoption, human and social factors, perceptions on agile methods, and comparative studies [6]. A framework was proposed a conceptual framework on different factors and represents the link between various predictor variables and agile development success [7].

Mahanti [8] mentioned six critical factors in agile methodology, during the survey conducted in four projects. He discussed several factors such as an office environment, team mind-set, mind-set toward documentation. Harnsen [9] mentioned different factors focusing on culture, stability, time variations, technology, stability, etc. Different factors and barriers of agile implementation were considered those significantly affecting the agile methods [10].

3 Different Factors in the Agile Development

In an agile environment, different technical (requirement volatility, requirement quality, technical dependency, non-functional requirement, etc.) and non-technical factors (communication, documentation, domain, hardware, customer involvement, etc.) are continually impacting in the agile environment. Figure 1 represents the various success and failure factors that are impacting on software development.

A. Success Factors:

There are certain success attributes which determine the overall observation of a particular project such as delivering a quality product and customer satisfaction, on-time delivery of product with the planned estimations. Ambler contends that in software development, the expert people are critical to make sure the success of the project while adopting the agile approaches [11]. In 2013 comparing software development paradigms, Ambler found the highest success rate of agile projects [12].

B. Failure Factors:

Boehm and Turner focus on management challenges in implementing the agile projects [13], whereas in another research Nerur et al. focused on management, people, technical, and process dimensions in agile projects [14].

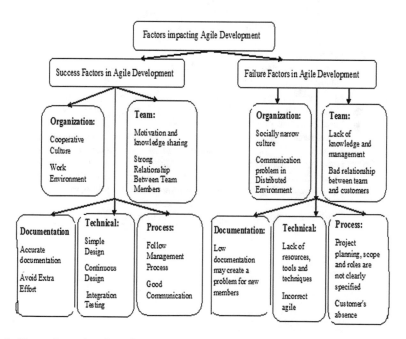

Fig. 1 Factors impacting the agile development

4 Strategies for Mitigating Factors Affecting Agile and Distributed Agile Development

There are different success factors on agile such as make training programs on higher priority, keep agile practices consistent, encourage team members, scale the infrastructure. Table 1 represents the different success, failure, and mitigation factors in agile software development.

Table 1 Success, failure, and mitigation factors based on different dimensions

Dimension	Success factor	Failure factor	Mitigation factors
Organization	1. Cooperative culture 2. Facilities for agile work environment	1. Organizational culture become socially narrow 2. Communication problem in distributed environment 3. Inaccurate estimations at initial stages	1. Provide a better technology infrastructure to support communication in a distributed environment
Team	1. Motivation between the team members 2. Teamwork reduces the work pressure and increases the knowledge 3. Strong relationship between the team members, stakeholders, and customer	1. Lack of knowledge and experience issue 2. Lack of management competence 3. Understanding issue between team members 4. A bad relationship with customers	1. Experienced people should be as a part of a team 2. There should be a proper time management and synchronize the working hours 3. Team collaboration 4. Build trust
Process	1. Team follow agile-oriented configuration, project management process 2. Good communication with daily meetings 3. Understanding the level of the project and its new issues	1. Customer's absence 2. Vague planning and project scope 3. Project roles are net clearly defined 4. Requirement prioritization becomes the major issue during the development of the process in a small team	1. The process should be clearly defined 2. Iterations should be implemented in fixed time-boxed 3. Work standards should be defined properly

(continued)

Table 1 (continued)

Dimension	Success factor	Failure factor	Mitigation factors
Technical	1. Following simple design 2. Continuous de faery of the software 3. Proper integration testing 4. The team is dynamic in nature and adapts new techniques according to demand	1. Lack of resources 2. Lack of the usage of new techniques and tools 3. Practices of incorrect agile approach	1. Availability of resources on time 2. Trainings or short-term courses should be provided for the awareness of new technologies and tools
Documentation	1. Accurate amount of documentation 2. Less documentation avoids extra effort	Less documentation may create a problem for new members	Documentation should be in appropriate form so the new users can be easily familiar with the project and its development

5 Case Study

Case study is based on the software project implementation during the training period of the students. Projects were divided into 5 teams and each team had 10 team members. Projects were based on the application development and Web site development for the customer. Projects were related to social implications such as safe cab car facility, e-voting system, women security app. Table 2 represents the team configuration, where different development processes of each team are mentioned, with the total number of team members involved in the development of project. The project implementation was implemented by waterfall, spiral, and the scrum (agile methodology). In the spiral implementation, each builds focused especially on risk analysis, including the requirement gathering and evaluation part. Scrum principles were followed by the team members for the requirement elicitation, daily meetings, and frequent changes. Daily meetings were conducted in a classroom and there was a customer interaction between the team members in a laboratory after every sprint cycle.

Table 2 Team configuration

Development process	Team members
Spiral	10
Scrum	10
Scrum	10
Waterfall	10
Scrum	8

Fig. 2 User stories of project 1

6 Findings

Initially, user stories were created by the customers and team members. Figure 2 shows the different user stories of project 1 by the team 1. Like project 1, other team members also build their different user stories as per customer and project requirement.

But due to the lack of experience, different responsibilities and environmental restrictions, it is really tough for students to follow this process. An analysis report was maintained on the success and failure factors of the projects. This analysis was done with the help of questionnaire and personal interaction with the team members. On the basis of a questionnaire, different factors were analyzed as:

1. Organization: Student had other responsibilities also and do not have a proper work environment; hence, there was a delay in delivery of the project.
2. Team: Team had a good relationship and trust between them, but as the beginner's team had a lack of experience about the methodology. Hence, they faced problems at the initial stage of development.
3. Process: Team followed the agile development process in which there was a proper group discussion between team members and also set sprint meetings with the customer. Project planning and roles were clearly defined. Team roles were rotated for the constant change in task prioritization to maintain the quality of the final product.
4. Technical: The team continuously tested the whole process with the strict TDD process. Students faced the technical issues such as new technical tool and techniques. Hence, free tools were used for the development of the project.
5. Documentation: As documentation, students maintain a daily diary on the regular basis, and at the end, report was generated.

6.1 Outcomes

During the analysis, it was observed that there were differences in non-functional activities with the different methods. Analysis was based on the efficiency,

Table 3 Factors based on different methodology

Methods	Efficiency	Accuracy	Time management	Risk analysis	Quality product
Waterfall	L	M	L	L	L
Spiral	M	L	M	H	M
Scrum	H	M	H	H	H

accuracy, time management, risk analysis, and product quality of the project. In the waterfall approach, team members approached to the customer after the delivery of the project. Development with waterfall approach had low efficiency, medium accuracy; low time management and product quality were less without the customer's involvement during the development. In the spiral method, students focused on risk analysis and quality of product. Projects had low accuracy in the spiral model as they created a prototype and did risk analysis. In the scrum methodology, results were better than waterfall and spiral model, where efficiency, product quality, and time management are high.

In Table 3, there is different parametric value that had major impact on success and failure of projects by using different approaches. Waterfall, spiral, and scrum methodology were used on different projects and all had different impacts. In Table 3, L represents the less/low value, M represents the medium value, and H represents the high value of different projects based on the usage of various approaches. Figure 3 represents the graphical representation of different factors using different methods, according to which agile methodologies have high performance rate and good quality of product on fixed time.

Fig. 3 Graphical representation of different factors using different methods

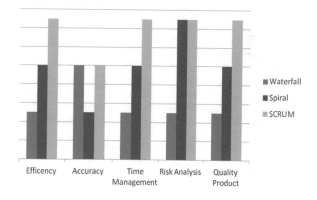

7 Conclusion

Paper is concluded with the success, failure, and mitigation factors in agile development projects. A case study was conducted based on the development of five projects. Projects were developed by the students as five different teams. It was observed that projects were developed using different development approaches such as waterfall, spiral, and agile approach and examined that there were differences in non-functional activities with different methods. Analysis was based on the efficiency, accuracy, time management, risk analysis, and product quality of the project. Finally, outcome was that in the scrum methodology results were better than waterfall and spiral model, where efficiency, product quality, and time management are high.

References

1. http://www.agilealliance.org/the-alliance/the-agile-manifesto/
2. Huisman, M., Iivari, J.: Deployment of systems development methodologies: perceptual congruence between IS managers and systems developers. Inf. Manag. **43**, 29–49 (2006)
3. Conboy, K., Coyle, S., Wang, X., Pikkarainen, M.: People over process: key people challenges in agile development. IEEE Softw. **99**, 47–57 (2010)
4. Williams, L.A., Cockburn, A.: Guest editors' introduction: agile software development: it's about feedback and change. IEEE Comput. **36**(6), 39–43 (2003)
5. Danillo, S., Bassi, D., Bravo, M., Goldman, A., Kon, F.: Agile projects: an imperial study (2006)
6. Byab, T., Dingsoyr, T.: Empirical studies of agile software development: a systematic review. Inf. Softw. Technol. (2008)
7. Misra, S.C., Kumar, V., Kumar, U.: Success factors of agile development method. J. Syst. Softw. (2009)
8. Mahanti, A.: Challenges in enterprise adoption of agile methods—a survey. J. Comput. Inf. Technol. 197–206 (2006)
9. Harnsen, F., Brand, M.V.D., Hillergerberg, J., Mehnet, N.A.: Agile methods for offshore information systems development. First Information Systems Workshop on Global Sourcing: Knowledge and Innovation (2007)
10. Asnawi, A.L., Gravell, A.M., Wills, G.B.: An empirical study—understanding factors and barriers for implementing agile methods in Malaysia. IDoESE (2010)
11. Ambler, S.: Agile adoption strategies: survey results. http://www.ambysoft.com (2011)
12. Ambler, S.: Agile adoption strategies: survey results. http://www.ambysoft.com (2013)
13. Boehm, B., Turner, R.: Management challenges to implement agile processes in traditional development organizations. IEEE Softw. **22**(5), 30–39 (2005)
14. Nerur, S., Mahapatra, R.K., Mangalaraj, G.: Challenges of migrating to agile methodologies. Commun. ACM **48**(5), 72–78 (2005)

Fuzzy Software Release Problem with Learning Functions for Fault Detection and Correction Processes

Deepak Kumar and Pankaj Gupta

Abstract Present-day software advancement has turned into an exceptionally difficult errand. The real difficulties included are shorter life cycles, expense invades and higher software quality desires. Notwithstanding these difficulties, the software developers have begun to give careful consideration on to the process of software advancement, testing and reliability analysis to bolster the procedure. A standout amongst the most essential choices identified with the software improvement is to focus the ideal release time of software. Software advancement procedure includes part of instabilities and ambiguities. We have proposed a software release time problem to overcome such vulnerabilities and ambiguities utilizing a software reliability growth model under fuzzy environment. Further we have talked about the fuzzy environment system to take care of the issue. Results are outlined numerically. Taking into account model and system, this paper particularly addresses the issue of when to release software under this condition.

Keywords Software reliability growth models · Fuzzy · Release time problem
Optimization problem · Membership function

1 Introduction

In the course of recent years, numerous software products unwavering software reliability growth models (SRGMs) have been proposed for estimation of reliability of software product. As personnel computer and its related software turn out to be more refined, whilst turning out to be more essential in our lives, individuals are progressively worried about its unwavering quality. Software reliability offers the

D. Kumar (✉)
Amity University, Noida 110025, Uttar Pradesh, India
e-mail: deepakgupta_du@redifmail.com

P. Gupta
Birla Institute of Technology, Mesra, Ranchi, India
e-mail: pgupta@bitmesra.ac.in

© Springer Nature Singapore Pte Ltd. 2019
M. N. Hoda et al. (eds.), *Software Engineering*, Advances in Intelligent Systems
and Computing 731, https://doi.org/10.1007/978-981-10-8848-3_63

655

most far-reaching cutting-edge procedures to measure the product quality and testing approaches. Software improvement forms normally concentrate on dodging mistakes, recognizing and redressing programming blames that do happen at any period of software advancement.

A wide range of SRGMs have been produced to depict the failure of software system. In the previous four decades, numerous software reliability development-based SRGMs [1–3] have been proposed in writing to gauge and anticipate the software dependability and number of shortcomings staying in the product.

A standout amongst the most critical utilizations of SRGMs is to focus on release time of the software. For the most part, the detection of faults included in enhancing the software reliability of a software comprises of an exceptionally prolonged and costly testing system. It is accounted for that much of the time, more than a large portion of the time and cost is spent in testing when creating software. Subsequently, one of the imperative issues in this testing is the point at which we ought to quit testing and are prepared to release the software.

In the writing, a wide range of methodologies have been created to focus the ideal release time of software, in view of distinctive SRGM. It could not be any more obvious, for case, Okumoto and Goel [4]; Kapur et al. [2, 5]; Jha et al. [6].

Parameters of the SRGM used to portray the failure are assessed from the watched testing information, different goals and limitations are situated by the administration and expense parameters included in the cost are resolved in the light of past experience and all are altered constants. Practically speaking, it is conceivable that the administration is not ready to situated exact estimations of the different cost parameters and targets to be met by the release time. It might likewise be conceivable that the administration itself does not set exact qualities keeping in mind the end goal to give some resilience on these parameters because of focused contemplations. This prompts vulnerability (fuzziness) in the problem. Fresh optimization problem ways to deal with take care of these issues give no instrument to evaluate these instabilities. The fuzzy procedures can be utilized as a part of such a circumstance.

The paper is composed as follows: first in Sect. 2.1, we have examined the SRGM using detection and correction of fault in the software. In Sect. 2.2, we have talked about the cost, and we defined the problem in Sect. 2.3. In Sect. 3.1, we have talked about the essential ideas of fuzzy problem and given a calculation to explain the fuzzy optimization problem. Further in Sect. 3.2, a method is shown with a numerical example. At last, we conclude in Sect. 4.

2 Formulation of Problem

2.1 Software Reliability Growth Models

SRGM based on non-homogeneous Poisson process (NHPP) model [3, 7, 8] is developed with following list of symbols and notations:

List of symbols:

a	Initial number of faults in the software.
$m_d(t)$	Expected number of fault detected by time t.
$m_c(t)$	Expected number of fault corrected by time t.
$b(t)$	Fault removal rate per remaining fault.
$R(x\|T)$	Pr{no failure happens during time $(T, T + x)$}
C_1	Cost acquired on testing before release of the software.
C_2	Cost acquired on testing after release of the software.
C_3	Testing cost per unit time.
C_0	Total cost spending plan.
T	Release time of the product.
α, β	Constant parameter in the learning ($a\alpha > 0$, $b\beta > 0$).
b, c	Constant parameter in the learning ($b > 0$, $c > 0$).

Assumption:

(1) Fault detection rate is proportional to the mean value of undetected faults.
(2) The number of faults in each of the individual interval is autonomous.
(3) Each time a failure happens; the fault that brought on it is perfectly fixed.
(4) No new fault is created.

The testing stage is a two-stage process. For first phase of testing process, the mean number of fault detected $m_d(t)$ is propositional to the mean number of undetected faults staying in the software and can be communicated by taking after differential mathematical equation:

$$m'_d(t) = b(t)(a - m_d(t)) \tag{2.1}$$

where

$$b(t) = \frac{\alpha + \beta t}{1 + bt}$$

Understanding comparison (2.1) with beginning $m_d(0) = 0$, we get

$$m_d(t) = a\left(1 - (1 + bt)^{\left(\frac{\beta}{b^2} - \frac{\alpha}{b}\right)} e^{-\left(\frac{\beta}{b}\right)t}\right) \tag{2.2}$$

It can be shown that as $t \to \infty, b(t) \to \frac{\beta}{b}$.

In the second stage, the fault correction rate is relative to the mean number of faults detected, however not yet fixed in the software. In this stage, fault correction rate is accepted as logistic learning capacity and it can be communicated as far as the differential equation as:

$$\frac{dm_c(t)}{dt} = b(t)(m_d(t) - m_c(t)) \tag{2.3}$$

where $b(t) = \dfrac{\left(\frac{\beta}{b}\right)}{1+c\,e^{-\left(\frac{\beta}{b}\right)t}}$.

Above mathematical Eq. (2.3) can be solved with beginning $m_c(0) = 0$; the mean number of fault correction is given by:

$$m_c(t) = \frac{a}{1+c\,e^{-\left(\frac{\beta}{b}\right)t}}\left(1 - \left(1 + \frac{(1+bt)^{\left(\frac{\beta}{b^2}-\frac{z}{b}+1\right)}-1}{\left(\frac{\beta}{b^2}-\frac{z}{b}+1\right)}\left(\frac{\beta}{b^2}\right)\right)e^{-\left(\frac{\beta}{b}\right)t}\right) \tag{2.4}$$

This model is due to Kapur et al. [9].

2.2 The Cost Model

The cost capacity incorporates cost of testing, fixing faults during testing and cost of failure and consequently removal of faults during testing and operational stage. Testing is performed under controlled environment. In this manner, utilizing the total cost of failure phenomenon the accompanying cost function can be defined to depict the aggregate expected cost of testing and debugging.

$$C(T) = C_1 m_c(T) + C_2(m_c(T+T_w) - m_c(T)) + C_3 T \tag{2.5}$$

Total cost shown in (2.5) is the most ordinarily utilized as a part of writing in ideal release time problem under blemished testing environment [2, 6, 7].

2.3 Problem Formulation

Utilizing the total cost capacity given by Eq. (2.5), the release time problem with minimizing the cost function subject to the reliability constraint is expressed as

$$\textbf{Min\~{i}mize} \quad C(T)$$

Subject to $R(T_S|T) \gtrsim R_0$

$$T \geq 0 \tag{P1}$$

where R_0 is the desired level of reliability by the release time, the management may not be prepared to acknowledge level of reliability lesser than R_0, called the lower resilience level of the reliability.

3   Problem Solution and Numerical Example

3.1   Problem Solution

Optimization problem (P1) can be solved by the Mathematical Programming methodology. As management may not be giving absolute value for cost and reliability and its aim to release software at earliest. Hence, we utilize fuzzy optimization techniques to comprehend the above problem. Problem P1 may be restated as

$$
\begin{aligned}
&\textbf{Find} \quad T \\
&\textbf{Subject to} \quad C(T) \le C_0 \\[6pt]
&\qquad\qquad R(T_W|T) \le R_0 \\
&\qquad\qquad T \ge 0
\end{aligned}
\tag{P2}
$$

Membership functions $\mu_i(T)$; $i = 1, 2$ for each of the fuzzy inequalities in problem P2 can be defined as

$$
\mu_1(T) = \begin{cases} 1; & C(T) \le C_0 \\ \frac{C_0^* - C(T)}{C_0^* - C_0}; & C_0 < C(T) \le C_0^* \\ 0; & C(T) > C_0^* \end{cases}
\tag{2.5}
$$

$$
\mu_2(T) = \begin{cases} 1; & R(T_W|T) \ge R_0 \\ \frac{R(T_W|T) - R^*}{R_0 - R^*}; & R^* \le R(T_W|T) < R_0 \\ 0; & R(T_W|T) < R^* \end{cases}
\tag{2.6}
$$

where C_0^* and R^* are the respective tolerances for the desired reliability and resources. Next we use Bellman and Zadeh's [10] principle to solve the problem P2. Crisp optimization problem can be written as

$$
\begin{aligned}
&\textbf{Max} \quad \alpha \\
&\textbf{Sub.to} \quad \mu_i(T) \ge \alpha \ \ i = 1,2,; \ \ \alpha \ge 0, \ T \ge 0
\end{aligned}
\tag{P3}
$$

Crisp mathematical programming approach can be used to find optimal solution.

3.2   Numerical Example

We have gathered real-time software data from Brooks and Motley [11] to evaluate the various parameters. The assessed estimations of parameters are $a = 1334.26$, $b = 0.119$, $c = 18.902$, $\alpha = 1.972$ and $\beta = 0.024$. Further it is accepted that estimations of C_1, C_2, C_3 and T_W are known. The release time issue in view of the

Fig. 1 Cost membership
values cost versus time

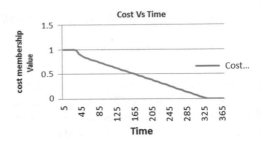

accompanying information could be dissected. Here we have $C_1 = 6$, $C_2 = 15$, $C_3 = 30$, $T_W = 5$. Further aggregate spending plan accessible to the management is $C_0 = 20,000$, and dependability prerequisite by the release time is $R_0 = 0.99$ with resistance levels on expense and reliability $C_0^* = 22,000$ and $R^* = 0.80$ (we have accepted these qualities for representation, however these qualities are situated by the management in the light of past experience).

After solving numerical problem with above method, we get following results. Figures 1 and 2 show cost membership value versus time and reliability versus time, respectively. Figure 3 demonstrates that the two curves cross at a point, which gives the ideal release time of the software.

From Fig. 3, we acquire ideal release time $T = 65$ and $\alpha = 0.87475$.

Fig. 2 Cost membership
values reliability versus time

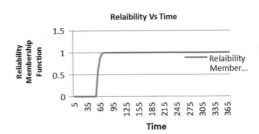

Fig. 3 Ideal software release
time

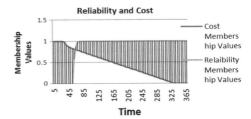

4 Conclusion

We have defined a fuzzy release time issue by minimizing the expense capacity subject to reliability limitation. We have also examined the fuzzy mathematical programming methodology for different type of learning function. The problem is then solved by fuzzy optimization method [12–16]. The numerical illustration is indicated for an achievable issue if there should arise an occurrence of an infeasible issue a fresh objective optimization problem is utilized to acquire a bargained arrangement. This is a fascinating subject of further study in fuzzy enhancement.

References

1. Goel, A.L., Okumoto, K.: Time dependent error detection rate model for software reliability and other performance measures. IEEE Trans. Reliab. **R-28**(3), 206–211 (1979)
2. Kapur, P.K., Garg, R.B.: Optimal release policies for software systems with testing effort. Int. J. Syst. Sci. **22**(9), 1563–1571 (1990)
3. Deepak, K., Sharma, S.G., Saini, S., Mrinal, N.: Development of software reliability S-shaped models. Rev. Bus. Technol. Res. **6**(1), 101–110 (2012)
4. Okumoto K. and Goel A.L., "Optimal release time for computer software", *IEEE Transactions On Software Engineering,* SE-9 (3), 323–327, 1983
5. Kapur, P.K., Aggarwal, S., Garg, R.B.: Bicriterion release policy for exponential software reliability growth model. RAIRO-Oper. Res. **28**, 165–180 (1994)
6. Jha, P.C., Deepak, K., Kapur, P.K.: Fuzzy release time problem. In: Proceedings of 3rd International Conference in Quality, Reliability and Infocomm Technology (ICQRIT'2006), pp. 304–310 (2006)
7. Kapur, P.K., Garg, R.B., Kumar, S.: Contributions to hardware and software reliability. World Scientific Publishing Co., Ltd., Singapore (1999)
8. Khatri, S.K., Deepak, K., Dwivedi, A., Mrinal, N.: Software reliability growth model with testing efforts using learning function. In: IEEE Explore Digital Library, Proceedings of International Conference on Software Engineering (Conseg 2012), Devi Ahilya Vishwavidhylaya, Indore, India, pp. 1–5 (2012)
9. Kapur, P.K., Jha, P.C., Deepak, K.: A general software reliability growth model with different types of learning functions for fault detection and correction processes. Commun. Dependability Qual. Manag. Int. J. **12**(1), 11–23 (2009)
10. Bellman, R.E., Zadeh, L.A.: Decision making in a fuzzy environment. Manag. Sci. **17**, 141–164 (1973)
11. Brooks, W.D., Motley, R.W.: Analysis of Discrete Software Reliability Models—Technical Report (RADC-TR-80-84). Rome Air Development Center, New York (1980)
12. Huang, C.Y., Lyu, M.R.: Optimal release time for software systems considering cost, testing-effort, and test efficiency. IEEE Trans. Reliab. **54**(4), 583–591 (2005)
13. Kapur, P.K., Deepak, K., Anshu, G., Jha, P.C.: On how to model software reliability growth in the presence of imperfect debugging and fault generation. In: Proceedings of 2nd International Conference on Reliability & Safety Engineering, pp. 515–523 (2006)
14. Pham, H.: System Software Reliability. Springer, Reliability Engineering Series (2006)
15. Xie, M.: A study of the effect of imperfect debugging on software development cost. IEEE Trans. Softw. Eng. **29**(5) (2003)
16. Zimmermann, H.J.: Fuzzy Set Theory and Its Applications. Academic Publisher (1991)

Reliability Assessment of Component-Based Software System Using Fuzzy-AHP

Bhat Jasra and Sanjay Kumar Dubey

Abstract Software reliability is one of the most commonly discussed research issues in the field of software engineering. Reliability of software concerns both the maker and the buyer of the software. It can be defined as a collection of attributes that check the capability of software to assure the needed performance in given conditions for a particular span of time. Most of the estimation models proposed till date have focused only on some conventional factors internal to the software. In this paper, we try to analyze the reliability of software using a FAHP approach. The proposed model considers the factors external to a component-based software that affects its reliability. Analysis shows that by considering these factors a more efficient model for estimating reliability in CBSE systems.

Keywords Fuzzy · AHP · CBSS · Reliability · Factors

1 Introduction

In this modern technology-driven world, role of computer systems has become more important than ever. And for any computer system to perform efficiently, quality of the underlying software system is a crucial concern. Quality of a software system is estimated using many factors such as software functionality, usability, efficiency, testability, and reliability as given in ISO/IEC 9126-1 software quality model. Among all these quality factors, software reliability is one of the most important factors. It can be defined as a collection of attributes that check the capability of software to assure the needed performance in given conditions for a

B. Jasra (✉) · S. K. Dubey
Amity University, Noida, Uttar Pradesh, India
e-mail: bhatjasra@gmail.com

S. K. Dubey
e-mail: skdubey1@amity.edu

© Springer Nature Singapore Pte Ltd. 2019
M. N. Hoda et al. (eds.), *Software Engineering*, Advances in Intelligent Systems and Computing 731, https://doi.org/10.1007/978-981-10-8848-3_64

B. Jasra and S. K. Dubey

particular span of time [1]. Software reliability consists of three main activities: prevention of error, detection and removing the faults, measures to increase the reliability [2]. Component-based software systems (CBSSs) are gaining importance because of various edges it provide over object-oriented technology in terms of design, development, flexible architecture maintenance, reliability, and reusability [3]. CBSS reliability is highly affected by the individual components in the system and interaction between these components which leads to interdependencies between them increasing the system complexity hence making estimation of reliability difficulty [4]. Other factors that play an important role in determining the reliability are deployment context, usage profiles, and component-environment dependencies [5]. There are lot of extrinsic factors that affect the performance and reliability of software [6]. In this paper, we propose a reliability evaluation model for component-based software systems based on fuzzy-AHP. It uses fuzzy evaluation with the capability of consistent evaluation of AHP. Fuzzy logic is used to deal with uncertain, vague data obtained from individual perception of humans providing more realistic and acceptable decisions. AHP handles diverse criteria by converging complex problem into less significant factors that are important for global decision making. Fuzzy-AHP uses goodness of both. AHP is used for weight metric assignment and complex evaluations at all the three layers, whereas fuzzy logic is used to evaluate and layer three weights [7, 8]. Using fuzzy-AHP approach, the uncertainties present in the data can be represented effectively to ensure better decision making [9].

2 Methodology

2.1 Identification of Factors

Reliability assessment is mostly confined to testing phase after the development of the whole software. But reliability is actually affected by factors from almost every stage of software's life cycle, i.e., analysis, development, testing, usage time [10]. To determine appropriate factors that affect reliability of CBSS, we identified relevant stakeholders, researchers, academicians, organizations, and other experts who deal with CBSSs. On the basis of these findings, we have selected following factors.

2.1.1 The Deployment Context

In a CBSS environment, one component has to interact with another, and these interactions increase dependency of component's reliability on each other, e.g., if a participating component fails, directly or indirectly the performance of other components is affected, thereby its reliability. Key factors of deployment context are unknown usage profile, unknown required context, and unknown operational profile.

2.1.2 Human Factor

Right from the requirement analysis to deployment and maintenance, humans are almost involved in every aspect of the software development. Key factors are programming skills, domain knowledge/expertise, and human nature.

2.1.3 Analysis and Design Factor

Analysis is the most important stage in life cycle of the software. An inefficient analysis and designing can have a severe effect on the reliability of the software. Some key factors influencing reliability in this aspect are missing requirements, misinterpreted requirements, conflicting/ambiguous requirements, design mismatch, and frequency of changes in requirement specifications.

2.1.4 Testing Factor

Testing is the most commonly used phase for reliability assessment of software. Efficient testing helps finding all possible shortcomings of the software and helps achieving higher efficiency as well as reliability. Some key factors comprising the effect of testing on reliability are tools methodology used for testing, testing resource allocation, testing coverage, testing effort, and testing environment.

2.2 Evaluation of Reliability Using Analytical Hierarchy Process

2.2.1 Building the Hierarchy

An indexed hierarchy of correlated assessment criteria is derived for the multi-criteria problem. Hierarchy for our model is given in Table 1.

2.2.2 Pair-Wise Comparisons

In this step, we find the relative significant of the criteria at both levels. Weight matrices are formed to determine the priority where every value of the matrix (A_{ij}) gives the comparative significance of Criteria I_i and I_j. The importance in marked on a scale of 1–9 where 1 means two equally significant criteria and 9 meaning I_i is highly significant than I_j. Let the two-level weight matrices for our model are given in Tables 2 and 3.

Similarly level 2 weight matrices are taken for all four sub-factors.

Table 1 Indexed hierarchy of factors for evaluation of reliability

Assessment quantity	Indexed selected criteria	Indexed sub-criteria
Reliability of component-based software systems	Deployment context (I_1)	Unknown usage profile (I_{11})
		Unknown required context (I_{12})
		Unknown operational profile (I_{13})
	Human factor (I_2)	Programming skills (I_{21})
		Domain knowledge (I_{22})
		Human nature (I_{24})
	Testing factor (I_3)	Test tools and methodology (I_{31})
		Testing coverage (I_{32})
		Testing environment (I_{33})
		Testing resource allocation (I_{34})
		Testing effort (I_{35})
	Analysis and design (I_4)	Missing requirements (I_{41})
		Misinterpreted requirements (I_{42})
		Conflicting/ambiguous requirements (I_{43})
		Design not to requirements (I_{44})
		Frequency of changes in requirement specifications (I_{45})

Table 2 Level 1 weight matrix for reliability

Reliability	I_1	I_2	I_3	I_4
I_1	1	4	1	2
I_2	0.25	1	0.33	1
I_3	1	3	1	4
I_4	0.5	1	0.25	1

Table 3 Level 2 weight matrix for I_1

Deployment context (I_1)			
I_1	I_{11}	I_{12}	I_{13}
I_{11}	1	0.5	1
I_{12}	2	1	2
I_{13}	1	0.5	1

2.2.3 Relative Weight Estimation

Based upon the above weight matrices, we calculate relative priorities of the factors using the eigenvector W corresponding to largest eigenvalue λ_{max}, such that

$$A \cdot W = \lambda_{max} \cdot W \qquad (1)$$

Table 4 Relative weights and ranking of factors

Criteria	Level 1 weight	Sub-criteria	Level 2 weight	Reliability value	Rank
I_1	0.3613	I_{11}	0.25	0.090323	4
		I_{12}	0.50	0.180646	1
		I_{13}	0.25	0.090323	4
I_2	0.1142	I_{21}	0.42317	0.048321	8
		I_{22}	0.484411	0.055314	7
		I_{23}	0.092418	0.010553	14
I_3	0.3963	I_{31}	0.211748	0.0839068	5
		I_{32}	0.306419	0.121421	2
		I_{33}	0.161894	0.064152	6
		I_{34}	0.230607	0.091379	3
		I_{35}	0.089332	0.035385	10
I_4	0.1283	I_{41}	0.33668	0.043183	9
		I_{42}	0.193926	0.024873	12
		I_{43}	0.137445	0.017629	13
		I_{44}	0.26405	0.033867	11
		I_{45}	0.067899	0.008709	15

Hence, the relative weight vector of level 1 criteria is $W = (0.361292, 0.114188, 0.396258, 0.128262)$. Similarly at level 2, $W_1 = (0.25, 0.50, 0.25)$, $W_2 = (0.42317, 0.484411, 0.092418)$, $W_3 = (0.2118, 0.3064, 0.1618, 0.2306, 0.0893)$, $W4 = (0.3367, 0.1939, 0.1374, 0.2641, 0.0679)$, and consistency $C.I. \leq 0.1$ for all matrices (Table 4).

2.3 Fuzzy Comprehensive Evaluation

In this qualitative method, we use following principles for reliability estimation.

2.3.1 Create Sets of Grade Factors and Elements

Let $U = \{u_1, u_2, u_3 \ldots, u_n\}$ be the factor set based on first-level criteria indexing and $V = \{V_1, V_2, V_3, V_4, V_5\}$, i.e., {high, higher, medium, lower, low} be the evaluation grades.

2.3.2 Derive a Single-Factor Evaluation Matrix R from U to V

To form the expert evaluation matrix, opinions of 25 experts were taken to decide the reliability of CBSS based on the suggested criterion. The values obtained are given in Table 5.

Table 5 Expert matrix

Sub-criteria	High	Higher	Medium	Low	Lower
I_{11}	5	6	4	8	2
I_{12}	9	6	4	3	3
I_{13}	6	8	5	2	4
I_{21}	2	5	8	1	9
I_{22}	3	5	7	7	3
I_{23}	1	3	6	8	7
I_{31}	4	3	9	5	4
I_{32}	4	8	5	3	5
I_{33}	7	2	6	4	6
I_{34}	7	4	3	5	6
I_{35}	4	7	8	4	2
I_{41}	3	6	7	3	6
I_{42}	5	2	5	8	5
I_{43}	1	5	6	9	4
I_{44}	5	7	3	4	6
I_{45}	2	3	4	7	9

If r_{ij} represents the degree of membership on U_j to V_i ($i = 1, 2, 3, 4$) for each U_j. $r_j = n/25$ where n is number of U_j. R is represented by the fuzzy matrix of U_j on grade factor V_i. The individual criteria reliability evaluation matrices are

$$U = \{I_1, I_2, I_3, I_4\}, \quad U_1 = \{I_{11}, I_{12}, I_{13}\},$$
$$U_2 = \{I_{21}, I_{22}, I_{23}\}, \quad U_3 = \{I_{31}, I_{32}, I_{33}, I_{34}, I_{35}\}$$
$$U_4 = \{I_{41}, I_{42}, I_{43}, I_{44}, I_{45}\}.$$

$$R_1 = \begin{bmatrix} 0.2 & 0.24 & 0.16 & 0.32 & 0.08 \\ 0.36 & 0.24 & 0.16 & 0.12 & 0.12 \\ 0.24 & 0.32 & 0.2 & 0.08 & 0.16 \end{bmatrix}$$

Similarly we calculated $R2$, $R3$, and $R4$.

2.3.3 Find Results of Comprehensive Evaluation

Evaluated results of reliability based on individual factors are: $B_i = W_i * R_i$ where $B_i = \{b_1, b_2, b_3, b_4, b_5\}$

Hence, $\mathbf{B_1} = W_1 * R_1$ i.e. $\{0.29, 0.26, 0.17, 0.16, 0.12\}$, $\mathbf{B_2} = \{0.0956, 0.1924, 0.2929, 0.1819, 0.2361\}$, $\mathbf{B_3} = \{0.2071, 0.3148, 0.2326, 0.3985, 0.1964\}$

$\mathbf{B_4} = \{0.1429, 0.2058, 0.2085, 0.2132, 0.2294\}$

### 2.3.4	Comprehensive Multi-level Fuzzy Evaluation

The synthetic evaluation results will be $B = W * R = \{b_1, b_2, b_3, b_4, b_5\}$ where $R = [B1 \ B2 \ B3 \ B4]^T$, and W are the relative weights of first-level criteria. From calculations $B = \{0.2161, 0.2671, 0.2138, 0.2639, 0.17763\}$.

### 2.3.5	Conclude Evaluation

Using maximum subordination principle, our synthetic evaluation shows maximum subordination in level "Higher" in set B. Therefore, the CBSS ranked by experts in terms of our given factors is having higher reliability according to our model.

## 3	Conclusion

Reliability of software plays very critical role for the success or failure of any organization. In this paper, we have proposed a reliability estimation model for component-based software systems. The proposed model considers a wider range of factors affecting the reliability. AHP is used to get the relative importance of each criterion, and comprehensive fuzzy evaluation method is used to evaluate reliability of a CBSS using the given criterion. The experimental results showed the effectiveness of evaluating criteria. In future, the experiments will be carried out at large scale and in the quantitative score.

References

1. Guo, Y., Wan, T.T., Ma, P.J., Su, X.H.: Reliability evaluation optimal selection model of component-based system. J. Softw. Eng. Appl. 4(7), 433–441 (2011)
2. Rosenberg, L., Hammer, T., Shaw, J.: Software metrics and reliability. In: 9th International Symposium on Software Reliability Engineering (1998)
3. Mishra, A., Dubey, S.K.: Fuzzy qualitative evaluation of reliability of object oriented software system. In: IEEE International Conference on Advances in Engineering & Technology Research (ICAETR-2014), 01–02 Aug 2014, Dr. Virendra Swarup Group of Institutions, Unnao, India, pp. 685–690. IEEE. ISBN: 978-1-4799-6393-5/14. https://doi.org/10.1109/icaetr.2014.7012813
4. Tyagi, K., Sharma, A.: Reliability of component based systems: a critical survey. ACM SIGSOFT Softw. Eng. Notes 36(6), 1–6 (2011)
5. Reussner, R.H., Heinz, W.S., Iman, H.P.: Reliability prediction for component-based software architectures. J. Syst. Softw. 66(3), 241–252 (2003)
6. Rahmani, C., Azadmanesh, A.: Exploitation of quantitative approaches to software reliability. Exploit. Quant. Approach Softw. Reliab. (2008)
7. Mishra, A., Dubey, S.K.: Evaluation of reliability of object oriented software system using fuzzy approach. In: 2014 5th International Conference on Confluence the Next Generation Information Technology Summit (Confluence), pp. 806–809. IEEE (2014)

8. Dubey, S.K., Rana, A.: A fuzzy approach for evaluation of maintainability of object oriented software system. Int. J. Comput. Appl. **41**, 0975–8887 (2012)
9. Gülçin, B., Kahraman, C., Ruan, D.: A fuzzy multi-criteria decision approach for software development strategy selection. Int. J. Gen. Syst. **33**(2–3), 259–280 (2004)
10. Zhang, X., Pham, H.: An analysis of factors affecting software reliability. J. Syst. Softw. **50**(1), 43–56 (2000)

Ranking Usability Metrics Using Intuitionistic Preference Relations and Group Decision Making

Ritu Shrivastava

Abstract The popularity of a Web site depends on the ease of usability of the site. In other words, a site is popular among users if it is user-friendly. This means that quantifiable attributes of usability, i.e., metrics, should be decided through a group decision activity. The present research considers three decision makers or stakeholders viz. user, developer, and professional to decide ranking of usability metrics and in turn ranking of usability of Web sites. In this process, each stakeholder gives his/her intuitionistic preference for each metric. These preferences are aggregated using intuitionistic fuzzy averaging operator, which is further aggregated using intuitionistic fuzzy weighted arithmetic averaging operator. Finally, eight considered usability metrics are ranked. The method is useful to compare Web site usability by assigning suitable weights on the basis of rank of metrics. An illustrative example comparing usability of six operational Web sites is considered.

Keywords Usability metrics · Intuitionistic fuzzy set · Intuitionistic preference Decision makers

1 Introduction

Every day, many new Web sites are hosted increasing thousands of pages on WWW. These Web sites are searched for information needs of user. E-commerce domain web sites like amazon.com, alibaba.com, snapdeal.com, flipkart.com are used for purchasing electronic goods, furniture, clothes, etc. People are using net banking for managing their accounts and making bill payments. However, it is well known that the popularity of a Web site depends on the ease of usability and authenticity of information. It is obvious that the quality of Web site and popularity

R. Shrivastava (✉)
Computer Science & Engineering, Sagar Institute
of Research Technology & Science, Bhopal, India
e-mail: ritushrivastava08@gmail.com

© Springer Nature Singapore Pte Ltd. 2019
M. N. Hoda et al. (eds.), *Software Engineering*, Advances in Intelligent Systems and Computing 731, https://doi.org/10.1007/978-981-10-8848-3_65

are related. Recently, Thanawala and Sakhardande [1] have emphasized that user experience (UX) is a critical quality aspect for software. They have pointed out that current UX assessments helped identify usability flaws, and they lacked quantifiable metrics for UX and suggested new user experience maturity models. It is obvious that user, developer, and professional have different perspectives of usability. Some amount of fuzziness is involved in selecting usability metrics due to the differences in perception of three stakeholders. In such situations, group decision making using intuitionistic fuzzy preference relations has been successfully applied [2–6]. The group decision making has proved very useful in medical diagnostic as well [7, 8]. As no exact numerical values are available, the intuitionistic fuzzy relations and group decision theory as proposed by Xu [9] are handy to rank usability metrics.

The author, in this research, proposes to apply group decision making using intuitionistic preference relations and the score and accuracy functions as proposed by Xu [9], to rank usability metrics. The three decision makers, viz. user, developer, and professional, have been used to provide their intuitionistic preferences for usability metrics.

2 Literature Survey

The ISO/IEC 9126 model [10] describes three views of quality, viz. user's view, developer's view, and manager's view. The users are interested in the external quality attributes, while developers are interested in internal quality attributes such as maintainability, portability. In a survey conducted by Web software development managers and practitioners by Offutt [11], they agreed at six quality attributes—usability, reliability, security, scalability, maintainability, and availability. Olsina and Rossi [12] identified attributes, sub-attributes, and metrics for measuring quality of e-commerce-based Web sites. They also developed a method called "WebQEM" for measuring metric values automatically. Olsina identified and measured quality metrics for Web sites of domain museum [13]. Shrivastava et al. [14] have specified and theoretically validated quality attributes, sub-attributes, and metrics for academic Web sites. They have developed a framework for measuring attributes and metrics [15]. In this framework, template for each metric has been developed so that metric value is measured unambiguously. Shrivastava et al. [16] used logical scoring of preferences (LSP) to rank six academic institution Web sites.

According to Atanassov [17, 18], the concept of intuitionistic fuzzy set is characterized by a membership function and a non-membership function, which is a general form of representation of fuzzy set. Chen and Tan [3] developed a technique for handling multi-criteria fuzzy decision-making problems based on vague sets (vague set is same as intuitionistic fuzzy set). They developed a score function to measure the degree of suitability of each alternative with respect to a set of criteria presented by vague values. It has been observed that a decision maker may not be able to accurately express his/her preference for alternatives, in real-life situations, due to various reasons. Thus, it is suitable to express the decision maker's preference values in terms of intuitionistic fuzzy values. As described in Sect. 1, the ranking of usability involves three stakeholders, who may not be sure of exact values of contribution of each metric, and therefore, it is natural to apply group decision making using intuitionistic fuzzy preference relations. These preferences are aggregated using intuitionistic fuzzy averaging operator, and then further aggregation is done using intuitionistic fuzzy weighted arithmetic averaging operator. In this research, the author has considered usability as the most important single attribute of quality which is crucial in Web applications from user's point of view and has tried to rank usability metrics using group decision-making process proposed by Xu [9]. Three decision makers, viz. user, developer, and professional, are considered.

The paper is organized as follows: Sect. 3 gives basics of group decision-making process and basic definitions. Section 4 deals with the description of usability metrics and four-step process to rank eight metrics. The process is empirically evaluated through an example in which usability is ranked for six Web sites of academic institutions. The conclusion and future work is given in Sect. 5.

3 Basics of Group Decision Making

Let $X = \{x_1, x_2 \ldots x_n\}$ be discrete set of alternatives in a group decision-making problem. Group decision makers generally provide preferences for each pair of alternatives x_i and then construct preference relations. A preference relation P on set X is defined as

$$\mu_P : X \times X \to D, \tag{1}$$

where D is the domain representing preference degrees.

A complementary matrix R is a fuzzy preference relation R on the set x and is given by

$$R = (r_{ij})_{n \times n} \subset X \times X \tag{2}$$

where $r_{ij} \geq 0$, $r_{ij} + r_{ji} = 1$, $r_{ii} = 0.5$ for all $i, j = 1, 2 \ldots, n$ and r_{ij} denotes preference degree of alternatives x_i over x_j. It is to be noted that $r_{ij} = 0.5$ indicates indifference between x_i and x_j; $r_{ij} > 0.5$ means x_i is preferred over x_j and $r_{ij} < 0.5$ means x_j is preferred over x_i.

The concept of intuitionistic fuzzy set characterized by a membership function and a non-membership function was introduced by Atanassov [17, 18]. The intuitionistic fuzzy set A is defined as

$$A = \{(x, \mu_A(x), \upsilon_A(x)) | x \varepsilon X\} \tag{3}$$

The A is characterized by a membership function μ_A

$$\mu_A : X \rightarrow [0, 1]$$

and a non-membership function υ_A

$$\upsilon_A : X \rightarrow [0, 1]$$

with the condition

$$0 \leq \mu_A(x) + \upsilon_A(x) \leq 1, \forall x \in X \tag{4}$$

Following Xu [9], the author introduces the concept of intuitionistic preference relation. An intuitionistic fuzzy relation B on X is a matrix defined by

$$
\begin{aligned}
B &= (b_{ij})_{n \times n} \subset X \times X \\
b_{ij} &= \{(x_i, x_j), \mu(x_i, x_j), v(x_i, x_j)\}, \forall i, j
\end{aligned}
\tag{5}
$$

In short, the author can write $b_{ij} = (\mu_{ij}, v_{ij})$, where b_{ij} is an intuitionistic fuzzy value representing certainty degree μ_{ij} to which x_i is preferred to x_j and certainty degree v_{ij} to which x_j is preferred to x_i. Further, μ_{ij} and v_{ij} satisfy the relation

$$0 \leq \mu_{ij} + v_{ij} \leq 1 \ \mu_{ji} = v_{ij} \ v_{ji} = \mu_{ij} \ \mu_{ii} = v_{ii} = 0.5 \tag{6}$$

Following Chen et al. [3] and Xu [9], score function Δ of an intuitionistic fuzzy value is defined as

$$\Delta(b_{ij}) = \mu_{ij} - v_{ij} \tag{7}$$

It is obvious that Δ will lie in the interval $[-1, 1]$. Hence, the greater the score $\Delta(b_{ij})$, the greater the intuitionistic fuzzy value b_{ij}.

As in [3, 9], the accuracy function H can be defined as

$$H(b_{ij}) = \mu_{ij} + v_{ij} \tag{8}$$

It evaluates degree of accuracy of intuitionistic fuzzy value b_{ij}. Clearly, the value of H will lie in the interval $[0, 1]$.

4 Application of Group Decision Making to Rank Usability Metrics

In the recent paper [14], the author has specified and theoretically validated usability metrics for Web sites of academic institutions. These metrics are reproduced below for reference

Usability Metrics, Global Site Under stability, *Site Map (Location Map), Table of Content, Alphabetic Index, Campus Map, Guided Tour, Help Features and On-line Feedback, Student Oriented Help, Search Help, Web-site Last Update Indicator, E-mail Directory, Phone Directory, FAQ, On-line in the form of Questionnaire, What is New Feature?*

For simplicity, the author considers eight metrics for ranking: x_1 = location map, x_2 = table of contents, x_3 = alphabetic index, x_4 = guided tour, x_5 = search help, x_6 = last update information, x_7 = e-mail directory, x_8 = what is new feature.

The usability metric ranking problem involves the following four steps:

Step 1: Let $X = \{x_1, x_2 \ldots x_8\}$ be a discrete set of alternatives in a group decision problem. Three decision makers are represented by $D = \{d_1, d_2, d_3\}$ with corresponding weights $\omega = (\omega_1, \omega_2, \omega_3)^T$ and having the property $\sum_{k=1}^{3} \omega_k = 1, \omega_k > 0$. The decision maker $d_k \in D$ provides his/her intuitionistic preferences for each pair of alternatives and then constructs an intuitionistic relation

$$B^{(K)} = (b_{ij}^{(K)})_{8 \times 8},$$

where

$$
\begin{aligned}
(b_{ij}^{(K)}) &= (\mu_{ij}^{(K)}, \upsilon_{ij}^{(K)}) \, 0 \leq \mu_{ij}^{(K)} + \upsilon_{ij}^{(K)} \leq 1 \\
\mu_{ji}^{(K)} &= \upsilon_{ij}^{(K)} \, \mu_{ij}^{(K)} = \upsilon_{ji}^{(K)} \, \mu_{ii}^{(K)} = \upsilon_{ii}^{(K)} = 0.5
\end{aligned}
\tag{9}
$$

In the present application, three decision makers have provided their intuitionistic preferences using relation (9) giving $B^{(1)} = (b_{ij}^{(1)})$ $B^{(2)} = (b_{ij}^{(2)})$ $B^{(3)} = (b_{ij}^{(3)})$. Values of these matrices are given in Appendix 1.

Step 2: The author now applies intuitionistic fuzzy averaging operator

$$b_i^{(K)} = \frac{1}{n} \sum_{j=1}^{n} b_{ij}^{(K)}, i = 1, 2 \ldots, n; n = 8 \tag{10}$$

Values of $b_i^{(K)}$ are given in Appendix 2.

3. Step 3: Now, use intuitionistic fuzzy weighted arithmetic averaging operator defined as

$$b_i = \sum_{K=1}^{3} w_k b_i^{(K)}, \quad i = 1, 2 \ldots, 8 \tag{11}$$

This will aggregate all $b_i^{(K)}$ corresponding to three DMs into a collective intuitionistic fuzzy value b_i of the alternative x_i over all other alternatives.

Using $\omega_1 = 0.4, \omega_2 = \omega_3 = 0.3,$, I get

$$b_1 = (0.6539, 0.1575), b_2 = (0.6075, 0.3450)$$
$$b_3 = (0.5298, 0.4101), b_4 = (0.5389, 0.4039)$$
$$b_5 = (0.4575, 0.4675), b_6 = (0.5053, 0.6289)$$
$$b_7 = (0.3739, 0.5651), b_8 = (0.2451, 0.6750)$$

Step 4: The author uses (7) to calculate score function Δ for each intuitionistic fuzzy value

$$\Delta b_1 = 0.4964, \Delta b_2 = 0.2625, \Delta b_3 = 0.1197$$
$$\Delta b_4 = 0.1350, \Delta b_5 = -0.01, \Delta b_6 = -0.1236$$
$$\Delta b_7 = -0.1912, \Delta b_8 = -0.4299$$

Thus, the following preference relation is obtained:

$$b_1 > b_2 > b_4 > b_3 > b_5 > b_6 > b_7 > b_8$$

If the symbol $\succ$ is used to represent preference of a usability metric over the other, then the following preference relation is obtained:

$$x_1 \succ x_2 \succ x_4 \succ x_3 \succ x_5 \succ x_6 \succ x_7 \succ x_8 \qquad (12)$$

This means that users prefer to see location map on Web site compared to table of contents, table of contents is preferred to guided tour of the campus, and so on. The relation (12) is useful in assigning weights to usability metrics so that overall usability of Web sites can be calculated.

5 Illustrative Example

In my work, I have applied group decision making in usability measurement and I have taken academic Web sites of six institutes, viz. Georgia Institute of Technology, Stanford University—School of Engineering, IIT Delhi, IIT BHU, MANIT Bhopal, and BITS Pilani. I have measured eight usability metric values for each institute using the methodology outlined by Shrivastava et al. in [15, 16]. The metric values were collected during March 2–6, 2015. I have used Eq. (12) that gives ranking of eight metrics to assign weights according to their ranks. Thus, assigned weights to x_1 through x_8 are 0.20, 0.18, 0.15, 0.13, 0.11, 0.10, 0.07, and 0.06. For assigned weights, the usability comparison is given in Fig. 1, where bars represent percentage usability of six sites. Figure 2 gives usability comparison for the case, where each metric is assigned equal weight or simple arithmetic average.

Fig. 1 Weighted usability (in %) comparison

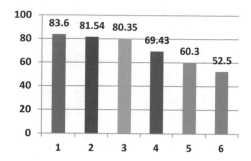

Fig. 2 Averaged usability (in %) comparison

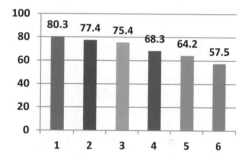

6 Conclusion

The present research uses intuitionistic preference relations and group decision theory to rank eight commonly used usability metrics. The group decision theory, described in Sects. 3 and 4, considers three decision makers, who provide their intuitionistic preferences for each metric. On the basis of theory developed, eight usability metrics are ranked and the result is given in Eq. (12). The main advantage of the method is that weights are assigned according to rank value to calculate overall usability of Web sites.

The usability of six Web sites (academic institute) has been calculated, and usability comparison is given in Fig. 1. Figure 2 also gives usability comparison in which usability is calculated using simple arithmetic average of metric values. It is observed that usability of good sites is going down compared to last two sites, where there is increase in usability value. This is somewhat unusual because either all values should increase or all should decrease. Hence, the method of group decision making using intuitionistic preference relations appears superior to simple aggregation.

1	2	3	4	5	6
Stanford	Georgia	IITD	IIT BHU	BITS	MANIT

Appendix 1

$B^{(1)} =$		x_1	x_2	x_3	x_4	x_5	x_6	x_7	x_8
	x_1	(0.5, 0.5)	(0.6, 0.2)	(0.5, 0.2)	(0.6, 0.4)	(0.6, 0.3)	(0.8, 0.1)	(0.7, 0.2)	(0.9, 0.1)
	x_2	(0.2, 0.6)	(0.5, 0.5)	(0.7, 0.2)	(0.6, 0.4)	(0.6, 0.3)	(0.8, 0.1)	(0.7, 0.1)	(0.7, 0.2)
	x_3	(0.2, 0.5)	(0.2, 0.7)	(0.5, 0.5)	(0.6, 0.3)	(0.7, 0.3)	(0.7, 0.2)	(0.8, 0.2)	(0.6, 0.3)
	x_4	(0.4, 0.6)	(0.4, 0.6)	(0.3, 0.6)	(0.5, 0.5)	(0.8, 0.1)	(0.7, 0.2)	(0.7, 0.3)	(0.6, 0.3)
	x_5	(0.3, 0.6)	(0.3, 0.6)	(0.3, 0.7)	(0.1, 0.8)	(0.5, 0.5)	(0.8, 0.1)	(0.6, 0.3)	(0.7, 0.2)
	x_6	(0.1, 0.8)	(0.1, 0.8)	(0.2, 0.7)	(0.2, 0.8)	(0.1, 0.8)	(0.5, 0.5)	(0.6, 0.4)	(0.7, 0.2)
	x_7	(0.2, 0.7)	(0.1, 0.7)	(0.2, 0.8)	(0.2, 0.7)	(0.3, 0.6)	(0.4, 0.6)	(0.5, 0.5)	(0.7, 0.1)
	x_8	(0.1, 0.9)	(0.2, 0.7)	(0.3, 0.6)	(0.3, 0.6)	(0.2, 0.7)	(0.2, 0.7)	(0.1, 0.7)	(0.5, 0.5)
$B^{(2)} =$		x_1	x_2	x_3	x_4	x_5	x_6	x_7	x_8
	x_1	(0.5, 0.5)	(0.6, 0.3)	(0.8, 0.2)	(0.7, 0.2)	(0.6, 0.3)	(0.7, 0.1)	(0.7, 0.2)	(0.8, 0.1)
	x_2	(0.3, 0.6)	(0.5, 0.5)	(0.8, 0.2)	(0.7, 0.3)	(0.6, 0.3)	(0.8, 0.1)	(0.6, 0.4)	(0.7, 0.2)
	x_3	(0.2, 0.8)	(0.2, 0.8)	(0.5, 0.5)	(0.6, 0.3)	(0.7, 0.2)	(0.8, 0.1)	(0.7, 0.3)	(0.6, 0.3)
	x_4	(0.2, 0.7)	(0.3, 0.7)	(0.3, 0.6)	(0.5, 0.5)	(0.8, 0.1)	(0.9, 0.1)	(0.7, 0.2)	(0.7, 0.2)
	x_5	(0.3, 0.6)	(0.3, 0.6)	(0.2, 0.7)	(0.1, 0.8)	(0.5, 0.5)	(0.8, 0.1)	(0.7, 0.3)	(0.6, 0.2)
	x_6	(0.1, 0.7)	(0.1, 0.8)	(0.1, 0.8)	(0.1, 0.9)	(0.1, 0.8)	(0.5, 0.5)	(0.6, 0.3)	(0.7, 0.2)
	x_7	(0.2, 0.7)	(0.4, 0.6)	(0.3, 0.7)	(0.2, 0.7)	(0.3, 0.7)	(0.3, 0.6)	(0.5, 0.5)	(0.8, 0.2)
	x_8	(0.1, 0.8)	(0.2, 0.7)	(0.3, 0.6)	(0.2, 0.7)	(0.2, 0.6)	(0.2, 0.7)	(0.2, 0.8)	(0.5, 0.5)
$B^{(3)} =$		x_1	x_2	x_3	x_4	x_5	x_6	x_7	x_8
	x_1	(0.5, 0.5)	(0.7, 0.2)	(0.8, 0.2)	(0.7, 0.3)	(0.6, 0.3)	(0.7, 0.1)	(0.5, 0.4)	(0.6, 0.3)
	x_2	(0.2, 0.7)	(0.5, 0.5)	(0.7, 0.1)	(0.7, 0.2)	(0.6, 0.4)	(0.8, 0.1)	(0.6, 0.3)	(0.7, 0.3)
	x_3	(0.2, 0.8)	(0.1, 0.7)	(0.5, 0.5)	(0.5, 0.4)	(0.7, 0.3)	(0.8, 0.2)	(0.6, 0.4)	(0.7, 0.2)
	x_4	(0.3, 0.7)	(0.2, 0.7)	(0.4, 0.5)	(0.5, 0.5)	(0.6, 0.3)	(0.7, 0.2)	(0.6, 0.4)	(0.8, 0.1)
	x_5	(0.3, 0.6)	(0.4, 0.6)	(0.3, 0.7)	(0.3, 0.6)	(0.5, 0.5)	(0.9, 0.1)	(0.6, 0.3)	(0.7, 0.2)
	x_6	(0.1, 0.7)	(0.1, 0.8)	(0.2, 0.8)	(0.2, 0.7)	(0.1, 0.9)	(0.5, 0.5)	(0.5, 0.4)	(0.6, 0.3)
	x_7	(0.4, 0.5)	(0.3, 0.6)	(0.4, 0.6)	(0.4, 0.6)	(0.3, 0.6)	(0.4, 0.5)	(0.5, 0.5)	(0.8, 0.2)
	x_8	(0.3, 0.6)	(0.3, 0.7)	(0.2, 0.7)	(0.1, 0.8)	(0.2, 0.7)	(0.3, 0.6)	(0.2, 0.8)	(0.5, 0.5)

Appendix 2

$$b_1^{(1)} = (0.65, 0.25), b_2^{(1)} = (0.60, 0.37), b_3 = (0.54, 0.38), b_4^{(1)} = (0.55, 0.40),$$
$$b_5^{(1)} = (0.45, 0.47), b_6^{(1)} = (0.32, 0.62), b_7^{(1)} = (0.32, 0.58), b_8^{(1)} = (0.28, 0.68)$$
$$b_1^{(2)} = (0.68, 0.25), b_2^{(2)} = (0.62, 0.32), b_3 = (0.53, 0.41), b_4^{(2)} = (0.55, 0.39),$$
$$b_5^{(2)} = (0.44, 0.47), b_6^{(2)} = (0.29, 0.62), b_7^{(2)} = (0.37, 0.59), b_8^{(2)} = (0.24, 0.67)$$
$$b_1^{(3)} = (0.64, 0.29), b_2^{(3)} = (0.60, 0.32), b_3 = (0.51, 0.44), b_4^{(3)} = (0.51, 0.42),$$
$$b_5^{(3)} = (0.50, 0.45), b_6^{(3)} = (0.29, 0.64), b_7^{(3)} = (0.44, 0.51), b_8^{(3)} = (0.26, 0.67)$$

References

1. Thanawala, R., Sakhardande, P.: Sotware user experience maturity model. CSI Commun. Knowl. Dig. IT Commun. **38**(8) (2014)
2. Atanassov, K., Pasi, G., Yager, R.R.: Intuitionistic fuzzy interpretations of multi-person multi-criteria decision making. In: Proceedings First International IEEE Symposium on Intelligent Systems, vol. I, Varna, pp. 115–119 (2002)
3. Chen, S.M., Tan, J.M.: Handeling multicriteria fuzzy decision-making problems based on vague set theory. Fuzzy Sets Syst. **67**, 163–172 (1994)
4. Szmidt, E., Kacprzyk, J.: Remarks on some applications of ituitionistic fuzzy sets in decision making. Note IFS **2**, 22–31 (1996)
5. Szmidt, E., Kacprzyk, J.: Group decision making under ituitionistic fuzzy preference relations. In: Proceedings of 7th IPMU Conference, Paris, pp. 172–178 (1998)
6. Szmidt, E., Kacprzyk, J.: Using ituitionistic fuzzy sets in group decision making. Cotrol Cybern. **31**, 1037–1053 (2002)
7. De, S.K., Biswas, R., Roy, A.R.: An application of ituitionistic fuzzy sets in medical diagnosis. Fuzzy Sets Syst. **117**, 209–213 (2001)
8. Xu, Z.S.: On correlation measures ituitionistic fuzzy sets. Lect. Notes Comput. Sci. **4224**, 16–24 (2006)
9. Xu, Z.: Intuitionistic preference relation and their application in group decision making. Inf. Sci. **177**, 2363–2379 (2007)
10. ISO/IEC 9126-1: Sotware Engineering—Product Quality Part 1 Quality Model (2000)
11. Offutt, J.: Quality attributes of Web software applications. IEEE Softw. 25–32 (2002)
12. Olsina, L., Rossi, G.: Measuring web-application quality with WebQEM. In: IEEE Multimedia, pp. 20–29, Oct–Dec 2002
13. Olsina, L.: Website quality evaluation method: a case study of museums. In: 2nd Workshop on Software Engineering Over Internet, ICSE 1999
14. Shrivastava, R., Rana, J.L., Kumar, M.: Specifying and validating quality characteristics for academic web-sites. Int. J. Compt. Sci. Inf. Secur. **8**(4) (2010)
15. Shrivastava, R., et al.: A framework for measuring external quality of web-sites. Int. J. Compt. Sci. Inf. Secur. **9**(7) (2011)
16. Shrivastava, R., et al.: Ranking of academic web-sites on the basis of external quality measurement. J. Emer. Trends Comput. Inf. Sci. **3**(3) (2012)
17. Atanassov, K.: Intuitioistic fuzzy sets. Fuzzy Sets Syst. **20**, 87–96 (1986)
18. Atanassov, K.: Intuitioistic Fuzzy Sets: Theory and Applications. Physica-Verlag, Heidelberg (1999)

Research Challenges of Web Service Composition

Ali A. Alwasouf and Deepak Kumar

Abstract Using semantic-based Web service composition based on functional and non-functional user requests promises to enable automatic dynamic assembly of applications. Apart from many advantages of such approaches, an effective automatic dynamic semantic-based Web service composition approach is still an open problem. Publishing, discovery, and selection mechanisms as well as heterogeneity and limitations of semantic languages have a major impact on the effectiveness of service composition approaches. This paper explores the major challenges related to semantic languages, Web service publishing, discovery, and selection techniques which affect the composition of the service. Additionally, it evaluates the effectiveness of automation, dynamicity, scalability, adaptation, and management strategies of the composition approaches.

Keywords Service-oriented architecture · Semantic-based Web service composition · Discoverability · Selection · Dynamic composition · Automatic composition Composition management

1 Introduction

Service is a milestone of service-oriented architecture (SOA) to develop rapid dynamic applications. Using widespread XML-based standards like simple object access protocol (SOAP), Web service description language (WSDL), semantics

A. A. Alwasouf (✉) · D. Kumar
Amity Institute of Information Technology, Amity University, Noida 110025,
Uttar Pradesh, India
e-mail: alialwasouf@gmail.com

D. Kumar
e-mail: deepakgupta_du@rediffmail.com

© Springer Nature Singapore Pte Ltd. 2019
M. N. Hoda et al. (eds.), *Software Engineering*, Advances in Intelligent Systems
and Computing 731, https://doi.org/10.1007/978-981-10-8848-3_66

(Web language ontology (OWL), resource description framework (RDF), ... etc.), and further WS-* specifications make SOA platform independent from underlying technologies.

The service is described using WSDL, semantic languages, and other WS-* specifications, published to a registry, i.e., Universal Description, Discovery and Integration (UDDI), and discovered by matchmaking, filtering, or any other search technique. The user query, preferences, QoS, user feedback, and rating [1] are used in many approaches to discover and select the best available service that fulfills users' requirements.

Composition techniques are classified to static versus dynamic and manual, semiautomatic or automatic techniques. Static composition is a predefined workflow which locates manually exact services at developing stage. Such techniques are very useful to an build enterprise application as they are much faster and where business process workflow is already predefined, i.e., BPEL4S. Meanwhile, dynamic approaches locate best services at run-time. It can be manual, semiautomatic, or automatic composition. Automatic dynamic composition is widely used to build Web applications where user requirements are undefined and unexpected.

Recently, some efforts have been done to provide semantic annotations through extending existing standards. WSDL-S, SAWSDL, OWL-S, METERO-S, and WSMO are the most prominent candidates. WSDL-S added some elements to extend WSDL in order to refer to semantic models. Using WSDL-S is considered to be more flexible than OWL-S and WSMO as developers are already familiars with WSDL. Also, WSDL-S specification has been extended to SAWSDL adding provisions for semantic annotations.

OWL-S is a semantic Web service description language, and it is an instance of OWL. OWL-S provides a model to describe both services and processes. A service ontology is defined in three parts: service profile to advertise the functionality of the service, service process to describe the workflow as well as data flow between services, and service grounding which provides all information related to how to access the composite service.

Another alternative to OWL-S is Web service modeling ontology (WSMO) and the combination of Unified Modeling Language (UML) and Object Constraints Language (OCL). WSMO defines four parts to describe a service: ontologies, Web services, goals, and mediators. WSMO differs with OWL as it employs object-oriented style of modeling using frames. WSMO prescribes the Web Service Modeling Language (WSML) as a tool to actually represent its elements. Unlike OWL-S [20], WSMO includes service and ontology specification formalisms, whereas OWL-S is OWL based as it uses OWL for ontology specifications and other languages for formal semantics.

In this paper, we present various existing semantic-based Web service composition techniques in Sect. 2. In Sect. 3, we discuss the major research challenges of semantic-based composition approaches. Finally, we present our main conclusion and introduce lines of our future research in Sect. 4.

2 Semantic-Based Composition Techniques

A considerable number of semantic-based compositions approaches have been proposed during recent years. Evaluation of such approaches must take into account some requirements need to be met. Since the focus of this survey is semantic-based approaches, we have to take into account the following composition requirements while evaluating approaches: (a) each semantic-based composition approach must provide an automated way to generate, at least partially, the composition workflow (automation), (b) it must also produce an abstract composition schema (dynamicity), (c) the richness of semantic description is fundamental to enhance the discovery and selection process of the services (discoverability and selection), (d) meanwhile, any approach may work correctly with a given set of services; there is no guarantee that it works with larger more complex composition (scalability), and (e) Finally, we have to study if the composition approach can adapt itself to the changes of real world (adaptation).

Ontology-based dynamic service composition is represented in [2]. The approach developed a prototype for service composition which has two elements: a composer and inference engine (OWL reasoner). Reasoner stores information of known services in knowledge base (KB) using RDF format. The composition workflow gets done by the user; the composer offers choices to the user at each step. This work suffers from scalability and availability problems. Also, it uses filtering on a set of pre-discovered services instead of dynamic matchmaking.

A semantic-based approach based on understanding the semantics of interactions of services is presented in [3]. Similar work has been proposed in [4]. The proposal supports reuse and composition of services through enabling ontologies to integrate models, languages, and activities.

Composing services on the basis of natural languages requests has been adopted by many researchers. In [15, 16], the authors propose architecture (SeGSeC) for semantics-based, context-aware, dynamic service composition inspired by the component model. They introduce CoSMoS, a semantic abstract model for both service components and users which is the basis for all required representations of their framework. The approach is based on parsing a natural language request from the user using preexisting natural language analysis technologies into a CoSMoS model instance. The workflow synthesis module creates an executable workflow by discovering and interconnecting components based on the request and the components' functional description. The workflow-based composition approach has evolved from offering only manual and static composition methods to support automation and dynamicity, but the resulting workflows are limited to sequential and parallel execution.

The solutions described in [5, 6] assume that the natural language is used to express requests with a controlled subset. Using templates, a flow model is created from a user request. Action and its parameters are identified by verbs. Well-defined keywords set are paired to service. Operation semantics and ontological classification are provide by OWL-S annotations. The operations act as nodes of a direct acyclic graph, and the relations among their IOPEs establish graph which is translated into an executable service. In [7], retrieval of relevant services is solved by defining conceptual distances using semantic concepts in order to measure the similarity between service definition and user request. Composition is done using retrieved services templates called aspects of assembly. Ubiquarium system is used to compose a service based on user request described by a natural language.

Another approach based on natural language proposed in [21]. The approach leverages description of known service operations catalog. Each request is processed with vocabulary that contains lexical constructs to cover semantics, in order to extract functional requirements emended in the request and link them to the Catalog. Additionally, the request interpreter extracts service logic, which is pre-defined as modular templates to describe control and data flow of operations. A composition specification is created, and each user request is associated to a composed service. The specification is transformed into an executable flow document to be used by composition engine.

Skogan et al. [18] proposed a method that uses UML activity diagrams to model service compositions. Executable BPEL processes are generated by using the UML diagrams which are used to generate XSLT transformations. While this work only uses WSDL service descriptions as input to the UML transformation, a follow-up work [19] eliminates this limitation by considering semantic Web service descriptions in OWL-S and WSMO as well as supporting QoS attributes. This enables dynamicity, since the BPEL processes that are generated are static and only invoke concrete services at run-time. Additionally, services are selected based on QoS properties when more than one service fulfill the requirements. Also, the work by Gronmo et al. presents only the methodology behind their model-driven approach without testing whether and how to implement such methodology. However, both works do not achieve full automation as the composition workflow is created manually.

In [12], the authors present a mixed framework for semantic Web service discovery and composition, with ability to user intervention. Their composition engine combines rule-based reasoning on OWL ontologies with Jess and planning functionality using GraphPlan algorithm. Reachability analysis determines whether a state can be reached from another state and disjunctive refinement resolves possible inconsistencies. Planning is used to propose composition schemas to the user, rather than enforce a decision, which is presented by authors to be the more realistic approach.

Graph-based planning is also employed by the work of Wu et al. [14] in order to realize service composition. The authors propose their own abstract model for service description which is essentially an extension of SAWSDL to more resemble OWL-S and WSMO. In addition, they model service requests and service compositions with similar semantic artifacts. Then, they extend the GraphPlan algorithm to work with the models defined. They also add limited support for determinism, by allowing loops only if they are identified beforehand. The final system takes a user request defned using the authors' models and extracts an executable BPEL flow.

In [13], the authors follow a similar approach, but they employ OWL-S descriptions (instead of creating their own services ontology), which are similarly translated to PDDL descriptions. They use a different planner, however, a hybrid heuristic search planner which combines graph-based planning and HTN. This combines the advantages of the two planning approaches, namely the fact that graph-based planning always finds a plan if one exists and the decomposition offered by HTN planning. The framework also includes a re-planning component which is able to re-adjust outdated plans during execution time.

3   Composition Research Challenges

All challenges presented in this section contribute to the same high-level goal to (a) provide rich and flexible semantic specifications, (b) automate discovery, selection, and composition process of Web services, and (c) achieve scalable, self-adaption, and self-management composition techniques.

3.1   Semantic Web Services Languages, Discovery, and Selection Challenges

The purpose of semantic Web services is to describe the semantic functional and non-functional attributes of a Web service with a machine-interpretable and also understandable way in order to enable automatic discovery, selection, and composition of services. The enormous number of semantic Web service languages, including OWL-S, WSMO, METERO-S, SAWSDL, and many others, resulted in overlap and difference in capabilities at conceptual and structural levels [20]. Such differences affect discovery, selection, and composition techniques. Therefore, composition of services implies to deal with heterogeneous terminologies, data formats, and interaction models.

Describing the behavior is a good progress for enriching service descriptions, but the adequate description of underlying service semantics beyond the abstract behavior models is still a challenging problem [1].

Current semantic Web service languages describe the syntactical aspects of a Web service, and therefore, the result is rigid services that cannot respond to unexpected user requirements and changes automatically, as it requires human intervention.

Input, output, effect, and precondition (IOEP) of each service are described in different semantic Web languages like OWL, SWRL [8], and many others. Composing services, described in different languages, is a complex process. Interoperations between composite services require mapping of IOEPs of each two service which is a complex process to get done automatically.

From composition point of view, discovery is an early step of composition. The discovery process should be based on matching a given description of the service and a description of the actual available service. This problem requires an algorithm to match descriptions and a language to describe capabilities of services. Also, enabling discovery of services involves publishing the service to a public registry. In spite of all efforts that have been done to add semantics to UDDI [9–11], such registries are still incapable to support different semantic languages and deal with their differences. On the other hand, standard registry structure is not suitable to combine the capabilities of semantic languages. The lack of semantic search capability of the registry is a major challenge for any semantic-based composition technique. Additionally, many approaches realize the QoS-based discovery and selection; registry support of QoS is important for automation of selection. For automated discovery of services, it is critical that a search engine can retrieve and perform reasoning on I/O parameters [17].

Automatic composition implies an automatic selection of the retrieved services. The approach must be able to choose the best available service that fulfills the composition requirements automatically based on the comparison of similarities and differences between the retrieved services. Thus, semantic languages of the service should enable such comparison. Some of the proposed approaches proposed an automatic selection based on QoS, rating, and user feedback. However, QoS and rating do not ensure that the best services will be selected. There is a need for richer description to distinguish among services.

To conclude, semantic languages initiatives do not enable automatic dynamic semantic-based Web service composition techniques and none of them achieve fully automated service discovery, selection, or composition. There is a need to abstract away differences among semantic languages and enrich them in order to (a) add different semantics support and semantic search capabilities to public registries to enable automatic discovery of services, (b) enable automatic interoperations and data flow in the composition workflow, (c) enable automatic selection of Web services those best fulfill the requirements. Such abstraction will benefit from the strength of each language and highlights the weakness of each individual language. On the other hand, registry search capabilities must be extended in order to enable semantic-based and QoS service matchmaking.

3.2 Composition Challenges

In general, while workflow-based composition approaches have evolved from offering only manual and static composition methods to supporting automation and dynamicity, the resulting workflows are limited to simple schemas such as sequential and parallel execution, or in other cases, automation is only supported during the execution and adaptation of the workflow, while the workflow design process is manual. This deficiency has been addressed by combining workflow-based methods with AI planning techniques. However, so far, the automated composition of the processes is still a difficult to be achieved: there no effective, easy-to-use, flexible support that can interact with the life cycle of processes.

3.3 Scalability, Adaptation, and Management

Composition approach must be scalable; the existing ones do not suggest how to describe, discover, and select a composite service. Any composition approach must suggest a solution to describe the composite services with the same standards automatically based on descriptions of services participating in the composition.

There is a lack of tools for supporting the evolution and adaptation of the processes. It is difficult to define compositions of processes that respond to the changes and differences of user requirements. Self-adapting service compositions should be able to respond to the changes of behaviors of external composite services. The need of human intervention for adapting services should be reduced to the minimum.

The composition approach must be self-healing, it should detect automatically that some service composition requirements have been changed and the implementation and react to requirement violations. On the other hand, the composition must detect automatically any collapse of a service participating in the composition, discover a new service that fulfills the exact same requirements then replace the discovered service and integrate it into the composition workflow.

Finally, any proposed approach must ensure that the advertisement of any service meets the actual result of service execution. The user must trust that the business rules are enforced into composition.

4 Conclusions and Future Work

In this paper, we explored many semantic-based composition approaches. The goal fully automated dynamic approach is still not achieved yet. The research challenges to achieve such approach include differences in the semantic languages capabilities which led to poor registry support of semantics. Thus, fully automated discovery and selection of services participating in composition have not met yet. At final, we highlighted many characteristics that any proposed approach has to satisfy in order to deliver a fully automated self-management composition process.

Currently, we are working to draft a new abstraction level of semantic languages which will enable compose services described in different semantic languages. This work is expected to add semantic support for different kinds of registry.

Next, we are going to propose a new kind of semantics that would enable auto-generation of workflow and auto-generation of composite services description in order to publish it for scalability purpose.

At last, we try to leverage the benefits of two previous works to suggest a new automatic dynamic composition approach based on natural language request for Web services on-fly composition. This work aims to achieve scalable, self-management, and self-healing composition approach.

References

1. Kritikos, K., Plexousakis, D.: Requirements for Qos-based web service description and discovery. IEEE T. Serv. Comput. **2**(4), 320–337 (2009)
2. Sirin, E., Hendler, J., Parsia, B.: Semi-automatic composition of web services using semantic descriptions. In: Web Services: Modeling, Architecture and Infrastructure workshop in ICEIS 2003 (2002)
3. Mrissa, M., et al.: Towards a semantic-and context-based approach for composing web services. Int. J. Web Grid Serv. **1**(3), 268–286 (2005)
4. Pahl, C.: A conceptual architecture for semantic web services development and deployment. Int. J. Web Grid Serv. **1**(3), 287–304 (2005)
5. Bosca, A., Ferrato, A., Corno, F., Congiu, I., Valetto, G.: Composing web services on the basis of natural language requests. In: IEEE International Conference on Web services (ICWS'05), pp. 817–818 (2005)
6. Bosca, A., Corno, F., Valetto, G., Maglione, R.: On-the-fly construction of web services compositions from natural language requests. J. Softw. (JSW), **1**(1), 53–63 (2006)
7. Pop, F.C., Cremene, M., Tigli, J.Y., Lavirotte, S., Riveill, M., Vaida, M.: Natural language based on-demand service composition (2010)
8. Horrocks, I., Patel-Schneider, P. F., Boley, H., Tabet, S., Grosof, B., Dean, M.: SWRL: a semantic web rule language combining OWL and RuleML, May, 2004, [Online]. Available: http://www.w3.org/Submission/2004/SUBM-SWRL-20040521/
9. Paolucci, M., Kawamura, T., Payne, T.R., Sycara, K.: Importing the semantic web in UDDI. In: Web Services EBusiness and the Semantic Web, vol. 2512 (2002)
10. Luo, J., Montrose, B., Kim, A., Khashnobish, A., Kang, M.K.M.: Adding OWL-S support to the existing UDDI infrastructure, pp. 153–162. IEEE (2006)
11. Paolucci, M., Kawamura, T., Payne, T.R., Sycara, K.: Importing the semantic web in UDDI. In: Web Services EBusiness and the Semantic Web, vol. 2512 (2002)
12. Rao, J., Dimitrov, D., Hofmann, P., Sadeh, N.M.: A mixed initiative approach to semantic web service discovery and composition: Sap's guided procedures framework. In: ICWS, pp. 401–410. IEEE Computer Society (2006)
13. Klusch M., Gerber, A.: Semantic web service composition planning with owls-xplan. In: Proceedings of the 1st International AAAI Fall Symposium on Agents and the Semantic Web, pp. 55–62 (2005)
14. Wu, Z., Ranabahu, A., Gomadam, K., Sheth, A.P., Miller, J.A.: Automatic composition of semantic web services using process and data mediation. Technical report, Kno.e.sis Center, Wright State University, 2007
15. Fujii, K., Suda, T.: Semantics-based dynamic web service composition. Int. J. Cooperative Inf. Syst. **15**(3), 293–324 (2006)
16. Fujii, K., Suda, T.: Semantics-based context-aware dynamic service composition. TAAS **4**(2), 12 (2009)
17. Ardagna, D., Comuzzi, M., Mussi, E., Pernici, B., Plebani, P.: Paws: a framework for executing adaptive web-service processes. IEEE Softw. **24**, 39–46 (2007)
18. Skogan, D., Gronmo, R., Solheim, I.: Web service composition in UML. In: Enterprise Distributed Object Computing Conference, IEEE International, pp. 47–57 (2004)

19. Gronmo R., Jaeger, M.C.: Model-driven semantic web service composition. In: APSEC'05: Proceedings of the 12th Asia-Pacific Software Engineering Conference, Washington, DC, USA,. IEEE Computer Society, pp. 79–86 (2005)
20. Lara, R., Roman, D., Polleres, A., Fensel, D.: A conceptual comparison of WSMO and OWL-S Web Services, pp. 254–269 (2004)
21. Pop, F.-C., Cremene, M., Tigli, J.-Y., Lavirotte, S., Riveill, M., Vaida, M.: Natural language based on-demand service composition. Int. J. Comput. Commun. Contr. 5(4), 871–883 (2010)

Automation Software Testing on Web-Based Application

Saru Dhir and Deepak Kumar

Abstract Agile testing is a software testing exercise, follows the rules of agile policy, and considers software improvement as a critical part like a client in the testing process. Automated testing is used to do this in order to minimize the amount of manpower required. In this paper, a traditional automation testing model has been discussed. A model has been proposed for automated agile testing, and an experimental work has also been represented on the testing of a Web application. Finally, outcomes are evaluated using the agile testing model, and there is a comparison between traditional and agile testing models.

Keywords Agile development and testing · Automation testing
Web application · Selenium tool

1 Introduction

A software test project can be successful, with a significant estimation and a complete execution in the software development life cycle [1]. Software testing is the main part of software development, where different level of testing is implemented, such as unit, integration, system, and acceptance testing according to the system behavior and client requirement, whereas unit and integration testing focus on individual modules, system and acceptance testing focus on overall behavior of system [2]. The adoption of the latest technology trends and development practices by the technology and software developers leads to polarization of opinions on the strengths and weaknesses of the technologies and software development practices [3]. Automation forms are one of the most important parts of agile testing; otherwise it is very difficult to keep pace with the agile development schedule.

S. Dhir (✉) · D. Kumar
Amity University, Noida 110025, Uttar Pradesh, India
e-mail: sdhir@amity.edu

D. Kumar
e-mail: dkumar8@amity.edu

© Springer Nature Singapore Pte Ltd. 2019
M. N. Hoda et al. (eds.), *Software Engineering*, Advances in Intelligent Systems and Computing 731, https://doi.org/10.1007/978-981-10-8848-3_67

The process of prioritization of defects identified by automation and their fixation during sprints is also determined at this stage. In the case of regression testing, efficiency increases with the automation testing, where test cases are implemented iteratively in the software [4].

In agile testing, generally the code is written during iteration and the testing process is done after each iteration. The developers and the testers work together to reduce the probability of error occurrences. Developers do the unit testing, and the rest system testing is done by the customer which is also known as acceptance testing and based on that clients provide their feedback which also gives a glance of excellence guarantee movement in agile [5].

2 Literature Review

In a survey result, it was revealed that only 26% of test cases are done through automation testing, which was considerably less than in comparison to the last years. The paper focused on to do more effort on automation testing and its tools [6]. According to a survey report, "State of agile development" showed that more than 80% of respondents' organizations had adopted agile testing methodology at some level and the other half of respondents indicated that their organization is using agile testing methodology for approximate two to three years [7]. Agile software development methods are these days widely extended and established. The main reason to adopt agile testing methodology is to deliver the product within a time limit, to increase efficiency, and to easily manage the frequently changing business requirements [8]. A survey report indicated that agile testing is mostly used development process. Agile testing provides small iterations (79%), regular feedback (77%), and the scrum meeting, which were on a daily basis (71%) were the most important factors [9]. Hanssen et al. [10] said that the use of agile testing methodology is global. Evaluation and scheduling are the main concern to the accomplishment of a software growth of a project of any dimension and consequences; agile software growth of a project has been the area under discussion of much conviction.

3 Automated Testing

In Fig. 1, automation testing model is mentioned in which different steps are specified [11]. After the implementation process, the testing environment is set, plan all of the test activities. In all of the planning, different test cases are created which is reviewed by senior testers. Test cases are executed, and bug report is generated. If the bugs are not generated, iterations are completed and backlog stories are ended [12].

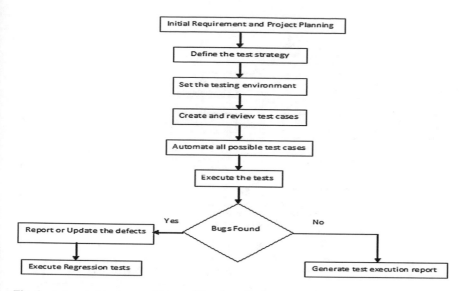

Fig. 1 Automated testing model in traditional environment

4 Proposed Method

In the agile environment, testing of the project is implemented with a proposed method to improve the accuracy of software. In an agile development, developers are also responsible for the testing. Hence, there is parallel and independent testing which is possible between developers and testers. Figure 2 is the proposed automation testing model using agile methodology.

Below algorithm is the pseudocode of automated agile testing to execute the test suites by the developers and testers. At line 2, quality assurance (QA) team initially involved in the project. Line 3 represents that the parallel testing is done by developers and testers, and stand meetings are also done to demonstrate the functionality of software. At line 4, testers generate the automation testing in different sprint cycles, and at line 5, verification test is build. At line 6 if the test suite result failed then at line 7, RCA (root cause analysis) is executed to remove the bugs. If at line 6, result successfully passed the validate the regression testing at line 10 and run the test and end. Finally at line 13 generate the report.

```
1.   Dd ← Set the delivery date
2.   QA ↔ P Involvement of QA team in project
3.   Deploy the build in the Pre-Production environment.
4.   t ↔ d    Testing and development both are implemented parallel.
5.   T → Generate automation test suite, in the sprint cycle.
6.   Release the 1ˢᵗ sprint and complete the BVT
7.    If d's and t's result failed then
```

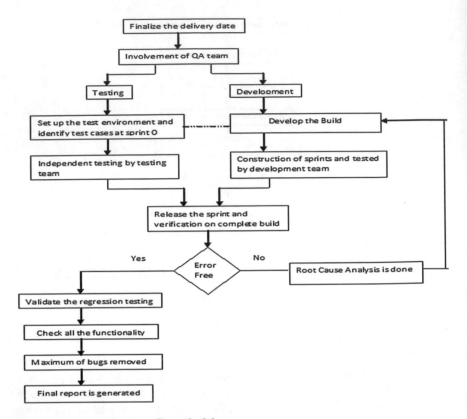

Fig. 2 Testing model using agile methodology

```
8.         do RCA ("remove the bugs in next sprint")
9.               GOTO step 3
10.     Else
11.   T → RT (validate the regression testing)
11.    Result ← T. runtest
12.    end if
13.   Generate the report
```

Whereas; *Dd: Delivery Date; QA: Quality Assurance Team; P: Project; T: Tester; D: Development; BVT: Build Verification Test; t: testing; d: development; RCA: root cause analysis; RT: regression testing.*

4.1 Experimental Work

During the implementation of Web application, project was developed and tested using the agile methodology. Product development and automation testing both were implemented in scrum. During the implementation in agile environment, developers and testing teams worked parallel. Automation test execution was implemented using the selenium tool in different steps. By using the steps of agile testing models, at the initial testing, bug was found as represented in Fig. 3. RCA was done, and then again a new sprint cycle was implemented. Bug was resolved as shown in Fig. 4 and validate the regression testing. Final result was evaluated as in Fig. 5, and maximum bugs were removed and a final report was generated.

Fig. 3 Failure in initial test and detect the bugs

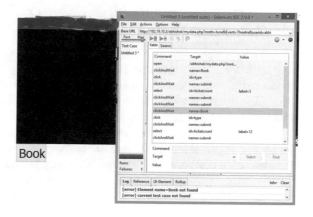

Fig. 4 Testing on a book button using selenium IDE

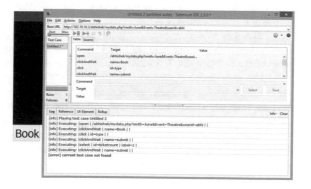

Fig. 5 Successfully booked
the tickets

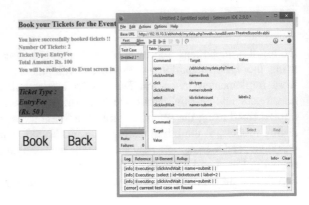

4.2 Comparison and Result Between Traditional and Agile Automated Testing Model

Web application was tested using the traditional and agile testing models vice versa. In the agile testing models, results were improved than the traditional model. During the testing implementation with or without agile methodology, results were observed as in Table 1:

A comparison between the testing in agile and traditional environments is represented in Fig. 6. Results in figure are based on different parameters per iteration. Parameters are cost, quality, detected bugs, and productivity.

Table 1 Comparison between agile model and automated testing model

Agile testing model	Automated testing model
According to the delivery date of the project, testing was done in parallel to the development process	Testing was implemented after the completion of development process
Due to the parallel testing from the initial stage of the development, less number of defects were evaluated at the end	Testing was done without the customer's involvement and took more time for customer satisfaction
As regression testing was executed frequently in a single sprint, it saved time and cost	After the completion of development process, test cases were created followed by automated test scripts
Productivity and quality of product were improved with the sequent involvement of customers	Less productivity with the low quality of product

Fig. 6 Testing parameters using agile implementation and traditional implementation

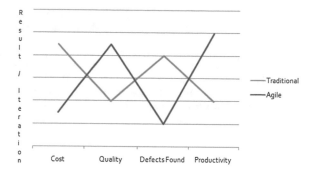

5 Conclusion

Paper concludes that the automation testing not only increases the test coverage but also reduces the cost and improves the delivery of the product. In this paper, an experimental work was discussed in which an automation testing was implemented on a Web application using agile environment and traditional development. The proposed agile testing model worked with productization team in a planned and organized manner to deliver the products in sprint. At the end, there is comparison between agile and traditional automated testing models, which specifies the results through the agile testing is better than traditional testing.

References

1. Sharma, M.A., Kushwaha, D.S.: A metric suite for early estimation of software testing effort using requirement engineering document and its validation. In: Computer and Communication Technology (ICCCT) 2nd International Conference, pp. 373–378 (2012)
2. Spillner, A., Linz, T., Schaefer, H.: Software Testing Foundation: A Study Guide for the Certified Tester Exam, 3rd ed. Rocky Nook (2011)
3. Aggarwal, S., Dhir, S.: Ground axioms to achieve movables: methodology. Int. J. Comput. Appl. **69**(14) (2013)
4. Karhu, K., Repo, T., Taipale, O., Smolander, K.: Empirical observations on software testing automation, international conference on software testing verification and validation (ICST'09). IEEE Computer Society, Washington, DC, USA, pp. 201–209. DOI = 10.1109/ ICST.2009.16 (2009)
5. Aggarwal, S., Dhir, S.: Swift tack: a new development approach. In: International Conference on Issues and Challenges in Intelligent Computing Techniques, IEEE (2014)
6. Kasurinen, J., Taipale, O., Smolander, K.: Software test automation in practice: empirical observations. Adv. Softw. Eng., Article 4 (2010)
7. http://www.versionone.com/pdf/2011_State_of_Agile_Development_Survey_Results.pdf
8. Rai, P., Dhir, S.: Impact of different methodologies in software development process. Int. J. Comput. Sci. Inf. Technol. **5**(2), 1112–1116 (2014). ISSN: 0975-9646
9. West, D., Grant, T.: Agile development: mainstream adoption has changed agility. Forrester Research Inc. (2010)

10. Hanssen, G.K., Šmite, D., Moe, N.B.: Signs of agile trends in global software engineering research: a tertiary study. In: 6th International Conference on Global Software Engineering, pp. 17–23 (2011)
11. Collins. E., Macedo. G., Maia. N., Neto. A. D.: An industrial experience on the application of distributed testing in an agile software development environment. In: Seventh International Conference on Global Software Engineering, IEEE, pp. 190–194 (2012)
12. Mattsson, A., Lundell, B., Lings, B., Fitzgerald, B.: Linking modeldriven development and software architecture: A case study. IEEE Trans. Softw. Eng. **35**(1), 83–93 (2009)

Automated Test Data Generation Applying Heuristic Approaches—A Survey

Neetu Jain and Rabins Porwal

Abstract Software testing is a systematic approach to identify the presence of errors in the developed software Pressman (Software Engineering A Practitioners Approach, Mc Graw Hill International Edition, 2010) [1], Beizer, Software Testing Techniques, Van Nostrand Reinhold Co, New York, 1990) [2], Beizer (Black Box Testing: Techniques for Functional Testing of Software and Systems, Wiley 1995) [3]. In this paper, we explore and present the challenges in software testing and how software testing techniques evolved over the period of time. Further software testing is tedious, time-consuming, cost-ineffective and does not guarantee reliability. Automation of software testing has been an area of most research in the field. Test cases play a vital role in achieving effective testing target, but generating effective test cases is equally challenging task. Heuristic approaches have gained the attention in different fields of computer science. In this paper, we discuss the need of automation of test data generation and heuristic algorithms or techniques to implement the same. We present an extensive survey of the work done in the related field by researchers and their results.

Keywords Software testing · Automated test data generation · Heuristic approaches

1 Introduction

Software development is a creative, intelligent, and a systematic process. Software construction can be summarized in four stages as *analysis, design, implementation, and testing*. Among these all four stages, *Software Testing* is considered as most

N. Jain (✉) · R. Porwal
Department of Computer Science, Faculty of Computer System Studies,
Mewar University, Chittorgarh, Rajasthan, India
e-mail: neetugupta78@gmail.com

© Springer Nature Singapore Pte Ltd. 2019
M. N. Hoda et al. (eds.), *Software Engineering*, Advances in Intelligent Systems
and Computing 731, https://doi.org/10.1007/978-981-10-8848-3_68

crucial and important task, wherein the output of all the other stages and their accuracy is evaluated and assured [1–3]. *Software testing* is a systematic approach to identify the presence of errors in the developed software. In software testing, the focus is to execute the program to identify the scenarios where the outcome of the execution is not as expected—this is referred as non-conformance with respect to the requirement and other specifications. Software testing can be thus termed as a process of repeatedly evaluating the software quality with respect to requirements, accuracy, and efficiency [1, 3–5]. For the conformance of the accuracy and quality of engineered software, it primarily goes through two level of testing—(i) *functional testing* or *black box* testing and (ii) *structural testing* or *white box* testing. *Functional testing* is performed in the absence of knowledge of implementation details, coding details an internal architecture of the software under consideration as stated by Pressman and Bezier in [1, 2]. *Structural testing* is performed with the adequate knowledge of internal details, program logic, implementation, and architecture of the software by actually executing the *source code* to examine the outcome(s) or behavior.

A vital component in software testing is test data. Test data is a value set of input variable that executes the few or more statements of the program. The success of any testing process is dependent on the effectiveness of the test data chosen to run the program. The test data selected should be such that it attains the high program coverage and meet the testing target. Manually deriving the test data to achieve specified code coverage and revealing the errors is tedious, time-consuming, and cost-ineffective. Also, the test data generated by programmers is ineffective and does not attain high coverage in terms of statement execution, branch execution, and path execution [6]. With the aim of reducing the cost and time in testing process, research on automation generation of test data has attracted the researchers and techniques has been tried and implemented.

Heuristic approaches have been applied in various areas to approximately solve a problem when an exact solution is not achievable using classical methods. Heuristic technique gives a solution that may not be the exact solution but seems best at the moment. Various heuristic techniques had been devised and tested in the different disciplines in computer science. Techniques like Hill Climbing, Swarm Optimization, Ant Colony Optimization, Simulated Annealing, and Genetic Algorithm have been used by researchers.

In this paper, we present the role of heuristic approaches in the field of software testing for the purpose of automatically generating the test data. Section 2 is an extensive literature review on automation of test data generation, how various heuristic algorithms have been applied in this direction and their results. In Sect. 3, detailed analysis of the work done in the area has been tabularized for the benefit of future researchers.

2 Literature Survey

2.1 Software Testing

References [1, 3–5] for the conformance of the accuracy and quality of an engineered software, it primarily goes through two different levels of testing—functional testing or black box testing and structural testing or white box testing. *Functional testing* is performed in absence of knowledge of implementation details, coding details, and internal architecture of the software under consideration as stated by Pressman and Bezier in [1, 2]. The sole aim is to run the implemented functions for the verification of their output as expected. It is strongly done in synchronization of the requirement specification. Further during the functional testing phase, purpose is to test the functionality in consent with the SRS and identify the errors those deviate from what is stated. Use cases are created during the analysis phase with conformance to functionality. Studying the use cases, the test cases are identified and generated. For a single use case, few test cases or a complete test suit is generated. The test suit should be sufficient enough to execute the software such that all the possible features have been tested and possible errors and unsatisfied functionality are identified. *Structural testing* is performed with the adequate knowledge of internal details, logic of the program, implementation details, and architecture of the software by actual execution of the *source code* to examine the outcome or behavior. This testing approach assures the accuracy of the code actually implemented to achieve desired functionally. A program consists of *control structures* in form of *loops, logical conditions, selective switch,* etc. With presence of control statements, a program is never a single sequence of statements executed from start to exit of the program it consists of multiple different sequences of statements depending upon the values of variables, and these different sequences are termed as *independent paths.* Execution of the independent paths decides the code coverage of program. Code coverage is important, and to achieve high code coverage, structural testing can be based upon *statement* testing, *branch* testing, *path* testing, and *data flow* testing depending upon the implementation details of the software [5, 7–10]. Test cases are to be identified to cover the all implemented paths in program [11]. The quality of test cases to much extent decides the quality of overall testing process hence of high importance [12]. An *adequacy criterion* is the test criterion that specifies how much and which code should be covered. It acts as the end point of the testing process which can be otherwise endless. Korel states that criterion could be *Statement coverage* requires execution all the statements of a program, *Branch coverage requires* all the control transfers are executed, *Path coverage* demands the execution of all the paths from start to end, and *Mutation coverage* is the percentage of dead mutants.

2.2 Test Data Generation

Test data is a value set of input variables that executes the few or more statements of the considered program. In testing, challenge for the programmers is to generate a minimal set of test data that can achieve high code coverage [6]. With the aim of reducing the cost and time invested in testing process, research on automation of generation of test data has attracted the researchers and significant techniques have been automated and implemented. Automatic test data approach is to generate the input variable values for a program with the help another program dynamically.

Korel [12] stated the idea of dynamic approach to test data generation. It is based on actually executing the program, analyzing the dynamic data flow, and using a function minimization method. Edvardsson [6] presented a survey stating that manual testing process is tedious, time-consuming, and less reliable. He focused on the need of automatically generated test data with the help of a program that can make testing cost and quality effective. Korel [13] divided the test data generation methods as *random, path oriented, and goal oriented*. Edvardsson [6] defines the test data generator as a program such that given a program P and a path u, the task of generator is to generate an input x belongs to S, such that x traverses the path u where S is the set of all possible inputs. The effectiveness depends on how paths are selected by the path selector. Path selection must achieve good coverage criteria which could be *Statement Coverage, Branch Coverage, Condition Coverage, Multiple-condition Coverage,* and *Path Coverage.* Pargas [14] found classical approaches like random technique, path-oriented technique inefficient as no knowledge of test target is taken as feedback and hence leads to the generation of widespread test data and infeasible paths test. He treated the test data generation as a search problem. Girgis [7] stated that an adequacy criterion is important. Latiu [4] took finding and testing each path in source code as an NP-complete problem. Test data generation is taken up as a *search problem*—A problem defined as finding the test data or test cases into a search space. Further, the set of test data generated should be small and enough to satisfy a target test *adequacy criterion*.

2.3 Heuristic Approaches

Heuristic approaches have been applied in various areas to approximately solve a problem when an exact solution is not achievable using classical methods. Primarily in the domain of artificial intelligence, scheduling problems, optimization problems, search problems, virus scanning problems, NP-complete problems, etc., heuristic approaches are being widely applied and proved to find an approximate solution [15, 16].

a. **Hill Climbing** is a local search algorithm for maximizing an objective function
b. **Simulated Annealing** [17, 18], a probabilistic that Kirkpatrick, Gelett, and Vecchi in 1983, and Cerny in 1985 proposed for finding the global minimum for a cost function that possesses several local minima values.
c. **Genetic evolutionary Algorithm** [19] is based on the natural process of selection, crossover, and mutation. It is a population of candidate solutions for the problem at hand and makes it evolve by iteratively applying a set of operators—selection, recombination, and mutation.
d. **Swarm Intelligence** [20–22] is an simulating the natural phenomenon of bird flocking or fish schooling. In PSO, the potential solutions in search space called particles fly through the problem space by following the current optimum particles. Two best values pbest, best position for each particle gbest, best position among all particles best position. Iteratively update velocity and position of ith particle as

$$V_i^d(t) = V_i^d(t-1) + c_1 \cdot r_{1i}^d \cdot \left(pbest_i^d - X_i^d(t-1)\right)$$
$$+ c_2 \cdot r_{2i}^d \cdot \left(gbest^d - X_i^d(t-1)\right) \qquad (1)$$

$$X_i^d(t) = X_i^d(t-1) + V_i^d(t) \qquad (2)$$

Here, $X_i = (X_{i1}, X_{i2},..., X_{iD})$ is ith particle position, $V_i = (V_{i1}, V_{i2}, ..., V_{iD})$ is the velocity of ith particle, c_1, c_2 are acceleration constants, and r_1, r_2 are two random numbers in the range of [0, 1]

2.4 Applying Heuristics in Test Data Generation

References [4, 7, 8, 14] popular heuristic approaches like data like Genetic Algorithm (GA), Simulating Annealing (SA), Particle Swarm Optimization, Ant Colony Optimization have been widely applied to search for effective test data. These approaches are verified to be more optimized than random technique. Studies suggest that though the test data generated achieves good code coverage the convergence toward the adequacy criteria is important. GA-, SA-based techniques are tested and found to be slow and takes more generations to generate the test data required to execute target path and achieve a foresaid code coverage [23, 24]. With an aim to achieve faster convergence, another heuristic approach Particle Swarm

Optimization (PSO) based on swarm behavior of insects, birds flocking has received a lot of attention due to it its comparatively simpler implementation and fast convergence [21, 25, 26]. Other versions of Particle Swarm Optimization— Binary PSO (BPSO) and Quantum PSO (QPSO)—have also been defined and tested for the effective test data generation [14]. Pargas treated test data generation as a search problem and applied GA, a heuristic approach to find an optimal solution, i.e., a set of *optimal test data*. His approach was based on *control dependency graph of* program. He implemented GA-based algorithm that generated test data (chromosomes) and calculated its fitness by comparing the predicates in the program actually executed by the test data with the set of predicates on the control dependency predicate paths of the target, assigning high fitness to test data that covered more predicates. His experiment on six programs concluded that GA-based approach outperformed RA [7]. Girgis implemented GA-based algorithm using *data flow dependencies* where the search was based on coverage of *def-use* associations of the variable to generate the test data that meets the *all-uses* criteria. A binary string represented chromosome such that $m = \sum m_{i,}$ *where i = 1 to k,* and m_i represents the value of $x_{i,}$ and fitness of chromosome was calculated as no of *def-use paths covered by v_i/total no. of def-use paths.* The experiment concluded that 12 out of 15 FORTRAN programs showed good performance with GA and 10 programs used less number of generations to achieve the same *def-use* coverage as compared to RA [8]. Girgis implemented GA based on d-u coverage percentage where a chromosome (binary vector) represents the edges in the DD graph of the considered program and length of the binary vector is number of edges plus two edges for entry–exit and number of edges contained in the loops. The set of test path was recorded that covered the d-u pairs. As a result, the 11 programs showed better performance in d-u coverage percentage by GA and in rest 4 programs both GA and RA showed 100% d-u coverage but GA needed less number of generations than RA.

Latiu [4] explored three evolutionary approaches, i.e., *Genetic Algorithm, Simulated Annealing,* and *Particle Swarm Optimization (PSO).* He worked on *target path* and used heuristics *approximation level* and *the branch distance* for evaluating the test data. The *approximation level* calculates how the actual test data is far away from target path branching condition and *Branch distance* is calculated as per the Korel's *Distance Function* which depends on the branching condition(s) of the node where the target node is missed. Fitness function used was sum of *approximation level* and normalized *branch distance.* He presented results in form of comparisons between convergences of algorithms (number of generations) for specified target path. SA converged earlier than GA and PSO. But in Sum and Prod, GA produced the fastest convergence test data and SA being the second. PSO is another heuristic approach to be studied for test data generation. Kennedy and Eberhart [20] proposed the PSO in 1995. Kennedy and Eberhart [21] in 1997 described a concept of BPSO. Agarwal [25] used BPSO and compared its performance with GA. Branch coverage was taken as adequacy criterion for the experiment. String was identified as a test case and fitness value was calculated as $f = 1/(|h - g| + \delta)$, where h and g were expected and the desired value of branch predicate, and a small quantity was chosen to avoid numeric overflow. The Soda Vending Machine simulator with total 27 branches was taken as the experiment problem and was run over hundred times with population size in range 5–50 to achieve 100% coverage. BPSO was better with small and large population while GA being effective in larger size and degraded for small size. Khushboo [26] used another variation QPSO and used the branch coverage as adequacy criterion. They made use of DFS with memory—if a test data traverse a branch for the first time, saved the test data and further injected this saved test data into the population for the sibling branch. Nayak [9] focused his research on PSO approach and compared it with. The work showed that GA converges in more generations than PSO. His work used *d-u path coverage* as fitness criteria and conducted experiment on fourteen FORTRAN programs and recorded *number of generations* and *d-u coverage* percentage. PSO technique took less number of generations to achieve a said *d-u coverage* percentage. The reason is—PSO chooses a *gbest* (global best) in each iteration and moves toward solution, whereas GA applies *selection, crossover,* and *mutation* in each iteration. In 2012 [23], *Chengying Mao implemented* PSO for test data generation and compared the same with GA. For PSO, initialized f(*pbest_i*) and f(gbest) to zero, and for each particle Xi, f(Xi) is calculated and *pbest_i/gbest* is updated. The function f() representing the fitness was based on *branch distance* based on Korel's and Tracey's theory. The experiment on five benchmark programs studied *Average converge, Successful rate, Average generations,* and Average Time for GA and PSO. PSO has higher converged rate and faster on convergence generations and time than a GA-based test cases. He opened the issues of more reasonable fitness function which can be future scope. In Sect. 3, we summarize the work in tabular form.

3 Heuristic Approaches Applied in Test Data Generation

(See Fig. 1).

S No.	Year	Work - Testing Approach and Fitness Function	Test Data, Experiment and Results
Genetic Algorithm			
1	[3]1999	CDG of program Predicates actually executed v/s predicates on the control dependency predicate paths of the target	6 C Programs. 32 runs of each program with TGen and RA 3 programs: TGen and RA gave equal statement coverage. 3 programs: RA required more iterations than GA to achieve 100% statement coverage
2	[4]2005	Data flow dependencies. *def-use coverage* % with test case. $$eval(v_i)=\frac{\#\ of\ d-u\ paths\ covered}{total\ d-u\ paths}$$	15 Fortran programs MaxGen = 100, pc = 0.8, pm = 0.15 GA used less generations to achieve a set d-u coverage compared to RA
3	[25] 2007	Two parts Framework : Program Analyzer System (BPAS), Automatic Test Cases Generation System (ATCGS). Data Flow Graph (DFG). Used all du paths	10 Java programs. LOC ranging from 20 to 200 # of if statements ranging from 1 to 5 $$F=\frac{Paths\,Covered}{Total\,\#of\,Paths}+\frac{Newly\,Covered\,Paths}{Paths\,Not\,Yet\,Covered}+\frac{Rarely\,Covered\,Paths}{Paths\,are-Covered}\ (1)$$
4.	[30] 2009		
5	[9] 2012	Basis Path Coverage Fitness function f(x) calculated as: a. *Path (statement) wise i.e.* V(x) = deviation b/w traversed & target path b. *Branch (predicate) wise i.e.* Dist(x) = Difference b/w execution track & target path in term of predicate values for the "unmatched node-branches as per Korel proposed branch function [30] $$V_r^*(x)=\sum w_i\times z_g(s(x))=\sum(m-i)\times z_g(s(x))$$ s(x) is execution character string of x tij(s(x)) is 1 or 0, jth bit encoding of s(x) and gi is same or not gi is ith target path in g(n) c. *Normalized Dist(x) if V is same*	4 benchmark programs and 4 industrial programs Recorded *Average evolutionary generations* Evolutionary time were found better and less in the approach implemented
6	[5] 2014	def-use (d-u) pairs. Searches for paths all-uses criterion. $$F(V_i)=\frac{\#\ of\ d-u\ paths\ covered}{total\ d-u\ paths}$$ Roulette wheel method to select Parents. MAXGENS=100, pc=0.8, pm=0.15 and POPSIZE=4.	15 (C#) object oriented & procedural programs. GA outperformed the RT technique in 11 out of the 15 programs in the d-u coverage percentage In 4 programs, the both techniques reached 100% d-u coverage. GA converged in less generations
PSO			
7	[10] 2007	PSO v/s GA Branch Coverage using CFG	25 artificial and 13 industrial programs PSO: particles = 40, w = 0.9 to 0.4 GA: stochastic universal Sampling, pc= 1.0 PSO is efficient, faster than GA
8	[7] 2010	Compared PSO with GA Data Flow testing. def-use coverage percentage $$eval\ (v_i)=\frac{\#\ of\ d-u\ paths\ covered}{total\ d-u\ paths}$$	14 small Fortran programs PSO converged in less number of generations than GA for same d-u coverage percentage.
9	[21] 2008	BPSO v/s GA. Branch coverage adequacy criteria $F(x) = 1/(|h-g|+\delta)$, h is and g are desired and actual branch predicate value	Soda Vending Machine simulator BPSO better than GA with small size of population.
10	[23] 2010	AQPSO, QPSO and GA. branch coverage adequacy criteria $f(x) = 1/(|h-g|+\delta)$,h and g are desired & actual branch predicate value	3 programs Triangle Classifier, Line in rectangle, Number of days between dates. QPSO it was possible to generate test cases for complete branch coverage with population size two also
11	[8]2012	Branch coverage Fitness $$fitness=1/\left[0.01+\sum w_i\cdot f(bch)_i\right]$$ s is no of branches $f(bch_i)$ is branch distance for i-th branch w_i is weight of ith branch where	Five programs with no of branch 5-20 GA: pc = 0.8, pm = 0.15 PSO: w ranges 0.2-1, c1=c2=-2.05, Vmax=24 PSO converged better than GA and faster
Simulated Annealing			
12	[6] 2012	SA, GA and PSO.CFG Based. Target path identified. Recorded algorithm convergence. Sum between the approximation level and normalized branch distance between actual path and target path	10 programs including Triangle Classification, Quadratic equation, minimum function, maximum function SA test data were more effective for complex programs to cover target path in lesser time

Fig. 1 Heuristic approaches applied in test data generation

4 Conclusion

Test data is vital for efficient software testing. Manually generated test data is costly, time-consuming, and ambiguous at times. Randomly generated test data does not achieve target paths or good code coverage. Automatic test data generation and use of heuristic approaches had shown good results. In this paper, we present a detail survey of work done in past for test data generation using heuristic approaches. Results show that GA outperforms the RA technique. Further work by researchers and their results presents that PSO is faster and efficient than GA. References [25, 26] applied variations of PSO, i.e., QPSO and BPSO and observed better results [27–32]. Future work will focus on testing more application and observing results using these algorithms.

References

1. Pressman, R.R.: Software Engineering A Practitioners Approch. Mc Graw Hill International Edition (2010)
2. Beizer, B.: Software Testing Techniques, 2nd Edn. New York: Van Nostrand Reinhold Co. 550 p. (1990). ISBN 0-442-20672-0
3. Beizer, B.: Black-Box Testing: Techniques for Functional Testing of Software and Systems. Wiley (1995)
4. Latiu, G.I., Cret, O.A., Vacariu, L.: Automatic test data generation for software path testing using evolutionary algorithms. In: Third International Conference on Emerging Intelligent Data and Web Technologies (2012)
5. Varshney, S., Mehrotra, M.: Search based software test data generation for structural. ACM SIGSOFT Soft. Eng. Notes, 38(4) (2013)
6. Edvardsson, J.: A survey on automatic test data generation. In Proceedings of the Second Conference on Computer Science and Engineering in Linkoping, ECSEL, pp. 21–28, October 1999
7. Girgis, M.R.: Automatic test data generation for data flow testing using a genetic algorithm. J. Univers. Comput. Sci. 11(6), 898–915 (2005)
8. Girgis, M.R., Ghiduk, A.S., Abd-Elkawy, E.H.: Automatic generation of data flow test paths using a genetic algorithm. Int. J. Comput. Appl. (0975–8887) 89(12) (2014)
9. Nayak, N., Mohapatra, D.P.: Automatic Test Data Generation for Data Flow Testing Using Particle Swarm Optimization. Springer (2010)
10. Jiang, S., Zhang, Y., Yi, D.: Test data generation approach for basis path coverage. ACM SIGSOFT Soft. Eng. Notes, 37(3) (2012)
11. Zhu, H., Hall, A.V.P., John, H.R.: Software unit test coverage and adequacy. ACM Comput. Surv. 29(4), 366–427 (1997)
12. Rapps, S., Weyuker, E.J.: Selecting software test data using data flow information. IEEE Trans. Software Eng. 11(4), 367–375 (1985)
13. Ferguson, R., Korel, B.: The chaining approach for software test data generation. IEEE Trans. Soft. Eng. 5(1), 63–86 (1996)

14. Pargas, R.P., Harrold, M.J., Peck, R.R.: Test-data generation using genetic algorithms. J. Soft. Test. Verification Reliab. (1999)
15. Nguyen, T.B., Delaunay, M., Robach, C.: Testing criteria for data flow software. In Proceedings of the Tenth Asia-Pacific Software Engineering Conference (APSEC'03), IEEE (2003)
16. Deng, M., Chen, R., Du, Z.: Automatic Test Data Generation Model by Combining Dataflow Analysis with Genetic Algorithm. IEEE (2009)
17. Kokash, N.: An introduction to heuristic algorithms. ACSIJ (2006)
18. Karaboga, D., Pham, D.: Intelligent Optimisation Techniques: Genetic Algorithms, Tabu Search, Simulated Annealing and Neural Networks. Springer
19. Bajeh, A.O., Abolarinwa, K.O.: Optimization: a comparative study of genetic and tabu search algorithms. Int. J. Comput. Appl. (IJCA), 31(5) (2011)
20. Kennedy, J., Eberhart, R.: Particle swarm optimization. Int. Conf. Neural Networks, Piscataway, NJ (1995)
21. Kennedy, J., Eberhart, R.C.: A discrete binary version of the particle swarm algorithm. IEEE International Conference on Systems Man, and Cybernetics (1997)
22. Eberhart, R., Shi, Y., Kennedy, J.: Swarm Intelligence. Morgan Kaufmann (2001)
23. Mao, C., Yu, X., Chen, J.: Swarm intelligence-based test data generation for structural testing. In: IEEE/ACIS 11th International Conference on Computer and Information Science (2012)
24. Windisch, A., Wappler, S., Wegener, J.: Applying Particle Swarm Optimization to Software Testing. In: Proceedings of the Conference on Genetic and Evolutionary Computation GECCO'07, London, England, United Kingdom, 7–11 July 2007
25. Agarwal, K., Pachauri, A., Gursaran: Towards software test data generation using binary particle swarm optimization. In: XXXII National Systems Conference, NSC 2008, 17–19 Dec 2008
26. Agarwal, K., Srivastava, G.: Towards software test data generation using discrete quantum particle swarm optimization. ISEC'10, Mysore, India, 25–27 Feb 2010
27. Frankl, P.G., Weyuker, E.J.: An applicable family of data flow testing criteria. IEEE Trans. Software Eng. 14(10), 1483–1498 (1998)
28. Korel, B.: Automated software test data generation. IEEE Trans. Software Eng. 16 (1990)
29. Mahajan, M., Kumar, S., Porwal, R.: Applying Genetic Algorithm to Increase the Efficiency of a Data Flow-based Test Data Generation Approach. ACM SIGSOFT, 37 (5), (2012)
30. Harrold, M.J., Soffa, M.L.: Interprocedural Data Flow Testing. ACM (1989)
31. Clarke, L.A., Podgurski, A., Richardson, D.J., Zeil, S.J.: IEEE Transactions on Software Engineering, 15(II) (1989)
32. Frankl, P.G., Weiss, S.N.: An experimental comparison of the effectiveness of branch testing and data flow testing. IEEE Trans. Soft. Eng. 19(8) (1993)

Comparison of Optimization Strategies for Numerical Optimization

Gopal Narayanam, Kartikay Ranjan and Sumit Kumar

Abstract According to the need and desire, various optimization strategies have been conceived and devised in past, particle swarm optimization (PSO), artificial bee colony (ABC), teacher–learner-based optimization (TLBO), and differential evolution(DE) to name a few. These algorithms have some advantages as well as disadvantages over each other for numerical optimization problems. In order to test these algorithms (optimization strategies), we use various functions which give us the idea of the situations that optimization algorithms have to face during their operation. In this paper, we have compared the above-mentioned algorithms on benchmark functions and the experimental result shows that TLBO outperforms the other three algorithms.

Keywords ABC · PSO · TLBO · DE

1 Introduction

According to mathematics, computer, and applied sciences, optimization is the process of selection of best candidates from a given set of candidates which may or may not be the solution to a particular problem, the process to find the maximum, or minimum obtainable value which could be attained by any given function within its domain. In simple words, optimization is finding the best suitable answer for a

G. Narayanam (✉) · K. Ranjan · S. Kumar
Krishna Institute of Engineering and Technology, Ghaziabad, India
e-mail: narayanam.gopal@gmail.com

K. Ranjan
e-mail: kartikey.ranjan30@gmail.com

S. Kumar
e-mail: sumitkumarbsr19@gmail.com

© Springer Nature Singapore Pte Ltd. 2019
M. N. Hoda et al. (eds.), *Software Engineering*, Advances in Intelligent Systems and Computing 731, https://doi.org/10.1007/978-981-10-8848-3_69

given problem in a given domain by systematically choosing various candidates and testing them for optimum performance. The problem of optimization revolves around determining such values for independent variables that satisfy the constraints and in the meanwhile also give the optimal value to the function which is being optimized. Optimization is fairly easy when dealing with simple mathematical problems, but when the problem get complex and involve a large number of invariants and dimensions, we need various optimization strategies or metaheuristic algorithms so as to seek out the optimum solutions of a given problem [1]. As optimization problems relate to various fields such as science, mathematics, engineering, and industry due to their real-life applicability and utility, there is always a need to formulate new optimization process/techniques which perform better than earlier ones, or to refine and modify the existing techniques in order to get optimum results with ensured quality and exploration of the domain [2]. Day by day, new and better algorithms are being devised or prior ones are being redefined in multiple variants; these new variants and algorithms often show better results than previous techniques. In order to ascertain oneself of the best optimization technique required for a particular problem, one needs to know about their comparative behavior and various attributes in a transparent and concise manner [3]. In order to achieve this objective, this paper compares few optimization techniques on mathematical benchmark functions for numerical optimization to learn about their comparative efficiency and effectiveness.

2 Related Work

Many optimization algorithms like GA, PSO, ABC, TLBO, and DE have been applied for numerical optimization problems. Genetic algorithm (GA) was the most initial optimization technique developed for numerical optimization [4], but its drawback is that as soon as the problem changes, the knowledge regarding the previous problem is discarded. Particle swarm optimization was discovered by Kennedy et al. [1]. PSO has its advantage of fast convergence and retaining of good solution due to memory capabilities, but its disadvantage is that it often gets stuck in local minima.

Artificial bee colony algorithm (ABC) was developed by Dervis Karaboga [5]. Its characteristic property is better exploration, ease to efficiently handle the cost with stochastic nature, but it had significant tradeoffs such as slow exploitation and missing of optimal solution in case of large swarm size. Differential evolution was formulated in 1995 by Price and Storm [5]. DE is simple to implement, but as PSO it also gets stuck in local minima. Teacher–learner-based optimization (TLBO) by Rao [6]. This metaheuristic algorithm is for solving continuous nonlinear optimization on large scale. The major disadvantage of TLBO is that it gets slow when dealing with problems having higher dimensions.

3 Proposed Work

In order to verify that which algorithm works efficiently under certain criteria, we have compared the four most common algorithms PSO, ABC, DE, and TLBO for numerical optimization problems. The details of these algorithms are as given below.

3.1 Particle Swarm Optimization

Particle swarm optimization (PSO) is an optimization algorithm which is based on the foraging and social habits of bird flocks and fish schools. Unlike traditional genetic operations, every particle in PSO moves by accounting on its own as well as the neighboring particles experience. PSO uses two equations, position and velocity update equations. These equations are modified in every successive run of particle swarm optimization to reach the required optimum solution. For a search space having n-dimensions, the swarm particles are given by a vector of n-dimensions, $X_i = (x_{i1}, x_{i2}... x_{in})$ T, whereas the velocity of the particles is given by another vector of similar dimensions $V_i = (v_{i1}, v_{i2}... v_{in})$ T. The best position visited by the ith particle previously is given as $P_i = (p_{i1}, p_{i2}, ..., p_{in})$ T, and "g" denotes the index of the particle having best value. Velocity and position update equations for ith particle are as

$$V_{id} = V_{id} + c_1 r_1 (p_{id} - x_{id}) + c_2 r_2 (p_{gd} - x_{id}) \tag{1}$$

$$X_{id} = X_{id} + V_{id} \tag{2}$$

where the dimension of the problem is represented by $d = 1, 2, ..., n$ and the swarm size is given by $I = 1, 2, ..., S$, while the constants $-c_1$ and c_2 are known as scaling and learning parameter, respectively, and acceleration parameters collectively. Generally, these two are generated randomly over a uniform distribution [3].

3.2 Artificial Bee Colony

The artificial bee colony algorithm often abbreviated as (ABC) is an optimization technique inspired by the intelligent behavior of honey bees while finding their food [5, 7]. This algorithm consists of three parts; each part is simulated by the different bees as employee bees, scout bees, and onlooker bees. In ABC algorithm, every iteration of the search process comprises of three steps, which can be categorized into, sending employee bees to their respective food sources (solutions) and calculating the nectar (fitness) values of these food sources. Second step consists of sharing the collected information pertaining to the food sources and selecting viable regions that contain food sources by onlooker bees and evaluating fitness value (nectar amount) of food sources. Thirdly, sending the scout bees randomly in the search space to scout and discover new sources of food.

The major steps of the algorithm are as:

1. Initializing the population
2. Placing the employee bees at their food sources
3. Placing onlooker bees on the food sources with respect to the nectar amount of the source
4. Sending scouts for discovering new food sources in the search area
5. The best food source so far is memorized
6. Repeat until termination condition is satisfied

Formulae used in ABC:

To produce a candidate food source for employee bees, ABC uses the formula.

$$V_{ij} = X_{ij} + \emptyset_{ij}(X_{ij} - X_{kj}) \tag{3}$$

where j and k are randomly chosen indices and $\emptyset$ is a constant.

Food source generation for onlooker bee:

$$p_i = \text{fit}_i \bigg/ \sum_{N-1}^{SN} \text{fit}_n \tag{4}$$

where p_i is the probabilistic value of that food particular source and fit_i is the fitness while SN represents the number of food sources.

New food generation for scouts is done by the below formula if the earlier food source gets exhausted

$$x_i^j = x_{min}^j + \text{rand}[0, 1](x_{max}^j - x_{min}^j) \tag{5}$$

3.3 Teacher–Learner-Based Optimization

This optimization technique has its formation basis in the phenomenon of the influence caused by a teacher on the outcome of the pupil. This method like other methods based on population uses a number of solutions in order to reach a global solution. The different parameters of TLBO are analogous to the different domains offered to the students, and the fitness function is resembled by their result, just like other population-based algorithms.

The best solution in TLBO is resembled by the teacher due to the consideration that the teacher is the most learned in the group. TLBO operation is divided into two sub-processes consisting of the "teachers phase" and the "learners phase", respectively. Teachers phase is analogous to learning from a teacher, and the second phase "Learners phase" represents peer to peer learning.

Formulae used in TLBO:

Initialization of population and filling up of parameters by random value:

$$x_{(i,j)}^0 = x_j^{min} + \text{rand} * \left(x_j^{max} - x_j^{min} \right) \tag{6}$$

$$x = \left[x_{(i,1)}^g, x_{(i,2)}^g, x_{(i,3)}^g, \ldots, x_{(i,j)}^g, \ldots, x_{(i,D)}^g \right] \tag{7}$$

The mean parameters of a learner at any generation g is given by

$$M^g = \left[m_1^g, m_2^g, m_3^g, \ldots, m_j^g, \ldots, m_D^g \right] \tag{8}$$

Improving the fitness/learning of candidates by using teacher is done by

$$Xnew_{(i)}^g = X_{(i)}^g + \text{rand} * \left(X_{\text{Teacher}}^g T_F M_g \right) \tag{9}$$

where T_f is known as teacher's factor and is decided by

$$T_F = \text{round}[1 + \text{rand}(0, 1)\{2 - 1\}] \tag{10}$$

Improving the fitness/learning of candidates by using other candidates is done by

$$Xnew_{(i)}^g = \begin{cases} X_{(i)}^g + \text{rand} * \left(X_{(i)}^g - X_{(r)}^g \right) & \text{if } f\left(X_{(i)}^g \right) < f\left(X_{(r)}^g \right) \\ X_{(i)}^g + \text{rand} * \left(X_{(r)}^g - X_{(i)}^g \right) \end{cases} \tag{11}$$

3.4 Differential Evolution

Differential evolution (DE) optimizes any given problem by creating new prospective solutions by combining the previously existing solutions on the basis of its formulae and retains only those solutions having improved fitness [8, 9]. DE consists of four parts, namely initialization, mutation, crossover, and selection. Initialization is carried out by randomly generating candidates according to the given formula

$$x^j_{(i,0)} = x^j_{\min} |\text{rand}(0,1) * \left(x^j_{\max} - x^j_{\min}\right)$$ (12)

After initialization, mutation is carried out to increase the fitness of the candidates

$$V_{i_1,G} = X_{r^{i,G}_1} + F\left(X_{r^{i,G}_2} - X_{r^{i,G}_3}\right)$$ (13)

Once mutation is performed [10], crossover is applied to each X with its corresponding V pair to generate a trial vector, and this phase is known as crossover phase

$$u^j_{(i,G)} = \begin{cases} v^j_{(i,G)}, & \text{if } (\text{rand}j[0,1) = \text{CR} \\ x^j_{(i,G)}, & \text{otherwise}(j = 1,2,\ldots,D). \end{cases}$$ (14)

Some of the newly generated trial vectors might consist of some parameters which violate the lower and/or upper bounds. Such parameters are reinitialized within the pre-specified range. After this, the values given by an objective function to each one of the trial vectors are evaluated and a selection operation is carried out.

$$X_{i,G+1} = \begin{cases} U_{i,G}, & \text{if } f(U_{i,G}) \leq f(X_{i,G}) \\ X_{i,G}, & \text{otherwise}. \end{cases}$$ (15)

3.5 Benchmark Functions

The functions used for testing various algorithms are often called as benchmark function due to their known solutions and behavioral properties [11]. We will be using three such benchmark functions in our study that is sphere function, Rastrigin function, and Griewank function which are mentioned in Table 1.

Table 1 Benchmark functions used

Function name	Function	Search domain	Optimal value
Sphere function	$f(x) = \sum_{i=1}^{d} x_i^2$	$-5.12 \leq x_i \leq 5.12$	0
Rastrigin function	$f(x) = A_n + \sum_{i=1}^{n} \left[x_i^2 - A\cos(2\pi x_i)\right]$	$-5.12 \leq x_i \leq 5.12$	0
Griewank function	$f(x) = \frac{1}{4000}\sum_{i=1}^{n} x_i^2 - \prod_{i=1}^{n} \cos\left(\frac{x_i}{\sqrt{i}}\right) + 1$	$-600 \leq x_i \leq 600$	0

4 Experimental Results and Analysis

To reach the conclusion, we compared the performance of PSO, ABC, TLBO, and DE on a series of benchmark functions that are given in Table 1. Dimensions, initial range, and formulation characteristics of these problems are tuned as given in the table. We used the above-mentioned benchmark functions in order to asses and compare their optimality and accuracy. We found that TLBO outperforms other algorithms by a significant difference evident by Table 2.

Parameter Tuning:

For the experiments, the values which are common in all algorithms that depict population size, iterations, and a number of functions, evaluations were kept constant. Population size was taken to be 20, iterations within a single run were carried out 20,000 times, and a total run of 30 was carried out in order to get a stable mean value. Parameter tuning of all algorithms is mentioned below.

After performing the above-given operations and experiments, the results have been tabulated and analyzed. The analysis shows the mean value of the solution that has been optimized after 30 runs containing number of iterations as 20,000 or until the function stops converging. Table 3 displays this data in a tabulated and easy format; Table 4 further summarizes the results as declarations.

Table 2 Parameter tuning

Algorithm	Parameter	Value
PSO	Acceleration constant	$C_1 = 2, C_2 = 2$
	Inertia weight	$W = 0.7$
DE	Variation constant	$F = 0.5 * (1 + rand(0,1))$

Table 3 Mean best value (optimized solution) over 30 runs

Algorithm used	Sphere	Rastrigin	Griewank
PSO	416.3412	0.9959	0.0660
ABC	9.505587e−016	9.156553e−010	9.129795e−016
TLBO	7.2500e−145	0	0
DE	5.8553e−005	34.3569	0.0030

Table 4 Performance table

Function	Best performance	Worst performance
Sphere	TLBO	PSO
Rastrigin	TLBO	DE
Griewank	TLBO	PSO

5 Conclusion

In this study, we applied four optimization algorithms on numerical optimization problem and the experimental results found out that TLBO significantly outperforms the other three algorithms (PSO, ABC, and DE) in numerical optimization by quality of the solution. We can test these algorithms performance on average time consumption and iterations of function evaluations.

References

1. Kennedy, J., Eberhart, R.C., et al.: Particle swarm optimization. In: Proceedings of IEEE International Conference on Neural Networks, vol. 4, pp. 1942–1948. Perth, Australia (1995)
2. Eberhart, R.C., Shi, Y.: Tracking and optimizing dynamic systems with particle swarms. In: Evolutionary Computation, 2001. Proceedings of the 2001 Congress on, vol. 1, pp. 94–100. IEEE (2002)
3. Shi, Y., Eberhart, R.C.: Parameter selection in particle swarm optimization. In: Lecture Notes in Computer Science Evolutionary Programming VII, vol. 1447, pp. 591–600 (1998)
4. Mitchell, M.: An introduction to genetic algorithm. MIT Press Cambridge USA (1998)
5. Dervis Karaboga, D.: An idea based on honey bee swarm for numerical optimization. Technical Report-TR06, Erciyes University, Engineering Faculty, Computer Engineering Department (2005)
6. Rao, R.V., Savsani, V.J., Vakharia, D.P.: Teaching learning-based optimization: a novel method for constrained mechanical design optimization problems. Comput. Aided Des. **43**(1), 303–315 (2011)
7. Hadidi, A., Azad, S.K., Azad, S.K.: Structural optimization using artificial bee colony algorithm. In: 2nd International Conference on Engineering Optimization, 2010, 6–9 September, Lisbon, Portugal
8. Storn, R., Price, K.: Differential evolution—a simple and efficient adaptive scheme for global optimization over continuous spaces. Technical Report, International Computer Science Institute, Berkley (1995)
9. Storn, R., Price, K.: Differential evolution—a simple and efficient heuristic for global optimization over continuous spaces. J. Global Optim. **11**(4), 341–359 (1997)
10. Rao, R.V., Savsani, V.J., Balic, J.: teaching learning based optimization algorithm for constrained and unconstrained real parameter optimization problems. Eng. Optim. **44**(12), 1447–1462 (2012)
11. Das, S., Abraham, A., Konar, A.. Automatic clustering using an improved differential evolution algorithm. IEEE Trans. Syst. Man Cyber. Part A: Syst. Humans **38**(1) (2008)

Sentiment Analysis on Tweets

Mehjabin Khatoon, W. Aisha Banu, A. Ayesha Zohra
and S. Chinthamani

Abstract The network of social media involves enormous amount of data being generated everyday by hundreds and thousands of actors. These data can be used for the analysis of collective behavior prediction. Data flooding from social media like Facebook, Twitter, and YouTube presents an opportunity to study collective behavior in a large scale. In today's world, almost every person updates status, shares pictures, and videos everyday, some even every hour. This has resulted in micro-blogging becoming the popular and most common communication tool of today. The users of micro-blogging Web sites not only share pictures and videos but also share their opinion about any product or issue. Thus, these Web sites provide us with rich sources of data for opinion mining. In this model, our focus is on Twitter, a popular micro-blogging site, for performing the task of opinion mining. The data required for the mining process is collected from Twitter. This data is then analyzed for good and bad tweets, i.e., positive and negative tweets. Based on the number of positive and negative tweets for a particular product, its quality gets determined, and then, the best product gets recommended to the user. Data mining in social media helps us to predict individual user preferences, and the result of which could be used for marketing and advertisement strategies to attract the consumers. In the present world, people tweet in English and regional languages as well. Our model aims to analyze such tweets that have both English words and regional language words pronounced using English alphabets.

Keywords Sentiment analysis · Social media · Blogs · Tweets

M. Khatoon · W. Aisha Banu (✉) · A. A. Zohra · S. Chinthamani
Computer Science and Engineering Department, B. S. Abdur Rahman University,
Chennai, India
e-mail: aisha@bsauniv.ac.in

M. Khatoon
e-mail: mehjabinkhatoon@gmail.com

© Springer Nature Singapore Pte Ltd. 2019
M. N. Hoda et al. (eds.), *Software Engineering*, Advances in Intelligent Systems
and Computing 731, https://doi.org/10.1007/978-981-10-8848-3_70

1 Introduction

All human activities are based on opinions. Opinions are one of the key factors that influence our behaviors. Our perception of reality, the choices we make, the products we buy, everything to a considerable amount, depend on how others see the world, i.e., opinion of others. Whenever we want to take a decision, we ask opinions of our friends and family before making the decision. This suits both for an individual as well as for an organization.

Businessmen and organizations always want to find out how well a particular product of theirs has reached the consumers. Individuals want to know how good a product is before buying it. In the past, when an individual wanted an opinion about some product, he/she asked their family and friends. Organizations conducted surveys and polls to collect information regarding the reach of a product among the consumers. In today's world, enormous amount of opinionated data is available on the Web. Organizations and individuals look up to these data when needed to make a decision.

Sentiment or opinion mining is the field of study that analyzes people's opinions, views, feelings, sentiments, and attitude toward a particular product, organization, individual, or service. It is a vast field with application in almost all the fields. The word opinion has a broader meaning. Here, we restrict it to those sentiments that imply either positive or negative feeling. The increased reach of social media has resulted in a large amount of data available on the Web for the purpose of decision making.

When one wants to buy a product, he/she is not restricted to the opinion of his/her family and friends. One can always read through the review of the product available online, submitted by the users of the product and also in discussion forums available on the Web. For an organization, it need not conduct polls and surveys since abundant of opinionated information is available online publicly. However, gathering the necessary information and processing it are a difficult task for a human. Hence, an automated sentiment analysis system is needed. Sentiment analysis is classifying a sentence to be positive, negative, or neutral. The early researches in this domain focused on factors like bag of words, support vectors, and rating systems. However, natural languages like regional languages require a more sophisticated approach for the purpose of analysis.

We identify the sentiment of a sentence based on sentiment words or opinion words, and these words imply either a positive or a negative opinion. Words like good, best, and awesome are examples of positive words, while bad, worse, and poor are examples of negative words. This can also include phrases that imply either a positive or a negative meaning. A list of such sentiment words and phrases is known as sentiment lexicon.

Micro-blogging allows an individual to post or share opinions from anywhere at any time. Some individual post false comments about a product either to make it reach to the masses or to compromise the analysis process. Such individuals are known as opinion spammers, and this process is known as opinion spamming. Opinion spamming poses a great challenge to the task of opinion mining. Hence, it is important to ensure that the data taken for analysis is from a trusted source and is free from opinion spamming. The next challenge is in identifying and processing factual sentences that may not have any sentiment words, but still imply a positive or negative meaning. For example, "The washer uses more water" is a factual sentence that implies negative opinion. Unlike facts, opinions and sentiments are subjective. Hence, it is important to ask opinion from multiple sources rather than a single source. The next challenge is identifying sentence that has a sentiment word but implies neither a positive nor a negative opinion. For example, the sentence "I will buy the phone if it is good" has the sentiment word 'good,' but it implies neither a positive nor a negative opinion.

2 Literature Survey

Sentiment mining has been an active area of research since the early 2000. Many have published scholarly articles on the same. Sentiment mining is nothing but feature-based analysis of collected data. It approximately follows the following steps:

- Keywords based on which the analysis is to be done are detected in the data.
- Sentiment words are searched for in the data.
- The sentiment words are then mapped to the keywords and assigned a sentiment score accordingly.
- The result can be displayed in visual format.

We refer to comprehensive summaries given in [7] for details about the first two steps. The sentiment words and the features can be extracted from external source or from a predefined list. It is important to associate the sentiment words with the keyword because certain words differ in meaning according to the domain in which they are used. For example, consider the word "fast" for the keyword or domain "laptop." In the sentence "The laptop processes fast," the word fast gives out a positive comment with respect to the laptop's processor. However, in the sentence "The laptop heats up fast," it gives out a negative comment.

There are different approaches for associating a sentiment word with the keyword. One approach is based on the distance in which the closer the keyword is to a sentiment word, the higher is its influence. These approaches can work on entire sentences Ding et al. [4], on sentence segments [3, 5] or on predefined words Oelke et al. [9]. Ng et al. [8] use subject–verb, verb–object, and adjective–noun relations for polarity classification. The feature and sentiment pairs can also be extracted based on ten dependency rules as done by Popescu and Etzioni [1].

All these approaches are based on parts of speech sequences only, rather than on typed in dependency. Analysis can also be done on reviews that are submitted directly to the company via the company's Web server Rohrdantz et al. [2]. Several methods are available for visualization of the outcome of analysis. The Opinion Observer visualization by Liu et al. [6] allows users to compare products with respect to the amount of positive and negative reviews on different product features.

3   Proposed System

All the past researches in the field of sentiment mining are based mostly on English. Our model is based on reviews that are typed in both English as well as the regional language. In our model, the analysis is based on tweets that are typed using both English and a regional language. The regional language words are spelled using English language characters rather than its characters.

In order to perform the analysis task, we need the data corpus on which the analysis is to be done. The data for analysis is extracted from the popular social networking site Twitter [10]. The tweets belonging to a particular hash tag or query are extracted and used for analysis. These tweets are then preprocessed, and then, sentiment words in each tweet are extracted. We compare these with a predefined list of words called bag of words. The bag of words consists of not only the dictionary form of words, but also their abbreviations and texting formats.

The sentiment words extracted from the preprocessed data are then compared with the bag of words. After comparison, each sentiment word is assigned a polarity according to the context in which it is used. The words are then combined with one another to determine the polarity of the entire sentence or tweet. The tweets are then classified as positive, negative, or neutral tweets based on the results of polarity determination.

4   Implementation

4.1   Tweets Extraction

As said earlier, the analysis task is done on the data extracted from the popular micro-blogging site Twitter. The comments, pictures, or anything that is being shared on Twitter is called as a 'tweet.' In order to extract these tweets, firstly we must create an application in Twitter and get it approved by the Twitter team. Twitter4j package is used for the extraction of tweets. When the application gets approved by the Twitter team, a unique consumer/secret key is given for the application. This consumer/secret key is needed to get authorization during the extraction process.

Once all these initial steps are done, we proceed with the extraction process. The tweets belonging to a particular hash tag are then extracted. This hash tag is given as a query in our code. When run, this module will generate an URL as the intermediary output, which has to be visited using a Web browser to get the session key. This key is copied and pasted in the output screen. Upon doing so, the tweets belonging to the given hash tag are extracted. Since the number of tweets for any hash tag may exceed thousands, we restrict the number of tweets to be extracted to 100 tweets. The extracted tweets are stored in a text file.

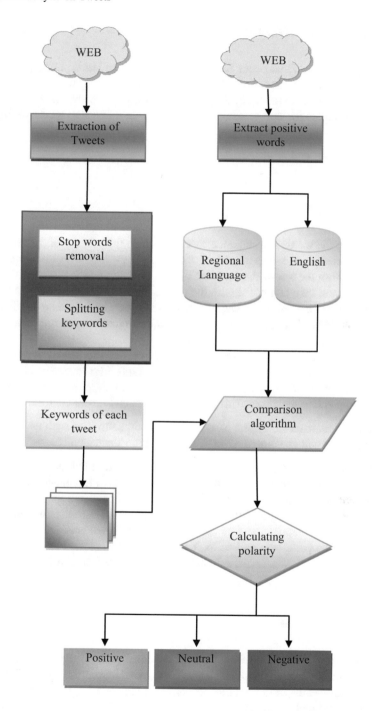

4.2 Stop Words Removal

Stop words are words that occur frequently in a sentence but do not represent any content of it. These words need to be removed before starting with the analysis as they are insignificant to the analysis process. Articles, prepositions, and some pronouns are examples for stop words. The following are a few stop words in English:

a, about, and, are, is, as, at, be, by, for, from, how, of, on, or, the, these, this, that, what, when, who, will, with, etc.

4.3 Split Keywords

Keywords are the words in a sentence based on which the polarity of the sentence is determined. Hence, it is important to remove the keywords, also known as sentiment words from the rest of the sentence. To do so, initially, the words in the tweet are extracted and then compared with the predefined list of words. When a word in the tweet matches a word in the bag of words, it is stored in a separate text file. This process is carried out until all the keywords in the extracted tweets are removed and stored separately.

For the splitting of words from the sentence, we use the 'initial splitting algorithm.' It parses the whole text file and splits paragraphs into sentences based on "." and "?" present in the input file. It uses the rule-based simplification technique to split paragraphs into sentences. This proposed approach follows the following steps:

I. Split the sentences from the paragraph based on delimiters such as "." and "?"
II. Delimiter such as comma,-,?,\,! is ignored from the sentences.

The text can be of any form, i.e., paragraphing format, individual sentences. The presence of delimiter such as "?" and "." is an important prerequisite as the initial splitting is done based on delimiters. Sentence boundary symbols (SBS) for sentence simplification simplify the paragraph into small simpler sentences. We defined the classical boundary symbols as (".","?"). This sentence boundary symbol goes through the paragraph and splits it into simple sentences when it encounters the symbols ".", "?". Words are split when a space is encountered.

4.4 Bag of Words

Bag of words is a predefined list of words collected prior to the analysis process. The words in the bag of words list are also extracted from the Web. The bag of words contains words from both the regional language and English language. Same words with different spellings are clustered together. These words are associated with a polarity.

4.5 Polarity Comparison

The keywords extracted from the tweets are then compared with the words in the bag of words list in order to associate each word with its polarity. The words in the bag of words are assigned polarity. The polarity of the input words is then found by comparing the keywords with the bag of words. The output of this module will be the words with their polarities heightened.

4.6 Calculating Polarity

In this, the polarity associated with each word is combined with one another and the polarity for the combined words is found using the "Basic Rules Algorithm," which contains a set of rules to be followed while calculating the polarity of two words combined. This process is continued till the polarity of the whole sentence is determined. The output of this module is the sentence with its polarity found.

After this, the sentences are classified into three groups, namely positive, negative, and neutral. The number of positive or negative tweets gives a collective opinion about the product, i.e., whether the product has more number of positive comments or more number of negative comments. The result is then visualized in the form of a graph in order to enable easy interpretation of the results.

5 Conclusion

In this paper, we use feature-based sentiment analysis approach to analyze and classify tweets that contain both English words and words in regional language. For our analysis, we used Tamil as the regional language. However, this approach is not restricted to Tamil language alone. It can be extended to any of the regional languages.

References

1. Popescu, A.-M., Etzioni, O.: Extracting product features and opinions from reviews. In: Proceedings of the Human Language Technology Conference and the Conference on Empirical Methods in Natural Language Processing (HLT/EMNLP) (2005)
2. Rohrdantz, C., Hao, M.C., Dayal, U., Haug, L.-E., Keim, D.A.: Feature-based Visual Sentiment Analysis of Text Document Streams (2012)
3. Ding, X., Liu, B.: The utility of linguistic rules in opinion mining. In: SIGIR'07: Proceedings of the 30th annual international ACM SIGIR conference on Research and development in information retrieval. pp. 811–812. ACM, New York, NY

4. Ding, X., Liu, B., Yu, P.: A holistic lexicon-based approach to opinion mining. In: Proceedings of the International Conference on Web Search and Web Data Mining, pp. 231–240 (2008)
5. Kim, S.-M., Hovy, E.: Determining the sentiment of opinions. In: COLING'04: Proceedings of the 20th International Conference on Computational Linguistics. Association for Computational Linguistics, Morristown, NJ, pp. 1367–1373 (2004)
6. Liu, B., Hu, M., Cheng, J.: Opinion observer: Analyzing and comparing opinions on the web. Proceedings of WWW (2005)
7. Liu, B.: Web Data Mining: Exploring Hyperlinks, Contents, and Usage Data. Springer (2006)
8. Ng, V., Dasgupta, S, Niaz Arifin, S.M.: Examining the role of linguistic knowledge sources in the automatic identification and classification of reviews. In: Proceedings of the COLING/ACL Main Conference Poster Sessions, Sydney, Australia, July 2006, pp. 611–618. Association for Computational Linguistics (2006)
9. Oelke, D. et al.: Visual Opinion Analysis of Customer Feedback Data. VAST (2009)
10. Zhou, X., Tao, X., Yong, J., Yang, Z.: Sentiment analysis on tweets for social events. In: Proceedings of the 2013 IEEE 17th International Conference on Computer Supported Cooperative Work in Design

Printed in the United States
By Bookmasters